SIXTH EDITION

Handbuch zur deutschen Grammatik

WIEDERHOLEN UND ANWENDEN

Jamie Rankin
Princeton University

Larry D. Wells
Late of Binghamton University

CENGAGE
Learning®

Australia • Brazil • Japan • Korea • Mexico • Singapore • Spain • United Kingdom • United States

CENGAGE Learning®

Handbuch zur deutschen Grammatik: Wiederholen und anwenden, Sixth Edition
Jamie Rankin and Larry D. Wells

Product Director: Beth Kramer

Senior Product Manager: Martine Edwards

Managing Developer: Katie Wade

Senior Content Developer: Harriet C. Dishman

Managing Media Developer: Patrick Brand

Associate Content Developer: Claire Kaplan

Product Assistant: Jacob R. Schott

Senior Content Project Manager:
  Aileen Mason

Senior Art Director: Linda Jurras

Manufacturing Planner: Betsy Donaghey

IP Analyst: Jessica Elias

IP Project Manager: Farah Fard

Production Service: MPS Limited

Cover Designer: Anne Dauchy

Compositor: MPS Limited

For product information and technology assistance, contact us at
Cengage Learning Customer & Sales Support, 1-800-354-9706

For permission to use material from this text or product, submit all requests online at **cengage.com/permissions**. Further permissions questions can be emailed to **permissionrequest@cengage.com**.

Library of Congress Control Number: 2014943691

Student Edition:

ISBN-13: 978-1-305-07884-0

ISBN-10: 1-305-07884-5

Instructor's Edition:

ISBN-13: 978-1-305-07897-0

ISBN-10: 1-305-07897-7

Cengage Learning
20 Channel Center Street
Boston, MA 02210
USA

Cengage Learning is a leading provider of customized learning solutions with office locations around the globe, including Singapore, the United Kingdom, Australia, Mexico, Brazil, and Japan. Locate your local office at: **international.cengage.com/region**

Cengage Learning products are represented in Canada by Nelson Education, Ltd.

For your course and learning solutions, visit **www.cengage.com.**

Purchase any of our products at your local college store or at our preferred online store **www.CengageBrain.com.**

Instructors: Please visit **login.cengage.com** and log in to access instructor-specific resources.

Printed in the United States of America
1 2 3 4 5 6 7 18 17 16 15 14

Contents

To the Student

If you have already learned some German, perhaps during several years of high school courses, in a college-level introductory program, or even on your own through online media, and you want to deepen your knowledge of German, this book is designed to help you do that. For language learners who do well on grammar tests but have trouble expressing themselves spontaneously in speaking and writing, this book has a wide range of interactive exercises for communicative use. For language learners who can already speak and write, but are not as proficient as they'd like to be, and are unsure of the rules underlying the grammatical structures they want to use, the book provides in-depth explanations of the syntax and grammar points used in everyday conversation as well as more formal modes of expression.

Here is what you will find in each chapter:

- **Grammatik.** The explanations of grammar are broken down into individual points, with examples in German that are glossed in English. Each chapter has a cultural focus for these examples, which is to say, the examples are "about something" in the context of each chapter, rather than randomly chosen bits of unrelated information. There are extensive cross-references in each section, so that you can easily find and review grammatical points that may not be clear to you.

- **Wortschatz.** This section is designed to expand your working vocabulary by focusing on contextually related words. In some chapters, the words revolve around a particular communicative function (for example, all the various ways that German has for saying *to go to* ... [Chapter 6]); in others, explanations are provided for words that have different nuanced meanings in English and German.

- **Übungen.** The exercises in this section allow you to work on the grammar as well as the vocabulary in the **Wortschatz** section, using a variety of approaches. There are tasks for matching forms and meaning, tasks that have you complete sentence stems, fill-in-the-blank kinds of tasks, as well as open-ended tasks that allow you to express your own ideas about a topic, using the grammar and vocabulary explained in the chapter.

- **Anwendung**. These tasks are specifically designed for classroom use, so you can interact with people in a class, or via Skype, or by any other means that lets you listen and respond to real people using real language.

- **Schriftliche Themen.** The exercises in this section foster competence in your written expression by incorporating new grammatical structures and vocabulary into your writing style. By guiding you through the processes of writing—giving you tips on what to include, how to structure your writing, how to improve it once you have a draft, and providing idioms that will allow you to express your ideas in a culturally appropriate way—the assignments will help you grow in your ability to express yourself clearly and accurately.

■ **Zusammenfassung.** Every chapter includes a brief summary of the most important grammatical rules explained in it, along with graphs and tables (**At a glance**) that provide a visually focused reference for the forms and words you need to know from the chapter.

The chapters themselves cover the grammar of German in a modular way. If you need to learn more about adjective endings, they are all covered in one chapter. If you're unsure how to form the passive voice or the subjunctive mood, those are explained in their respective chapters. The same is true for negation; comparative and superlative forms; each of the verb tenses; and every other topic that you'll need to know. All that to say: The book is designed to be a learning tool as well as a reference tool, so you can easily go back and review the topics you need to work on.

Components of the Program

The *Handbuch zur deutschen Grammatik* consists of the core textbook that you have in your hands, the *Arbeitsheft* or Student Activities Manual, as well as a Premium Website. On the Premium Website you will find the audio files for the *Arbeitsheft*, auto-graded web quizzes, as well as some animated German grammar tutorials that walk you through some basic German grammar topics.

Learning Vocabulary

Increasing your vocabulary is one of the most important things you can do at this point in your acquisition of German. You will find that the level of sophistication and precision of your spoken and written German depends in large measure on the range of words and idiomatic phrases at your disposal. Since many of the activities in this book are open-ended, it is impossible to predict all the words you will need. But you will be able to expand your repertoire of useful vocabulary by making good use of the suggested vocabulary (*Vokabelvorschläge*), themes (*Themenvorschläge*), and conversational gambits (*Redemittel*) that accompany many of the activities.

Here are a few tips for learning vocabulary:

■ Find a way to give yourself multiple exposures to new words—paper flashcards with German on one side, your own language on the other; online flashcards that you can create and manipulate yourself; online vocabulary systems that let you recycle new words randomly, or better, that detect which words you don't know and repeat them more often than others.

■ Use whatever review system works for you a little bit every day—rather than trying to cram vocabulary just before a quiz or test, which may help you in the short run, but will not lead to deep processing and retention.

■ As you learn new words and review the words you've learned, don't just glance at a word and say to yourself, "Yeah, I know that one." Instead, use as many modalities as you can to review it: say it out loud; picture it in your imagination, if it's something that can be visualized; use it in a few short sentences, either spoken or written, making use of whatever grammar you happen to be learning at the same time. In other words, allow yourself to process it as deeply as possible; the more modalities you use, the more connections you create that will help you remember it.

Learning Grammar

If your goal is to communicate in German through speaking or writing, then the grammar in this book should not be learned in isolation or merely for its own sake. You can, of course, work on particular grammar structures by consciously using them when talking or writing about things you have read, heard, or experienced—just as the examples found in the chapters all make use of the **zum Beispiel** cultural topics. You can also practice listening for particular structures when people speak or when you work with the SAM Audio Program that accompanies the Student Activities Manual. These habits will help you reach what should be your goal: meaningful, accurate communication in German.

Acknowledgments

As long as **Handbuch zur deutschen Grammatik** continues to be published, any-one working with it—including this co-author—should be mindful of the vision, insight, and sheer hard work that Larry Wells poured into it from the very beginning. For that we must all be grateful. It is my hope that he would be pleased with this Sixth Edition (not to mention excited that it has continued to thrive long after its beginning). Of course, he would be surprised at much of what you see here: when the book was first written, cell phones were the size of shoeboxes, e-mail was exotic, .mp3s did not exist, and the fall of the Berlin wall was fresh in everyone's memory. No one had heard even rumors of a spelling reform, so that **dass** was still spelled **daß**. Much has changed, indeed, yet the approach to language teaching that has informed **Handbuch zur deutschen Grammatik** from the beginning has proven its usefulness and validity over the years since the book's first appearance. This is the crux of the revision here: clarifying the grammatical nuances, strengthening the ties between language and culture, and updating the cultural and socio-pragmatic aspects of the text, providing relevant vocabulary, and stressing that all of this is done in the service of communicating in a meaningful, effective way.

It takes many people to produce a book, and a grammar textbook is no exception. I am grateful to my students and colleagues at Princeton University for their continuing input—in particular to Prof. Robert Ebert for his comments on successive drafts of the word-order sections, which were substantially rewritten for the Third Edition, and to Prof. Tom Levin for his help in identifying *Metropolis* as a useful component of Chapter 22. I want to thank Jason Adams for his enthusiastic contributions to the soccer terminology in Chapter 11; Jon Keller and Sean Rubin for their suggestions on how to squeeze *Harry Potter* into a graph of adjective endings; and Jens Klenner, Hannes Mandel, Julian Petri, Mareike Stoll, and Petra Spies for providing native-speaker intuitions on several critical questions of current usage. I am indebted to the editors, artists, designers, and assistants who were involved in this undertaking. I especially want to acknowledge the help of Senior Content Developer, Harriet C. Dishman, for her tireless and insightful attention to so many levels of detail in the development of this edition.

I also would like to thank the reviewers whose constructive comments have helped make **Handbuch zur deutschen Grammatik** such a rewarding project.

Mary Beth Bagg, *University of Indianapolis*

Thomas Baldwin

Barbara Bopp, *Las Vegas, Clark Country Library District*

Joanna Bottenberg, *Concordia University*

Barbara Bowlus

Elio Brancaforte, *Tulane University*

David Coury, *University of Wisconsin–Green Bay*

Ellen Crocker, *Massachusetts Institute of Technology*

Therese Decker

Walter Joseph Denk, *University of Toledo*

Margaret Devinney, *Temple University*

Eugene Dobson

Bruce Duncan, *Dartmouth College*

Esther Enns, *Saint Mary's University, Halifax*

Judith Fogle, *Pasadena City College*

Hildburg Herbst, *Rutgers, The State University of New Jersey*

Zsuzsanna Ittzes Abrams, *University of Texas–Austin*

Dr. John M. Jeep, *Miami University, Florida*

Anthony Jung, *University of Nebraska–Omaha*

George Koenig, *State University of New York–Oswego*

Hans Laetz

Andreas Lixl, *University of North Carolina–Greensboro*

Carla Love, *University of Wisconsin–Madison*

Timm Menke, *Portland State University*

Carol Miller, *University of Wisconsin–La Crosse*

Uwe Moeller, *Austin community College*

Matthew Pollard, *University of Victoria*

Julie Prandi, *Illinois Wesleyan University*

Donna Reeves-Marquardt, *Southwest Texas State University*

Walter von Reinhart, *University of Rhode Island*

Judith Ricker-Abderhalden, *University of Arkansas–Fayetteville*

Ann Rider, *Indiana State University*

Ruth Sanders

Wilhelm Seeger

Jane Sokolosky, *Brown University*

Richard Spuler, *Rice University*

Christian Stehr, *Oregon State University*

Karl Stenger, *University of South Carolina–Aiken*

Adam Stiener, *Salem College*

Wilfried Voge, *University of California–Berkeley*

Morris Vos, *Western Illinois University*

David Ward, *Norwich University*

Donald Watkins, *University of Kansas*

Helga Watt, *University of Denver*

—Jamie Rankin

zum Beispiel

Märchen

North Wind Picture Archives / Alamy

Märchen: The fairy tales used throughout this chapter were voted the most popular in a survey conducted in 2010 by **Südwestrundfunk**, a regional broadcasting corporation serving Baden-Württemberg and Rheinland-Pfalz, for their online readers. The top 10 list reads as follows: **Aschenputtel; Schneewittchen; Sterntaler; Der gestiefelte Kater; Rumpelstilzchen; Die Bremer Stadtmusikanten; Frau Holle; Der Froschkönig; Das hässliche Entlein; Hänsel und Gretel**. Some of these you no doubt know, but some are probably unfamiliar. Nine of them are used in this chapter as grammar examples. Given the clues from the examples, can you determine which one is missing?

Grammatik

The most prominent feature of German word order is the position of the verb. Each of the three major clause types in German—main clause, question, and subordinate clause—requires the conjugated verb to occupy a different place within the clause, which can differ considerably from English.

Main clause

Auf dem Fest **verliert** Aschenputtel ihren Schuh.	*At the ball, Cinderella **loses** her shoe.*

Question

Lügt der gestiefelte Kater immer?	*Does Puss-in-Boots always **lie**?*

Dependent clause

…, dass alle vier Tiere nach Bremen **gehen**.	*… that all four animals **go** to Bremen.*

But although the verb position varies from clause to clause, it is consistent within each clause type. It is important to remember which kind of clause you are constructing and how that dictates both the constraints and possible variations for word order within it.

1.1   WORD ORDER IN MAIN CLAUSES

A *main clause* statement in German normally consists of at least two, and up to five, basic components: (1) an initial element, referred to as the *front field*, followed by (2) a conjugated verb (these two are required to form a main clause); and then, as needed, (3) an assortment of noun and pronoun subjects and objects along with any accompanying modifiers, known as the *middle field*; all of which is followed by (4) any past participles or dependent infinitives associated with the conjugated verb. It is this split between the verbal elements and the way that they "surround" the middle field that leads to the term *verbal bracket*. On occasion, (5) an additional element is added after the end of the verbal bracket; this is sometimes called the *end field* (see below).

A. Elements in the front field

1. The *front field*, that is, the first element in a German sentence, is very often the grammatical subject.

Die Stiefmutter hat zwei Töchter.	*The stepmother has two daughters.*
Sie sind äußerlich schön aber innerlich grausam.	*They are outwardly beautiful, but inwardly cruel.*

2. Words directly modifying the first element are considered part of it and therefore remain in the front field.

Der Sohn *des Königs* sucht eine Frau.	*The son of the king is looking for a wife.*
Das Fest *im Schloss* soll drei Tage dauern.	*The celebration in the castle is supposed to last for three days.*

3. German speakers often put adverbial expressions or prepositional verbal complements (see Reference Chapter 3 [R.3]) in first position for the sake of style or emphasis, or to draw attention to this information as the actual "topic" of the statement. When this happens, the subject, which would normally be in first position, moves to a position after the conjugated verb. **NOTE:** Adverbial first elements are not set off by a comma in German, as they may be in English.

Auf das Fest freuen sich alle Mädchen. *(prepositional verbal complement)*	*All the girls are looking forward **to the celebration**.*
Vorher muss Aschenputtel geeignete Kleidung dafür finden. *(adverbial modifier)*	***Before that**, Cinderella must find appropriate clothes for it.*
Leider haben die Stiefschwestern ihr alles weggenommen. *(adverbial modifier)*	***Unfortunately**, the stepsisters have taken everything away from her.*

4. When direct and indirect objects, infinitives, and past participles appear in the front field, they have particularly strong emphasis. This emphasis is usually woven into the discourse context—for example, to answer a question, or to pick up on something mentioned in a previous statement, or to correct a mistake.

Dem armen Mädchen gibt der Vogel im Baum ein Kleid und Schuhe. *(indirect object)*	*The bird in the tree gives **the poor girl** a dress and shoes.*
Einen Schuh findet der Prinz auf der Treppe. *(direct object)*	*The prince finds **a shoe** on the stairs.*
Tanzen will der Prinz nur mit Aschenputtel. *(infinitive)*	*The prince wants **to dance** only with Cinderella.*
Gefunden hat er sie zu Hause. *(past participle)*	*He **found** her at home.*

5. Not just *any* element can appear first in a main clause, however. German speakers tend to avoid object pronouns such as **es**, **ihn**, **sie**, or **uns** in this position when these are unstressed, that is, when they merely repeat information from a previous utterance instead of conveying new or highlighted information. Similarly, the reflexive pronoun **sich** (see 10.1) and the negation element **nicht** (see 7.2) cannot stand alone in the front field.

6. Both in spoken and written German, there are words and phrases at the beginning of an utterance that are not considered part of the front field; they are set off by a comma to show this syntactic separation. Common examples are **ja** and **nein**.

Ja, Disney hat auch eine Version davon gemacht.	*Yes, Disney also made a version of it.*
Nein, das Ende der alten Version ist nicht wie im Disney-Film.	*No, the ending of the old version is not like the Disney film.*

There are also several idiomatic phrases that function as a kind of introduction to what follows, and are therefore not included in the front field.

Im Gegenteil, die alte Version endet mit einer brutalen Strafe.	*On the contrary, the old version ends with a violent punishment.*
Kurzum, sie betont Gerechtigkeit mehr als Magie und Zufriedenheit.	*In short, it emphasizes justice more than magic and happiness.*
Sehen Sie, heute finden viele Eltern die alte Version zu brutal für Kinder.	*You see, today many parents find the old version too violent for children.*
Wie gesagt, das Märchen endet mit Blindheit und Schmerzen.	*As I said, the fairy tale ends with blindness and pain.*
Wissen Sie, ich bin mir nicht sicher, was andere Leute denken.	*You know, I'm not sure what other people think.*
Aber unter uns gesagt, ich würde es kleinen Kindern nicht so erzählen.	*But between you and me, I wouldn't tell it to children like that.*

B. Position of the conjugated verb

1. The second sentence element in a main clause is normally the conjugated verb (V_1), regardless of which element occupies first position.

   „**Du *bist*** die Schönste im ganzen Land".

   „**Die Schönste *bist*** du im ganzen Land".   *"You are the fairest in all the land."*

   „**Im ganzen Land *bist*** du die Schönste".

2. Even if the first sentence element is a subordinate clause, the conjugated verb of the following main clause is still in second position within the overall sentence.

   $$\overline{\hspace{1cm}1\hspace{1cm}}\quad\overline{\hspace{0.3cm}2\hspace{0.3cm}}$$

   Obwohl Schneewittchen einen giftigen Apfel isst, *bleibt* sie nicht lange tot.
   Even though Snow White eats a poisonous apple, she doesn't remain dead for long.

3. The same applies to very short first elements, such as **dann**.

Dann *kommt* ein Prinz vorbei und sieht sie im Sarg.	*Then a prince comes along and sees her in the coffin.*

4. For purposes of word order, when two main clauses are connected by a coordinating conjunction (**aber, denn, oder, sondern, und**) (see R.2), the conjunction is not considered a first element of the second clause; thus the position of the conjugated verb in the second clause does not change.

Die böse Königin geht zur Hochzeit, ***aber*** dort **stirbt** sie.	*The wicked queen goes to the wedding, but she dies there.*

C. Elements in the middle field

1. The bracket formed by the conjugated verb (V_1) and verbal elements that appear later in the sentence (V_2) marks the boundaries of the *middle field*. The middle field includes subject nouns and pronouns if they are not in the front field, object nouns and pronouns (accusative and dative, including reflexive pronouns), negation elements, adverbial modifiers, and verbal complements.

2. If the subject of the main clause is not the first element, it usually appears at (or near) the beginning of the middle field. Subject *pronouns* must stand directly after V$_1$. Subject *nouns* can be preceded by unstressed personal pronouns or, if the subject is to be emphasized, by other elements as well.

Dann begegnete dem Mädchen **ein armer Mann ...**	*Then the girl met a poor man ...*
Dem armen Mann hat **sie** ihr letztes Stück Brot gegeben.	*To the poor man she gave her last piece of bread.*

3. The order of dative and accusative objects in the middle field (see 5.4 and 5.5) is determined in general by the level of emphasis desired: *The later one of these objects appears in the middle field, the greater the emphasis it receives.* In practice this means:

   ■ A pronoun object appears *before* a noun object.

Der junge Mann gab *ihm* **die neuen Stiefel**.	*The young man gave him the new boots.*
Der junge Mann gab *sie* **dem Kater**.	*The young man gave them to the cat.*

   ■ With two noun objects, the one being emphasized appears second.

Der gestiefelte Kater erzählte **den Leuten** *eine Lüge*.	*Puss-in-Boots told the people a lie.*
Die Leute erzählten dann **die Lüge** *dem König*.	*The people then told the lie to the king.*

   Some textbooks state that in such cases, the dative noun object should always precede the accusative noun object, but this oversimplifies the matter. If the accusative noun has already been mentioned (e.g., **Lüge** in the example above), and the speaker prefers to repeat it rather than use a pronoun, it should come first, thereby emphasizing the second noun, which is the dative indirect object (**König**).

A: Was hat der Kater mit **den Rebhühnern** gemacht?	*What did the cat do with the partridges?*
B: Der Kater hat *die Rebhühner* **dem König** geschenkt.	*The cat gave the partridges to the king.*

4. If both objects are personal pronouns, the accusative pronoun comes first, regardless of emphasis.

A: Wann denn?	*When (did he do that)?*
B: Er hat *sie* **ihm** gleich gegeben.	*He gave them to him right away.*

5. When they appear in the middle field, adverbial elements have no rigidly fixed position, though a general default order shows adverbials of manner coming after other adverbial elements. Many textbooks invoke the "TMP" rule (Time–Manner–Place) here, but this is an oversimplification. Phrases that indicate "Place" are very often verbal complements that specify direction or location in a way that is required by certain verbs, such as **stellen (sie stellt das + auf den Tisch)** and **wohnen (er wohnt + zu Hause)**. Verbal complements *always* appear after other adverbials, hence the common assumption that "Place" follows "Time" and "Manner." But when "Place" is not a verbal complement, it can precede "Manner," as in this example:

Der Kater hat *am See* (= wo) **ganz listig** (= wie) verhandelt.	*The cat negotiated quite cunningly at the lake.*

NOTE: The important thing to remember is the *emphasis rule*: The adverbial element to be stressed appears after elements that are less emphasized within the middle field, but never after verbal complements, including "Place" complements.

6. For rules concerning the position(s) of **nicht**, see 7.2.

7. Information that is required to "complete" the meaning of certain verbs (as in the examples in point 5 above) appears at the very end of the middle field. These *verbal complements* immediately precede V$_2$ (see D.1 below) or stand as the final element in a main clause with no V$_2$. Here are the most common types of verbal complements.

- Predicate nominatives (see 5.3):

Die Frau war **die Tochter eines Müllers**.	*The woman was the daughter of a miller.*

- Directional modifiers:

Der König brachte die Frau **in eine Kammer**.	*The king brought the woman into a chamber.*

- Separable prefixes (see R.5):

Jede Nacht kam das kleine Männlein **zurück**.	*Every night the little man returned.*

- Prepositional phrases that complete the meaning of certain verbs (see R.3):

Nach der Hochzeit dachte die Frau nicht mehr **an das Männlein**.	*After the wedding, the woman didn't think any more about the little man.*
Sie interessierte sich nur **für das Leben im Schloss**.	*She was interested only in life at the castle.*

- Object nouns, infinitives (see 11.3), and adverbs that combine with verbs to create specific meanings that extend beyond the literal meaning of the elements by themselves:

Die Frau **lief** *Gefahr*, ihr Kind zu verlieren.	*The woman ran the risk of losing her child.*
Als Mädchen **lernte** sie das Männlein im Schloss *kennen*.	*As a girl, she got to know the little man in the castle.*
Ihr Diener **lernte** den Namen des Männleins *auswendig*.	*Her servant learned the little man's name by heart.*

- Other examples include:[1]

Führerschein machen	*to get one's driver's license*
Farbe bekennen	*to take a stand, to show one's colors*
Kaffee trinken	*to drink coffee (also: have coffee together)*

---

[1]For additional examples and further explanation of verbal complements, see 7.2.B.

D. V₂ elements

1. The final portion of the verbal bracket (V_2) is formed with infinitives or past participles, and encloses the elements of the middle field.

Der Esel **hat** sein Heim **verlassen**, und drei andere Tiere **gefunden**.	*The donkey left his home and found three other animals.*
Sie **wollten** alle nach Bremen **gehen**.	*They all wanted to go to Bremen.*

2. Separable prefixes attach directly to the V_2 verb (see R.5), forming either an infinitive or a past participle together with the root verb. Notice that past participles formed with **-ge-** insert this element between the prefix and the root verb.

Der Hahn **ist** auf den Rücken des Hundes <u>**hinaufgeflogen**</u>.	*The rooster flew up onto the back of the dog.*
Dann **sind** alle vier ins Zimmer <u>**hineingestürzt**</u>.	*Then all four of them toppled into the room.*

E. Elements in the end field

1. While the first element, the verbal bracket, and the middle field contain almost all information in a main clause, some elements can appear after V_2 in informal, spoken discourse.

■ Adverbial modifiers added as an afterthought:

Die alte Frau hat sie heim geschickt **durch ein großes Tor**.	*The old woman sent her home through a large gate.*

■ Elements to be emphasized:

Also, beide Töchter sind auf der Wiese gelandet **bei Frau Holle**.	*So, both daughters landed on the meadow near Frau Holle's house.*

2. Placing information in the end field is common for both written and spoken German in the case of comparative phrases beginning with **als** or **wie**.

Die erste Tochter konnte viel besser arbeiten **als die zweite**.	*The first daughter was able to work much better than the second.*
Die zweite Tochter ist nicht so glücklich zurückgekommen **wie die erste**.	*The second daughter didn't return as happily as the first.*

1.2 **POSITIONS OF THE CONJUGATED VERB IN QUESTIONS**

1. In yes-no questions, the conjugated verb is in first position, followed by the middle field, including the subject.

Kennst du die Geschichte vom Froschkönig?	*Do you know the story about the frog prince?*

2. In information questions, the conjugated verb follows the interrogative word or expression (see 19.2).

Was **verspricht** die Prinzessin dem Frosch?	*What does the princess promise the frog?*
Was für Probleme **hat** sie später mit ihrem Vater, dem König?	*What kinds of problems does she have later with her father, the king?*

3. In indirect questions, the question itself is a subordinate clause (see 1.3) and the verb stands in final position within this clause.

Hast du gewusst, dass sie den Frosch nicht **küsst**, sondern gegen die Wand **wirft**?	*Did you know that she doesn't kiss the frog, but rather throws him against the wall?*

1.3   POSITIONS OF THE CONJUGATED VERB IN DEPENDENT CLAUSES

A. Types of dependent clauses

1. There are two kinds of dependent clauses: **subordinate** clauses, which begin with subordinating conjunctions such as **weil** and **dass** (see R.2.3); and **relative** clauses, which are connected to main clauses by means of relative pronouns (see 18.1). The conjugated verb (V_1) in dependent clauses follows final-position verbal elements (V_2).

Alles fängt an, <u>weil</u> die Familie nicht genug zu essen **hat**.	*It all begins because the family doesn't have enough to eat.*
Die Stiefmutter sagt, <u>dass</u> sie die Kinder im Wald lassen **sollten**.	*The stepmother says that they should leave the children in the forest.*
Die Eltern einigen sich auf einen Plan, <u>den</u> die Kinder **belauschen**.	*The parents agree on a plan that the children overhear.*

2. The only exception to this rule involves a double infinitive construction (see 11.6). The conjugated verb (V_1) in such cases immediately precedes the two infinitives.

Später denkt der Vater, dass sie die Kinder nicht ***hätten*** verlassen sollen.	*Later, the father thinks that they should not have abandoned the children.*

B. Subordinate clauses

1. In subordinate clauses, the conjugated verb (V_1) occupies final position, even if the subordinate clause is the first element in the sentence.

COMPARE:

Main clause

Die Hexe **ist** böse.	*The witch is wicked.*

Subordinate clause

Die Kinder haben Angst, weil die Hexe böse **ist**.	*The children are frightened because the witch is wicked.*
Weil die Hexe böse **ist**, haben die Kinder Angst.	*Because the witch is wicked, the children are frightened.*

2. As in English, the subordinating conjunction **dass** (*that*) may be omitted. When this happens the second clause is considered a main clause and the verb remains in second position.

   COMPARE:

Anfangs denken die Kinder, *dass* es keine Gefahr **gibt**.	*Initially, the children don't think that there's any danger.*
Anfangs denken die Kinder, es **gibt** keine Gefahr.	*Initially, the children don't think there's any danger.*

3. The normal word order in subordinate clauses (V_1 at the end) is sometimes changed to omit the **wenn** in conditional clauses, so that V_1 appears first, just as in English.

   COMPARE:

Wenn Gretel nicht so schnell gehandelt **hätte**, wäre die Hexe nicht tot.	*If Gretel had not acted so quickly, the witch wouldn't be dead.*
Hätte Gretel nicht so schnell gehandelt, wäre die Hexe nicht tot.	*Had Gretel not acted so quickly, the witch wouldn't be dead.*

C. Relative clauses

In relative clauses, the conjugated verb (V_1) likewise occupies final position, unless a double infinitive is in play.

   COMPARE:

Es ist eins von vielen Märchen, **in denen die böse Stiefmutter eine Rolle** *spielt*.	*It's one of many fairy tales in which the evil stepmother plays a role.*
War es nicht ihr Plan, **den der Vater** *hätte* **ablehnen sollen**?	*Wasn't it her plan that the father should have rejected?*

Wortschatz
Vokabeln zum Studium

The following words occur regularly in the direction lines for the exercises and activities in this text, and will also be useful for classroom discussion and questions.

Verben

ändern to change, modify	**ergänzen (durch)** to complete (with)
aus·drücken[2] to express, say	**erklären** to explain
zum Ausdruck bringen	**ersetzen** to replace, substitute
to express, say	**erzählen** to tell, narrate
sich äußern (zu) to express one's	**gebrauchen** to use, make use of
views (on), comment (on)	**mit·teilen** to communicate;
aus·tauschen to exchange	to impart, tell
beenden to end, complete	**übersetzen** to translate
berichten (über) + *accusative*	**um·formen** to transform, recast
to report (on), tell about	**unterstreichen** to underline
beschreiben to describe	**verbinden** to connect, combine
besprechen to discuss	**verwenden** to use, make use of
betonen to emphasize, stress	**wiederholen** to repeat
bilden to form (sentences)	**zusammen·fassen** to summarize
ein·setzen to insert, supply	
(missing words)	

Substantive *(Nouns)*

der Ausdruck, ⸚e expression	**die Lücke, -n** blank space
die Aussage, -n statement	**das Thema, die Themen** topic
der Gebrauch use	**der Vorschlag, ⸚e** suggestion
der Inhalt, -e content(s)	

Adjektive

fehlend missing	**passend** suitable, proper
fett gedruckt printed in boldface	**unterstrichen** underlined
kursiv gedruckt printed in italics	**verschieden** various

On the topic of classroom learning, it is important to know the distinction between **lernen** and **studieren**, and the use of *class* as opposed to **Klasse**.

1.   The verb **lernen** means *to learn* or *to acquire* specific subjects, skills, or information.

Was hast du in diesem Kurs **gelernt**?	*What did you learn in this course?*
Max **lernt** seit zwei Jahren Spanisch.	*Max has been studying Spanish for two years. (It is not his major.)*

2.   The verb **studieren** means *to study at a university-level institution*; it cannot refer to learning that takes place in elementary or high schools. **Studieren** also means *to study or major in a particular field or discipline*. Both meanings are too broad to refer to learning that precedes a test, as in *I have to study for a quiz tomorrow*. For this meaning, you should use **lernen** or (more casually) **büffeln** or **pauken**, colloquialisms that denote cramming or intense preparatory study.

Petra möchte in Heidelberg **studieren**.	*Petra would like to study in Heidelberg.*

---

[2]In the **Wortschatz** sections and exercises throughout this book, separable prefix verbs (see R.5) listed in infinitive form will be marked with a bullet (·) to distinguish between the prefix and the root verb.

| Ihr Bruder **studiert** Jura in Göttingen und muss im Sommer für seine Examen **lernen**. | *Her brother is studying law (as his major) in Göttingen and has to study this summer for his qualifying exams.* |

3. English *class* (in the context of a school) and German **die Klasse** are related in meaning, but not synonymous. German **Klasse** is used to refer to a *grade level* in school, as in **Das haben wir schon in der 4.** *Klasse* **gelernt**. It can also refer to the members of a school group: **Hier siehst du mich auf dem Bild mit meiner** *Schulklasse.* It does not refer to a particular classroom session, as in *In class today we talked about....* German has various ways of expressing this use of *class*, depending on the educational level in play (e.g., **das Gymnasium** vs. **die Universität**), and, in the case of the latter, the nature of the course.

- The most common way for German high school and university students to refer to their courses, when speaking of classroom sessions, is simply to use the name of the subject.

| Was habt ihr heute in **Bio** gemacht? | *What did you do in biology (class) today?* |

- Secondary school (i.e., pre-university) courses are sometimes referred to as **Unterricht (der)**.

| **Im Deutschunterricht** haben wir gestern einen Film gesehen. | *Yesterday in German class we saw a film.* |

- At the university level, a course is also referred to according to its status as a seminar (**das Seminar, -e**) or lecture (**die Vorlesung, -en**).

| **Im Seminar** haben wir einen sehr schweren Text behandelt. | *In class (i.e., a small, interactive class session) we dealt with a very difficult text.* |

| Heute war **die Vorlesung** aber komplett für die Füße. | *Class (i.e., a lecture-style presentation) today was totally useless. (lit.: "for the feet")* |

Beginning with the final years of secondary school and through the university program, **der Kurs, -e** is sometimes used to refer to a particular class (as a whole) and to identify the participants in it: **der Mathekurs; der Kursteilnehmer, -/die Kursteilnehmerin, -nen**.

Übungen

A **Die schwere Prüfung.**   Schreiben Sie die Sätze um. Setzen Sie das fett gedruckte Element an erste Stelle.

BEISPIEL   Wir haben **gestern** eine schwere Prüfung geschrieben.
Gestern haben wir eine schwere Prüfung geschrieben.

1. Schwere Fragen waren **in der Prüfung**.
2. Die Studenten konnten **die meisten dieser Fragen** nicht beantworten.
3. Die Professorin war **darüber** schwer enttäuscht.

4. Die Professorin hatte betont, **dass man das Material gut lernen sollte**.
5. Am Tag vor der Prüfung hatte die Professorin alles noch einmal **zusammengefasst**.
6. Ihre Studenten hatten allerdings *(certainly)* **etwas** gelernt.
7. Sie hatten **aber** einige wichtige Punkte nicht verstanden.
8. Jetzt wusste die Professorin, **dass sie die Lektion würde wiederholen müssen**.

B Antworten auf Fragen.   Beantworten Sie die folgenden Fragen. Stellen Sie die erwünschte Information an den Anfang Ihrer Antwort.

BEISPIEL   Wie alt sind Sie jetzt?
Achtzehn Jahre alt bin ich jetzt.

1. Seit wann lernen Sie Deutsch?
2. Wo wohnen Sie jetzt?
3. An welchen Tagen haben Sie einen Deutschkurs?
4. Was für Musik hören Sie besonders gern oder ungern?
5. Was werden Sie heute Abend nach dem Essen tun?   (z.B. lesen, fern·sehen, ein wenig schlafen usw.)

C Ein schöner Nachmittag.   Bilden Sie die Sätze um, aber ohne das Akkusativobjekt an den Anfang des Satzes zu stellen.

BEISPIEL   Am Vormittag machte Melanie einige Einkäufe im Kaufhaus.
Am Vormittag machte Melanie im Kaufhaus einige Einkäufe.

1. Am Nachmittag traf Melanie eine Freundin in der Stadt.
2. Sie entschlossen sich *(decided)* einen Spaziergang im Park zu machen.
3. Nach einer Weile machte Melanie den Vorschlag, irgendwo Kaffee zu trinken.
4. Im Park fanden sie einen gemütlichen Gartenpavillon.
5. Dort bestellten sie Kaffee und verschiedene Kuchen.
6. Nach dem Kaffee hat Melanie einen Kurs an der Uni erwähnt *(mentioned)*.
7. Besonders diese Vorlesung wollte sie ihrer Freundin beschreiben.
8. Sie verließen den Park gegen Abend und fuhren nach Hause.

D Fehlende Information.   Ergänzen Sie die Sätze durch die Wörter und Wortverbindungen in Klammern, und erklären Sie, welche Elemente besonders wichtig sind, je nach *(according to)* ihrer Position im Satz.

BEISPIEL   Wir fahren morgen nach Bern.   (mit dem Zug)
Wir fahren morgen mit dem Zug nach Bern.

1. Ich habe viel Zeit.   (heute)
2. Sie gingen mit der Familie.   (gestern; einkaufen)
3. Sie spricht mit anderen Passagieren.   (während der Fahrt)
4. Ich treffe dich.   (in der Stadt; in zwanzig Minuten)
5. Wir haben heute Morgen gelesen.   (mit großem Interesse; die Zeitung)
6. Sie muss heute eine Postkarte schicken.   (ihren Eltern)
7. Er hat vom Live-Konzert in Leipzig erzählt.   (uns)
8. Hat er seiner Freundin den Brief geschrieben? —Ja, er hat geschrieben.   (ihr; ihn)

Anwendung

A **Partnergespräch.** Erzählen Sie jemandem im Kurs Folgendes. Beginnen Sie Ihre Sätze mit der fett gedruckten Information.

was Sie **manchmal** denken
was Sie **in diesem Kurs** lernen möchten
was Sie **besonders gern** tun
was Sie gern tun, **wenn Sie Zeit haben**

was Sie **gestern** ...
was Sie **morgen** ...
usw.

B **Ein Bericht.** Berichten Sie im Kurs, was Sie in Anwendung A über Ihre Partnerin/Ihren Partner erfahren haben.

BEISPIEL *Meine Partnerin heißt Oksana. Manchmal denkt sie, dass Deutsch schwer ist. In diesem Kurs möchte sie mehr sprechen. Besonders gern geht sie abends ins Kino.*

Schriftliche Themen

Tipps zum Schreiben	**Beginning the Sentence**
	In German, using a variety of first-sentence elements is essential for effective writing. While sentence subjects often come first, it is considered good style to use adverbs, prepositional phrases, and subordinate clauses. As a rule, try not to begin more than two or three sentences in a row with the sentence subject. Remember that the first element is not merely a random choice, but a means of highlighting an element or using it to connect the ideas before and after it.

Leipzig: Geschichte einer Stadt. Ändern Sie den folgenden Text stilistisch, damit *(so that)* nicht jeder Satz mit dem Satzsubjekt beginnt.

Leipzig gilt[a] seit dem Herbst 1989 als die Stadt der friedlichen[b] Revolution, in der man den Zusammenbruch[c] des DDR-Sozialismus eingeleitet[d] hat. Die Stadt hat gleichzeitig[e] einen Ruf[f] als Messe[g]- und Buchstadt.

[a]*is considered* [b]*peaceful* [c]*collapse* [d]*began* [e]*at the same time* [f]*reputation* [g]*trade fair*

Johann Sebastian Bach engraved by Friedrich Wilhelm Nettling after Elias Gottlob Haussmann (1695–1774)/Bibliotheque Inguimbertine, Carpentras, France/Giraudon/The Bridgeman Art Library

Die Grundlagen[h] für das moderne Leipzig sind am Ende des Mittelalters zu finden. Martin Luther predigte[i] im Jahre 1539 in der Leipziger Thomaskirche. Es kam im Dreißigjährigen Krieg (1618–1648) um Leipzig herum zweimal zu großen Schlachten[j]. Leipzig erlebte in der Folgezeit[k] seine erste große Blüte[l]. Man las hier schon 1650 die erste Tageszeitung der Welt. Es gibt seit 1678 eine Börse[m] und ein Opernhaus. Johann Sebastian Bach wirkte[n] 1723–1750 an der Thomaskirche als Organist und Kantor. Weitere große Musiker, die aus Leipzig kommen oder hier gewirkt haben, sind Richard Wagner, Felix Mendelssohn Bartoldy, sowie Robert und Clara Schumann. Die Stadt war zu DDR-Zeiten[o] als Sitz der großen Karl-Marx-Universität bekannt. Die Uni besteht[p] noch heute unter einem anderen Namen. Die Stadt ist nach der friedlichen Revolution zu einem wichtigen kulturellen und kommerziellen Zentrum für ganz Deutschland geworden.

---

[h]*beginnings, foundations* [i]*preached* [j]*battles* [k]*ensuing years* [l]*blossoming* [m]*stock exchange* [n]*was engaged, active* [o]*in its GDR days* [p]*exists*

Zusammenfassung

Rules to Remember

1 In main clauses, the conjugated verb (V_1) is the second element.

2 In dependent clauses, the conjugated verb is the final element. **EXCEPTIONS:** In dependent clauses with double infinitive, V_1 comes before a double infinitive; in *if*-clauses where **wenn** is omitted, V_1 comes first.

3 In the middle field, *pronoun* subjects come immediately after the verb. *Noun* subjects can appear after unstressed object pronouns or, if the subject is to be emphasized, after other elements as well.

4 Adverbial modifiers in the middle field take on increasing emphasis the later they appear; the default position has adverbials of manner following other adverbial elements.

5 For direct and indirect noun/pronoun objects in the middle field:
- pronouns precede nouns
- the more emphasized of two noun objects goes to the right of the less emphasized
- direct-object pronouns precede indirect-object pronouns

6 Verbal complements, including "Place/Direction" complements, come at the very end of the middle field.

7 The conjugated verb (V_1) comes first in yes-no questions or immediately after interrogative elements in information questions.

At a Glance

Word order

Main clause				
front field	V_1	*middle field*	V_2	*(final elements)*
subject		pronoun subject/object		
direct object		noun subject/object	modal infinitive	
indirect object		adverbial modifiers	past participle	
adverbial modifier		**nicht**		
past participle		verbal		
modal infinitive		complements		
subordinate clause				

Question				
yes/no:				
V_1	*subject*	*middle field*	V_2	*(final elements)?*
open-ended:				
(interrogative)	V_1	*middle field (including subject)*	V_2	*(final elements)?*

Subordinate clause		
connector	*middle field (including subject)*	V_2 V_1
subordinating conjunction		
relative pronoun		
interrogative conjunction		
		V_1 double infinitive

2
Present tense

zum Beispiel

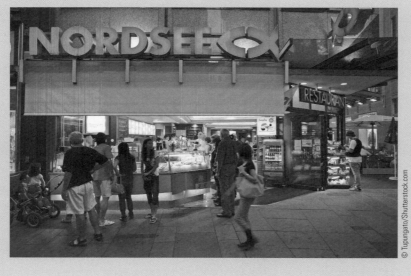

Fastfood

© Tupungato/Shutterstock.com

Fastfood has become a German word: **schnell verzehrbare kleinere Gerichte** (Duden). Anyone traveling in Germany cannot help but notice that McDonald's and Burger King seem to be everywhere; but a closer look shows how they have been adapted in specific ways to German culture. There are numerous German restaurant chains that have emerged as well, such as **Nordsee** and **Vapiano**. Yet the most popular fast food in Germany comes from Turkish immigrants: **Döner**. This consists of pita bread filled with sliced grilled lamb or chicken, lettuce, tomato, and a yogurt-based sauce.

Grammatik

A. Regular verbs

1. Most German verbs form the present tense (**das Präsens**) by dropping the **-en** from the infinitive and adding personal endings to the remaining stem.

Singular	**bestellen** (to order)	**bezahlen** (to pay for)
1st person	ich bestell **e**	ich bezahl **e**
2nd person: familiar	du bestell **st**	du bezahl **st**
2nd person: formal	Sie bestell **en**	Sie bezahl **en**
3rd person	er/sie/es bestell **t**	er/sie/es bezahl **t**
Plural		
1st person	wir bestell **en**	wir bezahl **en**
2nd person: familiar	ihr bestell **t**	ihr bezahl **t**
2nd person: formal	Sie bestell **en**	Sie bezahl **en**
3rd person	sie bestell **en**	sie bezahl **en**

2. Some verb stems require the insertion of an **-e-** between the stem and the personal endings **-t** and **-st** in order to facilitate pronunciation. This is the case with verbs whose stems end in:

   - **-d** or **-t** (such as **finden** or **arbeiten**)
   - **-m** or **-n,** when preceded by a consonant other than **-l-** or **-r-** (such as **atmen,** *to breathe*, or **begegnen,** *to meet*)

arbeiten (to work)		**öffnen** (to open)	
ich arbeit **e**	wir arbeit **en**	ich öffn **e**	wir öffn **en**
du arbeit **est**	ihr arbeit **et**	du öffn **est**	ihr öffn **et**
Sie arbeit **en**	Sie arbeit **en**	Sie öffn **en**	Sie öffn **en**
er/sie/es arbeit **et**	sie arbeit **en**	er/sie/es öffn **et**	sie öffn **en**

Verbs with these stem endings that also *change the stem vowel* when conjugated with **du, er, sie** (sing.), and **es** (see 2.1.B) do not add this extra **-e-,** and in some cases show other irregularities in the second- and third-person singular, as shown below.

Infinitive	ich	du	er/sie/es
gelten [als] (*to be considered*)	gelte	**giltst**	**gilt**
halten (*to stop, hold*)	halte	**hältst**	**hält**

laden (*to load*)	lade	**lädst**	**lädt**
raten (*to advise*)	rate	**rätst**	**rät**
treten (*to step*)	trete	**trittst**	**tritt**

3. A relatively small number of infinitives end with **-ern, -eln,** or a long vowel (other than **e**) plus **-n.** The stem of these verbs is formed by dropping the final **-n.** The verbs are conjugated by adding the usual personal endings to the stem, except that the **-en** ending is reduced to **-n.** With **-eln** verbs, the **-e-** preceding the first-person singular ending is optional.

ärgern (*to annoy, bother*)	**sammeln** (*to collect*)	**tun** (*to do*)
ich ärgere	ich **samm(e)le**	ich tue
du ärgerst	du sammelst	du tust
Sie **ärgern**	Sie **sammeln**	Sie **tun**
er/sie/es ärgert	er/sie/es sammelt	er/sie/es tut
wir **ärgern**	wir **sammeln**	wir **tun**
ihr ärgert	ihr sammelt	ihr tut
Sie **ärgern**	Sie **sammeln**	Sie tun
sie **ärgern**	sie **sammeln**	sie **tun**

4. If the verb stem ends in a sibilant (**-s, -ss, -ß, -tz, -x, -z**), the **s** of the second-person singular **-st** ending is absorbed into the preceding sibilant.

reisen (*to travel*)	**grüßen** (*to greet*)	**sitzen** (*to sit*)	**faxen** (*to send a fax*)
du reist	du grü**ßt**	du sit**zt**	du fa**xt**

B. Verbs with stem-vowel shifts

1. Some strong verbs (see 3.1) change a stem vowel **e** to **i** in the second- and third-person singular. (See Appendix 3 for a complete listing.)

brechen (*to break*)	
ich breche	wir brechen
du **brichst**	ihr brecht
Sie brechen	Sie brechen
er/sie/es **bricht**	sie brechen

Other common e → i verbs

Infinitive	du	er/sie/es
essen (*to eat*)	isst	isst
geben (*to give*)	gibst	gibt
gelten [als] (*to be considered*)	giltst	gilt

helfen *(to help)*	hilfst	hilft
nehmen *(to take)*	nimmst[1]	nimmt[1]
sprechen *(to speak)*	sprichst	spricht
sterben *(to die)*	stirbst	stirbt
treffen *(to meet)*	triffst	trifft
treten *(to step; to kick)*	trittst[1]	tritt[1]
vergessen *(to forget)*	vergisst	vergisst
werfen *(to throw)*	wirfst	wirft

2. Some strong verbs change a stem vowel **e** to **ie** in the second- and third-person singular.

sehen *(to see)*	
ich sehe	wir sehen
du **siehst**	ihr seht
Sie sehen	Sie sehen
er/sie/es **sieht**	sie sehen

Other common e → ie verbs

Infinitive	du	er/sie/es
befehlen *(to command)*	befiehlst	befiehlt
empfehlen *(to recommend)*	empfiehlst	empfiehlt
geschehen *(to happen)*	_____	es geschieht
lesen *(to read)*	liest	liest
stehlen *(to steal)*	stiehlst	stiehlt

3. Some strong verbs change a stem vowel **a** to **ä** in the second- and third-person singular.

fahren *(to drive, ride)*	
ich fahre	wir fahren
du **fährst**	ihr fahrt
Sie fahren	Sie fahren
er/sie/es **fährt**	sie fahren

Other common a → ä verbs

Infinitive	du	er/sie/es
an·fangen *(to begin)*	fängst an	fängt an
ein·laden *(to invite)*	lädst ein	lädt ein
fallen *(to fall)*	fällst	fällt
fangen *(to catch)*	fängst	fängt
gefallen *(to please)*	gefällst	gefällt

[1]Notice the additional consonant change.

halten *(to hold)*	hältst	hält
lassen *(to let; to leave)*	lässt	lässt
schlafen *(to sleep)*	schläfst	schläft
schlagen *(to hit, beat)*	schlägst	schlägt
tragen *(to carry; to wear)*	trägst	trägt
wachsen *(to grow)*	wächst	wächst
waschen *(to wash)*	wäschst	wäscht

4. Several strong verbs change their stem vowels as follows:

Infinitive	**du**	**er/sie/es**
laufen *(to run)*	läufst	läuft
saufen *(to drink, guzzle)*	säufst	säuft
gebären *(to give birth)*	gebierst	gebiert
stoßen *(to push, bump)*	stößt	stößt
erlöschen *(to go out [light, fire])*	erlischst	erlischt

C. Auxiliary verbs

The following frequently used verbs conjugate irregularly in the present tense.

sein *(to be)*	**haben** *(to have)*	**werden** *(to become)*
ich **bin**	ich habe	ich werde
du **bist**	du **hast**	du **wirst**
Sie **sind**	Sie haben	Sie werden
er/sie/es **ist**	er/sie/es **hat**	er/sie/es **wird**
wir **sind**	wir haben	wir werden
ihr **seid**	ihr habt	ihr werdet
Sie **sind**	Sie haben	Sie werden
sie **sind**	sie haben	sie werden

D. *Wissen* and the modal verbs

Wissen *(to know;* see **Wortschatz**, this chapter) and modal verbs such as **wollen, müssen,** and **können** have similar irregular conjugations in the present tense. The full conjugation in the present tense is given below for **wissen**; notice that the vowel change applies to all singular forms, and that the first- and third-person singular forms are identical.

wissen *(to know)*	
ich **weiß**	wir wissen
du **weißt**	ihr wisst
Sie wissen	Sie wissen
er/sie/es **weiß**	sie wissen

Modal verbs follow the same pattern of conjugation; they are discussed in detail in Chapter 9.

E. Prefix verbs

1. Verbs with the inseparable prefixes **be-**, **emp-**, **ent-**, **er-**, **ge-**, **miss-**, **ver-**, and **zer-** (see R.5.2) conjugate in the present tense just like their root verbs.

   COMPARE:

Er **stellt** die Cola aufs Tablett.	*He places the cola on the serving tray.*
Sie **bestellt** einen Big Mac.	*She orders a Big Mac.*

2. Verbs with separable prefixes (**an-**, **aus-**, **fort-**, **mit-**, **weg-**, etc.) conjugate just like their root verbs, but in the present and simple past tenses the prefix separates from the stem and moves to the end of the middle field (see 1.1.C and R.5.1).

Man **sieht** immer mehr Fastfood-Ketten in der Stadtmitte.	*You see more and more fast-food chains in the city center.*
Er **sieht** sich die Speisekarte **an**.	*He's looking at the menu.*

3. A separable prefix attaches to its root verb in a subordinate clause.

Ich frage mich, warum er sich die Speisekarte überhaupt **ansieht**.	*I wonder why he bothers to look at the menu at all.*

2.2   USES OF THE PRESENT TENSE

A. Present time

German has only one form to express the three aspects available in English for the present tense:

ich schreibe
- *I write* (present)
- *I am writing* (present progressive)
- *I do write* (present emphatic)

B. Continuing past actions

Unlike English, German uses the present tense with certain adverbial elements to express the idea of an action, process, or state that *began* in the past but *is still continuing* in the present. Thus a present tense German verb, in conjunction with any of the elements shown here

- the adverb **schon** + a time expression in the accusative

- the preposition **seit** + dative (see 6.3.I)

- **schon seit** + dative

expresses the idea in English of *have been _____ing* or *have* + past participle, with the duration or starting point expressed with *for* or *since*.

Die Kunden **warten** schon ***drei Stunden*** auf die Eröffnung des neuen Vapiano[2].	*The customers have been waiting (for) three hours for the opening of the new Vapiano.*
Ein Döner[3]-Imbiss **steht** *seit* zehn Jahren da.	*A "döner" takeaway has been there for ten years.*
Die „Nordsee"-Kette **serviert** Sushi ***schon seit*** 2006.	*The "Nordsee" (=North Sea) chain has been serving sushi since 2006.*

NOTE: German uses **haben** + the past participle to denote an action that *is no longer occurring* (see 3.2):

Die Kunden **haben** drei Stunden auf die Eröffnung **gewartet**.	*The customers waited three hours for the opening (but are no longer doing so).*
Ein Döner-Imbiss **hat** zehn Jahre dort **gestanden**.	*A "döner" takeaway was there for ten years (but now it's gone).*
Vor 2006 **hat** die „Nordsee"-Kette nur gebratenen Fisch **serviert**.	*Before 2006, the "Nordsee" chain sold only fried fish (but that's no longer the case).*

C. Narration

The present tense is used frequently when recounting jokes, episodes, and plots of films or books, even though the context is clearly past time.

Gestern habe ich einen Witz gehört, der geht so: Da sitzen zwei Männer in einem McDonald's, der eine aus München und der andere aus Hamburg. Fragt der Münchner den Hamburger: „Sagen Sie mal, Sie kommen aus Hamburg, oder? Heißt das etwa, dass …?"	*I heard a joke yesterday that goes like this. Two guys are sitting in a McDonald's, one of them from Munich and the other from Hamburg. The guy from Munich asks the fellow from Hamburg, "Say, you're from Hamburg, right? Does that mean …?"*

D. Future time

As in English, the German present tense can be used to indicate what someone *is doing* or *is going to do* in the future, provided that the discourse context or an adverb of time makes the time reference clear (see 24.1.B).

Wir **gehen** *morgen* einkaufen.	*We're going (to go) shopping tomorrow.*

In fact, German uses the present tense far more often than English to refer to the future. Many situations that require a future form in English are more colloquially correct in the present tense in German:

Wir sprechen später darüber.	*We**'ll** talk about it later.*

---

[2]**Vapiano** is a popular restaurant chain that started in Hamburg, Germany, in 2002. It offers reasonably priced, freshly made-to-order Italian cuisine (think Chipotle, but Italian, and more upscale and trendy in design).

[3]**Döner** is a shortened form of **döner-kebab**, a Turkish dish made from seasoned meat (usually beef, lamb, or chicken) cut from a revolving vertical rotisserie and wrapped in flatbread with lettuce, tomatoes and a sauce—something like a Greek "gyros." It has become Germany's most popular fast food.

Wortschatz
kennen | wissen

The verbs **kennen** and **wissen** provide a helpful contrast both in their conjugation patterns (regular as opposed to irregular), and in the range of meanings they express with regard to *"knowing."*

	kennen *(to know, be acquainted with)*	**wissen** *(to know)*
ich	kenne	**weiß**
du	kennst	**weißt**
Sie	kennen	wissen
er/sie/es	kennt	**weiß**
wir	kennen	wissen
ihr	kennt	wisst
Sie	kennen	wissen
sie	kennen	wissen

1. The verb **kennen** expresses knowledge or familiarity with someone or something. It is often used to express the English sense of *being acquainted with*:

   Kennst du die Leute da drüben? — *Do you know the people over there?*

   Ich **kenne** die französische Küche nicht besonders gut. — *I'm not particularly well acquainted with French cuisine.*

   Kennen is also used to denote knowledge of discrete bits of knowledge, such as telephone numbers, names, ages, and the like.

   Kennst du seine Adresse? — *Do you know his address?*

   —Nein, ich **kenne** nur seine Handy-Nummer. — *No, I only know his cell-phone number.*

2. The verb **wissen** also means *to know*, but *to know something as a fact*. It can never be used in the sense of knowing persons.

   Sie **weiß** die Antworten. — *She knows the answers.*

   Meine Freunde **wissen** viel über Musik. — *My friends know a lot about music.*

   Wissen can overlap with **kennen** in expressing knowledge of discrete bits of information.

   Weißt du seine Adresse?
   —Nein, ich **weiß** nur seine Handy-Nummer.

Wissen is used to introduce subordinate clauses, particularly indirect questions. **Kennen** is never used to introduce a subordinate clause.

Ich **weiß** nicht, wie du das essen kannst.	*I don't know how you can eat that.*
Weißt du, wo sie wohnt?	*Do you know where she lives?*

3. Neither **wissen** nor **kennen** can express *know* in the English sense of *knowing a language*; rather, the modal verb **können** takes on this meaning.

Kannst du Schwedisch?	*Do you know Swedish (i.e., can you speak/understand/read it)?*
—Nein, ich **kann** nur Deutsch und Englisch.	*No, I only know German and English.*

4. To express the idea *I know how to (do something)*, German uses one of two paraphrases: either an alternate version with **können**, particularly in straightforward questions, or a rephrasing of the idea with a clause using **man**.

Do you know how to cook?	**Kannst** du kochen?
I don't know how to help you.	Ich **kann** dir nicht helfen. Ich **weiß** nicht, wie **man** dir helfen soll.

Lerntipps	**Learning Words in Context**
	It may help you to retain new vocabulary terms if you associate them with words relating to a context. As you learn a new verb, associate two or three logical objects or verbal complements that combine with it meaningfully. For example: **an·kommen** *(to arrive):* am Bahnhof / mit Freunden / zu spät **OR:** **schreiben** *(to write):* eine E-Mail / einen Tweet / an Freunde

---

Übungen

A **In der Familie.**   Wer tut was?

BEISPIEL   kochen   (Vater)
         *Vater **kocht.***

1. manchmal fern·sehen   (die Mutter)
2. in einem Büro arbeiten   (der Vater)
3. Sport treiben   (die ältere Schwester)
4. stundenlang chatten   (die jüngere Schwester)
5. Gitarre spielen   (ich)
6. Feste feiern   (alle in der Familie)
7. viel über Politik reden *(talk)*   (der Onkel)

8. Videos illegal herunter·laden (*download*)   (der Bruder)
9. Bierdeckel (*beer coasters*) sammeln   (ich; die Tante)
10. verrückte (*crazy*) Dinge tun   (die Großeltern)
11. Bad und Toilette putzen   (niemand)
12. alles über die Nachbarn wissen   (die Mutter)

B **Immer zu viel oder zu wenig.** Thomas kritisiert alle Leute, die er kennt. Was sagt er zu diesen Personen?

BEISPIELE   zu seinem Vater: Taschengeld geben
„Papa, du gibst mir zu wenig Taschengeld."

zu seinen Eltern: arbeiten
„Liebe Eltern, ihr arbeitet zu viel."

1. zu seiner Mama: sein Zimmer nicht oft genug putzen
2. zu seinen Eltern: langweilige Ideen fürs Wochenende haben
3. zu seinem Freund Julian: Zeit verschwenden (*to waste time*)
4. zum Haushund: zu viel fressen
5. zu seiner Freundin: herum·sitzen und nichts tun
6. zu seinen Nachbarn: zu laut sein
7. zu seinen Mitspielern in der Fußballmannschaft: faul sein
8. zu seinen Lehrern: zu viele Hausaufgaben aufgeben

C **Einiges über andere.** Sie möchten einiges über andere Studenten im Kurs erfahren. Stellen Sie Fragen mit den folgenden Verben. Berichten Sie dann über die Antworten.

BEISPIELE   schlafen
*Wie lange **schläfst** du gewöhnlich?*

essen
*Was **isst** du gern[4] zum Frühstück?*

1. schlafen
2. essen
3. studieren
4. Kleidung ein·kaufen
5. tragen
6. sprechen
7. lesen
8. wissen (+ über)
9. auf Facebook sein
10. kennen

D **Einiges über Sie.** Bilden Sie mit den folgenden Verben Aussagen über sich selbst und andere Mitglieder (*members*) Ihrer Familie. Passen Sie bei den Präfixverben besonders gut auf!

BEISPIELE   ausgehen
*Ich **gehe** am Wochenende oft mit Freunden **aus**.*

verstehen
*Meine Eltern **verstehen** mich oft nicht.*

1. aus·geben (*to spend money*)
2. studieren

---

[4]For the use of **gern**, see Chapter 9, **Wortschatz**.

   3. fern·sehen
   4. helfen
   5. an·rufen
   6. verbringen *(to spend time)*
   7. fahren
   8. lernen

E **Wie lange schon?**   Erzählen Sie, wie lange/seit wann Sie Folgendes tun.

   BEISPIEL   Tennis spielen
   Ich spiele (schon) seit fünf Jahren Tennis.

   1. Deutsch lernen
   2. [eine Fremdsprache] können
   3. Auto fahren
   4. etwas besonders Interessantes tun
   5. [Freund/Freundin] kennen
   6. [noch eine Aktivität]

F **Welches Verb passt?**   Sagen Sie, ob Sie Folgendes **wissen, kennen** oder **können**.

   BEISPIELE   die Stadt Hamburg
   *Nein, die Stadt Hamburg **kenne** ich nicht.*

   wann Goethe gelebt hat
   *Ja, ich **weiß**, wann Goethe gelebt hat.*

   1. jemanden, der in Berlin wohnt
   2. das Geburtsjahr von Beethoven
   3. wann der Zweite Weltkrieg begonnen hat
   4. alle europäischen Länder, in denen man Deutsch spricht
   5. etwas Interessantes über die Schweiz
   6. den Namen Ihres Urgroßvaters
   7. das Alter *(age)* Ihres Deutschlehrers/Ihrer Deutschlehrerin
   8. eine andere Fremdsprache außer Deutsch

G **Die Stadt, in der ich jetzt wohne.**   Was **wissen** Sie über die Stadt, in der Sie jetzt wohnen? Was **kennen** Sie in dieser Stadt besonders gut? Machen Sie ein paar Aussagen mit jedem Verb.

Anwendung

A **Pläne für das Wochenende.**   Sprechen Sie mit jemandem im Kurs über Ihre Pläne für das kommende Wochenende. Verwenden Sie das Präsens.

REDEMITTEL

Das weiß ich noch nicht so genau.
Wahrscheinlich stehe ich am Samstag ... auf.
Zu Mittag esse ich ...
Am Nachmittag muss ich ...
Ich gehe dann am Abend ...
Und was hast *du* am Wochenende vor *(vor·haben: have in mind, intend to do)*?

B **Sich vorstellen und andere kennenlernen.** Erzählen Sie jemandem im Kurs von Ihren Hobbys, Interessen und Freizeitbeschäftigungen *(leisure time activities)*. Was tun Sie gern? Was tun Sie nicht so gern? Was tun Sie gern mit anderen Menschen zusammen? Merken Sie sich *(take note)*, was Ihre Partnerin/Ihr Partner erzählt (siehe **schriftliches Thema A**).

THEMEN- UND VOKABELVORSCHLÄGE

viel Sport treiben (z.B. Tennis, Golf, Fußball, Basketball spielen)
Rad fahren
angeln *(to fish)*
joggen gehen
reiten *(to go horseback riding)*
segeln *(to sail)*
inline·skaten
Musik hören
[musikalisches Instrument] spielen
sammeln (z.B. Briefmarken, Münzen, Sammelbilder von Sportlern)
fotografieren
Fitnesstraining machen
lesen (z.B. Bücher, Zeitungen, Zeitschriften)
auf Facebook herum·surfen
mit Freunden chatten/simsen (SMS senden)
mit Freunden zusammen etwas unternehmen, z.B. ein·kaufen gehen, ins Kino gehen,
    Videospiele/Brettspiele *(board games)*/Karten/Schach *(chess)*/Scrabble spielen

REDEMITTEL

Weißt du, was mir (besonders/echt) viel Spaß macht?
Ich [lese] besonders gern ...
Am liebsten [gehe] ich ... *(Most of all I like to [go] . . .)*
Mit guten Freunden ...
Abends gehe ich manchmal ...
Wenn ich viel Zeit habe, dann [fahre] ich ...

C   **Wo ich mich gern aufhalte *(spend time)*.**   Erzählen Sie anderen Studenten von einem Ort *(place)*, der Ihnen besonders gefällt. Erklären Sie, warum Sie diesen Ort so gern besuchen. Was gibt es dort? Was tut man dort?

THEMENVORSCHLÄGE

der/ein Strand *(beach)*
das/ein Café
der/ein Park
die/eine Bibliothek
das/ein Geschäft
das/ein Einkaufszentrum
zu Hause bei einem Freund

REDEMITTEL

Ich finde … ganz toll/super
Weißt du, was mir so daran gefällt?
Viele Leute kommen …
Dort sieht man auch, wie …
Manchmal gibt es …
Da findet man …
Besonders gut gefällt/gefallen mir … (+ *nominative*)

Schriftliche Themen

Tipps zum Schreiben

Using Familiar Words and Structures

Instead of translating English ideas directly into German with a string of new vocabulary items, try to use the words and grammatical structures you already know. Jot down your ideas in German, then look up a few words in a dictionary if necessary. To avoid misuse, cross-check the meaning of these words in German as well as in English. Avoid overusing **haben** and **sein**, when a specific verb will describe an activity more precisely. Try not to repeat words or idioms too often, unless you wish to emphasize a particular activity through repetition. A good variety of structures and vocabulary will make your writing more interesting.

A **Darf ich vorstellen?** Stellen Sie jemanden im Kurs schriftlich vor. Geben Sie Alter und Wohnort an. Erzählen Sie unter anderem *(among other things)* von ihren/seinen Hobbys, Interessen und Freizeitbeschäftigungen.

BEISPIEL *Christian ist 20 Jahre alt und kommt aus ... Im Sommer arbeitet er als Jugendberater* (youth counselor) *in einem Sportklub. Wenn er Zeit hat, segelt er gern mit seinen Freunden ... Abends gehen er und seine Freunde oft ... Seine Lieblingsband ist ... Später möchte er ... usw.*

B **Ein Arbeitstag.** Wie stellen Sie sich *(imagine)* einen Tag im Leben Ihrer Deutschlehrerin/Deutschprofessorin oder Ihres Deutschlehrers/Deutschprofessors vor? Erzählen Sie davon.

BEISPIEL *Meine Deutschprofessorin arbeitet sehr viel. Jeden Morgen fährt sie schon kurz nach acht Uhr zur Universität, wo sie zwei Stunden unterrichtet. Danach macht sie Mittagspause und isst oft in der Mensa. Am Nachmittag hat sie Sprechstunde und manchmal nimmt sie an einer Arbeitssitzung mit Kollegen teil. Wenn sie abends nach Hause kommt, ... usw.*

C **Alltägliche Menschen, alltägliches Leben.** Schildern Sie *(portray)* kurz die Arbeit oder den Tag eines Menschen, der mit seiner Arbeit zu unserem alltäglichen Leben gehört (z.B. die Busfahrerin, der Briefträger, der Verkäufer/die Verkäuferin im Geschäft, wo Sie sich manchmal etwas Kleines zum Essen holen usw.).

BEISPIEL der Schülerlotse *(school crossing guard)*
Jeden Morgen sieht man ihn an der Ecke stehen. Wenn die Schüler kommen, hält er die Autos an und die Schüler gehen über die Straße. An kalten Wintertagen hofft er, dass die letzten Schüler bald kommen. Er denkt oft (daran), dass er auch einmal klein war und ... Manchmal träumt er von ... usw.

Zusammenfassung

Rules to Remember

1 Conjugated verbs agree with their grammatical subjects in person and in number.

2 German has only one set of present-tense forms to express present, present progressive, and present emphatic.

3 When contextual cues refer to the future, e.g., *next week,* German usually prefers the present tense over the grammatical future tense.

At a Glance

Present-tense verb endings	
ich ___e	wir ___en
du ___(e)st	ihr ___(e)t
Sie ___en	Sie ___en
er/sie/es ___(e)t	sie ___en

Stem-vowel shifts
e → i
ich gebe → du gibst
e → ie
ich sehe → du siehst
a → ä
ich trage → du trägst
au → äu
ich laufe → du läufst

Auxiliary verbs and *wissen*			
sein	**haben**	**werden**	**wissen**
ich **bin**	habe	werde	**weiß**
du **bist**	**hast**	**wirst**	**weißt**
Sie **sind**	haben	werden	wissen
er/sie/es **ist**	**hat**	**wird**	**weiß**
wir **sind**	haben	werden	wissen
ihr **seid**	habt	werdet	wisst
Sie **sind**	haben	werden	wissen
sie **sind**	haben	werden	wissen

Present perfect tense

zum Beispiel

Wetten, dass…?

Arnd Wegmann/Getty Images

Wetten, dass…? (*Wanna bet?*) is a television show which in its heyday was the most popular TV entertainment in German-speaking Europe. The format is a hybrid of talk show and stunt show: People are brought in who claim they can do various oddball stunts (physical and mental), and an entertainment star (often from the USA) bets that they can (or cannot) pull them off. The stunts are attempted, and if the celebrity loses the bet, the stunt performers decide what the "punishment" will be. Hilarity ensues, overseen by a talkative MC—most notably Thomas Gottschalk, who successfully presided over the show for almost 20 years, until 2011, when a stunt performer was critically injured on live TV. Gottschalk left the show, and its status as a staple of German TV entertainment has been in flux ever since.

Grammatik

As in English, every German verb has three basic forms (often referred to as the "principal parts" of the verb), which can combine and change in various ways to form all tenses, voices, and moods of the verb.

- Infinitive   *do*   tun
- Simple past   *did*   tat
- Past participle *done*   getan

German verbs are classified as weak, strong, or irregular, depending on how they form their second (simple past) and third (past participle) part. With very few exceptions, these categories cannot be determined simply by looking at the infinitive itself, which makes it necessary to learn this along with the meaning(s) of the verb. **LEARNING STRATEGY:** Since most verbs are weak, learning the relatively shorter list of strong and irregular verbs will help you to recognize weak verbs by elimination.

A. Weak verbs

1. A weak verb forms the simple past with the insertion of a **-t-** before the personal ending, and its past participle by adding an unstressed **ge-** prefix and the ending **-t** to the infinitive stem. This characteristic, analogous to the *-ed* suffix in English, leads some grammar books to refer to it as a *t-verb*.

Infinitive	Simple past[1]	Past participle
lernen *(to learn)*	lernte	gelernt
tanzen *(to dance)*	tanzte	getanzt
reisen *(to travel)*	reiste	ist[2] gereist

2. Some weak verbs require the insertion of an **-e-** between the stem and the simple past ending, and between the stem and the final **-t** of the past participle in order to facilitate pronunciation (see 2.1.A). This is the case for verbs whose stems end in **-d** or **-t**, or in **-m** or **-n** preceded by a consonant other than **-l-** or **-r-**.

---

[1]Although this chapter focuses on past participles, it lists the simple past forms as well, since the principal parts of a verb are best learned together. Formation and use of the simple past tense is presented in Chapter 8.

[2]An **ist** before the past participle in tables and lists (see also Appendix 3) indicates that the present perfect tense is formed with the auxiliary verb **sein** instead of **haben** (see 3.2).

Infinitive	Simple past	Past participle
arbeiten *(to work)*	arbeitete	gearbeitet
atmen *(to breathe)*	atmete	geatmet
öffnen *(to open)*	öffnete	geöffnet

3. Verbs ending in **-ieren** are usually weak. (**EXCEPTION:** **frieren** *(to freeze)*: **fror, gefroren.**) If an infinitive ending in **-ieren** has more than two syllables, it does not take a **ge-** prefix in the past participle.

Infinitive	Simple past	Past participle
diskutieren *(to discuss)*	diskutierte	**diskutiert**
faszinieren *(to fascinate)*	faszinierte	**fasziniert**
studieren *(to study)*	studierte	**studiert**

BUT:

zieren *(to adorn, decorate)*	zierte	**geziert**

B. Strong verbs

1. The past participle of a strong verb, like that of weak verb, typically begins with an unstressed **ge-** prefix but always ends with **-n** rather than **-t**. (These are sometimes called *n-verbs*). A strong verb changes its stem vowel in the simple past form, and often in the past participle as well. While strong verbs are not as numerous as weak verbs in German, they denote common activities (**essen, trinken, sprechen, gehen, schlafen**) and therefore occur frequently in both spoken and written language. Their principal parts should be memorized. (See Appendix 3 for a more comprehensive list of strong verbs.)

Infinitive	Simple past	Past participle
beißen *(to bite)*	biss *(bit)*	gebissen *(bitten)*
fliegen *(to fly)*	flog *(flew)*	ist geflogen *(flown)*
geben *(to give)*	gab *(gave)*	gegeben *(given)*
singen *(to sing)*	sang *(sang)*	ist/hat gesungen *(sung)*

2. **Sein** and **werden** are strong verbs.

Infinitive	Simple past	Past participle
sein *(to be)*	war *(was)*	ist gewesen *(been)*
werden *(to become)*	wurde *(became)*	ist geworden *(become)*

3. Strong verbs may seem to change randomly in their simple past and past participles, but in most cases the vowel shifts follow a relatively small number of patterns. The following verb groups, for example, follow the patterns **i – a – u** and **e – a – e** respectively.

Infinitive	Simple past	Past participle
finden (to find)	fand (found)	gefunden (found)
springen (to jump)	sprang (jumped)	ist gesprungen (jumped)
trinken (to drink)	trank (drank)	getrunken (drunk)
zwingen (to force)	zwang (forced)	gezwungen (forced)
essen (to eat)	aß (ate)	gegessen (eaten)
lesen (to read)	las (read)	gelesen (read)
sehen (to see)	sah (saw)	gesehen (seen)
treten (to step)	trat (stepped)	ist/hat getreten (stepped)

Other recurring patterns:

a – ie – a	schlafen (to sleep)	schlief (slept)	geschlafen (slept)
a – u – a	fahren (to drive)	fuhr (drove)	ist[3] gefahren (driven)
e – o – o	heben (to lift)	hob (lifted)	gehoben (lifted)
ie – o – o	schieben (to push)	schob (pushed)	geschoben (pushed)
ei – i – i	beißen (to bite)	biss (bit)	gebissen (bitten)
ei – ie – ie	schreiben (to write)	schrieb (wrote)	geschrieben (written)

C. Irregular verbs

1. **Haben** is irregular in its simple past form.

Infinitive	Simple past	Past participle
haben (to have)	**hatte**	gehabt

2. A small number of verbs show both strong and weak characteristics. In their simple past forms and past participles they require a stem vowel change (strong); but the simple past forms include a -**t**- in the personal ending and the past participle ends with -**t** (weak). These are often called *irregular weak* or *mixed* verbs.

Infinitive	Simple past	Infinitive
brennen (to burn)	brannte	gebrannt
kennen (to know)	kannte	gekannt
nennen (to name)	nannte	genannt
rennen (to run)	rannte	ist gerannt
wissen (to know)	wusste	gewusst

3. Two irregular verbs show consonant changes as well.

Infinitive	Simple past	Past participle
bringen (to bring)	brachte	gebracht
denken (to think)	dachte	gedacht

---

[3]Depending on whether **fahren** takes a direct object or not, the auxiliary is **haben** or **sein**—but in actual usage, **sein** is more common.

4. Two verbs have interchangeable regular and irregular forms.[4]

Infinitive	Simple past	Past participle
senden *(to send)*	sendete/sandte	gesendet/gesandt
wenden *(to turn)*	wendete/wandte	gewendet/gewandt

5. A few strong verbs are irregular in that they show consonant, as well as vowel changes.

Infinitive	Simple past	Past participle
gehen *(to go)*	**ging**	ist ge**gang**en
nehmen *(to take)*	**nahm**	ge**nomm**en
stehen *(to stand)*	**stand**	ge**stand**en
tun *(to do)*	**tat**	get**an**

6. A small number of verbs are "mixed" in the sense that the simple past is formed as a "t-verb" while the past participle is formed like an "n-verb." In some cases, you may encounter weak and strong forms in the past participle, depending on regional dialects and era of literary usage.

Infinitive	Simple past	Past participle
backen (*to bake*)	backte	gebackt/gebacken
hauen (*to hit, cut, chop*)	haute	gehaut/gehauen
mahlen (*to grind, mill*)	mahlte	gemahlen

7. Modal verbs are also irregular in their past tense forms, as discussed in Chapter 9.

D. Prefix verbs

1. Verbs with *separable* prefixes (see R.5.1) insert **-ge-** between the separable prefix and the root verb to form the past participle. Separable prefixes can occur with weak, irregular, or strong verbs.

---

[4]The regular forms (**sendete, gesendet**) tend to be more literal, while the irregular forms (**sandte, gesandt**) can convey a metaphorical touch. The forms **sandte, gesandt,** for example, come across as slightly religious (as in the phrase **in die Welt** *gesandt*); but to express *to broadcast on radio or TV,* the weak forms of **senden** (**sendete, gesendet**) are used. Similarly, the weak forms of **wenden** mean *to turn over, inside out,* or *in the opposite direction,* while the participle **gewandt** can also mean *deft, adroitly,* and *suave,* that is, the irregular form takes on extended meanings beyond the concrete sense of *to turn.* Notice this usage in the examples below.

Übers Wochenende hat CNN Live-Bilder von der Katastrophe **gesendet.**	*Over the weekend CNN broadcast live pictures of the catastrophe.*
Zum Geburtstag hat sie mir einen Facebook-Gruß **gesendet/gesandt.**	*On my birthday she sent me a Facebook greeting.*
Ich habe das Blatt **gewendet** und schrieb dann weiter.	*I turned the page over and then continued writing.*
„Warum hast du dich nicht an uns **gewandt/gewendet?**" fragten die Eltern.	*"Why didn't you turn to us (for help)?" asked the parents.*

Infinitive	Simple past	Past participle
aus·atmen *(to exhale)*	atmete aus	aus**ge**atmet *(weak)*
ab·brennen *(to burn down)*	brannte ab	ab**ge**brannt *(irregular)*
mit·nehmen *(to take along)*	nahm mit	mit**ge**nommen *(strong)*

2. Verbs with the *inseparable* prefixes **be-, emp-, ent-, er-, ge-, miss-, ver-,** and **zer-** (see R.5.2) do not add **ge-** to form the past participle, since the participle already begins with an unstressed prefix. Inseparable prefixes can also occur with weak, irregular, or strong verbs.

Infinitive	Simple past	Past participle
besuchen *(to visit)*	besuchte	**besucht** *(weak)*
erkennen *(to recognize)*	erkannte	**erkannt** *(irregular)*
versprechen *(to promise)*	versprach	**versprochen** *(strong)*

3.2 PRESENT PERFECT TENSE

A. Formation

1. The German present perfect tense (**das Perfekt**) is formed with present-tense forms of **haben** or **sein** (V_1) and the past participle of the main verb (V_2).

haben + *past participle*		**sein** + *past participle*	
ich **habe**		ich **bin**	
du **hast**		du **bist**	
Sie **haben**		Sie **sind**	
er/sie/es **hat**	+ gesehen	er/sie/es **ist**	+ gekommen
wir **haben**		wir **sind**	
ihr **habt**		ihr **seid**	
Sie **haben**		Sie **sind**	
sie **haben**		sie **sind**	

2. As V_2, the past participle stands at the end of the main clause. In dependent clauses, however, the conjugated auxiliary (V_1) moves to final position.

Sie **hat** die Sendung aus Dresden **gesehen.** *(main clause)*	*She saw the show from Dresden.*
Wisst ihr, wer die Wette **gewonnen** <u>**hat?**</u> *(dependent clause)*	*Do you know who won the bet?*

B. *Haben* versus *sein*

1. Most verbs form the present perfect tense with a conjugated form of **haben.** In contexts where the verb takes a direct object or is used with a reflexive pronoun (see Chapter 10), **haben** is mandatory.[5]

Einmal bei *Wetten, dass...?* **hat** sich ein Mann auf den Boden **gelegt.**	*One time on* Wetten, dass . . .?, *a man lay down on the floor.*
Fünfzehn Autos **haben** ihn **überfahren.**	*Fifteen cars drove over him.*
Dabei **hat** er „O sole mio" **gesungen.**	*While that happened, he sang "O sole mio."*
Die Zuschauer **haben** maßlos gestaunt.	*The audience was utterly amazed.*

2. A small but important set of verbs requires **sein** as an auxiliary to form the perfect tense. These verbs are all *intransitive,* that is, they have no direct object in the accusative case (including accusative reflexive pronouns). They can be grouped as follows:

   a. The verbs **sein** and **bleiben:**

Vor einiger Zeit **ist** Tom Hanks als Gast dabei **gewesen.**	*A while ago, Tom Hanks was present as a guest.*
Es hat ihm sichtlich nicht gefallen, aber er **ist** trotzdem bis zum bitteren Ende **geblieben.**	*He obviously didn't enjoy it, but he stayed until the bitter end.*

   b. Verbs expressing motion from one location to another:

Vor ein paar Jahren **ist** ein Schwimmer 25 Meter **geschwommen,** während er eine Tasse Kaffee auf seiner Fußsohle balanciert hat.	*A few years ago, a swimmer swam 25 meters while he balanced a cup of coffee on the sole of his foot.*
Und einmal **ist** ein Mann von einem Heißluftballon in einen zweiten **gesprungen** – aber mit einem Fallschirm.	*And once, a man jumped from one hot air balloon into a second one—but with a parachute.*

   Typical verbs in this category include:

fahren *(to drive, ride)*	ist gefahren	kommen *(to come)*	ist gekommen
fliegen *(to fly)*	ist geflogen	laufen *(to walk, run)*	ist gelaufen
gehen *(to go)*	ist gegangen	reisen *(to travel)*	ist gereist

---

[5]Exceptions: Two verbs that use **sein** to form the present perfect—**werden** and **gehen**—take accusative direct objects when they appear with certain separable prefixes (**los·werden** *to get rid of*; **durch·gehen** *to go through, look over*), yet they still use **sein** when forming the present perfect tense:

Wir **sind** <u>ihn</u> endlich losgeworden!	*We finally got rid of him!*
Ich **bin** <u>diese Zahlen</u> dreimal durchgegangen und kann keine Fehler finden.	*I've gone over these numbers three times and can't find any mistakes.*

c. Verbs expressing a change of state, particularly the beginning or end of a process of change, as the examples below indicate:

Die Shows **sind** immer länger **geworden.**	*The shows have been getting longer and longer.*
Einmal **ist** Paris Hilton kurz vor dem Ende einer Show **erschienen.**	*One time, Paris Hilton appeared just before the end of a show.*
Und dann **ist** sie ohne Kommentar einfach **verschwunden.**	*And then, without saying anything, she just disappeared.*

This category also includes verbs such as:

auf·wachen *(to wake up)*	ist aufgewacht
ein·schlafen *(to fall asleep)*	ist eingeschlafen
sterben *(to die)*	ist gestorben
verschmelzen *(to melt)*	ist verschmolzen

d. Verbs relating to happenings, failure, and success:

passieren	Was **ist** bei der letzten Show **passiert?**	*What happened during the last show?*
vor·kommen	Es **ist** öfter **vorgekommen,** dass etwas schiefgeht.	*It has often happened/occurred that something has gone wrong.*
misslingen	Manche Versuche **sind** völlig **misslungen.**	*Some attempts have failed completely.*
gelingen	Andere **sind** auf erstaunliche Weise **gelungen.**	*Others have succeeded in astonishing ways.*

3. Some verbs of motion can take a direct object and thus take **haben** as the auxiliary (V$_1$). In this case they shift meaning, as shown in the sentence pairs below.

Fünfzehn Autos **sind** tatsächlich über den Mann **gefahren.**	*Fifteen cars actually drove over the man.*
Thomas Gottschalk, der Moderator der Sendung, **hat** keins von den Autos **gefahren,** so weit ich weiß.	*Thomas Gottschalk, the show's host, didn't drive any of the cars, as far as I know.*

4. Similarly, some verbs take on multiple and occasionally unrelated meanings, using **haben** or **sein** accordingly.

bekommen *(to agree with [food])*	**ist** bekommen
bekommen *(to receive, get)*	**hat** bekommen

Der Essig, den der Moderator einmal trinken musste, **ist** ihm bestimmt nicht **bekommen.**	*The vinegar that the host had to drink once certainly **didn't agree** with him.*
Der Mann, der „O sole mio" sang, **hat** einen kräftigen Applaus **bekommen.**	*The man who sang "O sole mio" **received** vigorous applause.*

folgen (*to follow*)	**ist** gefolgt
folgen (*to obey*)	**hat** gefolgt

Der Hund **ist** dem Mann auf die Tribüne **gefolgt.**	*The dog **followed** the man onto the podium.*
Der Hund **hat** dem Befehl des Mannes **gefolgt.**	*The dog **obeyed** the man's command.*

C. Use

1. The present perfect is primarily a *conversational tense* used when referring to actions in the past. It corresponds in meaning to several English forms.

    ich habe ... gehört = *I heard / I was hearing / I did hear / I have heard / I would hear*

2. In many cases, verbs in the present perfect tense (**ich habe ... gehört**) have the same meanings as their simple past tense equivalents (**ich hörte**). The present perfect, however, is used much more frequently in spoken German and in written contexts that mirror spoken speech, such as letters and diaries. (See 8.1.B.)[6]

3. As main verbs, **haben** and **sein** occur more often in the simple past than in the present perfect.

Cher, Madonna und Elton John **waren** öfter dabei.	*Cher, Madonna, and Elton John have been on [the show] quite often.*
Und einmal **hatte** Gottschalk den Schauspieler Hugh Grant als Gast.	*And once, Gottschalk had the actor Hugh Grant as a guest.*

Wortschatz
weil | da | denn

These three words—meaning *because* or *since* and used to introduce clauses that explain or show causality—can be confusing for non-native speakers of German. The following comments point out several distinctions in meaning, use, and the word order required in the clauses they introduce.

1. **weil**

    meaning and use:

    ■ **weil** means *because/since,* and introduces a clause expressing the *cause* of or *reason for* something

---

[6] The present perfect tense is more prevalent in southern Germany, Austria, and Switzerland, whereas in northern Germany the simple past tense is preferred for narration and sometimes even for conversation.

- only a **weil**-clause can stand alone as an answer to a **Warum?**-question
- in spoken (casual) German, a sentence can begin with a **weil**-clause, but in written (formal) German, **weil**-clauses usually follow the main clause, especially if the information in them provides background rather than a strong causal connection

word order:

- **weil** introduces a dependent clause, with V_1 at the end (see 1.3 and R.2.3)

Ich bin gestresst, **weil** ich morgen eine Prüfung **habe.**	*I'm stressed out because I have a test tomorrow.*
A: **Warum** warst du letzte Woche nicht so gestresst?	A: *Why weren't you as stressed out last week?*
B: **Weil** ich weniger Arbeit hatte, natürlich!	B: *Because I had less work, of course!*
Weil ich morgen eine Prüfung habe, bin ich gestresst.	*[It's] Because I have a test tomorrow [that] I'm stressed out.*

2. **da**

meaning and use:

- **da** can also mean *because/since,* but is usually used in written (rather than spoken) German, and therefore has a more formal tone than **weil**
- when a **da**-clause comes first in the sentence, its function is to provide *background* or *context* for what follows in the subsequent clause, as in *Since . . . / Seeing as . . .*
- **da** cannot be used to answer **Warum?**-questions

word order:

- **da** introduces a dependent clause, with V_1 at the end (see 1.3 and R.2.3)

Da es am folgenden Tag eine Prüfung geben sollte, war die ganze Klasse gestresst.	*Because there was supposed to be a test the following day, the whole class was stressed.*
Der Text lässt sich nicht gleich erschließen, **da** man ständig fragen muss, ob ...	*The text is not easily accessible since one must constantly ask whether . . .*
Da wir uns nicht entscheiden konnten, haben wir gar nichts gekauft.	*Seeing as we couldn't decide, we didn't buy anything at all.*

3. **denn**

meaning and use:

- **denn** means *since/for*
- it provides a *supplemental explanation* and thus always follows the information it's explaining, i.e., it cannot begin a sentence
- **denn** cannot be used to answer **Warum?**-questions

word order:

- introduces a main clause without affecting its word order, i.e., V_1 remains in second position (see 1.1.B.4)

Ich bin gestresst, **denn** wir haben morgen eine Prüfung.	*I'm stressed, since we're having a test tomorrow.*

Der Text lässt sich nicht gleich erschließen, **denn** man muss ständig fragen, ob ...

The text is not easily accessible, for one must constantly ask whether . . .

Wir haben gar nichts gekauft, **denn** wir konnten uns nicht entscheiden.

We didn't buy anything at all, since we couldn't decide.

4. **Weil** and **denn** are very close in meaning, but they are not entirely interchangeable. A **denn**-clause emphasizes the information in the clause that precedes it, to which the **denn**-clause adds an explanation. A **weil**-clause focuses on the cause or reason for whatever is stated in the other clause, resulting in an equal (or even greater) emphasis on the **weil**-clause itself.

Compare the following examples.

Ich kam spät zur Arbeit, **denn** mein Zug hatte Verspätung.

I came late to work, because my train was delayed. (The focus is on the late arrival, with a secondary focus on the explanation.)

Ich kam spät zur Arbeit, **weil** mein Zug Verspätung hatte.

I came late to work because my train was delayed. / The reason I came late to work was the delay of my train. (The focus shifts to the delay of the train as the cause of the late arrival.)

Thus situations can arise in which **denn** (*supplemental explanation*) will work, but not **weil** (*causality*).

Max muss müde sein, **denn** er trinkt viel Kaffee.

Max must be tired, seeing that he's drinking a lot of coffee.

Max isn't tired because he's drinking coffee; rather, the consumption of coffee explains why the observer thinks he's tired.

Übungen

A **Fragen im Perfekt.** Theo war heute Morgen nicht im Deutschkurs. Jetzt fragt er jemanden, was gemacht wurde. Welche Fragen stellt er?

BEISPIEL ihr / Test schreiben
Habt ihr einen Test geschrieben?

Schwache *(weak)* Verben

1. ihr / viel arbeiten
2. man / über das Gedicht von Rilke diskutieren
3. alle Studenten / ihre Hausarbeiten ein·reichen *(hand in)*
4. ich / etwas Wichtiges versäumen *(miss)*
5. ihr / die Reise nach Berlin planen
6. die Professorin / ein deutsches Musik-Video auf YouTube zeigen

Gemischte *(irregular)* Verben

7. die Professorin / denken, dass ich krank bin
8. du / wissen, wo ich war
9. Gabi / ihren Freund zur Stunde mit·bringen
10. ihr / nach dem Unterricht aus dem Zimmer rennen

Starke *(strong)* Verben

11. du / die Aufgabe für morgen auf·schreiben
12. jemand / beim Quiz durch·fallen *(to fail)*
13. ihr / ein neues Kapitel an·fangen
14. die Professorin / Infos über die Prüfung geben
15. ihr / die ganze Stunde nur auf Deutsch sprechen

B   Ordnen Sie zu!   Ordnen Sie die Sätze auf Englisch mit den Übersetzungen zu – und denken Sie ganz genau an die Nuancen in jedem Satz.

1. _____ *We used to watch the show, seeing as Gottschalk was the moderator.*

   a. Da Gottschalk der Moderator war, haben wir früher die Sendung angeschaut.

2. _____ *We used to watch the show because Gottschalk was the moderator.*

   b. Früher haben wir die Sendung angeschaut, denn Gottschalk war der Moderator.

3. _____ *Since Gottschalk was the moderator, we used to watch the show.*

   c. Früher haben wir die Sendung angeschaut, weil Gottschalk der Moderator war.

4. _____ *He quit in 2011 because there was a serious accident.*

   d. 2011 hat er aufgehört, weil es einen schweren Unfall gegeben hat.

5. _____ *He quit in 2011, seeing as there was a serious accident.*

   e. Da es 2011 einen schweren Unfall gegeben hat, hat er aufgehört.

6. _____ *Because there was a serious accident in 2011, he quit.*

   f. 2011 hat er aufgehört, denn es hat einen schweren Unfall gegeben.

C   Große Menschen, große Leistungen *(accomplishments)*.   Erzählen Sie, wie diese Menschen berühmt geworden sind. Verwenden Sie die angegebenen Verben aus dem Wortschatzkasten.

BEISPIEL   Alfred Nobel (das Dynamit)
Er hat das Dynamit erfunden.

bauen	erfinden *(to invent)*	schreiben	übersetzen
begründen *(to establish)*	erhalten *(to receive)*	singen	werden
entdecken *(to discover)*	komponieren		

1. Friedrich Schiller (das Drama *Wilhelm Tell*)
2. Elisabeth Kübler-Ross (die Sterbeforschung)
3. Rudolf Diesel (der Dieselmotor)
4. Marlene Dietrich (Lieder)

5. Clara Schumann (Klaviermusik)
6. Gottlieb Daimler (das erste Auto)
7. Maria Theresia (Kaiserin von Österreich)
8. Heinrich Schliemann (Troja)
9. Martin Luther (die Bibel)
10. Wilhelm Röntgen (der erste Nobelpreis für Physik)

D **Warum München?**   Welches Wort – **weil, da**, oder **denn** – passt in die Lücken? Passen Sie auf den Satzbau (*sentence structure*) in jedem Beispiel auf!

1. Letzten Sommer war ich in München, _____ ich wollte am Goethe-Institut einen Sprachkurs machen.
2. Warum im Sommer? _____ ich im Herbst studieren muss, natürlich!
3. Ich habe mich für München entschieden, _____ es nicht weit von den Bergen entfernt liegt.
4. _____ ich die Stadt gut erkunden (*explore*) wollte, bin ich von Anfang an mit Tram und U-Bahn viel herumgefahren.
5. Es war unmöglich, alles in nur einem Monat zu sehen, _____ es gibt so viele Museen, Parks und andere Sehenswürdigkeiten.
6. _____ ich gern joggen gehe, hat mir der Englische Garten besonders gut gefallen.
7. Ich war auch im Hofbräuhaus, _____ jeder muss das machen.
8. Aber andere Biergärten waren für mich viel interessanter, _____ es dort nicht so viele Touristen gab.

E **Auf dem Oktoberfest.**   Auf dem Oktoberfest ist Michaela Folgendes passiert. Erzählen Sie im Perfekt davon.

terrible
wallet
reports
gets lost
sees

Michaela kommt in München an. Nachdem sie in einer Pension ein preiswertes Zimmer findet, trifft sie Freunde und sie gehen zusammen zum Oktoberfest. Dort bleiben sie einige Stunden und alle sind sehr lustig. Sogar auf den Tischen tanzt man. Dann passiert aber etwas Schreckliches°. Die Kellnerin bringt die Rechnung, aber Michaela findet ihre Handtasche nicht. O je, auch das Portemonnaie° ist weg. Die Freunde bezahlen für sie und den Verlust meldet° sie bei der Polizei. Auf dem Heimweg verläuft sie sich° dann auch noch. Als sie endlich in der Pension ankommt, traut sie ihren Augen nicht. Was erblickt° sie auf dem Bett? Ihre Handtasche! Das Portemonnaie ist auch darin. Da freut sie sich, dass sie die Handtasche noch hat, und legt sich schlafen.

BEISPIEL   *Michaela ist in München angekommen ...*

F **Übung zu zweit: starke Verben.**   Schreiben Sie zehn starke Verbinfinitive auf (siehe Appendix 3) und tauschen Sie (*exchange*) Ihre Liste mit jemandem aus. Bilden Sie mit den Verben dieser Person wahre Aussagen oder Fragen im Perfekt. Beginnen Sie einige Aussagen mit den Redemitteln **Ich glaube, dass ..., Ich hoffe, dass ...** und **Weißt du, ob** (*whether*)...

BEISPIELE   finden
Weißt du, ob jemand meine Brille gefunden hat?

essen
Ich habe heute Morgen kein Frühstück gegessen.

Anwendung

A **Vom Aufstehen bis zum Schlafengehen.** Erzählen Sie jemandem von Ihrem gestrigen Tag *(yesterday)*. Machen Sie eine Aussage für jede Stunde, die Sie gestern wach waren. Wiederholen Sie keine Partizipien.

B **Aus meinem Leben.** Berichten Sie in einer Gruppe kurz über ein paar wichtige Daten, Ereignisse *(events)* oder bisherige Leistungen *(achievements)* aus Ihrem Leben. Haben Sie vielleicht einmal etwas Ungewöhnliches gemacht? Erzählen Sie!

REDEMITTEL

> Weißt du, was ich einmal gemacht habe?
> Ich glaube, ich habe dir nie erzählt, dass …
> Vor einigen Jahren ist mir etwas Unglaubliches passiert.
> Zu den wichtigsten Ereignissen meines Lebens gehört …
> Es hat sich nämlich so ereignet *(happened)*:

C **Ein berühmter Mensch.** Informieren Sie sich über einen berühmten Menschen. Schreiben Sie dann kurze Notizen, aber keine ganzen Sätze. (Wenn man Notizen macht, steht das Verb immer am Ende.) Berichten Sie mündlich und mit Hilfe Ihrer Notizen in ganzen Sätzen. Sagen Sie noch nicht, wer es war. Lassen Sie die anderen zuerst raten *(guess)*.

BEISPIEL **Notizen**
in Wien gelebt und dort Medizin studiert
1885–1886 in Paris studiert und gearbeitet
Psychiater geworden
die Lehre der Psychoanalyse mitbegründet *(co-founded)*
viele Werke zur Psychoanalyse verfasst *(wrote)*
1938 nach England geflohen
1939 in England gestorben

Mündlicher Bericht
„Er hat in Wien gelebt und dort Medizin studiert. 1885–1886 hat er in Paris studiert und dort gearbeitet. Er ist Psychiater geworden. Später hat er die Lehre der Psychoanalyse mitbegründet und viele Werke zur Psychoanalyse verfasst. 1938 ist er nach England geflohen und 1939 dort gestorben".

Wer war es?[7]

D **Texte im Perfekt.** Finden Sie ein paar kurze Texte (z.B. Märchen[8], Anekdoten oder Witze), die im Präsens oder Präteritum *(simple past)* geschrieben sind. Lesen Sie die Texte vor und ersetzen Sie beim Vorlesen alle Verben mit Perfekt-Formen.

---

[7]Answer: Sigmund Freud
[8]Texts of **Märchen**, and other tales are available online; search **Märchen / Kindermärchen / Grimm Erzählungen** to get started.

E **Zum ersten Mal.** Fragen Sie eine/einen oder mehrere Partnerinnen/Partner, wann sie/er zehn verschiedene Sachen zum ersten Mal gemacht hat/haben: „Wann hast du/bist du zum ersten Mal in deinem Leben _____?"

> **Tipps:** Rad fahren, eine große Stadt besuchen, ins Ausland reisen, Auto fahren

F **Das hat man (nicht) gemacht.** Nehmen Sie einen Text, den Sie im Deutschunterricht gelesen haben oder gerade lesen, und diskutieren Sie (mit Verben im Perfekt), was ein paar von den Charakteren gemacht haben (oder auch nicht gemacht haben) – und warum (nicht).

Schriftliche Themen

Tipps zum Schreiben	**Using the Present Perfect Tense** The present perfect tense is used primarily for conversational or informal writing. You can intersperse it with the simple past tense (see 8.1) in order to avoid repeated use of the auxiliary verbs **haben** and **sein,** or where the context is narration rather than explanation. Remember to link your ideas in terms of sequence with subordinating conjunctions (see R.2.3) or adverbial conjunctions (see 14.5), and to use **da, weil,** and **denn** appropriately to indicate the level of causality or explanation you want to express.

A **Ein Brief.** Schreiben Sie ein paar Sätze für ein Blog oder Tagebuch, in dem Sie erzählen, was Sie in den letzten Tagen gemacht oder erlebt haben.

BEISPIEL *In den letzten zwei Wochen war ich sehr beschäftigt (busy), denn ich hatte Prüfungen in drei Kursen. Ich habe sie alle mit „sehr gut" bestanden. Nicht schlecht, was? Am letzten Wochenende haben mich ein paar Freunde von zu Hause besucht und ich bin abends mit ihnen essen gegangen. Als wir im Restaurant saßen, ... usw.*

B **Danke.** Sie waren am Wochenende bei Bekannten *(acquaintances)* eingeladen. Jetzt schreiben Sie eine E-Mail, in der Sie sich bei Ihren Gastgebern bedanken und ganz kurz erzählen, wie Ihnen der Abend gefallen hat.

BEISPIEL *Hallo!*

Ich möchte mich für den schönen Abend bei euch[9] bedanken. Alle Gäste waren ganz nett und ich habe mich fast eine Stunde mit eurem Papagei (parrot) über

---

[9]According to the 2006 spelling reform rules, pronouns in letters and emails can be either capitalized or lowercase. See Appendix 2, *Rechtschreibreform 2006.*

Politik unterhalten. Besonders gut hat mir die schöne Atmosphäre bei euch gefallen. Dass ich ein volles Glas Rotwein über euer weißes Sofa gekippt (tipped over) *habe, tut mir natürlich leid. Hoffentlich gehen die Flecken* (spots) *weg. Die Brandlöcher im Orientteppich sind aber nicht von mir. Das war jemand anders. Ich hoffe, dass wir bald wieder Gelegenheit* (opportunity) *haben, ein paar nette Stunden zusammen zu verbringen. Nochmals vielen Dank!*

> *Herzliche Grüße,*
>
> *Peter*

Zusammenfassung

Rules to Remember

1   There are three types of verbs: weak, strong, and irregular.

2   Weak and irregular verb past participles end in **-t (gespielt, gewusst)**; strong verb past participles end in **-n (gefunden)**.

3   Verbs with an unstressed, inseparable prefix do not use **ge-** to form the past participle **(erfunden, begegnet)**.

4   The present perfect tense is formed with the conjugated auxiliary verb **(haben** or **sein)** and a past participle.

5   The auxiliary **haben** is used with most verbs **(hat gefunden)**, and is required for all verbs with a direct object (i.e., transitive verbs), including verbs with a reflexive accusative pronoun.

6   The auxiliary **sein** is used with intransitive verbs in the following categories: (a) **sein** and **bleiben**; (b) verbs expressing motion from one location to another **(ist gegangen)**; (c) verbs denoting a change of condition **(ist geworden)**; (d) certain verbs expressing meeting, success, and failure, such as **begegnen** and **gelingen**.

7   In a main clause, the conjugated auxiliary verb (V_1) is in second position and the past participle functions as V_2 after the middle field. In subordinate clauses, the auxiliary verb normally comes after V_2.

8   The present perfect tense refers to the "completed" past, be it five seconds or five centuries ago.

At a Glance

A. *Sein* and *haben*

Infinitive	3rd pers. present	Simple past	Present perfect
sein *(to be)*	ist	war	ist gewesen
haben *(to have)*	hat	hatte	hat gehabt

B. Past participles

weak		ge $\left[\dfrac{unchanged}{stem}\right]$ t
strong		ge $\left[\dfrac{changeable}{stem}\right]$ en
irregular	weak	ge $\left[\dfrac{changed}{stem}\right]$ t
	strong	ge $\left[\dfrac{changed}{stem}\right]$ en

kennen → gekannt	wissen → gewusst
bringen → gebracht	denken → gedacht
senden → gesendet/gesandt	wenden → gewendet/gewandt
nehmen → genommen	stehen → gestanden

No *ge-* in past participle	
1	Most verbs ending in **-ieren**
2	Inseparable prefixes: **be-** **ge-** **emp-** **miss-** **ent-** **ver-** **er-** **zer-**

C. *Sein* as present perfect auxiliary

1	bleiben, sein
2	gehen, fahren, reisen, ...
3	aufstehen, sterben, werden, ...
4	begegnen, gelingen, passieren, ...

4
Definite articles and *der*-words ▪ Indefinite articles and *ein*-words

zum Beispiel

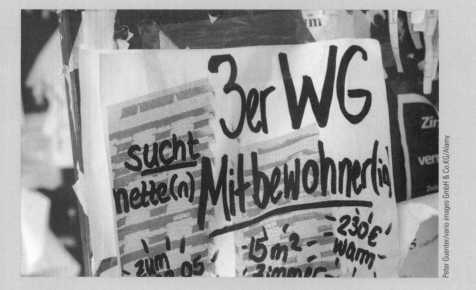

WG

Peter Guenter/vario images GmbH & Co.KG/Alamy

Wohngemeinschaften (WGs) are communal living arrangements, in which students rent an apartment together and share the common spaces, as well as chores such as cooking and cleaning. Considered one of the least expensive ways of finding housing, WGs have become something of a culture unto themselves among university students and are the topic of countless online discussions, magazine articles, and even films.

Grammatik

Chapters 4 and 5 both deal with the way German creates meaning with nouns and noun phrases, but they do so from two different perspectives. Chapter 4 focuses on the two systems in German for referring to nouns—the words used for *specific* reference (definite articles) and the system for more *general* reference (indefinite articles), along with words that follow the patterns of endings in these two systems—and how these systems differ from English. Chapter 5 cuts across these two systems to discuss how both of them use cases (nominative, accusative, dative, and genitive) to relate nouns and pronouns to each other and to other elements in a sentence. Depending on which perspective is more familiar or accessible to you, you may decide to work through Chapter 5 before Chapter 4; either way, the two chapters are designed to reinforce each other and deepen your understanding of how articles, nouns, and pronouns work together functionally.

4.1 ▶ DEFINITE ARTICLES

A. Declension

The definite article (**der bestimmte Artikel**)—English *the*—has masculine, feminine, neuter, and plural forms. It declines, or changes, according to the gender, number, and case of the noun it modifies (see 5.2).

	Masc.	Fem.	Neut.	Pl.
Nom.	**der** Wohnort[a]	**die** WG[b]	**das** Wohnheim[c]	**die** Mitbewohner[d]
Acc.	**den** Wohnort	**die** WG	**das** Wohnheim	**die** Mitbewohner
Dat.	**dem** Wohnort	**der** WG	**dem** Wohnheim	**den** Mitbewohner**n**
Gen.	**des** Wohnorts	**der** WG	**des** Wohnheims	**der** Mitbewohner

[a]*place of residence*   [b]WG = Wohngemeinschaft *(shared housing)*   [c]*dormitory*   [d]*housemate, apartment-mate; anyone sharing a living space*

B. Use

The use of German definite articles (also indefinite articles) overlaps to a great degree (some references say 85 percent) with English usage. But there are several important contexts in which German requires a definite article where English does not, and vice versa. The following rules provide guidance for cases where German and English differ.

1. German requires a definite article in the following contexts, where English normally does not.

    a. With names of days, months, seasons, and meals—particularly after prepositions (see R.4.3).

Der neue Mitbewohner ist **am** (= **an dem**) **Montag** eingezogen.	*The new housemate moved in on Monday.*
Im (= **in dem**) **Juli** hatte er wegen des Zimmers angefragt.	*In July he had made inquiries about the room.*
In Tübingen ist **der Juli** relativ heiß.	*In Tübingen, July is relatively hot.*
Deshalb haben wir mit ihm **vor dem Mittagessen** draußen geplaudert.	*That's why we chatted with him outside before lunch.*

NOTE: No article is used before days, months, and seasons if they follow **sein** or **werden**, or if they are preceded by an adjective such as **letzten, nächsten, vorigen,** etc.

Jetzt ist es schon wieder **Freitag.**	*It's Friday again already.*
Nächsten Oktober brauchen wir zwei Mitbewohner.	*Next October we'll need two housemates.*

b. With means of transportation.

Er fährt mit **dem** Zug, nicht mit **dem** Auto.	*He is traveling by train, not by car.*

c. With proper names of streets, intersections, squares, churches, schools, universities, etc., even when the names are in English. The same holds true for names of lakes, canyons, mountains, and rivers.

Unsere Wohnung in Tübingen ist **in der Münzgasse,** nicht weit **von der St. Georgs-Kirche.**	*Our apartment in Tübingen is on Münzgasse, not far from St. George's Church.*
Am Wochenende fahren wir alle **zum** (= **zu dem**) **Bodensee.**	*On the weekend, we're all driving to Lake Constance.*

Speakers of German tend to use English words for places in English-speaking countries, but with the same genders as their German equivalents.

in **der** Third Avenue = in **der** Straße

am Washington Square = **am [an dem]** Platz

d. With names of certain countries that are masculine or feminine in gender, or are plural. (In the case of several countries with masculine-gender names, the use of the article is optional.)

Masculine: **der Jemen, der Libanon, der Sudan, der Tschad; (der) Iran, (der) Irak**

Feminine: **die Mongolei, die Schweiz, die Slowakei, die Türkei, die Ukraine**

Plural: **die Niederlande, die Vereinigten Arabischen Emirate/die VAE, die Vereinigten Staaten/die USA**

Die Universität Basel ist die älteste Uni in **der** Schweiz.	*The University of Basel is the oldest university in Switzerland.*
Die USA **haben** auch gute Unis, aber keine sind so alt wie die in Basel oder Heidelberg.	*The USA also has good universities, but none are as old as those in Basel and Heidelberg.*

e. With geographical and proper names modified by preceding adjectives.

das alte Deutschland	*old Germany*
die junge Frau Scherling	*(the) young Mrs. Scherling*

f. With nouns that denote concepts, abstractions, and beliefs.

Lenin war ein bedeutender Kämpfer für **den** Kommunismus.	*Lenin was an important fighter for communism.*
Das Christentum hat im ersten Jahrhundert begonnen.	*Christianity began in the first century.*

g. With a number of words such as **Arbeit, Kirche, Schule,** and **Stadt,** particularly after prepositions.

Nach **der** Arbeit muss ich in **die** Stadt.	*After work I have to go into town.*
Nach **der** Schule musste er noch stundenlang Hausaufgaben machen.	*After school he still had to do homework for hours.*

h. With verbs used as nouns, which sometimes matches English usage.

Als Mitbewohner muss man **mit dem Aufräumen** konsequent bleiben.	*As a housemate, you have to be consistent about cleaning up.*
Das Meckern bei uns in der WG geht mir langsam auf die Nerven!	*The complaining in our apartment is slowly getting on my nerves!*

i. With proper names of mutual acquaintances. In colloquial German the definite article is sometimes used before first or last names (e.g., **der** Klaus, **die** Frau Messner) to indicate that both speaker and listener are acquainted with the person referred to.

Hast du **den** Klaus heute gesehen?	*Have you seen Klaus today (the one we both know)?*
Das Buch habe ich bei **der** Frau Messner geholt.	*I picked up the book at Mrs. Messner's house (the Mrs. Messner we both know).*

2. German speakers use the definite article in several situations where English speakers would use a possessive adjective.

a. When parts of the body are used as direct objects or objects of prepositions.

b. When parts of the body are the subject of the verb **wehtun**.[1]

c. When articles of clothing are used as direct objects or objects of prepositions.

A dative reflexive pronoun (see 10.1) can be used to clarify or emphasize personal reference.

Ich muss (mir) **die** Hände waschen.	*I have to wash **my** hands.*
Sie schüttelte **den** Kopf heftig.	*She shook **her** head vehemently.*

---

[1]According to the 2006 spelling reform, *to hurt, to cause pain* can be written either as **weh tun** or **wehtun**: Der Hals hat mir **weh getan/wehgetan**.

Beim Laufen tun (mir) **die** Knie weh.	*My knees hurt when I run.*
Sie zog sich sofort **den** Mantel aus.	*She took off **her** coat immediately.*

German does use possessive adjectives (**mein, dein,** etc.) with parts of the body and articles of clothing when these are the subject of the sentence, or when the context requires clarification.

„Ach, **deine** Augen sind so blau", sagte sie und legte **ihre** Hand auf **seine**.	*"Oh, **your** eyes are so blue," she said, and laid **her** hand on **his**.*

3. In a series of nouns with different genders, the definite article (or any other gender-specific determiner) must be repeated to indicate gender distinctions. Since plural nouns take the same article, regardless of gender, no such repetition is necessary.

Also, jetzt reicht's mir aber. Wer hat denn **meine** Nudeln und **meinen** Käse gegessen?	*OK, I've had it. Who ate my pasta and cheese?*
Die Flaschen und Dosen könnt ihr selber sortieren. Ich mach's nicht mehr.	*You all can sort the bottles and cans yourselves. I'm not doing it anymore.*

4. The definite article is always used in conjunction with the adjective **meist-**. English follows this pattern in the singular *(the most . . .)*, but German requires it in both singular and plural formations.

Singular: **Die meiste** Unordnung kommt wie immer von einem Mitbewohner.	*Most of the mess comes, as always, from one housemate.*
Plural: **Die meisten** von uns sind viel ordentlicher als Jens.	*Most of us are a lot neater than Jens.*

5. German generally omits the definite article before nouns that are used in conjunction with verbs to denote certain activities in general, rather than specific occurrences. In such cases, the noun functions as a verbal complement rather than a direct object (see 1.1.C and 7.2.B).

Und er spielt **Geige** ganz früh am Morgen, ...	*And he plays the violin early in the morning . . .*
... während andere schlafen, frühstücken oder **Zeitung** lesen wollen.	*. . . while others want to sleep, eat breakfast, or read the paper.*

BUT: When these nouns refer to specific objects, they normally require an article or possessive adjective.

Und **die Geige**, die er spielt, gehört ihm gar nicht, sondern einem anderen Mitbewohner.	*And the violin that he plays doesn't belong to him at all, but rather to another housemate.*

6. German normally omits the definite article with family names used as a collective plural, where English does include an article.

Schmitts, unsere Nachbarn von nebenan, haben sich oft darüber beschwert.	*The Schmitts, our neighbors next door, have often complained about it.*

4.2   **INDEFINITE ARTICLES**

A. Declension

The endings of the indefinite article (**der unbestimmte Artikel**)—English *a(n)*—are very similar to those of the definite article. They differ only in the masculine nominative singular and the neuter nominative and accusative singular, which have no endings.

	Masc.	**Fem.**	**Neut.**	**Pl.**
Nom.	ein ■ Stuhl	ein e Lampe	ein ■ Sofa	kein e² Möbel
Acc.	ein en Stuhl	ein e Lampe	ein ■ Sofa	kein e Möbel
Dat.	ein em Stuhl	ein er Lampe	ein em Sofa	kein en Möbeln
Gen.	ein es Stuhles	ein er Lampe ·	ein es Sofas	kein er Möbel

B. Use

1. Indefinite articles generally refer to nonspecific nouns—that is, *a* book as opposed to *the* book—just as in English. A nonspecific noun normally has no article in the plural.

Suchst du **ein Zimmer?**	*Are you looking for a room?*
Wir haben bei uns **Zimmer** frei.	*We have free rooms at our place.*

2. German does *not* use the indefinite article before nouns of *occupation, nationality,* or other markers that show membership in a *general* class (religious affiliation, military rank, marital status, etc.).

Camille ist **Französin,** und Julien ist **Belgier.** Sie verstehen sich gut.	*Camille is a French woman, and Julien is a Belgian. They get along well.*
Lukas ist **Physiker** und Jonas ist **Soziologe.** Sie verstehen sich nicht so gut.	*Lukas is a physicist, and Jonas is a sociologist. They don't get along so well.*
Warum nicht? Weil Lukas immer billige Nudelgerichte kocht, und Jonas **Feinschmecker** ist.	*Why not? Because Lukas always makes cheap pasta dishes, and Jonas is a gourmet.*

    But when the emphasis is on the specific individual rather than the group to which the individual belongs, the indefinite article can be used,[3] especially before adjectives.

Lukas wird entweder **ein berühmter Physiker** oder **ein *mittelmäßiger* Koch.**	*Lukas will become either a famous physicist or a mediocre cook.*

---

[2]Since **ein** has no plural form, **kein** is used here to show the plural endings.

[3]Thus it was entirely correct for John F. Kennedy to say, during his famous speech at the Berlin Wall in 1963, "Ich bin **ein** Berliner." The focus here was on his personal solidarity with the city of Berlin, not merely his inclusion in the population of the city, i.e., people who call themselves **Berliner.** (And nobody in Berlin that day thought he was describing himself as a jelly doughnut.)

3. Unlike English, German tends to avoid indefinite articles after **als** *(as)* in constructions such as the following:

Als Vegetarier isst Julien nur selten mit der Gruppe.	*As a vegetarian, Julien seldom eats with the group.*
Und **als überzeugte Veganerin** kocht Camille sowieso ihr eigenes Essen.	*And as a confirmed vegan, Camille cooks her own food anyway.*

4.3   DER-WORDS

A. Forms

1. The following article modifiers (**Artikelwörter**) take the same endings as the definite article. For this reason they are called **der**-words.

all-	*all* (s. and pl.)		**manch-**	*many a* (s.); *some* (pl.)
dies-	*this* (s.); *these* (pl.)		**solch-**	*such [a]* (s.); *such* (pl.)
jed-	*each, every* (s.)		**welch-**	*which* (s. and pl.)
jen-	*that* (s.); *those* (pl.)			

2. **Der**-words decline as follows:

	Masc.	**Fem.**	**Neut.**	**Pl.**
Nom.	dies **er** (der)	dies **e** (die)	dies **es** (das)	dies **e** (die)
Acc.	dies **en** (den)	dies **e** (die)	dies **es** (das)	dies **e** (die)
Dat.	dies **em** (dem)	dies **er** (der)	dies **em** (dem)	dies **en** (den)
Gen.	dies **es** (des)	dies **er** (der)	dies **es** (des)	dies **er** (der)

B. Use of *der*-words

1. **All-** by itself occurs mainly before plural nouns (see also 13.3.D, E); its use in the singular is somewhat less common.

Alle Zimmer in den Wohnheimen sind jetzt vergeben.	*All the rooms in the dorms are taken now.*
Wir haben **alle Hoffnung** aufgegeben.	*We have given up all hope.*

a. To express the idea of *all* or *all the* in the singular, German uses a definite article plus the adjective **ganz-**.

Ich habe **das ganze Wochenende** nach einer Wohnung gesucht.	*I hunted all weekend for an apartment.*

b. When followed by a **der**- or **ein**-word, **all-** takes no ending in the singular, and in the plural an ending is optional.

Aber **all** *meine Mühe* war umsonst.	*But all my effort was in vain.*
Aus **all(en)** diesen Versuchen ist gar nichts geworden.	*Nothing at all has come from all these attempts.*

2. **Jed-** occurs only in the singular.

    Jedes Semester ist das so.   *Every semester it's like this.*

3. **Jen-** is used mainly in contrast to **dies-**; it is fairly uncommon as a noun modifier.

    Nimmst du dieses Zimmer oder jenes   *Are you taking this room or that one?*
      (Zimmer)?

    NOTE: **Jen-** cannot be used as an exact equivalent for English *that*, as in *Who is **that** man?* To express this, German speakers often use the definite article, with intonational emphasis, and sometimes add an adverbial element to indicate position, such as **da,** e.g., that [one] there.

    Meinst du *das* Angebot da (**an der**   *Do you mean that offer there (on the*
      Pinnwand)?   *bulletin board)?*

4. **Manch-** is common in the plural, and means *a lot of, many*. It occurs much less frequently in the singular, where it means *many a . . .* —and sounds just as literary and archaic in German as the equivalent sounds in English. In the singular, **manch** is usually followed by **ein-**, as in **manch ein-**. In this construction, **manch** is not declined, and **ein-** takes indefinite article endings.

    Manche Leute lernen nie aus ihren Fehlern.   ***Some people** never learn from their*
                                                       mistakes.

    Ich kenne **manch eine Person (manche**   *I know many a person who is neater*
      Person), die ordentlicher ist als ich.   *than I am.*

5. **Solch-** is common in the plural, but less so in the singular, where speakers of German prefer **so ein-** or **solch ein-** *(such a, a [. . .] like that).*

    Solche Wohnungen sind schwer   *Such apartments (Apartments like*
      zu finden.   *that) are hard to find.*

    Gibt es überhaupt **so eine** Wohnung   *Is there even such an apartment (an*
      (**solch eine** Wohnung) in Tübingen?   *apartment like that) in Tübingen?*

6. **Welch-** is most commonly used as an interrogative article (see 19.2.C). The forms **welch ein-** or **was für ein-** occur also in exclamations.

    Welch ein großer Schlamassel.   ⎫
                                           ⎬ *What a big mess!*
    Was für ein großer Schlamassel!   ⎭

4.4 *EIN*-WORDS: POSSESSIVE ADJECTIVES

A. Forms

1. Every pronoun (see 17.1) and noun can be referred to with a corresponding possessive adjective (**das Possessivpronomen**).[4]

---

[4]What English grammarians classify as possessive adjectives (the term used in this book) are considered **Possessivpronomen** in German. A possessive adjective used as a pronoun (see 4.5.B) is a **substantiviertes Possessivpronomen**.

Pronoun	Noun	Possessive adjective	
ich		**mein**	*(my)*
du		**dein**	*(your [familiar])*
Sie		**Ihr**	*(your [formal])*
er →	**der**-*noun*	**sein**	*(his; its)*
sie →	**die**-*noun*	**ihr**	*(her; its)*
es →	**das**-*noun*	**sein**	*(his; its)*
man		**sein**	*(his; their)*
wir		**unser**	*(our)*
ihr		**euer**	*(your [familiar])*
Sie		**Ihr**	*(your [formal])*
sie →	*plural noun*	**ihr**	*(their)*

2. Possessive adjectives have the same endings as the indefinite article (see 4.2). For this reason they are called **ein**-words.

	Masc.	Fem.	Neut.	Pl.
Nom.	mein ∎	mein e	mein ∎	mein e
Acc.	mein **en**	mein e	mein ∎	mein e
Dat.	mein **em**	mein **er**	mein **em**	mein **en**
Gen.	mein **es**	mein **er**	mein **es**	mein **er**
Nom.	unser ∎	uns(e)r e	unser ∎	uns(e)r e
Acc.	uns(e)r **en**	uns(e)r e	unser ∎	uns(e)r e
Dat.	uns(e)r **em**	uns(e)r **er**	uns(e)r **em**	uns(e)r **en**
Gen.	uns(e)r **es**	uns(e)r **er**	uns(e)r **es**	uns(e)r **er**

3. Note that the -er of **unser** and **euer** is part of the adjective, not an ending. When these words have endings, the interior unstressed -**e**- is often dropped: **das Auto** *unsrer* **Eltern.**

B. Use

1. The choice of possessive adjective is determined by the noun or pronoun to which it refers; the *ending* depends on the case, number, and gender of the noun it modifies.

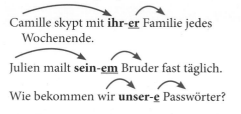

Camille skypt mit **ihr-<u>er</u>** Familie jedes Wochenende.

Camille Skypes with her family every weekend.

Julien mailt **sein-<u>em</u>** Bruder fast täglich.

Julien emails his brother almost daily.

Wie bekommen wir **unser-<u>e</u>** Passwörter?

How do we get our passwords?

2. Since **er, sie,** and **es** can refer to things as well as persons, the possessive forms **sein-** and **ihr-** can both mean *its* in English.

Eine WG hat **ihre** Vorteile.	*A shared apartment has **its** advantages.*
Aber ein Wohnheim hat auch **seine** Vorteile.	*But a dorm also has **its** advantages.*

4.5   *DER-* AND *EIN*-WORDS USED AS PRONOUNS

A. *Der*-word pronouns

1. When a noun is understood from context and thus not repeated, the accompanying definite article or **der**-word can function as a pronoun.

Hier sind zwei Wohnungsanzeigen. **Welche** Nummer willst du anrufen? —Ich nehme **diese** hier, du kannst **jene** nehmen.	*Here are two apartment ads. Which number do you want to call? —I'll take **this one** here, you can take **that one**.*

2. The pronouns **dies-** and **jen-** can express the idea of the *latter* and the *former,* respectively.

Na, was meinst du? Eigene Wohnung oder WG? —Keine Ahnung. **Diese** ist mir zu riskant, und **jene** ist mir zu teuer.	*So, what do you think? Apartment of your own or shared living space? —No idea. The latter is too risky for me, and the former is too expensive.*

3. **Dies-** and **jen-** also appear as pronouns in the phrase **dieses und jenes** *(this and that).*

Wir haben über **dieses und jenes** gesprochen.	*We spoke about this and that.*

4. The pronoun forms **dies** *(this, these)* and **das** *(that, those)* are commonly used as subjects with the verb **sein** when pointing out objects. In such cases, the verb takes its cue from what follows, not the subject, so that if the noun in the predicate is singular, **sein** is likewise singular (**ist**); and if the noun predicate is plural, **sein** is conjugated as **sind,** even though **dies/das** is singular.

Schau mal, **dies** ist mein Brot und **das** ist deins. Alles klar?	*Look here, this is my bread und that is yours. Got that?*
Ja, sicher, und **das** sind deine dreckigen Teller, Gläser und Pfannen im Spülbecken. Alles klar?	*Yeah, sure, and those are your dirty plates, glasses, and pans in the kitchen sink. Got that?*

B. *Ein*-word pronouns

Ein-words, including **so ein-, manch ein-,** and **was für ein-,** can also function as pronouns as long as they retain their endings. In the three instances where the article **ein-** has no ending, a **der**-word ending must be added to indicate number, gender, and case, as highlighted in the following chart. The genitive forms occur infrequently.

Ein-word pronoun declensions				
	Masculine	**Feminine**	**Neuter**	**Plural**
Nom.	meiner	meine	mein(e)s	meine
Acc.	meinen	meine	mein(e)s	meine
Dat.	meinem	meiner	meinem	meinen
Gen.	(meines)	(meiner)	(meines)	(meiner)

Ich kann meinen Schlüssel nicht finden. Hast du **deinen** dabei?	*I can't find my key. Do you have* ***yours*** *with you?*
Und wo ist mein Handy? —Was für **eins** hast du?	*And where's my cell phone?* —*What kind (of* ***one***) *do you have?*
Es ist ein iPhone, in einer Hülle. —In was für **einer**?[5]	*It's an iPhone, in a case.* —*In what kind (of* ***one***)?

Wortschatz
der Raum | der Platz | der Ort | die Stelle

Whether in a dorm, in an apartment, or at home, students need space to live in. But which word for *space* is appropriate when talking about this? Is it better described as **Raum** or **Platz**? Is where you live an **Ort** or a **Stelle**? The explanations below will help you distinguish among these words and identify the contexts in which they are properly used.

1. The noun **der Raum, ⁓e** means *space* or *room* as a general area or volume. It often occurs as a compound noun: **der Lebensraum** *(living space)*, **der Weltraum** *(outer space)*, **das Raumschiff** *(space ship)*, **die Raumfahrt** *(space travel)*. **Der Raum** can also mean *a room*, though **das Zimmer** is much more common.

Die Stadt braucht mehr **Raum** zum Bauen.	*The city needs more room for building.*
Wir müssen diesen kleinen **Raum** noch möblieren.	*We still have to furnish this small room.*

2. The noun **der Platz, ⁓e** also means *space* or *room*, but in a more specific sense than **der Raum**. It often denotes a definite *space* or *place* that someone or something occupies or where an activity takes place; one could say that **Platz** suggests a horizontal surface, whereas **der Raum** suggests a three-dimensional or cubic space. In this example, the speaker needs more horizontal space, such as space on a desk or on the floor.

Ich brauche mehr **Platz** für meine Sachen.	*I need more* ***room (space)*** *for my things.*

---

[5]The use of **für** in **was für** does not influence the case; the phrase is in the dative case because of the preposition **in** (see 6.4 and 19.2.D).

Platz occurs frequently as a compound noun:

der Arbeitsplatz *(place of work, work station)*	**der Spielplatz** *(playground)*
der Marktplatz *(marketplace)*	**der Tennisplatz** *(tennis court)*
der Parkplatz *(parking lot, parking space)*	

Der Platz can also refer to a *seat* (**Ist dieser Platz noch frei?**), or a *square* in a town (**der Mozartplatz**).

Ich brauche einen besseren **Platz** zum Arbeiten.	*I need a better place to work.*
Kannst du mich später am **Sportplatz** abholen?	*Can you pick me up later at the sports field?*
Dieser **Platz** ist besetzt.	*This seat is taken.*

3. The noun **der Ort, -e** can mean a *place, spot,* or *site* but does not denote an exact point. It can also refer to a city, town, or village.

Wir suchen einen **Ort**, wo wir allein sein können.	*We are looking for a place (spot) where we can be alone.*
Hier ist nicht **der Ort**, über solche Dinge zu sprechen.	*Here is not the place to talk about such things.*
Sein **Geburtsort** ist Salzburg.	*His birthplace is Salzburg.*

4. The noun **die Stelle, -n** refers to a precise *spot, place,* or *location,* usually on or within a larger entity, such as the human body. It can occasionally occur interchangeably with **der Ort**, but always refers to a more defined *spot*. **Die Stelle** can also mean *stead* (that is, in someone's place). Finally, **die Stelle** can denote a *passage* in a book, or a *job* or *position.*

An dieser **Stelle** im Wald wachsen besonders große Pilze.	*Particularly large mushrooms grow in this spot in the woods.*
An dieser **Stelle** (an meinem Arm) tut es weh.	*This spot (on my arm) hurts.*
An deiner **Stelle** würde ich anders handeln.	*In your position (If I were you) I would act differently.*
Lesen Sie diese **Stelle** im Buch noch einmal.	*Read this passage in the book once more.*
Sie sucht eine bessere **Stelle**.	*She is looking for a better job/position.*

5. Although the uses of **Ort, Stelle,** and **Platz** overlap to some degree, they do have subtle differences in meaning.

An dieser **Stelle** haben sie sich verliebt. *(the specific spot)*

An diesem **Ort** haben sie sich verliebt. *(the general location)*

ALSO:

In diesem **Ort** haben sie sich verliebt. *(village or town)*

Auf diesem **Platz** haben sie sich verliebt. *(the place/seat where they were sitting)*

Übungen

A   **Welches Wort passt?**   Ergänzen Sie die Sätze mit den passenden Substantiven. (Ab und zu passt mehr als ein Wort hinein!)

> Raum   Ort   Platz   Stelle

1. Der Kommissar fuhr zu d- _____ des Mordes.
2. Wer Golf spielen will, braucht ein- _____ zum Spielen.
3. Sie erzählt gern von d- _____, wo sie aufgewachsen ist.
4. In vielen deutschen Städten gibt es kaum noch _____ zum Bauen.
5. An Ihr- _____ hätte ich das nicht gesagt.
6. An dies- _____ ist der Unfall passiert.

B   **Von großer Bedeutung.**   Nennen Sie jeweils zwei Orte und zwei Plätze, die für Sie große Bedeutung haben oder hatten.

BEISPIEL   *Seattle bedeutet mir viel, denn in diesem **Ort** bin ich geboren und aufgewachsen.*

C   **Die Hansestadt[6] Hamburg.**   Ergänzen Sie die Sätze durch passende Formen von **der** oder **ein**.

1. Im 9. Jahrhundert wurde die Festung „Hammaburg" an _____ Elbe *(f.)* gegründet.
2. Im Mittelalter entwickelte sich _____ Ort zu _____ wichtigen Handelsmetropole *(f.)*.
3. Mit _____ Aufkommen _____ Dampfschifffahrt *(steamboat travel)* galt Hamburg als wichtiger Hafen für Seefahrer aus _____ ganzen Welt.
4. Trotz seines Alters ist Hamburg _____ moderne Stadt.
5. _____ Bombenangriffe *(bombing raids)* im Juli 1943 zerstörten _____ Stadtzentrum.
6. Heute umfasst *(encompasses)* _____ Hafen _____ Gebiet *(n.)* von 16 km Länge.
7. In _____ Stadtteil Stellingen gibt es _____ sehenswerten Tierpark.
8. Im Westen _____ Stadt liegt _____ Hafenviertel St. Pauli mit _____ vielbesuchten Reeperbahn[7] *(f.)*.
9. Mit mehr als 1,7 Millionen Einwohnern gehört Hamburg zu _____ Weltstädten Europas.

---

[6]During the Middle Ages, Hamburg was a member of the Hanseatic League, a powerful alliance of key port cities along the North and Baltic Seas. It is still often referred to as **die Hansestadt Hamburg,** and the license plate numbers of all cars registered there begin with **HH.**

[7]The **Reeperbahn** is a street known for its bars, nightclubs, arcades, and adult entertainment.

D **Gewohnheiten.** Was machen Sie in der Regel **vor, während** und/oder **nach** den folgenden Aktivitäten?

BEISPIEL   die Deutschstunde
Vor der Deutschstunde lerne ich gewöhnlich neue Vokabeln.

1. das Frühstück
2. die Schule
3. die Vorlesungen
4. die Arbeit
5. das Abendessen

E **Modefragen.** Lesen Sie die Sätze und dann ergänzen Sie sie mit den passenden Artikelwörtern aus dem Wortschatzkasten (und mit passenden Endungen, natürlich!). Verwenden Sie dabei jedes Artikelwort.

BEISPIEL   Kauf dir doch _____ Pullover.
*Kauf dir doch **diesen** Pullover.*

> all- dies- jed- so ein- solch- welch-

1. Soll ich mir _____ Hemd kaufen oder nicht?
2. Und wenn ja, dann in _____ Farbe?
3. Eigentlich habe ich _____ Hemd ja schon, aber ich könnte doch noch eins gebrauchen, oder?
4. _____ Freund von mir hat drei oder vier davon.
5. Hmm ... warum tragen eigentlich _____ meine Freunde die gleiche Kleidung?
6. An _____ Fragen sollte man im Kleidungsgeschäft lieber nicht denken.

F **Jeder für sich.** Bilden Sie mit jedem der folgenden Pronomen oder Substantive einen Satz, der auch ein Possessivpronomen enthält. Wiederholen Sie dabei kein Verb.

BEISPIELE   sie
*Sie schreibt **ihrem** Freund.*

der Vogel
*Der Vogel baut **sein** Nest in einem Baum.*

1. ich
2. du
3. die Katze
4. der Mensch
5. das Mädchen
6. wir
7. ihr
8. die Arbeiter
9. Sie
10. man

Anwendung

A   **Bei uns zu Hause.**   Erzählen Sie einer Partnerin/einem Partner über das Leben bei Ihnen zu Hause. Berichten Sie dann jemand anders, was Sie erfahren haben.

> **REDEMITTEL**
>
> Bei uns zu Hause muss jeder sein-/ihr- (eigenes) …
> Vater hat sein- …
> Mutter hat ihr- …
> Von unserem … muss ich auch erzählen.
> Und wie ist es bei euch?
> Habt ihr auch … ?

B   *Sein* **und** *ihr.*   Vergleichen Sie zwei Bekannte – eine Frau und einen Mann. Schreiben Sie mindestens fünf Sätze darüber, was bei den beiden alles unterschiedlich *(different)* ist: Eigenschaften *(personality traits)*, Gewohnheiten *(habits)*, Familien, Interessen, Hobbys usw. Verwenden Sie dabei **sein-** und **ihr-** mit passenden Endungen.

BEISPIEL   *Ihre Eltern wohnen in New York, **seine** Eltern in Cleveland.*
             ***Ihr** Zimmer im Studentenwohnheim sieht immer ordentlich aus,*
             ***sein** Zimmer, als ob ein Orkan (hurricane) gerade vorbeigezogen wäre.*

C   **Charaktere.**   Schreiben Sie eine Liste mit Charakteren aus ein paar Texten auf, die Sie in Ihrem Deutschunterricht gelesen haben. Machen Sie dann mit einer Partnerin/einem Partner ein paar Aussagen über jeden Charakter mit Vokabeln wie **sein-, ihr-, jed-, dies-, so ein-** usw.

Schriftliche Themen

Tipps zum Schreiben	**Editing Your Writing** When preparing an introduction to or a description of a person or place, read aloud what you have written. Do the sentences provide essential information in a manner that is easy for your listeners to comprehend? Are you varying word order and have you tried to avoid beginning every sentence with the name of the person or place or with the subject pronouns **er** and **sie?** When you use the possessive adjectives **sein** and **ihr,** do they match the nouns to which they refer in number and gender?

A **Wir stellen vor.** Kennen Sie jemanden aus einem anderen Land, der jetzt in Ihrer Heimat studiert oder arbeitet? Stellen Sie diese Person in einem kurzen Bericht vor. Erwähnen *(mention)* Sie Nationalität, Beruf, Wohnort, Adresse (in welcher Straße, bei wem), Beruf der Eltern, besondere Interessen und Leistungen *(accomplishments)* usw.

BEISPIEL *Ich möchte meinen Freund Ting-Fung Jiang vorstellen. Er ist Chinese und Student. Abends arbeitet er manchmal als Kassierer in einem Studentencafé am University Square. Sein Vater ist Ingenieur in Beijing, seine Mutter Lehrerin. Nach seinem Studium möchte er Wirtschaftsberater (business consultant) oder vielleicht Journalist werden, weil er meint, dass … usw.*

B **Ortskundig.** Beschreiben Sie einen Ort, den Sie gut kennen. Geben Sie Informationen über die Sehenswürdigkeiten *(places of interest)* und die Geschichte und alles, was diesen Ort sonst noch interessant macht. Benutzen Sie dabei Vokabeln aus dem ganzen Kapitel, wie **so ein, jed-, all-, dies-, mein, dein, unser** und auch **Ort, Platz, Stelle** und **Raum**.

BEISPIEL *In dem Dorf, wo mein Vater aufwuchs, gibt es eigentlich recht viel zu sehen. Der interessanteste Platz ist sicher die Festung (fort), die 10 Jahre vor der Amerikanischen Revolution dort am Flussufer (river bank) gebaut wurde. So eine Festung hat nicht jeder Ort in den USA! Hinter dieser Festung steht ein kleines Museum, wo mein Vater im Sommer gearbeitet hat. Am Marktplatz gibt es immer noch … usw.*

Zusammenfassung

Rules to Remember

1 There are two types of articles: **der**-words and **ein**-words.

2 Articles mark the case, number, and gender of nouns.

3 The **der**-words are **all-, dies-, jed-, jen-, manch-, solch-,** and **welch-**.

4 The **ein**-words are the possessive adjectives **mein, dein, sein, ihr, unser, euer,** and **Ihr** plus the negating element **kein**.

5 **Der**-words and **ein**-words can be used as pronouns.

At a Glance

Definite articles

	Masc.	Fem.	Neut.	Pl.
Nom.	der	die	das	die
Acc.	den	die	das	die
Dat.	dem	der	dem	den
Gen.	des	der	des	der

Indefinite articles

	Masc.	Fem.	Neut.	Pl.
Nom.	ein	eine	ein	(keine)
Acc.	einen	eine	ein	(keine)
Dat.	einem	einer	einem	(keinen)
Gen.	eines	einer	eines	(keiner)

Der-words

all-	all (s. and pl.)
dies-	this (s.); these (pl.)
jed-	each, every (s.)
jen-	that (s.); those (pl.)
manch-	many a (s.); some (pl.)
solch-	such [a] (s.); such (pl.)
welch-	which (s. and pl.)

Ein-word pronoun declensions

	Masc.	Fem.	Neut.	Pl.
Nom.	meiner	meine	mein(e)s	meine
Acc.	meinen	meine	mein(e)s	meine
Dat.	meinem	meiner	meinem	meinen
Gen.	meines	meiner	meines	meiner
so ein-		manch ein-		was für ein-

Pronoun	Noun	Possessive adjective	
ich		**mein**	(my)
du		**dein**	(your [familiar])
Sie		**Ihr**	(your [formal])
er →	**der**-noun	**sein**	(his; its)
sie →	**die**-noun	**ihr**	(her; its)
es →	**das**-noun	**sein**	(his; its)
man		**sein**	(his; their)
wir		**unser**	(our)
ihr		**euer**	(your [familiar])
Sie		**Ihr**	(your [formal])
sie →	plural noun	**ihr**	(their)

zum Beispiel

Das Leben der anderen

Creado Film/Br/Arte/The Kobal Collection

Das Leben der anderen (2006) won an Oscar in 2007 for Best Foreign Film and catapulted its writer/director, Florian Henckel von Donnersmarck, to fame in Germany and beyond. Here are a few key plot elements in the movie. **Georg Dreyman** is a celebrated playwright in the DDR, and **Christa-Maria Sieland** is an equally celebrated stage actress. Georg and Christa-Maria love each other deeply and live together in East Berlin. **Gerd Wiesler** *(pictured above)* is a **Stasi** worker who has been assigned to conduct surveillance on Dreyman and his apartment, not because Dreyman is an enemy of the state, but to find some excuse to denounce him and thereby secure Christa-Maria for a powerful functionary in the DDR government. **Grubnitz** is Wiesler's immediate superior, who oversees the surveillance operation. The **Stasi** was the official secret police of East Germany, and much of its work involved spying on DDR citizens.

Grammatik

Every German noun has *number* (singular or plural), *gender* (masculine, feminine, or neuter; see R.1), and *case*. The case of a noun indicates its function within a sentence. There are four cases in German, and each can indicate multiple grammatical functions.

Nominative | *Accusative* | *Dative* | *Genitive*

Case in German is usually indicated by an *article* accompanying the noun, or, if there is no article, by an *adjective* whose ending takes on the function of that article. A word group comprised of a noun and these modifiers (articles and adjectives) is referred to as a *noun phrase*.

Knowing the gender, number, and case of a noun may seem merely pedantic to English speakers, but in German, this knowledge is critical to understanding the meaning of a sentence. In English, the grammatical function of a noun is indicated primarily by position: the sentence subject typically comes right before the verb, which is then followed by objects and other modifiers. Fluent speakers and readers line these elements up in order to make their relational functions clear. By contrast, German places nouns and noun phrases in positions one would not expect in English, and uses inflections (i.e., changes) in the noun phrase to show whether the noun is the subject or an object, what kind of an object, or how it otherwise stands in relation to the rest of the sentence elements. Learning to associate these inflections with functional meaning is essential to communicating in German.

COMPARE:

Diese Schauspielerin kennt **den Mann** seit Jahren.
This actress has known the man for years.
(**den** signals that **Mann** is the direct object; default word order)

Diese Schauspielerin kennt **der Mann** seit Jahren.
The man has known this actress for years.
(**der** signals that **Mann** is the subject; direct object is highlighted in the front field)

As the following chart indicates, the greatest amount of inflection across gender, number, and case appears in the articles preceding the nouns. But nouns themselves also show changes in several contexts, notably the plural form (like English), the dative plural (with the addition of -**n**), and masculine and neuter genitive singular (with the addition of -**s** or -**es**).

	Masc.	Fem.	Neut.	Pl.
Nom.	der Mann	die Frau	das Theater	die Probleme
Acc.	den Mann	die Frau	das Theater	die Probleme
Dat.	dem Mann	der Frau	dem Theater	den Problemen
Gen.	des Mannes	der Frau	des Theaters	der Probleme

The discussion in this section focuses on changes to nouns themselves, depending on case and context.

1. In the dative singular, monosyllabic masculine and neuter nouns have an optional -**e** ending that is usually omitted, except in a few set expressions; and even in these (as indicated by parentheses) the -**e** can be dropped.

   auf dem Land(**e**)   *in the country*

   im Grund**e** genommen   *basically, fundamentally*

   im Jahr(**e**) 1749   *in the year 1749*

   im Lauf(**e**) (des Jahres/des Tages)   *in the course (of the day/the year)*

   in diesem Sinn(**e**)   *in this sense*

   nach dem Tod(**e**)   *after death*

   nach Haus**e**   *(back) home (with verbs of motion)*[1]

   zu Haus**e**   *(at) home (denoting location, not motion)*[1]

2. Unless a noun plural already ends in -**n**, an -**n** must be added in the dative plural (**die Leute** ⟶ **mit den Leuten**).

   EXCEPTION: Noun plurals ending in -**s** do not add the dative plural -**n** (**die Autos** ⟶ **mit den Autos**).

3. Masculine and neuter nouns in the genitive case add either -**s** or -**es**.

   - The -**s** is preferred when the noun has more than one syllable (**das Rad** ⟶ **des Rades** BUT: **das Fahrrad** ⟶ **des Fahrrads**), or ends in a vowel (**der Schrei** ⟶ **des Schreis**) or silent **h** (**der Schuh** ⟶ **des Schuhs**).

   - The -**es** is preferred when a noun is monosyllabic (**das Geld** ⟶ **des Geldes**), and is required when the noun ends in -**s**, -**sch**, -**ß**, -**x**, or -**z** (**der Schreibtisch** ⟶ **des Schreibtisches**). Nouns ending in -**nis** add an -**s** before the -**es** (**das Missverständnis** ⟶ **des Missverständnisses**).

---

[1]For details on the use of **nach Hause** and **zu Hause,** see the **Wortschatz** section of Chapter 6.

EXCEPTIONS:

- Foreign nouns ending in **-s** usually do not take the **-s/-es** genitive ending: **des Chaos, eines Index, trotz des Sozialismus, wegen eines Zirkus.**

- Singular masculine or neuter nouns following a genitive preposition (see 6.5) but with no accompanying articles or modifying adjectives can (but do not necessarily) omit the **-s** or **-es**: **wegen Verrat/trotz Regen** (but also: **wegen Verrats/trotz Regens**).

4. Masculine nouns that add **-(e)n** in all cases except the nominative singular—sometimes referred to as *weak nouns*—are discussed in R.1.3.

5.3 NOMINATIVE CASE

If German cases show relationships among words in a sentence, then the nominative case is the least "relational"—it is never used to connect nouns with prepositions, as are the other cases—and it is the most neutral, since it is the default case when nouns are used with no grammatical context. Its chief functions are to signal the subject of a sentence or clause, and to link the subject with words or phrases in the predicate, known as *predicate nominatives*.

A. Words in isolation

The nominative case is the default for noun phrases or pronouns that stand by themselves, either absolutely or syntactically.

Ein guter Mann, der Georg.	*A good man, that Georg.*
Und **ihr,** was meint ihr dazu?	*And you all, what do you think of it?*

B. Subjects

1. A noun or pronoun used as the *sentence subject* takes the nominative case. A singular subject requires a singular verb; a plural subject requires a plural verb.[2]

Singular

Die Geschichte fängt mit einem Verhör an.	*The story begins with an interrogation.*
Im Hörsaal erklärt **ein Stasi-Mitarbeiter** einer Gruppe Studenten den Vorgang.	*In a lecture hall, a Stasi agent explains the process to a group of students.*

Plural

Zwei Leute sitzen auf dem Balkon und schauen zu.	*Two people sit in the balcony and watch.*

---

[2]This rule bends a bit when "pointers" such as **dies, das,** or **es** appear as the subject in the front field followed by the verb **sein.** In such cases, the noun *following* the verb determines whether **sein** will be conjugated as **ist** or **sind,** even though what appears to be the subject in the front field is singular: **Das sind** schöne Blumen! **Es sind** die kleinen Dinge, die mich nerven. (See 4.5.A)

2. In German, the subject does not necessarily precede the conjugated verb, as it often does in English (see 1.1.C).

Mit einem Fernglas *beobachtet* **Wiesler** die anderen Zuschauer.	*With a pair of binoculars, Wiesler <u>observes</u> the other spectators.*
Sehr skeptisch *äußert* **er** sich über Dreyman, den Autor des Stückes.	*Very skeptically, he <u>expresses his opinion</u> about Dreyman, the author of the play.*

C. Predicate nominatives

A noun or noun phrase following V_1 that renames or describes the subject is called the *predicate nominative* and, like the subject, takes the nominative case. The verb used with the predicate nominative is a linking verb, which functions more or less like an equal sign.

bleiben   *to stay, remain*
gelten [+ als]   *to be regarded as*
heißen   *to be called or named*
scheinen   *to seem*
sein   *to be*
werden   *to become*

Die Inszenierung *ist* **eine Katastrophe,** meint Dreyman.	*The production is a catastrophe, in Dreyman's opinion.*
Aber Schwalber *bleibt* **der Regisseur.**	*But Schwalber remains the director.*

5.4   ACCUSATIVE CASE

The accusative case has a wider range of functions in German than the nominative. Not only is it the marker for direct objects, but it also connects nouns with certain prepositions, indicates length and duration, and completes the phrase **es gibt** _____.

A. Direct objects

1. A noun or pronoun used to complete the activity of verbs other than linking verbs is called an *object*. Many verbs take a *direct object,* also known as an *accusative object.*

Dreyman besucht **einen alten Freund** in seiner Wohnung.	*Dreyman visits an old friend in his apartment.*
Leider kann er **keinen Schlips** binden und muss **seine Nachbarin** um Hilfe bitten.	*Unfortunately, he can't tie a tie and has to ask his neighbor for help.*

2. Two accusative objects may be used after the verbs **fragen, kosten,** and **lehren.**

Wiesler fragt **sie** *etwas Wichtiges.*	*Wiesler asks her something important.*
Es kostet **sie** *große Mühe,* ihm nicht zu antworten.	*She finds it very difficult not to answer him.*

B. Other uses of the accusative

1. The accusative is used with verbs of motion to express a distance covered, or to show a measurement or amount.

Dreyman läuft **die Treppe** herunter.	*Dreyman runs down the stairs.*
Wiesler sitzt nur **vier Meter** direkt über Dreymans Wohnung.	*Wiesler sits only four meters directly above Dreyman's apartment.*

2. The accusative is used in many conventional greetings and wishes, indicating that these phrases are the accusative objects of *I wish you ___* or *I offer you ___*.

    Guten Morgen/Tag/Abend; **Gute** Nacht.   *Good morning/day/evening. Good night.*
    Herzlichen Glückwunsch.   *Congratulations.*
    Angenehme Reise.   *Have a nice trip.*
    Vielen Dank.   *Many thanks.*
    Gute Besserung.   *Get well soon.*

3. The accusative is used after the expression **es gibt** (see 20.3.B); after two important groups of prepositions (see 6.2: accusative prepositions; and 6.4: two-way prepositions); and in some time expressions denoting a *period* of time or a *point* in time (see R.4.3).

5.5   DATIVE CASE

Of all the German cases, the dative has the widest range of use. In its most familiar function—signaling indirect objects—it completes the picture of *someone* (the subject: nominative) giving *something* (the direct object: accusative) *to someone* (the indirect object: dative). In addition, it is the required case for objects of various kinds of verbs; it can serve as a "dative of reference" that indicates how the verb is connected (by perspective or possession) with another element of the sentence; and it is used with specific prepositions, certain adjectives, and time expressions.

A. Indirect objects

1. The noun or pronoun that indicates the person (*or less often:* the thing) *to whom* or *for whom* an activity is done is called the *indirect object*. An indirect object is in the dative case; it normally requires an accusative object or subordinate clause to complete its meaning.

    DAT. OBJ.   ACC. OBJ.
    Jerska schenkt **dem Autor** ein Musikstück.   *Jerska gives the author a piece of music.*

    DAT. OBJ.   SUB. CLAUSE
    Hauser erklärt **ihm**, **warum er Position beziehen muss.**   *Hauser explains to him why he has to take a stand.*

2. Indirect objects usually precede direct object nouns, unless extra emphasis is required (see 1.1.C).

Dreyman zeigt **seinen Freunden** das Manuskript.	*Dreyman shows his friends the manuscript.*
Hessenstein bringt **ihm** eine neue Schreibmaschine.	*Hessenstein brings him a new typewriter.*

3. Indirect objects always follow direct object pronouns.

Dreyman zeigt **es <u>seinen Freunden</u>.**   *Dreyman shows it to his friends.*

Hessenstein bringt **sie <u>ihm</u>.**   *Hessenstein brings it to him.*

4. Indirect (dative) and direct (accusative) objects often occur together with the following types of verbs:

Verbs of giving: **bringen, geben, leihen** *(to lend),* **reichen** *(to hand, pass),* **schenken** *(to give as a gift),* **spendieren** *(to buy, pay for, treat)*

Verbs of showing: **bei·bringen** *(to teach),* **beweisen** *(to prove),* **erklären, zeigen**

Verbs of telling: **beschreiben** *(to describe),* **erzählen, mit·teilen** *(to inform),* **sagen**

Verbs of recommending: **empfehlen** *(to recommend),* **vor·schlagen** *(to suggest)*

Dreyman empfiehlt **<u>ihnen</u> seine Wohnung** als sicheren Ort.   *Dreyman recommends his apartment to them as a safe place.*

Hauser schlägt **<u>den Verschwörern</u> einen Test** vor.   *Hauser suggests a test to the conspirators.*

Es ist wichtig, **<u>ihnen</u> die Sicherheit** der Wohnung zu beweisen.   *It's important to prove to them the security of the apartment.*

5. Where English uses *to* as well as word order to indicate some indirect objects, German uses the dative case, rather than **zu** + an object, to express the idea of doing something *to* or *for* someone.

COMPARE:

*The dentist sold **her** the drugs.*
*The dentist sold the drugs **to her**.*   Der Zahnarzt verkaufte **ihr** die Drogen.

B. Verbs with dative objects

A significant number of verbs in German take a dative object instead of an accusative object to complete the action of the verb. Commonly used verbs of this type include the following.

ähneln *to resemble*	helfen *to help*
antworten *to answer*	imponieren *to impress*
begegnen *(aux.* sein*)* *to encounter, meet*	nutzen/nützen *to be of use to*
danken *to thank*	passen *to suit, fit*
ein·fallen *(aux.* sein*)* *to occur to, come to mind*	passieren *(aux.* sein*)* *to happen*
folgen *(aux.* sein*)* *to follow*	raten *to advise*
folgen *to obey*	schaden *to harm*
gehorchen *to obey*	schmecken *to taste, taste good*
gehören *to belong to*	schmeicheln *to flatter*
genügen *to suffice*	trauen *to trust*
geschehen *(aux.* sein*)* *to happen*	weh·tun/weh tun *to hurt, cause pain*
gratulieren *to congratulate*	widersprechen *to contradict*

Es fällt **dem Stasi-Mitarbeiter** ein, dass er **den beiden** helfen kann.	*It occurs to the Stasi worker that he can help both of them.*
Er begegnet **der Frau** in einer Kneipe.	*He meets the woman in a bar.*
Er war **ihr** tagelang gefolgt.	*He had followed her for days.*
Er will **der Frau** nicht schmeicheln, sondern ihr die Wahrheit sagen.	*He doesn't want to flatter the woman, but rather to tell her the truth.*
Er rät **ihr**, zu Dreyman zurückzugehen.	*He advises her to return to Dreyman.*
Dreyman liebt sie, und ihre Untreue tut **ihm** unsäglich weh.	*Dreyman loves her, and her infidelity is unspeakably painful to him.*

2. The verb **glauben** takes a dative object with persons but an accusative object with things.

Wieslers Chef glaubt **ihm** nicht mehr.	*Wiesler's boss no longer believes him.*
Zumindest glaubt er **die Erklärung** für Wieslers Bitte nicht.	*At least, he doesn't believe the explanation for Wiesler's request.*

3. With several commonly used verbs, the dative object in German is expressed in English as the subject (see also *impersonal es,* 20.3.A).

fehlen	Christa-Maria fehlt **ihm**. *He misses Christa-Maria.*
gefallen	Es gefällt **einem Studenten** nicht, wie der Häftling verhört wird. *One student doesn't like how the prisoner is being interrogated.*
gelingen	Es gelingt **Dreyman**, Christa von seiner Liebe zu überzeugen. *Dreyman succeeds in convincing Christa of his love.*
leid·tun	Frau Meineke tut **mir** besonders leid. *I'm especially sorry for Mrs. Meineke.*
reichen[3]	Nach Wieslers Verrat reicht es **seinem Chef**, und Wiesler wird versetzt. *After Wiesler's betrayal,* ***his boss*** *has had enough, and Wiesler is transferred.*

4. Verbs of motion with the prefixes **ent-** (inseparable) and **nach-** (separable) take dative objects. The most common combinations occur with **gehen, kommen,** and **laufen.**

entgehen	*to escape, elude, avoid*
entlaufen	*to run away from*
nach·gehen	*to pursue, investigate; to follow*
nach·kommen	*to come, follow after*

Es scheint, dass **der Stasi** kein Detail entgehen kann.	*It seems that no detail can escape the Stasi.*
Wieslers Chef muss **der Sache** mit dem Zeitschriftenartikel nachgehen.	*Wiesler's boss must pursue the matter of the magazine article.*

---

[3]Like many verbs, **reichen** can take several meanings. When it means *I've had enough,* it takes the dative, as shown above; but it can also mean *to reach or stretch,* which can be intransitive with no object: Das Geld **reicht** nicht für ein neues Auto.

5. Some commonly used verbs with the separable prefixes **bei-** and **zu-** also take dative objects.

bei·stehen   *to help, aid*
bei·treten   *to join (a party, club, etc.)*
zu·hören   *to listen to*
zu·lächeln   *to smile at*
zu·reden   *to (try to) persuade, urge*
zu·sagen   *to be to one's liking; to accept (an invitation)*
zu·sehen   *to watch, witness*
zu·stimmen   *to agree with*

Jerskas Freunde wollen **ihm** beistehen, aber sie können sehr wenig für ihn tun.	*Jerska's friends want to help (support) him, but there's very little they can do for him.*
Wiesler hört **dem Klavierspiel** ganz bewegt zu.	*Wiesler listens with great emotion to the piano playing.*

C. The "dative of reference"

1. Many English speakers think of the dative case as synonymous with *to whom* (as in **dem Mann** = *to the man*), and in many situations this is true. It certainly applies to the use of the dative with indirect objects, as discussed above, and it holds for many of the dative verbs, such as **danken,** which can be thought of as *to give thanks to someone*; **ein·fallen,** *to occur to someone*; or **gehören,** *to belong to someone*. But there are many situations in which German uses the dative case to link verbs and objects in a way that does not fit this English pattern; this usage is sometimes referred to as the "dative of reference."

2. A "dative of reference" establishes a connection between an action and the person or thing affected by that action—the person or thing to which the action "refers." Notice how this connection is made in the examples below—and the way that *for whom*, rather than *to whom*, becomes the most viable way to express it.

Sie öffnete **ihren Freunden** die Tür.	*She opened the door for her friends.*
Der Kellner füllte **ihm** das Glas.	*The waiter filled the glass for him.*
Er spielte **ihr** das Lied vor.	*He played the song for her.*
Sie schrieb es **mir** auf.	*She wrote it down for me (for my sake).*

3. Sometimes this connection requires a translation other than *for whom/for whose sake*, since the idea being expressed is not *on someone's behalf*, but rather *from someone's perspective, affecting someone*, or *with respect to someone*, either positively or negatively, as the following examples show.

Ihnen war das Wetter zu heiß.	*The weather was too hot for them (from their perspective).*
Aber **mir** war's gerade richtig.	*But it was just right for me (from my perspective).*
Der Firma geht's gut.	*It's going well for the firm (i.e., with respect to the firm).*

Ihr ist die Uhr stehen geblieben.	*The watch stopped on her (i.e., that affected her).*
Die Stasi verwanzt **ihm** die ganze Wohnung.	*The Stasi bugs his whole apartment (and that affects him).*

D. Other uses of the dative

1. You may have noticed that in several of the examples above it is possible to translate the German dative with an English possessive, when the "reference" serves to connect a person with an element belonging to that person.

Ihr ist die Uhr stehen geblieben.	*Her watch stopped.*
Die Stasi verwanzt **ihm** die ganze Wohnung.	*The Stasi bugs **his** whole apartment.*

This capacity of the dative to show possession is used in German in conjunction with body parts, clothing, and other objects, where German sometimes prefers to use the definite article rather than a possessive pronoun (see also 4.1.B).

Ich habe **mir** die Hände gewaschen.	*I washed **my** hands.*
Sie knöpfte **ihm** das Hemd auf.	*She unbuttoned **his** shirt.*
Die Frau ist **dem Mann** vors Auto gelaufen.	*The woman ran in front of the **man's** car.*

2. The dative is also used with two important groups of prepositions (see 6.3: dative prepositions; and 6.4: two-way prepositions), and it appears in time expressions with certain prepositions (see R.4.3) and some adjectives (see 13.4.A).

5.6 ▶ GENITIVE CASE

Some will say that the genitive case is falling into disuse,[4] but in many contexts it is still essential: to show a particular relation between two nouns, especially possession; as the object of certain verbs; to indicate the object of certain prepositions; to formulate time expressions; and to form phrases with **sein** and an adjective.

A. General use

1. The genitive case in German is often used to indicate a relationship between two nouns—one noun is part of, connected to, belongs to, or depends on the other noun. In English, such a relationship can be expressed with an *of*-phrase (with the genitive noun following the other noun) or with the possessive *-'s* (with the genitive noun preceding the other noun). German favors the former of these two, with the genitive noun phrase *following* the first noun. In a few special cases (see point 2 on next page) the pattern is reversed; the genitive noun precedes the other noun. The usual form is shown here.

---

[4]Witness the (slightly) tongue-in-cheek title of the book series *Der Dativ ist dem Genitiv sein Tod* (Kiepenheuer & Witsch), by Bastian Sick—a must-read for anyone interested in German grammar.

der Schreibtisch **des Mannes**	*the **man's** desk*
das Geheimnis **der Freundin**	*the **girlfriend's** secret*
die Zerstörung **der Mauer**	*the destruction **of the wall***
die Farbe **der Tinte**	*the color **of the ink***

2. With proper names and family-member terms used as names (usually reserved for **Vater, Mutter, Großmutter, Großvater**), German adds an **-s** (*without* an apostrophe) and positions the genitive noun before its related noun, as in English.

Dreymans Entscheidung	*Dreyman's decision*
Wieslers Entschlossenheit	*Wiesler's determination*
Mutters Verschwiegenheit	*mother's discretion*
Vaters Angst	*father's anxiety*

The addition of an article or other determiner before a family-member term, as in *the father's computer* or ***my** father's computer,* changes the term from a name to a noun, for which the "genitive second" structure is required: Der Computer **meines Vaters.**

3. If the name ends in an **s** sound (**-s, -ß, -z, -tz**), no **-s** is added in the genitive. In writing, the omission of this **-s** is indicated by an apostrophe. In speech, a construction with **von** + dative is often used instead of the genitive (see section C below).

Grubitz' Büro *or* das Büro **von Grubitz**

4. The genitive is *not* used after units of measurement (such as **Gruppe**, **Tasse**, **Flasche**), as in English.

| Wiesler trinkt **ein Glas Wodka.** | *Wiesler drinks a **glass of vodka.*** |
| Hempf, der Minister, steht mitten in **einer Gruppe Künstler.** | *Hempf, the cabinet minister, is standing right in the middle of a **group of artists.*** |

B. Genitive verbs

1. At one time, a significant number of German verbs took genitive objects, similar to English *to have need **of something*** or *to make use **of something.*** In recent years, most of these have been replaced by other verbs and prepositional phrases, but the following genitive verbs are still in use:

einer Sache bedürfen *to have need of something*

sich einer Sache bedienen *to make use of something*

sich einer Sache bemächtigen *to take control of something*

sich einer Sache erwehren *to resist (doing) something*

sich einer Sache erfreuen *to enjoy, be the beneficiary of something*

| Als der Film „Das Leben der anderen" im Kino erschien, erfreute er sich **großer Beliebtheit.** | *When the film* The Lives of Others *appeared in theaters, it enjoyed tremendous popularity.* |
| Der Regisseur bedient sich **einer Filmtechnik,** die die Geschichte umso emotionaler macht. | *The director makes use of a film technique that renders the story all the more emotional.* |

C. *Von* as a substitute for the genitive case

1. The word **von** + dative is often used as a genitive substitute.

   der Name **des Häftlings** } *the name of the prisoner/the prisoner's name*
   der Name **vom Häftling**

2. **Von** is always used if there is no article or adjective that can be inflected to indicate the genitive case.

   die Witze **von Stasi-Mitarbeitern**   *the jokes of Stasi co-workers*

   die Wirkung **von Politik**   *the effect of politics*

3. **Von** is used with personal pronouns to show connections, where English uses *of* + possessive pronoun.

   ein Feind **des Staates,** aber ein   *an enemy of the state, but a friend*
       Freund **von ihm**   *of his*

4. In the examples above, **von** is used like English *of* to express a connective relationship. **Von** and *of* are also used in phrases referring to a part (or multiple parts) of a larger group or entity, such as *two* **of** *their friends* or *much* **of** *his time.*

   When these phrases begin with numbers, plural modifiers, or nouns, German allows either **von** or a genitive construction to be used.

   [zwei] **von** ihren Freunden }
   [zwei] **ihrer** Freunde   } *[two] of their friends*

   einige **von** seinen Mitarbeitern }
   einige **seiner** Mitarbeiter   } *some of his co-workers*

   ein Teil **von** dem Problem }
   ein Teil **des** Problems   } *one part of the problem*

   But when these phrases begin with singular modifiers, such as **viel, etwas, welches** and **nichts,** only **von** can be used.

   viel **von** seiner Zeit (*rather than* **seiner Zeit**)   *much of his time*

   nichts **von** ihrem Talent (*rather than*   *nothing of her talent*
       ihres Talents)

D. Genitive after *sein* and other uses

1. Genitive noun phrases can be used after conjugated forms of **sein** as complements of the subject. This is similar to English constructions such as *I am of the opinion*, both in structure and in the whiff of sophistication this usage carries.

   Ich bin **der Meinung**, dass ...   *I'm of the opinion that . . .*

   Bist du also **der Ansicht**, dass ... ?   *So you're of the view that . . .?*

   Wir sind **der festen Überzeugung**, dass ...   *We are of the firm conviction that . . .*

   Sie war **guter Laune**, weil ...   *She was in a good mood because . . .*

Die zwei sind **gleichen Alters.**	*The two (of them) are of the same age.*
Dieses Märchen ist wohl **französischen Ursprungs.**	*This fairy tale is probably of French origin.*

2. The genitive case is used with certain adjectives and adverbs (see 13.4.B), after prepositions (see 6.5), and in some time expressions (see R.4.3).

Wortschatz
machen

1. **Machen** can mean *to do,* synonymous with **tun.**

Was **macht** er aber, wenn die Schreibmaschine entdeckt wird?	*But what will he do if the typewriter is discovered?*

2. **Machen** can mean *to make,* in the sense of *to produce, create,* or *build.*

Der Sektkorken **macht** ganz schön viel Lärm.	*The champagne cork makes a whole lot of noise.*
Hat Christa-Maria die Häppchen fürs Fest selber **gemacht?**	*Did Christa-Maria make the hors d'oeuvres for the party herself?*

3. **Machen** can mean *to make,* as in *to cause to be.*

Christa-Marias Verhaftung **macht** alles viel komplizierter.	*Christa-Maria's arrest makes everything more complicated.*
Grubitz' Bemerkung **macht** den jungen Mitarbeiter am Tisch sehr nervös.	*Grubitz's remark makes the young co-worker at the table very nervous.*

4. **Machen** also occurs with a wide variety of direct-object complements. Some of these mirror English usage (**eine Ausnahme machen** = *to **make** an exception*), but others express ideas for which English uses a different verb (**Schulden machen** = *to **incur** debts*). Pay close attention to this second group as you learn these expressions.

Wie auf Englisch

eine Ausnahme machen   *to make an exception*
eine Aussage machen   *to make a statement*
einen Fehler machen   *to make a mistake*
Fortschritte machen   *to make progress*
jemandem *(dat.)* **eine (große) Freude machen**   *to make someone (very) happy*
Lärm machen   *to make noise*
Musik machen   *to make music*
jemandem *(dat.)* **Platz machen**
   to make room for someone

Nicht wie auf Englisch

einen Abschluss machen   *to graduate*
einen Ausflug machen   *to go on an outing*
ein Foto machen   *to take a picture*
Mach doch!   *Hurry up! Get on with it!*
eine Pause machen   *to take a break*
eine Reise machen   *to take a trip*
einen Schritt machen   *to take a step*
Schulden machen   *to incur debts*
jemandem *(dat.)* **Sorgen machen**
   to cause someone to worry

einen Unterschied machen	*to make a difference, draw a distinction; to discriminate*	**einen Spaziergang machen**	*to go for a walk*
ein Vermögen machen	*to make a fortune*	**Unsinn machen**	*to do something stupid*
einen Versuch machen	*to make an attempt; to conduct an experiment*	**Urlaub machen**	*to go on vacation*

All of these expressions are negated with **kein-.**

Boris wird **keine** Ausnahme machen. *Boris won't make an exception.*

Mach doch **keinen** Unsinn! *Don't do anything foolish!*

Übungen

A **Berlin: Kulisse *(backdrop)* für den Film.**   Lesen Sie den Text und markieren Sie die Fälle *(cases)* aller Substantive (**N** für Nominativ, **A** für Akkusativ, **D** für Dativ und **G** für Genitiv).

Die Kulisse, vor der sich die ganze Geschichte abspielt, ist Ost-Berlin, damals die Hauptstadt der Deutschen Demokratischen Republik (DDR). Heute ist Berlin wieder die Hauptstadt vom vereinigten Deutschland; von 1871 bis 1945 war sie die Hauptstadt des Deutschen Reiches. Vor dem Zweiten Weltkrieg gehörte die Stadt mit mehr als 4,5 Millionen Einwohnern zu den wichtigsten Metropolen Europas. Nach dem Krieg aber lag die Stadt in Trümmern°. Die alliierten Mächte° teilten° die Stadt nach ihrem Sieg° in vier Besatzungszonen°. Während der Berliner Blockade von 1948–1949 wurde die Ostzone der Stadt Teil der DDR. Dreizehn Jahre später baute man die Berliner Mauer°, um die Flucht° von Bürgern aus der DDR zu verhindern. Berlin blieb bis zum Fall der Mauer im November 1989 eine geteilte Stadt. Wenige Monate später wurden die DDR und Ost–Berlin Teil eines neuen vereinigten Deutschlands. Der Film verbindet sozusagen zwei Epochen der Stadt, indem er das Leben vor und nach dem Mauerfall darstellt.

rubble
powers / divided / victory / occupation zones
wall
flight

B **Anders machen.**   Drücken Sie die Sätze mit dem Verb **machen** anders aus.

1. Wir kommen mit der Arbeit schnell voran.
2. Euer Besuch hat uns sehr gefreut.
3. Darf ich dich fotografieren?
4. Die Stasi will den Ruf *(reputation)* von Jerska zerstören.
5. In ihrem Examen hat Michelle alles richtig gehabt.
6. Lukas borgt Geld und kauft allerlei Dinge.
7. Wir wollen im Sommer für ein paar Wochen in die Schweizer Alpen fahren.
8. Christine hat vor Gericht *(court)* gegen den Angeklagten *(defendant)* ausgesagt.
9. Im Laufe der Jahre wurde sie sehr reich.
10. Jan soll zur Schule gehen, aber er geht stattdessen einkaufen.

C **Das habe ich gemacht.** Machen Sie mit jedem Verb und einem passenden *(appropri-ate)* Objekt – Akkusativ oder Dativ – eine Aussage darüber, was Sie heute oder gestern gemacht (oder auch nicht gemacht) haben.

BEISPIEL *Ich habe **einen Freund** in der Mensa getroffen.*

begegnen   bekommen   essen   kaufen   lernen   schmeicheln   schreiben
treffen   trinken   widersprechen

D **In der Stadt.** Wer macht was? Verwenden Sie Nominativ, Akkusativ und Dativ mit Vokabeln von der Liste und aus dem Wortschatzkasten. Erzählen Sie dabei eine Geschichte.

BEISPIEL Sie lesen: *Der Kellner bringt* _____.
Sie nehmen *Mutter* und *Eis* und schreiben: *Der Kellner bringt der Mutter ein Eis.*

Mutter   Vater   Sohn   Tochter   Tante   Onkel   Familie   Großeltern

Bier   Cola   Dom   Eis   Kaufhaus   Leute   Pizza *(f.)*   Rathaus   Stadtplan *(m.)*
Touristen *(pl.)*   Wein

1. Zuerst zeigt der Vater _____.
2. Auf dem Markt kauft _____.
3. Dann bringt _____.
4. Beim Mittagessen bestellt _____.
5. Danach begegnet _____.
6. Der Vater macht _____ eine große Freude, weil er _____.
7. Beim Kaffeetrinken um vier Uhr empfiehlt _____.
8. Zum Abendessen bringt der Kellner _____.
9. Die Tochter macht den Eltern Sorgen, weil sie _____.
10. Zum Schluss empfiehlt die Mutter _____, dass _____ kaufen soll.

E **Durch Pronomen ersetzen.** Ersetzen Sie in den Sätzen von **Übung D** zuerst alle Dativobjekte durch Pronomen, dann alle Akkusativobjekte durch Pronomen und zum Schluss beide Objekte durch Pronomen.

BEISPIEL Der Kellner bringt der Mutter ein Eis.
*Der Kellner bringt **ihr** ein Eis.*
*Der Kellner bringt **es** der Mutter.*
*Der Kellner bringt **es** **ihr.***

F **Der hilfreiche Hans.** Hans ist immer hilfsbereit. Erzählen Sie, was er heute alles gemacht hat. Drücken Sie die Sätze mit einem Dativ anders aus.

BEISPIEL Hans macht ein Frühstück für seine Frau.
*Hans macht **seiner Frau** ein Frühstück.*

1. Er hat einen Brief an seine Eltern geschrieben.
2. Er hat Blumen für seine Frau mitgebracht.
3. Er hat den Computer für seinen Chef repariert.

4. Er hat ein Märchen für seine Kinder erzählt.
5. Er hat den Wagen für seinen Freund Andreas gewaschen.

G   **Anders ausdrücken.**   Verwenden Sie die folgenden Verben aus dem Wortschatzkasten mit Dativobjekten.

BEISPIEL   Das ist mein Buch.
*Das Buch gehört **mir**.*

ähneln   danken   gehören   gehorchen   schmeicheln   widersprechen

---

1. Dreymans Wohnung sieht nicht aus wie die Wohnung von Jerska.
2. Du sollst tun, was ich dir sage.
3. Das ist der Wagen von meinem Lehrer.
4. Wenn der Professor *ja* sagt, soll man nicht zu schnell *nein* sagen.
5. Tobias sagt allen Leuten immer das, was sie gern über sich hören.
6. Ich möchte ihm meinen Dank für das nette Geschenk aussprechen.

H   **Worterklärungen.**   Erklären Sie die Wörter und verwenden Sie dabei den Genitiv.

BEISPIELE   der Familienvater
*Das ist **der Vater der Familie**.*

die Hosentaschen
*Das sind **die Taschen einer Hose**.*

1. die Bleistiftspitze
2. der Berggipfel
3. der Hausbesitzer
4. der Mauerfall
5. der Arbeiterstreik
6. die Lastwagenfahrer
   (der Lastwagen = *truck*)
7. die Lehrbuchpreise
8. der Schlossgarten
9. der Familienname
10. der Filmregisseur (*director*)
11. der Autounfall
12. die Handynummer

Anwendung

A   **Fragen zum Überlegen.**   Diskutieren Sie mit jemandem in Ihrem Kurs über die folgenden Fragen. Berichten Sie dann dem ganzen Kurs Ihre Ideen.

1. Welche Dinge sind im Leben von Studenten am wichtigsten?
2. Welche größeren Käufe würden Sie machen, wenn Sie das Geld dafür hätten?
3. Welche vier Dinge würden Sie unbedingt (*absolutely*) haben wollen, wenn Sie alleine auf einer kleinen Südseeinsel wären?
4. Welche fünf Erfindungen haben der Menschheit am meisten geholfen?

B **Ich kenne jenen Ort.** Jemand im Kurs hat vor *(plans),* einen Ort (z.B. eine Stadt, einen Park) zu besuchen, den Sie gut kennen. Erzählen Sie ihr/ihm, was es dort alles zu sehen gibt und was man da alles machen kann.

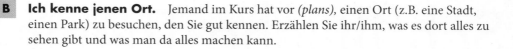

REDEMITTEL

Du musst unbedingt … sehen.
Vielleicht kannst du auch … besichtigen.
Dort gibt es …
Dort findet man auch …
Der … ist dort besonders gut/bekannt …
Empfehlen kann ich dir auch …

C **Familienverhältnisse *(family relationships).*** Bringen Sie Familienfotos zum Deutschunterricht mit. Zeigen Sie Ihre Bilder und erklären Sie die Familienverhältnisse.

VOKABELVORSCHLÄGE: FAMILIENMITGLIEDER

der Schwager	*brother-in-law*	die Schwägerin	*sister-in-law*
der Stiefvater	*stepfather*	die Stiefmutter	*stepmother*
der Stiefbruder	*stepbrother*	die Stiefschwester	*stepsister*
der Halbbruder	*half-brother*	die Halbschwester	*half-sister*
die Großeltern	*grandparents*	das Enkelkind	*grandchild*

REDEMITTEL

Unsere Familie besteht aus [fünf] Personen…
Das sind …
Auf diesem Bild siehst du …
[X] ist der/die … von …

D **Sei doch so nett!** Denken Sie darüber nach, wie Sie jemandem eine kleine Freude machen könnten – und dabei ein paar Akkusative und Dative benutzen. Das bedeutet natürlich, dass Sie jemandem etwas schenken oder schreiben, oder dass Sie für jemanden etwas Nettes tun.

BEISPIELE *Ich könnte meiner Mutter eine E-Mail schreiben.*
Ich könnte meiner Freundin Blumen schenken.

Was könnten *Sie* wohl machen?

Schriftliche Themen

> **Tipps zum Schreiben**
>
> **Checking for Correct Cases**
>
> After writing a first draft of any composition in German, be sure to check whether all the nouns and pronouns are in the correct cases. Read through each sentence and mark each noun or pronoun for its function: Is it the subject? Direct object? Indirect object? Object of a preposition? Remember that nouns in the predicate linked to the sentence subject with **sein, werden, bleiben,** and **heißen** are nominative, not accusative.

A   **Beziehungen.**   Wie sieht das aus, wenn es in einer Familie gute Beziehungen zwischen Eltern und Kinder gibt? Was können Freunde tun, um ihre Freundschaft zu vertiefen oder verbessern? Verwenden Sie in Ihrem Aufsatz ein paar Redewendungen mit **machen: jemandem Sorgen machen, einen Versuch machen, Lärm machen, Fortschritt machen, einen Fehler machen** usw. Wenn Sie den Film „Das Leben der anderen" gesehen haben, können Sie auch über das Thema „Beziehung" im Film schreiben.

B   **Witze!**   Im Film „Das Leben der anderen" spielen Witze eine Rolle, und unten finden Sie zwei DDR-Witze aus dieser Zeit. Können Sie einen Witz auf Deutsch erzählen? Nehmen Sie einen Witz, den Sie schon kennen, und suchen Sie die Vokabeln dafür auf Deutsch. Passen Sie bei den Fällen – Nominativ, Akkusativ, Dativ, Genitiv – gut auf und versuchen Sie dabei, Redewendungen mit **machen** zu benutzen.

BEISPIELE   A: „Können Sie mir den Kapitalismus erklären?"
　　　　　　　B: „Kapitalismus ist die Ausbeutung *(exploitation)* des Menschen durch den Menschen."
　　　　　　　A: „Und wie ist es mit dem Sozialismus?"
　　　　　　　B: „Da ist es genau umgekehrt *(the other way around)*!"

　　　　　　　Stasi-Mitarbeiter auf der Straße: „Was halten Sie von der aktuellen *(current)* politischen Lage *(situation)*?"
　　　　　　　Passant *(passerby)*: „Ich denke ... "
　　　　　　　Stasi-Mitarbeiter: „Das genügt *(suffices)* – Sie sind verhaftet *(arrested)*!"

Zusammenfassung

Rules to Remember

1 There are four cases in German: nominative, accusative, dative, and genitive.

2 Preceding articles and other modifiers (see 4.1–4 and 13.3) indicate the case of the noun that follows.

3 Pronouns indicate case by themselves (see 17.1).

4 The nominative case signals the subject of a sentence or a predicate nominative.

5 The accusative and dative cases signal objects of various kinds—direct, indirect, objects of prepositions—as well as several special uses (see "At a Glance" below).

6 The genitive case shows a special relationship between two or more nouns, often one of possession, and is also required by certain prepositions and verbs (see "At a Glance" below).

At a Glance

Nominativ		
der Mann	1	Sentence subject
die Frau	2	Predicate nominative follows:
das Geld		**sein** **heißen**
die Probleme		**bleiben** **scheinen**
		werden **gelten** [+ **als**]

Akkusativ		
den Mann	1	Direct object
die Frau	2	Accusative prepositions (6.1)
das Geld	3	Two-way prepositions: motion (6.3)
die Probleme	4	Measured distances and amounts (R.4)
	5	Time expressions (R.4)
	6	**Es gibt** _____ (20.3)

Dativ		
dem Mann(e)	1	Indirect object
der Frau	2	Verbs with dative objects
dem Geld(e)	3	Dative prepositions (6.3)
den Problem**en**	4	Two-way prepositions: position (6.4)
	5	"Dative of reference"
	6	Time expressions (R.4)
	7	With adjectives (13.4)

Genitiv		
des Mannes	1	Connection between nouns, usually denoting possession
der Frau	2	Genitive object of verbs
des Geld(**e**)s	3	After **sein**
der Probleme	4	Genitive prepositions (6.5)
	5	With adjectives and adverbs (13.4.B)
	6	Time expressions (R.4)

zum Beispiel

Eurovision Song Contest

AXEL HEIMKEN/AFP/Getty Images/Newscom

Eurovision is an annual song contest with an enormous and avid pan-European fan base. A singer (or a group of singers) representing each of the countries served by the European Broadcasting Union competes on live TV in front of a large and boisterous crowd, while the TV audiences in the various countries vote for their favorite performers from any of the other countries represented, i.e., you can't vote for your own country. Begun in 1956 with just a handful of participants, it now embraces most of Europe, extending to Ukraine, Turkey, and some countries in North Africa and the Middle East. Austria has won twice (1966, 2014), as have Switzerland and Germany, in 1956/1988 and 1982/2010, respectively. Winning the **Eurovision** contest has led to international careers for several artists, including ABBA and Céline Dion.

85

Grammatik

A preposition with its object and any related articles and modifiers is called a *prepositional phrase*. Some prepositional phrases function adverbially by telling *how* (**ohne deine Hilfe**), *when* (**nach dem Seminar**), or *where* (**auf der Straße**) something occurs, and follow the word order rules of the middle field (see 1.1.C). Some function as verbal complements (**denken + an dich**), and come at the very end of the middle field. Prepositional phrases can also describe persons and things (**die Kellnerin mit den müden Augen**), provide explanation (**wegen des Wetters**), or take on other functions.

All German prepositions require a specific case for their noun or pronoun objects, depending on the preposition and its use. Prepositions are said to "govern" a case, which means that each preposition dictates the case of the associated noun and its modifiers. The prepositions listed below, following an introductory discussion of contractions, are grouped according to the case(s) they govern for their objects. Keep in mind as you read that the meanings given in this chapter for each preposition are its most basic, or default, meanings. Like most words, prepositions can take on many meanings, and frequently they do so in combination with nouns, verbs, and adjectives, for example, **Interesse *an*** *(interest in)*, **warten *auf*** *(to wait for)*, **fähig *zu*** *(capable of)*. It is important to notice the context in which prepositions occur, and learn to associate these combinations with their correct meanings.

6.1   PREPOSITIONS AND CONTRACTIONS

In the examples throughout this chapter, you will notice that many of the prepositions appear in contracted form with articles, e.g., **im (in + dem)** and **ums (um + das)**. Commonly used contractions will be listed for each group of prepositions in the following sections of the chapter. But the question inevitably arises: When are the contracted forms appropriate, and when should one use the separate elements? This is not just a matter of informal vs. formal style. When the focus of attention is on the noun following the preposition, and especially when that noun is particularized by a subsequent modifying clause, the noncontracted form is preferable.

COMPARE:

Ins Düsseldorfer Stadion strömten 24.000 kreischende Fans.

Twenty-four thousand screaming fans poured into the stadium. (emphasis on the fans)

Die Fans strömten **in das** Stadion, wo am 14. Mai das Finale stattfinden sollte.

The fans poured into the stadium where the final would take place on the 14th of May. (emphasis on the stadium itself)

Unless there is a need to particularize the noun, however, the contracted form should be used in phrases where this is the norm, as in these examples.

beim Lesen (i.e., with any infinitive used as a noun)
beim Frühstück, **beim** Mittagessen, **beim** Abendessen
im April, **am** Montag, **am** Wochenende
ins Kino, **ins** Bett
zum Geburtstag, **zum** Glück, **zum** Beispiel

6.2 ACCUSATIVE PREPOSITIONS

A. Forms

1. The accusative prepositions (**die Präposition, -en**) are as follows:

bis	*until, to, as far as, by*	**ohne**	*without*
durch	*through*	**um**	*around; at*
für	*for*	**wider**	*against*[1]
gegen	*against; toward*		

2. The following contractions with accusative prepositions are quite common:

    durchs (durch das)   **fürs** (für das)   **ums** (um das)

B. Use

An accusative preposition is followed by an object noun or pronoun in the accusative case. The accusative case must be shown by the noun itself, if possible (this happens with weak masculine nouns; see R.1.3), and any articles or modifiers connected to it in the noun phrase.

C. *Bis*

1. **Bis** means *until, as far as, up to,* or *by a certain point or time.*

Der Wettbewerb beginnt am Donnerstag, und die Proben gehen **bis** Mittwoch.	*The competition begins on Thursday, and the rehearsals go until Wednesday.*
Bis Donnerstagabend muss alles fertig sein.	*By Thursday evening, everything has to be ready.*
Von 1966 **bis** 1973 musste das Lied in der offiziellen Landessprache gesungen werden.	*From 1966 until 1973, the song had to be sung in the official language of the country.*

---

[1]**Wider** is used as a preposition very infrequently, appearing only in a few idiomatic phrases such as **wider Erwarten** (*against all expectation*). It is more often used as a variable verb prefix (see Reference 5.3.5). Be careful not to confuse it with the **wieder**, which is used as an adverb (*again*) and as a verb prefix, meaning *back*.

2. **Bis** is frequently used in combination with other prepositions. In such constructions the case of the following noun phrase is determined by the other preposition, not by **bis.**

Bis vor 10 Jahren haben 37 Länder daran teilgenommen, aber jetzt sind es mehr als 50.	*Up until 10 years ago, 37 countries participated in it, but now there are more than 50.*
Jedes Lied darf **bis zu** drei Minuten dauern.	*Every song is allowed to last up to three minutes.*
Das Finale dauert immer **bis** spät **in die** Nacht.	*The Grand Finale always lasts until late into the night.*
2014 mussten die Fans **bis nach** Dänemark reisen.	*In 2014, the fans had to travel all the way to Denmark.*
Bis zu sechs Personen dürfen für jeden Auftritt auf der Bühne sein.	*Up to six people are allowed to be on stage for each performance.*

D. *Durch*

Durch means *through.*

Nach dem Finale feiern die Fans und die Musiker **durch** die Nacht.	*After the Grand Finale, the fans and the musicians celebrate through the night.*
Die Teilnehmerliste liest sich wie eine Tour **durch** Europa.	*The list of participants reads like a tour through Europe.*
Popmusiker wie ABBA und Céline Dion sind **durch** ihren Erfolg bei Eurovision bekannt geworden.	*Pop musicians such as ABBA and Céline Dion became famous through (by means of) their success at Eurovision.*

E. *Für*

1. **Für** means *for.*

Für die Musiker bietet Eurovision eine große Chance.	*For the musicians, Eurovision offers a great opportunity.*
Die Gastgeberstadt muss ein Stadion **für** alle Musiker und Fans bieten.	*The host city has to provide a stadium for all the musicians and fans.*

2. **Für** can be used to indicate duration, as in English *for a week,* but only when the time element is unrelated to the main verb. This is the case, for example, in the following sentence:

2011 fuhren die Delegationen von 43 Ländern **für** zwei Wochen nach Düsseldorf.	*In 2011, the delegations from 43 countries traveled for two weeks to Düsseldorf.*

Für zwei Wochen tells you not how long it took to get there (**fuhren**), but rather how long the delegations intended to stay.

3. When the duration does apply to the verb, **für** is *not* used, but rather an accusative time expression without any preposition (see R.4), as in the following example.

Die Live-Übertragung dauert mindestens **drei Stunden**.	*The live broadcast lasts at least three hours.*

4. When a prepositional phrase is used to indicate *how long* an activity has been going on, German uses **seit** (+ dative) or **schon,** rather than **für,** in conjunction with the *present tense* (see 2.2.B).

Seit ungefähr 15 Jahren kann man das Finale auch online sehen.	*For about 15 years people have been able to watch the Grand Finale online as well.*

F. *Gegen*

1. **Gegen** means *against* or *in exchange for*.

Die Türkei war **gegen** die Aufnahme von Italien in die „Big Five"-Gruppe[2].	*Turkey was against the induction of Italy into the "Big Five" group.*
1956 hat die Schweiz **gegen** alle Erwartung gewonnen.	*Against all expectations, Switzerland won in 1956.*
Viele Länder waren **gegen** das neue Wahlkonzept.	*Many countries were against the new voting concept.*
Jemand hatte einem Mann ein Hotelzimmer in Düsseldorf im Tausch **gegen** ein Ticket fürs Finale gegeben.	*Someone had given a man a hotel room in Düsseldorf in exchange for a ticket to the Grand Finale.*

2. **Gegen** can also be used in a very narrow sense to mean *into* in relation to directional motion, as in *driving into* or *running into*.

Der Mann fuhr **gegen** die Garagentür.	*The man drove into the garage door.*
Sie lief **gegen** ein Fenster.	*She ran into a window.*

3. English uses *against* to describe locations, as in *The cabinet was against the back wall*. German usage with **gegen** is more restricted than this, and is usually reserved for motion toward something, as in the examples above. An exception is its usage with **lehnen** (*to lean*), which can indicate position (when used without a direct object), or with a direct object to show motion toward something.

Eine Leiter lehnte **gegen** die Wand.	*A ladder was leaning against the house.*
Ich lehnte die Leiter **gegen** die Wand.	*I leaned the ladder against the wall.*

4. In time expressions, **gegen** means *toward* (see R.4.3.B).

Gegen Mitternacht wurden die Fans unruhig.	*Toward midnight the fans became restless.*

---

[2]Only 26 participants are allowed to compete in the final round. Five countries that provide major financial support for the event—the so-called "Big Five"—are guaranteed a spot among those 26 finalists: The United Kingdom, France, Germany, Spain, and (since 2011) Italy.

G. *Ohne*

Ohne means *without.*

Bis 1973 mussten die Lieder live, d.h. **ohne** Playback-Musik gesungen werden.	*Until 1973 the songs had to be sung live, i.e., without a soundtrack.*
Das Spektakel zählt viel, aber **ohne** einen guten Song kann niemand gewinnen.	*The spectacle counts for a lot, but without a good song, no one can win.*

H. *Um*

1. **Um** means *around* and is often used with an optional **herum.**

Um die Bühne **(herum)** ist immer viel los.	*There's always a lot going on around the stage.*
Er verließ das Stadion und ging **um** die Ecke ins Hotel.	*He left the stadium and went around the corner into the hotel.*

2. For the use of **um** in time expressions, see R.4.3.

6.3   DATIVE PREPOSITIONS

A. Forms

1. The dative prepositions are as follows:

aus	*out of, (made) of, from*	**mit**	*with, by*
außer	*except for, besides; out of*	**nach**	*to, toward; after; according to*
bei	*by, near, at; with, in case of, during; upon, when, while doing*	**seit**	*since, for*
		von	*from, of; by; about*
gegenüber	*across from, opposite*	**zu**	*to; at*

2. The following contractions are quite common:

beim (bei dem)	**zum** (zu dem)
vom (von dem)	**zur** (zu der)

B. Use

Dative prepositions are followed by objects in the dative case.

C. *Aus*

1. **Aus** means *out of, (made) of,* or *from the point of origin.*

Sänger **aus** ganz Europa machen mit.	*Singers from all of Europe participate.*
Lena, die deutsche Preisträgerin 2010, kommt **aus** Hannover.	*Lena, the German winner in 2010, comes from (i.e., grew up in) Hannover.*
Die deutsche Gruppe „Cascada" bestand **aus** drei Sängern.	*The German group "Cascada" consisted of three singers.*

2. When **aus** is used with a city or country, it signifies origin (especially in conjunction with **kommen** or **sein** in the present tense). It can also refer simply to a point of departure. But to describe an itinerary (traveling from A to B), the point of departure is expressed with **von**, and the destination with **nach/zu** (see the **Wortschatz** section of this chapter for more details).

Die Band kommt **aus** London.	*The band comes from London. (The band originated in London; its roots are in London.)*
Die Band ist gerade **aus** London gekommen.	*The band just came from London. (The band was in London, then came here; nothing else is implied about its relationship to London.)*
Die Band ist gestern **von** London **nach** Zürich geflogen.	*The band flew from London to Zurich yesterday.*

D. *Außer*

1. **Außer** usually means *except (for), besides,* or *in addition to.*

Außer einem Lied hat mir die Musik gar nicht gefallen.	*Except for one song, I didn't like the music at all.*
Außer der Schweiz haben noch andere Länder mehr als einmal gewonnen.	*Besides (in addition to) Switzerland, several countries have won more than once.*

2. In a few idiomatic expressions **außer** means *out of.*

Ich bin jetzt **außer Atem.**	*I am now out of breath.*
Der Lift ist **außer Betrieb.**	*The elevator is out of order.*

E. *Bei*

1. When used with geographical locations, **bei** means *near* or *by.*

1983 fand das Programm in Sendling-Westpark **bei** München statt.	*In 1983, the program took place in Sendling-Westpark, near Munich.*

2. Used in conjunction with the name of a store or restaurant, **bei** means *at;* with the name of a company it means *for.*

Habt ihr **bei** McDonald's gegessen?	*Did you all eat at McDonald's?*
Sie kauft alles **bei** H&M in München.	*She buys everything at H&M in Munich.*
Seit wann arbeitest du **bei** BMW?	*Since when have you been working for BMW?*

3. Used with a person's name or a personal pronoun, **bei** means *at that person's home* (e.g., **bei Julia** = *at Julia's place;* **bei uns** = *at our place*). Likewise, **zu** followed by a

person's name or a personal pronoun indicates going *to where the person lives* (see 3.K below).

Letztes Jahr sah ich die Show **bei Julia.**	*Last year I watched the show at Julia's place.*
Dieses Jahr aber kommen alle **zu mir.**	*This year, however, everybody is coming over to my place.*

4. **Bei** can express the idea of *in case of, during,* or *with.*

Bei seinem ersten Auftritt hat ein Sänger einen furchtbaren Patzer gemacht.	*During his first performance, one singer made a horrific mistake.*
Bei einem Unentschieden gibt es ein komplexes Entscheidungsverfahren.	*In case of a tie, there's a complex decision process.*

5. **Bei** can also be used in conjunction with a verb to give the meaning *in the course of* or *while doing an activity.* In this usage, the verb is used as a noun and the definite article (see 4.1.B) contracts with the preposition to form **beim.**

Beim Wählen warten die Zuschauer gespannt.	*During the voting the spectators wait anxiously.*
Ich bin **beim** Zuschauen eingeschlafen.	*I fell asleep while watching.*

F. *Gegenüber*

1. **Gegenüber** means *across from* or *opposite.* Pronoun objects usually precede this preposition.

Sie saß **ihm** gegenüber.	*She sat across from him.*

Noun objects can either precede or follow **gegenüber.**

Er saß **seiner Frau** gegenüber. Er saß gegenüber **seiner Frau.**	*He sat across from his wife.*

2. **Gegenüber** is often joined with **von,** in which case the object—noun or pronoun—follows **von.**

Gegenüber von den Sängern standen viele Fans.	*A lot of fans were standing across from the singers.*

G. *Mit*

1. In its most basic meaning, **mit** means *with.*

Früher hat man **mit** tragbaren Mikros gesungen, aber jetzt benutzt man Kopfbügelmikros.	*They used to sing with hand-held microphones, but now they use headsets.*

2. **Mit** also indicates the instrument or means with which an activity is performed (see also 12.1.C).

Sag mal, wie hat Dänemark 2013 **mit** dem absurden Lied gewonnen?	*Tell me, how did Denmark win in 2013 with (by means of) that absurd song?*

3. When describing means of transportation, **mit** means *by* and is normally used with a definite article (see 4.1.B).

Bist du **mit** *dem* Auto oder **mit** *der* Bahn nach Düsseldorf gereist?	*Did you travel to Düsseldorf by car or by train?*

H. *Nach*

1. **Nach** often means *(going) to* and is used with proper names of geographical locations such as towns, cities, countries, and continents. It is also used with directions and points of the compass.

2012 sind Zehntausende **nach** Malmö im Süden von Schweden gereist.	*In 2012, tens of thousands traveled to Malmö, in southern Sweden.*
2014 sind genau so viele Leute **nach** Dänemark gereist.	*In 2014, just as many people traveled to Denmark.*
Die Straße führt zuerst **nach** rechts, dann scharf **nach** links und dann geradeaus **nach** Norden.	*The street goes first to the right, then sharply to the left, and then straight ahead to the north.*

2. In some contexts, **nach** can also indicate motion *toward* a place or object.

Alle Zuschauer blickten gespannt **nach** der Bühne.	*All of the spectators were looking expectantly toward the stage.*

3. **Nach** can mean *after* in either a temporal or a spatial sense.

Die Ansage des Siegers kommt immer **nach** einer ziemlich langen Pause.	*The announcement of the winner always comes after a rather long break.*
Nach dem Eingang siehst du die Treppe zum Balkon. Wir sind oben links.	*After the entrance you'll see the stairs to the balcony. We're upstairs on the left.*

4. **Nach** sometimes means *according to* or *judging by;* in this case **nach** usually follows its object.

Einigen Kritikern **nach** besteht die Show nur noch aus Spektakel.	*According to some critics, the show consists of nothing but spectacle.*
Aber dem Publikum **nach** hat sie nichts an Beliebtheit verloren.	*But according to the audience, it hasn't lost any popularity.*

5. **Nach** occurs in a number of idiomatic expressions.

nach Bedarf   *as needed*
nach Belieben   *at one's discretion*
nach dem Gehör   *by ear* (as in *playing the piano by ear*)
nach Hause   *(to go) home*
nach Wunsch   *as you wish, as desired*
(nur) dem Namen nach kennen   *to know by name (only)*
nach und nach   *little by little, gradually*
nach wie vor   *now as ever, the same as before*

I. *Seit*

1. **Seit** indicates *for how long* or *since when* an action that started in the past *has* or *had been going on.* German uses **seit** with the present tense, where English requires the present perfect (see 2.2), and **seit** with the simple past tense where English uses the past perfect. **Seit** often occurs with the adverb **schon.**

Seit 1977 *versucht* Frankreich, noch einmal zu gewinnen.	France **has been trying** since 1977 to win again.
Den Wettbewerb *gab* es erst **seit** zwei Jahren, als die Schweiz gewonnen hat.	The competition had only been around for two years when Switzerland won.

2. **Seit** also functions colloquially as a shortened form of **seitdem** (see R.2), a subordinating conjunction that introduces a dependent clause. **NOTE:** One must be careful to discern the function of **seit** in a sentence. As a preposition, it requires the dative case for nouns associated with it; as a conjunction, it has no effect on the case of following nouns.

   COMPARE:

Preposition: Seit **dem** Lied „Rise like a Phoenix" hat Österreich mehr Siege als Belgien.	*Ever since the song "Rise like a Phoenix," Austria has had more wins than Belgium.*
Conjunction: Seit Conchita Wurst **das** Lied „Rise like a Phoenix" gesungen hat, hat Österreich mehr Siege als Belgien.	*Ever since Conchita Wurst sang the song "Rise like a Phoenix," Austria has had more wins than Belgium.*

J. *Von*

1. **Von** means *from* a source, but not *out of* a point of origin (see **aus,** 3.C above).

Die Idee für das ganze Unternehmen kam **von** der European Broadcasting Union.	*The idea for the whole enterprise came from the European Broadcasting Union.*
Die echten Fans fahren jedes Jahr **von** Land zu Land.	*The real fans travel every year from country to country.*
Lädst du deine Musik **vom** Internet runter oder kaufst du noch CDs?	*Do you download your music from the Internet or do you still buy CDs?*

2. **Von** means *of* when it expresses a relationship of *belonging* between two nouns. It is often a substitute for the genitive case, and must be used if there is no modifier to signal the genitive (see 5.6.D).

Die Sängerin **von** „Cascada" war Natalie Horler.	*Cascada's singer was Natalie Horler.*

3. **Von** can also mean *by* (authorship) or *about* (topic of discussion).

Das Lied „Glorious" ist **von** Yann Peifer und Manuel Reuter.	*The song "Glorious" is by Yann Peifer and Manuel Reuter.*
Die europäischen Medien schreiben gern **von** jedem Skandal im Wettbewerb.	*The European media likes to write about every scandal in the contest.*

4. **Von** in combination with **aus** indicates a vantage point or motion away from a particular location; **aus** has no direct English equivalent in this usage.

Von unserem Stehplatz **aus** hat man gar nichts gesehen.	*From where we were standing, you couldn't see anything at all.*
Von Berlin **aus** ist man in etwa fünf Stunden mit dem Auto in Düsseldorf.	*From Berlin you can be in Düsseldorf in about five hours by car.*

5. **Von** in combination with **an** indicates a point from which an activity starts and continues; in this usage, **an** translates into English as *on*.

Von jetzt **an** bitte keine schmalzigen Lieder mehr!	*From now on, no more corny songs, please!*

K. *Zu*

1. **Zu** means *to* and is used with persons, objects, locales, and events. (See the **Wortschatz** section in this chapter for more details.)

Einige von diesen Sängern sollten **zu** einem Gesangslehrer gehen ...	*Some of these singers should go to a voice teacher . . .*
... und andere **zum** Tanzcoaching.	*. . . and others to a dance coach.*
Gehst du heute Abend **zu** Natalie?	*Are you going to Natalie's (home) tonight?*

2. The contracted form **zum** commonly occurs with infinitives used as nouns (see 4.1.B).

Hast du etwas **zum** Essen oder Trinken mitgebracht?	*Did you bring something along to eat or drink?*
Ich habe nichts **zum** Anziehen.	*I don't have anything to wear.*

3. **Zu** occurs in a number of idiomatic expressions.

zu dritt, zu viert usw.   *in threes, in fours, etc.*
zu Ende   *over, at an end*
zu Fuß   *on foot*
zu Hause   *at home (compare with* nach Hause*)*
zu Ihnen/dir   *(to go) to your place*
zu Eva   *(to go) to Eva's place; cf.* bei Eva
zu Mittag   *at noon*
zu Weihnachten, zu Ostern   *for/at Christmas, for/at Easter*

zum Beispiel   *for example*
zum Essen, zum Schreiben usw.   *for eating, for writing, etc.*
zum Frühstück, zum Mittagessen   *for/at breakfast/the midday meal*
zum Geburtstag   *for one's birthday*
zum Kaffee (nehmen)   *(to take) with one's coffee*
zum Schluss   *in conclusion*
zum Wohl!   *(here's) to your health!*

4. **Zu** is sometimes used in the names of eating establishments.

   (Gasthaus) zum Roten Bären   *the Red Bear Inn*

5. **Zu** should *not* be used with **geben** and other verbs of giving. Such verbs require an indirect object in the dative case (see 5.5.B).

   Sie gibt es **ihrem** Freund.   *She gives it to her friend.*

6.4 VARIABLE PREPOSITIONS

A. Forms

1. The following prepositions are called two-way or variable prepositions (**Wechselprä-positionen**) because they can take either the accusative or the dative, depending on how they are used.

an	*at, on, to*	**über**	*over, across; above; about*
auf	*on, upon, at*	**unter**	*under, beneath, below; among*
hinter	*behind*	**vor**	*before, in front of; ago*
in	*in, into, inside*	**zwischen**	*between*
neben	*beside, next to*		
entlang	*along*		

2. The following contractions are very common and are preferred to the separated forms, unless the following noun is being emphasized.

Accusative	**Dative**
ans (an das)	**am** (an dem)
aufs (auf das)	
ins (in das)	**im** (in dem)

3. The following contractions are considered colloquial.

Accusative	**Dative**
hinters (hinter das)	**hinterm** (hinter dem)
übers (über das)	**überm** (über dem)
vors (vor das)	**vorm** (vor dem)

B. Use

1. Variable prepositions take the *dative case* when the context indicates *location*.

   Wo steht sie?   *Where is she standing?*
   —**Im** Garten.   —*In the garden.*

2. Variable prepositions take the *accusative case* when the context indicates *direction or motion toward an object or place*.

   Wohin geht er?   *Where is he going?*
   —**In den** Garten.   —*Into the garden.*

3. Motion itself does not necessarily mean that the object must be in the accusative. The motion can be taking place within the area of the object, in which case the object is in the dative, since there is no change of position with respect to this location.

Wo laufen die Kinder?	*Where are the children running (around)?*
—**Im** Garten.	—*In the garden.*

4. Variable prepositions are widely used in a variety of idiomatic expressions that have nothing to do with the "position vs. motion" distinction; the expressions themselves determine whether the object of the preposition will be in the accusative or dative case. In a sentence such as **Ich habe Angst vor dieser Schlange** *(I'm scared of this snake),* for example, the dative is necessary not because of position, but because the phrase **Angst haben vor** *(to be scared of)* stipulates a dative object for the preposition **vor.** Such phrases must be learned with the appropriate case assignments for their prepositions. The following definitions, examples, and comments are restricted to the spatial meanings of the variable prepositions. For additional uses in idiomatic phrases, see 10.2, 13.5, and especially R.3.

C. *An*

An can mean *to* with the accusative and *at* with the dative when used with some verbs; it can mean *on* with reference to vertical surfaces.

Sie ging **an die** Anzeigetafel.	*She walked **to** the scoreboard.*
Das Ergebnis stand **an der** Anzeigetafel.	*The result was **on** the scoreboard.*

D. *Auf*

1. **Auf** means *on* (that is, located on a horizontal surface) with the dative, and *onto* (that is, moving toward a horizontal surface) with the accusative.

Das Duo tanzte **auf die** Bühne. *(direction)*	*The duo danced **onto** the stage.*
Das Duo tanzte **auf der** Bühne. *(location)*	*The duo danced **on** the stage.*

2. **Auf** can be used in certain contexts to express *going to a specific location,* as explained in the **Wortschatz** section of this chapter.

Nach dem Finale gingen wir alle **auf eine** Party. *(direction)*	*After the grand finale, we all went **to** a party.*
Nach dem Finale war ich **auf einer** Party. *(location)*	*After the grand finale, I was **at** a party.*

3. German uses **auf** with pictures, signs, or posters, where English uses *in* or *on.*

Wer steht **auf** dem Foto neben der Siegerin?	*Who is standing next to the winner in the picture?*
Auf der Webseite stand, dass das Programm um 20.00 Uhr beginnt.	*On the website it said that the program begins at 8:00 PM.*

E. *Hinter*

Hinter means *behind*.

Zwei Männer tanzten **hinter der** Sängerin. *(location)*	*Two men danced behind the singer.*
Dann lief die Sängerin **hinter die** Tänzer. *(direction)*	*Then the singer ran behind the dancers.*

F. *In*

1. **In** means *in* with the dative and *into* with the accusative. It is also used in certain contexts where English uses *at* or *to*.

Schon am Nachmittag strömten Tausende **ins** Stadion. *(direction)*	*In the afternoon, thousands of people were already pouring into the stadium.*
Am Abend waren mehr als 20.000 Menschen **im** Stadion. *(location)*	*In the evening, there were more than 20,000 people in the stadium.*

2. **In** is used in combination with certain venues (see the **Wortschatz** section in this chapter for examples) to indicate *going* to a place for a specific activity, e.g., movie theater, concert, café, etc. **Zu** can also be used in these phrases, but this changes the meaning slightly, depending on the phrase in play. ***Ins* Konzert gehen,** for example, implies going to a formal concert, with classical music; ***zum* Konzert gehen** is used for a rock concert. ***Ins* Kino gehen** means *going to see a movie*; ***zum* Kino gehen** means going to the building, but not necessarily going inside.

3. **In** is used with media where English uses *on*.

im Fernsehen	*on TV*
im Netz, **im** Internet	*on the Web, on the Internet*
BUT: **am** Telefon, **am** Handy	*on the telephone, on the cell phone*
auf/bei Facebook, **auf/bei** Twitter	*on Facebook, on Twitter*

G. *Neben*

Neben means *beside* or *next to*.

Wir stellten uns direkt **neben die** Bühne. *(direction)*	*We positioned ourselves right next to the stage.*
Wir blieben den ganzen Abend **neben der** Bühne. *(location)*	*We stayed the whole evening next to the stage.*

H. *Über*

1. **Über** means *over, above, across,* or *about*.

Über dem Publikum schwebte die Beleuchtung. *(location)*	*The lighting was suspended above the audience.*
Man hatte sogar fahrbare Kameras **über das** Publikum hingestellt. *(direction)*	*They had even placed mobile cameras above the audience.*

2. **Über** appears in many idiomatic expressions that include a preposition (see 10.2 and R.3.2 for examples), and usually means *about*. In such cases it always takes the accusative case.

Die Presse hat tagelang **über die** deutsche Niederlage geschrieben.	*The press wrote for days about the German defeat.*

I. *Unter*

1. **Unter** means *under, beneath,* or *below.*

In Schweden fand die ganze Show **unter einer** riesigen Betonmuschel statt. *(location)*	*In Sweden the entire show took place under a giant concrete shell.*
Man hatte die technische Ausrüstung **unter den** Zuschauerraum hingestellt. *(direction)*	*They had put the technical equipment underneath the spectator area.*

2. **Unter** can also mean *among.*

Keine Sorge! Sie sind hier **unter** Freunden.	*Don't worry! You're among friends here.*

J. *Vor*

1. **Vor** means *in front of* or *ahead of.*

Wir treffen uns **vor** dem Stadion. *(location)*	*We'll meet in front of the stadium.*
Eine weiße Limousine fuhr **vor das** Stadion. *(direction)*	*A white limousine drove up in front of the stadium.*

2. In a temporal sense, **vor** means *before* and takes the dative.

Alle Länder müssen ihre Lieder einige Monate **vor dem** Wettbewerb bekanntgeben.	*All the countries have to announce their songs several months before the competition.*
Welches Land kommt **vor der** Schweiz?	*Which country comes (= plays) before Switzerland?*

3. With units of time (years, weeks, days, etc.) **vor** means *ago* and takes the dative case. Notice that unlike English, the preposition *precedes* rather than follows the time unit.

Vor mehr als **zehn Jahren** ist die Türkei dazugekommen.	*Turkey joined in more than **10 years ago.***
Man hat den Sieger **vor einer Stunde** bekanntgegeben.	*They announced the winner **one hour ago.***

K. *Zwischen*

Zwischen means *between.*

Die Sängerin aus Kroatien stand **zwischen den** Tänzern. *(location)*	*The singer from Croatia stood between the dancers.*

| Ein Tänzer aus Norwegen stellte sich dann **zwischen die** zwei Sängerinnen. *(direction)* | *A dancer from Norway then placed himself between the two singers.* |

L. *Entlang*

Entlang means *along*. It normally *precedes* a noun in the dative case when indicating *position* along an object, but it *follows* a noun in the accusative case when indicating *direction* along an object.

| Die Fans standen **entlang der** Straße hinter dem Stadion. *(location)* | *The fans were standing along the road behind the stadium.* |
| Die Straße führte **den** ganzen Parkplatz **entlang.** *(direction)* | *The road led along the entire parking lot.* |

6.5   GENITIVE PREPOSITIONS

A. Forms

Frequent

(an)statt   *instead of*
außerhalb   *outside of*
innerhalb   *inside of*
trotz   *in spite of*
während   *during*
wegen   *because of, on account of*

Less frequent

diesseits   *this side of*
jenseits   *that side of*
oberhalb   *above, on the upper side of*
unterhalb   *beneath, on the bottom side of*

There are also some fifty more genitive prepositions generally restricted to official or legal language: **angesichts** *(in light of)*, **mangels** *(in the absence of)*, etc.

B. *(An)statt, trotz, während, wegen*

1. **(An)statt, trotz, während,** and **wegen** are normally followed by objects in the genitive case, though in colloquial German the dative is also quite common.

| Früher hatte man **trotz des** Verbots/**dem** Verbot auf Englisch gesungen. | *They used to sing in English in spite of the prohibition.* |
| Aber ich möchte **statt dieser** Lieder/**diesen** Liedern auf Englisch lieber etwas in der Landessprache hören. | *But I'd rather hear something in the national language instead of these songs in English.* |

2. When genitive prepositions are followed by masculine or neuter nouns without articles, the genitive **-s** can be (but is not necessarily) dropped (see 5.2).

Wegen Schnee (Wegen Schnees) wird das Programm abgesagt.	*Because of snow, the program is being cancelled.*

3. Genitive prepositions are used infrequently with pronouns. The one exception is **wegen,** which either takes dative pronouns or combines with special pronoun forms, for example:

wegen mir or **meinetwegen**	*as far as I'm concerned/because of me*
wegen dir or **deinetwegen**	*as far as you're concerned/because of you*
wegen uns or **unseretwegen**	*as far as we're concerned/because of us*
Ich tue es **seinetwegen.**	*I am doing it on his account/on account of him.*
Wegen mir brauchst du dir keine Sorgen (zu) machen.	*You don't have to worry on my account.*

4. The form **meinetwegen** is used idiomatically to mean *for all I care* or *it's okay by me.* It often occurs all by itself in response to a question.

Papa, kann ich nächstes Jahr zum Wettbewerb?	*Dad, can I go to the competition next year?*
—**Meinetwegen**.	*—It's okay with me.*
Mama, was meinst du?	*Mom, what do you think?*
—**Meinetwegen** kannst du gehen, aber das musst du selbst bezahlen.	*—As far as I'm concerned you can go, but you'll have to pay for it yourself.*

C. *Außerhalb, innerhalb, oberhalb, unterhalb; diesseits, jenseits*

1. **Diesseits, jenseits,** and the prepositions with **-halb** can be followed by either the genitive or by **von** + dative.

Jenseits der/von der Grenze sind die Leute genauso enthusiastisch.	*Beyond (on the other side of) the border, people are just as enthusiastic.*
Außerhalb der/von der European Broadcasting Union darf kein Land mitmachen.	*No country outside of the European Broadcasting Union is allowed to participate.*
Oberhalb der/von der Bühne ist Spektakel pur – Feuer, Nebel und Computergrafik.	*Above the stage, it's pure spectacle— fire, fog, and computer graphics.*

2. In the plural, however, **von** + dative must be used if there is no article to indicate case.

Die Ergebnisse des Televotings sind immer **innerhalb von** Minuten da.	*The results of the TV voting are always ready within minutes.*

Wortschatz
Wie sagt man *to go to...?*

English uses the preposition *to* for most situations denoting motion toward a destination (traveling, walking, going). This can cause problems for English speakers learning German, because German distinguishes among possible destinations by using different prepositions. Here are the some of the most commonly used combinations.

a. *going to a country*

nach [*country name*]	Frank und Marc fahren **nach Marokko.**

in [*country names that include an article, such as*]
    die Schweiz
    die Türkei
    der Iraq / der Iran
    die USA (*plural*)
	Sie fährt mit der Bahn **in die Schweiz.**
	Daniel und Julia sind **in die Türkei** gefahren.
	
	Freunde von mir reisen im Sommer **in die USA.**

b. *going to a city*

nach [*city name*]	Morgen fahren wir **nach** Budapest.

c. *going to a specific site or locale*

generic name of an enclosed space	**in** (+ *acc.*)[3]	Wir gehen gern ins Café.
		            ins Restaurant.
		            ins Konzert.
		            ins Museum.
		            ins Stadion.
		            ins Kino.
		            in die Kirche.
		            in die Oper.

proper name; job title as location; unenclosed space	**zu** (+ *dat.*)	Ich gehe jetzt zu Aldi.[3]
		            zu Burger King.
		            zum Bäcker (*baker's*).
		            zum Friseur (*barber's*).
		            zum Alexanderplatz.
		            zum Markt.

"official" locales such as government offices, banks, post offices	**auf** (+ *acc.*)	Sie muss auf die Bank gehen.
		            auf die Post.
		            auf das (aufs) Arbeitsamt.

---

[3]In colloquial speech, Germans also use **zu** with generic stores: **Ich geh' noch schnell zur Drogerie.** It is primarily in established idioms such as **ins Kino gehen** that the use of **zu** implies *going up to, but not necessarily into* (see 6.4.F).

including this very specific locale

to go to the WC, bathroom, toilet	**auf** (+ *acc.*)	Entschuldigung, … ich muss auf das (aufs) WC (gehen). auf das (aufs) Klo (gehen).

d. *going to a celebratory event*

parties, festivals, weddings	**auf** (+ *acc.*)	Er geht mit uns auf die Party. auf das (aufs) Fest. auf eine Hochzeit.

e. *going (to someone's) home*

to go home (default: going to the home of the sentence subject)	**nach Hause**	Wann musst du nach Hause gehen? *(i.e., to where you live)* Wann muss Max nach Hause gehen? *(i.e., to where he lives)*
to go to [X's] home (i.e., to the home of someone other than the sentence subject)	**zu [X]** **zu [X] nach Hause**	Wir gehen zu Max. Wir gehen zu Max nach Hause. *(i.e., to where he lives)*

Since these examples all involve *going to a destination*, the variable prepositions **in** and **auf** require the accusative case. But when the situation denotes being *at the destination*, these prepositions require the dative case:

Ich war **auf der Party**.

Arbeitet sie **im Café**?

Similarly, the idiom **zu Hause** means *at home* and is used with verbs that denote position or activity at that location (e.g., **sein, essen, schlafen, arbeiten**), as opposed to verbs that denote *going home*. As in English, the default interpretation of *at home* assumes the home of the sentence subject:

Ich arbeite meistens **zu Hause**.	*I work mostly at home. (i.e., where I live)*
Anna arbeitet immer **zu Hause**.	*Anna always works at home. (i.e., where she lives)*

But if the home in question is not that of the sentence subject, **bei [X]** must be used, either by itself or in conjunction with **zu Hause**:

Ich arbeite heute *bei Anna* (**zu Hause**).	*I'm working today at Anna's house / Anna's place / where Anna lives.*

Übungen

A **Wie oft gehe ich …?** Ergänzen Sie die Sätze unten mit einem Element von **Liste A** und einem Element von **Liste B** – natürlich mit der richtigen Präposition dafür!

Liste A	**Liste B**
oft	[ein Land]
nicht oft	[eine Stadt]
jeden Tag	[Hause]
alle [zwei] Tage	Bank
(every two days)	Bibliothek
manchmal	Café
einmal, zweimal, dreimal, …	Party
noch nie	Hochzeit
im Sommer	Kino
im Monat	Kirche
(ganz) selten	Konzert
	Oper

1. Dieses Semester bin ich _____ gegangen / gefahren / geflogen.
2. Letzte Woche bin ich _____ gegangen / gefahren / geflogen.
3. Am Wochenende bin ich _____ gegangen / gefahren / geflogen.
4. In den letzten zwei Jahren bin ich _____ gegangen / gefahren / geflogen.
5. Ich gehe _____.
6. Meine Familie geht _____.
7. Meine Freunde und ich fahren _____.
8. Nächstes Jahre möchte ich _____ gehen / fahren / fliegen.

B **Welche Präposition passt?** Ergänzen Sie die Sätze durch passende Dativpräpositionen und Endungen.

BEISPIEL *Sie arbeitet **bei** Siemens.*

aus	außer	bei	gegenüber	mit	nach	seit	von	zu

1. Bist du _____ dein-_____ Wohnung zufrieden?
2. Ich habe gerade einen Tweet _____ Deutschland bekommen.
3. Das Postamt befindet sich _____ d-_____ Hauptbahnhof.
4. Wir gehen heute Abend _____ unser-_____ Freund Andreas.
5. Du kriegst so viele E-Mails _____ dein-_____ Facebook-Freunden!
6. Sie bauen ihr Haus _____ Holz.
7. Wir warten schon _____ ein-_____ Monat auf eine Antwort.
8. Die Kinder kommen heute sehr früh _____ d-_____ Schule _____ Hause.
9. Ich hole dir etwas _____ d-_____ Kühlschrank.
10. Sagt es niemandem _____ eur-_____ Eltern!

C **Aussagen.** Machen Sie wahre Aussagen über Ihre Kurse dieses Semester mit fünf der folgenden Präpositionen:

> bis   durch   für   gegen   ohne   um

BEISPIEL   *Ich habe **für** meine Kurse sehr viel zu tun.*

D **Fragen zu Ihrer Person.**   Beantworten Sie die Fragen mit den folgenden Präpositionen. Verwenden Sie jede Präposition mindestens einmal. Stellen Sie diese Fragen an andere Personen im Kurs, dann berichten Sie der ganzen Gruppe, was Sie dabei erfahren haben.

> aus   bei   mit   nach   seit   von   zu

1. Woher kommen Ihre Vorfahren (z.B. Ihre Großeltern) väterlicher- und mütterlicherseits?
2. Wie lange lernen Sie schon Deutsch?
3. Wohin würden Sie im Winter besonders gern in Urlaub fahren?
4. Wo arbeiten Ihre Eltern?
5. Wohin gehen Sie gern, wenn Sie abends ausgehen?
6. Wie kommen Sie jeden Tag zur Schule oder zur Uni?
7. Bei welchen Aktivitäten müssen Sie viel, wenig oder überhaupt nicht denken?

E *Aus, von, nach oder zu?*   Wie können die Sätze weitergehen?

1. Cellos baut man ...
2. Wenn man Löwen und Elefanten sehen will, dann muss man ...
3. Die Astronauten Aldrin und Armstrong flogen ...
4. Die besten/teuersten Autos der Welt kommen ...
5. Wenn du eine wunderschöne Stadt sehen willst, dann musst du ...
6. Nach meinen Vorlesungen gehe ich manchmal ...

F **Wechselpräpositionen.**   Bilden Sie kurze Beispielsätze mit den folgenden präpositionalen Ausdrücken.

BEISPIELE   ins Stadtzentrum
   Wir fahren ins Stadtzentrum.

   neben dem Haus
   Die Kinder spielen neben dem Haus.

1. hinter dem Supermarkt
2. in die Stadt
3. über dem Tisch
4. aufs Land
5. vor einem Computer
6. unter den Zeitungen
7. neben die Teller
8. den Rhein entlang
9. ans Meer
10. zwischen die Schiffe

G **Ich möchte…, also gehe ich…**   Wohin geht man für diese Sachen? Ergänzen Sie die Sätze mit einem Verb wie **gehen/fahren/fliegen** und mit einem Element von der Liste.

> Berlin   Bibliothek   Café   Hause   Kino   McDonald's   Museum   Oper   Stadion die Türkei   Wien   Zürich

1. Ich möchte die größte Stadt der Schweiz besuchen, also _____.
2. Ich brauche ein bestimmtes Buch, um eine Arbeit für einen Kurs zu schreiben, also _____.
3. Ich möchte mit einer Freundin Kaffee trinken, also _____.
4. Ich habe Lust auf einen Big Mac, also _____.
5. Ein paar Freunde und ich wollen einen Film sehen, also _____.
6. Ich möchte zu einem Profi-Fußballspiel gehen, also _____.
7. Richard Wagner ist mein Lieblingskomponist, und heute Abend steht „Tristan" auf dem Programm, also _____.

H **Dativ oder Akkusativ?**   Ergänzen Sie die Sätze mit passenden präpositionalen Ausdrücken. Ziehen Sie die Wechselpräpositionen und Artikel zusammen, wenn es geht.

1. Der Hund legt sich unter …
2. Ein Stein fiel in …
3. Stellen Sie die Bücher neben …
4. Unser Professor spricht morgen über …
5. Anita holt Briefmarken auf …
6. Oma spaziert jeden Tag eine halbe Stunde in …

I **Was macht Onkel Helmut?**   Gehen Sie rechts um den Kreis herum. Bilden Sie einen Satz mit einer der Wechselpräpositionen. Wenn Sie zur nächsten Präposition kommen, bilden Sie einen weiteren Satz. Wenn Sie aber den ersten Satz mit einer Präposition *im Dativ* gebildet haben, dann sollen Sie mit der zweiten Präposition *den Akkusativ* verwenden, und umgekehrt *(vice versa)*. Und so geht es zwischen Dativ und Akkusativ weiter, bis Sie einmal um den ganzen Kreis gegangen sind. Bei dieser Übung sollen Sie auch kein Verb wiederholen!

BEISPIELE   *Onkel Helmut steht **am** Fenster.*
*Er schaut **auf den** Garten hinunter.*

J **Anders ausdrücken.** Drücken Sie die Sätze mit den folgenden Genitivpräpositionen anders aus.

BEISPIELE Die Arbeit war gefährlich, aber er machte sie.
Trotz der Gefahr *machte er die Arbeit.*

(an)statt	außerhalb	innerhalb	trotz	während	wegen/[-et]wegen

1. Annika blieb, weil ihre Familie es wollte.
2. Die Arbeit war in weniger als zehn Tagen fertig.
3. Wir können im Sommer reisen.
4. Das Wetter ist schlecht, aber wir gehen wandern.
5. Ich habe nichts dagegen, wenn du mitkommst.
6. Seine Firma ist nicht direkt in der Stadt.
7. Ihre Freunde sagten, sie sollte Französisch lernen, aber sie lernte Deutsch.

K **Einiges über Sie.** Machen Sie Aussagen über sich mit vier der Präpositionen in **Übung J.**

BEISPIELE *Ich werde **während** des Sommers arbeiten.*
***Innerhalb** der nächsten Woche muss ich vier Aufsätze schreiben.*

L **Wohin?** Wohin gehen Sie, wenn Sie während des Semesters Folgendes tun wollen?

BEISPIELE billig essen
Ich gehe ins Wendys.

schwimmen
Ich gehe ins Hallenbad an der Universität.

1. im Internet surfen
2. wandern
3. Fitnesstraining machen
4. tanzen
5. mit Freunden aus·gehen
6. Hausaufgaben machen
7. Zeit vertreiben *(pass)*
8. Videospiele spielen
9. Geld holen
10. allein sein

M **Otto fuhr und fuhr und fuhr.** Mit wie vielen verschiedenen Präpositionen können Sie diesen Satz zu Ende schreiben? **Otto fuhr …** Schreiben Sie mindestens zwölf Sätze. Vergessen Sie auch den Genitiv nicht!

BEISPIELE *Otto fuhr **in** den Park.*
*Otto fuhr **nach** Hamburg.*
*Otto fuhr **mit** seinen Freunden.*

Anwendung

A   Wie kommt man dorthin?   Jemand im Kurs möchte Sie in den Ferien besuchen. Erklären Sie ihr/ihm, wie man zu Ihnen hinkommt.

Wie komme ich (am besten) zu dir hin?
Wie fährt / kommt man von hier zum / zur / nach / in ...?
Nimm die [dritte] Straße rechts/links.
Fahre ...
    etwa eine halbe Stunde
    geradeaus
    nach links / nach rechts
    rechts / links in die [_____]straße
    noch zwei Straßen weiter
    bis zur ersten Ampel *(traffic light)*
    bis zur Kreuzung *(intersection)*
Dort siehst du dann auf der linken / rechten Seite ...

B   Rollenspiel: Auskunft geben.   Sie arbeiten bei der Touristeninformation im Zentrum Ihres Heimatorts. Jemand im Kurs ist Touristin/Tourist und stellt Ihnen viele Fragen. Verwenden Sie Präpositionen in Ihren Antworten.

Wo kann ich hier [Blumen / Medikamente usw.] bekommen?
Wo finde ich hier [eine Kirche / eine Synagoge / eine Moschee]?
Können Sie hier in der Nähe [ein Restaurant / ein Kaufhaus usw.] empfehlen? Wie komme ich dorthin?
Wann schließen hier die Geschäfte?
Wo gibt es hier in der Nähe [eine Bank / eine Tankstelle usw.]?
Wir suchen [den Zoo / die Polizei / eine Bibliothek usw.].
Kann man hier irgendwo [baden / einkaufen / sich hinsetzen usw.]?
Wie komme ich am besten von hier [zur Bushaltestelle / zum Flughafen / zum Bahnhof usw.]? Ich bin ohne Auto unterwegs.
Wie lange arbeiten Sie schon hier?

C   Ausarbeitung eines Planes.   Sie haben morgen frei und wollen mit drei oder vier anderen Personen im Kurs etwas unternehmen (z.B. einen Ausflug machen, an einem Projekt arbeiten, Sport treiben). Diskutieren Sie, wohin Sie gehen wollen, was Sie dort machen können und wann Sie es machen wollen. Teilen Sie anderen Gruppen im Kurs Ihren Plan mit. Verwenden Sie dabei so viele Präpositionen wie möglich!

REDEMITTEL

Ich schlage vor, dass wir ...
Wollen wir nicht ... ?
Wir können auch ...

Habt ihr nicht Lust, ... ?
Was haltet ihr davon, wenn wir alle ... ?

Schriftliche Themen

Tipps zum Schreiben

Adding Information Through Prepositions

Prepositions are important linking words within sentences, and prepositional phrases can add both color and detail to your writing. For example, **Die Frau lachte ...** is much less descriptive and interesting than **Die Frau *in Rot* lachte *vor Vergnügen*** *(delight)*. When used at the beginning of a sentence, a prepositional phrase can provide a setting (a time and/or place) for the main action: **An einem kalten Schneetag in Berlin ging Herr Moritz mit seinem blauen Hut spazieren.** Remember that in German, initial prepositional phrases are not followed by a comma, as they may be in English (see 1.1.A).

A **Beim Friseur.** Erzählen Sie – im Präsens oder Präteritum – die Bildergeschichte und verwenden Sie dabei so viele Präpositionen wie möglich.

VOKABELVORSCHLÄGE

sitzen	gießen	die Biene, -n	rennen (wohin?)
der Friseur	sehr froh	fliegen/kreisen	nach·fliegen
die Flasche	riechen	denken	stecken
das Haarwasser	gehen (wohin?)	Angst haben	das Waschbecken

B   **Verlaufen.**   Haben Sie sich je verlaufen *(taken the wrong way),* sodass Sie Ihr Ziel nur mit großen Schwierigkeiten oder gar nicht erreicht haben? Erzählen Sie davon! Beschreiben Sie auch, wie Sie sich dabei gefühlt haben. Verwenden Sie präpositionale Ausdrücke und auch Adjektive (siehe Kapitel 13), um alles noch genauer zu schildern *(depict).*

Zusammenfassung

Rules to Remember

1   Prepositions determine the case of the nouns that follow.

2   Prepositions that can form contractions (**im, am, zur,** etc.) do so as long as the noun that follows is not emphasized, but remain separate when that noun is a focus of attention.

3   The prepositions **bis, durch, für, gegen, ohne, um** (and **wider**) require the accusative case.

4   The prepositions **aus, außer, bei, mit, nach, seit, von, zu,** and **gegenüber** require the dative case.

5   The variable prepositions **an, auf, hinter, in, neben, über, unter, vor, zwischen,** and **entlang** take the accusative when they indicate *change of position* and the dative when they indicate *location.*

6   The prepositions **(an)statt, außerhalb, innerhalb, trotz, während, wegen,** and a number of other less common prepositions take a genitive object.

NOTE: Prepositions are discussed in this chapter in their most literal meanings. Many prepositions, particularly the variable prepositions, have idiomatic meanings dependent upon the verbs, nouns or adjectives they complement. These are listed in R.3.

At a Glance

Accusative prepositions	
bis	ohne
durch	um
für	(wider)
gegen	
durchs fürs ums	

Dative prepositions	
aus	nach
außer	seit
bei	von
gegenüber	zu
mit	
beim zur vom zum	

Variable prepositions	
an	entlang
auf	über
hinter	unter
in	vor
neben	zwischen
ans aufs ins am im	

Genitive prepositions	
Frequent	**Less frequent**
(an)statt	diesseits
außerhalb	jenseits
innerhalb	oberhalb
trotz	unterhalb
während	
wegen	

7

Negation

zum Beispiel

Rad fahren

ARochau/Fotolia

Rad fahren is more than just *riding a bicycle* in German-speaking Europe—it's an important element of everyday life, on multiple levels. Cycling as a competitive sport has a long history in Germany, Switzerland, and Austria, where the Tour de France and similar races are popular media events. Riding one's bike as a means of everyday transportation—in urban centers as well as smaller towns—is much more common there than one finds in most parts of North America. Biking as a leisure activity, on weekends and vacations, is growing in popularity, as the continually expanding network of **Radwege** throughout these countries shows. A recent survey indicated that 80% of Germans own a bicycle, and that almost 11% of the total distance traveled on any given day in Germany is done on a bike.

Grammatik

1. **Kein-** is used to negate indefinite nouns, that is, nouns that are preceded either by **ein-** or by no article at all, although they may be preceded by adjectives. In meaning, **kein-** corresponds to English *not a / not any / no* ___ . Structurally, it is the negative form of the indefinite article **ein-** and takes the same endings (see 4.2).

   The following chart shows the complete declension for **kein-**, in all cases, numbers, and genders:

	der Reifen[a]	**die Bremse**[b]	**das Fahrrad**	**die Pedale**
Nom.	kein■ Reifen	keine Bremse	kein■ Fahrrad	keine Pedale
Acc.	keinen Reifen	keine Bremse	kein■ Fahrrad	keine Pedale
Dat.	keinem Reifen	keiner Bremse	keinem Fahrrad	keinen Pedalen
Gen.	keines Reifens	keiner Bremse	keines Fahrrads	keiner Pedale

[a]*tire* [b]*brake*

Hast du **einen** Dachträger für dein Fahrrad?
—Nein, ich habe **keinen** Dachträger.

Do you have a roof rack for your bike?
—No, I don't have a roof rack. (I have no roof rack.)

Nimmst du Ersatzventile mit?
—Nein, ich nehme **keine** Ersatzventile mit.

Are you taking along spare valves?
—No, I'm not taking any spare valves along.

2. **Kein-** cannot be used to negate a noun preceded by a **der**-word or a possessive adjective. In these contexts, **nicht** is the appropriate negating element.

   COMPARE:

   Er hat **kein** Fahrrad.

   He has no (doesn't have a) bicycle.

   Sie benutzt <u>mein</u> Fahrrad **nicht.**

   She doesn't use my bicycle.

   Ich kaufe <u>dieses</u> Fahrrad **nicht.**

   I'm not buying this bicycle.

A. *Nicht, nie,* and *niemals*

Nicht *(not)* and **nie/niemals** *(never)* are used to negate sentence information in general. Like **kein-**, they can be used to negate specific sentence elements, except when those elements are preceded by **ein-** or by no article at all.

The position of **nicht** in a clause depends on which level of negation is in play—that is, whether **nicht** relates to the clause in general (clause-level negation), or focuses on a particular piece of information within it (element-level negation). **Nie** and **niemals** follow the same position rules as **nicht**.

1. In *clause-level negation,* the position of **nicht** is determined by the grammatical context.

   a. **Nicht** *follows* conjugated verbs, dative and accusative objects, and most adverbial modifiers.

Für längere Strecken benutze ich **mein Velo[1] *nicht.*** *(accusative object)*	*For longer distances, I don't use my bicycle.*
Ein schneller Reifenwechsel gelingt **mir *nie.*** *(dative object)*	*I'm never successful at changing a tire quickly.*
Wegen des Regens fahren wir **morgen *nicht.*** *(time modifier)*	*Because of the rain, we're not riding tomorrow.*

   b. **Nicht** *precedes* adverbial modifiers of manner (such as **gern** in the example above), predicate nominatives and predicate adjectives, verbal complements (see 1.B below), and V₂ structures (see 1.1.C).

Ich fahre gern, aber ich fahre ***nicht* besonders schnell.** *(adverb of manner)*	*I like to ride, but I don't ride especially fast.*
Das ist ***nicht* mein *Fahrrad.*** *(predicate nominative)*	*That's not my bicycle.*
Die Fahrräder im 19. Jahrhundert waren ***nicht* sehr effizient.** *(predicate adjective)*	*The bicycles in the 19th century weren't very efficient.*
Warum machst du bei der Radtour ***nicht* mit?** *(separable prefix)*	*Why aren't you coming along on the bike trip?*
Wir haben unsere Velos ***nicht* mitgenommen.** *(past participle)*	*We didn't take our bikes along.*

2. In *element-level negation,* however, where a specific element is to be negated, **nicht** precedes this element directly, and the element receives intonational emphasis when spoken. Contrasting (that is, corrective) information following the negated element is usually introduced by **sondern**.

Clause-level negation

positive: Er organisiert unsere Radtour *(bike trip).*

negative: Er organisiert unsere Radtour **nicht.**

---

[1]**das Velo, -s** is used in German-speaking Switzerland for **Fahrrad.**

Element-level negation

positive: Er organisiert unsere Radtour.

negative: Er organisiert doch **nicht** unsere Radtour, oder? Das wäre ja katastrophal.
*(with emphasis on either **unsere** or **Radtour,** depending on intended emphasis; either way, one can assume, the results would be catastrophic)*

With contrasting information

Er organisiert **nicht** *unsere* Radtour, **sondern** eine Radtour für Schulkinder.
Er organisiert **nicht** unsere *Radtour,* **sondern** unsere Bustour nach Wien.

B. *Nicht* with verbal complements

1. The position of **nicht** with respect to verbal complements is both simple and complicated: simple, in that the rule itself is easy enough—**nicht** precedes verbal complements—but complicated, in that it can be difficult for nonnative speakers to know when a noun is a verbal complement and when it is a direct object.

   Take **Rad fahren** *(riding a bicycle)*, for example.

Nur im Sommer **fährt** sie **Rad.**	*She rides her bike only in the summer time.*

   Is **Rad** in this sentence a direct object? It may seem to be, but notice the changes one must make to render the phrase into English. If you translate **fahren** as *ride,* then the element *her* must be added to *bike.* Alternately, if you follow the German by using no article before *bike,* then the verb has to change from *rides* to *riding.* The point is this: If it were simply a direct object, such maneuvering would not be necessary. In this phrase, in fact, **Rad** is a verbal complement—meaning that it functions as part of the verb rather than as a separate noun object.

   The same is true of these verbal complements.

Farbe bekennen	*to show one's colors (i.e., take a stand)*
Gefahr laufen	*to be in danger, run the risk of . . .*
Klavier spielen	*to play the piano (not a specific piano, but in general)*

   As verbal complements, **Rad, Farbe, Gefahr,** and **Klavier** combine with verbs to create meanings that are different from what the individual components mean on their own—a function that is hinted at by the absence of a preceding article. Notice how this plays out in a sentence context:

Du musst endlich **Farbe bekennen!**	*You've got to show your true colors!*
Wir **laufen Gefahr,** alles zu verlieren.	*We run the risk of losing everything.*

   German negates these verb + complement combinations by placing **nicht** directly before the complement:

Im Winter **fährt** sie *nicht* **Rad.**	*In the winter she doesn't ride her bike.*
Ich will *nicht* **Farbe bekennen!**	*I don't want to show my true colors!*
Wir laufen gar *nicht* **Gefahr,** alles zu verlieren.	*We're not at all in danger of losing everything.*

2. Here are other examples of verbal complements that are negated according to this model (see 1.1.C).

- Phrases that complete the action of motion verbs:

nach Hause gehen	auf das Regal stellen
in die Stadt fahren	ins Kino gehen
nach Berlin fliegen	nach Heilbronn wandern

- Phrases that complete the idea of position verbs:

zu Hause bleiben	im Bett liegen
auf dem Lande wohnen	bei Schmidts übernachten
in der Ecke sitzen	

- Prepositional phrases that form specific meanings with verbs:

auf jemand warten	sich für etwas interessieren
an etwas denken	sich vor etwas (*or* vor jemandem) fürchten
über jemand schimpfen	

- Noun objects that join with verbs to form specific meanings:
  Sturm laufen (*to be up in arms*)
  Zeitung lesen (*to sit down and read a newspaper*)

- Noun objects used to denote playing a game or an instrument:

Fußball spielen	Gitarre spielen
Poker spielen	Klavier spielen

- Adverbs that join with verbs to form specific meanings:
  auswendig lernen

The negation of all such constructions—in the case of clause-level negation—is formed by placing **nicht** before the verbal complement. But bear in mind that with noun objects used as complements, some German speakers will treat the complement as a direct object and use **kein-** instead.

7.3 KEIN- ... MEHR/NICHT MEHR

1. English joins *no* + *more* to inject an added dimension into negative statements involving plural and non-count nouns (see R.1.2).

COMPARE:

*We have **no** time.* ⟶ *We have **no more** time.*

*I **don't** want **any** interruptions.* ⟶ *I **don't** want **any more** interruptions.*

In both pairs, the second sentence indicates a limit to something already present.

The German counterpart to this is similar in vocabulary (**kein-** + **mehr**), but differs in structure, since the object of **kein-** splits the two elements.

Wir haben **keine** Zeit. ⟶ Wir haben **keine** Zeit **mehr.**

Ich will **keine** Unterbrechungen. ⟶ Ich will **keine** Unterbrechungen **mehr.**

MORE EXAMPLES:

Ich will **keine** Fahrradschlösser **mehr** kaufen.	I don't want to buy **any more** bike locks.
Aber ich habe **keine** Lust **mehr,** mein Fahrrad zu verlieren.	But I don't have **any more** desire to lose my bike.
Und trotz eines Schlosses hatte ich mal nach einer Vorlesung **keinen** Sattel **mehr.**	And in spite of a lock, once after a lecture I didn't have a bicycle seat **anymore.**
Schade, dass der Campus **kein** sicherer Platz **mehr** ist.	Too bad that the campus isn't safe **anymore.**

2. German uses **nicht + mehr** and **nicht + länger** to express *not any more* or *not any longer* in relation to a verb (as opposed to a noun); this structure is similar to English. Like English, **nicht länger** is used in contexts where time is a factor; otherwise, **nicht mehr** is appropriate.

Wir sollten uns **nicht länger** nur auf Autos verlassen.	We should **no longer** rely just on cars. / We shouldn't rely just on cars **anymore.**
Hast du das Rennrad **nicht mehr,** das deine Eltern dir geschenkt haben?	Don't you have the racing bike **anymore** that your parents gave you?

Wortschatz
Negationselemente

The most common expressions of negation include the following words and phrases:

kein-   *no, not any*
nicht   *not*
nichts   *nothing, not anything*
nie, niemals   *never*
niemand   *no one, not anyone*
nirgends, nirgendwo   *nowhere, not anywhere*
nicht einmal   *not even, not once*
nicht nur (sondern auch)   *not only (but also)* (see R.2.2)
noch nicht   *not yet*
noch kein-   *not any . . . yet*
noch nie   *not ever (yet)*
ich nicht   *not me/not I*
ich auch nicht   *me neither, nor (do) I*
gar nicht, überhaupt nicht   *not at all*
gar nichts, überhaupt nichts   *nothing at all*
gar kein-, überhaupt kein-   *not any . . . at all*
lieber nicht   *(preferably) not, (would) rather not*
weder ... noch   *neither . . . nor* (see R.2.2)
durchaus nicht, keinesfalls   *by no means, not at all*
auf keinen Fall   *by no means*

Übungen

A   **Zimmerinventar.**   Lesen Sie die Liste durch und markieren Sie die Sachen (*things*), die es in Ihrem Zimmer zu Hause oder im Studentenwohnheim gibt. Dann berichten Sie – schriftlich oder mündlich mit jemandem im Kurs – was Sie auf der Liste haben (**ich habe ein- … /es gibt ein- …**) und was Sie nicht haben (**aber es gibt kein- … /ich habe kein- …**).

der:	**die:**	**das:**
_____ Schreibtisch, -e	_____ Lampe, -n	_____ Poster, -
_____ Computer, -	_____ Kommode, -n	_____ Fenster , -
_____ Sessel, -	_____ Kiste, -n (*box*)	_____ Bett, -en
_____ Kühlschrank, ⸚e	_____ Flasche, -n	_____ Bücherregal, -e
_____ Kleiderschrank, ⸚e	_____ Dose, -n (*can*)	_____ Sofa, -s
_____ Teppich, -e	_____ Pflanze, -n	_____ Bild, -er

Extra:

_____ verfaultes (*rotten*) Essen im Kühlschrank

_____ Klamotten (*clothes, stuff*) überall auf dem Boden

_____ vergessene Hausaufgaben

_____ (die) Pizza vom Wochenende

_____ leere Flaschen

B   **Alles falsch.**   Berichtigen Sie die Aussagen. Verwenden Sie **kein-**, **nicht** oder **nie**, und wenn Sie können, geben Sie die richtige Information mit **sondern** an (*provide*).

BEISPIEL   Mein Nachbar ist ein Idiot.
*Mein Nachbar ist **kein** Idiot, sondern ein Genie!*
OR:
***Nicht** mein Nachbar, sondern mein Mitbewohner ist ein Idiot.*

1. Fische haben lange Beine.
2. Montreal ist die Hauptstadt von Kanada.
3. Immanuel Kant hat an einer Universität in Japan studiert.
4. Barack Obama war früher Bundeskanzler (*chancellor*) von Deutschland.
5. Es schneit oft in Honolulu.
6. Kaninchen (*rabbits*) fressen gern Mäuse.
7. Schüler und Studenten schreiben ihre Arbeiten gern per Hand.
8. Frankfurt liegt im Norden von Deutschland.
9. Computer-Viren findet man heute selten.
10. **Alle** in diesem Deutschkurs werden gute Noten bekommen.

C **Der ewige Neinsager.** Markus sieht alles negativ. Wie wird er wohl auf diese Fragen antworten?

BEISPIELE Markus, macht dir dein Studium Spaß?
Nein, mein Studium macht mir **keinen** *Spaß.*

Markus, liest du gern?
Nein, ich lese **nicht** *gern.*

1. Bekommst du interessante E-Mails?
2. Hast du ein Lied heruntergeladen *(downloaded)*?
3. Verstehst du meine Fragen?
4. Möchtest du Sportler werden?
5. Kannst du deine Hausaufgaben morgen abgeben?
6. Bekommst du in Deutsch gute Noten?
7. Gehst du morgen mit uns schwimmen?
8. Folgst du jemandem auf Twitter?
9. Interessierst du dich für Musik?
10. Spielst du Fußball?

D **Das mache ich nicht.** Gibt es Dinge, die Sie nicht haben, nicht oder nie tun, oder nicht gern tun? Machen Sie sieben Aussagen.

BEISPIELE *Ich spiele kein Musikinstrument.*
Ich tanze nicht gern.
Ich habe keinen Plasmafernseher.

E **Überhaupt nicht. Völlig falsch.** Machen Sie Aussagen über sich *(yourself)* in Bezug auf dieses Semester mit den folgenden Ausdrücken.

BEISPIELE *Ich habe gar nicht genug geschlafen.*
Ich habe mein Zimmer bis jetzt niemals aufgeräumt (cleaned up).

1. noch nicht
2. gar kein-/überhaupt kein-
3. niemand
4. durchaus nicht
5. weder ... noch
6. auf jeden Fall
7. nirgendwo
8. kein- ... mehr

F **Filmrezension – richtig oder falsch?** Unten finden Sie eine Rezension *(critique)* eines bekannten deutschen Filmes, *Lola rennt* (1998), der am Anfang fast wie ein Computerspiel aussieht, aber am Ende ein sehr menschliches Herz hat. Lesen Sie den Text zuerst gut durch. Dann berichtigen Sie die (falschen) Aussagen, die darauf folgen, mit **nicht** oder **kein,** und denken Sie dabei an *clause-level negation.*

BEISPIEL Sie lesen: Lola rennt ist ein französischer Film.
Sie schreiben: *Lola rennt ist kein französischer Film.*

shallow / qualifies
case study

Lola rennt war einer der größten internationalen Erfolge des deutschen Films der letzten Jahre [...]. Zu gleichen Teilen originell und flach° taugt° der Film als Fallbeispiel° deutschen Massengeschmacks, reflektierte er doch die jungen Deutschen und wie sie die Welt sahen, oder besser, sehen wollten: Als Computerspiel.

red-head

"short work"
"source" = viel Geld
ability to convince /
monosyllabic way
of speaking /
wrong

Rotschopf° Lola (Franka Potente) hat es eilig, denn ihr Freund Manni (Moritz Bleibtreu) hat 100.000 DM in der (Berliner) U-Bahn vergessen. Die muss er aber bis 12 Uhr seinem Kleingangsterboss übergeben. Wenn nicht, macht der Boss mit ihm kurzen Prozess°. Lolas erste Idee: Papa. Denn Papa ist Bankdirektor, sitzt also direkt an der Quelle°. Schade, dass er sein Töchterlein nicht wirklich liebt und schade, dass Lolas Überzeugungskraft° unter ihrer Einsilbigkeit° zusammenbricht, kurz: Irgendwie geht alles schief°. Doch als es das tut, geht's wieder von vorne los, denn Lola kriegt heute nicht nur eine, sondern drei Chancen. [...]

Source: http://www.filmrezension.de/filme/lola_rennt.shtml/11May2009; leicht bearbeitet

Aussagen zum Film

1. Der Autor der Rezension findet den Film unoriginell.
2. Der Film ist ein Fallbeispiel für die heutige Perspektive der älteren Generation.
3. Lola ist Blondine.
4. Manni hat das Geld auf dumme Weise verschenkt *(gave away)*.
5. Mannis Boss ist ein sehr netter und verständnisvoller Mann.
6. Lolas erste Idee ist ein Bankraub.
7. Ihr Papa ist Fußballtrainer.
8. Papa liebt sein Töchterlein.
9. Lola spricht fließend und viel.
10. Lolas Versuch, ihrem Freund zu helfen, gelingt ihr *(she succeeds)* sofort *(right away)*.

Anwendung

 A   **Faule Menschen.**   Wer kann den faulsten Menschen beschreiben? Erzählen Sie von einem wirklichen oder erfundenen *(imaginary)* Menschen, der gar nichts hat und gar nichts tut.

> **REDEMITTEL**
>
> Da kenne <u>ich</u> vielleicht eine faule Person!²
> Sie/Er ist so faul, dass sie/er ...
> Weil sie/er nie ... [tut], hat sie/er auch kein- ...
> Natürlich [tut] sie/er auch kein- ...
> Meistens [tut] sie/er ... und [tut] gar nicht(s).
> Sie/Er will nicht einmal *(not even)* ...

---

² *"Boy, do* <u>I</u> *know a lazy person!"* See R.6 for this use of **vielleicht**.

B **Das hast du nicht? Ich habe noch weniger!**   Machen Sie ein Rollenspiel mit jemandem im Kurs, um zu zeigen, dass Sie noch weniger haben als die Partnerin/der Partner. Beginnen Sie mit einer kurzen negativen Aussage, dann fügen Sie jedes Mal noch eine negative Aussage dazu *(add)*.

BEISPIEL   A: Ich habe keine Zeit.
B: Keine Zeit? Ich habe keine Zeit und kein Geld.
A: Wirklich? Ich habe keine Zeit, kein Geld und keine Energie.
B: Aber ich habe weder... noch...

Schriftliche Themen

Tipps zum Schreiben	**Writing First Drafts and Checking for Common Errors** Always jot down a few ideas in German before beginning a composition. Then write a first draft. Read through this draft to see whether you have used a variety of verbs. This is also a good time to check for common errors such as misspellings, uncapitalized nouns, verbs not in second position, and the use of **nicht ein-** instead of **kein-** (see 7.1). Are your sentences concise and to the point, or do they ramble on and on and on? When writing a second or final draft, be sure to vary your style by starting some sentences with elements other than the sentence subject.

A **Selbstanalyse.**   Schreiben Sie eine Selbstanalyse mit dem folgenden Titel: „Was ich nicht bin, nicht habe, nicht tue und nicht will." (Siehe auch den **Wortschatz**.)

BEISPIEL   *Ich bin kein fauler Mensch, aber ich will nicht immer arbeiten. Ich will auch nicht ... Natürlich habe ich auch keine Lust ... usw.*

B **Reicher Mensch, armer Mensch.**   Man kann sich leicht das Leben eines reichen Menschen vorstellen *(imagine)*. Wie sieht es aber bei einem armen Menschen aus, der wenig oder nichts hat? Erzählen Sie davon mit Elementen aus dem **Wortschatz**.

Auf der Straße achtet **niemand** auf ihn ...
Zum Frühstück hat sie manchmal **nicht einmal** ...
Heime *(shelters)* für Obdachlose *(homeless people)* gibt es schon, aber er möchte **lieber nicht** ...

C **Ach, diese Stadt!**   Gibt es Dinge, die Ihnen an der Stadt, in der Sie jetzt wohnen, nicht gefallen? Erzählen Sie aus einer etwas negativen Sicht davon. Verwenden Sie einige der Ausdrücke aus dem **Wortschatz.**

BEISPIEL   *Diese Stadt gefällt mir nicht so sehr. Es gibt keine netten Studentenlokale und nirgendwo kann man sich abends im Stadtzentrum gemütlich treffen. Aber ich gehe abends sowieso lieber nicht in die Stadt, denn es fahren nach zehn Uhr keine Busse zur Universität zurück. Außerdem gibt es nicht einmal ... usw.*

Zusammenfassung

Rules to Remember

1 **Kein-** negates nouns preceded by **ein-** or no article at all.

2 **Nicht** negates nouns preceded by definite articles, other **der**-words, and possessive adjectives (see 4.3-4); as well as verbs and modifiers. In doing so it follows word order rules that sometimes differ from English.

3 Word order in element-level negation: **nicht** *precedes* the element to be negated, as in English.

4 When corrective information is provided following element-level negation, it is introduced by the coordinating conjunction **sondern:** *not X, but rather Y.*

5 Word order in clause-level negation:
   a. **Nicht** appears in the middle field *after* direct and indirect object nouns and pronouns, and after most adverbial modifiers (except adverbial phrases of manner).
   b. **Nicht** *precedes* all other elements in the middle field, such as predicate adjectives, predicate nominatives, adverbs of manner, separated prefixes, and verbal complements; **nicht** also *precedes* V_2 elements, such as modal infinitives and past participles.

At a Glance

Nicht: Element-level negation

nicht	x	(...)	sondern	y

Nicht: Clause-level negation

first elements	V_1	objects	most adverbials	nicht	adverbials of manner; predicate nominatives; verbal complements	V_2

Simple past tense · Past perfect tense

zum Beispiel

Bus

KurzFilmAgentur Hamburg

By way of a disarmingly simple story, the short film **"Bus"** raises an intriguing question: How should one respond if people step in unbidden to help—and then present a bill for payment? Is gratitude in order? Or resentment? With minimal dialogue, **"Bus"** depicts a group of people who travel around in a minivan (**der Kleinbus**) in order to "help" people: fixing a car, cleaning public toilets, pitching in to hoe a garden. Our expectations of what constitutes "help," "work," and "fair play" influence our reactions to these scenes; we may well decide that the demand for money in these situations is wrong. Or not. But along the way another question arises: If we decide that taking money from the "helped" is ethically dubious, what should we think of someone who takes money from the "helpers"?

Grammatik

| 8.1 | SIMPLE PAST TENSE |

A. Formation

1. The simple past tense (**das Präteritum**) is the second principal part of the verb (see 3.1). The simple past tense of *weak verbs* is formed by adding a -**t** plus a set of personal endings to the infinitive stem.

   If the infinitive stem ends in -**d**, -**t**, or in a single -**m** or -**n** preceded by a consonant other than **l** or **r**, then an **e** is added before the -**t** to facilitate pronunciation.

	sagen	**retten** *(to save)*	**atmen** *(to breathe)*
ich	sagt **e**	rettet **e**	atmet **e**
du	sagt **est**	rettet **est**	atmet **est**
Sie	sagt **en**	rettet **en**	atmet **en**
er/sie/es	sagt **e**	rettet **e**	atmet **e**
wir	sagt **en**	rettet **en**	atmet **en**
ihr	sagt **et**	rettet **et**	atmet **et**
Sie	sagt **en**	rettet **en**	atmet **en**
sie	sagt **en**	rettet **en**	atmet **en**

2. *Strong verbs* (see also 3.1.B) form the past-tense stem by changing the vowel and some-times also the consonant of the infinitive stem; they *do not* add a -**t** to this stem, as do the weak verbs. There are no endings in the first- and third-persons singular of strong verbs.

	fahren	**gehen**	**sitzen**
ich	fuhr ■	ging ■	saß ■
du	fuhr st	ging st	saß est[1]
Sie	fuhr en	ging en	saß en
er/sie/es	fuhr ■	ging ■	saß ■
wir	fuhr en	ging en	saß en
ihr	fuhr t	ging t	saß t
Sie	fuhr en	ging en	saß en
sie	fuhr en	ging en	saß en

For a listing of strong and irregular verbs, see Appendix 3.

---

[1]Past-tense stems ending in -**s**, -**ss**, and -**ß** require an **e** before the -**st** in the second-person singular. This **e** often occurs with many other strong verbs as well, particularly in poetry: **du fand(e)st; du hielt(e)st; du schnitt(e)st;** BUT **du kamst; du lagst; du warst.**

3. *Irregular verbs* (see 3.1.C) form the simple past tense like weak verbs, but in addition, they change their stem vowel. The verbs **bringen** and **denken** have consonant changes as well. (The modal verbs are also irregular; their tense formation is discussed in Chapter 9.)

wissen	
ich wuss<u>t</u> e	wir wuss<u>t</u> en
du wuss<u>t</u> est	ihr wuss<u>t</u> et
Sie wuss<u>t</u> en	Sie wuss<u>t</u> en
er/sie/es wuss<u>t</u> e	sie wuss<u>t</u> en
ALSO: brennen ⟶ brannte	nennen ⟶ nannte
bringen ⟶ bra**ch**te	rennen ⟶ rannte
denken ⟶ da**ch**te	senden ⟶ sandte/sendete[2]
kennen ⟶ kannte	wenden ⟶ wandte/wendete[2]

4. **Sein** conjugates like a strong verb in the simple past; **werden** and **haben** are irregular, adding the weak verb personal endings to the altered stem forms **wurd-** and **hatt-.**

	sein	werden	haben
ich	war ■	wurde	hatte
du	warst	wurdest	hattest
Sie	waren	wurden	hatten
er/sie/es	war ■	wurde	hatte
wir	waren	wurden	hatten
ihr	wart	wurdet	hattet
Sie	waren	wurden	hatten
sie	waren	wurden	hatten

5. In the simple past tense, separable prefixes function exactly as they do in the present tense (see 2.1.E). In main clauses, the prefix moves to the end of the middle field; in dependent clauses, the prefix reconnects to the root verb to form a single word. Consider the verb **ein·steigen** *(to climb in, get in)*:

Zuerst **stiegen** die Arbeiter in den Minibus **ein.**	*First, the workers climbed into the minibus.*
Sie sagten kein Wort, als sie alle **einstiegen.**	*They didn't say a word as they all got in.*

B. Use

1. The German simple past tense is sometimes called the *narrative past;* it has several English equivalents.

---

[2]For the use of these verb forms, see 3.1.C, footnote 3.

Sie **fuhren** auf der Autobahn. =	*They*	*drove*	*on the highway.*
		were driving	
		did drive	
		used to drive	
		would (often) drive	

2. In German, both the simple past and present perfect tense refer to actions and events that have taken place in the past. In general, the *present perfect* is used in conversational renditions of past events (hence its designation by some as the *conversational past*), while the *simple past* is more common in certain kinds of writing (and therefore often referred to as the *narrative past*). Sometimes they are interchangeable: speakers in northern Germany use the simple past in some situations to express the same information that speakers from southern Germany convey with the present perfect tense. The following comparison, however, points out several important differences.

Present perfect tense

- Refers to events just prior to the moment of speaking.

Warum **haben** mich diese Leute **angehalten?**	*Why did these people stop me (just now)?*

- Refers to past events that are linked (often by consequence) to the present.

Sie **haben** mein kaputtes Bremslicht **repariert.**	*They've fixed my broken brake light (so it's fixed now).*
Sie **haben** die Autofenster **geputzt.**	*They've washed the car windows (now they're clean).*
Aber jetzt **haben** sie mir eine Rechnung dafür **gegeben!**	*But now they've given me a bill for it!*

Simple past tense

- Lends a sense of sequence and connection, if used consistently in a series of sentences.
- Suggests moving through narrative time, rather than standing in the present looking back.

Zuerst **deckten** sie den Tisch fürs Picknick draußen.	*First, they set the table for the outdoor picnic (and then they...).*
Dann **verlangten** sie Geld von den Leuten am Tisch.	*Then they demanded money from the people at the table (which then led to...).*

3. The simple past tense of **haben, sein,** and the modal verbs (see 9.1) is preferred over the present perfect tense, even in conversation (see 3.2.C).

Die Gruppe **hatte** eine Tasche fürs Geld.	*The group had a bag for the money.*
Der Mann auf dem WC **war** total verblüfft.	*The man in the restroom was totally bewildered.*
Warum **wollten** sie die Frau nicht mitnehmen?	*Why didn't they want to take the woman along?*

4. In actual practice, spoken German is usually a mixture of the two tenses—past and present perfect—dictated by a sense of rhythm and style.

Heute **ist** mir etwas Komisches **passiert**. Ich **war** im Auto auf dem Weg ins Büro, und auf einmal **habe** ich direkt neben mir einen Minibus **bemerkt** mit 5-6 Leuten darin. Zuerst **habe** ich **gedacht**, naja, das geht mich nichts an. Aber dann **stellten** sie ein Warnlicht ins Fenster, so dass ich **dachte**, aha, die sind wohl von der Polizei. Also **fuhr** ich auf die Seite und **hielt an**. Der Minibus **hielt** hinter mir **an**, ein Mann **stieg aus**, und **sagte** mir: „Ihr Bremslicht ist kaputt". Ich **sagte** nichts, aber dann **habe** ich **gesehen**, wie alle anderen aus dem Minibus **ausstiegen** und **anfingen** zu arbeiten. Der eine **hat** mir das Bremslicht **ausgewechselt**, der andere **putzte** die Autofenster, eine Frau **machte** alles sauber. Schön, **dachte** ich, das ist wirklich sehr nett. Aber dann **kam's**: der Mann, der zuerst mit mir gesprochen hatte, **gab** mir einen Papierzettel. Was ist denn das, **habe** ich mich **gefragt**. Dann **schaute** ich aufs Papier und alles **wurde** klar. Es **war** eine Rechnung! Sie **haben** mich **angehalten**, haben mir **geholfen** – und dann **wollten** sie noch Geld dafür. So eine Frechheit!

5. With the exception of **haben, sein,** and the modal verbs, the second-person singular and plural forms **(Sie, du, ihr)** seldom occur in the simple past.

8.2 PAST PERFECT TENSE

A. Formation

The *past perfect* tense (**das Plusquamperfekt**) is a compound tense; it is formed with the *simple past* of either **haben** or **sein** + the past participle. The choice of **haben** or **sein** follows the same rules as in the present perfect (see 3.2.B). The participle is placed at the end of the clause, as V_2 (see 1.3.A).

haben + *past participle*			sein + *past participle*	
ich	hatte		war	
du	hattest		warst	
Sie	hatten		war	
er/sie/es	hatte	+ **gewaschen**	war	+ **gefahren**
wir	hatten		waren	
ihr	hattet		wart	
Sie	hatten		waren	
sie	hatten		waren	

B. Use

1. The German past perfect tense corresponds to the English past perfect; it shows that an action has taken place *prior* to some other past-time event. The past perfect tense therefore does not occur by itself; there is always some other past-time context, whether expressed or implied.

Die Frau im Auto hielt an, weil sie das Warnlicht im Minibus **gesehen hatte.**	*The woman in the car stopped because she had seen the warning light in the minibus.*
Sie **hatte** wohl **gedacht,** dass es sich um eine Polizeiaktion handelte.	*She probably had thought that it had to do with a police operation.*
Hinterher konnte sie kaum glauben, dass es tatsächlich **passiert war.**	*Afterwards she could hardly believe that it had actually happened.*

2. The past perfect tense is *not* used when describing a sequence of events, even though some actions occurred prior to others, since the sequence itself indicates their order of occurrence.

Auf einmal **erschienen** sie, dann **fingen** sie **an** zu putzen, **brachten** alles in Ordnung und **verlangten** Geld dafür.	*All at once they appeared, then they began to clean, got everything in order, and demanded money for it.*
Zuerst **waren** die Leute verwirrt, aber dann **zahlten** sie doch – bis auf einen Mann.	*At first, the people were confused, but then they ended up paying anyway— all except for one man.*

3. The past perfect is very common in dependent clauses introduced by **nachdem.**

Nachdem sie ihm im Garten **geholfen hatten,** wollte er nicht zahlen.	*After they had helped him in the garden, he didn't want to pay.*
Hinterher klaute man ihnen das Geld, nachdem sie **eingeschlafen waren.**	*After that, somebody stole their money after they had fallen asleep.*

Wortschatz
bekommen | erhalten | kriegen | holen

1. **Bekommen** means *to get or receive*. Note that it does <u>not</u> mean to *become*.

Verschiedene Leute haben unerwartete Hilfe **bekommen.**	*Various people received unexpected help.*
Wie viel Geld **bekam** die Gruppe jedes Mal?	*How much money did the group get every time?*

2. **Erhalten** is close in meaning to **bekommen** but somewhat more formal.

Wir haben Ihr Paket gestern **erhalten.** *We received your package yesterday.*

Sie **erhielten** zwei Jahre im Gefängnis. *They received two years in prison.*

3. **Kriegen** is synonymous with **bekommen,** but very colloquial. You should not use it in formal contexts, either written or spoken.

Du **kriegst** 50%, ich **kriege** 50%, klar? *You get 50%, I get 50%, is that clear?*

Ich habe mindestens 30 SMS in den letzten 10 Minuten **gekriegt.** *I've gotten at least 30 texts in the last 10 minutes.*

4. **Holen** means *to (go and) get* or *to fetch* and is often used with the dative, indicating *for whom* something has been gotten.

Hol (mir) bitte einen Eimer. *Please (go and) get (me) a bucket.*

Der Mann **holte** zwei Kaffeetassen, aber die Frau war schon weg. *The man fetched two coffee cups, but the woman was already gone.*

Übungen

A **Hans und die Bohnenranke.** Unten finden Sie den Anfang eines bekannten Märchens, und wie bei vielen Erzählungen stehen viele Verben darin im Präteritum. Lesen Sie den Text gut durch – Sie werden wohl nicht alle Vokabeln kennen, aber doch genug, um die Handlung (*plot*) zu verstehen – und dann arbeiten Sie an den Aufgaben, die darauf folgen.

ES WAR EINMAL eine arme Witwe, die hatte einen Sohn, der Hans hieß, und eine Kuh, die sie Milchweiß nannten. Und sie hatten nichts als die Milch der Kuh, um ihr Leben zu fristen. Jeden Morgen trugen sie die Milch zum Markt und verkauften sie. Aber eines Tages gab Milchweiß keine Milch mehr, und nun wussten sie nicht, was sie tun sollten.

„Was sollen wir nur anfangen, was sollen wir nur anfangen?" klagte die Witwe.

„Sei guten Mutes, Mutter, ich werde fortziehen und Arbeit suchen", sagte Hans.

„Das hast du ja schon einmal versucht", sagte die Mutter, „aber niemand hat dich nehmen wollen. Wir müssen Milchweiß verkaufen und mit dem Geld ein Geschäft anfangen oder sonst etwas."

„Gut, Mutter", sagte Hans, „heute ist Markttag, da werde ich Milchweiß gut verkaufen können. Dann wollen wir sehen, was sich machen lässt" Und Hans band die Kuh an einen Strick und ging fort mit ihr.

Auf dem Weg zum Markt begegnete ihm ein seltsam anmutendes altes Männlein, das sagte zu ihm: „Guten Morgen, Hans!"

„Auch einen schönen guten Morgen", sagte Hans und wunderte sich, wieso das Männlein seinen Namen kannte.

„Nun, Hans, wohin des Weges?" fragte das Männlein.

„Auf den Markt, die Kuh verkaufen."

„Du schaust mir gar nicht danach aus, als ob du Kühe verkaufen könntest", sagte das Männlein, „Ich glaube, du weißt nicht einmal, wie viele Bohnen fünf ergeben."

„Zwei in deiner Hand und eine in deinem Mund", sagte Hans eilig.

„Richtig", sagte das Männlein, „und da hast du auch schon die Bohnen." Und darauf zog es aus seiner Tasche eine Handvoll seltsam aussehender Bohnen.

„Weil du so schlau bist", sagte es, „so habe ich nichts dagegen, mit dir einen Handel zu machen. Gib mir die Kuh, ich geb dir die Bohnen."

„So dumm bin ich nun wirklich nicht", sagte Hans.

„Ah, du weißt nicht, was für Bohnen das sind", sagte der Mann. „Wenn du sie am Abend einpflanzt, so sind sie am Morgen bis zum Himmel hinauf gewachsen."

„Ist das wahr, was du da sagst?" fragte Hans.

„Ja, es ist wahr, und wenn es nicht so ist, so kannst du deine Kuh zurück haben."

„Gut", sagte Hans und gab ihm den Strick mit der Kuh und steckte die Bohnen in die Tasche.

Hans ging nun heimwärts, und kam gerade nach Haus, bevor es dunkel wurde ...

Aufgaben

1. Unterstreichen Sie die Präteritum-Verben, die in den ersten vier Sätzen stehen. Geben Sie die entsprechenden Infinitivformen an.
2. In der ersten Hälfte dieses Textes findet man Verben im Präteritum wie auch im Perfekt. In welchem Kontext kommen die Verben im Perfekt vor? Warum?
3. Setzen Sie die Sätze ohne Dialog in das Perfekt.
4. Wenn Sie die Geschichte kennen, erzählen Sie sie weiter, mit Verben im Präteritum.

B **Heute Morgen stand ich auf ...** Benutzen Sie die Liste von Aktivitäten, die unten stehen, und erzählen Sie von Ihren Erfahrungen gestern. Wenn es Ihnen hilft, markieren Sie zuerst die Aktivitäten, die auf Sie zutreffen (*apply*), schreiben Sie noch etwas Information dazu (z.B. *was* Sie gegessen haben), ordnen Sie sie chronologisch und dann fangen Sie an.

_____ Wecker hören
_____ auf·stehen
_____ auf·wachen
_____ sich waschen/duschen
_____ sich rasieren/kämmen
_____ frühstücken: _____ essen und _____ trinken
_____ E-Mails lesen/SMS schicken/_____ an·rufen
_____ zu Vorlesungen eilen/gehen/rennen
_____ sich verspäten

_____ Notizen machen/Arbeiten schreiben
_____ zu·hören/ein·schlafen
_____ Mittagessen/Abendessen essen: bei _____/mit _____
_____ Sport treiben: _____ spielen/joggen gehen/schwimmen
_____ Schläfchen machen
_____ fern·sehen
_____ Musik: _____ spielen/singen
_____ Videospiele spielen
_____ sich entspannen (relax)
_____ sich ärgern/freuen
_____ Aufgaben schreiben/erledigen
_____ müde werden
_____ ins Bett gehen

C **Zu ihrer Zeit.** Oma erzählt von ihrer Jugend. Damals machte man natürlich alles besser, oder? Was sagt sie?

BEISPIEL   meine Mutter / uns jeden Morgen das Frühstück machen
Meine Mutter **machte** uns jeden Morgen das Frühstück.

1. junge Leute / nicht so viel rauchen
2. wir / mehr im Freien spielen
3. Studenten / nicht so oft und nicht so wild feiern
4. ich / mehr in der Schule auf·passen
5. Schüler / mehr Hausaufgaben machen
6. Teenager / nicht denken / dass / mehr wissen als die Eltern
7. wir / öfter Museen und Theater besuchen
8. Leute / fleißiger arbeiten
9. Kinder / ihren Eltern besser zu·hören
10. Familien / mehr Kinder haben

Was werden Sie Ihren Kindern (falls Sie später welche haben) von Ihrer Jugend erzählen? Machen Sie bitte fünf Aussagen.

BEISPIEL   _Als ich ein Kind war, war alles nicht so teuer wie heute._

D **Amadeus.** Ergänzen Sie die Sätze durch die folgenden Verben im Präteritum.

arbeiten	hören	machen	spielen
bringen	kennen lernen	reisen	sterben
geben	kommen	schreiben	werden
heiraten	komponieren	sein	ziehen + nach (to move to)

Mozart (1) _____ 1756 in der Stadt Salzburg zur Welt. Schon mit drei Jahren (2) _____ er Klavier. Wenig später (3) _____ Wolfgang sein erstes Musikstück. Sein musikalisches Talent (4) _____ ihn berühmt. Als Wunderkind (5) _____ er mit seiner Schwester durch Europa. In vielen aristokratischen

Häusern (6) _____ man ihn spielen. Im Jahre 1780 (7) _____ er nach Wien.
Dort (8) _____ er als Musiklehrer und (9) _____ private Konzerte. Er
(10) _____ Konstanze Weber im Jahre 1782. Bald danach (11) _____ er
Haydn (12) _____ und sie (12) _____ gute Freunde. Zwischen 1782 und 1791
(13) _____ er Sinfonien und Opern, wie z.B. *Die Zauberflöte.* Diese Werke (14)
_____ ihm Ruhm *(fame).* Als er 1791 (15) _____, (16) _____ er erst 35 Jahre alt.

E Eine tolle Party.   Erzählen Sie mit Verben im Präteritum über eine (fiktive?) Party in
Ihrem Zimmer oder sonst irgendwo auf Ihrem Campus oder in der Stadt, wo Sie wohnen.
Verwenden Sie dabei die Präteritumformen für **kriegen** und **holen.** Seien Sie kreativ!

BEISPIEL   Als die Party **anfing, wusste** ich, dass der Abend interessant werden würde.
Florian **erschien** mit drei Freundinnen, dann **kamen** Jana und Kemal mit
noch mehr Leuten. Ich **holte** schnell noch etwas zu trinken vom Laden an
der Ecke, und dann **kriegten** wir sogar Besuch von…

F Plusquamperfekt: Und wie war es vorher?   Setzen Sie die Sätze in die Vergangenheit.

BEISPIEL   *Jasmin spielt ein Lied, das sie heruntergeladen* (downloaded) *hat.*
*Jasmin **spielte** ein Lied, das sie **heruntergeladen hatte.***

1. Jemand, der noch nichts gesagt hat, hebt *(raises)* seine Hand.
2. Lena sitzt im Garten und ruht sich aus *(relaxes).* Sie ist den ganzen Tag Rad gefahren.
3. Herr und Frau Kuhnert können ins Konzert gehen, weil sie Karten bekommen haben.
4. Ein Mann putzt die Autofenster, nachdem das Auto angehalten hat.
5. Nachdem du Tennis gespielt hast, gehst du wohl nach Hause.
6. Sara beginnt ihr Referat. Sie hat drei Bücher zum Thema gelesen.

G Von Märchen, Sagen und Heldentaten.   Was war schon vorher geschehen? Ergänzen Sie die Sätze.

BEISPIEL   Dornröschen schlief ein, nachdem … (Finger stechen)
Dornröschen schlief ein, nachdem sie sich in den Finger gestochen hatte.

1. Als Rotkäppchen das Haus der Großmutter erreichte, … (der Wolf/Großmutter fressen)
2. Die Nibelungen machten Siegfried zu ihrem König, weil … (er/den Drachen Fafnir erschlagen)
3. Dornröschen wachte erst auf, nachdem … (hundert Jahre vergehen)
4. Die böse Hexe *(witch)* verbrannte, nachdem … (Gretel/sie in den Backofen stoßen)
5. Der Rattenfänger bekam die tausend Taler nicht, die *(which)* … (der Stadtrat *[city council]* von Hameln/ihm versprechen)

H **Welches Verb passt?** Ergänzen Sie die Sätze mit dem passenden Verb.

bekommen   erhalten   holen   kriegen

1. Eure E-Mail haben wir _____, nachdem wir losgefahren waren.
2. Wo kann ich Karten für den Vortrag *(lecture)* _____?
3. _____ dir etwas zu essen und setz dich hin.
4. Katie _____ jetzt immer bessere Noten in Deutsch.
5. Ich _____ eine Wut *(rage)*, wenn ich so was sehe.

I Sehen Sie sich den Kurzfilm („**Bus**") an, und erzählen Sie die Geschichte mit Verben im Präteritum. Unten finden Sie einige Vokabeltipps.

warten + auf	bar *(in cash)* bezahlen	mit·nehmen
Geld verlangen	aufwecken *(to wake s.o. up)*	stehlen
sauber machen	anhalten	waschen
das Zelt, -e *(tent)*	der Garten	die Toilette
der Minibus	das Bremslicht	
verweigern *(to refuse)*	die Rechnung	

Anwendung

Tipps zum mündlichen Erzählen	**Telling Stories** Telling stories has nearly become a lost art. This is too bad, as it provides excellent language practice. You should prepare for oral narratives by making only the most necessary chronological notes in outline format, with verb infinitives last (e.g., **ins Auto steigen, Motor starten, Gas geben, schnell rückwarts statt vorwärts fahren usw.**). For now, tell your story in many short, simple sentences, and avoid complex structures such as subordinating conjunctions or relative pronouns. The oral topics of activities A, B, and C can also be written as compositions.

A   **Aus meinem Leben.**   Erzählen Sie anderen Leuten von einem besonderen Ereignis aus Ihrem Leben oder aus dem Leben eines anderen Menschen, den Sie kennen.

> **THEMENVORSCHLÄGE**
>
> eine unvergessliche Begegnung *(encounter)*
> das Schlimmste, was mir je passierte
> eine große Dummheit von mir
> ein unglaubliches Erlebnis *(experience)*
> der schönste Tag meines Lebens
> eine große Überraschung *(surprise)*

> **REDEMITTEL**
>
> Einmal / einst war(en) ...
> Früher [wohnte] ich ...
> Eines Tages / eines Morgens / eines Abends / eines Nachts ...
> Schon vorher waren wir ... [gegangen].
> Ich hatte auch vorher ... [getan].
> Und plötzlich ...
> Na ja, wie gesagt, ich ...
> Später ...
> Zu meinem Entsetzen *(horror)* / zu meiner Überraschung ...
> Kurz danach ...
> Zum Schluss ...

B   **Es war einmal.**   Erzählen Sie im Kurs ein bekanntes Märchen oder eine von Ihnen erfundene Geschichte.

C   **Erzählen Sie mal!**   Nehmen Sie ein Blatt Papier und schreiben Sie darauf sechs Verben und sechs andere Wörter (Adjektive, Adverbien usw.). Dann geben Sie einer Partnerin/ einem Partner das Papier und sie/er muss sich eine Erzählung mit diesen Vokabeln im Präteritum ausdenken!

D   **Nacherzählung.**   Die Beispiele in diesem Kapitel stammen aus *(come from)* dem Kurzfilm **„Bus"**, den Sie hoffentlich gesehen haben. Sie kennen bestimmt andere Geschichten – aus Filmen oder Theaterstücken, Romanen *(novels)* oder Opern, zum Beispiel. Erzählen Sie die Handlung *(plot)* von einer dieser Geschichten in der dritten Person *(„Die Frau dachte, dass..."),* oder aus der Perspektive einer Figur in der Geschichte *(„Ich dachte, dass...").*

Schriftliche Themen

Tipps zum Schreiben	**Choosing Precise Verbs**
	Verbs are the key to good writing! Avoid general verbs such as **haben, sein,** and **machen** in favor of verbs that convey the actions or events you are describing with more precision. For example, **gehen** denotes activity but does not describe it. Consider how many different ways there are to *go* in English: *walk, run, stumble, hobble, limp, race,* etc. just as there are in German. If you want to express a precise English verb, look up its German equivalent. Then cross-check this verb as a German entry, to see whether it really means what you think it does. Have in mind a person (not necessarily your instructor) for whom you are writing, and continually ask yourself how you can make your narrative more interesting to this reader.

A   **Eine Bildgeschichte: Der Verdacht.**   Erzählen Sie die Bildgeschichte auf Seite 136 im Präteritum. Benutzen Sie dabei die Erzählskizze.

> bei Nacht • tragen • das Paket • die Brücke • ins Wasser werfen • Polizist sehen • glauben • stehlen • verhaften *(arrest)* • andere Polizisten • kommen • fest·halten • telefonieren • das Baggerschiff • heraus·fischen • herauf·holen • auf·schneiden • eine Bowle • kitschig aus·sehen • erzählen • schenken • um Entschuldigung bitten • wieder ins Wasser werfen

B   **Lebenslauf.**   Schreiben Sie einen Lebenslauf von sich oder von einem bekannten *(well-known)* Menschen. Der Lebenslauf muss nicht lang sein, aber er soll die wichtigsten Informationen enthalten.

BEISPIEL   *Helga Schütz wurde 1937 im schlesischen Falkenhain geboren und wuchs dann in Dresden auf. Nach einer Gärtnerlehre machte sie an der Potsdamer Arbeiter- und-Bauern-Fakultät ihr Abitur und studierte Dramaturgie an der Deutschen Hochschule für Filmkunst in Potsdam Babelsberg. Für die DEFA[3] schrieb sie Dokumentar- und Spielfilme – zum Beispiel „Die Leiden des jungen Werthers".*

> *1970 erschien ihr erster Prosaband: „Vorgeschichten oder Schöne Gegend Probstein", eine Chronik von kleinen Leuten in der niederschlesischen Provinz. Im Westen erschienen im Luchterhand-Verlag ihre Erzählung „Festbe-leuchtung" und die Romane „In Annas Namen" und „Julia oder Erziehung zum Chorgesang".*

> *Helga Schütz wurde mit dem Heinrich-Greif-Preis, dem Heinrich Mann-Preis und dem Theodor-Fontane-Preis ausgezeichnet.*

---

[3]**DEFA: Deutsche Film-Aktiengesellschaft.** The official film company of the former German Democratic Republic.

Zusammenfassung

Rules to Remember

1 The simple past is primarily a narrative tense; it is used to tell stories, recite anecdotes, etc.

2 Weak and irregular verbs add **-t** + personal endings to their respective stems to form the simple past (**ich lernte, ich rannte;** *pl.* **wir lernten, wir rann<u>ten</u>**). Irregular verbs also change their stem vowel and in some cases a consonant.

3 Strong verbs form the simple past by changing the stem vowel and in some cases a consonant, and by adding endings where needed (**singen → sang → wir sangen**). The first- and third-person singular forms take no ending (**singen → sang → ich/er/sie sang**).

4 The second-person simple past tense forms of most verbs **du lerntest (ranntest, gingst); ihr lerntet (ranntet, gingt)** are seldom used.

5 The past perfect tense is formed by combining the simple past forms of **sein** or **haben** with the past participle: **ich <u>war</u> gelaufen; er <u>hatte</u> vergessen.**

6 The past perfect tense is never used in isolation, but rather within the context of some other past time event that it precedes chronologically.

At a Glance

Simple past: Auxiliaries		
haben	**sein**	**werden**
ich hatte	war ■	wurde
du hattest	warst	wurdest
Sie hatten	waren	wurden
er/sie/es hatte	war ■	wurde
wir hatten	waren	wurden
ihr hattet	wart	wurdet
Sie hatten	waren	wurden
sie hatten	waren	wurden

Simple past: Weak verbs	
lernen	**arbeiten**
ich lernte	arbeitete
du lerntest	arbeitetest
Sie lernten	arbeiteten
er/sie/es lernte	arbeitete
wir lernten	arbeiteten
ihr lerntet	arbeitetet
Sie lernten	arbeiteten
sie lernten	arbeiteten

Simple past: Strong verbs

	fahren	gehen	sitzen
ich	fuhr ■	ging ■	saß ■
du	fuhrst	gingst	saßest
Sie	fuhren	gingen	saßen
er/sie/es	fuhr ■	ging ■	saß ■
wir	fuhren	gingen	saßen
ihr	fuhrt	gingt	saßt
Sie	fuhren	gingen	saßen
sie	fuhren	gingen	saßen

Simple past: Irregular verbs

	wissen	denken	kennen
ich	wusste	dachte	kannte
du	wusstest	dachtest	kanntest
Sie	wussten	dachten	kannten
er/sie/es	wusste	dachte	kannte
wir	wussten	dachten	kannte
ihr	wusstet	dachtet	kanntet
Sie	wussten	dachten	kannten
sie	wussten	dachten	kannten

Past perfect: Forms

hatte + *past participle*		war + *past participle*	
ich hatte ... gelernt		ich war ... gegangen	
du hattest ... gelernt		du warst ... gegangen	
Sie hatten ... gelernt		Sie waren ... gegangen	
er/sie/es hatte ... gelernt		er/sie/es war ... gegangen	
wir hatten ... gelernt		wir waren ... gegangen	
ihr hattet ... gelernt		ihr wart ... gegangen	
Sie hatten ... gelernt		Sie waren ... gegangen	
sie hatten ... gelernt		sie waren ... gegangen	

Modal verbs

zum Beispiel

An der Uni

Caro/Alamy

Uni/Universität may seem to need no explanation, since so many university experiences—lectures, study, tests, anxiety, social interaction—are shared by students in many cultures. But like all cultural phenomena, the concept of Universität in Germany, Austria, and Switzerland differs markedly from what North Americans may associate with it. Most German high school students wouldn't know what is meant by a "safety school," for example, since the admissions process is so different in Europe; most German students would be surprised at the cost of higher education in the USA and the resulting problems of college debt; and many would be baffled by the lengths to which North American colleges and universities go to provide not only housing for students, but to organize their social life as well.

139

Grammatik

9.1 ▶ PRESENT AND PAST TENSES OF MODAL VERBS

A. Forms

1. Present-tense modal verbs conjugate irregularly with **ich, du,** and **er/sie/es.** With the exception of **sollen,** the infinitive stem of each modal verb undergoes a vowel change with all of these forms. First- and third-person singular forms take no endings, similar to strong verbs in the simple past tense (see 8.1.A). All plural forms, as well as singular **Sie,** are regular in their conjugation.

Present tense of modal verbs					
dürfen	**können**	**mögen**	**müssen**	**sollen**	**wollen**
ich **darf** ■	kann ■	mag ■	muss ■	soll ■	will ■
du **darfst**	kannst	magst	musst	sollst	willst
Sie dürfen	können	mögen	müssen	sollen	wollen
er/sie/es **darf** ■	kann ■	mag ■	muss ■	soll ■	will ■
wir dürfen	können	mögen	müssen	sollen	wollen
ihr dürft	könnt	mögt	müsst	sollt	wollt
Sie dürfen	können	mögen	müssen	sollen	wollen
sie dürfen	können	mögen	müssen	sollen	wollen

2. Modal verbs form the simple past tense like weak verbs (see 8.1.A), except that there are no umlauts carried over from their infinitive stems, and **mögen** undergoes a consonant change.

Simple past tense of modal verbs					
dürfen	**können**	**mögen**	**müssen**	**sollen**	**wollen**
ich durfte	konnte	mochte	musste	sollte	wollte
du durftest	konntest	mochtest	musstest	solltest	wolltest
Sie durften	konnten	mochten	mussten	sollten	wollten
er/sie/es durfte	konnte	mochte	musste	sollte	wollte
wir durften	konnten	mochten	mussten	sollten	wollten
ihr durftet	konntet	mochtet	musstet	solltet	wolltet
Sie durften	konnten	mochten	mussten	sollten	wollten
sie durften	konnten	mochten	mussten	sollten	wollten

B. Use

A modal verb combines with another verb, often called the *dependent infinitive,* to indicate the speaker's attitude or disposition toward the action or state expressed by the infinitive. A speaker may say, for example:

Ich schreibe mich an der Uni ein.	*I'm enrolling at the university.*

A modal verb adds a subjective element to this statement.

Ich **muss** mich bald einschreiben.	*I **need** to enroll soon at the university.*
Das heißt, ich weiß, ich **soll** mich einschreiben.	*That is, I know I'm **supposed** to enroll.*
Aber ich bin nicht sicher, wo ich studieren **will.**	*But I'm not sure where I **want** to study.*

The main differences between German and English modal usage involve word order, allowable deletions, and the meanings that modal verbs can take on in specific contexts.

1. Modal verb constructions in main clauses make use of the same "bracket" structure as does the present perfect tense (see 1.1 and 3.2). The modal verb functions as V_1 and the dependent infinitive serves as V_2, just like a past participle.

Felix **will** unbedingt in Heidelberg **studieren.**	*Felix really wants to study in Heidelberg.*

2. In dependent clauses, the conjugated verb (V_1) moves to final position.

Meinst du, dass ich auch einen Platz dort **kriegen kann?**	*Do you think that I can also get a spot there?*

3. If a modal verb and a dependent infinitive occur in an infinitive **zu**-phrase (see 11.1–2), they appear at the end of the phrase in this order: dependent infinitive + **zu** + modal verb (in infinitive form).

Wäre es besser, an der Humboldt-Universität in Berlin **studieren *zu* können?**	*Would it be better to be able to study in Berlin at the Humboldt university?*

4. Like English, German allows the dependent infinitive to be deleted, or replaced by **das** or **es,** if the meaning is obvious from the immediate context.

Papa, darf ich irgendwo in Kalifornien studieren?	*Dad, may I study somewhere in California?*
—Nein, das **darfst** du nicht. Punkt.	*—No, you may not. Period.*

5. If a sentence contains verbal complements or separable prefixes that indicate motion in a direction (such as **nach Hause, aufs WC, zurück,** or **hin**), German allows dependent infinitives such as **gehen, fahren, fliegen,** and **laufen** to be deleted. (This differs from English.) **Machen** and **tun** can sometimes be deleted as well, if the context clearly points to those verbs.

Was **soll** ich denn jetzt?	*What am I supposed to do now?*
Wir **müssen** morgen hin.	*We have to go there tomorrow.*

German also has several idiomatic phrases in which other dependent infinitives can drop out, assuming the context makes them clear.

Was soll das? [+ bedeuten]	*What's the point? What's that supposed to mean?*
Ich kann nicht mehr. [+ weitermachen]	*I can't go on/continue.*
Mir kann keiner was! [+ antun OR + vormachen]	*No one can get the better of me! No one can fool me!*

6. In all of the preceding examples, the dependent infinitive refers to the same time as the modal verb—i.e., in a sentence such as **Du kannst hereinkommen,** both **kannst** and **hereinkommen** refer to present time; and in **Ich konnte ihm nicht helfen,** the verbs **konnte** and **helfen** refer to ability and action in the past. In some contexts, however, a speaker wants to distinguish between a modal verb that refers to the present, and an action or state that is already completed. To express this distinction, German uses a present-tense modal verb and a *perfect infinitive*. Perfect infinitives (discussed in more detail in 24.2) are formed by the past participle of a verb plus the infinitive of the appropriate auxiliary (see 3.2).

gegessen haben	*to have eaten*
gesagt haben	*to have said*
ausgeflippt sein	*to have flipped out*
geblieben sein	*to have stayed*
weggelaufen sein	*to have run away*

Present-tense modals with perfect infinitives express a present-tense attitude or disposition regarding a past-tense action or state.

Ich **muss** das zu Hause **gelassen haben.**	*I must have left that at home.* (present speculation—past action)
Das **kann** er doch nicht **gesagt haben**!	*He can't have said that!* (present incredulity—past action)
Das **muss** ja furchtbar **gewesen sein.**	*That must have been terrible.* (present reaction—past state)

Compare these with modal verbs in the simple past tense, which signify that the modality and the action or state both refer to the past.

Ich **musste** das zu Hause **lassen.**	*I had to leave that at home.*
Er **konnte** das nicht **sagen.**	*He wasn't able to/couldn't say that.*
Das **musste** furchtbar **sein.**	*That had to be (i.e., inevitably was) terrible.*

MEANINGS OF MODAL VERBS

A. *Dürfen* (Permission)

1. **Dürfen** means *to be allowed, to have permission,* or *may* (relating to permission, not possibility; see section A.4 below). It is commonly used in polite requests.

Wer **darf** an einer deutschen Uni studieren?	*Who's allowed to study at a German university?*
Normalerweise **dürfen** nur Leute da studieren, die das Abitur[1] gemacht haben.	*Normally, only people who have done the* Abitur *are allowed to study there.*
Darf ich mich als Ausländer bewerben?	*May I apply as a foreigner?*

2. English speakers sometimes confuse **dürfen** with verbs that confer permission, such as **erlauben** *(to allow)* or **lassen** *(to let; see 11.4).* **Dürfen,** by contrast, is used when permission is (or is not) being granted *to* the sentence subject, rather than coming *from* the subject.

    COMPARE:

Kunstakademien **lassen** Leute auch ohne Abitur studieren.	*Art academies allow people to study even without* Abitur.
Das heißt, man **darf** studieren, solange man qualifiziert ist.	*That is to say, you're allowed to study as long as you're qualified.*

3. In the negative (with **nicht** or **kein-**), **dürfen** means *must not* or *may not.* (Compare with **müssen nicht** in section C.)

Nicht-Studenten **dürfen keine** Vorlesungen besuchen.	*Non-students are not permitted to attend any lectures.*
Und im ersten Semester **darf** man **nicht** an Seminaren teilnehmen.	*And during the first semester, you're not allowed to participate in seminars.*

4. Besides expressing permission, English *may* can denote possibility, as in *She may be waiting for us outside.* To convey this meaning, German uses adverbs such as **vielleicht** *(maybe)* or **möglicherweise** *(possibly)* in conjunction with the verb, rather than **dürfen.**

    COMPARE:

Sie **darf** sich einschreiben.	*She may enroll (i.e., she has permission to do so).*
Vielleicht schreibt sie sich ein.	*She may enroll (i.e., there's a possibility she will).*

---

[1]The **Abitur** is the comprehensive final exam taken at the conclusion of one's studies at a German **Gymnasium,** the highest level of secondary school. It varies somewhat from region to region, but as a rule it covers multiple subjects, in four or five separate exams (each lasting up to three hours), and usually one of the subjects is tested orally before a panel of teachers. A similar exam in Switzerland and Austria is called the **Matura.**

B. *Können* (Ability; possibility)

1. **Können** means *can* or *to be able to* and expresses the idea of ability.

Kannst du diese Vorlesungen verstehen?
—Verstehen? Ich **konnte** den Professor
heute gar nicht hören.

Can you understand these lectures?
—Understand? I couldn't even hear
the professor today.

2. **Können** can also express possibility.

Das **kann** vorkommen, wenn der
Hörsaal so überfüllt ist.

That can happen when the lecture
hall is so overcrowded.

3. **Können** also has a special meaning of *to know* a language or *to know how to do* something, and normally stands alone (without a dependent infinitive) when used in this sense.

Sie **kann** Deutsch.

She knows German. (She can speak
German.)[2]

Kannst du diesen Trick?

Do you know how to perform this trick?

4. **Können** is sometimes used interchangeably with **dürfen,** just as *can* and *may* are often confused in English. Strict grammarians of German (and English) still regard this usage as substandard.

Wohin **kann** man sich überhaupt
setzen?

Where can you/are you allowed to sit
anyway?

C. Müssen (Necessity; probability)

1. **Müssen** is the equivalent of English *must* or *have to* and expresses the idea of necessity.

Manchmal **müssen** einige Studenten im
Hörsaal auf dem Boden sitzen.

Sometimes a few students have to/must
sit on the floor in the lecture hall.

Genau. Das **musste** ich gestern machen.

Exactly. I had to do that yesterday.

2. **Müssen** can express probability, the speculation that something must be or probably is true.

Dieser Kurs **muss** sehr gut sein.

This course must be very good.

Oder der Hörsaal **muss** wohl zu
klein sein.

Or the lecture hall must be too small.

3. **Müssen** can also be used to mean *need to,* but particular care is in order when dealing with the three-way correspondence involving *need,* **müssen,** and the other German word for *need,* **brauchen.** First, one must distinguish between *need* as a transitive verb with an object *(I need that)* and as a modal verb with a dependent infinitive *(I need to leave),* and then between positive and negative uses of the modal usage *(I need to leave; I don't need to leave).*

---

[2]Like the verbs of motion (see 9.1.B), the verb **sprechen** is understood and therefore usually omitted in this context.

- For *need* as a transitive verb, positive or negative, only **brauchen** is appropriate.

Ich **brauche** deine Hilfe.	*I need your help.*
Ich **brauche** sie doch nicht.	*I don't need it after all.*

- For *need* as a modal verb in the *positive* sense, only **müssen** is correct.

Ich **muss** noch ein Seminar belegen.	*I need to take one more seminar.*

- For *need* as a modal verb in *negative* usage, both **brauchen nicht (+ zu)**[3] and **müssen nicht** can be used.

Das **brauchst** du wirklich **nicht (zu)** machen. ⎱
Das **musst** du wirklich **nicht** machen. ⎰ *You really don't need to do that.*

4. *Must not* is not the same thing as **müssen nicht.** In German, **müssen** with a negator (**nicht** or **kein-**) is restricted in meaning to *don't need to* or *don't have to.* To express the more forceful *must not,* use **dürfen nicht** (see section A).

COMPARE:

Du **musst nicht** aufstehen.	*You don't have to stand up.*
Mitten in der Vorlesung **darf** man **nicht** aufstehen.	*You mustn't stand up in the middle of the lecture.*

5. **Müssen** + perfect infinitive suggests a strong sense of probability assumed by the speaker or writer regarding an action or state that has already happened.

Die Uni **muss** doch **gewusst haben,** wie viele Studenten sich eingeschrieben haben.	*The university must have known how many students enrolled.*
Oder mehr Studenten **müssen** in den Hörsaal **gekommen sein** als geplant.	*Or more students must have come into the lecture hall than planned.*

D. *Sollen* (Obligation)

1. **Sollen** means *supposed to* or *is to.* It implies a relatively strong order or obligation.[4]

Mediziner **sollen** Physik, Chemie und Anatomie machen.	*Medical students are supposed to do physics, chemistry, and anatomy.*
Welche Kurse **soll** man für Geschichte belegen?	*Which courses are you supposed to sign up for in history?*
Im 19. Jahrhundert **sollten** alle Studenten Latein können.	*In the 19th century, all students were supposed to be proficient in Latin.*

---

[3]The use of **brauchen nicht** without **zu** was originally considered colloquial but is now acceptable.

[4]The subjunctive II form **sollte(n)** *(should)* is normally used instead of the indicative to express suggestion or recommendation (what one *should* or *ought to do*), as opposed to obligation (what one *is supposed to do*).

Du **sollst** hier bleiben. *(obligation)*	*You are (supposed) to stay here.*
Du **solltest** hier bleiben. *(recommendation)*	*You ought to stay here.*

2. **Sollen** can also mean *to be said to,* indicating that the statement is hearsay and thus may or may not be true. In this sense it is used with *present infinitives* to refer to hearsay about present actions or states, and with *perfect infinitives* to refer to hearsay about past actions or states.

Münster und München **sollen** die besten Unis für Jura sein.	*Münster and Munich are supposed to be the best universities for law.*
Goethe **soll** Jura studiert – und gehasst – haben.	*Goethe is said/supposed to have studied law and hated it.*

3. Used in the simple past tense, **sollen** can take on the meaning of *would* in statements such as *He would soon discover that (. . .).* This is sometimes called the "future-in-the-past," since it refers to a point in the "future" with respect to the narrated context, but which is in the "past" from the perspective of what happens even later in the narration.

Erst später **sollte** er darüber schreiben.	*It was only later that he would write about it.*
Bismarck hat auch Jura studiert, und **sollte** danach der erste Kanzler von Deutschland werden.	*Bismarck also studied law, and after that would become the first Chancellor of Germany.*

E. *Wollen* (Desire; wanting; intention)

1. **Wollen** means *to want to* or *to intend to.* In some contexts its meaning is very close to the future tense (see 24.1), but it always emphasizes intention over prediction.

Heute **wollen** sehr viele junge Leute Betriebswirtschaftslehre (BWL) studieren.	*Today, many young people want to study business management.*
Ich dachte, du **wolltest** Psychologie studieren.	*I thought you wanted to study psychology.*
Willst du jetzt Geschäftsfrau oder Beraterin werden?	*Do you want to become a businesswoman or a consultant now?*

2. **Wollen** can also mean *to claim to.* Like other modal verbs with speculative or figurative meanings, **wollen** with *present infinitives* refers to a claim about present actions or states, while with *perfect infinitives* it refers to a claim about past actions or states.

Die Uni-Köln **will** die größte deutsche Uni sein.	*The University of Cologne claims to be the largest German university.*
Und Heidelberg **will** die meisten deutschen Nobelpreisträger **ausgebildet haben.**	*And Heidelberg claims to have educated the most German Nobel Prize winners.*

3. **Wollen** is often used as a main verb with a direct object.

Jede Uni **will** gute Studenten und Studentinnen[5].	*Every university wants good students.*
Und alle Studierenden **wollen** gute Noten.	*And all students want good grades.*

4. **Wollen** is sometimes used in the first-person plural to introduce a polite suggestion.

Wollen wir jetzt Kaffee trinken?	*Shall we go get some coffee?*

5. In an English sentence such as *She wants him to return her book,* the word *him* is less the direct object of *wants* and more the subject of the subsequent idea that "he should return her book"—which is what she wants, after all. German deals with this ambiguity by turning the pseudo-object in this structure into the subject of a dependent clause beginning with **dass.** In such cases, **wollen** can take either the present or simple past tense, depending on when the desiring occurred, but the verb in the **dass**-clause normally remains in the present.

Meine Eltern **wollten** immer, dass **ich** Arzt werde.	*My parents always wanted me to become a doctor.*
Ich **will,** dass **sie** mich entscheiden lassen.	*I want them to let me decide.*
Wollen sie nicht, dass **ich** glücklich bin?	*Don't they want me to be happy?*

F. *Mögen* (Liking)

1. The verb **mögen** is used mainly in the subjunctive form **möchte(n)** (Subjunctive II; see 21.2.E) to express a wish or request, and can be translated as *would like* or *want.* It is the preferred way to express *want* in polite contexts, since **wollen** sounds more forceful and blunt in German than *want* does in English, especially in the first-person singular: **Ich will.** **Möchte** is often combined with **gern** in a positive wish or request.

Ich **möchte** von Medizin zu Biologie wechseln.	*I'd like to switch from medicine to biology.*
Und ich **möchte** (gern) wissen, ob man das machen darf.	*And I'd like to know if you're allowed to do that.*

2. In its indicative form, **mögen** means *to like* or *to want,* but only in certain contexts.

- When used by itself—that is, with no dependent infinitive—**mögen** takes a direct object and means *to like,* very often with reference to people, food, and places.

Ich **mag** dich.	*I like you.*
Magst du Kaffee?	*Do you like/Do you want (some) coffee?*

---

[5]The word **Student** illustrates how gender issues are encoded in linguistic forms. Though used by some speakers in the plural to refer to both male and female students, **Studenten** technically denotes only male students. Consequently, some writers use the word **StudentInnen** (with the medial "I" capitalized) as a plural noun that refers to both men and women; others prefer the participial forms, thus avoiding specifically masculine and feminine references: **Studierende** *(students),* **die Studierenden** *(the students).*

Diesen Kurs **mag** er einfach nicht.   *He just doesn't like this course.*

„Manche **mögen's** heiß"   *"Some Like It Hot" (movie title)[6]*

- When used with an infinitive, **mögen** often combines with a negator such as **nicht** or **kein** to express dislike: *to (not) like to* or *to (not) want to.*

Nein, ich **mag** keinen Kaffee trinken.   *No, I don't want to drink any coffee.*

Er **mochte** nicht mehr allein sein.   *He didn't want be alone any more.*

Ich **mag** nicht lernen.   { *I don't want to study (right now).*
{ *I don't like to study.*

Notice in this last example that the first meaning is localized: *I don't want to study (at the moment),* while the second meaning is general: *I don't like to study (at all).* **Mögen** can be used for both, but only when they are negative. For *positive,* general expressions of *liking to [with a verb],* German uses the "verb + **gern**" structure (see the **Wortschatz** in this chapter).

COMPARE:

Felix **tanzt** sehr **gern.**   *Felix really likes to dance.*

Sophie **tanzt** *nicht* **gern/mag**   *Sophie doesn't like to dance, but*
   nicht **tanzen,** aber manchmal   *sometimes she goes along to the*
   geht sie trotzdem mit zum Tanzclub.   *dance club anyway.*

3. Like other modal verbs, **mögen** can take on a speculative, conjectural sense. With *present infinitives,* it is used to attach the idea of *may* or *might* to present actions or states.

Das **mag** schon sein.   *That may very well be.*

Das **mag** schon stimmen, aber …   *That might be true, but . . .*

With *past infinitives,* the speculation refers to events or states in the past.

Ich **mag** das vielleicht einmal   *I may perhaps have thought that*
   gedacht haben, aber …   *once, but . . .*

Sie **mag** das schon früher **gesagt haben.**   *She may have already said that earlier.*

4. As is the case with **wollen** (see E.5 above), if the subject of a sentence would like someone else to do something, then a **dass**-clause must be used.

Ich möchte dir helfen.   *I would like to help you.*

Ich möchte, **dass du mir hilfst.**   *I would like you to help me.*

---

[6]A 1959 comedy film by Billy Wilder (1906–2002), an Austrian who became famous in Hollywood as a screenwriter, director, and producer.

9.3 ▸ PERFECT TENSES OF MODAL VERBS

A. Formation

1. The present perfect and past perfect of modal verbs are formed like those of other verbs.

haben + past participle (no dependent infinitive)	
Er hat/hatte es { gedurft.	He has/had been permitted to do it.
gekonnt.	He has/had been able to do it.
gemocht.	He has/had liked it.
gemusst.	He has/had had to do it.
gesollt.	He was/had been supposed to do it.
gewollt.	He has/had wanted to do it.

2. In practice, however, modal verbs normally appear with infinitives, which means that both verbs must be taken into account when a modal verb is in the present perfect or past perfect tense. One might expect to see the auxiliary as V_1, with the dependent infinitive and the past participle of the modal verb functioning together as V_2. But in this case, German prefers to have both V_2 verbs—the dependent infinitive as well as the modal—in infinitive form, creating a *double infinitive* construction. The auxiliary used with modal double infinitives is always **haben,**[7] regardless of the dependent infinitive, since the auxiliary is connected with the modal verb.

haben + double infinitive[8]	
Sie hat/hatte es { machen dürfen.	She was/had been permitted to do it.
machen können.	She was/had been able to do it.
machen müssen.	She had to/had had to do it.
machen sollen.	She was/had been supposed to do it.
machen wollen.	She wanted/had wanted to do it.

3. In dependent clauses, the conjugated auxiliary **haben** precedes the two infinitives.

Leider weiß ich gar nicht, was wir für Montag *haben* lesen sollen.

Unfortunately, I have no idea what we were supposed to read for Monday.

B. Use

1. In the present perfect tense, modals can occur without accompanying infinitives when these can be inferred from the context (see 1.B.5 above).

---

[7]Some speakers use an infinitive structure (**ich habe es dürfen/können,** etc.) *without* an accompanying main verb infinitive; such usage is considered regional.

[8]**Mögen** is excluded here and in 9.4, since it is extremely rare in a double infinitive construction.

Hat Lina gestern in die Stadt **gemusst**?	*Did Lina have to go into town yesterday?*
Kannst du Französisch?	*Do you know French?*
—Ja, aber früher habe ich es besser **gekonnt**.	*—Yes, but I used to know it better.*

2. There is virtually no difference in meaning between the simple past tense and the present perfect tense of modals, but the simple past tense is much more common.

Ich **habe** leider nicht zum Vortrag **gehen**
  können.

MORE COMMON:

Ich **konnte** leider nicht zum Vortrag **gehen.**

Unfortunately, I wasn't able to go to the talk.

9.4   FUTURE TENSE OF MODAL VERBS

1. The future tense of modal verbs (e.g., *I **will have to** study, they **will be able to** study, he **will be allowed to** study*) is formed by using the conjugated auxiliary **werden** (see 24.1) as V_1, with V_2 consisting of the dependent infinitive and the modal verb in infinitive form, i.e., a double infinitive construction.

werden + double infinitive		
Er/Sie wird es {	**machen dürfen.** **machen können.** **machen müssen.** **machen sollen.** **machen wollen.**	He/She will { *be permitted to do it.* *be able to do it.* *have to do it.* *be supposed to do it.* *want to do it.*

COMPARE:

***Muss** ich eine Hausarbeit[9] **schreiben?** (present tense)*	*Do I have to write a research paper?*
Werde ich eine Hausarbeit **schreiben müssen?** *(future tense)*	*Will I have to write a research paper?*

2. In dependent clauses, the conjugated future auxiliary is placed directly *before* the double infinitive, not at the end of the clause.

Ich glaube nicht, dass wir eine Hausarbeit **werden schreiben *müssen*.**[10]	*I don't believe we'll have to write a research paper.*

---

[9]**Hausarbeit** is not the same as *homework*, but rather a research paper written in a very specific format, and submitted as the final project for a seminar or other university-level course.

[10]In some parts of southern Germany and Austria, the future auxiliary (**werden**) is placed between the main verb and the modal verb in this construction, rather than in front of it, so that the example here would be rendered: ..., dass wir eine Hausarbeit **schreiben *werden* müssen.**

Wortschatz
Wie sagt man *to like?*

gern haben	mögen/möchten
lieben	hätte(n) gern
gefallen	würde(n) gern tun
gern tun	Lust haben auf/zu

How do you distinguish in German between *I like pizza* and *I like you*, or between *I love pizza* and *I love you*? As you can imagine, choosing the right word for the right meaning is crucial here!

1. The expressions **gern haben** and **mögen** mean *to like* in the sense of affection or approval. They express the emotions of someone toward the person or thing liked.

   Sie **hat** dich **gern.**
   Sie **mag** dich. } *She likes you.*

   Ich **habe** es nicht **gern,** wenn du so sprichst.
   Ich **mag** es nicht, wenn du so sprichst. } *I don't like it when you talk like that.*

   Here is a list of expressions for *liking*, arranged in increasing degrees of emotional affection.

   Ich habe dich gern = *I'm fond of you.*

   Ich mag dich = *I like you.*

   Ich habe dich lieb = *I'm really fond of you/I care about you.*

   Ich liebe dich = *I love you.*

   And going in the opposite direction, according to one blogger:

   Ich liebe dich ⟶ **Ich habe dich lieb** ⟶ **Ich mag dich sehr** ⟶ **Ich mag dich** ⟶ **Ich mag dich ja noch** ⟶ **Also irgendwie mag ich dich schon noch ...**

2. **Gefallen** (*to please; to be pleasing*) can also express *liking*, and overlaps with **mögen** a bit, but usually conveys a more critical, detached liking, as in *I like that film*. It also involves an important grammatical distinction. Whereas **gern haben** and **mögen** express the liking of the subject for the direct object (**Ich habe das gern/Ich mag das**), it is the (dative) *object* of **gefallen** that does the liking, while the subject represents what is liked: **Das gefällt mir** (*That is pleasing to me = I like that*). English speakers must keep in mind that **gefallen** is singular or plural depending on the subject (the thing

liked), regardless of whether the "liker" (which would be the subject in English) is singular or plural.

Dieser Film **gefällt** mir.	*I like this film. (It pleases me.)*
Diese Filme **gefallen** mir.	*I like these films. (They please me.)*
Dieser Film **gefällt** vielen Leuten.	*Many people like this film. (It pleases many people.)*
Diese Filme **gefallen** vielen Leuten.	*Many people like these films. (They please many people.)*

3. To express *to like [food],* German uses **schmecken** (in its meaning *to taste good*) with the dative.

Ich muss zugeben, Sauerkraut **schmeckt mir** gar nicht.	*I have to admit I don't like sauerkraut at all.*
Schmeckt dir das Essen in der Mensa?	*Do you like the food in the (university) cafeteria?*

While Germans no doubt love their food as much as Americans love theirs, Germans tend to use **lieben** far less often to express culinary rapture. When they do, it is usually to show enthusiasm for a category in general, e.g., **Ich liebe Schokoladenkuchen,** and not a specific example, as in *I love **this** chocolate cake.* To indicate an exceptional appreciation for food, one can add various modifiers to **schmecken,** all of which can be enhanced with **sehr** or **wirklich.**

wunderbar	*wonderful*
köstlich	*delicious/delectable*
hervorragend	*superb/outstanding*

4. **Lieben** can be used to indicate profound enjoyment of other things as well as food, but similar to its usage with food, it normally does so in a general rather than specific sense. Notice in the following examples how German distinguishes between the specific and the general.

Ich **liebe** klassische Musik.	*I love classical music.*
Das Konzert gestern Abend **hat mir** sehr gut/ super **gefallen.**	*I loved the concert last night.*
Er **liebt** die vielen Farben des Frühlings.	*He loves the many colors of spring.*
Sie **findet** die Farben dieser Vorhänge genial.	*She loves the colors of these curtains.*

5. The adverb **gern** used with a verb other than **haben** means *to like to do* the activity expressed by the verb, i.e., in general. To express this idea in the negative (*to **not** like to do something*), German uses both **nicht gern** and **nicht mögen.**

Wir **wandern gern.**	*We like to hike.*
Ich esse **nicht gern** allein im Restaurant.	*I don't like to eat by myself in a restaurant.*
Sie **mag nicht** immer fernsehen.	*She doesn't like to watch TV all the time.*

6. The subjunctive forms **möchten (tun), hätten gern,** and **würden gern tun** (see 21.2) are polite ways of expressing inclination or asking what someone *would like (to do),* i.e., at the moment.

Ich **möchte** einen Kaffee.
Ich **hätte gern** einen Kaffee. } *I would like a (cup of) coffee.*

Möchten Sie mitfahren?
Würden Sie **gern** mitfahren? } *Would you like to come along?*

7. The expression **Lust auf/zu etwas haben** is commonly used to express what someone *feels like having or doing.* It is close in meaning to **möchte(n)** and can be made more polite by using the subjunctive form **hätte(n)** instead of **haben** (see 21.2).

■ When the goal in question is an object, the preposition **auf** (+ accusative) is used.

Hast du **Lust auf** eine Tasse Kaffee? *Do you feel like (having) a cup of coffee?*

Oder **hättest** du **Lust auf** eine Tasse Tee? *Or would you like to have a cup of tea?*

■ When the goal is an activity, an infinitive phrase with **zu** is used (see 11.1).

Wir **haben** keine **Lust zu** tanzen. *We do not feel like dancing/have no desire to dance.*

Wir **haben** keine **Lust,** diesen Film noch einmal **zu** sehen. *We don't feel like seeing/have no desire to see this film again.*

Übungen

A **Ratschläge (*advice*) mit Modalverben.** Wie viele Ratschläge können Sie in den folgenden Situationen geben? Wer hat die besten Ratschläge?

BEISPIELE Günther Schulz will einen Marathon laufen. (Er ...)
*Er **soll/sollte** sich Laufschuhe kaufen.*
*Er **muss** jeden Tag trainieren.*

Ihre Freundin Monika sucht eine Arbeitsstelle. (Du ...)
*Du **kannst** zum Arbeitsamt gehen.*
*Du **sollst/solltest** die Annoncen in der Zeitung lesen.*

1. Ich habe hohes Fieber und fühle mich nicht wohl. (Du ...)
2. Eine Bekannte von Ihnen sucht ohne Erfolg eine neue Wohnung. (Sie ...)
3. Freunde von Ihnen wollen im Restaurant essen, aber sie haben ihr Geld zu Hause vergessen. (Ihr *[you]*...)
4. Wir (du und ich) haben morgen eine schwere Prüfung in Deutsch. (Wir ...)
5. Ein Bekannter von Ihnen hat einen schrecklichen Minderwertigkeitskomplex (*inferiority complex*). Es wird jeden Tag schlimmer mit ihm. (Er ...)
6. Ihre Nachbarn fliegen nächste Woche zum ersten Mal nach Europa. (Sie *[they]* ...)

B   **Gefällt's Ihnen?**   Was meinen Sie zu den folgenden Themen? Verwenden Sie Ausdrücke aus dem Wortschatz, um Ihre Meinung auszudrücken.

BEISPIEL   tanzen/heute Abend tanzen
*Ich tanze **gern**. Ich **habe** aber **keine Lust,** heute Abend zu tanzen.*

1. die Universität, an der Sie jetzt studieren
2. Jimmy Fallon auf Twitter folgen
3. Joghurt zum Frühstück essen
4. fern·sehen
5. Rechtsanwältin/Rechtsanwalt *(lawyer)* werden
6. wenn jemand Ihnen Ratschläge *(advice)* gibt
7. bei Facebook herum·schnüffeln *(to snoop around)*
8. zu einem Heavy-Metal-Konzert gehen
9. ein Studiensemester im Ausland verbringen
10. der letzte Film, den Sie gesehen haben
11. die politische Stimmung im Lande/an Ihrer Uni
12. inline·skaten *(rollerblading)*

C   **Mit Modalverben geht's auch.**   Drücken Sie den Inhalt dieser Sätze mit Modalverben aus.

BEISPIEL   Hier ist Parkverbot.
Hier darf man nicht parken.

1. Jean-Luc spricht und versteht Französisch.
2. Die Studenten verstanden die Leseaufgabe nicht.
3. Man sagt, dass zu viel Sonne ungesund ist.
4. Den Rasen *(lawn)* bitte nicht betreten!
5. Machen Sie das lieber nicht!
6. Ich habe gehört, dass das Nietzsche-Seminar sehr gut ist.
7. Jonathan behauptet immer, dass er alles besser weiß.
8. Erlauben Sie, dass ich eine Frage stelle?
9. Während des Fluges ist das Rauchen verboten.
10. Es ist dringend *(urgently)* nötig, dass du deine Eltern anrufst!

D   **So bin ich.**   Erzählen Sie von sich und Ihren Meinungen mit Modalverben und Ausdrücken aus dem **Wortschatz.**

1. Was Sie überhaupt nicht gern haben
2. Was Sie besonders gut machen können
3. Wozu Sie im Moment Lust haben
4. Was/Wen Sie mögen
5. Was jede Studentin/jeder Student machen soll/wissen sollte
6. Was Sie heute Abend machen möchten
7. Was Ihnen an Ihrer Uni (nicht) gefällt
8. Was Sie am Wochenende machen müssen/sollen/wollen

E **Forderungen (demands)!** Jeder will etwas von mir! Was wollen oder möchten Leute von Ihnen? Machen Sie bitte vier Aussagen.

BEISPIELE *Meine Mutter **will, dass** ich gute Noten bekomme.*
*Mein Freund **möchte, dass** ich ihn jeden Abend anrufe.*

Eltern	Lehrerinnen/Lehrer oder Professorinnen/Professoren
Freunde	Mitbewohnerinnen/Mitbewohner *(roommates)*
Chef/Chefin	der Staat *(government)*

Und was müssen Sie zum Glück *nicht* machen? Machen Sie drei Aussagen.

BEISPIELE *Ich **muss nicht** auf meine kleine Schwester aufpassen.*
*Ich **brauche nicht** beim Kochen **(zu)** helfen.*

F **Alles nur vom Hörensagen.** Ist es wahr, was andere vom Hörensagen berichten? Machen Sie vier Aussagen, die mit **sollen** in diesem Sinne gebildet sind. Lesen Sie Ihre Aussagen im Unterricht vor.

REAKTIONEN

Das stimmt gewiss.	Unsinn!
Das mag sein.	Quatsch!
Sehr unwahrscheinlich!	

BEISPIELE *Es soll mehr als 25 Millionen Facebooknutzer in Deutschland geben.*
Die Präsidentin/Der Präsident unserer Uni soll früher bei Starbucks gearbeitet haben.

G **Damals.** Drücken Sie die Sätze im Perfekt aus.

BEISPIEL *Als Kind wollte ich oft meinen Eltern helfen.*
*Als Kind **habe** ich oft meinen Eltern **helfen wollen.***

1. Früher musste ich oft meinen Eltern helfen.
2. Manchmal durfte ich nicht ausgehen, wenn ich ihnen nicht geholfen hatte.
3. Es stimmte aber nicht, dass ich ihnen nicht helfen wollte.
4. Aber manchmal konnte ich es nicht, weil ich etwas anderes machen musste.
5. Das konnten meine Eltern nicht immer verstehen.

H **Er liebt sie, aber sie mag ihn nicht, weil ...** Nehmen Sie Vokabeln aus dem Wortschatz **(gern, möchte, lieben** usw.) und erzählen Sie von der Handlung und besonders von den Beziehungen *(relationships)* in einer Fernsehsendung, einem Film oder einem Roman, den Sie kennen. Wer macht was (nicht) gern? Wer möchte …? Wer liebt wen? Wer mag wen nicht? Was gefällt einer Figur an einer anderen Figur in der Geschichte? Machen Sie 5–6 Aussagen – aber wenn Sie einen Jane Austen-Roman oder *Game of Thrones* als Beispiel wählen, dann darf's ruhig mehr sein!

I   **Eine schöne Zukunft?**   Erzählen Sie davon.

BEISPIEL   Heute muss ich noch (nicht) ..., aber in zwei Jahren ...
Jetzt **muss** *ich noch* **studieren**, *aber in 10 Jahren* **werde** *ich nicht mehr* **studieren müssen**.

1. Heute muss ich (nicht) ..., aber in vier Jahren ...
2. Heute kann ich (nicht) ..., aber ich weiß, dass ich in acht Jahren ...
3. Heute will ich (nicht) ..., aber in zwölf Jahren ...
4. Heute darf ich (nicht) ..., aber ich hoffe, dass ich in zwanzig Jahren ...
5. Heute soll ich (nicht) ..., aber in 30 Jahren ...

Anwendung

A   **Rollenspiel: Machen Sie mit?**   Sie wollen etwas tun, aber Sie wollen es nicht allein tun. Versuchen Sie, jemanden dazu zu überreden *(persuade)*. Diese andere Person will nicht und hat viele Ausreden *(excuses)*.

THEMENVORSCHLÄGE

Heute Abend zum Essen oder zu einer Party gehen
Mit Ihnen *World of Warcraft* spielen
Mit Ihnen zusammen eine Hausaufgabe machen
An einer Protestaktion teil·nehmen

REDEMITTEL

für	**gegen**
Du, ich habe eine tolle Idee!	Oh, das klingt interessant, aber ...
Wir können/sollen ...	Leider kann ich nicht, denn ...
Wir müssen nicht ...	Ach weißt du, ich möchte schon, aber ...

B   **Gebote *(commands)* und Verbote.**   Als Kind gab es sicher manches, was Sie (nicht) tun **durften, konnten, mussten** oder **sollten,** aber doch (nicht) tun **wollten.** Erzählen Sie in einer Gruppe davon. Fragen Sie auch Ihre Professorin/Ihren Professor, wie es in ihrer/seiner Kindheit war. Machen Sie einige Aussagen im Präteritum (**ich musste ... tun**) und einige Aussagen im Perfekt (**ich habe ... tun müssen**).

THEMENVORSCHLÄGE

beim Essen	auf Reisen
in der Schule	mit Freunden
im Haushalt	

Schriftliche Themen

Tipps zum Schreiben	**Providing Explanations**
	To link ideas by explaining *why* something happens, make use of adverbial conjunctions such as **daher, darum, deshalb,** and **deswegen,** (*therefore, for that reason, that's why;* see 14.5), rather than **Das ist warum** (*That's why*). These conjunctions can either begin a clause or occur elsewhere in it, and sound more authentically German. Ich habe keine Zeit, (und) **daher/deshalb** kann ich nicht kommen. Ich habe keine Zeit und (ich) kann **daher/deshalb** nicht kommen. *I don't have any time, and therefore/that's why I can't come.*

A **Bildgeschichte.** Erzählen Sie die folgende Bildgeschichte im Präteritum. Verwenden Sie mehrere Modalverben und benutzen Sie dabei die Erzählskizze.

> der Drachen • in den Baum fliegen • hängen bleiben • der Pförtner (*gatekeeper*) • das Tor • nicht hinein • gehen • nach Hause • Vater bitten • holen • sich fein an·ziehen • denken, dass • auf den Baum klettern • der Junge wird in Zukunft ... [*Modalverb im Futur*]

B **Sich entschuldigen.** Schreiben Sie eine E-Mail, in der Sie sich bei jemandem dafür entschuldigen, dass Sie etwas *nicht tun können* oder *nicht getan haben* (z.B. nicht zurückgemailt; nicht angerufen; nicht auf seine Facebook-Einladung reagiert). Nennen Sie die Gründe dafür. (Siehe Appendix 1, *Formats for Written Communication*.)

BEISPIEL *Hi Lena! Du, es tut mir echt leid, dass ich nicht geschrieben habe. Weißt du, ich war übers Wochenende bei Verwandten auf dem Land, und die hatten kein W-LAN (Wi-Fi). Unglaublich! Drei Tage offline!! Aber jetzt bin ich wieder zu Hause ... usw.*

C   **Die zehn Gebote *(commandments).***   Schreiben Sie eine Liste mit zehn Geboten für eine der folgenden Personen: eine Politikerin/einen Politiker; eine Studentin/einen Studenten; einen Gebrauchtwagenhändler *(used car salesman);* ein Fotomodell; eine Mitbewohnerin/einen Mitbewohner. Benutzen Sie dabei das Modalverb **sollen**!

BEISPIEL   (für einen Professor)
1. Sie sollen uns übers Wochenende keine schwierigen Aufgaben stellen.
2. Sie sollen bei der Benotung der Prüfungen etwas Gnade (mercy) *zeigen.*
usw.

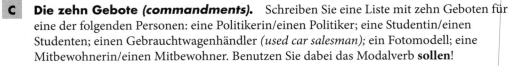

Zusammenfassung

Rules to Remember

1   Modal verbs conjugate irregularly in the present-tense singular for **ich/du/er/sie** (sing.)/**es,** but they conjugate like other verbs in the present-tense plural as well as **Sie** (sing.).

2   *Must not* is **dürfen nicht; müssen nicht** means *not to have to.*

3   **Ich will/möchte gehen** means *I want/would like to go.* **Ich will/möchte, dass** *sie* **geht** means *I want/would like* **her** *to go.*

4   Modal verbs conjugate like weak verbs in the past tense, but without any infinitive stem umlauts (**können → konnte; müssen → musste**).

5   German speakers use the simple past tense of modals more often than the present perfect.

6   The future tense and the perfect tenses of modals require a double infinitive construction if there is also a dependent infinitive involved (**Sie hat** *gewollt,* BUT **Sie hat** *gehen wollen*).

At a Glance

A. Conjugation of modal verbs

Present tense						
	dürfen	**können**	**mögen**	**müssen**	**sollen**	**wollen**
ich	darf ■	kann ■	mag ■	muss ■	soll ■	will ■
du	darfst	kannst	magst	musst	sollst	willst
Sie	dürfen	können	mögen	müssen	sollen	wollen
er/sie/es	darf ■	kann ■	mag ■	muss ■	soll ■	will ■
wir	dürfen	können	mögen	müssen	sollen	wollen
ihr	dürft	könnt	mögt	müsst	sollt	wollt
Sie	dürfen	können	mögen	müssen	sollen	wollen
sie	dürfen	können	mögen	müssen	sollen	wollen

Simple past tense						
	dürfen	**können**	**mögen**	**müssen**	**sollen**	**wollen**
ich durfte		konnte	mochte	musste	sollte	wollte
du durftest		konntest	mochtest	musstest	solltest	wolltest
Sie durften		konnten	mochten	mussten	sollten	wollten
er/sie/es durfte		konnte	mochte	musste	sollte	wollte
wir durften		konnten	mochten	mussten	sollten	wollten
ihr durftet		konntet	mochtet	musstet	solltet	wolltet
Sie durften		konnten	mochten	mussten	sollten	wollten
sie durften		konnten	mochten	mussten	sollten	wollten

B. Sentence structure

Present/Simple past

Main clause

_____ | kann / konnte | _____ | machen |

Dependent clause

(main), _____ | machen | kann / konnte |

Present perfect

Main clause

_____ | habe | _____ | machen | können |

Dependent clause

(main), _____ | habe | machen | können |

Future

Main clause

_____ | werde | _____ | machen | können |

Dependent clause

(main), _____ | werde | machen | können |

Reflexive pronouns ▪ Reflexive verbs ▪ *Selbst* and *selber* ▪ *Einander*

zum Beispiel

Albrecht Dürer

The Art Archive / Alamy

Albrecht Dürer (1471–1528) was renowned throughout Europe for his groundbreaking work in engraving techniques, printmaking, and painting, as well as his treatises on geometry and proportion. He was one of the first artists who consciously worked (and succeeded) at establishing a "brand." Born into an artistic family in Nuremberg, Germany—his father was a successful goldsmith—he apprenticed under several of the best-known European artisans of his time, traveled and worked extensively in Italy, and returned to Nuremberg to create art in multiple media (woodcuts, copper engravings, watercolors, oil) using a variety of subjects (landscape, portraits, religious symbolism). Several of his most famous works can be seen in the **Alte Pinakothek**, a museum in Munich, Germany.

Grammatik

10.1 **REFLEXIVE PRONOUNS**

A. Forms

In English, reflexive pronouns are indicated by adding *-self* or *-selves* to the object or possessive pronoun: *He drew himself. / Many artists draw themselves.* In German, the reflexives for the first-person (**ich, wir**) and second-person (**du, ihr**) pronouns are the same as regular accusative and dative forms; all third-person forms plus the formal **Sie** take the reflexive **sich.**[1]

	Nom.	Acc.	Dat.	
1st pers. sing.	ich	mich	mir	*myself*
1st pers. plural	wir	uns	uns	*ourselves*
2nd pers. sing.: familiar	du	dich	dir	*yourself*
2nd pers. sing.: formal	Sie	sich	sich	*yourself*
2nd pers. plural: familiar	ihr	euch	euch	*yourselves*
2nd pers. plural: formal	Sie	sich	sich	*yourselves*
3rd pers. sing.	er (der Mann)	sich	sich	*himself*
	sie (die Frau)	sich	sich	*herself*
	es (das Kind)	sich	sich	*itself*
3rd pers. plural.	sie (die Leute)	sich	sich	*themselves*

B. Positions of reflexive pronouns

1. When the sentence subject—noun or pronoun—is the first element in the sentence, the reflexive pronoun comes directly after the conjugated verb.

   Dürer hat **sich** als Maler und Grafiker einen Namen gemacht.
   Dürer made a name for himself as a painter and graphic artist.

   Er hat **sich** oft selbst gezeichnet.
   He drew himself often.

2. When a *subject noun* is in the middle field, it can precede or follow a reflexive pronoun; a *subject pronoun* always follows directly after the conjugated verb and precedes a reflexive pronoun (see 1.1.C).

---

[1]The interrogative pronouns **wer** and **was** (see 19.2) and the indefinite pronouns (**man, jemand, niemand, etwas, jedermann,** etc; see 17.2) are third-person pronouns and also take the reflexive **sich.**

Schon mit 13 hat *Dürer* **sich** dreimal selbst gezeichnet.	*Even as a 13-year-old, Dürer drew himself three times.*
Schon mit 13 hat **sich** *Dürer* dreimal selbst gezeichnet.	
Schon mit 13 hat *er* **sich** dreimal selbst gezeichnet.	*Even as a 13-year-old, he drew himself three times.*

10.2 ▶ REFLEXIVE VERBS

A pronoun in the accusative or dative case is reflexive when it refers to (i.e., "reflects") the sentence subject.

„Ich schaute **mich** im Spiegel an", hat er aufs Bild geschrieben.	*"I looked at myself in the mirror," he wrote on the drawing.*
Als Erwachsener malte er drei Ölgemälde von **sich.**	*As an adult, he painted three oil paintings of himself.*

Both English and German make use of reflexive pronouns, but German does so even more, thanks to a category of verbs in German that are "inherently" reflexive—they require a reflexive pronoun in order to convey certain meanings.[2] Thus German makes use of reflexive pronouns in multiple ways:

- As accusative or dative objects that refer to the sentence subject (as in the examples above).

- With verbs that require a reflexive pronoun, sometimes called *reflexive verbs.*

- With certain verbs of activity that translate as passive constructions.

The following discussion takes up these multiple contexts for reflexives, first with accusative objects and then with dative objects.

A. Accusative reflexives with verbs

1. An accusative reflexive pronoun can be used with virtually any transitive verb if the subject directs an activity at himself/herself/itself. The accusative reflexive pronoun functions as a *direct* object (see 5.4) and refers to the sentence subject.

---

[2]English has comparatively few such verbs, but one example is *to enjoy oneself.* In English you can say *I enjoyed the food last night,* with *the food* as the direct object of *enjoy.* But with a reflexive pronoun, as in *I enjoyed myself/They enjoyed themselves at the party,* the verb conveys a different meaning: *to have a good time personally.*

COMPARE:

Nonreflexive	**Reflexive**
Er zeichnete einmal einen Hasen.	Er zeichnete sich selbst[3] öfter.
He once drew a rabbit.	*He drew himself quite often.*
Man kann es da im Bild sehen.	Ich kann mich da im Bild sehen.
You can see it there in the drawing.	*I can see myself there in the drawing.*
Wie hat er die Pinsel vorbereitet?	Wie hat er sich vorbereitet?
How did he prepare the (paint)brushes?	*How did he prepare himself?*
Er stellte alles genau hin.	Er stellte sich genau hin.
He positioned everything precisely.	*He positioned himself precisely.*

2.   Several German verbs are more consistently transitive than their English equivalents: they require an object no matter what. If the sentence has no direct object, they use a reflexive object to fulfill this function, whereas in English they remain intransitive in such cases. Typical verbs of this category are listed below.

(sich) ändern   *to change*
(sich) bewegen   *to move*
(sich) drehen   *to turn*
(sich) öffnen   *to open*

COMPARE:

A breeze moved the curtain. (direct object)	Ein leichter Wind bewegte **den Vorhang.**
The curtain moved. (no object)	**Der Vorhang** bewegte **sich.**
The trip to Italy changed everything. *(direct object)*	Die Reise nach Italien änderte **alles.**
Everything changed. (no object)	**Alles** änderte **sich.**

3.   With certain meanings, a significant number of German verbs *always* take an accusative reflexive, and are therefore referred to as *reflexive verbs*. Reflexive verbs always take the auxiliary **haben** in the perfect tenses, since a reflexive verb by definition always has a direct object (see 3.2.B). Here are some common examples.

sich amüsieren *to enjoy oneself*	sich langweilen *to be bored*
sich ausr·uhen *to take a rest*	sich (hin·)legen *to lie down*
sich beeilen *to hurry*	sich setzen *to sit down*
sich benehmen *to behave*	sich um·sehen *to take a look around*
sich entschuldigen *to apologize*	sich verlaufen *to get lost, go the*
sich erholen *to recover*	*wrong way*
sich erkälten *to catch a cold*	sich verspäten *to be late, come too*
sich (wohl/schlecht) fühlen *to feel well/ill*	*late*

---

[3]See section 10.3.2 below for commentary on the use of **selbst** in this context.

Vanessa **amüsiert sich** immer in Kunstmuseen.	*Vanessa always enjoys herself / has fun in art museums.*
Sie geht von Raum zu Raum und **sieht sich** überall um.	*She goes from room to room and looks around everywhere.*
„Es macht mir Spaß, **mich** in einem Museum zu **verlaufen**", sagt sie.	*"I think it's fun to get lost in a museum," she says.*
„Wie kann man **sich** da nur **langweilen?**"	*"How can one possibly be bored there?"*

4. Many reflexive verbs complete their meaning with a prepositional phrase. In the following examples, **sich** (the direct object referring to the subject) is always accusative, while the case following the preposition may be either accusative, dative, or even genitive, depending on the preposition rather than the reflexive pronoun. (For more examples, see R.3.)

sich ärgern über *(acc.)*   *to be annoyed at*
sich beschäftigen mit   *to be occupied with*
sich erinnern an *(acc.)*   *to remember*
sich freuen auf *(acc.)*   *to look forward to*
sich freuen über *(acc.)*   *to be happy about*
sich fürchten vor *(dat.)*   *to be afraid of*
sich gewöhnen an *(acc.)*   *to get used to*
sich interessieren für   *to be interested in*
sich konzentrieren auf *(acc.)*   *to concentrate on*
sich kümmern um   *to attend to, concern oneself with*
sich um·sehen nach   *to look around for*
sich verlieben in *(acc.)*   *to fall in love with*
sich verstecken vor *(dat.)*   *to hide from*
sich wundern über *(acc.)*   *to wonder about*

Erinnern Sie **sich an** Dürers Reisen nach Italien?	*Do you remember Dürer's trips to Italy?*
Er **interessierte sich** besonders **für** die Werke von Bellini.	*He was especially interested in the works of Bellini.*
Und er hat **sich mit** Geometrie und Proportionen **beschäftigt.**	*And he occupied himself with geometry and proportions.*

5. **Sich** can also be used in certain contexts with a nonacting subject, creating an idea that is expressed in English in the passive voice (see 12.3.B).

Die Pose im Selbstporträt **findet sich** sonst nur in Christus-Darstellungen.	*The pose in the self-portrait is otherwise found only in portrayals of Christ.*
Seine Briefe **lesen sich** nicht so leicht.	*His letters are not very easy to read / not very easily read.*
Sein Interesse an der Natur **versteht sich** von selbst.	*His interest in nature can be understood on its own (i.e., it's obvious).*

B. Dative reflexives with verbs

1. Dative reflexive pronouns and accusative direct objects may both appear with nonreflexive verbs when the subject is acting on his/her/its own behalf. When the context is clear, the dative reflexive is optional, as in English.

Kaufst du (**dir**) etwas im Museumsladen?	*Are you buying something (for yourself) in the museum shop?*
Nein, aber ich habe (**mir**) Schauertes neue Dürer-Biographie bestellt.	*No, but I've ordered (for myself) Schauerte's new biography of Dürer.*

2. Some verbs require dative reflexives to convey particular meanings.

sich etwas an·hören	*to listen intentionally to something*
sich etwas an·sehen	*to take a look at something*
sich etwas ein·bilden	*to imagine or think something*
sich etwas leisten	*to afford something*
sich etwas merken	*to take note of something*
sich etwas überlegen	*to think something over*
sich etwas vor·stellen	*to imagine, conceive of something*

In the expressions above, the **sich** stands for a reflexive pronoun in the dative case, while the **etwas** can be a direct object in the accusative case or information in the form of a clause, either an infinitive clause (see 11.1) or a **dass**-clause (see R.2.3). In the following examples, the reflexive verb is highlighted in bold and the information corresponding to **etwas** is bold italic.

Wir haben **uns** *das Dürer-Haus* in Nürnberg **angesehen.**	*We took a look at the Dürer House in Nuremberg.*
Hast du **dir** *den Audio-Guide* genau **angehört?**	*Did you listen carefully to the audio guide?*
Ich habe **mir** *seine Werkstatt* ganz anders **vorgestellt.**	*I pictured his workshop very differently.*
Leider konnte ich es **mir** nicht **leisten,** *ein Andenken zu kaufen.*	*Unfortunately I couldn't afford to buy a souvenir.*

3. German tends to avoid possessive adjectives when referring to body parts and clothing in conjunction with certain verbs and uses dative reflexives instead to clarify the reference (see 4.5 and 5.5). This usage is so common that such verbs are frequently listed as reflexive verbs: **sich die Zähne putzen.** But if the context is clear, the reflexive "dative of reference" is optional.

Für das Selbstporträt von 1500[4] zog er (**sich**) einen Mantel mit Pelzkragen an.	*For the self-portrait of 1500, he put on a coat with a fur collar.*
„Albrecht, das Essen ist fertig! Hast du (**dir**) die Hände gewaschen?"	*"Albrecht, we're ready to eat! Have you washed your hands?"*

---

[4]Probably the most famous of Dürer's self-portraits, the *Self-Portrait of 1500* (also known as the *Self-portrait with Fur-trimmed Collar*) can be seen in the **Alte Pinakothek** in Munich.

4. With **anziehen, waschen,** and related verbs, an accusative reflexive is normally used when referring to the activity in general (such as *getting dressed* or *washing*), but the reflexive is dative when a direct object is specified.

Zieh **dich** doch an!	*Come on and get dressed!*
Zieh **dir** *etwas Anständiges* an!	*Put on something decent!*
Du siehst aber aus – wasch **dich** doch!	*You look a sight—go wash up!*
Nach dem Malen solltest du **dir** *die Hände* waschen.	*After painting you should wash your hands.*

10.3 ▸ *SELBST* AND *SELBER*

1. **Selbst** and **selber** both mean *-self;* they are intensifying adverbs, not reflexive pronouns. They can occur either by themselves or in combination with reflexive pronouns.

Wenn er *sich* nicht **selbst/selber** darum kümmern konnte, führte seine Frau Agnes das Geschäft.	*When he could not attend to it himself, his wife Agnes was in charge of the business.*
Er sah *sich* **selbst/selber** im Spiegel.	*He saw himself in the mirror.*
Die Symbolik in einigen seiner Werke erklärt *sich von* **selbst/selber.**	*The symbolism in several of his works explains itself.*

2. With verbs that take a dative object (see 5.5.B), **selbst** or **selber** is used to emphasize a reflexive pronoun object. **Selbst/selber** are similarly used in contexts in which a verb that normally takes a non-reflexive object is being used reflexively, such as **zeichnen.**

Hat er *sich* durch diese Porträts **selbst/selber** gratuliert?	*Was he congratulating himself by means of these portraits?*
Du widersprichst *dir* **selbst/selber.**	*You're contradicting yourself.*
Wie oft hat Dürer *sich* **selbst/selber** gezeichnet?	*How often did Dürer draw himself?*

3. **Selbst** and **selber** are used after reflexive pronouns that serve as the objects of a prepositional phrase following a reflexive verb, i.e., to emphasize one reflexive pronoun over another when two of them appear in close proximity.

Bei einem Selbstporträt kann man **sich** nicht vor *sich* **selbst** verstecken.	*In the case of a self-portrait, you can't hide from yourself.*
Im Gegenteil: Man muss **sich** auf *sich* **selbst** konzentrieren.	*On the contrary: You have to concentrate on yourself.*

4. **Selbst** and **selber** can be used interchangeably except in one instance. When **selbst** precedes the words it intensifies, it means *even.* **Selber** cannot be used this way.

Selbst in Italien wurden seine Werke begehrt.	*Even in Italy his works were sought after.*
Selbst Galileo und Kepler haben sein Buch über Mathematik zitiert.	*Even Galileo and Kepler quoted his book on mathematics.*

| 10.4 | THE RECIPROCAL PRONOUN *EINANDER* |

1. Plural reflexive pronouns can be used to express reciprocal actions, that is, actions done by persons **to** *each other* or *one another*. This structure, however, may result in ambiguity, which is best eliminated by using **einander** *(each other)*.

Wir kauften **uns** im Museumsladen kleine Reiseandenken.

> *We bought **each other** little travel souvenirs in the museum shop.*
> *We bought **ourselves** little travel souvenirs in the museum shop.*

Wir kauften **einander** kleine Reiseandenken.

*We bought **each other** little travel souvenirs.*

2. When used with prepositions, **einander** attaches to the preposition to form one word.

Haben Dürer und Martin Luther mal **miteinander** gesprochen?

Did Dürer and Martin Luther ever speak with each other?

Dürer und die Stadt Nürnberg haben viel **füreinander** getan.

Dürer and the city of Nuremberg did a lot for each other.

Wortschatz
Wie sagt man *to decide?*

(sich) entscheiden	eine Entscheidung treffen
sich entschließen	einen Entschluss fassen
beschließen	

1. **Entscheiden** means *to decide (for or against)* or *to settle a question intellectually.*

Ein Richter muss diesen Fall **entscheiden**.   *A judge must decide this case.*

2. **Sich entscheiden** means *to decide, make up one's mind,* or *choose among various options.* **Sich entscheiden (für)** means *to decide on one option, to choose.*

Hast du **dich entschieden,** ob du mitfahren willst oder nicht?

Have you decided whether or not you want to ride along?

Ich habe **mich** doch **für** den grünen Mantel **entschieden**.

I decided on the green coat after all.

3. **Eine Entscheidung treffen** means *to come to a decision*. It is roughly synonymous with **(sich) entscheiden,** though stylistically more emphatic.

Hast du schon **eine Entscheidung getroffen,** wo du studieren möchtest?	*Have you come to a decision as to where you want to study?*

4. **Sich entschließen** means *to decide to take a course of action* or *to make up one's mind to do something.*

Er konnte **sich** nicht (dazu)[5] **entschließen,** ein neues Auto zu kaufen.	*He could not make up his mind to buy a new car.*

5. **Einen Entschluss fassen** means *to make a decision or resolution*. It is roughly synonymous with **sich entschließen,** but more emphatic.

Sie hat **den Entschluss gefasst,** ein anderes Studium anzufangen.	*She made the decision to begin a different course of study.*

6. **Beschließen** means *to resolve to take a course of action* or *to pass a resolution by virtue of some authority.*

Wir haben **beschlossen,** eine neue Wohnung zu suchen.	*We have decided to look for a new apartment.*
Der Bundestag hat **beschlossen,** das neue Einwanderungsgesetz zu verabschieden.	*The German parliament has resolved to pass the new immigration bill.*

Übungen

A **Nicht reflexiv → reflexiv.** Machen Sie die Sätze reflexiv, indem Sie die fett gedruckten Wörter ersetzen.

BEISPIEL Narzissus sah **Bäume** im Wasserspiegel.
*Narzissus sah **sich** im Wasserspiegel.*

1. Man sollte **die Sachen** regelmäßig waschen.
2. Ich habe **die Zeitung** auf das Sofa gelegt.
3. Sie zog **ihre Kinder** immer sehr schick an.
4. Zieh **ihm** die Jacke aus.
5. Wir legten **die Decken** in die Sonne.
6. Kinder, seht ihr **das Haus** im Spiegel?
7. Was hat sie **ihm** gekauft?
8. Haben Sie **die Kinder** schon angezogen?
9. Niemand konnte **der Polizei** den Unfall erklären.
10. Der Arzt hat **ihm** den Arm verbunden.

---

[5]The anticipatory **dazu** (see 20.2) is optional with **sich entschließen.**

B **Anders gesagt.** Drücken Sie die folgenden Sätze mit Hilfe von Reflexivverben in diesem Kapitel anders aus.

BEISPIEL   In fünf Minuten geht's los, und ich bin noch nicht fertig!
Ich muss mich beeilen.

1. Jetzt muss ich endlich mit ihr sprechen!
2. Die Tür ging langsam auf.
3. Eigentlich sollte das Essen um sieben Uhr beginnen, aber wir kamen erst um Viertel vor acht an.
4. Fünf Jahre nach meinem Abschluss war ich mal wieder auf dem Campus meiner Uni, aber da war inzwischen alles anders.
5. Die Party war furchtbar. Die Musik war doof und ich kannte überhaupt niemanden.
6. Was sagst du ihr denn nun, ja oder nein? Irgendwann musst du ihr ja irgendetwas sagen.
7. Entschuldigung, können Sie mir helfen? Ich muss zum Bahnhof, aber anstatt nach rechts bin ich nach links gelaufen und jetzt weiß ich überhaupt nicht mehr, wo ich bin.
8. Das Theaterstück war toll! Ich habe nie im Leben so viel gelacht!

C **Wer die Wahl *(choice)* hat, hat die Qual *(torment).*** Beantworten Sie die Fragen.

BEISPIEL   Was war die schwerste Entscheidung in Ihrem Leben?
Ich musste mich entscheiden, an welcher Universität ich studieren wollte.

1. Was war die beste/schlechteste Entscheidung, die Sie je getroffen haben?
2. Wann ist es für Sie schwer/leicht, sich zu entscheiden?
3. Haben Sie sich je zu etwas entschlossen, was Sie später bereut *(regretted)* haben?
4. Haben Sie einmal einen ganz klugen Entschluss gefasst?
5. Wofür würden Sie sich nie entscheiden?

D **Situationen.** Beenden Sie die Sätze. Verwenden Sie die folgenden Verben.

sich amüsieren	sich erkälten	sich bewerben um *(to apply for)*
sich aus·ruhen	sich um·sehen	sich entschuldigen *(to apologize)*
sich beeilen		sich irren *(to be mistaken)*

BEISPIEL   Der Hund von nebenan bellt seit Stunden. Vielleicht sollte Herr Franzen ...
Vielleicht sollte Herr Franzen sich bei seinem Nachbarn oder bei der Polizei beschweren.

1. Lukas lief letzte Woche dauernd ohne Mantel im Regen herum. Kein Wunder also, dass ...
2. Der Schulbus fährt in zehn Minuten und die Kinder ziehen sich noch an. „Kinder, ... !"
3. Lufthansa hat jetzt Stellen frei und Nadine sucht Arbeit. Vielleicht kann sie ...
4. Die Arbeit im Büro ist wie immer sehr langweilig. In der Pause will sie ...
5. „Es tut mir leid, Marcel, aber das stimmt nicht. Ich glaube, dass ... "
6. Verkäuferin im Kleidungsgeschäft: „Suchen Sie etwas Bestimmtes?" „Nein, ich will ... "
7. Timm hat seinen Kollegen beleidigt *(insulted)*. Jetzt möchte er ...
8. „Ich bin sehr müde." „Dann solltest du ... "

E   **Früher.**   Machen Sie fünf Aussagen über Ihr vergangenes Leben. Verwenden Sie reflexive Verben mit Präpositionen und Verben aus dem Wortschatz. Beginnen Sie zwei Ihrer Aussagen mit: **Ich glaube, dass...**

BEISPIEL   *Früher habe ich mich vor Schlangen gefürchtet.* OR:
Ich glaube, dass ich mich als Kind vor Schlangen gefürchtet habe.

F   **Akkusativ → Dativ.**   Bilden Sie Sätze mit Reflexivpronomen im Dativ.

BEISPIEL   Du wäschst dich.   (Hände)
Du wäschst dir die Hände.

1. Zieh dich aus!   (die Schuhe)
2. Habt ihr euch gewaschen?   (die Füße)
3. Ich muss mich abtrocknen *(to dry).*   (die Hände)
4. Sie kämmt sich.   (die Haare)
5. Sie sollen sich anziehen.   (andere Sachen)

G   *Einander.*   Drücken Sie die Sätze anders aus.

BEISPIEL   Wann habt ihr euch kennengelernt?
*Wann habt ihr **einander** kennengelernt?*

1. Die zwei haben sich geliebt.
2. Die Schüler helfen sich mit den Hausaufgaben.
3. Habt ihr euch nicht geschrieben?
4. Yasmin und Finn machen sich oft kleine Geschenke.

H   **Selbst Supermann könnte nicht ...**   Niemand kann alles. Wählen Sie 5 Personen von der Liste – alle haben schon sehr viel gemacht und sind dafür bekannt – und sagen Sie, was selbst *diese* Personen nicht schaffen oder immer noch schwierig finden. Gehört die Person einer anderen Epoche an, dann müssen Sie den Satz im Präteritum bilden. (Und wenn Sie über andere bekannte Leute sprechen wollen, dann geht das natürlich auch!)

BEISPIEL   Bill Gates
Selbst Bill Gates muss sich morgens anziehen und die Zähne putzen.

Angela Merkel	Mahatma Gandhi	Oprah Winfrey
Charles Lindbergh	Lady Gaga	St. Nikolaus
Cleopatra	Napoleon Bonaparte	der Papst *(pope)*
die „Spinne" *(Spider-Man)*		

Anwendung

A   **Beim Aufstehen und vor dem Schlafengehen.**   Erzählen Sie jemandem im Kurs, wie Sie sich morgens nach dem Aufstehen und abends zum Schlafengehen fertig machen. Was machen Sie zuerst? Was kommt danach? Was machen Sie zuletzt? Was machen Sie nicht? Berichten Sie dann, was jemand Ihnen erzählt hat.

sich an·ziehen/aus·ziehen

(sich) duschen

sich die Haare kämmen

sich rasieren

sich Kleider aus·suchen *(to pick out clothes)*

sich strecken *(stretch)*

sich schminken *(put on makeup)*

sich ab·trocknen

sich waschen

Kleider auf·hängen

B **Gefühle, Interessen und Reaktionen.**   Erkundigen Sie sich bei jemandem nach der folgenden Information, dann berichten Sie darüber. Fragen Sie ...

1. wann sie/er sich besonders ärgert.
2. wovor sie/er sich fürchtet.
3. wofür sie/er sich besonders interessiert.
4. woran sie/er sich (un)gern erinnert.
5. worauf sie/er sich ganz besonders freut.
6. worüber sie/er sich ganz besonders freut.

C **Na und? (So?)**   Egal, was Ihre Partnerin/Ihr Partner gesehen, gedacht oder gekauft hat, Sie haben's besser gemacht! Bilden Sie Sätze und benutzen Sie dabei die folgenden Verben: **sich etwas an·sehen, sich entschließen, sich erinnern an, sich etwas kaufen** und **sich etwas leisten.** Mit wie vielen Aussagen können Sie Ihre Partnerin/Ihren Partner übertrumpfen?

BEISPIEL A: *Du, ich war letzten Sommer in Deutschland und habe mir das Schloss in Heidelberg angesehen.*
B: *Na und? Ich war ja auch in Heidelberg und habe mir das Schloss gekauft! Dann habe ich ein Glas Wein getrunken.*

Schriftliche Themen

Tipps zum Schreiben	**Using Process Writing in German** Writing effectively in a foreign language requires an intentional approach to gathering, organizing, and expressing your thoughts. A few tips: Once you've chosen a topic, make a list of verbs that you associate with it. Then write short statements about the topic with these verbs, using a basic subject-verb-object format. Next, expand these sentences with descriptive phrases and modifiers, and put them in a meaningful sequence. Now and then, place elements other than the sentence subject in the front field to improve the overall style.

A **Nacherzählung.** Erzählen Sie die folgende Bildgeschichte *in der Vergangenheit* nach. Gebrauchen Sie Verben mit Reflexivpronomen.

VOKABELVORSCHLÄGE

die Straßenbahn	sich das Gesicht ein·reiben
die Werbung, -en *(advertisement)*	sich die Zähne putzen
sich vor·stellen	sich freuen (auf)
sich etwas kaufen/holen	sich interessieren (für)
sich waschen	sich fragen
sich im Spiegel an·schauen	

© Cengage Learning

B **Selber gemacht!** Haben Sie in Ihrem Leben etwas ohne Hilfe von jemand getan oder gemacht? Vielleicht etwas gebaut, erfunden, geschrieben oder komponiert? Schreiben Sie darüber!

BEISPIEL *Als ich 8 Jahre alt war, habe ich ein Lied selber komponiert. Nun, ich war nicht Mozart und das Lied war nichts Besonderes, aber ich war stolz darauf, dass ich es selbst gemacht hatte ...*

C **Menschenbeschreibung.** Kennen Sie jemanden, der sehr begabt, exzentrisch oder eigenartig ist? Beschreiben Sie diesen Menschen! Womit beschäftigt sie/er sich? Wie verhält sie/er sich? Wofür interessiert sie/er sich? Worüber ärgert sie/er sich?

BEISPIEL *Mein Freund David ist sehr exzentrisch. Er langweilt sich nie, denn dauernd beschäftigt er sich mit Fragen, die ich mir nicht einmal vorstellen kann. Er hat z.B. einmal ausgerechnet, dass ein Mensch sich im Laufe seines Lebens mehr als hundertmal erkältet. Obwohl er sich einbildet, ... usw.*

Zusammenfassung

Rules to Remember

1 A reflexive pronoun is an object pronoun, either accusative or dative, that refers to the sentence subject.

2 The dative and accusative reflexive form of all third-person pronouns and **Sie** is **sich**. COMPARE: **Er sieht sie.** *(He sees her.)* **Er sieht sich.** *(He sees himself.)*

3 Some German verbs always require a reflexive pronoun, even though the English equivalent may not: **Ich erinnere mich.** *(I remember.)*

4 Many reflexive verbs complete their meaning with a prepositional complement: **Ich erinnere mich <u>an ihn</u>.** *(I remember him.)*

At a Glance

	Nominative	Accusative	Dative	
1st pers. sing.	**ich**	**mich**	**mir**	*myself*
1st pers. plural	**wir**	**uns**	**uns**	*ourselves*
2nd pers. sing.: familiar	**du**	**dich**	**dir**	*yourself*
2nd pers. sing.: formal	**Sie**	**sich**	**sich**	*yourself*
2nd pers. plural: familiar	**ihr**	**euch**	**euch**	*yourselves*
2nd pers. plural: formal	**Sie**	**sich**	**sich**	*yourselves*
3rd pers. sing.	**er** (der Mann)	**sich**	**sich**	*himself*
	sie (die Frau)	**sich**	**sich**	*herself*
	es (das Kind)	**sich**	**sich**	*itself*
3rd pers. plural	**sie** (die Leute)	**sich**	**sich**	*themselves*

Reflexive verbs + prepositional complements

sich ärgern + über *(acc.)*	sich konzentrieren + auf *(acc.)*
sich beschäftigen + mit *(dat.)*	sich kümmern + um *(acc.)*
sich erinnern + an *(acc.)*	sich um·sehen + nach *(dat.)*
sich freuen + auf/über *(acc.)*	sich verlieben + in *(acc.)*
sich fürchten + vor *(dat.)*	sich verstecken + vor *(dat.)*
sich interessieren + für *(acc.)*	sich wundern + über *(acc.)*

11

Infinitives

zum Beispiel

Fußball

AP Images/Martin Meissner

Fußball: It would be difficult to overstate the role that **Fußball** plays in the cultural life of Germany, Austria, and Switzerland. Soccer is easily the most popular sport in these countries; in Germany, more people attend soccer matches on average than in any other country—for any sport—in the world. Nearly every town in German-speaking countries, no matter how small, has its own **Sport-/Fußballverein** (*sport/soccer club*), which fields teams at all age and skill levels, right up through the powerhouse professional teams of major cities. In Germany, about 8% of the population is actively involved in more than 26,000 of these clubs, sponsoring 178,000 teams. Ever since Germany's memorable victory in the 1954 World Cup, dramatized in the film *Das Wunder von Bern* (2003), it has been a dominant presence in international competition, winning the World Cup most recently in 2014. In recent decades the German women's national soccer team has likewise become a world power, and hosted the Women's World Cup competition in 2011. Thanks to its international appeal, soccer has taken on an important role in integrating diverse ethnic groups in all of these countries.

Grammatik

1. An infinitive clause can be as basic as two words: **zu** + infinitive.

Fußball ist doch leicht **zu verstehen**.	*Soccer is actually easy to understand.*

But it can also include various objects and modifiers that precede **zu** and follow the word order rules of the middle field (see 1.1.C).

Fußball ist die Kunst, **mit 44 krummen Beinen eine luftgefüllte Lederkugel in zwei große Netze <u>zu dreschen</u>.**[1]	*Soccer is the art of slamming an air-filled leather sphere into two nets by means of 44 crooked legs.*

Notice in the examples above that in English, the infinitive follows closely on the heels of the word or phrase that introduces it *(easy to understand/art of slamming . . .)*, with connected objects and modifiers trailing behind; while in German, the infinitive comes at the very end of its own clause, following any such elements, and is always preceded by **zu**. Notice also that German infinitive structures sometimes translate into English with *to* ___, and sometimes with an *-ing* construction.

2. In the case of separable-prefix verbs (see R.5.1 and 7.2.B), **zu** is inserted between the prefix and the stem verb, forming one word.

Ein Team versucht, das andere **anzugreifen** und **zu überlisten**.	*One team tries to attack and outsmart the other.*

3. When an infinitive clause includes a verbal complement (see 7.2.B), **zu** is placed between the complement and the infinitive.

Es ist nicht einfach, eine solche Niederlage **in Kauf zu nehmen.**	*It's not easy to accept a defeat like that.*

This also applies to modal verbs with dependent infinitives, such as **gewinnen können** = *to be able to win.*

FC Bayern München hofft, die Meisterschaft wieder **gewinnen zu können.**	*FC Bayern Munich hopes to be able to win the championship game again.*

4. An infinitive clause usually follows the main clause, rather than being framed by it, though a small number of verbs (**anfangen** and **versprechen,** for example) allow for embedding.

Alle Spieler *fingen* gleichzeitig **zu** **streiten** *an*.	*All the players began arguing at the same time.*

---

[1]This sentence is actually the title of a popular book about soccer in Germany, by Funcke and Schneider (Tomus Verlag, München).

If the infinitive clause functions as the subject of the sentence, it precedes the main clause.

In die zweite Bundesliga abzusteigen, wäre für den Hamburger SV eine große Blamage.	*To drop down into the second-tier league would be a huge embarrassment for the Hamburg team.*
Ein Eigentor zu schießen, kann manchmal gefährlich sein, wie ein kolombianischer Spieler 1994 erfuhr.	*To score a goal in your own net can sometimes be dangerous, as a player from Colombia found out in 1994.*

5. A comma is used to separate the main and infinitive clauses in the following situations:

   a. If the infinitive clause is linked to a noun in the introductory clause.

   b. If the infinitive clause begins with **als, außer, ohne, statt,** or **um** (see 11.2 below).

   c. If the introductory clause contains an anticipatory **da**-compound or **es** (see 20.2–3).

   d. If the sentence could be misunderstood without the comma.

   WITH COMMA:

Der Spieler hat sich vorgenommen, noch aggressiver **zu spielen.**	*The player decided to play more aggressively.*
Es gibt nichts Besseres, **als** im entscheidenden Moment einen Fallrückzieher **zu sehen.**	*There's nothing better than seeing a bicycle kick at a decisive moment.*
Ich freue mich jedes Wochenende **darauf,** Real Madrid spielen **zu sehen.**	*I look forward every weekend to seeing Real Madrid play.*
Sie lief etwas langsamer, **um** ein Abseits zu vermeiden.	*She ran a bit more slowly in order to avoid being offsides.*

   WITHOUT COMMA:

Er entschied sich nur **zu sitzen** und **zuzuschauen.**	*He decided just to sit and watch.*

6. Some English infinitive constructions require an altogether different construction in German.

   a. English statements containing *like to* ___ are usually expressed in German with **gern:** *Every fan **likes to** wear his team's colors* = **Jeder Fan *trägt gern* die Farben seiner Mannschaft** (see 9.2.F and Chapter 9 **Wortschatz**).

   b. Constructions in English such as *We want them to win* cannot be expressed in German with an infinitive; instead, they require **wollen, dass ...** with a subject and a conjugated verb (see 9.2.E): ***We want** Dortmund to win this year* = ***Wir wollen, dass*** Dortmund dieses Jahr gewinnt.

7. In English, an infinitive clause often follows a predicate adjective, completing the idea conveyed by the adjective about the subject of the main clause: *The sight was <u>terrible</u> to behold. That idea is <u>bound</u> to fail.* German uses this construction only if the verb in the infinitive clause takes a direct object (that is, it cannot be a dative verb), and only with a small number of adjectives: **einfach, interessant, leicht, schwer,** and **schwierig.**

*Brazil's playing style is **interesting to observe**.*	Der Spielstil Brasiliens ist ***interessant* zu beobachten.**
*An offsides is a little **difficult to explain**.*	Ein Abseits ist etwas ***schwer* zu erklären.**

BUT:

*Their defense wasn't **easy to avoid**.*	Es war nicht **einfach,** ihrer Abwehr **auszuweichen.** (*avoid* = **aus·weichen** + Dativ)

11.2 ADVERBIAL PHRASES WITH *UM ... ZU, OHNE ... ZU,* AND *(AN)STATT ... ZU*

To express English *in order to* ____, *without* ____*-ing,* and *instead of* __*-ing,* German uses infinitive clauses beginning with **um, ohne,** or **(an)statt.** (Note: In **(an)statt,** the **an** is optional; adding it renders the word slightly more formal.) In each case, the clause begins with the preposition, followed by an optional middle field with any additional information, and finally **zu** + infinitive. A comma always separates these clauses from the main clause.

Keine Mannschaft kann gewinnen, **ohne zu trainieren.**	*No team can win without training.*
(An)statt in Richtung Tor **zu schießen,** hat er sich entschieden weiterzudribbeln.	*Instead of shooting toward the goal, he decided to keep on dribbling.*

11.3 INFINITIVES WITHOUT *ZU*

1. Infinitives accompanying modal verbs, as in *I want to . . .* (see 9.1) and the future auxiliary **werden,** as in *I am going to . . .* (see 24.1), do not take a preceding **zu.**

2. The verbs of perception **fühlen, hören, sehen, spüren** *(to perceive, feel),* as well as the verbs **heißen** (here: *to bid* or *command*) and **lassen** (see 11.4), can function like modal verbs as V₁ of the verbal bracket, and in this use can be considered *semi-modals.* Infinitives accompanying them function as V₂, without **zu.**

Der Verteidiger **hat** den Schiedsrichter pfeifen *hören*.	*The defender heard the referee blow his whistle.*
Der Schiedsrichter **sah** den Verteidiger im Strafraum ein Foul *begehen*.	*The referee saw the defender committing a foul in the penalty area.*

3. Infinitives accompanying the semi-modals **helfen, lehren,** and **lernen** can occur either with or without **zu.**

Bei einem Eckstoß **helfen** die Spieler dem Torwart, das Tor **zu verteidigen.**

OR:

Bei einem Eckstoß **helfen** die Spieler dem Torwart das Tor **verteidigen.**

On a corner kick, the players help the goalie defend the goal.

4. With **fühlen, hören, sehen, spüren,** and also with **lernen** and **lehren,** a subordinate clause is often used instead of an accompanying infinitive clause.

EITHER:

Der Stürmer **fühlte,** wie der Verteidiger hinter ihm **herlief.**

The striker felt how the defender ran right behind.

OR:

Der Stürmer **fühlte** den Verteidiger hinter ihm **herlaufen.**

The striker felt the defender running right behind him.

EITHER:

Alle **sahen,** dass sie ein Foul **beging.**

Everyone saw that she committed a foul.

OR:

Alle **sahen** sie ein Foul **begehen.**

Everyone saw her commit a foul.

5. The verb **gehen** is also often used with a following infinitive without **zu.**

Vor dem Spiel **gehen** viele Fans Schals, Fahnen und Trikots **einkaufen.**

Before the game, many fans go shopping for scarves, flags, and jerseys.

11.4 LASSEN + INFINITIVE

1. **Lassen** has numerous meanings, depending on the objects and infinitives to which it is (or is not) attached. These include:

to leave: **Ich lasse den Ball hier** (see the **Wortschatz** in this chapter)
to let someone do something: **Lässt er mich endlich spielen?**
to have something done: **Ich lasse meine Fußball-Klamotten waschen.**

2. When **lassen** is connected with an infinitive, its meaning is determined by the use of direct objects in the clause and by context. Here are the most common meanings and their configuration.

a. *to let/have someone do something*

■ **lassen** + direct object (person) + infinitive

Der Trainer **lässt** den jungen Spieler endlich **spielen.**

The coach is finally letting/having the young player play.

- **lassen** + direct object (person) + direct object + infinitive

Der Torwart **ließ** die Gegner das letzte Tor **kriegen**.

*The keeper **let** the opposing team **get** the final goal. [Note: "had" is not appropriate here because it changes the meaning]*

Mit einer zweiten Gelben Karte **ließ** der Schiedsrichter den Spieler den Platz **verlassen**.

*With a second yellow card, the referee **had** the player **leave** the field. [Note: "let" is not appropriate here because it changes the meaning]*

b. *to let/have something (be) done*

- **lassen** + direct object + infinitive

Vor dem Spiel **lassen** wir den Spielplatz nochmal **mähen**.

Before the game we're having the field mowed again.

Ich **lasse** auch die Stadionuhr nochmal **kontrollieren**.

I'll have the stadium clock checked again too.

3. A "dative of reference" (see 5.5) is sometimes used with **lassen** to indicate *to whom* or *for whom* an action is done.

Der Teamarzt **ließ** *dem verletzten Spieler* einen Krankenwagen rufen.

OR:

Der Teamarzt **ließ** *für den verletzten Spieler* einen Krankenwagen rufen.

The team doctor had an ambulance called for the injured player.

4. The dative reflexive pronoun (see 10.1) is commonly used with **lassen**.

Einige Fans **lassen** *sich* einen Ball oder ein Programm **unterschreiben**.

Some fans have a ball or a program autographed (for themselves).

Nach der Niederlage musste *sich* das Team einige Buhrufe gefallen **lassen**.

After the defeat, the team had to put up with some booing.

11.5 INFINITIVES AS NOUNS

Virtually any German infinitive can be capitalized and used as a neuter noun. Such nouns usually correspond to English gerunds (the *-ing* form).

Das Verteidigen ist manchmal noch anstrengender als **das Angreifen**.

Defending is sometimes more demanding than attacking.

Ich wünschte, der Schiedsrichter würde **mit seinem Pfeifen** aufhören!

*I wish the referee would stop **his whistling!***

11.6   **DOUBLE INFINITIVES**

A. Double infinitives with the perfect tenses

1. Like modal verbs, **fühlen, hören, sehen, spüren,** and **lassen** generally form the perfect tenses with a so-called *double infinitive* construction rather than with a past participle (see 9.3).[2]

   COMPARE:

Beim Einwurf **hat** eine Spielerin den Ball gar nicht **gesehen.**	*At the throw-in, one player didn't see the ball at all.*
Beim Einwurf **hat** eine Spielerin den Ball gar nicht **kommen sehen.**	*At the throw-in, one player didn't see the ball coming at all.*
Der Torwart **hat** den Ball nicht in den Strafraum **gelassen.**	*The goalie didn't let the ball into the penalty area.*
Der Torwart **hat** den Ball nicht in den Strafraum **rollen lassen.**	*The goalie didn't let the ball roll into the penalty area.*

2. The verb **helfen** can also form its perfect tense with a double infinitive. However, the tendency among German speakers is to use the past participle in combination with an infinitive clause including **zu.**

   POSSIBLE:

   Bei einem gefährlichen Eckball haben zwei Spieler ihrem Torwart das Tor **verteidigen helfen.**

   PREFERRED:

   Bei einem gefährlichen Eckball haben zwei Spieler ihrem Torwart geholfen, **das Tor zu verteidigen.**

   On one dangerous corner kick, two players helped their goalie defend the goal.

3. German speakers often avoid a double infinitive construction by using the simple past tense instead.

Den Ball **ließ** der Schiedsrichter dort **liegen,** wo er das Foul gesehen hatte.	*The referee left the ball lying where he had seen the foul.*
Und natürlich **sah** er nur unser Team ein Foul **begehen,** nicht unsere Gegner.	*And of course he only saw our team commit a foul, not our opponents.*

4. In dependent clauses, the auxiliary verb comes before a double infinitive.

---

[2]When using the verbs of perception (**fühlen, hören, sehen,** and **spüren**) in the perfect tense, some German speakers use an infinitive + participle construction in subordinate clauses (**Wir haben ihn kommen *gehört***), but this usage is considered substandard.

B. Double infinitives with the future tense

The future tense of all verbs accompanied by infinitives without **zu** (that is, modals and semi-modals) results in a double infinitive construction, with **werden** as V$_1$ and the double infinitive as V$_2$. In dependent clauses, **werden** precedes the double infinitive (see 24.1.A).

Wird sich der Fußball in den USA als Volkssport **durchsetzen können?**	*Will soccer be able to gain acceptance in the United States as a sport for everyone?*
Ich bezweifle sehr, dass dein Team jemals **wird** gewinnen können.	*I really doubt that your team will ever be able to win.*

Wortschatz
Wie sagt man *to leave*?

1. **Lassen** followed by a noun or pronoun object but no subsequent infinitive means *to leave someone or something in a place or condition.*

„**Lass** den Ball, wo er ist!" rief der Schiedsrichter.	*"Leave the ball where it is!" shouted the referee.*

2. **Verlassen** means *to leave or depart from a person, place, or activity,* and always takes a direct object.

Es wurde chaotisch, als 80 000 Fans anfingen, das Stadion zu **verlassen.**	*Things became chaotic as 80,000 fans began to leave the stadium.*
2013 haben Boateng und sein Team aus Protest gegen Rassismus den Platz **verlassen.**	*In 2013, Boateng and his team left the field as a protest against racism.*

Verlassen can also connote emotional (and by implication, long-term) separation.

„Ich **verlasse** dich nie", hatte Ollie Kahn[3] zu Simone gesagt. Dann traf er Verena.	*"I'll never leave you," Ollie Kahn[3] had said to Simone. Then he met Verena.*

COMPARE:

Ich **verlasse** dich!	*I'm leaving you!* (implied: *forever*)
Ich **lasse** dich auf der Tribüne.	*I'll leave you here in the stands.* (implied: *I'll come back for you*)

---

[3]**Ollie Kahn** is a sports celebrity in Germany, having been named **Fußballer des Jahres** in Germany twice and **Torhüter** *(goalie)* **des Jahres** in Germany six times during his career, with a World Cup title and multiple national and European titles to his credit.

3. **Weg·gehen** means to *leave, depart,* or *go away.* This verb cannot be used with a direct object.

„Wir **gehen** nicht **weg,** bis wir ein Autogramm kriegen!"

"We're not leaving till we get an autograph!"

„**Geht** doch **weg**", sagte der Spieler mürrisch nach der peinlichen Niederlage.

"Go away," said the player sullenly to the reporters after the embarrassing defeat.

COMPARE:

Leave!

Gehen Sie **weg!**

Leave this room at once!

Verlassen Sie sofort *dieses Zimmer!*

Leave me here while you shop!

Lass mich hier, während du einkaufen gehst!

Übungen

A **Ich habe vor...**   Beenden Sie die Sätze einmal mit **zu** plus Infinitiv und einmal mit einer längeren Infinitivgruppe.

BEISPIEL   Ich habe vor ...   (arbeiten)
Ich habe vor zu arbeiten.
Ich habe vor, im Sommer zu arbeiten.

1. Die Touristen haben die Absicht (*intention*) ...   (weiterfahren)
2. Wann fängst du an ...?   (übersetzen)
3. Der Kapitän hat vor, die Mannschaft...   (retten: *to save*)
4. Es scheint jetzt ...   (regnen)
5. Mein Nachbar versucht ...   (singen)
6. Vergiss auch nicht ...   (schreiben)

B **Treiben Sie auch Sport?**   Erzählen Sie von Ihren Erfahrungen (*experiences*) mit Fußball oder einer anderen Sportart (positiv oder negativ!), indem Sie die Satzteile unten mit Infinitivgruppen ergänzen.

1. Ich war _____ Jahre alt, als ich zum ersten Mal versuchte, ... zu ...
2. Es machte mir [großen/keinen] Spaß, ... zu ...
3. Bei dieser Sportart (*particular sport*) ist das Ziel, ... zu ...
4. Dabei ist es sehr wichtig, ... zu ...
5. Und man muss aufpassen, ... zu ...
6. Alle Spieler versuchen, ... zu ...
7. Es ist bei dieser Sportart besonders schwer, ... zu ...
8. Einmal gelang es mir (*I succeeded in*), ... zu ...

C ***Lassen, verlassen* oder *weggehen*?** Ergänzen Sie die Sätze durch passende Verben.

1. Die Frau hat ihren Ehemann und ihre Kinder _____.
2. Frau Engler hat ihre Kinder für ein paar Tage in Bern _____.
3. Herr Weber hat sein Smartphone im Büro _____.
4. Tut mir leid, aber du musst jetzt _____.
5. Ach, warum hat er mich nur _____?
6. Eines Tages wird Peter von hier _____.

D **Anders ausdrücken.** Drücken Sie die Sätze anders aus. Verwenden Sie die Präpositionen **um, ohne** und **(an)statt** mit Infinitiven.

BEISPIEL   Ich lerne Deutsch, weil ich es mit meinen Verwandten sprechen will.
            Ich lerne Deutsch, um es mit meinen Verwandten zu sprechen.

1. Manche Menschen denken nicht, wenn sie reden.
2. Ich verlasse dich nicht, ich bleibe bei dir.
3. Die meisten Menschen arbeiten, damit sie essen können.
4. Wie kann man im Ausland studieren, wenn man die Sprache des Landes nicht versteht?
5. Die meisten Studenten schreiben ihre Notizen nicht per Hand, sondern auf ihrem Laptop.
6. Und viele Studenten benutzen ihren Laptop nicht für Notizen, sondern sie surfen online.

E **Aussagen.** Machen Sie mit den Präpositionen **um, ohne** und **(an)statt** und einer Infinitivgruppe jeweils eine Aussage über sich selbst oder andere Menschen, die Sie kennen.

BEISPIEL   *Meine Schwester redet manchmal, ohne zu denken.*

F **Sätze mit Infinitiven.** Machen Sie aus zwei Sätzen einen Satz.

BEISPIEL   Julia spielt Fußball. Ich sehe es.
            Ich sehe Julia Fußball spielen.

1. Philip kocht das Essen. Niemand hilft ihm.
2. Ihr Herz schlägt kräftig *(heavily)*. Sie fühlt es.
3. Jemand klopft an die Tür. Ich höre es.
4. Der Baum fiel im Sturm um. Niemand sah es.
5. Markus lernt gern. Er lernt, wie man Schach spielt.
6. Ein Mann im Bus liest *kicker*.[4] Die anderen Passagiere sehen ihn.
7. Sie macht einen Fehler. Niemand hört es.
8. Maya ließ ihre Schlüssel im Auto. Tobias sah es.

Schreiben Sie Ihre Sätze jetzt im Präteritum.

BEISPIEL   *Ich sah Julia spielen.*

---

[4]***kicker*** is the best-selling sports magazine in Germany. Published since 1920, it covers all sports, but as the title suggests, it focuses on soccer. You can find it online at **www.kicker.de.**

G **Einiges über mich.** Ergänzen Sie die Aussagen. Verwenden Sie Infinitive.

BEISPIEL Morgens höre ich ...
Morgens höre ich meine Eltern frühstücken.

1. Ich sehe gern ...
2. Wenn ich morgens aufwache, höre ich als erstes ...
3. Als ich noch ganz klein war, lehrte mich jemand ...
4. Gestern habe ich ... (sehen/hören)
5. Ich würde gern ... lernen.

H **Anders ausdrücken.** Drücken Sie Ihre Aussagen in **Übung G** durch den Gebrauch von Nebensätzen *(subordinate clauses)* anders aus.

BEISPIEL *Morgens höre ich, wie meine Eltern frühstücken.*

I **Man kann doch nicht alles selber machen.** Beantworten Sie die Fragen. Verwenden Sie das Verb **lassen.**

1. Was machen Sie, wenn Ihre Haare zu lang sind?
2. Was muss man machen, wenn man Kaffee oder Tee über den Computer verschüttet *(spills)*?
3. Was haben Sie in der letzten Woche machen lassen?
4. Was ließen Ihre Eltern Sie früher nicht machen?
5. Was lassen Sie gern machen?
6. Was würden Sie gern machen lassen?
7. Was würden Sie nie machen lassen?

Anwendung

A **Ungewöhnliche Erfahrungen und Erlebnisse.** Tauschen Sie *(exchange)* ungewöhnliche Erfahrungen mit anderen Studenten im Kurs aus. Wer hat das Ungewöhnlichste gesehen oder gehört?

B **Zeit oder keine Zeit? Spaß oder kein Spaß?** Was meint Ihre Partnerin/Ihr Partner zu diesen Fragen? Sie/Er soll mit Infinitivkonstruktionen darauf antworten.

1. Wofür hast du immer Zeit?
2. Wofür hast du keine Zeit?
3. Wofür möchtest du mehr Zeit haben?
4. Wofür brauchst du keine Zeit?
5. Welche Hobbys machen dir Spaß?
6. Was macht dir überhaupt keinen Spaß?
7. Was würde dir dieses Wochenende viel Spaß machen?

Schriftliche Themen

Tipps zum Schreiben	**Expressing Your Own Views**
	To let readers know that you are expressing your opinions rather than indisputable facts, use phrases such as the following:
	ich finde, (dass)
	ich glaube, (dass)
	meiner Meinung/Ansicht nach
	ich halte es für [wichtig/notwendig/möglich/wahrscheinlich], …

A **Verpflichtungen (obligations).** Was wollen oder sagen andere Leute (z.B. Ihre Eltern oder Lehrer), dass Sie machen sollen? Macht es Ihnen Spaß, das zu machen? Tun Sie es ungern? Was lassen Ihre Eltern Sie nicht tun? Verwenden Sie in Ihrem Aufsatz grammatische Strukturen aus diesem Kapitel.

BEISPIEL *Meine Eltern sagen immer, dass ich ihnen mehr helfen soll. Okay, sie lassen mich die Aufgaben selber aussuchen, die ich machen will, aber trotzdem gefällt es mir nicht immer. Nun, ich finde es schön, zum Haushalt etwas beizutragen* (contribute), *aber ich habe keine Lust, das jeden Tag zu tun. Schließlich will ich mein eigenes Leben führen, und ich lasse mir nicht gern sagen, …*

B **Was man ungern tut.** Müssen Sie manchmal etwas machen, was Sie als besonders schwierig oder unangenehm empfinden? Erzählen Sie davon.

BEISPIEL *Ich finde es besonders unangenehm, in eine neue Wohnung umzuziehen. Natürlich versuche ich Leute zu finden, die mir dabei helfen, aber wenn meine Freunde mich kommen sehen … usw.*

Zusammenfassung

Rules to Remember

1   Infinitive clauses are formed by placing **zu** before the infinitive, before the final element of a compound infinitive, or by inserting **zu** between a separable prefix and its root verb infinitive.

2   The **zu** + infinitive structure is always at the end of an infinitive clause, preceded by any modifiers or accusative or dative objects the clause may contain.

3   Infinitive clauses usually follow the main clause, rather than being embedded in it.

4   Infinitives used in conjunction with modal verbs (**können, wollen,** etc.) and semi-modal verbs such as **fühlen, heißen, hören, lassen, sehen,** and **spüren** function as V_2 in the verbal bracket, with no preceding **zu.**

5   Infinitives used in combination with semi-modal verbs such as **helfen, lehren,** and **lernen** can either form an infinitive clause with **zu** or function as V_2 in the verbal bracket, with no preceding **zu.**

6   **Fühlen, hören, sehen, spüren,** and **lassen** used in combination with other verbs normally form the present perfect tense with an infinitive rather than a participle: Das habe ich *kommen sehen* (NOT: *gesehen*).

At a Glance

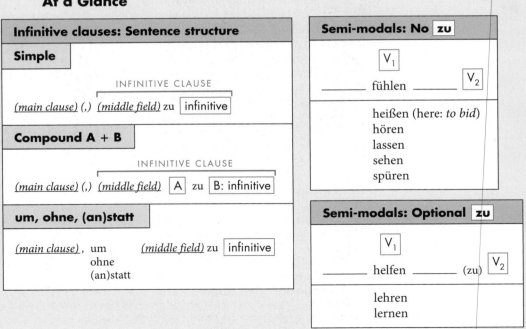

Infinitive clauses: Sentence structure
Simple
INFINITIVE CLAUSE
(main clause) (,) *(middle field)* zu infinitive
Compound A + B
INFINITIVE CLAUSE
(main clause) (,) *(middle field)* A zu B: infinitive
um, ohne, (an)statt
(main clause) , um   *(middle field)* zu infinitive
ohne
(an)statt

Semi-modals: No zu
V_1
_____ fühlen _____ V_2
heißen (here: *to bid*)
hören
lassen
sehen
spüren

Semi-modals: Optional zu
V_1
_____ helfen _____ (zu) V_2
lehren
lernen

zum Beispiel

Stuttgart 21

© S. Kuelcue/Shutterstock.com

Stuttgart 21: Planned for over a decade, and with construction projected to continue through at least 2020, **Stuttgart 21** is a massive, multi-billion euro railway and urban development project. When completed, the train tracks in the Stuttgart station will have been turned 90° from their original orientation and run through underground tunnels, freeing up considerable space in the city and expediting rail commerce between Vienna and Paris. From its inception, the project has been a lightning rod for criticism from all points along the political spectrum. Activists in the local Green Party have protested against its environmental impact; fiscal conservatives decry the billions of euros in cost overruns; many locals opposed the partial demolition of the landmark train station of the 1920s; and over 50,000 people came out on October 1, 2010, to protest the use of water cannons and pepper spray used by police the day before to disperse a demonstration.

Grammatik

| 12.1 | PASSIVE VOICE |

A. Formation

1. German expresses the passive as a process, as something "becoming" done (**das Vorgangspassiv**). Thus the passive voice is formed with the verb **werden** *(to become)* + a past participle.

Trotz der Proteste **wird** das Bahnprojekt *Stuttgart 21* also doch **durchgeführt.**

Despite protests, the railway project Stuttgart 21 is being implemented after all.

Present tense		
ich **werde...**	informiert	*I am informed/being informed*
du **wirst ...**	informiert	*you (sing.) are informed/being informed*
Sie **werden ...**	informiert	
er/sie/es **wird ...**	informiert	*he/she/it is informed/being informed*
wir **werden ...**	informiert	*we are informed/being informed*
ihr **werdet ...**	informiert	*you (all) are informed/being informed*
Sie **werden...**	informiert	
sie **werden...**	informiert	*they are informed/being informed*
Simple past tense		
ich **wurde...**	informiert	*I was informed/being informed*
du **wurdest...**	informiert	*you (sing.) were informed/being informed*
Sie wurden...	informiert	
etc.		
Present perfect tense		
ich **bin...**	informiert worden[1]	*I was informed/have been informed*
du **bist...**	informiert worden	*you (sing.) were informed/have been informed*
Sie **sind...**	informiert worden	
etc.		
Past perfect tense		
ich **war...**	informiert worden	*I had been informed*
du **warst...**	informiert worden	*you (sing.) had been informed*
Sie **waren...**	informiert worden	
etc.		

---

[1]**worden:** a shortened form of the past participle **geworden,** which only appears in passive constructions.

Future tense		
ich **werde...**	informiert werden	*I will be informed*
du **wirst...**	informiert werden	*you (sing.) will be informed*
Sie **werden...**	informiert werden	
etc.		

2. Notice in the charts above that V$_1$ changes constantly, as **werden** undergoes shifts in conjugation and tense (e.g., **werde, wirst, wird, wurde**), while the past participle of the verb (V$_2$) remains constant—just as in English.

   Notice also that V$_2$ does not always consist of a past participle alone. As the preceding charts indicate, there are three different V$_2$ configurations possible in a passive sentence, all of which involve the past participle.

   ■ *a past participle,* standing alone: $\longrightarrow$ **informiert**   *informed*

   ■ *a passive participle,* formed with the past participle + **worden,** with **sein** as its auxiliary: $\longrightarrow$ **informiert worden**   *been informed*

   ■ *a passive infinitive,* formed with the past participle + **werden** (see D.1 below): $\longrightarrow$ **informiert werden**   *be informed*

   Regardless of which structure is used, V$_1$ is inflected to show number, tense, and mood, but V$_2$ does not change.

3. In main clauses, V$_1$ stands, as usual, in second position and V$_2$ is positioned at the end of the clause. In subordinate clauses, V$_1$ follows V$_2$ as the final element.

..., dass er ***informiert* wird**	*that he's being informed*
..., dass er ***informiert worden* ist**	*that he has been informed*
..., dass er ***informiert werden* wird**	*that he will be informed*

4. Placing various sentence elements in first position (even V$_2$ itself, which is not possible in English but can occur in German) changes the emphasis in a passive sentence.

***Das Projekt* wurde** 1994 der Öffentlichkeit **vorgestellt.**	*The project was presented to the public in 1994.* (front field = subject)
***Von Öko-Aktivisten* wurde** massive Kritik daran **geäußert.**	*On the part of environmental activists, massive criticism was raised about it.* (front field = agent)
***Bei Protesten im September 2010* sind** Hunderte **verletzt worden.**	*In the course of protests in September 2010, hundreds of people were injured.* (front field = adverbial complement)
***Angehoben* wurden** die prognostizierten Kosten immer wieder.	*What was elevated again and again were the projected costs.* (front field = V$_2$)

B. Use

1. Using the passive voice allows a speaker or writer to refer to an action without identifying who or what performs it. This makes the passive particularly useful when the agent is unknown or irrelevant, or when the speaker or writer simply does not want to mention the agent.

Im Sommer 2010 ist der Nordflügel vom Bahnhof abgerissen worden.	*During the summer of 2010, the north wing of the train station was torn down.*
Bei den Protesten danach sind Demonstranten und Polizisten verletzt worden.	*At the protests following that, protesters and policemen were injured.*
„Schlichtungsgespräche" wurden kurz darauf durchgeführt.	*"Reconciliation discussions" were conducted shortly after that.*
Und im November 2011 wurde ein Volksentscheid abgehalten.	*And in November 2011, a referendum was held.*
Dabei wurde eine Kündigung des Projekts abgelehnt.	*The result: A cancellation of the project was rejected.*

2. Passive and active constructions are linked by the relation of subject to object. The (nominative) subjects in the passive sentences above are the (accusative) direct objects of equivalent sentences in the active voice below.

- X hat den **Nordflügel** abgerissen.

- X hat **Demonstranten und Polizisten** verletzt.

- X führte die **Schlichtungsgespräche** durch.

- X hat **einen Volksentscheid** abgehalten.

- X lehnten **die Kündigung des Projekts** ab.

In the first example, X (i.e., whoever tore down part of the station) is not nearly as important as the fact that it was torn down. In the second example, X is ambiguous—it could refer to the people who were responsible for the injuries, or the means by which the injuries were inflicted—as well as politically volatile, and perhaps for both reasons is better left unsaid. In the third and fourth examples, the organizers of the discussions and the popular referendum are secondary in importance, or perhaps unidentifiable. And in the final example, the focus of attention is rightly on the outcome of the referendum, rather than on "the people who voted." It makes sense, therefore, to frame all of these sentences with passive constructions. The object of the action becomes the passive subject, making it structurally unnecessary to mention the agent. It follows that sentences like these can only be formed with verbs that take accusative objects (i.e., transitive verbs).[2]

3. In fact, the *only* permissible subject in a passive sentence is the element that would be the accusative object of an equivalent active sentence. This has important consequences when transferring meanings from English to German:

a. *When indirect objects function as subjects in the passive.* With certain verbs, English allows the indirect object of an active sentence to become the subject of a passive sentence.

active: Someone showed **the city council** the new plans.

passive: **The city council** was shown the new plans.

But in German, only an *accusative* object can become the subject of a passive sentence. Indirect objects must remain in the dative case.

COMPARE:

active: Jemand zeigte **dem Stadtrat** <u>die neuen Pläne</u>.

passive: <u>Die neuen Pläne</u> wurden **dem Stadtrat** gezeigt.

Depending on what the writer or speaker wishes to emphasize, the passive sentence may begin with either the subject or the indirect object.

subject: <u>Die neuen Pläne</u> wurden **dem Stadtrat** gezeigt.

indirect object: **Dem Stadtrat** wurden <u>die neuen Pläne</u> gezeigt.

The second example above may seem odd to an English speaker who reads **Stadtrat** in this context as a singular noun and therefore expects a singular verb, as one finds in *The city council **was** shown....* But remember: The subject of the sentence is still the plural noun **Pläne,** not the singular indirect object **Stadtrat,** and the verb is therefore conjugated in the plural.

In sentences like these, an impersonal **es** can be used as a "place holder" in the front field, thereby allowing the writer to move all the other elements into the middle field, but the subject remains nonetheless **Pläne,** and the verb must be conjugated in the plural to agree with it.

Es wurden **dem Stadtrat** die neuen Pläne gezeigt. *The city was shown the new plans.*

b. *German dative verbs.* English verbs such as *to help, to answer,* or *to congratulate* take objects and can easily be reconstructed as passives in English. However, their

---

[2]While most transitive German verbs can be expressed in the passive, there are a few exceptions. Verbs such as **bekommen** (and its synonym **erhalten**), **besitzen** *(to own),* **haben,** and **wissen** do not form the passive, even though they take accusative objects and can be expressed by passive constructions in English. To translate English passive sentences with these verbs into German requires either the active voice or an altogether different expression.

*That **wasn't known** at the time.* Man hat das damals nicht gewusst.

*For years, the property **had been owned** by German Railways.* Seit Jahren hatte das Grundstück der Deutschen Bahn gehört.

German equivalents take *dative* objects (jemand half **dem Mann;** man gratulierte **den Politikern;** see 5.5.B), which cannot become passive subjects. As with the indirect objects in section 3.a above, the dative objects of such verbs remain in the dative. But here there are no accusative objects to become passive subjects, which means that *a passive sentence formed with a dative verb will have no grammatical subject.* In this case, the verb defaults to the third-person singular, and the dative object routinely takes first position.

Dem Demonstranten wurde geholfen.	*The protester was helped.*
Den Politikern wurde gratuliert.	*The politicians were congratulated.*

If the first example does not seem awkward to an English speaker, the second most likely does, for the same reasons discussed in section 3.a above. **Dem** Demonstranten **wurde geholfen** begins with a singular noun in what English speakers think of as the "subject" position, followed by a singular verb, so that there appears to be subject-verb agreement. But in the second example, **den Politikern** is plural, followed by singular **wurde,** which seems to violate that rule. In fact, neither sentence has subject-verb agreement, since there is no subject. The verb in both examples is third-person singular by default, regardless of what precedes it. As in other passive constructions, an impersonal **es** can be used as a "place holder" in first position, moving the dative object into the middle field, but **es** is not the subject and has no influence on how the verb is conjugated.

Es wurde **dem** Demonstranten geholfen.	*The protester was helped.*
Es wurde **den Politikern** gratuliert.	*The politicians were congratulated.*

C. Agents with the passive

1. Though it is not necessary to do so, the agent of the action in a passive construction can be expressed by a prepositional phrase, usually introduced by **von** or **durch,** and sometimes **mit.**

2. **Von** *(by)* + dative is used to indicate the agent(s) or performer(s) of an action—most often a person—but sometimes an inanimate agent, carrying out an action.

Am 2. Februar 2010 wurde der Baubeginn **von vielen Beteiligten** gefeiert.	*On February 2, 2010, the beginning of the construction was celebrated by many of the parties involved.*
Ein paar Monate später sind Wasserwerfer **von der Polizei** eingesetzt worden.	*A few months later, water cannons were deployed by the police.*
Und die Polizei selbst wurde **von Flaschen** getroffen.	*And the police themselves were hit by (glass) bottles.*

3. **Durch** *(by, by means of, through)* is used to indicate the process or means by which something happens; it often expresses an involuntary cause and is generally less personal or volitional than **von;** it is used with people only when they are acting as intermediaries.

Die Innenstadt von Stuttgart wird **durch die Bauarbeiten** drastisch verändert.	*The city center of Stuttgart is being changed drastically by (means of) the construction work.*

Die Vorteile des Gesamtplans wurden **durch eine Studie** aus der Schweiz bestätigt.	*The advantages of the overall plan were confirmed by (means of) a study out of Switzerland.*

4. **Mit** *(with)* is used to indicate the instrument or tool—physical as well as conceptual—with which an action is carried out.

Die S21-Gegner werden mit **Twitter, Facebook und Blogs** über Demos und andere Veranstaltungen informiert.	*The anti-S21 people are informed about demonstrations and other meetings by Twitter, Facebook, and blogs.*

D. Passives with modal verbs

1. While modal verbs themselves are rarely formed into passives, they combine easily and frequently with passive structures, using the conventional format of modal auxiliary + infinitive (see 9.1).

Das **muss** heute noch *gemacht werden.*	*That must be done today.*

The important difference here is that the infinitive is no longer the familiar active infinitive **(machen),** but rather a *passive infinitive*, formed by joining a past participle with **werden: gemacht werden.** Passive infinitives always appear in this form, and these components cannot be changed or separated.

gebaut werden	*(to) be built*
weitergeführt werden	*(to) be continued*
überschritten werden	*(to) be exceeded*
informiert werden	*(to) be informed*

2. As in any modal verb construction, the modal verb serves as V_1, with the passive infinitive as V_2. And as always, it is the modal verb rather than the infinitive that undergoes changes to indicate variations in number, tense, and mood.

Die eine Seite sagt: „Stuttgart 21 **muss** unbedingt **gebaut werden!"** *(present indicative; singular)*	*One side says: "Stuttgart 21 absolutely must be built!"*
Die andere Seite fragt: „**Könnte** der Bahnhof nicht für weniger als 6,5 Milliarden Euro **modernisiert werden?"** *(present subjunctive; singular)*	*The other side asks: "Couldn't the train station be modernized for less than 6.5 billion euros?"*
Während der Proteste **konnten** die Bauarbeiten nicht **weitergeführt werden.** *(simple past indicative; plural)*	*During the protests, the construction work could not be continued.*

3. The future passive tense makes use of the same structure, with **werden** as V_1 and a passive infinitive as V_2.

Die Polizei **wird** darüber **informiert werden.**   *The police will be informed about it.*

4. When passive constructions with modal verbs occur in compound tenses, such as the perfect, past perfect, future, or past subjunctive, they follow the same rules as all compound modal structures: auxiliary + infinitive + modal (infinitive) (see 9.3–4; 21.4.C). The only difference is that an active infinitive (e.g., **machen**) is replaced by a passive infinitive (e.g., **gemacht werden**). Compare the active and passive constructions below.

ACTIVE:

Man **hat** das schnell *entscheiden* **können.**	*One was able to decide that quickly.* (perfect tense)
Man **wird** das später *entscheiden* **müssen.**	*One will have to decide that later.* (future tense)
Man **hätte** das gleich am Anfang *entscheiden* **sollen.**	*One should have decided that right at the outset.* (past subjunctive mood)

PASSIVE:

Das **hat** schnell *entschieden werden* **können.**	*That was able to be decided quickly.* (perfect tense)
Das **wird** später *entschieden werden* **müssen.**	*That will have to be decided later.* (future tense)
Das **hätte** gleich am Anfang *entschieden werden* **sollen.**	*That should have been decided right at the outset.* (past subjunctive mood)

E. Passives with no subjects

German passive constructions do not require a grammatical subject, as explained in the case of dative verbs in section 1.B above. In fact, there are several additional contexts in which passives use no subject.

1. *With prepositional complements.* German verbs that take prepositional phrase complements (see R.3), rather than direct objects, can form passives. The conjugated verb in such sentences defaults to third-person singular. In some cases, English translates these verbs with a direct object, which then becomes the passive subject in the English equivalent.

Über die Risiken muss noch diskutiert werden.   *The risks still have to be discussed.*

Warum wurde nicht früher **daran** gedacht?   *Why wasn't that thought of earlier?*

2. *With verbs, both transitive and intransitive, that denote an activity in general.* This construction capitalizes on the anonymity of a subjectless sentence to express an activity *per se*, with no reference to who or what performs it or "receives" the action. In this case, V_1 can be either **werden** or a modal verb, conjugated in any tense in the default third-person singular. Verbs used in this construction either take no object (i.e., they

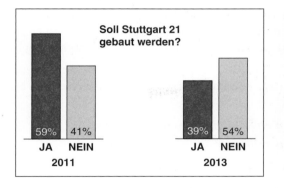

Soll Stuttgart 21
gebaut werden?

Marijan Murat/dpa/picture-alliance/Newscom

are intransitive, like **schlafen**), or can function without an object (i.e., transitive verbs used intransitively, such as **rauchen**). There is no equivalent structure for this in English, though English has ways of conveying similar meanings.

Im Sommer 2011 haben viele gefragt: **Wird** jetzt **weitergebaut** oder nicht?	*During the summer of 2011, many were asking: Will the construction continue or not?*
Am Anfang **wurde kritisiert,** dass …	*At the beginning, there was criticism that… / people criticized the fact that…*
Bei den „Schlichtungsgesprächen" **wurde** 60 Stunden lang **diskutiert.**	*In the course of the "reconciliation discussions," discussions went on for 60 hours.*
Im Moment **wird** öffentlich nicht viel **protestiert.**	*At the moment, there's not much protesting in public.*

12.2 TRUE PASSIVE VS. STATAL PASSIVE

German has constructions that resemble the passive, but in fact they are different in meaning and form.

COMPARE:

true passive: Der alte Bahnhof **wird abgerissen.**	*The old train station is being torn down.* (process)
statal passive: Der alte Bahnhof **ist abgerissen.**	*The old train station is torn down.* (result)

The first sentence uses the combination of **werden** + past participle to express the (ongoing) process of *tearing down*. The second sentence uses **sein** along with a past participle to indicate the result of a process, i.e., that something is (already) *torn down*. This second usage is known as a *statal passive* (**das Zustandspassiv**), since it uses the past participle as an adjective to describe the *state* of the sentence subject.

English distinguishes clearly enough between process and result, true passive and statal passive, in the present tense. When something is *being done*, the process is not yet complete (and presumably part of the train station is still standing); but when something is *done*, the consequences are in evidence, i.e., the train station is gone.

But in the past tense, English is not as clear, since both the process and the result can be expressed by the same construction:

> **The old train station was torn down** *while the protesters watched.* (process)
>
> **The old train station was torn down** *by the time they arrived.* (result)

In German, that distinction is easily made by using either a true passive (**werden +** past participle) or a statal passive (**sein +** past participle) in the past tense:

> Der alte Bahnhof **wurde abgerissen,** während die Demonstranten zuschauten.
>
> Der alte Bahnhof **war** (schon) **abgerissen,** als sie ankamen.

12.3 ▸ SUBSTITUTES FOR THE PASSIVE VOICE

Since repeated use of the passive voice is considered poor style, one of several active-voice equivalents is often substituted.

A. *Man*

Man is a common alternative to the passive when no specific subject performs the action.

Jetzt baut **man** weiter. (Jetzt wird weitergebaut.)	*The construction is continuing now.*
Wie macht **man** das? (Wie wird das gemacht?)	*How is that done? How does one do that?*

B. Reflexive verbs

Reflexive constructions are used occasionally in place of the passive (see 10.2.A5).

Das **lernt sich** ganz schnell. (Das wird ganz schnell gelernt.)	*That can be learned quite quickly.*
Vielleicht **findet sich** eine Lösung.	*Maybe a solution can be found.*
Wie **schreibt sich** Ihr Name? (Wie wird Ihr Name geschrieben?)	*How is your name spelled? How do you spell your name?*

C. *Sich lassen*

The use of reflexive **sich lassen** with an infinitive expresses the idea that something can be done or that someone lets something be done (see **lassen,** 11.4).

Das **lässt sich** leicht **sagen,** aber... (Das wird leicht gesagt, aber...)	*That's easy to say, but...* (lit., *That lets itself be easily said*)

Die Argumente dagegen **ließen sich** nicht pauschal **abtun.**	*The arguments against it could not be dismissed out of hand.*

D. *Sein ... zu* + infinitive

Sein ... zu + an infinitive can replace the passive to express that something can or must be done.

Die „Schlichtungsgespräche" **sind** am besten so **zu verstehen**: ... (Die „Schlichtungsgespräche" können am besten so verstanden werden:...)	*The "reconciliation discussions" can best be understood like this:…*
Das Baugebiet **ist** jetzt nur mit einer Genehmigung **zu betreten.** (Das Baugebiet darf jetzt nur mit einer Genehmigung betreten werden.)	*The construction area may only be entered with a permit.*
Die Reaktion **war** kaum **zu glauben.** (Die Reaktion konnte kaum geglaubt werden.)	*The reaction could hardly be believed.*

Wortschatz
schaffen

---

schaffen, schaffte, geschafft
schaffen, schuf, geschaffen

---

1. As a weak verb, **schaffen (schaffte, hat geschafft)** means *to manage to do* or *accomplish* a task, often with considerable effort.

Sie wollten die Arbeit bis sechs Uhr beenden, und sie haben es **geschafft.**	*They wanted to finish the work by six o'clock, and they managed to do so.*
Wir haben's **geschafft!**	*We did it!*

In southern Germany, **schaffen** is also used to mean *to work hard*, especially in reference to manual labor.

Bauarbeiter **schaffen** schon seit 2010 an diesem Projekt.	*Construction workers have been working on this project since 2010.*

Schaffen sometimes means *to bring* or *get* an object to a particular place.

Zur Baustelle hat man bis jetzt mehr als 1,5 Millionen m³ Beton **geschafft.**	*Up to now, more than 1.5 million cubic meters of concrete have been transported to the construction site.*

2. When used as a strong verb, **schaffen (schuf, hat geschaffen)** means *to create, make,* or *bring about.*

Gott soll die Welt in sechs Tagen **geschaffen** haben.	*God is said to have created the world in six days.*
In sechs Tagen kann ich nicht einmal Ordnung im eigenen Zimmer **schaffen.**	*In six days I can't even create order in my own room.*

3. The strong participle **geschaffen** occurs often as an adjective meaning *made* or *cut out for* something.

Sie ist für diese Rolle wie **geschaffen.**	*She was made for this role. (i.e., it is the ideal role for her)*

Übungen

A **Das Passiv kann manipuliert werden!**   Nehmen Sie den Mustersatz *(model sentence)* und bilden Sie damit Passivsätze mit den angegebenen Zeiten und Elementen.

Mein Zimmer wird verwüstet. *(My room is being trashed.)*

 BEISPIEL   nächstes Semester *(Futur)*
Nächstes Semester wird mein Zimmer verwüstet werden.

1. letztes Jahr *(Imperfekt)*
2. meine Mitbewohner machen das *(von wem)*
3. es könnte sein *(mit einem Modalverb im Konjunktiv)*
4. jemand hat es letztes Wochenende gemacht *(Perfekt)*
5. durch _____ *(wie)*
6. wie oft? warum?
7. *(mit einem Modalverb)*

B *Geschaffen oder geschafft?*   Ergänzen Sie die Sätze durch das richtige Partizip.

1. Wir hatten für das Examen zwei Stunden Zeit. Hast du es ge-_____?
2. Haben die Kinder den Schnee vor der Haustür weg-_____?
3. Die Diskussionen in Stuttgart haben eine bessere Atmosphäre ge-_____.
4. Dieser Posten ist wie für ihn ge-_____.
5. Ludwig van Beethoven hat viele unsterbliche Werke ge-_____.

C **Selber geschafft.**   Was haben Sie bisher in Ihrem Leben **geschaffen** und **geschafft**? Machen Sie zwei Aussagen mit jedem Partizip.

BEISPIELE   *Ich habe mehr Ruhe in meinem Leben **geschaffen.***
Ich habe es gerade noch (just barely) ***geschafft**, alle meine Prüfungen im vergangenen Semester zu bestehen* (pass).

D **Kleinanzeigen.** Erklären Sie die Kleinanzeigen *(short advertisements)* im Passiv Präsens.

BEISPIEL   Autoreparatur – billig!
Autos werden billig repariert.

1. Neuer Plasmafernseher? Wir installieren!
2. Alter VW Käfer *(Beetle)* zu verkaufen!
3. Ankauf *(purchase)* von Antiquitäten!
4. Fahrradverleih! (verleihen = *to rent*)
5. Mensa stellt Koch ein! (ein·stellen = *to hire*)
6. Studienprobleme? Wir beraten dich! (beraten = *to advise*)
7. Zimmervermittlung! (vermitteln = *to act as a broker or intermediary*)

E **Große Leistungen *(accomplishments).*** Was wurde von wem gemacht? Antworten Sie im Passiv. Verwenden Sie die Verben im Kasten – als Partizipien natürlich!

BEISPIEL   das Dynamit
Das Dynamit wurde im Jahre 1867 von Alfred Nobel erfunden.

bauen	besiegen	beschreiben	brechen	entdecken
erfinden	erreichen	gründen	komponieren	verfassen

Was?	**Von wem?**
1. das *Kommunistische Manifest* (1848)	Henri Dunant
2. das *Weihnachts-Oratorium* (1734)	Michael Phelps
3. die Buchdruckerkunst (1445)	Roald Amundsen
4. der Südpol (1911)	Karl Marx
5. das Rote Kreuz (1864)	Jane Goodall
6. das Leben von Schimpansen (1960)	J. S. Bach
7. der Tuberkel-Bazillus (1882)	Johannes Gutenberg
8. die Römer im Teutoburger Wald (9 nach Chr.)	Robert Koch
9. Weltrekord *(m.)* für Goldmedaillen bei den Olympischen Spielen	Schweizer Ingenieure *(engineers)*
10. der längste Bahntunnel der Welt (2016)	Hermann der Cherusker (Arminius)

F **Historisches.** Wählen Sie aus fünf verschiedenen Jahrhunderten jeweils ein Jahr, in dem ein historisches Ereignis stattfand. Erzählen Sie im Präteritum davon.

BEISPIELE   1066: *England wurde im Jahre 1066 von den Normannen erobert (conquered).*

1914: *Der Erzherzog* (Archduke) *Franz Ferdinand von Österreich wurde 1914 in Sarajevo erschossen.*

G **Veränderungen.** Erzählen Sie im Perfekt von drei oder vier Veränderungen der letzten paar Jahre, die die Lebensqualität in Ihrer Heimatstadt oder an Ihrer Universität oder Schule verbessert oder verschlechtert haben.

BEISPIELE *Viele neue Häuser sind gebaut worden.*
Mein Studentenwohnheim ist renoviert worden.

Welche Veränderungen sind für die Zukunft geplant? Machen Sie bitte Aussagen im Futur oder mit Modalverben.

BEISPIELE *Ich glaube, dass ein neues Einkaufszentrum bald gebaut werden wird.*
Es soll auch ein neues Parkhaus eröffnet werden.
Ich weiß nicht, was sonst noch gemacht werden wird.

H **Was alles gemacht werden musste.** Stellen Sie sich mal vor *(just imagine)*, einige Studenten fanden eine ziemlich heruntergekommene *(run-down)* Wohnung. Was musste alles gemacht werden, bevor sie einziehen konnten? Verwenden Sie das Passiv der Vergangenheit mit oder ohne **es.**

BEISPIELE Fenster ersetzen
Zwei kaputte Fenster mussten ersetzt werden.

Vorhänge *(curtains)* aufhängen
Es mussten auch Vorhänge aufgehängt werden.

1. die Küche sauber machen
2. die Gardinen *(drapes)* reinigen
3. das Badezimmer putzen
4. eine Tür reparieren
5. den Keller auf·räumen

I **Das müsste bald gemacht werden.** Wie sieht es in Ihrer Wohnung oder in Ihrem Haus aus? Was könnte oder müsste *(would have to)* dort bald gemacht werden?

BEISPIEL *Die Wände müssten bald gestrichen werden.*

J **Was wird dort gemacht?** Beschreiben Sie, was gemacht wird. Benutzen Sie das Passiv, mit oder ohne Subjekt.

BEISPIELE in einer Bibliothek
Dort werden Bücher ausgeliehen.
Dort wird gelesen.

1. an einem Kiosk *(newsstand)*
2. in einer Vorlesung um 9 Uhr morgens
3. in einer Autowerkstatt *(car repair shop)*
4. in einem Kino
5. an einer Tankstelle *(gas station)*
6. auf Netzwerken wie Facebook, LinkedIn oder Twitter
7. in einer Sporthalle
8. in einem Restaurant

K **Passiv mit dem Dativ.** Drücken Sie die Sätze mit dem Passiv anders aus.

BEISPIEL Man hat der alten Frau geholfen.
Der alten Frau ist geholfen worden.
OR: *Es ist der alten Frau geholfen worden.*

1. Man erzählte den Kindern nichts davon.
2. Man hat den Gastgebern *(hosts)* gedankt.
3. Uns empfiehlt man dieses Buch.
4. Mir haben viele Leute zum Geburtstag gratuliert.
5. Man wird der Frau wahrscheinlich raten, nichts zu sagen.

L **Anders ausdrücken.** Drücken Sie die Sätze durch andere Konstruktionen aus.

BEISPIELE Das kann man nicht mit Sicherheit sagen.
Das lässt sich nicht mit Sicherheit sagen.
OR: *Das kann nicht mit Sicherheit gesagt werden.*
OR: *Man kann das nicht mit Sicherheit sagen.*

1. Wie schreibt man dieses Wort?
2. Auto fahren ist leicht zu lernen.
3. Es konnte festgestellt *(ascertained)* werden, dass ...
4. Solche Behauptungen *(assertions)* lassen sich nicht so einfach beweisen *(prove)*.
5. Änderungen an der chemischen Verbindung *(compound)* waren nicht zu erkennen *(recognize)*.
6. Das Wasser muss mindestens zwanzig Minuten gekocht werden.

Anwendung

Klischeevorstellungen. Über fast jedes Volk und jedes Land auf der Welt gibt es Klischees. In China z.B. soll angeblich *(supposedly)* immer gearbeitet werden, in Amerika wird nur noch ferngesehen, in Deutschland wird viel Bier getrunken usw. An welche Klischees denken Sie? Welche Klischees halten Sie für richtig, welche für falsch? Diskutieren Sie mit anderen Personen darüber. Konzentrieren Sie sich dabei auf das Passiv und auch auf das Pronomen **man** als Ersatz für das Passiv.

REDEMITTEL
Es wird behauptet, dass in Amerika/Deutschland ... [gemacht] wird.
Manche meinen, es wird in der Schweiz/in Deutschland ... [gemacht].
Es wird ja oft gesagt, dass ...
In Österreich/Deutschland soll angeblich *(supposedly)* viel ... [gemacht] werden.
Man kann nicht behaupten, dass ...

Da kann ich nur zustimmen *(agree)*.
Das halte ich für nicht ganz richtig/falsch.
Das finde ich (nicht) richtig.
Das ist ja Unsinn!
Das lässt sich nicht einfach so behaupten.
Das kann man auch anders sehen.

Schriftliche Themen

Tipps zum Schreiben

Practicing the Passive

The traditional wisdom that one should fundamentally avoid the passive is not always the best advice. When the agent of an action is not known or not important, or if the action is meant to be described in general rather than in a specific application, then the passive voice is preferred, in both English and German. In addition, German regularly uses the passive to express ideas such as *There was dancing and singing* with **Es wurde getanzt und gesungen.**

At this point in your writing, you should use the passive whenever you think it might fit, since English-speaking learners, faced with the complexities of German passive constructions, often shy away from employing them even when they would be appropriate. Practice forming passives in various tenses, moods, and with modal verbs. For even more effective writing in German, you should use the various alternatives to the passive (see 12.3), which provide good stylistic variation. In any case, pay attention to German writers and speakers to see how the passive is actually used.

A **Eine interessante Veranstaltung *(organized event).*** Erzählen Sie von einer Veranstaltung, bei der Sie einmal mitgemacht haben. Sie sollen nicht so sehr davon erzählen, **wer** was getan hat, sondern lieber davon, **was** geschah oder gemacht wurde.

BEISPIEL   *Einmal nahm ich an einer Protestaktion teil. Am Anfang organisierte man ... Es wurden Transparente* (banners) *verteilt* (distributed) *... Es wurde viel geredet ... Gegen Ende der Aktion marschierte man ... Zum Schluss mussten alle Demonstranten ... zurückgebracht werden.*

B **Bessere Lebensqualität.** Was könnte oder müsste getan werden, um die Atmosphäre und die Lebensqualität an Ihrer Universität oder in Ihrer Stadt attraktiver zu machen?

BEISPIEL *Meiner Meinung nach könnte die Lebensqualität an dieser Universität durch renovierte Unterrichtsräume erheblich (substantially) verbessert werden. Man müsste auch mehr Räume einrichten (set up), in denen man sich auch außerhalb der Unterrichtszeit treffen könnte. Vielleicht sollten auch mehr Parkplätze geschaffen werden, damit ...*

Zusammenfassung

Rules to Remember

1. The passive voice is used mainly to express occurrences and actions where no agent is to be specified.

2. The passive voice is formed with variations of **werden** + past participle.

3. Agents of a passive action are expressed with the preposition **von** + the agent (**von der Polizei**). The means or processes through which an action is accomplished are expressed with **durch** + noun (**durch lange Diskussionen**). The instrument used to accomplish an action is shown with **mit** + noun (**mit einem Wasserwerfer**).

4. The passive expresses a process (**Das Haus *wird* verkauft**); the so-called statal passive describes a condition (**Das Haus *ist* verkauft**).

At a Glance

werden + past participle
V₁ + V₂

ich werde	⎫	
du wirst		
Sie werden		
er/sie/es wird	⎬ informiert	
wir werden		
ihr werdet		
Sie werden		
sie werden	⎭	

Passive: Tenses	Passive with modals
Present	**Present**
Wir **werden informiert.**	Das Gebäude *muss* renoviert werden.
Simple past	**Simple past**
Wir **wurden informiert.**	Das Gebäude *musste* renoviert werden.
Present perfect	**Present perfect**
Wir **sind informiert worden.**	Das Gebäude *hat* renoviert werden *müssen.*
Past perfect	**Past perfect**
Wir **waren informiert worden.**	Das Gebäude *hatte* renoviert werden *müssen.*
Future	**Future**
Wir **werden informiert werden.**	Das Gebäude *wird* renoviert werden *müssen.*
Subjunctive: Present	**Subjunctive: Present**
Wir **würden informiert (werden).**	Das Gebäude *müsste* renoviert werden.
Subjunctive: Past	**Subjunctive: Past**
Wir **wären informiert worden.**	Das Gebäude *hätte* renoviert werden *müssen.*

zum Beispiel

Harry auf Deutsch

JENS SCHLUETER/AFP/Getty Images

Harry Potter hardly needs an introduction, but the popularity of the book series in Germany, Austria, and Switzerland deserves some attention. The first volume, *Harry Potter und der Stein der Weisen,* appeared in German in 1998, and quickly became a success. Hundreds of thousands of German-speaking fans were just as impatient as their counterparts in the UK and North America for the arrival of each volume, judging from the long lines outside bookstores. Numerous fan sites attest to the series' ongoing popularity: *Harry-Potter-Fanclub, Harry auf Deutsch, Harry Potter Xperts, Viola Owlfeathers Harry-Potter-Kiste,* and so on. The success of the books eventually led to controversy, as some school districts decided to replace canonical English readings (Shakespeare, Joyce, Wilde) with the Harry Potter stories. Not everyone was excited about those authors, of course, but as one critic (who readily admits he never finished reading his English assignments) put it: *"Es macht einen gravierenden Unterschied, ob man nicht weiß, wer King Lear ist oder wer Hagrid ist …"*

205

Grammatik

13.1 ADJECTIVES WITHOUT ENDINGS

1. Adjectives (**das Adjektiv, -e**) provide additional information about nouns and pronouns. When they provide this information via linking verbs such as **sein, werden, bleiben**, and **gelten** [+ **als**] (see 5.3.C) as *predicate adjectives,* they do not have endings.

Auch in Deutschland *sind* die *Harry* Potter-Bücher sehr **beliebt**.	*The Harry Potter books are very popular in Germany too.*
Junge Leser *sind* außerordentlich **enthusiastisch geworden.**	*Young readers have become extremely enthusiastic.*
Sogar in akademischen Kreisen *gilt* das Potter-Phänomen *als* **wichtig**.	*Even in academic circles, the Potter phenomenon is considered important.*

2. In German, many adjectives can also be used without endings as adverbs.

Dieses Medien-Ereignis fing zwar **langsam** an.	*This media event began slowly, to be sure.*
Aber es hat sich **erstaunlich schnell** entwickelt.	*But it developed astonishingly quickly.*

13.2 ADJECTIVES WITH ENDINGS

When adjectives precede the nouns they modify, they are called *attributive adjectives* and require endings. Just which ending is needed depends on whether the accompanying article in the noun phrase provides the required grammatical information. Definite articles (**der/die/das**) and related words (**dieser/jeder/welcher**) always provide it; indefinite articles (**ein/eine**) and related words (**mein/ihr/sein/kein**) sometimes do but sometimes don't. Of course if there is no article, no grammatical information can be given. German has developed two sets of adjective endings to cover these contingencies: *weak endings* for contexts in which the information is already provided by the article; and *strong endings* for contexts when the article does not supply it, or when there is no article in the noun phrase. The two sets are presented below in chart format, and the discussion that follows explains how these two sets are applied to the three basic configurations of adjectives in noun phrases: adjectives following **der**-words; adjectives following **ein**-words, and adjectives with no preceding article.

Weak endings

	Masc.	Fem.	Neut.	Pl.
Nom.			-e	
Acc.				-en
Dat.				
Gen.		-en		

Strong endings

	Masc.	Fem.	Neut.	Pl.
Nom.	-er	-e	-es	-e
Acc.	-en	-e	-es	-e
Dat.	-em	-er	-em	-en
Gen.	-en	-er	-en	-er

A. Adjectives after *der*-words

Since **der**-words supply the maximum amount of grammatical information possible, adjectives following **der**-words require only a weak ending. This is true for all **der**-words—the definite articles, as well as **dieser, jeder, jener, mancher, solcher,** and **welcher** (see 4.3)—in all cases.

	Singular		
	Masc.	**Fem.**	**Neut.**
Nom.	**der** junge Zauberer[a]	**die** weiße Eule[b]	**das** magische Schwert[c]
Acc.	**den** jungen Zauberer	**die** weiße Eule	**das** magische Schwert
Dat.	**dem** jungen Zauberer	**der** weißen Eule	**dem** magischen Schwert
Gen.	**des** jungen Zauberers	**der** weißen Eule	**des** magischen Schwerts
	Plural		
Nom.	**die** eifrigen[d] Hauselfen		
Acc.	**die** eifrigen Hauselfen		
Dat.	**den** eifrigen Hauselfen		
Gen.	**der** eifrigen Hauselfen		

---

[a]*wizard, magician*   [b]*owl*   [c]*sword*   [d]*diligent, eager*

B. Adjectives following *ein*-words

Adjectives after **ein**-words—**ein** and **kein**, as well as **mein, dein, sein, ihr, unser, euer, ihr**, and **Ihr** (see 4.4)—are not as straightforward, since these words vary in the amount of grammatical information they supply. You know that **ein**-words make no distinction between masculine and neuter nominative (e.g., **dein** Freund ist nett *vs.* **dein** Buch kostet zu viel), whereas **der**-words do (e.g., **dies**<u>er</u> Freund ist nett *vs.* **dies**<u>es</u> Buch kostet zu viel). Since German tries to clarify this gender distinction wherever possible, adjectives following **ein**, **dein,** and **mein** and the other **ein**-words require the strong endings. After words such as **ein**<u>em</u> and **ein**<u>er</u>, however, whose endings already exhibit grammatical information, the weak endings are sufficient. Notice in the chart below how these noun phrases make use of both the weak and strong endings.

Singular		
Masc.	**Fem.**	**Neut.**
ein schnell**er** Besen[a]	**eine** schreckliche Kammer[b]	**ein** verzaubertes[c] Tagebuch[d]
einen schnell**en** Besen	**eine** schreckliche Kammer	**ein** verzaubertes Tagebuch
einem schnell**en** Besen	**einer** schrecklich**en** Kammer	**einem** verzauberten Tagebuch
eines schnell**en** Besens	**einer** schrecklich**en** Kammer	**eines** verzauberten Tagebuchs

(row labels: Nom. / Acc. / Dat. / Gen.)

Plural
keine guten Horkruxe
keine guten Horkruxe
keinen guten Horkruxe
keiner guten Horkruxe

(row labels: Nom. / Acc. / Dat. / Gen.)

[a]*broom*   [b]*chamber*   [c]*enchanted*   [d]*diary*

As the chart shows, the only instances in which an **ein**-word does *not* provide sufficient information are the three cases where **ein**-words in the singular have no endings to distinguish gender: *masculine nominative, neuter nominative* and *neuter accusative.* Except for these three instances, **ein**-words, like **der**-words, take *weak endings.*

C. Adjectives with no preceding articles

When a noun phrase consists solely of one or more adjectives and nouns—that is, without an article—then the adjective ending takes on the function of an article. Indeed, the strong endings clearly resemble the definite articles (-**er** for **der**, -**es** for **das**, -**em** for **dem**, etc.). The only apparent exceptions to this pattern are the endings for *masculine and neuter genitive singular,* which are -**en** instead of the expected -**es**. But even these conform to principle: Since genitive masculine and neuter nouns show number and case with the -**(e)s** ending on the noun itself, the adjectives preceding them do not need to emphasize this information, as in **ein Zeichen besonderen Mutes** (*a sign of particular courage*). Notice in the following examples how the adjective endings stand in for the article that would be appropriate if an article were included.

Nominative:	der Mut[a]:	groß**er** Mut
Nominative/Accusative:	die Angst:	lähmende[b] Angst
	Zaubertränke[c]:	giftig**e** Zaubertränke
Dative:	das Interesse:	mit wachsend**em**[d] Interesse
	die Freundschaft:	aus alt**er** Freundschaft
	Häuser *(pl.)*:	in verschieden**en** Häusern

[a]*courage*   [b]*paralyzing*   [c]*potions, pl.*   [d]*growing*

D. Summary of adjective endings

At least one modifier before a noun—either an article or an adjective—must show information regarding number, gender, and case. Compare the following examples, and notice the similarity of articles and endings.

Singular		
der-word	**ein-word**	**No article**

	der-word	ein-word	No article
Nom.	dies**er** neue Mut	sein neu**er** Mut	neu**er** Mut
Nom.	d**as** echte Glück *(luck)*	ein echt**es** Glück	echt**es** Glück
Nom./Acc.	jed**e** große Macht *(power)*	ihr**e** große Macht	groß**e** Macht
Dat.	(mit) d**er** neuen Kraft *(strength)*	sein**er** neuen Kraft	neu**er** Kraft

Plural		

	der-word	ein-word	No article
Nom.	dies**e** starken Feinde *(enemies)*	ihr**e** starken Feinde	stark**e** Feinde
Dat.	(mit) **den** treuen Freunden	ihr**en** treuen Freunden	treu**en** Freunden
Gen.	(wegen) **der** großen Gefahr *(danger)*	ihr**er** großen Gefahr	groß**er** Gefahr

E. Additional rules

1. All adjectives in a series take the same ending.

   Am Anfang ist Harry ein **unglücklicher, einsamer** Junge.

   At the outset, Harry is an unhappy, lonely boy.

   Hermine ist ein **kluges, wissbegieriges** aber auch manchmal **unsicheres** Mädchen.

   Hermione is a smart, inquisitive girl, but also unsure of herself sometimes.

2. Adjective stems ending in -**er** and -**el** drop the stem **e** when they have adjective endings.

   teuer: ein teu**res** Buch
   dunkel: ein dun**kler** Korridor

3. The adjective **hoch** drops the **c** when it has an adjective ending.

hoch:	**hohes** Interesse	*great (lit.: high level of) interest*
	sehr **hohe** Gefahr	*very great (lit.: high level of) danger*

4. The adjectives **beige, lila** *(lilac),* **orange, rosa** *(pink),* and **prima** *(great)* are invariable; they do not take endings.

Hermine trägt ein **rosa** Kleid zum Ball, oder?	*Hermione wears a pink dress to the ball, doesn't she?*
Das war eine **prima** Idee!	*That was a brilliant idea!*

5. The adjectives **halb** and **ganz** do not take endings before names of towns, countries, and continents, unless the name requires an article (see 4.1).

    halb Hogsmeade *(half of Hogsmeade)*
    ganz England *(all of England)*

    BUT:

    die **halbe** Schweiz *(half of Switzerland)*
    die **ganze** Türkei *(all of Turkey)*
    die **ganzen** USA *(the whole U.S.)*

6. Adjectives of nationality behave like other descriptive adjectives (**EXCEPT: die Schweiz,** see below). They are capitalized only when used in proper names.

für die **deutsche** Übersetzung	*for the German translation*
französische Ausgaben	*French editions*
von einem **russischen** Verlag	*from a Russian publisher*

    BUT:

    die **Deutsche** Bank   die **Französischen** Eisenbahnen

7. Adjectives based on the names of cities or towns take no endings and are formed by adding the suffix **-er** to the noun. All capitalization is retained. The adjective of nationality based on **die Schweiz** also follows this rule.

Der erste Film wurde in einem **Berliner** Kino gezeigt.	*The first film was shown in a Berlin movie theater.*
In einem **Londoner** Bahnhof findet man tatsächlich das besondere Gleis.	*In a London train station, you can in fact find the special track.*
Ich vermute, Rowling hat ein **Schweizer** Bankkonto.	*I suspect Rowling has a Swiss bank account.*

13.3 LIMITING ADJECTIVES

A. *Wenig, etwas, genug, viel*

The singular limiting adjectives **wenig** *(little)*, **etwas** *(some)*, **genug** *(enough)*, and **viel** *(much, a lot of)* are used only with singular nouns. Since these words take no endings themselves,[1] the adjectives following them require *strong* endings.

Für einen Vielsaft-Trank beginnt man mit etwas **heißem** Wasser, und dann ...	*For a Polyjuice Potion you begin with some hot water, and then ...*
Aber gibt es genug **gemahlene** Baumschlangenhaut dafür?	*But is there enough shredded Boomslang skin for it?*

B. *Ein paar*

The plural limiting phrase **ein paar** *(a few, a couple of)*, used with plural nouns, likewise takes no ending, so that any following adjectives require *strong* endings.

Sie hatte **ein paar gute** Freunde.	*She had a couple of good friends.*
Sie sprach mit **ein paar guten** Freunden.	*She spoke with a couple of good friends.*

C. *Wenige, andere, einige, mehrere, viele*

1. Other plural limiting adjectives, such as **wenige** *(few)*, **andere** *(other)*, **einige** *(some, several)*, **mehrere** *(several, a number of)*, and **viele** *(many)*, function as adjectives themselves. Like all adjectives, their endings depend on the preceding article or (as is often the case with these words) the absence of an article. All subsequent adjectives take the same ending.

Einige enthusiastische Schulleiter haben sich für *Harry Potter* als Lektüre eingesetzt.	*Several enthusiastic school principals promoted Harry Potter for the reading syllabus.*
Das wurde von **mehreren kritischen** Stimmen infrage gestellt.	*That was called into question by a number of critical voices.*
Die vielen jungen Fans in den Schulen waren aber sehr dafür.	*But the many young fans in the schools were very much in favor of it.*

2. Notice that in English, *a lot* can apply to both singular and plural nouns: *a lot of time/a lot of books*. In German, by contrast, the singular meaning can only be expressed with **viel,** which normally takes no endings; and the plural meaning must be expressed with **viele,** which requires adjective endings.

viel Zeit	$\longrightarrow$	mit **viel** Zeit
viele Bücher	$\longrightarrow$	mit **vielen** Büchern

---

[1]Occasionally **viel** and **wenig** do occur in the accusative and dative with optional endings: **mit viel (vielem) Ärger** *(with much aggravation)*; **nach wenig (wenigem) Erfolg** *(after little success)*. The ending is not optional in the expression **vielen Dank.**

D. *All-*

1. In the plural, **all-** functions like a **der**-word (see 4.3); any adjectives following **all-** take the weak ending -**en.**

    Die Dementoren können **alle guten**   *The dementors can destroy all good*
      Erinnerungen und **alle glücklichen**   *memories and all happy feelings.*
      Gefühle vernichten.

2. When **all-** precedes an article or possessive adjective, its ending is often omitted—usually when **all-** is plural, and always when **all-** is singular. In the plural, any **der**-words or possessive adjectives following **all-** take the same endings added to **all-**; if no endings are added to **all-**, any **der**-words or possessive modifiers preceding the noun still require normal endings.

all(e) die komischen Sachen	*all the strange things*
all(e) seine neuen Freunde	*all his new friends*
mit **all(en) seinen neuen** Freunden	*with all his new friends*
all sein Mut	*all his courage*

E. *Ganz* **instead of** *all-*

Instead of **all-** (singular and plural), German sometimes uses an article or possessive pronoun followed by **ganz-** *(all, whole, complete).* In this usage, **ganz-** functions like any other adjective and takes weak and strong endings. Note, however, that **all-** and **ganz-** are not simply interchangeable, and do not correspond directly to English usage with *all* and *whole.*

In the singular, German prefers **ganz-**, while *all* and *whole* are equally acceptable in English, at least in most cases. When **all-** occurs in the singular, it takes no ending and is followed by an article or possessive adjective.

Den ganzen Sommer haben die Fans   *The fans waited all summer/the whole*
  auf den letzten Band gewartet.   *summer for the final volume.*

Als er endlich erschien, haben ihn viele   *When it finally appeared, many children*
  Kinder **die ganze** Nacht gelesen.   *read it all night/the whole night.*

BUT:

Einige haben **ihr ganzes** Taschengeld
  dafür ausgegeben.   *Some spent all their pocket money*
                                                                                 on it.
Einige haben **all ihr** Taschengeld dafür
  ausgegeben.

In plural usage, German allows either **all-** or **ganz-**, whereas English only allows *all*.

All(e) ihre Schulkameraden haben das gleiche gemacht.	*All their school classmates did the same thing.*
Ihre ganzen Schulkameraden haben das gleiche gemacht.	

Kennt jemand **all(e) die geheimen** Räume in Hogwarts?	*Does anyone know all the secret rooms at Hogwarts?*
Kennt jemand **die ganzen geheimen** Räume in Hogwarts?	

13.4 ADJECTIVES GOVERNING CASES

A. Adjectives with the dative or with *für* + accusative

1. The following adjectives normally require a noun or pronoun object in the dative when used as predicate adjectives. The adjective is positioned at the end of the middle field (see 1.1.C).

(un)ähnlich	*(dis)similar, (un)like*	(un)klar	*(un)clear*
(un)bekannt	*(un)known*	nahe	*near, close*
(un)bequem	*(un)comfortable*	schuldig	*in debt (to owe)*
(un)bewusst	*(un)aware*	teuer	*expensive, valuable*
(un)dankbar	*(un)grateful*	überlegen	*superior*
fremd	*strange, alien*	wert	*worth, of value*
gehorsam	*obedient*		

Ist er *seinem Vater* sehr **ähnlich**?	*Is he very much like his father?*
Sie ist *ihren Schulkameraden* in vielen Dingen **überlegen**.	*She is superior to her classmates in many things.*
Dem Schulleiter sind sie eine Erklärung **schuldig.**	*They owe the principal an explanation.*

2. Some common adjectives can be used either with the dative or with **für** + the accusative.

(un)angenehm	*(un)pleasant*	nützlich	*useful*
leicht	*easy*	peinlich	*embarrassing*
(un)möglich	*(im)possible*	(un)wichtig	*(un)important*

Die Aufgabe war *ihm/für ihn* sehr **unangenehm**.	*The task was unpleasant for him.*
Ist es *ihr/für sie* wirklich **möglich**, gleichzeitig an zwei Orten zu sein?	*Is it really possible for her to be in two places at the same time?*
Es war *ihnen/für sie* sehr **wichtig** zu wissen, wer auf ihrer Seite war.	*It was very important for them to know who was on their side.*

B. Adjectives with the genitive

Another group of adjectives normally requires a genitive noun or pronoun when they are used as predicate adjectives. The adjective follows the noun or pronoun. The three adjectives marked with an asterisk are also used with the dative, but with slightly different meanings (see A, above). Like other uses of the genitive, this structure conveys a relatively formal, elevated tone.

*sich *(dat.)* bewusst *conscious of, aware of*	*(un)schuldig *(not) guilty of*
gewiss *certain of, sure of*	*wert *worth, worthy of*
müde *tired of*	

War Snape sich **der Folgen** seiner Taten **bewusst?**

Was Snape aware of the consequences of his actions?

Harry ist sich **seines Sieges** über Durmstrang **gewiss.**

Harry is certain of his victory over Durmstrang.

Hermine war **des Hin- und Herlaufens müde.**

Hermione was tired of running back and forth.

13.5   ADJECTIVES WITH PREPOSITIONAL COMPLEMENTS

1. Some adjectives occur in combination with a complementing prepositional phrase, which may come before or after the adjective. Since the German preposition is often different from what one might expect in English (COMPARE: **sicher *vor*** = *safe **from***), it should be learned along with the adjective to convey the phrase's special meaning.

arm/reich an *(dat.)*   *poor/rich in*
gewöhnt an *(acc.)*   *accustomed to*
interessiert an *(dat.)*   *interested in*

böse auf *(acc.)*   *angry at*
gespannt auf *(acc.)*   *in suspense about*
neidisch auf *(acc.)*   *envious of*
neugierig auf *(acc.)*   *curious about*
stolz auf *(acc.)*   *proud of*
wütend auf *(acc.)*   *furious at*

durstig/hungrig auf *(acc.)* / nach   *thirsty/hungry for*
verrückt auf *(acc.)* /nach   *crazy about (someone)*

abhängig von   *dependent on*
begeistert von   *enthusiastic about*
überzeugt von   *convinced of*

blass vor *(dat.)*   *pale from/with*
sicher vor *(dat.)*   *safe from*

bereit zu   *ready to do*
fähig zu   *capable of (doing)*

Kinder in Deutschland waren genauso **verrückt nach** den Büchern wie in den USA.	*Children in Germany were just as crazy about the books as in the USA.*
Einige Soziologen sind **an** den Gründen dafür **interessiert.**	*Several sociologists are interested in the reasons for this.*

2. Many of these adjectives can also be used with an anticipatory **da**-construction (see 20.2). Note that the **da**-compound is often optional.

Viele Eltern waren **begeistert (davon),** dass ihre Kinder wieder Spaß am Lesen hatten.	*Many parents were thrilled that their children were having fun reading again.*
Aber einige waren **böse (darauf),** dass Shakespeare im Englischunterricht von *Harry Potter* ersetzt wurde.	*But some were angry that Shakespeare was being replaced in English class with* Harry Potter.

13.6 ▶ SUFFIXES THAT FORM ADJECTIVES

Many descriptive adjectives are formed by adding suffixes to noun stems (and sometimes verb stems). Each suffix allows some quality or aspect of the stem word to function descriptively. Knowing these suffixes can help you determine the meanings of adjectives. Keep in mind that these suffixes are part of the adjective, and not endings. Adjectives formed with these suffixes must still be declined with endings according to their grammatical context, as discussed above.

A. The suffixes *-ig, -lich, -isch*

These three suffixes denote *having the quality* expressed by the noun stem. Some nouns used with these suffixes require an umlaut.

1. **-ig** often corresponds to English *-y.*

das Blut	**blutig**	*bloody*
der Hunger	**hungrig**	*hungry*
die Lust	**lustig**	*funny*
der Schatten	**schattig**	*shadowy*
der Schlaf	**schläfrig**	*sleepy*

2. **-lich** indicates that the adjective has the quality or appearance denoted by the noun stem.

der Ärger	**ärgerlich**	*annoying*
der Frieden	**friedlich**	*peaceful*
die Gefahr	**gefährlich**	*dangerous*
die Natur	**natürlich**	*natural*

COMPARE:

der Geist: **geist<u>lich</u>** *spiritual*   **geist<u>ig</u>** *intellectual*

3. **-isch** often corresponds to English *-cal, -ish,* or *-ic*. It is also commonly used with nationalities and religions.

die Chemie	**chemisch**	*chemical*
der Narr	**närrisch**	*foolish*
der Franzose	**französisch**	*French*
der Jude	**jüdisch**	*Jewish*
der Katholik	**katholisch**	*Catholic*

COMPARE:

das Kind:	**kind<u>isch</u>**	*childish*	**kind<u>lich</u>**	*childlike*

B. Other common suffixes

1. **-bar** corresponds to English *-ful, -ible,* or *-able*. It is often added to nouns or verb stems.

der Dank	**dankbar**	*thankful*
die Sicht	**sichtbar**	*visible*
lesen	**lesbar**	*legible*
tragen	**tragbar**	*portable, bearable*
trinken	**trinkbar**	*drinkable*

2. **-(e)n** and **-ern** are used to create adjectives from nouns for materials, such as wood, metal, or cloth. Some of these nouns require an umlaut in the adjective form.[2]

das Glas	**gläsern**	*of glass*	der Stahl	**stählern**	*of steel*
das Holz	**hölzern**	*wooden*	die Wolle	**wollen**	*woolen*
das Silber	**silbern**[3]	*of silver*			

3. **-haft** (*from* **haben**) denotes *having the quality or nature* of the stem noun.

der Meister	**meisterhaft**	*masterful/masterly*
die Fabel	**fabelhaft**	*fabulous*
die Tugend	**tugendhaft**	*virtuous*

4. **-los** indicates a *complete lack* of the quality expressed by the stem. It corresponds to English *-less*.

die Hoffnung	**hoffnungslos**	*hopeless*
die Kraft	**kraftlos**	*powerless*

5. **-reich** and **-voll** mean *full of* the quality expressed by the stem.

die Hilfe	**hilfreich**	*helpful*
die Lehre	**lehrreich**	*instructive*
die Liebe	**liebevoll**	*loving*
der Wert	**wertvoll**	*valuable*

---

[2]With some materials, German speakers often prefer a compound word to an adjective + noun.

ein Glasauge (*instead of* **ein gläsernes Auge**)
ein Holzbein (*instead of* **ein hölzernes Bein**)

[3]But: **silbrig** *silvery*

6. **-sam** sometimes corresponds to English *-some*. It normally indicates a tendency to do the action expressed by a verb or noun stem.

biegen	**biegsam**	*flexible, pliable*
die Mühe	**mühsam**	*tiresome, laborious*
sparen	**sparsam**	*thrifty, frugal*

Wortschatz
gut | schlecht

1. The following adjectives and adverbs describe very positive reactions and emotions. The cues in parentheses are indications of register (formal to informal), and like all such indications, are subjective and highly dependent on social context.

ausgezeichnet *excellent*
erstklassig *first-rate*
fabelhaft *fabulous, marvelous*
fantastisch *fantastic*
genial *brilliant, inspired, ingenious*
glänzend *splendid, magnificent, brilliant* (relatively formal; **glänzend** gespielt)
großartig *splendid, magnificent, wonderful*
herrlich *splendid, magnificent, lovely* (relatively formal)
klasse *great*
prächtig *splendid, magnificent, sumptuous* (formal; often an adverb: gedeiht **prächtig**)
prima *great, first-rate*
toll *fantastic, incredible, terrific* (relatively informal)
vorzüglich *exquisite, superior, excellent* (very formal)
wunderbar *splendid, wonderful, marvelous*

2. The following adjectives and adverbs describe very negative reactions and emotions.

abscheulich *disgusting, revolting, repulsive*
armselig *poor, pitiful, wretched, miserable* (relatively literary)
böse *bad, evil, wicked* (also: *angry*)
entsetzlich, fürchterlich, furchtbar, schrecklich *dreadful, frightful, horrible, awful, terrible*
erbärmlich *pitiful, miserable, wretched* (relatively literary)
gehässig *spiteful, hateful, malicious*
grässlich/grauenhaft *dreadful, ghastly, hideous*
grausig *ghastly, gruesome, horrid*
hässlich *ugly, nasty, hideous*
lächerlich *ridiculous, ludicrous, absurd*
scheußlich *abominable, revolting, foul*
widerlich *disgusting, repugnant, repulsive, nauseating*

Übungen

A **Welche Endung fehlt?** Ergänzen Sie die Adjektive durch die fehlenden Endungen.

1. der jung ____ Nachbar; unser toll ____ Lehrer; ein erstklassig ____ Musiker
2. aus einem voll ____ Glas; aus der leer ____ Flasche; aus warm ____ Milch
3. durch ein groß ____ Feld; durch das hoh ____ Gras; durch tief ____ Wasser
4. trotz der bös____ Mächte; trotz der groß ____ Angst; trotz eines klein ____ Missverständnisses
5. die reich ____ Familien; ihre verwöhnt ____ *(spoiled)* Kinder; gehässig ____ Leute
6. während der lang ____ Nächte; keine warm ____ Nachmittage; herrlich ____ Wintertage
7. sein unsichtbar ____ Buch; ihr nächst ____ Plan; ein ungewöhnlich ____ Spiel

B **Anders ausdrücken.** Beenden Sie die Sätze. Verwenden Sie Adjektive ohne Artikelwörter.

BEISPIEL Der Wein, den er trinkt, ist sehr herb. Er trinkt …
            Er trinkt herben Wein.

1. Das Wetter ist heute fabelhaft. Wir haben heute …
2. Die Blumen in meinem Garten sind sehr schön. In meinem Garten wachsen …
3. Die Leute, bei denen er wohnt, sind sehr freundlich. Er wohnt bei …
4. Der Schnee vor dem Haus ist sehr hoch. Vor dem Haus liegt …
5. Wenn das Wetter schlecht ist, wandern wir nicht. Wir wandern nicht bei …

C **Kluge Sprüche.** Die folgenden Sprüche sind noch nicht ganz richtig. Berichtigen Sie die Sprüche, indem Sie passende Adjektive aus der Liste einsetzen.

BEISPIEL Liebe rostet nicht.
            Alte Liebe rostet nicht.

alt	kurz
geschenkt *(given as a gift)*	still
gut	voll

1. Ein Bauch *(m.; belly)* studiert nicht gern.
2. Rat *(m.; advice)* ist teuer.
3. Lügen haben Beine.
4. Einem Gaul *(m.; horse)* schaut man nicht ins Maul.
5. Wasser sind tief.

D **Nützliche Ausdrücke.** Ergänzen Sie die Ausdrücke durch passende Adjektive aus der Liste.

BEISPIEL Freunde haben
            nette Freunde haben

best-	gut	laut	offen
falsch	hoch	nett	schön
groß	lang	niedrig	zweit-

1. ein Gesicht machen
2. Schulden (debts) machen
3. Menschen kennenlernen
4. einen Nachmittag verbringen
5. mit Stimme schreien
6. in den Jahren sein
7. wegen des Preises kaufen
8. mit Karten spielen
9. eine Note bekommen
10. die Geige spielen
11. aufs Pferd setzen
12. Lärm (noise) machen

E **Ein toller Mensch.** Ersetzen Sie in jedem Satz die Adjektive *gut* und *schön* mit Adjektiven aus dem Wortschatz – positiv oder negativ, wie Sie wollen!

BEISPIEL   Sie schreibt gute Bücher.
*Sie schreibt **geniale** Bücher.*
*Sie schreibt **lächerliche** Bücher.*

1. Sie wohnt jetzt in einem schönen Haus.
2. Sie hat eine gute Fantasie (*imagination*).
3. Man hat gute Filme aus ihren Büchern gemacht.
4. Es gibt gute Parodien von diesen Büchern.
5. Mit ihrem Geld hat sie wohl einen schönen Wagen gekauft.
6. Was ist der schönste Moment in den Büchern?

F **Altersstufen.** Wie geht's weiter? Verwenden Sie Adjektive mit oder ohne Artikelwörter.

BEISPIEL   Mit fünf Jahren spielt man mit ...
Mit fünf Jahren spielt man mit vielen Spielsachen.

1. Mit zehn Jahren freut man sich auf (*acc.*) ...
2. Zwanzig kommt, und man träumt von ...
3. Dreißigjährige hoffen auf (*acc.*) ...
4. Vierzig ist man und plant ...
5. Mit fünfzig Jahren kann man ...
6. Mit sechzig genießt man ...
7. Was hat man mit siebzig schon alles gesehen! Zum Beispiel, ...
8. Achtzig Jahre zählt man und denkt an (*acc.*) ...
9. Wer neunzig wird, freut sich über ...

G **Ein prima Leben.** Für Angelika gibt es immer nur das Beste. Ergänzen Sie die Sätze mit Adjektiven aus dem Wortschatzkasten.

BEISPIEL   Ihre Kleidung kommt direkt aus Paris. Sie trägt _____ Kleidung.
*Sie trägt **Pariser** Kleidung.*

ganz	hoch	holländisch	lila	Paris	prima	Schweizer	teuer

1. Ihr Geld hat sie auf einem _____ Sparkonto in Zürich.
2. Sie trägt Schuhe von _____ Qualität.
3. Für Kleidung gibt sie sehr viel Geld aus. Selbstverständlich trägt sie einen _____ Ledermantel.
4. Der Käse, den sie kauft, kommt aus Holland, denn sie isst _____ Käse besonders gern.

5. Letzte Woche war sie in Frankreich und hat *Die Zauberflöte* in der _____ Oper gesehen.
6. Sie fährt einen _____ BMW.
7. Auf ihren Einkaufstouren reist sie jedes Jahr durch _____ Europa.
8. Angelika führt ein _____ Leben!

H **Ob *viel* oder *wenig*, Graz hat's!** Ergänzen Sie die Endungen.

In der Grazer Altstadt gibt es viel____ sehr gut____ Restaurants. Dort kann man vor allem im Sommer einig____ nett____ Stunden im Freien sitzen und mit Leuten plaudern. Abends sucht man vielleicht am besten einig____ der nicht wenig____ gemütlich____ Studentenkneipen auf, wo eine gut____ Stimmung herrscht (*prevails*). Die viel____ Touristen, die nach Graz kommen, können die Landeshauptstadt der Steiermark mit wenig____ Geld aber viel____ Zeit schon richtig genießen.

I **Alles und ganz.** Machen Sie fünf Aussagen mit **all-** + Possessivpronomen (**mein-**, **dein-** usw.). Dann drücken Sie Ihre Aussagen durch den Gebrauch von **ganz-** anders aus.

BEISPIELE *Ich habe **mein ganzes** Geld für dieses Semester schon ausgegeben.*
__Alle meine__ Freunde sehen Reality-TV.
__Meine ganzen__ Freunde sehen Reality-TV.

J **Dativ oder Genitiv?** Drücken Sie die Sätze durch den Gebrauch von Adjektiven aus dem Wortschatzkasten anders aus. Einige Adjektive müssen Sie mehr als einmal benutzen.

BEISPIEL Dieser Vorschlag hilft den Leuten wenig.
Dieser Vorschlag ist den Leuten nicht sehr nützlich.

(un)bekannt   dankbar   fremd   gewiss   müde   nützlich   (nicht) schuldig   wert

1. Von den finanziellen Schwierigkeiten unseres Nachbarn wussten wir nichts.
2. Der Angeklagte (*defendant*) konnte beweisen, dass er den Mord nicht begangen (*committed*) hatte.
3. Er muss einem Sportgeschäft noch viel Geld zahlen.
4. Wir sind sehr froh, dass du uns geholfen hast.
5. Deine Ausreden (*excuses*) möchten wir uns nicht mehr anhören.
6. Ihr Verständnis für seine Probleme bedeutete ihm viel.
7. An eine solche Arbeitsweise war die Frau nicht gewöhnt.
8. Sie zweifelte nicht an ihrem Erfolg.
9. Sein neuer Roman verdient (*merits*) unsere Aufmerksamkeit.

K **Welche Präposition?** Schreiben Sie Modellsätze mit den folgenden Adjektiven + Präposition.

BEISPIEL interessiert
*Ich bin **an** der europäischen Politik interessiert.*

1. neugierig
2. verrückt

   3. überzeugt
   4. stolz
   5. gewöhnt
   6. begeistert
   7. wütend
   8. gespannt

L **Exportdefizite.** Welche ausländischen Produkte kaufen oder benutzen Sie und Ihre Familie? Machen Sie fünf Aussagen.

BEISPIELE *Wir haben einen japanischen Fernseher.*
Zu Hause essen wir gern holländischen Käse.

M **Was ist das?** Suchen Sie eine passende Aussage aus der zweiten Spalte *(column)*.

BEISPIEL ein schweigsamer Mensch
Er spricht nicht viel.

1. sparsame Menschen	a. Vorsicht!
2. eine friedliche Epoche	b. Das Leben ist immer schön.
3. ein lehrreicher Satz	c. 25 Jahre!
4. ein bissiger Hund	d. Davon kann man etwas lernen.
5. traumhafter Schnee	e. Sie sind sicher nicht faul.
6. eine lustige Person	f. Endlich keine Kriege mehr!
7. ein sportlicher Mensch	g. Wer den Pfennig nicht ehrt ...
8. sorgenlose Kinder	h. Es gibt immer etwas zu lachen.
9. arbeitsame Menschen	i. Er ist fit und gesund.
10. silberne Hochzeit	j. Ja, Pulver *(powder)* bis zu den Knien!

N **Anders ausdrücken.** Wiederholen Sie die neuen Vokabeln in 13.6, dann drücken Sie den Inhalt der Sätze mit Adjektiven anders aus.

BEISPIELE Manche Wörter kann man nicht übersetzen.
*Manche Wörter sind nicht **übersetzbar.***

Meine Eltern sparen viel.
*Meine Eltern sind sehr **sparsam.***

   1. Man kann dieses Radio leicht tragen.
   2. Es hat keinen Sinn, mehr Atomwaffen zu produzieren.
   3. Die Zahl 12 kann man durch 2, 3, 4 und 6 teilen.
   4. Während einer Rezession haben manche Menschen keine Arbeit.
   5. Ein gutes Medikament wirkt sofort.
   6. Die Kuppel *(dome)* vom renovierten Reichstagsgebäude in Berlin ist aus Glas.
   7. Wir fuhren gestern auf einer Bergstraße mit vielen Kurven.
   8. Gedanken kann man nicht sehen, aber man kann sie denken.

Anwendung

A **Alles verrückt!** Vielleicht kennen Sie die Geschichte auf Englisch, die so beginnt: *There was a crooked man and he went a crooked mile.* Erzählen Sie eine solche Geschichte mündlich und mit dem Adjektiv *merkwürdig* oder *lustig,* oder mit einem anderen Adjektiv, das Ihnen besonders gefällt.

> **BEISPIEL** *Es waren einmal ein merkwürdiger Mann und eine merkwürdige Frau. Sie wohnten in einem merkwürdigen Haus und hatten merkwürdige Kinder. Ihre merkwürdigen Kinder gingen in eine merkwürdige Schule, wo sie mit anderen merkwürdigen Kindern spielten. Sie trugen auch ...*

B **Sich etwas genau merken.** Arbeiten Sie mit einer Partnerin/einem Partner. Sie/Er zeigt Ihnen etwa zehn Sekunden lang ein Bild. Was können Sie mit Adjektiven noch genau beschreiben, wenn Sie das Bild nicht mehr sehen?

C **Gute Geschichten, schlechte Geschichten.** Diskutieren Sie mit anderen Leuten im Kurs über die Handlung (*plot*) und Charaktere in einem Buch oder einem Film. Wenn Sie die Bücher von J.K. Rowling kennen, dann können Sie darüber diskutieren – oder wählen Sie eine andere Geschichte (Film oder Buch), die Sie kennen.

- Was ist besonders gut oder schlecht?

- Finden Sie etwas dabei großartig? Oder grausig?

REDEMITTEL	
POSITIV	**NEGATIV**
Ich finde, das Buch ist ...	Nein, das sehe ich ganz anders.
Besonders [schön] finde ich ...	Es gibt zu wenig/wenige ...
Die vielen ... finde ich [genial]	Besonders [grauenhaft] finde ich ...
Mir gefällt/gefallen vor allem ...	Es stört mich, dass ...
Die Szene von ... ist [herrlich]	Die vielen ... finde ich [schrecklich]

D **Ach, die schöne Schweiz!** Wählen Sie ein Land und teilen Sie Ihrer Partnerin/Ihrem Partner mit, welches Land Sie gewählt haben. Ihre Partnerin/Ihr Partner bildet dann vier oder fünf kurze Wortverbindungen mit Adjektiven, die sie/er mit diesem Land assoziiert.

> **BEISPIEL** A: die Schweiz
> B: *hohe Berge, viel weißer Schnee, viele alte Städte, guter Käse, ein schöner Urlaub ... usw.*

E **Freunde.** Beschreiben Sie für jemand eine gute Freundin/einen guten Freund von Ihnen und verwenden Sie dabei so viele Adjektive aus dem Wortschatz wie möglich! Denken Sie an das Aussehen (*appearance*), aber auch an Hobbys, Kleidung, Familie, Meinungen, besondere Talente usw. Wie lang können Sie über sie/ihn sprechen?

Schriftliche Themen

Tipps zum Schreiben	**Making Writing More Vivid with Adjectives**
	A text with just nouns and verbs is like a picture in black and white; adjectives can help turn it into color. With adjectives you can convey *how* you view or react to the persons, things, or events you write about. When beginning these compositions, write the first draft without adjectives. Next, check to see that all articles and nouns are in the proper cases. Then add the adjectives that best describe your topics and situations.

A **Werbung.**   Sie studieren ein Jahr an einer deutschsprachigen Universität und organisieren eine Ferienreise für interessierte Studenten. Sie müssen eine kurze Werbeschrift *(prospectus)* zusammenstellen. Beschreiben Sie das Ferienziel so positiv wie möglich.

BEISPIEL   *Wir fliegen im April nach Menorca! Unser preiswertes Hotel – selbstverständlich mit Vollpension! – liegt an einem traumhaft schönen Strand in der Nähe des sonnigen Städtchens Ciutadella. Tag und Nacht bietet das Hotel ein reiches Angebot an Sport- und Unterhaltungsmöglichkeiten. Auch für seine vorzügliche Küche ist das Hotel weit und breit bekannt ... usw.*

B **Ein merkwürdiger *(odd, strange)* Traum.**   Beschreiben Sie einen merkwürdigen Traum, den Sie einmal hatten. Wenn Sie sich an keinen Ihrer Träume erinnern, können Sie vielleicht einen tollen Traum erfinden.

BEISPIEL   *Einmal hatte ich einen ganz merkwürdigen Traum. Ich fuhr an einem warmen Sommerabend in einem kleinen Boot auf einem dunklen See. Um den See herum waren hohe Berge und im Westen ging die Sonne gerade hinter den Bergen unter—aber die Sonne war grün statt rot. Wie ich nun dort saß, erschien* (appeared) *plötzlich über mir ein riesiger* (gigantic) *schwarzer Vogel mit ... usw.*

C **Bildhaft beschreiben.**   Gehen Sie an einen Ort, der Ihnen gut gefällt. Nehmen Sie Papier und etwas zum Schreiben mit. Beschreiben Sie diesen Ort. Beginnen Sie Ihre Beschreibung mit *einem* Gegenstand an diesem Ort. Erweitern Sie dann Ihr Blickfeld allmählich *(gradually)*, bis Sie in die Ferne blicken. Nennen Sie erst im letzten Satz Ihrer Beschreibung diesen Ort.

BEISPIEL   *An diesem Ort steht ein kleiner Baum mit graugrünen Nadeln. Der Baum ist so groß wie ein erwachsener Mensch und umgeben von einem breiten Rasen. Hinter dem Rasen ragt ein steinernes Haus mit einem hübschen Blumengarten hervor. Vom Haus aus hat man einen Ausblick auf ... usw.*

Zusammenfassung

Rules to Remember

1 Predicate adjectives do not take endings; attributive adjectives require endings.

2 If an adjective is preceded by an article that shows number, case, and gender (**der**-words in all cases, and most cases of **ein**-words), the adjective takes a *weak* ending.

3 If there is no preceding **der**-word or **ein**-word, or if the **ein**-word does not show gender explicitly (masculine nominative singular/neuter nominative and accusative singular), the adjective takes a *strong* ending.

4 Some adjectives take noun complements in the dative and the genitive case; with some adjectives the noun complement precedes the adjective.

5 An adjective can combine with a complementing prepositional phrase to convey a particular meaning.

At a Glance

Adjectives: Weak endings

	Masc.	Fem.	Neut.	Pl.
Nom.			-e	
Acc.				-en
Dat.			-en	
Gen.				

Adjectives: Strong endings

	Masc.	Fem.	Neut.	Pl.
Nom.	-er	-e	-es	-e
Acc.	-en	-e	-es	-e
Dat.	-em	-er	-em	-en
Gen.	-en	-er	-en	-er

Limiting words

Singular

wenig etwas genug viel	• No endings • Subsequent adjectives take strong endings

Plural

ein paar	• No ending • Subsequent adjectives take strong endings
wenige andere einige mehrere viele	• Function like adjectives • Subsequent adjectives take same endings
all-	• Singular: no endings • Plural: strong endings; ending is optional if followed by article or possessive adjective • Articles and possessive adjectives following it are unaffected

zum Beispiel

Mauerfall

Dave Cameron / Alamy

Mauerfall: When the German Democratic Republic opened its borders on November 9, 1989, it meant the fall of two walls: one stretching 1378 kilometers along the border between East and West Germany; and one that ran for 168 kilometers around West Berlin. The latter section, which most non-Germans associate with the **Mauerfall,** formed only a very small part. Since then it has become routine (even cliché) to note that the cultural, political, and economic walls dividing the two states cannot be removed so easily. Since 1989, both West and East have struggled to come to terms with the new reality, and while progress has been made, there has been finger pointing and accusations of exploitation on both sides. Some in the East have thrived, some have left the East in order to secure jobs in the West, and it is still the case that unemployment remains higher in the East than in the West. The result in some circles—especially among older adults in the East—is a kind of **Ostalgie** (*Ost + Nostalgie*) for the former times, which figures in films such as *Sonnenallee* (1999) and *Good Bye Lenin!* (2003).

225

Grammatik

Adverbs convey information about verbs, adjectives, and other adverbs—how or where an activity takes place, for example, or the particular intensity of a modifier—and can take the form of a single word or a phrase, including a prepositional phrase (see 6.1).

14.1   DESCRIPTIVE ADVERBS

1. A descriptive adverb (**das Adverb, -ien**) looks like a descriptive adjective without an ending. When such an adverb modifies a verb, it often indicates *how, in which manner,* or *to what degree* an activity is done.

Am 9. November 1989 tanzten Hunderte von Berlinern **fröhlich** auf der Mauer.	*On November 9, 1989, hundreds of people in Berlin danced happily on top of the wall.*
Es wurde aber **schnell** klar, dass eine Wiedervereinigung nicht so einfach ist.	*But it soon became obvious that reunification isn't so easy.*

2. Descriptive adverbs can modify adjectives.

   COMPARE:

Laute Stimmen und **laute** Musik waren überall zu hören. *(adjectives—with endings—modify the nouns)*	*Loud voices and loud music could be heard everywhere.*
Laut hupende Trabis aus dem Ostteil fuhren in den Westteil der Stadt. *(adverb—with no ending—modifies the adjective)*	*Honking loudly, Trabis[1] from the eastern section drove into the western section of the city.*

3. Adverbs can also modify other adverbs.

Man hatte die Demonstrationen in Leipzig davor **besonders** ängstlich angeschaut.	*One had watched the demonstrations in Leipzig before that with particular worry.*
Aber der Mauerfall selbst ist *erstaunlich* **friedlich** verlaufen.	*But the fall of the wall itself proceeded astonishingly peacefully.*

4. Some adverbs of *manner* have no adjective equivalents.

Ich wäre selber **gern** dort gewesen.	*I would have liked to have been there.*
Ich habe es **kaum** geglaubt.	*I hardly believed it.*

---

[1]**Trabi:** tiny trademark car of the GDR

5. A few descriptive adverbs conveying attitude or reaction are formed by adding the suffix -**erweise** to descriptive adjectives.

bedauerlicherweise *regrettably*	glücklicherweise *fortunately*
dummerweise *foolishly, stupidly*	möglicherweise *possibly*
erstaunlicherweise *amazingly*	überraschenderweise *surprisingly*

Überraschenderweise hörte man von ganz wenigen Störungen oder Problemen gleich nach dem Mauerfall.	*Surprisingly, one heard of very few complications or problems right after the fall of the wall.*
Der wirtschaftliche Aufschwung danach war **bedauerlicherweise** nicht gleich in allen Teilen des Landes.	*The economic recovery afterwards was regrettably not the same in all parts of the country.*

Some descriptive adverbs are formed by adding the suffix -**weise** to nouns.

fallweise *case by case*	stückweise *piece by piece*
paarweise *in pairs*	teilweise *partially*

Die Mauer wurde **stückweise** an Millionen verkauft.	*The wall was sold to millions of people piece by piece.*
Man hat sie an ein paar Stellen **teilweise** stehen lassen, um als Erinnerung zu dienen.	*It was left partially standing in a few places, in order to serve as a reminder.*

14.2 ADVERBS OF TIME

1. Some adverbs of time tell *when* or *how often* an activity occurs. Some examples are:

ab und zu *now and then*	nie *never*
bald *soon*	oft *often*
immer *always*	schon *already*
manchmal *sometimes*	wieder *again*

2. Some adverbs of time indicate *when an activity begins* and are particularly useful for introducing narratives.

anfangs *in the beginning*	einst *once* (past); *some day* (future)
damals *(back) then*	einmal *one time*
eines Abends *one evening* (see R.4.3)	neulich/vor kurzem *recently*
eines Morgens *one morning*	zuerst/zunächst *(at) first*
eines Tages *one day*	

3. Some adverbs of time help establish *sequences within narratives.*

auf einmal/plötzlich *suddenly*	inzwischen/mittlerweile/unterdessen *meanwhile*
bald darauf *soon (thereafter)*	
bis dahin *up until then; by then*	kurz darauf *shortly thereafter*
da/dann *then*	nachher *afterwards*
danach *after that*	später *later*
immer noch *still*	vorher *first, beforehand*

Ich erfuhr davon im Fernsehen, und **kurz darauf** rief ich einen Freund in Deutschland an. **Bis dahin,** sagte er, hatte er nur davon geträumt. Und dann **plötzlich** ist es zur Wirklichkeit geworden.	*I heard about it on TV, and shortly afterwards I called up a friend of mine in Germany. Up until then, he said, he had only dreamed about it. And then suddenly it became a reality.*

4. Some adverbs of time indicate the *conclusion of an activity or narrative.*[2]

am Ende/zum Schluss   *finally, in the end, in conclusion*
endlich   *finally, at long last*
schließlich   *finally, in the final analysis*
seitdem/seither   *(ever) since then, (ever) since that time*
zuletzt   *at last, finally; last*

Seitdem denkt er gern an diese Tage zurück, auch wenn die Wiedervereinigung viele Probleme mit sich gebracht hat.	*Ever since then, he likes to think back on those days, even though reunification has brought with it many problems of its own.*

14.3   ADVERBS OF PLACE

1. Adverbs of place tell *where.* Some common examples are:

anderswo/irgendwo anders   *somewhere else*
da   *there*
(da) drüben   *over there*
hier/dort   *here/there*
innen/außen   *(on the) inside/(on the) outside*
irgendwo   *somewhere, anywhere*

links/rechts   *(on the) left/(on the) right*
nirgends/nirgendwo   *nowhere*
oben/unten   *above/below*
überall   *everywhere*
vorn/hinten   *in front/behind*

„**Drüben**" hatte vor 1989 eine ganz bestimmte Bedeutung.	*Before 1989, "over there" had a very particular meaning.*

2. Some adverbs of place combine with the prefixes **hin-** and **her-** (see R.5.1.) to indicate direction *to* or *from*: **anderswohin** *(to someplace else),* **überallher** *(from everywhere),* **irgendwohin** *(to somewhere/anywhere).*

3. Some adverbs of place are used with the prepositions **nach** and **von** to indicate *to* or *from where.*

nach links/rechts   *to the left/right*
von links/rechts   *from the left/right*
nach oben   *upward, (to go) upstairs*
nach unten   *downward, (to go) downstairs*
nach/von vorn(e)   *to/from the front*
von oben   *from above*
von unten   *from below/beneath*

---

[2]See **Wortschatz** in this chapter for further explanation.

4. The distinction in English between *somewhere* and *anywhere*, which is often clear (e.g., *I must have put it somewhere, but it could be anywhere*) but sometimes quite subtle (e.g., *Did you go anywhere? Did you go somewhere?*) does not correspond neatly with two words in German. German uses **irgendwo(hin)** to refer to generally unspecified or unknown locations or directions (i.e., both *somewhere* and *anywhere*). For references that emphasize a lack of specificity (as in *She could find a job anywhere*), German uses **überall**. Since **überall** can also mean *everywhere*, the context must indicate which meaning is appropriate in a given situation.

*Are you going **anywhere/somewhere**?*	Gehst du **irgendwohin**?
*I know it's here **somewhere**.*	Ich weiß, es ist hier **irgendwo**.
*It could be **anywhere**!*	Es könnte ja **überall** sein!
*I looked for it **everywhere**!*	Ich hab's ja **überall** gesucht!

14.4 POSITION OF ADVERBS AND ADVERBIAL PHRASES

1. When adverbial modifiers express *how, when,* or *where,* the default sequence is to place modifiers of time and place (not including verbal complements of direction or position; see 1.1.C) before modifiers of manner.

                          TIME   PLACE

   Am 9. November 1989 tanzten viele Menschen **stundenlang oben auf der Mauer.**
   On November 9, 1989, many (people) danced for hours up on top of the wall.

           PLACE   MANNER

   Pablo Casals hat **an der Mauer spontan** Cello gespielt.
   Pablo Casals spontaneously played the cello at the wall.

   Keep in mind, however, that in practice a speaker or writer usually includes these modifiers in response to a question or to emphasize them for some other reason, and that the "emphasis rule" trumps the default sequence: The further to the right in the middle field, the greater the emphasis.

2. General time precedes specific time, which is not always the case in English.

         GEN. TIME   SPEC. TIME

   Erst **an dem Abend um 20 Uhr** konnte ich's im Fernsehen anschauen.
   Not until 8 PM that night was I able to see it on TV.

3. German adverbs and adverbial phrases often appear at the beginning of a sentence; they are not set off by a comma, as they often are in English.

Bedauerlicherweise konnte ich nicht dabei sein.	*Regrettably, I wasn't able to be there.*
Seither wünschte ich mir, ich hätte es persönlich erleben können.	*Ever since then, I've wished I could have experienced it personally.*

14.5   ADVERBIAL CONJUNCTIONS

German has a number of adverbs that link sentences or clauses by signaling additional information, explanation, or contrast. They do not affect word order as do coordinating or subordinating conjunctions (see R.2.1 and R.2.3); rather, they normally appear as the first element in a main clause, or take their place in the middle field.

außerdem *moreover, furthermore (additional information)*

daher
darum
deshalb   *therefore, thus, for this/that reason (explanation)*
deswegen
aus diesem Grunde

dennoch   *nevertheless, yet (contrast)*
stattdessen   *instead (contrast)*
trotzdem   *in spite of this/that*

Dank der geöffneten Grenze zwischen Ungarn und Österreich konnten DDR-Bürger auch so in den Westen, und **darum/deshalb** musste etwas geschehen.	*Thanks to the open border between Hungary and Austria, GDR citizens could also get into the West that way, and thus something had to happen.*
Dennoch war es bis zum 9. November 1989 nicht klar, dass die DDR-Regierung den Mauerfall friedlich anerkennen würde.	*Nevertheless, it was not clear until November 9, 1989, that the government of the GDR would recognize the fall of the wall peacefully.*
Man hatte auf einen schnellen Zusammenschluss gehofft, aber **stattdessen** arbeitet man schon seit Jahrzehnten daran.	*People had hoped for a quick fusion, but instead they've been working on it for decades.*

Wortschatz
Ende | Schluss | zuletzt | endlich | schließlich

1. **Am Ende** and **zum Schluss** express the idea of conclusion in general terms and are synonymous in most instances.

Erich Honegger war bis dahin der wichtigste Mann der DDR gewesen, aber **am Ende/zum Schluss** verließen ihn auch seine früheren Freunde.	*Up until then, Erich Honegger had been the most important man in the GDR, but in the end, even his former friends left him.*

2. **Zuletzt** usually introduces the final event in a series.

In Leipzig fanden zuerst kleine Demonstra-
tionen in den Häusern statt, dann in vielen
Kirchen, und **zuletzt** auf dem großen
Augustusplatz.

*In Leipzig, small demonstrations took
place first in homes, then in many
churches, and finally in the large
(open air) Augustus Square.*

3. **Schließlich** and **endlich** can both express the idea that after a considerable period of
time or series of events, something *finally* happens.

Nach den vielen Jahren konnten
Familien **endlich** wieder
zusammenkommen, und
schließlich durfte man reisen,
wohin man wollte.

*After all those years, families were
finally able to get back together
again, and people could finally
travel wherever they wanted to go.*

4. **Schließlich** (like **zuletzt**) can mean *finally* when introducing the last element in a
discourse such as a speech, sermon, or argument; this meaning derives from **schließen**
(to close). **Schließlich** can also mean *in the final analysis* or *after all*.

Schließlich sagte Reagan: „Herr Gorbatschow,
reißen Sie diese Mauer nieder!"[3]

*Finally, Reagan said: "Mr. Gorbachev,
tear down this wall!"*

Dabei haben viele Zuhörer und
Zuschauer gespottet. **Schließlich**
glaubte kein Mensch, dass die
Russen es je zulassen würden.

*Many listeners and viewers scoffed
at that. After all, no one believed
the Russians would ever permit it.*

5. **Endlich,** when stressed, is stronger than **schließlich** and conveys the idea that something has *finally* or *at (long) last* happened.

Aber im November 1989 war es für
die deutsche Einheit **endlich** so weit.

*But in November 1989, the time for
German unity had finally come.*

Übungen

A **Zeitadverbien.** Erzählen Sie etwas über sich und verwenden Sie dabei die folgenden
Adverbien.

BEISPIEL neulich
Neulich habe ich einen guten Film gesehen.

1. ab und zu
2. bisher *(up until now)*
3. stets *(continually, always)*
4. niemals *(never)*
5. endlich
6. kürzlich/vor kurzem *(recently)*

---

[3]Spoken by Ronald Reagan, then president of the USA, in a speech in front of the Brandenburg Gate
in West Berlin on June 12, 1987.

B   **Wie geht es weiter?**   Vervollständigen Sie die Sätze. Verwenden Sie adverbiale Ausdrücke aus dem **Wortschatz**.

BEISPIEL   Wir arbeiteten den ganzen Tag, doch ...
*Wir arbeiteten den ganzen Tag, doch **am Ende** war unser Projekt immer noch nicht fertig.*

1. Wir warten schon seit Stunden, aber jetzt möchte ich ...
2. Die Party wird bis Mitternacht gehen, und ...
3. Wir sollten uns nicht über ihn ärgern. Er hat uns ...
4. Ich habe heute einiges vor. Zuerst muss ich arbeiten, dann muss ich einkaufen, danach muss ich zur Uni, und ...
5. Sie dachte, sie würde das Geld für ein Auto nie auftreiben *(come up with)* können, aber ...

C   **Meinungen.**   Bilden Sie Aussagen mit den folgenden Adverbien.

BEISPIEL   vergebens *(in vain)*
*Ich finde, die meisten Menschen suchen **vergebens** nach Glück.*

1. auswendig *(by heart)*
2. sicherlich *(certainly, for sure)*
3. hoffentlich *(hopefully)*
4. glücklicherweise *(fortunately)*
5. leider *(unfortunately)*
6. zufällig *(by chance)*

D   **Wortstellung der Adverbien.**   Schreiben Sie fünf Sätze, die adverbiale Ausdrücke der Zeit, des Ortes und der Beschreibung enthalten. Schreiben Sie die Sätze noch einmal, indem Sie *einen* adverbialen Ausdruck an eine andere Stelle setzen.

BEISPIEL   Wir gehen oft mit Freunden im Park spazieren.
***Mit Freunden** gehen wir oft im Park spazieren.*

E   **Adverbiale Konjunktionen.**   Machen Sie fünf Aussagen über Aktivitäten, Situationen oder Gedanken und die Folgen *(results)* davon. Verwenden Sie die angegebenen adverbialen Konjunktionen: **aus diesem Grunde, dennoch, deswegen/daher, stattdessen, trotzdem.**

BEISPIELE   *Ich habe für meine Deutschprüfung intensiv gelernt, und **deswegen** werde ich eine gute Note bekommen.*

*Sie hatten sich aus großer Not gerettet, aber **trotzdem** starben die Seeleute am Ende.*

Anwendung

A   **Wann? Wo? Wie?**   Sie und eine Partnerin/ein Partner stellen jeweils drei Listen mit je fünf Adverbien (Wörter und Wortverbindungen) zusammen. Machen Sie erst eine Liste für Zeitadverbien (wann), dann eine für adverbiale Ausdrücke des Ortes (wo/wohin) und eine für adverbiale Ausdrücke der Beschreibung (wie). Tauschen Sie dann Ihre Listen miteinander aus und bilden Sie einige Sätze mit Elementen aus allen drei Listen. Achten Sie auf die richtige Wortstellung und seien Sie so kreativ wie möglich!

B **Es kam aber ganz anders.** Erzählen Sie von einem Ereignis oder Unternehmen *(undertaking)* aus Ihrem Leben, das anders verlief als geplant. Verwenden Sie Zeitadverbien und Adverbien, die Ihre Reaktionen zum Ausdruck bringen.

REDEMITTEL

Einmal wollte ich …　　　　　　　　　Wir konnten aber trotzdem …
Ich habe zuerst gedacht …　　　　　　Glücklicherweise hat niemand gemerkt …
Leider war es so, dass …　　　　　　　Wir mussten dann schließlich …

C **Das mache ich so.** Beschreiben Sie, in welcher zeitlichen Folge Sie etwas machen oder sich auf etwas vorbereiten *(prepare)*.

THEMENVORSCHLÄGE

eine schwere Prüfung　　　　　　　　　eine Wohnung suchen
eine schriftliche Arbeit für einen Kurs　　eine Ferienreise planen
ein Auto suchen und kaufen

BEISPIEL　eine schwere Prüfung
Zuerst frage ich die Professorin, was dabei besonders wichtig ist. Dann lese ich meine Notizen gut durch. Danach wiederhole ich die wichtigsten Kapitel, und zum Schluss überlege ich mir ein paar mögliche Fragen.

D **Wie komme ich … ?** Beschreiben Sie für eine Partnerin/einen Partner, wie man von Punkt A nach Punkt B kommt. Ein paar Vorschläge: von Ihrem Zimmer im Studentenheim zur Mensa; von dem Zimmer, wo Sie jetzt sind, zu der nächsten Toilette. Verwenden Sie dabei so viele von den folgenden Adverbien wie möglich.

nach links • nach oben • geradeaus • nach draußen *(outside)* • da drüben • durch eine Tür • um ein Gebäude • durch ein Zimmer • vorsichtig *(carefully)* • dann • nachher

Schriftliche Themen

Tipps zum Schreiben	**Establishing a Sequence of Events**
	To establish a chronology of events from one sentence or clause to another, you should use adverbs of time. Remember that time expressions normally precede expressions of manner and place and can also begin a sentence. You can also use adverbial conjunctions to establish logical links of explanation or contrast between sentences and clauses.

Der Verlauf eines wichtigen Ereignisses *(event)*.   Berichten Sie über ein wichtiges Ereignis (z.B. eine politische Wende, eine Katastrophe, die Karriere eines berühmten Menschen). Verwenden Sie dabei Adverbien, die den Verlauf und die Folgen davon verdeutlichen.

BEISPIEL   *Im Jahre 1906 ereignete sich in San Francisco ein schreckliches Erdbeben. Anfangs spürte man nur leichte Erschütterungen* (tremors), *aber kurz darauf kam … Und überall sah man …*

B **Aus meinem Leben.**   Erzählen Sie auf ähnliche Weise von einem Erlebnis *(experience)* aus Ihrem eigenen Leben. Wie verlief es? Was waren die Folgen davon?

Zusammenfassung

Rules to Remember

1 A descriptive adverb looks like an adjective without an ending (**schnell, fleißig**).

2 When no emphasis is intended, modifiers of time and place (not including verbal complements of position and direction) usually precede modifiers of manner.

3 When emphasis is intended, that modifier appears as far as possible toward the end of the middle field.

4 A few adverbs (**deshalb, trotzdem,** etc.) function like conjunctions and link thoughts in two separate clauses or sentences.

At a Glance

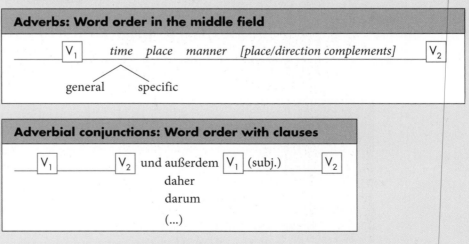

Comparative and superlative

zum Beispiel

Berlin | Bern | Wien

Berlin, Bern, Wien: Though they share similarities in their function as capitals, these cities are three very different urban spaces, and they lend themselves handily to comparisons. The chapter illustrates some of the many differences you'll encounter if you visit them or read about their history: which one is the largest, which has the tallest buildings, or the oldest cafés? We'll start off with a few random facts: Berlin has 1,700 bridges (more than Venice!); Bern has almost 4 miles of arcade-style (covered) sidewalks in its Old City; and Vienna has over 770 miles of bike lanes on its streets. For more information, keep reading!

Grammatik

15.1   COMPARATIVE AND SUPERLATIVE FORMS

A. Regular forms

1. In German, almost all adjectives and adverbs, regardless of length, add **-er** to form the comparative and **-(e)st** to form the superlative.

2. German does *not* have forms equivalent to English *more* and *most* used with adjectives and adverbs of more than two syllables.

wichtig	*important*
wichtig**er**	*more important*
wichtig**st-**	*most important*

3. German does occasionally use the comparative **weniger** + adjective, which corresponds to English *less*.

   Als Touristenziel ist Bern **weniger bekannt**,   *As a tourist destination, Bern is less*
       hat aber viel zu bieten.   *well-known, but it has much to offer.*

4. Adjectives and adverbs ending in **-e** add only an **r** in the comparative, while adjectives and adverbs ending in **-el** or **-er** drop the interior **e** in the comparative, but not in the superlative.

leise *quiet(ly), soft(ly)*	dunkel *dark*	teuer *expensive*
leise**r**	dunk**ler**	teu**rer**
leis**est-**	dunk**elst-**	teu**erst-**

5. If an adjective or adverb ends in **-s, -ß, -x, -z,** or **-haft,** the superlative form always requires **-est** (plus whatever ending is appropriate):

harmlos	*harmless*	harmlos**est-**
süß	*sweet*	süß**est-**
fix	*quick*	fix**est-**
stolz	*proud*	stolz**est-**
boshaft	*malicious*	boshaft**est-**

6. Adjectives and adverbs ending in **-d, -t,** and **-sch** add the **-est** ending if the syllable containing these sounds is stressed (which is always the case if there is only one syllable).

rund	*round*	rund**est**-
gesund	*healthy*	gesund**est**-
sanft	*gentle*	sanft**est**-
berühmt	*famous*	berühmt**est**-
frisch	*fresh*	frisch**est**-

But if they have more than one syllable, and the final syllable is unstressed, they take the **-st** ending:

frustrierend	*frustrating*	frustrierend**st**-
logisch	*logical*	logisch**st**-

7. Adjectives and adverbs ending with a vowel or diphthong can take either **-st** or **-est:**

früh	*early*	früh**st**- / früh**est**-
scheu	*shy*	scheu**st**- / scheu**est**-

B. Umlauted and irregular forms

1. A limited number of short adjectives and adverbs take an umlaut in the comparative and superlative.

alt *old*	älter	ältest-
arm *poor*	ärmer	ärmst-
dumm *dumb*	dümmer	dümmst-
gesund *healthy*	gesünder[1]	gesündest-
grob *coarse, rough*	gröber	gröbst-
hart *hard*	härter	härtest-
jung *young*	jünger	jüngst-
kalt *cold*	kälter	kältest-
klug *smart*	klüger	klügst-
krank *sick*	kränker	kränkst-
kurz *short*	kürzer	kürzest-
lang *long*	länger	längst-
scharf *sharp*	schärfer	schärfst-
schwach *weak*	schwächer	schwächst-
schwarz *black*	schwärzer	schwärzest-
stark *strong*	stärker	stärkst-
warm *warm*	wärmer	wärmst-

Berlin hat eine **lange** Geschichte, und Berns Geschichte ist noch **länger**. Aber Wien ist die **älteste** der drei Städte.	*Berlin has a long history, and Bern's history is even longer. But Vienna is the oldest of the three cities.*

---

[1]**Gesund** can also take the forms **gesunder/gesundest-** (without umlaut), as seen above in A.6, but these are less common than the umlauted forms.

2. Several adjectives have alternate comparative and superlative forms, with or without an umlaut, and both versions are acceptable.

blass *pale*	blässer/blasser	blässest-/blassest-
krumm *crooked, bent*	krümmer/krummer	krümmst-/krummst-
nass *wet*	nässer/nasser	nässest-/nassest-
rot *red*	röter/roter	rötest-/rotest-
schmal *narrow*	schmäler/schmaler	schmälst-/schmalst-

3. Several adjectives and adverbs have an irregular comparative or superlative or use different forms altogether.

bald *soon*	**eher**	**ehest-**
groß *big, large*	**größer**	**größt-**
gut *good; well*	**besser**	**best-**
hoch *high; tall*[2]	**höher**	höchst-
nahe *near*	näher	**nächst-**
viel *much*	**mehr**	meist-

Der Turm vom Berner Münster ist **hoch** (100 m), aber der Turm vom Stephansdom in Wien ist noch **höher** (137 m). Das **höchste** Gebäude in den drei Städten ist der Berliner Fernsehturm (368 m).

The tower of the Bernese cathedral is tall (100 meters), but the tower of St. Stephan's cathedral in Vienna is taller (137 meters). The tallest building in the three cities is the Berlin television tower (368 meters).

4. The adverb **gern** (used with verbs to express the idea of *liking to do something;* see **Wortschatz,** Chapter 9) has a comparative and a superlative derived from the adjective **lieb** (*dear*).

gern   *gladly*   **lieber**   **am liebsten**

In Wien gehe ich **gern** durch die Parks spazieren, ich besuche noch **lieber** die Museen, aber **am liebsten** verbringe ich einen Nachmittag im Café Central.

In Vienna, I like to stroll through the parks, I like even more to visit the museums, but most of all I like to spend an afternoon in Café Central.

---

[2]In English, *tall* can apply to inanimate as well as animate nouns (*a tall mountain; the tallest person*), but German distinguishes between these with different adjectives. For inanimate nouns, *tall* (as well as *high*) is expressed with **hoch**: ein **hoher** Baum, der **höchste** Berg); but with people and animals, **groß** is used: eine **große** Frau, ein **größerer** Mann, die **größte** Person). In colloquial speech, you may also hear **lang** used for *tall*: ein ganz **langer** Kerl (*a really tall guy*).

15.2 USES OF THE COMPARATIVE AND SUPERLATIVE

A. Comparative of adjectives and adverbs

1. Comparative forms of adverbs and predicate adjectives do not take endings.

Man sagt, die Berner sprechen **langsamer** als andere Schweizer. *(adverb)*	*They say that people in Bern speak more slowly than other Swiss.*
Man sagt auch, dass die Stadt etwas **konservativer** ist als andere Schweizer Städte. *(predicate adjective)*	*They also say that the city is somewhat more conservative than other Swiss cities.*

2. Comparative adjectives used attributively, that is, before nouns, take the same weak or strong endings as any other adjective (see 13.2).

Auf jeden Fall hat Bern eine **größere** historische Innenstadt als andere Schweizer Städte.	*In any case, Bern has a larger historic city center than other Swiss cities.*
Aber welche Stadt hat den **älteren** Dom, Bern oder Zürich?	*But which city has the older cathedral, Bern or Zurich?*

3. **Mehr** and **weniger** do not take adjective endings.

Zürich hat zwar **mehr** Einwohner als Bern, aber **weniger** politische Bedeutung.	*Zurich has more inhabitants than Bern, to be sure, but less political significance.*

B. Superlative of adjectives

1. Attributive adjectives in the superlative take the same weak or strong endings as any other adjective (see 13.2).

Wien ist vielleicht nicht die **älteste** Stadt in Österreich.	*Vienna is perhaps not the oldest city in Austria.*
Aber es hat die **ältesten** Kaffeehäuser.	*But it has the oldest cafés.*

2. If the noun after an adjective in the superlative is omitted but understood, the adjective still requires an ending.

Viele europäische Städte haben einen Dom, aber der Stephansdom ist einer der **schönsten**, finde ich.	*Many European cities have a cathedral, but St. Stephen's Cathedral is one of the most beautiful (ones), I think.*

3. The prefix **aller-** *(of all)* can be added to superlatives for emphasis without any comparison necessarily implied.

Gestern habe ich im Wiener Musikverein die **allerschönste** Musik gehört!	*Yesterday I heard the most beautiful music in the Viennese Musikverein!*

4. The superlative adjective **meist-** requires a definite article in situations where English *most* does not.

Die meisten Touristen in Wien wollen Schloss Schönbrunn besichtigen.	*Most tourists in Vienna want to see Schönbrunn Palace.*

C. Superlative of adverbs and predicate adjectives

1. Adverbs in the superlative require the prepositional construction **am [-]sten.**

Von den drei Städten habe ich Berlin **am häufigsten** besucht.	*Of the three cities, I've visited Berlin the most often.*
Welche kennst du **am besten?**	*Which one do you know the best?*

2. When an adverb in the superlative (or comparative, for that matter) modifies an adjective, it takes the normal superlative or comparative forms and is embedded in the noun phrase like any other element:

eine **schön** gestaltete Stadt	*a beautifully laid out city*
die **schöner** gestaltete Stadt	*the more beautifully laid out city*
die **am schönsten** gestaltete Stadt	*the most beautifully laid out city*

The endings used with the adverbs here (**schöner, schönsten**) are independent of the adjective endings (**die ... gestaltete Stadt**), and the use of the **am [-]sten** construction is only permissible because it is a superlative *adverb*, not a superlative *adjective*, that follows the article. Superlative adjectives following an article must use the attributive construction with appropriate endings.

das **häufigste** Problem	*the most frequent/common problem*
das **am häufigsten** erwähnte Problem	*the most frequently/commonly mentioned problem*

3. The **am [-]sten** construction is also used with predicate adjectives in the superlative, as is the attributive construction. Notice that adjectives in the **am [-]sten** construction are never capitalized.

Welche Zeit war für Berlin **am schwersten?**	*Which period was the most difficult for Berlin?*
Welche Zeit war für Berlin **die schwerste?**	*Which period was the most difficult (one) for Berlin?*

4. Whether to use **am [-]sten** or the article + [-]st- construction in the predicate depends on the following rules:

a. If the comparison is reflexive *(at its most _____)*, or if there is no clearly implied noun, the **am [-]sten** construction is used.

In der Weimarer Zeit war Berlin politisch **am brisantesten.**	*During the Weimar period, Berlin was at its most volatile (point) politically.*
Viele würden aber sagen, dass es gleichzeitig **am kreativsten** war.	*But many would say that it was simultaneously at its most creative.*

b. If a noun is implied after the adjective, then either construction is acceptable.

Welche Filmemacher der Weimarer Republik waren **am berühmtesten?**	*Which filmmakers of the Weimar Republic were the most famous?*
Wer von ihnen war **der/die Berühmteste?**	*Which of them was the most famous (one)?*

Notice how the attributive construction requires a gender distinction (**der** Berühmteste/**die** Berühmteste) unlike **am [-]sten.**

c. If a noun is not merely implied but in fact follows the superlative, the article + [-]st-construction must be used.

Fritz Lang, der Regisseur von *Metropolis*, war wohl **der berühmteste** der Weimarer Filmemacher.	*Fritz Lang, the director of* Metropolis, *was probably the most famous of the Weimar filmmakers.*

5. Why is **der Berühmteste** (in 4.b) capitalized, while **der berühmteste** (in 4.c) is not? It all depends on the presence or absence of a reference noun in the sentence. If the context includes such a noun (such as **Filmemacher** in 4.c above), the adjective in an attributive construction is not capitalized; if the context includes no reference noun, as in **Wer von ihnen war ... ?,** then the adjective following the article must be capitalized. This applies to comparative as well as superlative adjectives.

Von den zwei Stadtteilen nach 1945 war Ost-Berlin **der kleinere.**	*Of the two parts of the city after 1945, East Berlin was the smaller (one).*
Aber die Gebäude auf der Ostseite waren **die wichtigsten.**	*But the buildings on the east side were the most important (ones).*

BUT:

Das Tragischste, was Berlin nach dem Krieg passierte, war die Teilung der Stadt durch eine Mauer.	*The most tragic thing that happened to Berlin after the war was the division of the city by means of a wall.*
Beim Mauerfall haben viele eine Rolle gespielt, aber Gorbatschow war wohl **der Wichtigste** dabei.	*Many (people) played a role in bringing down the wall, but Gorbachev was probably the most important man in the process.*

D. Absolute comparatives and superlatives

1. Comparatives can be used with no explicit comparison implied, and in some cases do not translate with a comparative form in English.

Unser Fremdenführer in Bern war ein **älterer** Herr.	*Our tour guide in Bern was an elderly gentleman.*
Er hat einen **längeren** Vortrag über „Bären" und den Namen „Bern" gehalten.	*He gave a lengthy talk about "bears" and the name "Bern."*

Notice that in such cases, the comparative form paradoxically means *less than* the positive form, even if the English equivalent doesn't always make this clear: **ein älterer Mann** is younger than **ein alter Mann,** and **ein längerer Vortrag** shorter than **ein langer Vortrag.**

2. Superlatives can be used to express an intense subjective reaction, with no objective comparison implied.

An klaren Tagen hat man von Bern aus den **schönsten** Blick auf die Alpen.	*On clear days, you have the most beautiful view of the Alps from Bern.*
In den Geschäften findet man die **leckerste** Schokolade.	*In the shops you find the most delicious chocolate.*
Und überall hört man den **interessantesten** Dialekt.	*And everywhere you hear the most interesting dialect.*

E. Comparison with *als*

1. German makes comparisons by combining the comparative with **als** *(than).*

Wien ist **kleiner als** Berlin.	*Vienna is smaller than Berlin.*
Wiens historische Innenstadt ist **besser** erhalten **als** in Berlin.	*Vienna's historic city center is better preserved than in Berlin.*

2. In comparisons, the **als** phrase normally comes after all middle field and V₂ elements, and after infinitive phrases (see 1.1.E and 11.1).

Die Bahnverbindungen nach Berlin sind jetzt viel besser **als** vor 20 Jahren.	*Rail connections to Berlin are much better now than 20 years ago.*
Aber es ist immer noch schneller, Berlin per Flugzeug zu erreichen **als** per Bahn.	*But it's still faster to reach Berlin by plane rather than by train.*

F. Comparisons with *so ... wie, immer, je ... desto*

1. German makes comparisons *without* the comparative by using **(nicht) so ... wie** *([not] as/so . . . as).*

Ist die Lebensqualität in Berlin **so** gut **wie** in Wien? Was meint ihr?	*Is the quality of life as good in Berlin as in Vienna? What do you (both) think?*

This type of comparison can be modified by other adverbs such as **ebenso, genauso, fast, gar nicht so, nicht ganz so, zweimal so,** etc.

Berliner: Wir haben **zweimal so** viele Clubs **wie** ihr!	*We have twice as many clubs as you!*
Wiener: Mag sein. Aber ihr habt **gar nicht so** viele Tage mit Sonnenschein **wie** wir.	*Could be. But you don't have nearly as many days with sunshine as we (do).*
Berliner: Quatsch. Das Wetter ist **genauso** gut in Berlin **wie** bei euch.	*Rubbish. The weather is just as good in Berlin as where you are.*

WIENER: Auf jeden Fall verdient man in Berlin **nicht so** gut **wie** in Wien.

In any case, people don't earn as much in Berlin as in Vienna.

BERLINER: Jaja – „arm aber sexy".[3]

Yeah, yeah, "poor but sexy."

2. German expresses the equivalent of English phrases like *better and better, more and more, faster and faster* with **immer** + an adjective or adverb in the comparative.

Die Mieten in Berlin waren mal spottbillig, aber sie werden jetzt **immer teurer.**

Rental rates in Berlin were ridiculously cheap at one point, but they're becoming more and more expensive.

Günstige Wohnmöglichkeiten sind vor allem für Studenten **immer schwieriger** zu finden.

Reasonable living spaces for students in particular are more and more difficult to find.

3. German uses **je** + the comparative, followed by **desto** or **umso** and another comparative to express comparisons of the type: *"The more, the better"* or *"The bigger they are, the harder they fall."*

Je beliebter der Stadtteil, **desto/umso** höher die Mieten.

The more popular the urban area, the higher the rents.

The **je**-clause in such comparisons is a dependent clause; any conjugated verb in this clause is in final position. The verb in the follow-up clause comes immediately after **desto/umso** + comparative.

Je mehr Leute dort wohnen *wollen*, **desto knapper** werden die Wohnungen.

The more people want to live there, the scarcer apartments will become.

15.3   COMPARISONS WITH COMPOUND ADJECTIVES

German has a number of adjectives that consist of an adverbial modifier and a participial adjective, similar to *good-looking* or *long-standing* in English. English normally treats the first element in a compound adjective as a separate word, and changes it as needed to produce comparative and superlative forms: *better looking, longer-standing.* But the recent spelling reform has made this problematic in German, since "split" forms, as well as "fused" (one-word) forms, are now allowed for many of these compounds.[4]

gut aussehend / gutaussehend	*good-looking*
gut bezahlt / gutbezahlt	*well-paid*
hoch industrialisiert / hochindustrialisiert	*highly industrialized*
hoch qualifiziert / hochqualifiziert	*highly qualified*
tief greifend / tiefgreifend	*profound, extensive*

---

[3]In 2004, the mayor of Berlin, Klaus Wowereit, was famously quoted for saying in a television interview: "Berlin ist arm, aber sexy."

[4]The examples and rules here conform to the 2006 revision of the *Rechtschreibreform*. But the rules for deciding which compound adjectives can be fused or split (or both) are quite detailed, and users are advised to consult the latest edition of *Duden: Die deutsche Rechtschreibung* (Dudenverlag) in the case of compound adjectives besides the ones listed here.

viel sagend / vielsagend	*significant, telling*
viel versprechend / vielversprechend	*promising, encouraging*
weit reichend / weitreichend	*far-reaching, extensive*

1. Producing the comparative and superlative forms of these adjectives depends on the first element in the compound.

   a. If the first element requires no changes other than the addition of -**er** and -**(e)st** to create its comparative and superlative forms (e.g., **weit** ⟶ **weiter/weitest**-), then two different sets of comparative and superlative forms are possible, one with an inflected first element for the split version, and one with an inflected fused form.

Positive:	weit reichend / weitreichend
Comparative:	weit**er** reichend / weitreichend**er**
Superlative:	am weite**sten** reichend / am weitreichend**sten**

Positive:	tief greifend / tiefgreifend
Comparative:	tief**er** greifend / tiefgreifend**er**
Superlative:	am tief**sten** greifend / am tiefgreifend**sten**

   b. If the first element in the compound requires more than just the addition of -**er** or -**(e)st** to form the comparative or superlative (e.g., **gut** ⟶ **besser** or **hoch** ⟶ **höher**), only the split version can be used to form the comparative and superlative forms, with one important exception.

Positive:	gut aussehend / gutaussehend
Comparative:	**besser** aussehend
Superlative:	**am besten** aussehend

Positive:	**hoch** qualifiziert / hochqualifiziert
Comparative:	**höher** qualifiziert
Superlative:	**am höchsten** qualifiziert

   EXCEPTION: When **viel** is the first element in a compound adjective, only the fused version can be used for the comparative and superlative forms.

Positive:	viel sagend / vielsagend
Comparative:	**vielsagender**
Superlative:	**am vielsagendsten**

Positive:	viel versprechend / vielversprechend
Comparative:	**vielversprechender**
Superlative:	**am vielversprechendsten**

Sie hatte einen **noch vielsprechenderen** Vorschlag.	*She had an even more promising suggestion.*

2. Since the first element of a compound adjective is an adverb, not an adjective, it takes no adjective endings when the split form is used. The participial adjective modified by that adverb, however, declines like any other adjective according to its grammatical context (see 13.2). If the fused form is used, it declines just as any other adjective in that context.

Positive:	ein **tief greifender** / **tiefgreifender** Vergleich
Comparative:	ein **tiefer greifender** / **tiefgreifenderer** Vergleich
Superlative:	der **am tiefsten greifende** / **am tiefgreifendste** Vergleich

BUT:

Positive:	eine **viel versprechende** / **vielversprechende** Entwicklung
Comparative:	eine **viel versprechendere** Entwicklung
Superlative:	die **viel versprechendste** Entwicklung

In den letzten Jahren hat Berlin die **vielsprechendsten** Entwicklungen erlebt.	*In recent years, Berlin has experienced the most promising developments.*

15.4 OTHER SUPERLATIVE CONSTRUCTIONS

1. The following superlative adverbs occur frequently in German:

frühestens   *at the earliest*
höchstens   *at (the) most*
meistens/meist   *mostly*
mindestens   *at least (with amounts)*
möglichst   *as . . . as possible*
spätestens   *at the latest*
wenigstens/zumindest   *at (the very) least*

Tipps für einen kurzen Besuch in Wien:

✔ **möglichst** viele Kaffeehäuser besuchen   *visit as many cafés as possible*

✔ **wenigstens** ein- oder zweimal zum Naschmarkt[5] gehen   *go at least once or twice to the Nasch-markt (outdoor marketplace)*

✔ **spätestens** 8 Uhr morgens für die Tour von Schönbrunn losfahren   *leave no later than 8 AM for the tour of Schönbrunn*

✔ **höchstens** ein Stück Sachertorte   *no more than one slice of Sacher torte*

---

[5]The **Naschmarkt** (naschen = *to nibble, snack*) is a large open-air market in the center of Vienna, with over 120 market stands and shops selling fruits, vegetables, candy, meat, fish, and delicacies from around the world. There are also restaurants and bistros offering a variety of international cuisines, and on Saturdays a flea market is added to this colorful mix.

2. The adverb **mindestens** is used with amounts only; **wenigstens** (or **zumindest**) is used in all other contexts.

    COMPARE:

    Gut, Bern ist nicht so aufregend wie Berlin oder Wien, aber du hättest es **mindestens einmal** besuchen können.

    *OK, Bern isn't as exciting as Berlin or Vienna, but you could have visited it **at least once.***

    Gut, Bern ist nicht so aufregend wie Berlin oder Wien, aber du hättest es **wenigstens** einmal **besuchen** können.

    *OK, Bern isn't as exciting as Berlin or Vienna, but you could have **at least visited** it once.*

3. The adverbs **äußerst** (*extremely, most*) and **höchst** (*highly*) add superlative emphasis to the base forms of adjectives, but are used mostly in writing, and sound stilted in spoken language.

    Ich finde es **äußerst** wichtig, alle drei Städte besucht zu haben.

    I think it's extremely important to have visited all three cities.

Wortschatz
Adjektiv → Substantiv

A number of common German feminine nouns ending in **-e** are derived from adjectives. Most of these nouns indicate dimension, size, strength, or personal quality.

breit	*wide, broad*	**die Breite**	*width, breadth*
flach	*flat, level*	**die Fläche**	*surface*
groß	*large, great*	**die Größe**	*size, greatness*
gut	*good*	**die Güte**	*goodness*
hart	*hard*	**die Härte**	*hardness*
hoch	*high*	**die Höhe**	*height*
kalt	*cold*	**die Kälte**	*cold*
kurz	*short*	**die Kürze**	*shortness, brevity*
lang	*long*	**die Länge**	*length*
nah	*near*	**die Nähe**	*nearness, proximity*
schwach	*weak*	**die Schwäche**	*weakness*
stark	*strong*	**die Stärke**	*strength*
tief	*deep*	**die Tiefe**	*depth*
warm	*warm*	**die Wärme**	*warmth*
weit	*far, wide*	**die Weite**	*distance, width*

Übungen

A **Formen üben.** Setzen Sie die Ausdrücke zuerst in den Komparativ, dann in den Superlativ.

BEISPIELE ein alter Freund sein
ein **älterer** Freund sein; **der älteste** Freund sein

schnell laufen
schneller laufen; **am schnellsten** laufen

1. leise sprechen
2. mit großem Interesse zu·hören
3. teure Kleidung tragen
4. starken Kaffee trinken
5. gern bleiben

6. viel verdienen
7. spannende Bücher lesen
8. komplizierte Sudokus lösen (solve)
9. in einem schönen Haus wohnen
10. fleißig arbeiten

B **Aussagen.** Machen Sie wahre Aussagen mit mindestens acht Substantiven aus dem Wortschatz.

BEISPIELE Ich habe eine **Schwäche** für komische Klingeltöne (ring tones).
Das Matterhorn hat eine **Höhe** von mehr als 4.000 Metern.
In der **Kürze** liegt die Würze (spice). (= Brevity is the soul of wit.)

C **Vergleiche.** Machen Sie jeweils **zwei** vergleichende Aussagen, eine mit **(nicht) so … wie** und eine mit **als** + Komparativ. Verwenden Sie die angegebenen Kategorien!

BEISPIEL zwei Tiere
Ein Nilpferd ist **nicht so** groß **wie** ein Elefant.
Eine Spinne hat **mehr** Beine **als** eine Biene.

1. zwei Tiere
2. zwei Automarken (makes of car)
3. zwei Filmschauspieler(innen)
4. zwei Politiker(innen)
5. zwei Sportler(innen)
6. zwei Menschen, die Sie kennen
7. zwei Reality-Shows
8. zwei Kurse, die Sie belegt haben

D **Mehr Vergleiche.** Bilden Sie fünf Aussagen mit attributiven Adjektiven im Komparativ. Verwenden Sie dabei immer ein anderes Verb.

BEISPIELE Wir fahren ein **größeres** Auto als unsere Nachbarn.
Meine Mutter verdient **mehr** Geld als mein Vater.

E **Anders ausdrücken.** Drücken Sie die Sätze anders aus, indem Sie die Adjektive mit Substantiven aus dem **Wortschatz** ersetzen.

> BEISPIEL   Dieser Brunnen *(well)* ist fünf Meter **tief.**
> *Dieser Brunnen hat eine **Tiefe** von fünf Metern.*

1. Er wohnt ganz **nah** bei einem Supermarkt.
2. Das Paket darf höchstens 60 cm **breit** sein.
3. Wir mögen es nicht, wenn es so **kalt** ist.
4. Ein Diamant ist unglaublich **hart.**
5. Wir haben kein Hemd, das für Sie **groß** genug ist.

F **Unsere moderne Welt.** Die Welt ändert sich! Wird sie **immer besser** oder **immer schlechter?** Geben Sie drei Argumente für jeden Standpunkt.

> BEISPIEL   Besser: *Die Menschen leben jetzt immer länger.*
> Schlechter: *Aber immer mehr Menschen werden ärmer.*

G **Sprüche machen.** Wie geht der Spruch weiter?

> BEISPIEL   Je älter ...
> *Je älter man wird, desto mehr weiß man.*

1. Je größer ...
2. Je mehr man ...
3. Je länger ...
4. Je weniger ...
5. ein Spruch, der **Sie** besonders gut charakterisiert
6. ein Spruch, der eine Bekannte oder einen Bekannten von Ihnen treffend *(accurately)* charakterisiert
7. ein Spruch, der Ihre Professorin/Ihren Professor gut charakterisiert

H **Eine Welt der Superlative.** Machen Sie mindestens acht Aussagen. Verwenden Sie kein Adjektiv und kein Adverb mehr als einmal.

> BEISPIELE   *Mount Everest ist **der höchste** Berg der Welt.*
> *Der Jaguar läuft **am schnellsten,** aber der Elefant hat **den längsten** Rüssel (trunk).*

> **THEMENVORSCHLÄGE**
>
> Edelsteine und Metalle: der Diamant, das Gold, das Platin usw.
> Tiere: der Elefant, der Strauß *(ostrich)*, der Walfisch *(whale)* usw.
> Geografie: Berge, Seen, Länder, Flüsse, Meere, Wüsten *(deserts)* usw.

I **Möglichst viele!** Machen Sie mindestens fünf wahre Aussagen mit Adverbien im Superlativ (siehe 15.4).

> BEISPIELE   *Ich stehe am Wochenende **meistens** erst sehr spät auf.*
> *Ich finde, man sollte **mindestens** eine Fremdsprache lernen.*

Anwendung

A **Enthusiastischer Bericht.** Haben Sie kürzlich etwas besonders Schönes oder Interessantes erlebt? Erzählen Sie jemandem davon. Übertreiben *(exaggerate)* Sie ruhig ein bisschen, indem Sie Komparative und Superlative verwenden! Je enthusiastischer, desto besser! (Siehe auch den **Wortschatz.**)

BEISPIEL *Du, ich habe einen ganz interessanten Tag erlebt! Wir waren in den tollsten Geschäften und haben die schönsten Sachen gesehen. Es war alles noch viel schöner, als ich es mir vorher vorgestellt hatte. Das Beste habe ich aber noch gar nicht erwähnt ... usw.*

THEMENVORSCHLÄGE

eine Person	ein Film	eine Reise
ein Ort	eine Party	eine Anschaffung *(purchase)*

B **Eine bessere Alternative.** Versuchen Sie jemanden im Kurs von einem Vorhaben *(plan of action)* abzubringen, indem Sie „eine bessere Alternative" vorschlagen.

THEMENVORSCHLÄGE

ein bestimmtes *(particular)* Auto kaufen
an einer bestimmten Universität studieren
eine bestimmte Fremdsprache lernen
in einer bestimmten Stadt wohnen
eine bestimmte Reise machen
Urlaub in einem bestimmten Land machen
ein Buch über ein bestimmtes Thema schreiben
eine Beziehung mit einer bestimmten Person ein·gehen *(enter into)*

REDEMITTEL

Ich finde ... viel schöner/interessanter/usw. als ...
Ich glaube, das ist nicht so ... wie ...
Würdest du nicht lieber ... ?
Allerdings hat ... schönere/nettere/interessantere/usw. ...
Eigentlich ist ... besser/schöner/usw.

KONZESSIONEN UND GEGENARGUMENTE

Das mag wohl richtig sein, aber ...
Na gut, aber meinst du nicht, dass ... ?
Das schon *(well yes, that's true)*, aber du musst auch ...

C **Wer hat's am besten?**   Sprechen Sie mit einer Partnerin/einem Partner und entscheiden Sie, (1) wer von Ihnen das bessere (oder das schlechtere) Zimmer hat. Vergleichen Sie die Größe der Zimmer, die Nähe zu wichtigen Gebäuden auf dem Campus, die Möbel usw. mit so vielen Komparativen wie möglich; und dann (2) wer von Ihnen dieses Semester die besseren Kurse belegt hat (außer Deutsch, natürlich!). Diskutieren Sie mit Komparativen und Superlativen über die Stärken und Schwächen Ihrer Kurse.

D **Unvergleichlich!**   Sie und eine Partnerin/ein Partner schreiben für sich mindestens fünf Gegenstände und Personen auf, die mit dem gleichen Buchstaben beginnen – aber Sie sagen einander nicht, welchen Buchstaben Sie gewählt haben. Sie schreiben z.B. **Ei, Elvis, Elefant** usw. Ihre Partnerin/Ihr Partner schreibt aber Wörter, die alle mit „M" beginnen: **Maus, München, Milch** usw. Dann lesen Sie einander je ein Wort von der Liste vor (z.B. **Ei + Maus**) und vergleichen die zwei Wörter mit Komparativen. Je verrückter, desto besser!

BEISPIEL   Ei + Maus
Ein Ei schmeckt besser als eine Maus.
Ein Ei ist härter als eine Maus.
Eine Maus hat mehr Haare als ein Ei.

Schriftliche Themen

Tipps zum Schreiben	**Comparing and Contrasting**
	There are various ways to point out similarities and contrasts between objects of comparison. You can alternate between them, sentence by sentence, showing how they match up and how they differ. Or you can deal first with one object at length and then switch to the second object, thereby dividing your paragraph into two contrasting halves. In both methods, you can use the comparative of adjectives and adverbs to measure and contrast two objects with respect to each other. To express your opinion rather than absolute fact, you should indicate this situation with phrases such as **ich finde, meiner Meinung nach,** or **mir scheint es.**

A **Größer oder kleiner?**   Möchten Sie nach dem Studium lieber in einer großen oder in einer kleinen Stadt leben? Führen Sie überzeugende *(convincing)* Argumente an. Verwenden Sie in Ihrem Argument möglichst viele Beispiele von Komparativ und Superlativ.

BEISPIEL   *Ich würde lieber in einer größeren Stadt leben als in der Stadt, in der ich aufgewachsen bin. Bei uns zu Hause gab es wenig zu tun, und in einer größeren Stadt könnte man bessere Restaurants, mehr Clubs, interessantere Leute und besser bezahlende Jobs finden. In einer großen Stadt gibt es mindestens … In einer kleineren Stadt findet man dagegen (on the other hand)…*

B   **Lieber Tierfreund!**   Schreiben Sie eine E-Mail an die Zeitschrift *Der Tierfreund,* in der Sie erzählen, warum sich Ihrer Meinung nach ein bestimmtes Tier (z.B. eine Katze) als Haustier besser eignet *(is suited)* als ein anderes (z.B. ein Hund).

BEISPIEL   *Lieber Tierfreund,*
meiner Meinung nach sind Fische die besten Haustiere, denn sie sind viel ruhiger als Hunde, sie miauen nicht so laut wie Katzen und fressen weniger als die meisten anderen Haustiere. Außerdem (moreover) *sind Fische besonders ... Aus diesem Grunde empfehle ich ... usw.*

C   **Heute und früher.**   Ist Ihr Leben oder das Leben überhaupt im Laufe der letzten Jahre besser, schlechter, einfacher, komplizierter usw. geworden? Begründen Sie Ihre Antwort mit Vergleichen.

BEISPIEL   *Ich glaube, dass es mir im Vergleich zu früher jetzt viel besser geht. Mir macht das Studium mehr Spaß als die Jahre in der Schule und ich lerne interessantere Menschen kennen. Allerdings muss ich jetzt viel intensiver lernen. Im großen und ganzen aber finde ich ... usw.*

Zusammenfassung

Rules to Remember

1   The comparative is formed by adding **-er** to the stem of an adjective or adverb (**klar, klarer**).

2   The superlative is formed by adding **-(e)st** to the stem of an adjective or adverb (**klar-, klarst-**).

3   The comparative and superlative forms of adjectives take adjective endings according to the normal adjective ending rules.

4   Adverbs must use the **am [-]sten** construction in the superlative (**am ältesten**). Predicate adjectives may use this construction as well.

5   Compound adjectives that can be written in split or fused versions form their comparatives and superlatives on the basis of the first element in the compound.

At a Glance

Comparative and superlative: Normal formation			
	Positive	**Comparative**	**Superlative**
Adjective	interessant	interessant**er**	am interessante**sten** der die } interessante**ste** das
Adverb	schnell	schnell**er**	am schnell**sten**

Comparative and superlative: Add umlaut			Optional umlaut
alt	jung	scharf	blass
arm	kalt	schwach	krumm
dumm	klug	schwarz	nass
gesund	krank	stark	rot
grob	kurz	warm	schmal
hart	lang		

Comparative/Superlative: Irregular forms
bald ⟶ **eher/ehest-**
groß ⟶ größer/**größt-**
gut ⟶ **besser/best-**
hoch ⟶ **höher**/höchst-
nahe ⟶ näher/**nächst-**
viel ⟶ **mehr/meist-**

Capitalization

- Reference noun included in context: NO CAPITALIZATION
  Von den drei Hauptstädten ist Bern wohl die **gemütlichste**.

- No reference noun included in context: CAPITALIZATION
  Was ist **das Interessanteste**, was du in Wien und Berlin gesehen hast?

Superlative predicate of adjectives/adverbs: *am [-]sten or (der) [-]st-*		
Adverbs	All contexts	am [-]sten
Adjectives	• Implied noun	am [-]sten *or* der [-]st-
	• No implied noun • Reflexive comparison	am [-]sten
	• Subsequent noun	der [-]st-

Compound adjectives: Comparative and superlative forms		
First element	Comparative form	Superlative form
tief weit	tiefer gehend / tiefgehender weiter reichend / weitreichender	am tiefsten gehend / am tiefgehendsten am weitesten reichend / am weitreichendsten
gut hoch	besser aussehend höher bezahlt	am besten aussehend am höchsten bezahlt
viel	vielsagender	am vielsagendsten

16
Adjectival nouns ▪ Participial modifiers

zum Beispiel

Urlaub

zixia/Alamy

For people who associate Germany, Austria, and Switzerland with an obsession for work and industry, it may come as a surprise to hear how much **Urlaub** (*vacation time*) their workers get. German law provides for six weeks of paid vacation time each year (similar to its neighbors Denmark and France); Austrian workers get a mandated five weeks; and Switzerland gives its workers four weeks a year. (And before you feel sorry for the Swiss, in 2012 voters in Switzerland actually turned down a proposal for two more weeks of federally mandated vacation time.) In Germany, vacation time is closely associated with travel. While Germany itself remains the favorite destination of German tourists, Germans travel more to other countries (per capita) than anyone else in the world. Germany represents about 1% of the world's population, yet manages to make up more than 10% of the world's vacation travel budget, and for decades has been considered the **Reiseweltmeister.** Spain—particularly Spanish islands such as Majorca and Ibiza—is the favorite destination, followed by Italy and Turkey. To find out more about this side of German life, do a Google search of **Deutsche + Mallorca**, and decide for yourself how much this resembles a German version of spring break.

Grammatik

A. Masculine and feminine adjectival nouns

1. Masculine and feminine nouns designating persons are sometimes formed from adjectives or from participles used as adjectives. Such nouns are capitalized and require the same weak or strong endings that they would have as adjectives (see 13.2).

	Masc.	Fem.	Pl. *(preceded/unpreceded)*
Nom.	der Deutsche (ein Deutscher)	die Deutsche (eine Deutsche)	die Deutschen/Deutsche (keine Deutschen)
Acc.	den Deutschen	die Deutsche	die Deutschen/Deutsche
Dat.	dem Deutschen	der Deutschen	den Deutschen/Deutschen
Gen.	des Deutschen	der Deutschen	der Deutschen/Deutscher

Die **Deutschen** reisen sehr gern.	*Germans really like to travel.*
Wenn ein **Deutscher** in Urlaub fährt, ...	*When a German (man) goes on vacation, ...*
Aber wenn eine **Deutsche** in Urlaub fährt, ...	*But when a German (woman) goes on vacation, ...*
Mehr als 10 Millionen **Deutsche** fahren jedes Jahr nach Mallorca.	*More than 10 million Germans travel every year to Majorca.*

2. While many adjectives and participles can be used in this construction, the following adjectival nouns have become the preferred means for certain references:

Adjectives

alt *(old)*	→	**der/die Alte** *(old person)*
blind *(blind)*	→	**der/die Blinde** *(blind person)*
deutsch *(German)*	→	**der/die Deutsche** *(German person)*
fremd *(strange, foreign)*	→	**der/die Fremde** *(foreigner, stranger)*
krank *(sick)*	→	**der/die Kranke** *(sick person)*
tot *(dead)*	→	**der/die Tote** *(dead person)*

Participles (past and present)[1]

angestellt *(employed)*	→	**der/die Angestellte** *(employee)*
bekannt *(well-known)*	→	**der/die Bekannte** *(acquaintance)*

---

[1]See 16.2 on p. 258.

erwachsen (grown)	→	der/die Erwachsene (grown-up, adult)
reisend- (traveling)	→	der/die Reisende (traveler)
studierend- (studying)	→	die Studierenden (students; usually in the plural)
verlobt (engaged)	→	der Verlobte (fiancé)/die Verlobte (fiancée)
verwandt (related)	→	der/die Verwandte (relative)
vorgesetzt (placed in front of)	→	der/die Vorgesetzte (supervisor, superior)

Viele **Reisende** ziehen das eigene Auto vor.	*Many travelers prefer their own car.*
Letztes Jahr sind wir mit **Verwandten** an die Ostsee gefahren.	*Last year we drove with relatives to the Baltic Sea.*

3. In the case of **der Beamte** (*tenured civil servant*), which derives from the participial form **beamtet** (*given permanent civil service status*), only the masculine form functions as an adjectival noun. The feminine singular form (**die Beamtin**) is fixed, and has no endings; the feminine plural form is **Beamtinnen**.

B. Neuter adjectival nouns

1. The adjectival nouns in section A above all refer to people. But adjectives can become neuter nouns as well, referring to ideas, collective concepts, or abstractions. To do so, they combine with neuter articles in the singular (normally definite articles) and take the corresponding adjective endings, or, in contexts where no article is needed, they simply take strong adjective endings. The resulting nouns and noun phrases (for example, **neu**) can translate in various ways into English: *the new, what is new, new things*.

	Neuter	
Nom.	das Neue	Neues
Acc.	das Neue	Neues
Dat.	dem Neuen	Neuem
Gen.	des Neuen	——

Ich erlebe gern **Neues** im Urlaub.	*I like to experience new things on vacation.*
Gerade **das Ungewohnte** ist **das Interessante** im Ausland, finde ich.	*The unfamiliar is precisely what's interesting in a foreign country, I think.*
Aber einige Touristen haben Angst vor **Neuem**.	*But some tourists are scared of new things.*
Natürlich will man immer **das Richtige** machen, aber manchmal ...	*Of course, you always want to do the right thing, but sometimes . . . .*

2. Sometimes neuter nouns are formed using comparative or superlative forms of adjectives (see 15.1).

Wir haben **unser Äußerstes** getan, uns im Urlaub zu entspannen.	*We did our utmost to relax on vacation.*
Wegen der Online-Bewertungen habe ich eigentlich **Besseres** erwartet.	*Because of the online ratings, I was actually expecting better things.*

3. Adjectives following **etwas, nichts, viel,** or **wenig** become neuter nouns with endings. Notice that in some contexts, the English equivalent uses a plural form in place of the German singular.

Nom.	etwas Gutes
Acc.	etwas Gutes
Dat.	etwas Gutem
Gen.	——

Tun Sie was Gutes.

Wir wollten dieses Jahr **etwas Neues** probieren.	*We wanted to try something new this year.*
Unsere Nachbarn meinten, es gibt **nichts Schöneres** als Venedig im Sommer.	*Our neighbors said there's nothing more beautiful than Venice in the summertime.*
Wir haben dort **viel Interessantes** erlebt.	*We experienced a lot of interesting things there.*
Und übers Hotel hatten wir **viel Positives** und nur **wenig Negatives** zu berichten.	*And regarding the hotel, we had lots of positive things and only a few negatives to report.*

4. The adjective **ander-** *(other)* is often used as a neuter adjectival noun, but it is usually not capitalized.

Das Hotelzimmer buchen wir jetzt und **das andere** erledigen wir später.	*We'll book the hotel room now and take care of the other (stuff) later.*

It can also be used with **etwas** in the sense of *something else.*

Noch einmal Schwarzwald? Bitte, machen wir dieses Jahr doch lieber **etwas anderes!**	*The Black Forest again? Please, let's do something else this year!*

5. After the declinable pronoun **alles** *(everything)*, adjective nouns take weak neuter endings.

Nom.	alles Mögliche
Acc.	alles Mögliche
Dat.	allem Möglichen
Gen.	alles Möglichen

In seinem Reiseblog lässt er sich täglich über **alles Mögliche** aus.	*In his travel blog, he rants and raves every day about all sorts of things.*

16.2 ▶ PARTICIPLES AS MODIFIERS

A. Present participle modifiers

The present participle (**das Partizip Präsens**) is formed by adding **-d** to the infinitive; the resulting **-(e)nd** ending corresponds to English *-ing*. A present participle can stand alone to describe actions taking place at the same time as the main verb, or it can function as an attributive adjective (with appropriate endings), or as an adverb.

Lachend liefen die Kinder zum Schwimmbecken.	*The children ran laughing to the pool.*
Ihre Eltern wollten ein paar Tücher auf die **herumstehenden** Liegen legen.	*Their parents wanted to lay a few towels on the lounge chairs standing around.*
Aber die anderen im Hotel hatten die Liegen **überraschend** schnell reserviert.	*But the others in the hotel had reserved the lounge chairs surprisingly fast.*

B. Past participle modifiers

1. Past participles (**das Partizip Perfekt;** see 3.1) occur often as predicate adjectives.

Das Hotel ist im traditionellen Stil **gebaut.**	*The hotel is built in a traditional style.*
Es ist direkt am Strand **gelegen.**	*It's located directly on the beach.*
Leider waren alle Zimmer schon **gebucht.**	*Unfortunately, all the rooms were already booked.*

2. Past participles can also be used attributively to modify nouns.

ein neu **entdecktes** Urlaubsziel	*a newly discovered vacation spot*
das **empfohlene** Hotel	*the recommended hotel*
die schnell **gepackten** Koffer	*the quickly packed suitcases*
unterhaltende Abendprogramme	*entertaining evening programs*
ein im Voraus **gebuchtes** Zimmer	*a room booked in advance*

16.3 ▶ EXTENDED MODIFIERS

A. Extended participial modifiers

1. The last example cited above—**ein im Voraus gebuchtes Zimmer**—illustrates a particularly German syntactic feature: the extended participial modifier (**die erweiterte Partizipialkonstruktion**). Extended participial modifiers consist of a primary modifier in the form of a participle (**gebucht**) preceded by one or more secondary modifiers (**im Voraus**) that modify the participle. English also uses primary and secondary modifiers, but it normally does so by placing the primary modifier after the noun, followed by the secondary modifier (*a room booked in advance*)—though certain combinations

appear in English as they do in German, such as *a newly discovered vacation spot.* German allows longer strings of modifying elements, including prepositional phrases, to precede the participle and the noun, and in doing so creates phrases quite unlike what one would expect in English.

This syntactic feature is normally reserved for formal usage, and the longer the extended modifier, the more formal the tone.

Compare how German and English render the following (actual!) book title, and pay attention to where the information appears with respect to the noun in each version.

eine **Forschungsreise**	*a research trip*
eine ausgeführte **Forschungsreise**	*a research trip undertaken*
eine in den Jahren 1904–06 ausgeführte **Forschungsreise**	*a research trip undertaken in the years 1904–06*
eine im Auftrag der Humboldt-Stiftung in den Jahren 1904–06 ausgeführte **Forschungsreise**[2]	*a research trip undertaken in the years 1904–06 on behalf of the Humboldt Foundation*

Note the following factors:

a. The basic noun phrase (**eine Forschungsreise**) consists of an article and a noun.

b. The adjective ending added to the participial adjective (**ausgeführte**) is dictated by the article (**eine**), regardless of how far the article and the participle are separated from each other, and regardless of any other cases and endings that may appear in the intervening phrases.

c. The modifiers that come between the article (**eine**) and the primary modifier (**ausgeführt**) provide additional information about that modifier—in the case just cited, to explain *when* and *on whose behalf* the trip was *undertaken*. English shows this relationship by placing the primary modifier after the noun, with the secondary modifiers trailing behind it, using virtually the same word order as a relative clause. German reverses that order in these constructions.

d. As a result, extended modifiers are most easily *read*—and they are almost always read, since they appear very rarely in spoken German—by starting with the basic noun phrase and then working backwards, first to the participial adjective and from there sequentially through the modifiers, all the way back to the modifier closest to the article.

Another example, this time showing more typical (and current) journalistic usage[3]:

„Die Nordsee ist **ein für den Urlaub am Meer beliebtes Reiseziel**…"	*"The Baltic Sea is a popular destination for a seaside vacation."*

---

[2]In fact, the complete title of this work is: **Eine** im Auftrag der Humboldt-Stiftung der Königlichen Preussischen Akademie der Wissenschaften zu Berlin in den Jahren 1904–06 ausgeführte **Forschungsreise**.

[3]Source: http://www.ferienhausmiete.de/reise/Nordsee-Ostfriesland-s80.html

> *Core phrase:*   **ein Reiseziel** *(a travel destination)*
> *Primary modifier:*   **beliebt** *(popular, beloved)*
> *Secondary modifiers:*   **für den Urlaub** *(for a vacation)*
>   **am Meer** *(seaside, at the sea)*

2. For English-speaking readers, the juxtaposition of an *article* and a *preposition* is the clearest indication that an extended modifier is present in a German text.

das *vor* zwei Jahren gebaute **Ferienhaus**	*the vacation home built two years ago*
in **einem *am*** Flughafen gemieteten **Auto**	*in a car rented at the airport*

3. A participial modifier may appear with no article in the noun phrase, making it particularly difficult to read for novice readers, since the "signal" of article + preposition is missing.

vom Hotelpersonal völlig ignorierte **Gäste**	*guests (who are) completely ignored by the hotel staff*
kleine über das Jahr verteilte **Kurzurlaube**	*short vacations (that are) spread out over the year*

4. Extended modifiers can also have regular (i.e., nonparticipial) adjectives as the primary modifiers before the noun, though this is less common.

in **einem** für dieses Gebiet *typischen* **Zustand**	*in a condition (that is) typical for this region*

5. As mentioned above, the use of extended modifiers is generally restricted to writing, particularly journalistic prose, academic writing, and legal documents, and the longer the modifier, the more elevated the register. Compare the effect of extended modifiers to more informal, spoken registers while expressing similar information:

INFORMAL: Buchen Sie eine Ferienwohnung in einem Palazzo aus dem 18. Jahrhundert!

MORE FORMAL: Buchen Sie eine Ferienwohnung, die in einem Palazzo aus dem 18. Jahrhundert gelegen ist.

MOST FORMAL: Buchen Sie eine in einem Palazzo aus dem 18. Jahrhundert gelegene Ferienwohung!

B. Extended modifiers with *zu* + present participle

In formal contexts, one finds extended modifiers that make use of the **sein** + **zu** + infinitive structure (see 12.3.D), which translates into an English passive. As part of an extended modifier, the infinitive following **zu** becomes a present participle with appropriate adjective endings, and **sein** disappears.

COMPARE:

Construction with *sein* + *zu*	As an extended modifier
Die Reaktion der Hotelgäste auf die winzigen Zimmer **war zu erwarten.**	Man konnte **die zu erwartende Reaktion** der Hotelgäste in den Online-Bewertungen finden.
The reaction of the hotel guests to the tiny rooms was to be expected.	*One could find the reaction expected of the hotel guests in the online ratings.*

Wortschatz

lernen | erfahren | herausfinden | entdecken | feststellen

1. **Lernen** (see also **Wortschatz,** Chapter 2) means *to acquire knowledge or ability* through study or experience.

Das ganze Semester **lernt** man fleißig, dann will man eine Pause machen.	*You study hard the whole semester, then you want to take a break.*
Nach und nach habe ich **gelernt**, Online-Hotelbewertungen nicht immer zu vertrauen.	*Gradually, I've learned not to trust online hotel ratings all the time.*

2. **Erfahren** means *to learn* or *find out* without any study or searching necessarily implied.

Von meinen Nachbarn habe ich gerade **erfahren**, dass sie morgen nach Ibiza fliegen.	*I've just heard from my neighbors that they're flying to Ibiza tomorrow.*
Hoffentlich **erfahren** meine Kollegen nicht alles, was in Monte Carlo passierte.	*I hope my colleagues don't find out about everything that happened in Monte Carlo.*

3. **Heraus·finden** means *to learn, find out,* or *discover* through effort or inquiry.

Hast du **herausgefunden**, ob das Hotel noch Platz für uns hat?	*Have you found out if the hotel still has room for us?*
Irgendwie müssen wir **herausfinden**, wie man zur Jugendherberge kommt.	*Somehow we've got to figure how to get to the Youth Hostel.*

4. **Entdecken** means *to discover*.

Letzten Sommer haben wir ein wunderbares Hotel in der Züricher Altstadt **entdeckt**.	*Last summer we discovered a wonderful hotel in the historic district of Zurich.*

5. **Fest·stellen** can be used informally to express *to realize*, in the sense of becoming aware of something by means of insight or perception. It also is used more formally to mean *ascertain* or *determine*, i.e., to find out by means of directed effort or inquiry.

Eine Umfrage hat **festgestellt**, was deutsche Touristen im Urlaub am meisten stört:	*A survey has determined what upsets German tourists most on vacation:*
■ ein schmutziges Badezimmer	■ *a dirty bathroom*
■ nicht genug Auswahl beim Frühstücksbuffet	■ *not enough selection at the breakfast buffet*
■ unfreundliches Hotelpersonal[4]	■ *unfriendly hotel staff*
Wir waren schon am Flughafen, als wir **feststellten**, dass wir unsere Pässe vergessen hatten.	*We were already at the airport when we realized that we had forgotten our passports.*

Übungen

A **Adjektiv → Substantiv.** Ergänzen Sie die Sätze durch passende Adjektivsubstantive. Achten Sie dabei auf die Adjektivendungen!

BEISPIEL In unseren Großstädten gibt es viele _____.
In unseren Großstädten gibt es viele **Fremde.**

angestellt   arm   blind   erwachsen   fremd   reich   tot   verliebt *(in love)*
verlobt   verwandt

1. Kennen Sie den Kultfilm „Nacht der lebenden *(living)* _____?"
2. Er hat kürzlich erfahren, dass ein paar seiner _____ aus Deutschland sind.
3. Robin Hood nahm Geld von den _____ und gab es den _____.
4. Wir haben den Schlüssel zum Zimmer von der _____ an der Hotelrezeption geholt.
5. Sie gingen ins Restaurant als _____ und kamen als _____ heraus.
6. Dem _____ half ein netter Junge die Straße überqueren.
7. Solche Bücher gefallen sowohl _____ als auch Kindern.

---

[4] Source: http://www.welt.de/reise/article118807800/Das-Beschwerde-Ranking-der-deutschen-Urlauber.html

B **Anders ausdrücken.** Verwenden Sie Adjektive als Substantive im Neutrum.

BEISPIEL   Er hat etwas gesagt, was sehr gut war.
*Er hat etwas **sehr Gutes** gesagt.*

1. Wir wünschen, dass euch nur gute Dinge passieren.
2. Auf unserer Reise durch die Schweiz haben wir viele interessante Dinge gesehen.
3. Alles, was wichtig ist, wird dir der Chef erklären.
4. Der Politiker spricht von nichts, was neu ist.
5. Die Tagesschau *(evening TV news)* brachte wenige neue Nachrichten.
6. Was machst du jetzt? —Nichts, was besonders wäre.
7. Für sie ist etwas nur schön, wenn es teuer ist.
8. Hoffentlich habe ich mich richtig verhalten.

C **Das passende Verb.** Welche Verben aus dem **Wortschatz** könnte man mit den folgenden Wörtern oder Ausdrücken verwenden?

BEISPIEL   ein neues Videospiel
ein neues Videospiel entdecken

1. etwas Neues über Computer
2. einen Fehler im Softwareprogramm
3. woher der Fehler im Softwareprogramm kommt
4. wo man Computer am günstigsten reparieren lässt
5. dass es meistens zu viel kostet, einen älteren Computer reparieren zu lassen
6. wie man einen Computer selbst repariert

D **Was passt am besten?** Ergänzen Sie die Substantive durch passende Partizipien des Präsens.

BEISPIEL   die Sonne
*die **aufgehende** Sonne*

1. die Temperatur	3. viele Kinder	5. das Schiff
2. ein Wald	4. alle Zuschauer	6. Blumen

E **Länger und noch länger machen.** Erweitern Sie die Ausdrücke in **Übung D** zuerst durch einen adverbialen Ausdruck, dann durch mehrere Wörter.

BEISPIEL   die aufgehende Sonne
*die **am Morgen** aufgehende Sonne*
*die **ganz früh am Morgen im Osten** aufgehende Sonne*

F **Partizip Präsens → Partizip Perfekt.** Nehmen Sie die folgenden Wortverbindungen mit dem Partizip Präsens und bilden Sie Wortverbindungen im Partizip Perfekt.

BEISPIEL   die abfallenden Blätter
*die **abgefallenen** Blätter*

1. ein abbrechender Ast *(branch)*	4. die aufgehende Sonne
2. wachsende Städte	5. ein inspirierender Mensch
3. aussterbende Kulturen	6. eine motivierende Lehrerin

G **Länger machen.**   Erweitern Sie die Wortverbindungen aus **Übung F** (sowohl mit dem Partizip Präsens als auch mit dem Partizip Perfekt) durch weitere Elemente.

BEISPIELE   die abfallenden Blätter
*die **schnell** abfallenden Blätter*

die abgefallenen Blätter
*die **während des Sturms** abgefallenen Blätter*

H **Partizipialkonstruktionen.**   Drücken Sie die Relativkonstruktionen durch Partizipialkonstruktionen (entweder Partizip Präsens oder Partizip Perfekt) anders aus.

BEISPIELE   der Zug, der schnell abfährt
der schnell abfahrende Zug

ein Bus, der schon abgefahren ist
ein schon abgefahrener Bus

1. die Steuern *(taxes),* die dauernd steigen
2. der Preis, der rasch gesunken war
3. der Brief von einer Professorin, die in Dresden arbeitet
4. in einem Auto, das gerade repariert wurde
5. eine Autorin, die von Millionen gelesen wird

I **Erweiterte Partizipialkonstruktionen.**   Analysieren Sie die folgenden Sätze: Wo stehen die Partizipialkonstruktionen? Aus welchen Elementen bestehen sie? Versuchen Sie, einige von den Konstruktionen mit Relativsätzen umzuschreiben.

BEISPIEL   Die in Rostock geborene Langstreckenschwimmerin *(long-distance swimmer)* nimmt den Wettkampf bereits zum fünften Mal in Angriff, Lampenfieber *(jitters)* vor den bis zu neuneinhalb Stunden langen Rennen *(races)* in den Flüssen hat sie deshalb nicht. [Aus: *Der Spiegel*]

Partizipialkonstruktionen: *Die ... Langstreckenschwimmerin/vor den ... Rennen*
Elemente: *in Rostock geborene/bis zu neuneinhalb Stunden lang*
Relativsätze: *Die Langstreckenschwimmerin, die in Rostock geboren ist/vor den Rennen, die bis zu neuneinhalb Stunden lang sind*

1. Endlich rief das seit Jahren brutal unterdrückte *(suppressed)* Volk zur Revolution auf.
2. Der wegen mehrerer Schneelawinen *(avalanches)* vorübergehend *(temporarily)* geschlossene Sankt-Gotthard-Pass soll heute Abend gegen 18 Uhr für den Verkehr wieder freigegeben werden.
3. „[Gregor Samsa] sah, wenn er den Kopf ein wenig hob, seinen gewölbten, braunen, von bogenförmigen Versteifungen geteilten Bauch ...“ [aus Kafkas *Verwandlung*]
4. „Seine vielen, im Vergleich zu seinem sonstigen Umfang kläglich dünnen Beine flimmerten ihm hilflos vor den Augen.“ [aus Kafkas *Verwandlung*]
5. Achtung, Achtung, eine Durchsage! Der Intercity-Zug 511 wird wegen in der Nähe von Prag noch nicht abgeschlossener Gleisreparaturen *(track repairs)* mit zwanzigminütiger Verspätung auf Gleis 7 ankommen.

Anwendung

A **Sind Sie neugierig (curious)?**   Was möchten Sie über Ihre Schule oder Uni herausfinden? Wählen Sie fünf Punkte aus, und bilden Sie damit Sätze. Die anderen in der Gruppe lesen dann ihre Sätze vor. Vielleicht weiß jemand, was Sie wissen wollen!

> **BEISPIEL**   *Ich möchte herausfinden, wie viel Geld die Präsidentin/der Präsident dieser Uni verdient. Ich möchte auch gerne wissen, wo unsere Deutschprofessorin/unser Deutschprofessor geboren und aufgewachsen ist.*

B **Eigene Erfahrungen.**   Was haben Sie in diesem Semester erfahren, herausgefunden, entdeckt oder festgestellt? Machen Sie eine Aussage mit jedem Verb.

> **BEISPIEL**   *Ich habe festgestellt, dass Deutsch nicht immer leicht ist.*

C **Partizipialkonstruktionen im Gebrauch.**   Suchen Sie aus Zeitungen, Zeitschriften oder anderen Quellen *(sources)* drei bis fünf erweiterte Partizipialkonstruktionen heraus. Stellen Sie diese Konstruktionen im Kurs vor.

Schriftliche Themen

<table>
<tr><td>Tipps zum Schreiben</td><td>Using Extended Modifiers
Lengthy extended modifiers are usually found only in very official documents and reports. Shorter extended modifiers, however, can be used to good effect even in less formal writing to avoid short relative clauses that might interrupt the flow of a sentence. From a German point of view, the phrase der von Gleis fünf abfahrende Intercity-Zug is simply more to the point than the relative clause construction der Intercity-Zug, der von Gleis fünf abfährt, particularly when additional information is still to come.</td></tr>
</table>

A **Eine Mitteilung (notification).**   Sie arbeiten für ein Studentenreisebüro und schreiben eine Mitteilung auf Amtsdeutsch *("officialese")* über eine geplante Reise an die Adria *(Adriatic Sea)*, die aus verschiedenen Gründen nicht mehr stattfinden kann.

Eine Ferienreise an die Adria war geplant.
Diese Reise kann nicht mehr stattfinden.
Man konnte nicht alle Hotelzimmer buchen, die nötig waren.
Hinzu *(in addition)* kamen auch einige Schwierigkeiten bei der Buchung des Fluges.
Diese Schwierigkeiten waren unerwartet.
Deswegen hat Ihr Reisebüro die Reise abgesagt *(cancelled)*.
Für die Reise nach Kreta [Griechenland] sind noch einige Plätze frei.
Diese Reise findet auch zu Ostern statt.

B   **Eine Meldung *(announcement)*.**   Schreiben Sie auf Amtsdeutsch eine Meldung über Ihren Deutschkurs oder über Ihre Schule/Universität. Benutzen Sie dabei ruhig ein bisschen Humor.

BEISPIEL   *Unser von allen Studenten bewunderter und geliebter Deutschprofessor wird in Zukunft seinen mit Arbeit überlasteten (overburdened) Studenten keine schweren Prüfungen mehr geben. Er hat außerdem mitgeteilt, dass ... usw.*

Zusammenfassung

Rules to Remember

1   Many adjectives and participles can be capitalized and made into nouns.

2   Masculine adjectival nouns always refer to male persons, female adjectival nouns to female persons, and neuter adjectival nouns to abstractions: **der Reisende** *(traveler, male)*; **die Reisende** *(traveler, female)*; **das Seltsame** *(the strange thing, what's strange, that which is strange)*.

3   Adjectival nouns take the same weak or strong endings they would as adjectives.

4   Present and past participles can function as adjectives: **eine alleinstehende Mutter, der unausgesprochene Wunsch.**

5   Most extended modifiers contain either a present participle or a past participle that stands immediately before the modified noun.

6   The modifiers within an extended modifier construction follow normal word order rules for the middle field, with the participle (functioning as predicate adjective) in final position before the noun: **die von der Professorin korrigierten Arbeiten** *(research papers)*; **der in Wut** *(rage)* **geratene Chef.**

At a Glance

Adjectival nouns: Masculine and feminine

	Masculine	Feminine	Plural
Nom.	der Fremde	die Fremde	die Fremden/Fremde
	(ein Fremder)	(eine Fremde)	(keine Fremden)
Acc.	den Fremden	die Fremde	die Fremden/Fremde
Dat.	dem Fremden	der Fremden	den Fremden/Fremden
Gen.	des Fremden	der Fremden	der Fremden/Fremder

Adjectival nouns: Neuter

Nom.	das Gute	ein Gutes	Gutes
Acc.	das Gute	ein Gutes	Gutes
Dat.	dem Guten	einem Guten	Gutem
Gen.	des Guten	eines Guten	——

etwas, nichts, viel, wenig + adjective

Nom.	etwas Schreckliches
Acc.	etwas Schreckliches
Dat.	etwas Schrecklichem
Gen.	——

alles + adjective

Nom.	alles Denkbare
Acc.	alles Denkbare
Dat.	allem Denkbaren
Gen.	alles Denkbaren

Present participle: Form

infinitive + **d** (+ ending)

17
Personal, indefinite, and demonstrative pronouns

zum Beispiel

Erlkönig

Postcard illustrating the song 'Erlkonig' by Franz Peter Schubert (1797-1828), early 20th century (colour litho), Austrian School, (20th century) / Private Collection / Archives Charmet / The Bridgeman Art Library

"**Erlkönig**" (1782), a ballad by Johann Wolfgang von Goethe (1749–1832) remains one of the best-known poems in German. Working from a translation of a Danish folktale by Johann Gottfried Herder (1744–1803), Goethe wove four distinct narrative voices—that of the narrator, the father, the son, and the *Erlkönig* himself—into a compelling drama. But who (or what) is an *Erlkönig*? Goethe chose to keep that word ambiguous, rather than following the Danish for *elf*, and the glosses here retain that choice. Over the centuries the poem has found its way into cultural expressions on many levels. Various composers have set it to music, the best-known version being that of Franz Schubert (1815), whose rendition has been recorded by Dietrich Fischer-Dieskau, Jessye Norman and many others, and was adapted by Hope Lies Within, a progressive metal band, in 2012. There are also paintings and prints, echoes in literature (Nabokov, Angela Carter), parodies (by Marco Rima, for example, a Swiss stand-up comic), and even an episode of the cable TV series *Boardwalk Empire* (2013).

Erlkönig

Wer reitet° so spät durch Nacht und Wind?   *rides*
Es ist der Vater mit seinem Kind.
Er hat den Knaben° wohl in dem Arm,   *boy*
Er faßt ihn sicher°, er hält ihn warm.   *securely*

Mein Sohn, was birgst° du so bang° dein Gesicht?   *are hiding / anxiously*
Siehst, Vater, du den Erlkönig nicht?
Den Erlenkönig mit Kron'° und Schweif°?   *crown / retinue, train (of*
Mein Sohn, es ist ein Nebelstreif°.   *a robe) / wisp of fog*

Du liebes Kind, komm geh' mit mir!
Gar schöne Spiele spiel ich mit dir,
Manch bunte Blumen sind an dem Strand°,   *beach*
Meine Mutter hat manch gülden Gewand°.   *robe*

Mein Vater, mein Vater, und hörest du nicht,
Was Erlenkönig mir leise° verspricht?   *softly*
Sei ruhig°, bleibe ruhig, mein Kind,   *calm, quiet*
In dürren° Blättern° säuselt° der Wind.   *withered / leaves / rustles*

Willst feiner Knabe du mit mir geh'n?
Meine Töchter sollen dich warten schön,
Meine Töchter führen° den nächtlichen Reihn°   *lead / dance*
Und wiegen° und tanzen und singen dich ein°.   *rock (in one's arms) / sing to sleep*

Mein Vater, mein Vater, und siehst du nicht dort
Erlkönigs Töchter am düsteren° Ort?   *gloomy*
Mein Sohn, mein Sohn, ich seh' es genau:
Es scheinen die alten Weiden° so grau.   *willow trees*

Ich liebe dich, mich reizt° deine schöne Gestalt°, *entices, provokes / form*
Und bist du nicht willig, so brauch ich Gewalt°!   *force, violence*
Mein Vater, mein Vater, jetzt faßt er mich an°,   *grabs*
Erlkönig hat mir ein Leids getan°.   *hurt, harmed*

Dem Vater grauset's°, er reitet geschwind°,   *is horrified / quickly*
Er hält in den Armen das ächzende° Kind,   *moaning*
Erreicht den Hof° mit Mühe und Not°   *farm, courtyard / just barely*
In seinen Armen das Kind war tot.

—Johann Wolfgang von Goethe

Grammatik

A. Forms

Personal pronouns (**das Personalpronomen**, -) have four cases.

	Nom.	**Acc.**	**Dat.**	**Gen.**[1]
1ˢᵗ **person sing.**	ich	mich	mir	(meiner)
2ⁿᵈ **person sing. (familiar)**	du	dich	dir	(deiner)
(formal)	Sie	Sie	Ihnen	(Ihrer)
3ʳᵈ **person sing.**	er	ihn	ihm	(seiner)
	sie	sie	ihr	(ihrer)
	es	es	ihm	(seiner)
1ˢᵗ **person pl.**	wir	uns	uns	(unser)
2ⁿᵈ **person pl. (familiar)**	ihr	euch	euch	(unser)
(formal)	Sie	Sie	Ihnen	(Ihrer)
3ʳᵈ **person pl.**	sie	sie	ihnen	(ihrer)

B. Use

Sie and **du**: *"You can say 'you' to me . . ."* This literal translation of **Sie können gern „du" zu mir sagen**—cited in English by Germans as a joke—points out the lack of distinctions in English for the pronoun *you* compared with German. But the choice of which pronoun to use when addressing a German—**du, ihr,** or **Sie**—is anything but humorous. At best, a mistake here is regarded by Germans as touristic fumbling; at worst, it can be perceived as an ethnic slur. The use of second-person pronouns has shifted over the years in German-speaking countries, often in differing degrees within various subcultures, so that sometimes even native speakers are unsure of what is correct in unfamiliar social contexts. Thus the following guidelines are not exhaustive, but they will point you in the right direction. In any case, it is wise to listen very carefully for native speaker cues and to let a German speaker take the lead in determining the correct form of address in a given situation.

1. **du**

   a. On one level, **du** signals inclusion in a group of social equals, with attendant overtones of affection, intimacy, and solidarity. It is used in this sense with family members, close friends, fellow schoolmates and students (acquainted or not), members of

---

[1]Although genitive case pronoun forms have become archaic, they do form the basis for the possessive adjectives (see 4.4).

a club, or colleagues with whom one has explicitly agreed to use **du.** A special case of this sense is its appropriateness when speaking to God, based on biblical language.

Siehst, Vater, **du** den Erlkönig nicht? *Father, don't you see the Erl-king?*

b. Outside of such contexts, its use connotes condescension. Thus it is considered appropriate when addressing children under 14 or so (as strangers), inanimate objects, and animals. But the same condescension can be perceived as profound rudeness, for example in addressing a store clerk, in contexts where lack of familiarity dictates **Sie** rather than **du.**

Du liebes Kind ... *You dear child . . .*

c. Using **du** correlates in most cases with using a person's first name. A German who states as part of a greeting, **Ich heiße Johann,** is indirectly conveying the message *Let's use "du" with each other.* One shouldn't expect this often from older adults: Germans use first names much more selectively than do Americans, and it is not uncommon for co-workers who have spent years in the same office to remain on a last-name (and therefore **Sie**) basis. In schools, on the other hand, it has become common for teachers to use **Sie** with pupils in the upper grades, while continuing to address them by their first names. University students routinely use **du** and first names with each other; however, beyond the university the social guidelines for **du** are sometimes ambiguous.

2. **ihr**

a. **Ihr** is the plural form of **du,** used when addressing a group consisting of people with whom one would use **du** on an individual basis.

b. If a group is "mixed," comprising people one would address with both **du** and **Sie,** then **ihr** can be used to cover both cases. Since it is both familiar and plural, it avoids the pompousness that **Sie** would convey to friends, as well the inappropriately familiar overtones of a misdirected **du.** This is the pronoun you would use, for example, when addressing a gathering that included your classmates from school (with whom you would use **du** individually and **ihr** in a group) along with their parents (with whom you would most likely use **Sie**).

„Also, ich möchte **euch** alle recht herzlich grüßen und bin sehr froh, dass **ihr** heute Abend ..."

c. **Ihr** can be used instead of **Sie** when referring to people as representatives of a group rather than individuals.

Wie erklärt ihr Eltern euren Kindern ...? *How do you parents explain to your children . . .?*

3. **Sie**

a. **Sie** is used for all social situations in which **du/ihr** would be inappropriate. Thus it is the default mode of address among adults who meet for the first time (beyond university), and conveys a respect for privacy and social position by implying a polite distance.

b. While **Sie** is grammatically plural, it is used to address one person as well as a group. If a distinction must be made (addressing only one person within a group, for example), other cues are necessary, such as mention of the addressee's name or extra-linguistic cues. The plural can be stressed through the addition of **alle.**

Sie wissen **alle,** was ich meine.   *You all know what I mean.*

c. Just as **du** correlates in most cases with first-name use, **Sie** is associated with the last name. As long as a German speaker addresses you as **Frau** _____ or **Herr** _____, the implication is clear: **Wir sind per Sie** *(We should use "Sie" with each other).* In some circles, adults will use first names and **Sie,** perhaps indicating a compromise between relaxed attitudes toward formality and a desire nonetheless for some social distance.

4.   The third-person pronouns **er, sie,** and **es** can refer to persons. However, they also substitute for all **der-, die-,** and **das**-nouns respectively, whether persons or things. Thus, depending upon the noun, **er, sie,** or **es** can all be equivalent to English *it.* (For other uses of **es,** see 20.3.)

Vater, hörst du den Wind?   *Father, do you hear the wind?*
—Ja, ich höre **ihn. Er** säuselt durch die   *—Yes, I hear it. It's rustling through*
  Blätter.   *the leaves.*
Und siehst du die Krone?   *And do you see the crown?*
—Nein, mein Kind, ich sehe **sie** nicht.   *—No, my child, I don't see it.*

5.   Pronouns used after prepositions are subject to the same case rules as nouns (see 6.1-5). However, if a third-person pronoun refers to something other than a person, German generally requires a **da**-construction instead of the preposition + pronoun structure (see 20.1).

COMPARE:

Kennst du Dietrich Fischer-Dieskau[2]?   *Do you know Dietrich*
—Na klar, ich habe viele Aufnahmen   *Fischer-Dieskau?*
  von ihm.   *—Of course. I have many recordings*
                                                of him.

Kennst du seine Aufnahmen von Schuberts   *Are you acquainted with his*
  „Erlkönig"?   *recordings of Schubert's "Erlkönig"?*
—Ja, ich habe zwei **davon.**   *—Yes, I have two of them.*

17.2   **INDEFINITE PRONOUNS**

A. Forms

The following indefinite personal pronouns (**das Indefinitpronomen,** -) are masculine in form, but they refer to persons of either sex. Their possessive is **sein,** their reflexive **sich.** For **jedermann, jemand,** and **niemand,** the relative pronoun is the masculine **der** (see 18.2).

---

[2]Dietrich Fischer-Dieskau (1925–2012) was a German baritone, renowned for his nuanced interpretations of art songs, operas, and oratorios, and for his exceptionally wide repertoire—which included several famous recordings of Schubert's **"Erlkönig"**.

	man *(one)*	**jedermann** *(everyone)*	**jemand** *(someone)*	**niemand** *(no one)*
Nom.	man (einer)	jedermann (jeder)	jemand	niemand
Acc.	(einen)	jedermann (jeden)	jemand(en)	niemand(en)
Dat.	(einem)	jedermann (jedem)	jemand(em)	niemand(em)
Gen.	(_____)	jedermanns (_____)	jemands	niemands

B. Use

1. **Man** is normally used where English uses *one, you, they,* or *people* in general. It often occurs as a substitute for the passive voice (see 12.3.A). **Man** is a subject form only; in other grammatical cases the pronoun forms **einen** (accusative) or **einem** (dative) must be used.

    Man weiß nie, was **einem** passieren kann.　　*You/One never know(s) what can happen to you/one.*

2. When **man** is used in a sentence, it cannot be subsequently replaced by **er.**

    Wenn **man** Schuberts Vertonung hört, versteht **man** (*not:* **er**) den Text noch besser.　　*When you hear Schubert's setting, you understand the text even better.*

3. **Jedermann** (*everyone, everybody*) and **jeder** are interchangeable in general statements, although **jeder** is more common.

    Fast **jedermann/jeder,** der das Lied hört, ist am Ende tief berührt.　　*Almost everyone who hears the song is deeply moved at the end.*

4. When referring to women, German speakers sometimes avoid **jedermann** and instead use **jede** (feminine) with the possessive **ihr-** or the relative pronoun **die.**[3] This makes the reference specific rather than general.

    Jede, *die* es jetzt singt, muss sich an der Aufnahme von Jessye Norman messen.　　*Everyone (i.e., every woman) who sings it now has to measure herself against Jessye Norman's recording.*

5. **Jemand** (*somebody, someone, anybody, anyone*) and **niemand** (*nobody, no one*) can be used with or without endings in the accusative and dative. They take no endings when followed by forms of **anders.**

    Der Vater sagt immer wieder, es gibt **niemand(en)** da.　　*The father says again and again there's no one there.*

    Das Kind spricht mit **niemand(em)** außer dem Vater.　　*The child speaks with no one besides the father.*

    Wie hätte **jemand anders** in dieser Situation gehandelt?　　*How would someone else have acted in this situation?*

---

[3]**Jemand** and **niemand** are also used occasionally with the feminine possessive **ihr-** and the feminine relative pronoun **die** (instead of the masculine **der**).

6. The word **irgend** (*any, some*) is often combined with **jemand** to stress the latter's indefiniteness (compare with **irgendwo** and **irgendwohin**, 14.3).

Kann mir **irgendjemand** erklären, was ein Erlkönig ist?	*Can anyone (at all) explain to me what an "Erl-king" is?*

7. **Irgend** is also used alone and in the following combinations.

Natürlich will der Vater das Kind retten, wenn **irgend** möglich.	*Of course the father wants to save child if at all possible.*
Zuerst muss er das Kind **irgendwie** beruhigen.	*First, he has to calm the child somehow (or other).*
Aber **irgendetwas** sagt uns, dass der Vater nicht ganz recht hat.	*But something (or other) tells us that the father isn't quite right.*
Irgendwann muss er zugeben, dass seine Antworten nicht helfen.	*At some point (or other) he has to admit that his answers aren't helping.*
Und **irgendwo** auf der Strecke ist es dann zu spät.	*And somewhere along the way, it's too late.*

17.3   DEMONSTRATIVE PRONOUNS

A. Forms

The demonstrative pronoun (**das Demonstrativpronomen**, -) is essentially a definite article used as a pronoun. Only the forms of the genitive and the dative plural differ slightly from those of the definite article, and in fact are identical with the relative pronouns (see 18.2).

	Masc.	Fem.	Neut.	Pl.
Nom.	der	die	das	die
Acc.	den	die	das	die
Dat.	dem	der	dem	**denen**
Gen.	**dessen**	**deren**	**dessen**	**deren**

B. Use

1. Demonstrative pronouns are used instead of personal pronouns to indicate stress or emphasis. German speakers often use them when pointing out someone or something, frequently with intonational emphasis or in combination with a strengthening **da** or **hier.**

Papa, siehst du den Mann?	*Daddy, do you see the man?*
—Welchen Mann meinst du?	*—Which man do you mean?*
—**Den hier,** gleich neben uns.	*—This one, right next to us.*
Ich sehe auch seine Töchter. **Die da** hat mit mir gesprochen.	*I see his daughters too. That one there spoke to me.*

2. Demonstratives are also used in informal, colloquial contexts to indicate familiarity with specific persons or things. In such instances, they are often in the front field of a sentence—a position of relative emphasis that is generally inappropriate for pronoun objects unless they are stressed or are accompanied by other elements, such as prepositions (see 1.1.A).

COMPARE:

Hörst du den Mann?	*Do you hear the man?*
—Nein, ich höre **ihn** nicht.	*—No, I don't hear him.*
Hörst du den Mann?	*Do you hear the man?*
—Nein, **den** höre ich nicht.	*—No, [that man] I don't hear.*

BUT:

Kind, was sagen dir die Mädchen?	*Child, what are the girls saying to you?*
—Ich soll mit **denen** tanzen.	*—I'm supposed to dance with them.*

OR:

Kind, was sagen dir die Mädchen?	*Child, what are the girls saying to you?*
—Ich soll mit **ihnen** tanzen.	*—I'm supposed to dance with them.*

3. The genitive demonstratives **dessen** *(his)* and **deren** *(her)* are used mainly to eliminate the ambiguity of **sein** or **ihr** when they could refer to either of two preceding nouns of the same gender. **Dessen** and **deren** refer only to the last previously mentioned masculine noun or feminine noun.

COMPARE:

Beethoven hörte Schubert **sein** neues Lied aufführen.	*Beethoven heard Schubert performing his (Beethoven's? Schubert's?) new song.*
Beethoven hörte Schubert **dessen**[4] neues Lied aufführen.	*Beethoven heard Schubert performing his (Schubert's) new song.*

COMPARE:

Sarah diskutierte mit Lena über **ihre** Interpretation des Gedichts.	*Sarah had a discussion with Lena about her (Sarah's? Lena's?) interpretation of the poem.*
Sarah diskutierte mit Lena über **deren** Interpretation des Gedichts.	*Sarah had a discussion with Lena about her (Lena's) interpretation of the poem.*

---

[4]Literally, **dessen Lied** means *the song of that one,* that is, the latter-mentioned person.

C. The demonstrative *derselbe*

1. The demonstrative pronoun **derselbe** *(the same one[s])* consists of two parts: the first part (**der-/die-/das-**) declines as a definite article, the second part (**selb-**) and any subsequent adjectives take weak adjective endings (see 13.2).

	Masc.	Fem.	Neut.	Pl.
Nom.	derselbe	dieselbe	dasselbe	dieselben
Acc.	denselben	dieselbe	dasselbe	dieselben
Dat.	demselben	derselben	demselben	denselben
Gen.	desselben	derselben	desselben	derselben

Viele Komponisten haben **dasselbe** Gedicht vertont, aber ganz unterschiedliche Lieder geschrieben.

Many composers have set the same poem to music, but have written very different songs.

2. **Derselbe** is used adjectivally (as if it were *article + adjective*) to mean *the very same [X]*. **Der gleiche,** by contrast, means *an [X] that is similar*. Both are declined according to the noun(s) they modify. Strictly speaking, **derselb-** and **der gleich-** are different in meaning: **derselb-** refers to one concrete (often physical) entity (*in the same house*), while **der gleich-** refers to similarity between two or more entities (*wearing the same dress*), including repetitions of words or ideas over time (*he kept saying the same thing*). But colloquially, German speakers often use **derselb-** to cover both meanings. You should be aware of the distinction and observe it at least in writing.

Vater und Sohn reiten auf **demselben** Pferd.

Father and son are riding on the same horse.

Vater und Sohn tragen **den gleichen** Umhang.

Father and son are wearing the same cloak (i.e., the same kind of cloak = multiple cloaks)

BUT:

Vater und Sohn teilen **denselben** Umhang.

Father and son are sharing the same cloak (i.e., one cloak)

Wortschatz
nur | erst | ein ander- | noch ein-

1. **Nur** means *only* in the sense of *that is all there is*.

Er ist **nur** fünf Jahre alt geworden.

He lived only to the age of 5.

Sie haben **nur** ein paar Minuten.

They have only a few minutes.

2. **Erst** means *only* in the sense of *up until now* or *so far* and implies that more is to come.

Schubert war **erst** 18 Jahre alt, als er
Goethes Gedicht vertonte.

*Schubert was only 18 years old when he
set Goethe's poem to music.
(implied: he lived longer)*

Erst can also mean *only* in the sense of *not until.*

Wir haben **erst** gestern vom Liederabend
erfahren.

*We only heard about the song recital
yesterday. / We didn't hear … until
yesterday.*

„Erlkönig" kam **erst** am Ende des
Programms.

*"Erlkönig" didn't come until the end of
the program.*

3. **Ein ander-** and **noch ein-** can both mean *another (an other)*, but **ein ander-** implies *another kind* and **noch ein** *an additional one.*

Die Sängerin hat **ein anderes** Lied
gesungen.

*The singer sang another (different)
song.*

Die Sängerin hat **noch ein** Lied gesungen.

*The singer sang another (additional)
song.*

NOTE: This is an important distinction when asking for more of something to eat
or drink.

Ich hätte gern **noch ein** Glas Wein.

*I'd like another (i.e., **additional**) glass
of wine. (implied: I like it and want
more)*

Ich hätte gern **ein anderes** Glas Wein.

*I'd like another (i.e., **different**) glass
of wine. (implied: I don't like the one
I have)*

Übungen

A **Welches Pronomen passt?**   Ergänzen Sie durch Personalpronomen.

1. Heinz und Heidi brauchen Hilfe und fragen: „Wer hilft _____?"
2. Daniel fühlt sich missverstanden und lamentiert: „Ach, niemand versteht _____.
   Und nur meine Mutter ruft _____ an."
3. Lena ist total begeistert von ihrem neuen Freund: „Er liebt _____ und spricht
   immer nur von _____."
4. Die Kinder fragen: „Wer will mit _____ spielen?"
5. Die Lehrerin fragt: „Kinder, wie geht es _____?"
6. Ich schreibe: „Markus, wir besuchen _____ erst am Wochenende."
7. „Herr Keller, wann kommen _____ uns besuchen?"
8. Ich möchte mit Frau Seidlhofer sprechen: „Frau Seidlhofer, darf ich mit _____
   sprechen?"

B **Situationen: *du, ihr* oder *Sie*?** Welche Anredeform gebrauchen Sie in den folgenden Situationen in einem deutschsprachigen Land?

1. Sie sprechen im Zugabteil *(train compartment)* mit einer Mutter und ihrer kleinen Tochter.
2. Sie sprechen mit einer Verkäuferin im Kaufhaus.
3. Sie sind in ein Studentenheim eingezogen und treffen einige Studentinnen zum ersten Mal.
4. Sie treffen zum ersten Mal die 20-jährige Schwester eines Studienfreundes.
5. Sie spielen Volleyball im Sportverein, aber Sie kennen die anderen Spieler nicht. Es sind Jugendliche und Erwachsene dabei.
6. Sie haben gerade ein wunderbares Liederkonzert gehört, und wollen jetzt der Sängerin gratulieren.
7. Bei einer Party im Studentenwohnheim wollen Sie sich mit einer Studentin unterhalten *(engage in conversation)*, die Sie noch nicht kennen.
8. Sie sprechen mit den Tieren im Tierpark.

C **Fragen.** Beantworten Sie die folgenden Fragen. Ersetzen Sie in Ihren Antworten die **fett** gedruckten Wörter durch Pronomen oder Demonstrativpronomen.

BEISPIEL   Kennen Sie **die Romane von Ian Fleming?**
Ja, ich kenne sie./Ja, die kenne ich.

1. Wie hieß **der erste Star-Trek Film?**
2. Haben Sie **diesen Film** gesehen?
3. Kennen Sie einen James-Bond Film mit **Sean Connery?**
4. Lesen Sie oft **Filmrezensionen** *(film reviews)*?
5. Wie heißt **Ihre Lieblingsband?**
6. Haben Sie **diese Band** im Konzert gesehen?

D **Personalpronomen.** Machen Sie über jeden Gegenstand <u>eine</u> Aussage mit einem Pronomen im Nominativ und <u>eine</u> mit einem Pronomen im Akkusativ.

BEISPIEL   mein Computer
Er ist drei Jahre alt.
*Ich finde **ihn** noch ganz gut.*

1. mein Bett im Studentenwohnheim
2. mein Lieblingshemd
3. meine Armbanduhr
4. mein Handy (das)
5. die Schuhe, die ich im Moment trage
6. mein Studentenwohnheim

E **Was bedeuten diese Sprüche?** Können Sie die Sprichwörter erklären oder anders ausdrücken? Verwenden Sie Strukturen mit **man, jemand** oder **niemand.**

BEISPIEL   Morgenstund' hat Gold im Mund.
Wenn man früh aufsteht, kann man den Tag besser nutzen.

1. Wer im Glashaus sitzt, soll nicht mit Steinen werfen.
2. Es ist noch kein Meister vom Himmel gefallen.
3. In der Kürze liegt die Würze.

4. Kleider machen Leute.
5. Zu viele Köche verderben *(ruin)* den Brei *(porridge)*.
6. Wer die Wahl *(choice)* hat, hat die Qual *(torment)*.

F **Erst oder nur?** Welches Wort passt in die Lücke?

1. Tut mir leid, aber das Essen ist noch nicht fertig. Wir können _____ um zwei essen.
2. Beeile dich doch! Wir haben _____ zwanzig Minuten, bis es zu spät ist!
3. Das Buch gefällt mir überhaupt nicht … Ich habe zwar _____ das erste Kapitel gelesen, aber das hat mir voll gereicht.
4. Was, heute schon ein Test darüber? Aber wir haben doch _____ gestern damit angefangen!
5. Kannst du mir etwas Geld leihen? Ich muss einkaufen und habe _____ zwei Dollar bei mir.

G **Wer ist gemeint?** Ändern Sie die Sätze so, dass klar wird, dass mit dem Possessivpronomen die zuletzt genannte Person gemeint ist.

BEISPIEL   Sie fuhren mit Freunden in ihrem Auto.
            *Sie fuhren mit Freunden in **deren** Auto.*

1. Annette saß mit Monika in ihrem Zimmer.
2. Die Kinder sahen zwei fremde Kinder mit ihrem Spielzeug spielen.
3. Herr Rubin rief seinen Nachbarn an und sprach mit seiner Tochter.
4. Johanna sprach mit ihrer Mutter in ihrem Schlafzimmer.
5. Eberhard sprach mit Detlev über seine Kinder.

H **Ich auch.** Felix macht und erlebt immer dasselbe, was andere machen und erleben. Das sagt er jedenfalls immer. Was sagt er, wenn er Folgendes hört?

BEISPIEL   Sandra hat gute Noten bekommen.
            *Ich habe **dieselben** guten Noten bekommen.*

1. Alexander hat einen dummen Fehler gemacht.
2. Nicole hat ein Lied von Schubert aufgeführt.
3. Micha hat die Frau eines berühmten Schauspielers gesehen.
4. Wir haben heute nette Leute aus Österreich kennengelernt.
5. Das sage ich ja immer.

I **Ein ander- oder noch ein-?** Was sagen Sie in den folgenden Situationen?

BEISPIEL   In der Kleiderabteilung probieren Sie ein Hemd an, aber der Schnitt *(cut)* des Hemdes gefällt Ihnen nicht.
            *Ich möchte bitte **ein anderes** Hemd anprobieren.*

1. Ein Stück Kuchen hat so gut geschmeckt, dass Sie Lust auf ein zweites Stück haben.
2. Sie haben für vier Eintrittskarten für den Liederabend bezahlt, aber nur drei Karten bekommen.
3. Sie wollen in den zoologischen Garten gehen, aber man hat Ihnen eine Karte für das Aquarium gegeben.
4. Ihr Zimmer ist für Sie zu klein geworden.

Anwendung

A   **Das habe ich mitgebracht.**   Bringen Sie etwas (oder ein Foto davon) mit, was Sie im Kurs gern zeigen würden. Erklären Sie anderen Studenten diesen Gegenstand, und stellen Sie Fragen über die Gegenstände anderer Studenten.

> **REDEMITTEL**
>
> Ich möchte dir/euch mein- … zeigen/vorstellen.
> Er/Sie/Es ist/kann …
> Sein-/Ihr- … sind aus Holz/Metall/usw.
> Ich habe ihn/sie/es … bekommen/gekauft/gebaut/usw.
> Hast du auch … ?
> Wie sieht dein … aus? Hast du ihn/sie/es auch dabei?
> Und nun möchte ich dir/euch etwas anderes zeigen.

B   **So macht man das.**   Suchen Sie jemanden im Kurs, der etwas nicht macht oder machen kann, was Sie können. Geben Sie Ihrer Partnerin/Ihrem Partner eine genaue Anleitung *(instruction)* für diese Tätigkeit *(activity)*.

> **THEMENVORSCHLÄGE**
>
> ein Video auf YouTube hochladen *(upload)*   eine App herunterladen *(download)*
> Kleidung/Schuhe online kaufen   ein Videospiel spielen
> eine Reise planen   ein Brettspiel spielen
> eine SMS schicken

C   **Was ist es?**   Jede Partnerin/Jeder Partner macht Aussagen über einen Gegenstand mit passenden **der**-Wörtern, aber sagt nicht direkt, was „es" ist. Die andere Partnerin/Der andere Partner muss erraten, welcher Gegenstand gemeint ist.

BEISPIEL   *Er ist klein. Er ist lang und dünn. Man benutzt ihn zum Schreiben, aber er ist normalerweise nicht aus Holz …*

D   **Könnt ihr mir sagen…?**   Bilden Sie Gruppen mit drei oder mehr Studentinnen und Studenten. Stellen Sie einander Fragen und benutzen Sie dabei die Pronomen *ihr* und *euch* so oft wie möglich.

BEISPIELE   *Wo wohnt ihr? Wie gefällt euch das Leben hier auf dem Campus? Was für Kurse habt ihr dieses Semester belegt?*

Schriftliche Themen

Tipps zum Schreiben	**Using Pronouns in German** Germans generally use the indefinite pronoun **man** instead of the editorial *we* or *you* characteristic of English *(If you want to succeed, you have to . . .)*. Remember, however, that if you use **man** in a sentence, you cannot shift to **er** or to **du/Sie** later on in the same sentence. Keep in mind too that other general reference words that could be used here (such as **jeder** or **jemand**) are masculine, and that German requires consistency in number and gender distinctions. This means that the colloquial English trick of avoiding sexist possessive pronouns *(Everyone has their own goals)* will not work in German, since the only appropriate possessive pronoun for **jeder, jemand,** or **man** is the masculine **sein,** and the pronoun is **er.** If you find this usage awkward or restrictive, you can avoid it by using plural reference words such as **Menschen: Wenn** *Menschen* **erfolgreich sein wollen, müssen** *sie* **fleißig arbeiten.**

A **Kommentar.** Äußern Sie sich im Allgemeinen *(in general)* zu einer Tätigkeit, einer Handlung oder einer Handlungsweise.

	THEMENVORSCHLÄGE
Menschen, die immer ... die Politik einer Regierung Fremdsprachen lernen	gesund/ungesund leben umweltbewusst leben wie man Glück im Leben findet

BEISPIEL *Wer dauernd vorm Fernseher hockt* (colloquial: sits) *und Kartoffelchips isst, lebt ungesund. Aber leben Menschen, die täglich joggen und so ihre Knie ruinieren, auch nicht genauso ungesund? Zwar behauptet man, dass Joggen gesund ist, aber dasselbe könnte man vielleicht auch vom ständigen* (constant) *Fernsehen sagen. Jedenfalls kenne ich niemanden, der sich beim Fernsehen die Knie verletzt hat oder von einem Hund gebissen wurde. Irgendjemand hat einmal geschrieben, dass ... usw.*

B **Das sollte man nicht tun.** Erklären Sie, warum man gewisse Dinge lieber nicht machen soll. Begründen Sie, warum.

BEISPIEL *Ich glaube, man sollte nicht Fallschirm* (parachute) *springen. Wenn jemand aus einem Flugzeug abspringt und der Fallschirm sich nicht öffnet, hat er großes Pech gehabt. Man kann sich auch beim Landen verletzen* (injure) *und ... usw.*

Zusammenfassung

Rules to Remember

1 **Du** (*you,* sing.) and **ihr** (*you,* pl.) are informal; **Sie** (*you,* sing. and pl.) is formal and always takes a plural verb form.

2 The pronouns **er, sie,** and **es** refer to **der-, die-,** and **das**-nouns respectively; **sie** refers to all plural nouns.

3 The pronoun **man** refers to persons in general without gender distinction; its subsequent use in a sentence cannot be replaced by **er. Man** does, however, use **sein** as its possessive pronoun.

4 The demonstrative pronouns **der, die, das,** and **die** are often used instead of the personal pronouns **er, sie, es,** and **sie** when referring to persons and things with which one is familiar.

At a Glance

Personal pronouns					
Singular			**Plural**		
Nom.	**Acc.**	**Dat.**	**Nom.**	**Acc.**	**Dat.**
ich	mich	mir	wir	uns	uns
du	dich	dir	ihr	euch	euch
er	ihn	ihm	sie	sie	ihnen
sie	sie	ihr	Sie	Sie	Ihnen
es	es	ihm			

Indefinite pronouns				
	man	**jedermann**	**jemand**	**niemand**
Nom.	man	jedermann (jeder)	jemand	niemand
Acc.	einen	jedermann (jeden)	jemand(en)	niemand(en)
Dat.	einem	jedermann (jedem)	jemand(em)	niemand(em)
Gen.	_____	jedermanns	jemands	niemands

Demonstrative pronouns

	Masc.	Fem.	Neut.	Pl.
Nom.	der	die	das	die
Acc.	den	die	das	die
Dat.	dem	der	dem	**denen**
Gen.	**dessen**	**deren**	**dessen**	**deren**

Derselbe / dieselbe / dasselbe

	Masc.	Fem.	Neut.	Pl.
Nom.	derselbe	dieselbe	dasselbe	dieselben
Acc.	denselben	dieselbe	dasselbe	dieselben
Dat.	demselben	derselben	demselben	denselben
Gen.	desselben	derselben	desselben	derselben

18

Relative pronouns

zum Beispiel

Krimi

pashabo/Shutterstock.com

Krimi: One finds just as much interest in **Krimis** (short for **Kriminalfilme** and **Kriminalromane,** stories about murder mysteries and crime detection) in Germany, Switzerland, and Austria as in Britain, the USA, Scandinavia, and elsewhere. While the Swiss author Friedrich Glauser (1896–1938) is often considered the first German-language detective story writer, early 19th-century authors such as E.T.A. Hoffmann (*Das Fräulein von Scuderi,*1829) and Adolf Müllner (*Der Kaliber. Aus den Papieren eines Criminalbeamten,* 1828) explored the genre almost two centuries ago, and German-speaking literature has its own versions of Sherlock, Poirot, and Rebus. One of the first (of many) **Kriminalfilme** in German is the classic Weimar film *M—eine Stadt sucht einen Mörder* (1931). German, Swiss, and Austrian TV producers offer a variety of detective programs, notably *Tatort,* a crime show that has been broadcast on Sunday evenings continually since 1970. And of course there's *Cluedo*—a popular German-language adaptation of *Clue,* the murder-mystery board game.

Grammatik

18.1 RELATIVE CLAUSES

Relative clauses (**der Relativsatz, ̈e**), like adjectives and prepositional phrases, are modifiers. What distinguishes them from other modifiers is the inclusion of a conjugated verb; and while it is true that a relative clause can provide more descriptive information than adjectives and adverbial phrases because of its potential length, it is primarily the verb itself that makes a relative clause necessary to convey certain information.

COMPARE:

die Frau

die **junge** Frau *(the new information is expressed with an adjective)*

die Frau **mit zwei Kindern** *(the new information involves a noun, hence a phrase is necessary)*

die Frau, **die bei der Polizei arbeitet** *(the new information revolves around a verb, and thus requires a relative clause)*

18.2 RELATIVE PRONOUNS

A. Forms

A relative clause in German is introduced by a pronoun (**das Relativpronomen, -**) that shows number, gender, and case. The relative pronouns are nearly identical in form to the definite articles, except for the dative plural and the genitive forms;[1] they are in fact identical to the demonstrative pronouns (see 17.3).

	Masc.	Fem.	Neut.	Pl.
Nom.	der	die	das	die
Acc.	den	die	das	die
Dat.	dem	der	dem	**denen**
Gen.	**dessen**	**deren**	**dessen**	**deren**

---

[1]German sometimes uses the declined forms of **welch-** as relative pronouns to avoid repetition: **Ich meine die, welche** (instead of another **die**) **noch nichts gesagt haben.** But this usage is relatively rare, especially in current spoken German.

B. Use

1. Relative clauses provide information about the preceding clause and usually about a specific noun or pronoun in that clause, called the *antecedent*.

*That's the man **who** <u>is investigating this case.</u>*	(**who** refers to the antecedent noun "*man*")
*Where is the knife **that** <u>was on the table</u>?*	(**that** refers to the antecedent noun "*knife*")
*The inspector worked tirelessly with those **who** <u>needed her help</u>.*	(**who** refers to the antecedent demonstrative pronoun "*those*")

    In German, the bond between the relative pronoun and its antecedent consists of *number* and *gender*; the relative pronoun must show whether the antecedent is plural or singular, and, if singular, whether it is masculine, feminine, or neuter.

Das ist der Mann, **der** *<u>in diesem Fall ermittelt</u>*.	(**der** reflects the masculine singular **Mann**)
Wo ist das Messer, **das** *<u>auf dem Tisch war</u>*?	(**das** reflects the neuter singular **Messer**)
Die Kommissarin arbeitete unermüdlich mit denen, **die** *<u>ihre Hilfe benötigten</u>*.	(**die** reflects the plural **denen**)

    If there are multiple antecedents separated by **oder,** the relative pronoun takes the number and gender of the final antecedent.

War es **der Mann** oder **die Frau,** *die* ihn angelogen hat?	*Was it the man or the woman who lied to him?*

2. But *number* and *gender* provide only part of the information that determines which relative pronoun should be used. The additional factor is *case,* and here it is the relative clause itself, rather than the antecedent, that is decisive: *the case of the relative pronoun depends on its grammatical function within its own clause, not on the case of the antecedent.* The relative pronoun may be the subject (as in all the examples above), or a direct or indirect object, or the object of a preposition, or a genitive, and its case must indicate that function. German relative pronouns are very precise, and English speakers must be careful to avoid the common mistake of defaulting to **das**—a handy translation of English *that*—as an all-purpose connector.

3. The examples in the chart on page 287 show how antecedent and grammatical function determine which relative pronoun is correct in a given context. The "Relative clause" column shows the forms for each case of the three genders and the plural: N (nominative), A (accusative), D (dative), G (genitive). The "Function" column makes use of demonstrative pronouns (which are identical to relative pronouns, as stated above) to show how each pronoun would appear in a main clause to serve that particular function.

Antecedent	Relative clause	Function of relative pronoun
ein Mann, …[2]	N: **der** in München lebte A: **den** jemand erschossen hat D: **dem** man nicht vertrauen kann G: **dessen** Mord untersucht wird	*subject:* **Der** lebte in München. *direct object:* Jemand hat **den** erschossen. *dative object of* **vertrauen**: Man kann **dem** nicht vertrauen. **Mord** *is the subject, and* **dessen** *indicates possession (whose):* **Sein** Mord wird untersucht.
eine Frau, …	N: **die** aus Thailand kommt A: für **die** es viele Probleme gibt D: von **der** man nicht viel weiß G: **deren** Kind in Gefahr (*danger*) ist	*subject:* **Die** kommt aus Thailand. *accusative object of* **für**: Es gibt viele Probleme für **die**. *dative object of* **von**: Man weiß nicht viel von **der**. *genitive (possession):* **Ihr** Kind ist in Gefahr.
ein Thema, …	N: **das** für viele unbequem ist A: **das** man besprechen sollte D: vor **dem** die Autoren nicht zurückschrecken (*shy away*) G: **dessen** Wichtigkeit klar wird	*subject:* **Das** ist für viele unbequem. *direct object:* Man sollte **das** besprechen. *dative object of* **vor**: Die Autoren schrecken vor **dem** nicht zurück. *genitive (possession):* **Seine** (*its*) Wichtigkeit wird klar.
viele Fragen, …	N: **die** hier auftauchen (*emerge*) A: **die** man sich stellen muss D: mit **denen** die Sendung sich beschäftigt (*deals*) G: **deren** Bedeutung sich entfaltet (*unfolds, develops*)	*subject:* **Die** tauchen hier auf. *direct object:* **Die** muss man sich stellen. *dative object of* **mit**: Die Sendung beschäftigt sich mit **denen**. *genitive (possession):* **Ihre** (*their*) Bedeutung entfaltet sich.

4. The examples above demonstrate two important structural features of relative clauses: first, the conjugated verb (V_1) moves to the end of the clause, as it normally does in subordinate clauses; and second, relative clauses are set off from other clauses by commas. Notice, too, that relative clauses are placed as close as possible to their antecedents; in most cases, the only intervening elements are V_2 structures (modal infinitives, past participles) and separated verb prefixes that would sound awkward if left dangling by themselves.

---

[2]The examples in this chart derive from the 332nd episode of *Tatort* from 1995 (its 25th anniversary year), entitled *Frau Bu lacht*. The episode won widespread acclaim from film and TV critics for its unsettling questions about child abuse and exploitation in Germany. Christian Buß, writing in *Spiegel online*, called it a *Meisterstück*: "Viele halten den Krimi für den besten 'Tatort' aller Zeiten" (*Spiegel online*, October 25, 2013).

Hast du die **Folge** gesehen, von **der** ich dir gerade erzählte?	*Did you see the episode I just told you about?*
Tatort fängt mit einem **Bild** an, **das** sich seit 40 Jahren nicht verändert hat.	*Tatort begins with an image that hasn't changed in 40 years.*

5. Relative pronoun or no relative pronoun? The difference between the German and the English in the two examples above points to a recurrent problem for English speakers. Because English allows the relative pronoun in a clause to be dropped if it functions as an object, English speakers sometimes forget to include relative pronouns in German. In other words, English speakers who might say *the book **about which** I told you*, or (more likely), *the book **that** I told you **about***, can just as well say, *the book I told you **about***, and hardly notice that the relative pronoun has evaporated into thin air. In German, however, relative pronouns *must* be included, whether subject or object.

… die Folge, **die** Sherlocks Tod darstellt.	*… the episode that depicts Sherlock's death.*
… die Folge, **die** wir immer wieder angeschaut haben.	*… the episode (that) we watched again and again.*
die Folge, von **der** ich dir erzählte, …	*… the episode (that) I was telling you about.*

To take another example, in a sentence such as *What's in the text message he sent them?* the clause *he sent them* consists of a Subject–Verb–Indirect Object structure, with a dropped direct-object pronoun. In the German equivalent of that sentence, that pronoun must be restored: **Was steht in der SMS, <u>die</u> er ihnen geschickt hat?**

6. When a preposition is used in conjunction with a relative pronoun (**… der Fall** (*case*), **an dem** sie arbeitet), the preposition must precede the pronoun and take its place as the first element in the relative clause. This poses a problem for some English speakers, to whom *the case that she's working **on*** sounds more acceptable (or at least less stilted) than *the case **on** which she's working*, and who are therefore tempted to place **an** in final position in German. But German allows no variation here: In a relative clause, the preposition *must* precede the relative pronoun, which in turn cannot be dropped, as discussed above.

der Fall, **an dem** sie arbeitet $\begin{cases} \textit{the case } \textbf{\textit{on which}} \textit{ she's working} \\ \textit{the case } \textbf{\textit{that}} \textit{ she's working } \textbf{\textit{on}} \\ \textit{the case she's working } \textbf{\textit{on}} \end{cases}$

7. When a preposition precedes a genitive relative pronoun, the preposition determines the case of only the following *noun* (and any associated adjectives), not the relative pronoun. The relative pronoun will be **deren** or **dessen,** depending on the number and gender of the antecedent, and will remain a fixed form in the relative clause, regardless of the case surrounding it or the gender of the noun following it.

der Detektiv, ohne **dessen** Hilfe die Polizei diesen Fall nicht gelöst hätte	*the detective without whose help the police wouldn't have solved the case*
eine Straftat, von **deren** schrecklich**em** Ausgang wir erst später erfahren	*an offense whose horrible outcome we don't find out about until later*

18.3 ▶ WAS AND WO-COMPOUNDS AS RELATIVE PRONOUNS

A. Was

1. **Was** is used as a relative pronoun to refer to the indefinite antecedents **etwas, nichts, alles, viel(es), wenig(es), manches, einiges,** and the demonstratives **das** and **dasselbe.**

Es gibt fast **nichts**, *was* mich überrascht.	*There is almost nothing that surprises me.*
Er tut **dasselbe**, *was* die anderen tun.	*He does the same thing (that) the others do.*

2. **Was** is used to refer to neuter adjectival nouns (see 16.1.B), usually in the superlative, and to neuter ordinal numbers.

Das ist **das Beste**, *was* Friedrich Glauser je geschrieben hat.	*That is the best thing (that) Friedrich Glauser ever wrote.*
Das Erste, *was* Wachtmeister Studer tun muss, ist Folgendes: ...	*The first thing (that) Constable Studer must do is the following: ...*

3. **Was** is used when the "antecedent" is not merely a noun or pronoun, but the information conveyed by the entire preceding clause.

   COMPARE:

Jemand hat ein Verbrechen begangen, das zu erwarten war.	*Someone committed a crime that was to be expected. (i.e., the crime itself was to be expected)*
Jemand hat ein Verbrechen begangen, **was** zu erwarten war.	*Someone committed a crime, which was to be expected. (i.e., the committing of the crime was to be expected)*

B. Wo-compounds

1. If the *preposition + relative pronoun* structure is called for, and **was** is the appropriate relative pronoun, then **wo**-compounds (**worauf, wodurch, womit,** etc.; see 19.2.B) are used in place of *preposition + was.*

Einige Episoden sind viral geworden, **worauf** die Produzenten sehr stolz sein müssen.	*Several episodes have gone viral, which the producers must be very proud of.* (**auf** + **was** = **worauf**)
Das Erste, **woran** man denkt, ist die psychologische Komplexität der Handlungen.	*The first thing (that) one thinks about is the psychological complexity of the plots.* (**an** + **was** = **woran**)

2. A **wo**-compound may also be used in place of the *preposition + relative pronoun* structure when the antecedent is not a person. However, the *preposition + relative pronoun* structure is generally preferred.

ACCEPTABLE:

| Wo ist das Handy, **womit** das Opfer die SMS geschickt hat? | *Where's the cell phone that the victim sent the text message with?* |

PREFERABLE:

| Wo ist das Handy, **mit dem** das Opfer die SMS geschickt hat? | *Where's the cell phone that the victim sent the text message with?* |

3. Neither **da**-compounds (see 20.1) nor **wo**-compounds can be used when the antecedent is a person.

18.4   THE INDEFINITE RELATIVE PRONOUNS *WER* AND *WAS*

A. *Wer* and *was* (who/what)

1. The indefinite relative pronoun **wer (wen, wem, wessen)** meaning *who (whom, whose)* is used when there is no antecedent referring to a specific person.

Am Anfang von *M* weiß weder die Polizei noch die Berliner Unterwelt, **wer** der Serienmörder ist. *(nominative)*	*At the beginning of M, neither the police nor the Berlin underworld knows who the serial killer is.*
Aber bald ist dem Zuschauer klar, **wen** sie festnehmen sollten. *(accusative)*	*But soon it's clear to the movie viewer whom they should arrest.*
Am Pfeifen erkennt der Blinde, mit **wem** er's zu tun hat. *(dative)*	*The blind man knows from the whistling who he's dealing with.*
Man fragt sich dabei, **wessen** Methoden besser sind – die der Kriminellen oder die der Polizei. *(genitive)*	*One is left wondering in the process whose methods are better—those of the criminals or those of the police.*

2. **Was** functions like **wer** but refers to things or concepts.

| Der Mörder beschreibt in einem Brief, **was** er fühlt und denkt. | *The murderer describes in a letter what he feels and thinks.* |

B. *Wer* and *was* (whoever/whatever)

1. **Wer** and **was** can also be used to mean *whoever (he/she who)* and *whatever* respectively. In this usage, the first clause begins with **wer** or **was,** and the second clause generally begins with an optional demonstrative pronoun (see 17.3).

| **Wer** Hans Beckert zuerst findet, **(der)** darf ihn richten. | *Whoever finds Hans Beckert first is allowed to judge him.* |

2. The demonstrative pronoun must be used if it is not in the same case as **wer.**

| **Wer** solche Verbrechen begeht, **dem** verzeiht man nie. | *Whoever commits such crimes, one never pardons (that person).* |

3. Both **wer** and **was** occur frequently in proverbs and sayings.

Wer nicht hören will, muss fühlen.	*Whoever won't listen, will have to feel (i.e., learn the hard way).*
Wer mich liebt, liebt auch meinen Hund.	*Whoever loves me, also loves my dog. (i.e., If you want me, you have to accept everything about me.)*
Was ich nicht weiß, (das) macht mich nicht heiß.	*What I don't know doesn't upset me. (i.e., Ignorance is bliss.)*

18.5 OTHER FORMS OF RELATIVIZATION

1. When the antecedent is a place, the subsequent relative clause can begin with **in** _____ (formal) or **wo** (less formal). But in either case, some form of connection is required, even where English allows such connectors to disappear.

Das Zimmer, in dem Dr. Schwarz ermordet wurde, ...³

Das Zimmer, wo Dr. Schwarz ermordet wurde, ...

- *The room in which Dr. Black was murdered ...*
- *The room Dr. Black was murdered in ...*
- *The room where Dr. Black was murdered ...*

2. When the antecedent involves a time reference, written German often uses prepositions with relative pronouns, and **als** or **wenn** (depending on tense) as more colloquial alternatives.

... der verregnete Nachmittag, **an dem/als** wir stundenlang *Cluedo* spielten.

... *the rainy afternoon (when) we played* Clue *for hours.*

Wo can be used similarly, but is considered very colloquial.

... der Moment, **wo** ich genau wusste, wie, wo und von wem Dr. Schwarz ermordet wurde.

... *the moment (when) I knew exactly how, where and by whom Dr. Black was murdered.*

3. To express relativization of manner, as in English *the way (in which) this happened*, German uses **die Art + wie**.

Die Art, wie du die Lösung erraten hast, war erstaunlich!

The way (that) you guessed the solution was amazing!

---

³Just in case you ever find yourself playing *Clue* in Germany: The German version was revised in 2008 to include nine weapons rather than six, and the names of the suspects and the rooms have been updated. In place of the library, for example, there's a home theater (*Heimkino*), and the conservatory has given way to a fitness room (*Wellnessraum*). Time marches on.

Wortschatz

Kategorien

The following words designate general categories of nouns. They are useful when classifying or defining items.

der Apparat, -e/das Gerät, -e *apparatus, tool, device, piece of equipment*

die Einrichtung, -en *layout, setup, contrivance; furnishings*

das Fahrzeug, -e *vehicle*

das Gebäude, - *building*

der Gegenstand, ⸚e *object, thing, item*

das Instrument, -e *instrument*

die Krankheit, -en *illness*

die Maschine, -n *machine*

das Medikament, -e *medicine, drug*

das Mittel, - *means, medium*

das Möbel, - *(piece of) furniture*

das Spiel, -e *game*

das Brettspiel, -e *board game*

das Kartenspiel, -e *card game*

das Spielzeug, -e *toy*

der Stoff, -e *material, cloth, fabric*

das Transportmittel, - *means of transportation*

das Werkzeug, -e *tool, implement*

Übungen

A **Am Rhein.** Verbinden Sie die beiden Sätze durch Relativpronomen.

BEISPIEL Der Rhein ist ein Fluss. Er fließt durch mehrere Länder.
Der Rhein ist ein Fluss, der durch mehrere Länder fließt.

1. Am Rhein stehen viele alte Burgen *(castles)*. Sie stammen aus dem frühen Mittelalter.
2. Hoch oben auf einem Felsen *(cliff)* am Rhein sitzt eine Frau. Sie heißt Loreley. Sie singt ein altes Lied.
3. Auf beiden Seiten des Rheins wächst der Wein. Den trinken die Rheinländer so gern.
4. Der Rhein fließt durch einige große Städte. In ihnen gibt es jetzt viel Industrie und auch viel Umweltverschmutzung *(pollution)*.
5. Die Mosel mündet *(flows)* bei der Stadt Koblenz in den Rhein. Die Stadt ist über zweitausend Jahre alt.
6. Touristen können mit Schiffen auf dem Rhein fahren. Sie wollen die Romantik dieses Flusses erleben.

B **Eine gute Wanderausrüstung.** Sie und ein paar Freunde wollen eine Woche in den Bergen wandern. Sie sprechen mit dem Verkäufer im Sportgeschäft.

BEISPIEL   Wir brauchen Anoraks *(parkas)*, _____ wasserdicht sind.
*Wir brauchen Anoraks, **die** wasserdicht sind.*

1. Wir brauchen Bergschuhe, _____ aus Leder sind.
2. Wir suchen Rucksäcke, _____ leicht sind und in _____ man viel tragen kann.
3. Gibt es Medikamente, _____ bei Höhenkrankheit *(altitude sickness)* helfen?
4. Wir möchten eine Wanderkarte, auf _____ auch schwierige Touren eingezeichnet *(marked)* sind.
5. Es wäre auch eine gute Idee, ein paar Kartenspiele mitzunehmen, mit _____ wir uns abends die Zeit vertreiben *(pass the time)* können.
6. Ein Kompass *(m.)*, _____ man auch im Dunkeln lesen kann, wäre auch ganz praktisch.
7. Es gibt bestimmt ein paar Werkzeuge, _____ wir noch brauchen.
8. Haben Sie ein Zelt, in _____ drei Personen schlafen können?
9. Wir müssen auch alle eine Brille tragen, _____ unsere Augen vor der Höhensonne schützt *(protects)*.

C **Personenbeschreibung.** Was erfahren wir über Julia und Daniel? Verwenden Sie Relativpronomen.

Julia

BEISPIEL   Sie kann mehrere Sprachen.
Sie ist eine Frau, die mehrere Sprachen kann. [oder]
Sie ist eine Person, die mehrere Sprachen kann.

1. Alle Leute mögen sie.
2. Sie spricht gern über Politik.
3. Sie treibt viel Sport.
4. Zu ihr kann man kommen, wenn man Probleme hat.
5. Daniel könnte ohne sie nicht glücklich sein.
6. Ihr Lachen ist ansteckend *(contagious)*.

Daniel

BEISPIEL   Er arbeitet sehr fleißig.
Er ist ein Mann, der sehr fleißig arbeitet. [oder]
Er ist jemand, der sehr fleißig arbeitet.

1. Alle Leute mögen ihn.
2. Mit ihm kann man sich gut unterhalten *(engage in conversation)*.
3. Er arbeitet gern an seiner Website.
4. Man hört über ihn nur Positives.
5. Seine Freunde schicken ihm mindestens 100 SMS jeden Tag.
6. Sein Englisch ist recht gut.

Beschreiben Sie jetzt jemanden, den Sie kennen. Schreiben Sie fünf bis sechs Sätze mit verschiedenen Relativpronomen.

D   **Gerümpel *(junk)* oder Schätze *(treasures)*?**   In Ihrer Garage gibt es noch viel altes Gerümpel, das Sie gern loswerden möchten. Versuchen Sie andere Leute zum Kauf dieser Dinge zu überreden *(persuade)*.

BEISPIELE   *Hier ist ein Fahrrad, **das** noch gut fährt.*
*Hier sind ein paar alte Hobby-Zeitschriften, **in denen** interessante Artikel stehen.*

1. ein Kinderwagen mit nur drei Rädern
2. Plakate *(posters)*
3. ein leeres Aquarium
4. verrostete Werkzeuge
5. Autoreifen *(tires)*
6. ein altes Spielzeug aus Holz
7. ein künstlicher *(artificial)* Weihnachtsbaum
8. ein kleines U-Boot aus Kunststoff *(plastic)*

Und was für andere unwiderstehliche *(irresistible)* Dinge haben Sie denn noch so in Ihrer Garage?

E   **Tolle Dinge erfinden.**   Welche fünf Dinge möchten Sie erfinden? Je toller (oder verrückter), desto besser!

BEISPIELE   *Ich möchte einen Hut erfinden, **der** sich automatisch vom Kopf hebt, wenn sein Besitzer „Guten Tag" sagt.*
*Ich möchte eine Brille erfinden, **die** Scheibenwischer hat.*

F   **Ein Handy? Das ist ein Gerät, mit dem man …**   Stellen Sie sich vor, Sie treffen jemand, der die Erfindungen *(inventions)*, Geräte *(gadgets)* und vor allem die Kommunikationsmittel der letzten 30 Jahre gar nicht kennt, und viele Fragen darüber hat. Wie würden Sie diesem Menschen alles erklären? Benutzen Sie dabei die Kategorien aus dem Wortschatz und Relativpronomen, wie in dem Beispiel.

BEISPIEL   Was ist ein Handy?
*Das ist ein Gerät, **mit dem** man drahtlos (without a wire, cord) telefonieren kann.*

1. Was ist ein „Laptop?"
2. Was ist „Twitter"? Und wie „twittert" man?
3. Und ein „MP3-Spieler"?
4. Ich habe etwas über einen „iPod" gelesen. Was ist das denn?
5. Ich habe natürlich einen Fernseher – aber was ist ein „Plasmafernseher"?
6. Was bedeutet denn „streaming"? Hat das mit Wasser zu tun?
7. Neulich habe ich jemand von einem „Hybrid-Auto" erzählen hören. Was für ein Auto ist das?
8. Was für ein Gebäude ist ein „grünes" Gebäude?

G   **Was ist das?**   Schreiben Sie Definitionen. Verwenden Sie Relativsätze oder substantivierte Infinitive (siehe 11.5) mit Vokabeln aus dem **Wortschatz**.

BEISPIELE   ein Klavier
Ein Klavier ist ein (Musik)instrument, das 88 Tasten (keys) hat.

eine Schere *(scissors)*
Eine Schere ist ein Werkzeug zum Schneiden.

1. eine Kirche
2. ein Motorrad
3. (das) Poker
4. eine Uhr
5. eine Vuvuzela

6. (die) Baumwolle *(cotton)*
7. eine Schlaftablette
8. eine Erkältung
9. eine Bibliothek
10. *Die Siedler von Catan*

Schreiben Sie fünf weitere Definitionen für Gegenstände aus fünf verschiedenen Kategorien.

H **Tipps für Europabesucher.**   Machen Sie aus zwei Sätzen einen Satz mit Relativpronomen im Genitiv.

BEISPIEL   Auf dem Land gibt es viele Pensionen. Ihre Zimmer sind nicht so teuer.
*Auf dem Land gibt es viele Pensionen, **deren** Zimmer nicht so teuer sind.*

1. Im Herbst fahren viele Touristen in den Kaiserstuhl (Weingebiet in Südbaden). Seine Weine genießen einen besonders guten Ruf.
2. Man muss unbedingt auf den Dachstein (im Land Salzburg) hinauffahren. Von seinem Gipfel *(summit)* aus hat man einen herrlichen Panoramablick auf die umliegende Alpenwelt.
3. Im Sommer pilgern viele Touristen zum Kitzsteinhorn (einem Berg in Österreich). Auf seinen Gletschern *(glaciers)* kann man sogar im Sommer Skilaufen.
4. Zu den großen Natursehenswürdigkeiten *(natural attractions)* Europas gehört die Adelsberger Grotte in Slowenien. Ihre Tropfsteine *(stalactites)* bewundern Tausende von Besuchern jedes Jahr.
5. Besonders beliebt sind die Kurorte *(health resorts)* im Alpengebiet. Ihre Bergluft ist besonders gesund.

Gibt es denn auch in Ihrem Land oder in anderen Ländern, die Sie kennen, Sehenswürdigkeiten, die man unbedingt besuchen sollte? Schreiben Sie bitte drei Sätze mit **dessen** oder **deren**.

I *Der, die, das, was oder wo?*   Beenden Sie die Sätze mit passenden Relativsätzen.

BEISPIELE   Ich habe eine Arbeit, ...
*Ich habe eine Arbeit, **die** nächste Woche fällig (due) ist.*

Ich mache alles, ...
*Ich mache alles, **was** ich will.*

1. Ich möchte etwas machen, ...
2. Ameisen *(ants)* sind Insekten, ...
3. Ich kenne Menschen, ...
4. Deutsch ist eine Sprache, ...
5. Liechtenstein ist ein Land, ...
6. Es gibt viele Dinge, ...

7. Ich lese heutzutage viel, ...
8. Eine schwere Krankheit wäre das Schlimmste, ...
9. Ein Mercedes ist ein Auto, ...
10. Ich möchte an einen Ort reisen, ...

J **Was ich alles möchte.** Ergänzen Sie die Sätze. Verwenden Sie entweder Präpositionen aus dem Kasten mit Relativpronomen oder **wo** plus Präposition.

BEISPIELE Ich brauche einen Freund, ...
*Ich brauche einen Freund, **mit dem** ich über alles sprechen kann.*

Ich möchte nichts tun, ...
*Ich möchte nichts tun, **wofür** ich mich später schämen müsste.*

an	bei	durch	für	in	mit	über	von	zu

1. Ich möchte Professoren haben, ...
2. Ich möchte etwas studieren, ...
3. Ich möchte gern ein Buch schreiben, ...
4. Ich würde gern einen Beruf erlernen, ...
5. Ich möchte eine Wohnung finden, ...
6. Ich möchte später viel(es) sehen, ...
7. Ich möchte später in einer Stadt wohnen, ...
8. Ich hätte gern ein Haustier *(pet),* ...

K **Was die Eltern nicht wissen ...** Es gibt bestimmt einiges, was Ihre Eltern über Sie nicht wissen. Erzählen Sie in etwa fünf Sätzen davon. Verwenden Sie **was** und Formen von **wer**.

BEISPIEL Meine Eltern wissen nicht, ...
*Meine Eltern wissen nicht, **wer** meine feste Freundin/mein fester Freund ist.*
***mit wem** ich jeden Tag zu Mittag esse.*
***was** ich abends mache, wenn ich keine*
Hausaufgaben habe.

L **Sprüche und Antisprüche.** Was bedeuten diese bekannten Sprüche? Erfinden Sie eigene Varianten (Antisprüche!) dazu. Je lustiger, desto besser!

BEISPIEL Wer im Glashaus sitzt, soll nicht mit Steinen werfen.
*Wer im Glashaus sitzt, **(der)** soll keinen Krach* (noise, racket) *machen.*
***den** sieht jeder.*
***(der)** braucht gute Vorhänge* (curtains).

1. Wer *a* sagt, muss auch *b* sagen.
2. Wer den Pfennig *(penny)* nicht ehrt *(respects),* ist des Talers[4] nicht wert.
3. Wer nichts wagt *(dares),* gewinnt nichts.
4. Wer zuletzt lacht, lacht am besten.

---

[4]**Taler:** older unit of German currency, cognate with *dollar*

5. Was Hänschen (*"little Hans"*) nicht lernt, lernt Hans nimmermehr (*never*).
6. Was man nicht im Kopf hat, muss man in den Beinen haben.

Erfinden Sie ein paar „weise" Sprüche dieser Art!

Anwendung

A **Fotos.** Bringen Sie ein paar Fotos oder Videos von einer Reise oder einer Episode aus Ihrem Leben zur Unterrichtsstunde mit. Erklären Sie die Orte und Menschen auf Ihren Bildern. Sie sollen dabei selbstverständlich Relativpronomen verwenden!

> **REDEMITTEL**
>
> Hier seht ihr ..., die/das/der ...
> Die Leute auf diesem Bild ..., die ...
> Links/Rechts im Bild sind die ..., die wir ...
> Das war in einem [Hotel], in dem/wo ...

B **Zukunftswünsche.** Diskutieren Sie mit anderen Studenten über ihre Wünsche für die Zukunft.

> **REDEMITTEL**
>
> Ich suche vor allem einen Beruf, ...
> Natürlich möchte ich Kollegen haben, ...
> Vielleicht kann ich in einer Stadt/in einer Gegend wohnen, wo ...
> Hoffentlich lerne ich eine Frau/einen Mann kennen, ...
> Ich möchte auch noch eine Familie haben, ...
> Ich möchte übrigens auch nichts/etwas erleben, was ...

C **Gut und nicht so gut.** Was für Dinge (Menschen, Gegenstände, Ideen usw.) finden Sie gut oder nicht so gut? Diskutieren Sie mit anderen Studenten darüber. Verwenden Sie Relativpronomen.

> **REDEMITTEL**
>
> Gut finde ich die [Kurse], die/in denen ...
> Nicht so gut finde ich das, was ...
> Ich halte viel/nichts von [Menschen], die ...
> Ich mag [Städte] (nicht), wo/in denen ...

D **Eindrücke und Meinungen.** Fragen Sie andere in Ihrem Kurs, was sie von bestimmten bekannten oder berühmten Persönlichkeiten halten. Diskutieren Sie darüber.

Was denkst du (denken Sie)/hältst du (halten Sie) von ... ?
Was ist dein/Ihr Eindruck von ... ?
Ich halte sie/ihn für eine Person, die/der/deren ...
Nun, (ich finde,) das ist ein Mensch, der/den/dem/dessen ...
Sie/Er kommt mir vor wie jemand, die/der ...
Meiner Meinung nach hat sie/er etwas gemacht, was ...
Nun, wer so etwas macht, der/den/dem ...

Schriftliche Themen

Tipps zum Schreiben	**Using and Avoiding Relative Clauses**
	Relative clauses work well in all kinds of writing; they enrich your prose by providing additional information about the persons and things you wish to discuss. However, since relative clauses tend to interrupt the flow of a sentence, you should use them carefully, particularly in fast-paced narratives or in compositions where the emphasis is on action(s) rather than explanation. Often a descriptive prepositional phrase can convey the same information (see **Tipps zum Schreiben,** Chapter 10). For example, **die Familie, die in der nächsten Straße wohnt,** is expressed more succinctly by **die Familie in der nächsten Straße.** A relative clause with **haben** (for example, **die Studentin, die das Buch hatte**) can usually be replaced by a simpler prepositional phrase **(die Studentin mit dem Buch).** Relative clauses with the verb **sein (die Preise, die sehr hoch waren)** are even less desirable, since an adjective construction **(die sehr hohen Preise)** usually supplies the same information. (See also **Tipps zum Schreiben** in Chapter 16.)

A **Zurück in die Zukunft.** Was für technische Erfindungen *(inventions)* des 20. oder 21. Jahrhunderts würde jemand aus dem 18. Jahrhundert gar nicht verstehen? Wie könnte man solche Erfindungen erklären? Verwenden Sie dabei die Kategorien aus dem **Wortschatz,** wie bei **Übung G.**

BEISPIEL das Surfbrett
Ein Surfbrett ist ein Stück Holz oder Kunststoff, **mit dem** *man im Stehen* (while standing) *auf den Wasserwellen im Meer herumgleiten* (glide) *kann.*

das Auto, -s
der Fernseher, -
das Flugzeug, -e
die Glühbirne, -n *(light bulb)*
das Penizillin
die Rolltreppe, -n *(escalator)*
der Satellit, -en *(weak noun, see R.1.3)*
die Spülmaschine, -n *(dishwasher)*
das Telefon, -
die U-Bahn, -en

B **Charakterbeschreibung.** Beschreiben Sie eine Person, die Sie kennen, oder einen unvergesslichen Charakter aus einem Buch oder einem Film.

BEISPIEL *Oskar ist ein Mensch, der die Welt anders sieht als andere Menschen. Er redet auch dauernd von Dingen, die andere Menschen überhaupt nicht interessieren. Wenn er z.B. ...*

C **Der Mensch.** Schreiben Sie einen Aufsatz mit diesem Titel. Vielleicht gibt Ihnen der folgende Textauszug *(excerpt)* ein paar Anregungen *(ideas)*.

BEISPIEL *Man könnte den Menschen geradezu (frankly) als ein Wesen (being) definieren, das nie zuhört ... Jeder Mensch hat eine Leber, eine Milz (spleen), eine Lunge und eine Fahne[5]... Es soll Menschen ohne Leber, ohne Milz und mit halber Lunge geben; Menschen ohne Fahne gibt es nicht ... Menschen miteinander gibt es nicht. Es gibt nur Menschen, die herrschen (rule), und solche, die beherrscht werden ... Im Übrigen (in other respects) ist der Mensch ein Lebewesen, das klopft, schlechte Musik macht und seinen Hund bellen lässt ... Neben den Menschen gibt es noch Sachsen (Saxons) und Amerikaner, aber die haben wir noch nicht gehabt und bekommen Zoologie erst in der nächsten Klasse.* [Kurt Tucholsky, 1890–1935]

---

[5]**Fahne** = *flag;* but **Er hat eine Fahne** = *You can smell alcohol on his breath.*

Zusammenfassung

Rules to Remember

1 The relative pronouns agree with the word(s) they refer to in *gender* and *number*, but the *case* of the relative pronoun depends on its function within its own clause.

2 A relative clause is a subordinate clause; the conjugated verb (V_1) normally occupies final position.

3 English relative clauses often omit object pronouns and move prepositions to final position. German relative clauses must include a relative pronoun or equivalent connector (such as **wo**, **wie**, **wenn**, or **als**), and any preposition related to the relative pronoun must precede it: *the film I'm thinking of* = **der Film, <u>an den</u> ich denke.**

4 The neuter relative pronoun **was** is used instead of the relative pronoun **das** to refer to concepts (as opposed to specific objects) and entire clauses (**das Beste, <u>was</u> ... ; sie liest gern Krimis, <u>was</u> ich auch gern mache**).

5 A **wo**-compound may be used in casual speech instead of a *preposition + relative pronoun* construction to refer to inanimate things (**der Bleistift, <u>womit</u>** [or **<u>mit dem</u>**] **ich schreibe**), and always replaces the *preposition + relative pronoun* construction when the pronoun is **was** (**alles, <u>woran</u> ich denke**).

At a Glance

Relative pronouns: Forms				
	Masc.	**Fem.**	**Neut.**	**Pl.**
Nom.	der	die	das	die
Acc.	den	die	das	die
Dat.	dem	der	dem	**denen**
Gen.	**dessen**	**deren**	**dessen**	**deren**

Antecedents taking *was* as relative pronoun		
etwas	manch(es)	das Beste
nichts	einiges	das Erste, Zweite, ...
alles	das	*[entire preceding clause]*
viel(es)	dasselbe	

Relative pronouns: Structure

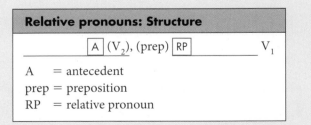

A = antecedent
prep = preposition
RP = relative pronoun

zum Beispiel

Dufte

Source: Dufte, directed by Ingo Rasper

Dufte (Kurzfilm): The short film **Dufte** is based on a true story. It tells the tale of four people traveling by train from West Berlin to Leipzig in 1952. The title of the film is a play on word associations: On one level, **Dufte** is similar to **Düfte,** the plural form of **der Duft** *(aroma, pleasant smell)*, which has an important role in the plot; on another level, it's a slang word from that era meaning *great, neat, awesome.* Though simple on its surface, the story reflects some of the complex tensions in Germany during the decades following WWII. West Berlin had become an island of prosperity surrounded by East German scarcity, with easy access to what were then considered luxury goods: coffee, cigarettes, and alcohol. This led to a thriving black market between West Berlin and the cities surrounding it in East Germany, which the East German government tried its best to suppress by placing heavy restrictions on the transport of these items, even when they were meant simply as gifts for friends and family. "Transport police" and East Germans working undercover for the *Stasi* (the East German internal intelligence service) would search through every compartment of trains leaving West Berlin, leading not only to the stress of the inspections themselves, but also to distrust of one's fellow passengers, any of whom might be a *Stasi* informant. In this particular train compartment, it turns out that each passenger has something to hide—and not just the roasted coffee beans confiscated by the policeman.

Grammatik

19.1 YES-NO QUESTIONS

1. Questions intended to elicit a *yes* or *no* answer begin with the conjugated verb (V_1), with the rest of the sentence following normal word order rules for subjects in the middle field (see 1.1.C).

    ■ Subject *nouns* normally appear directly after V_1, unless the verb element includes a reflexive pronoun (see 10.1.B).

Hat **die Frau** einen Koffer dabei?	*Does the woman have a suitcase with her?*
Freut *sich* **die Frau** auf ihren Besuch in Leipzig?	*Is the woman looking forward to her visit in Leipzig?*

    ■ Subject nouns can also appear even later after V_1, following adverbial modifiers, if the subject is to be emphasized.

Arbeitet denn tatsächlich **der alte Mann** für die Stasi?	*Is it really the old man who is working for the Stasi?*

    ■ Subject pronouns, by contrast, always follow directly after V_1, with no intervening elements.

Freut **sie** sich auf ihren Besuch?	*Is she looking forward to her visit?*
Arbeitet **er** denn tatsächlich für die Stasi?	*Does he actually work for the Stasi?*

2. In conversation, yes-no questions are frequently posed as statements followed by **nicht wahr?**[1], **nicht?**, or **oder?** (*right?, isn't it?, don't you?, haven't they?*, etc.).

Er sieht doch verdächtig aus, **oder?**	*He looks suspicious, doesn't he?*

3. German uses the particle **doch** (see R.6.2.E) to provide a *yes* answer to a question posed negatively.

Gibt es denn wirklich keinen Kaffee in der Tasche?	*Is there really no coffee in the bag?*
—**Doch!**	*—Of course there is!*

---

[1]In southern Germany and Austria, **gelt?** or **gell?** are often used instead of **nicht wahr?**—but these are restricted to casual, spoken language and are considered highly regional elsewhere.

Du kommst morgen, **gell?**	*You're coming tomorrow, aren't you?*

19.2 INTERROGATIVE WORDS

Questions intended to elicit content information begin with an interrogative word, followed immediately by the conjugated verb (V_1). The rest of the question, including the subject and any subsequent middle field or V_2 elements, follows normal word order as described above.

Wer *sitzt* schon im Zugabteil, wenn die zwei Männer ankommen?	*Who is already sitting in the train compartment when the two men arrive?*
Wann *sind* die zwei Männer *eingestiegen?*	*When did the two men get on the train?*
Wie *wollen* sie das *verstecken?*	*How do they want to hide it?*

A. *Wer* and *was*

1. The interrogative pronoun **wer** *(who)* has masculine case forms only, but it refers to people of either gender. **Was** *(what)* has only one form, which is both nominative and accusative. Its use with prepositions is limited to the genitive prepositions and a few prepositions governing the accusative and dative cases (**außer, hinter, ohne, seit, zwischen**), but with most accusative and dative prepositions it is replaced by a **wo**-compound, as discussed in 19.2.B below.

	Persons		Objects or ideas	
Nom.	wer?	*who?*	was?	*what?*
Acc.	wen?	*who(m)?*	was?	*what?*
Dat.	wem?	*(to) who(m)?*	**(mit)** was?	*(with) what?*
Gen.	wessen?	*whose?*	**(wegen)** was?	*(on account of) what?*

Wer ist der alte Mann? *(subject → nominative)*	*Who is the old man?*
Wen wollen sie vermeiden? *(direct object → accusative)*	*Who(m) do they want to avoid?*
„**Wem** gehört der Koffer da oben?" *(indirect object → dative)*	*"Who does the suitcase up there belong to?" / "To whom …?"*
Wessen Kaffee ist das? *(possession → genitive)*	*Whose coffee is that?*
Was passiert dann? *(subject → nominative)*	*What happens then?*
„**Was** haben Sie in der Tasche?" *(direct object → accusative)*	*"What do you have in the bag?"*

2. **Wer** and **was** can be used with either singular or plural forms of the verb **sein,** depending upon whether the subsequent subject is singular or plural.

Wer *ist* nervöser, die Männer oder die Frau?	*Who is more nervous, the men or the woman?*
Wer/Was *waren* „IMs"[2] bei der Stasi?	*Who/What were "IM's" with the Stasi?*
Was *sind* die Konsequenzen, wenn man erwischt wird?	*What are the consequences if you're caught?*

3. Prepositions are placed directly before the forms of **wer.** They cannot occur at the end of the sentence in interrogatives, as frequently happens in colloquial English.

Vor wem hat sie Angst?	*Who is she afraid of? / Of whom…?*
Für wen ist das Paket?	*Who is the package for? / For whom…?*

4. **Wessen** is a genitive form, but the noun following it is not necessarily genitive. That noun's case is determined, as always, by its function in the sentence (subject, direct object, indirect object, or object of a preposition), independent of **wessen.**

Subject: Wessen **Paket** ist im Koffer?	*Whose package is in the suitcase?*
Direct object: Wessen **Kaffee** kann der Polizist riechen?	*Whose coffee can the policeman smell?*
Object of preposition: Aus wessen **Tasche** nimmt er den Kaffee?	*From whose bag does he take the coffee? / Whose bag … from?*

Adjectives following **wessen** must be declined to agree with the noun they modify, not **wessen.**

Wessen **verstecktes Paket** ist im Koffer?	*Whose hidden package is in the suitcase?*
Wessen **versteckten Kaffee** kann er riechen?	*Whose hidden coffee can he smell?*
Aus wessen **versteckter Tasche** nimmt er etwas?	*From whose hidden bag does he take something? / Whose hidden bag… from?*

In current spoken language, **wessen** is considered relatively stilted, and most German speakers prefer a paraphrase that uses **gehören + wem.**

„**Wessen** Kaffee ist das?"	*"Whose coffee is that?"*

PREFERRED:

„**Wem gehört** dieser Kaffee?"	*"Who does this coffee belong to?" / "To whom does belong?"*

---

[2]**IMs** (= Inoffizielle Mitarbeiter) were civilians paid by the *Stasi* (short for **Ministerium für Staatssicherheit:** *ministry of security*) to inform on neighbors, co-workers, and in some cases family members.

B. *Wo*-compounds

1. When a question begins with **was** as the object of a preposition (*"About what . . . ?"* or *"With what . . . ?"*), German often uses a prepositional **wo(r)**[3]-compound as the interrogative element in first position. With some verb + preposition combinations, such as **denken + an** and **sprechen + über,** both forms are used (**Woran denkst du? An was denkst du?**), but in writing **wo**-compounds are preferred. Like **da(r)**-compounds (see 20.1), **wo(r)**-compounds refer to things and ideas, not to people; in other words, the **wo(r)** element translates as **was,** not **wen** or **wem.**

Wovor haben die zwei Männer Angst?	*What are the two men scared of?*
Womit haben sie nicht gerechnet?	*What didn't they reckon with?*
Woran denkt der alte Mann?	*What is the old man thinking about?*
An was denkt der alte Mann?	

BUT:

Vor wem haben sie Angst?	*Who(m) are they afraid of?*
Mit wem haben sie nicht gerechnet?	*Who(m) didn't they reckon with?*
An wen denkt er?	*Who(m) is he thinking about?*

2. **Außer, gegenüber, hinter, neben, ohne, seit, zwischen,** and the genitive prepositions cannot be used in **wo**-compounds. On the rare occasion when one might wish to pose a question with one of these prepositions, **was** should be used instead.

Hinter was hat der Polizist alles gefunden?	*Behind what did the policeman find everything?*

C. *Welch-*

The interrogative article **welch-** *(which, what)* is a **der**-word and declines like the definite article (see 4.3.B) to indicate gender, number, and case.

Welcher Koffer gehört dem alten Mann?	*Which suitcase belongs to the old man?*
Und mit **welchem** Koffer fängt der Polizist an?	*And which suitcase does the policeman start with?*

D. *Was für (ein)*

1. The preposition **für** in **was für (ein)** *(what kind of [a])* does not affect the case of a following article and noun; their case is determined by their function within the sentence. Notice that in its use with singular nouns, **was für** requires the article **ein-,** whereas in English, the corresponding *a* can be optional.

Was für ein Polizist ist er? *(subject)*	*What kind of (a) policeman is he?*
Was für Waren durfte man mitnehmen? *(direct object)*	*What kind of goods was one allowed to bring along?*

---

[3]When the preposition begins with a vowel, an **-r-** is inserted for pronunciation purposes: wo + an = **woran.**

<u>In</u> **was für einer** Situation befinden sie sich jetzt? *(object of preposition)*	*What kind of (a) situation do they find themselves in now? / In what kind...?*
Was für Mitreisenden kann man vertrauen? *(dative plural)*	*What kind of fellow travelers can you trust?*

2. When **was für** is the initial interrogative element in a question (that is, not following a preposition), **was** and **für** are sometimes separated, as long as the meaning is clear. This often occurs in spoken German, and occasionally in written language as well.

„**Was für** einen Plan hast du, Thomas?	*"What kind of a plan do you have, Thomas?"*
„**Was** hast du **für** einen Plan, Thomas?"	

„Kein Problem, Frank. **Was für** eine Tasche hast du da?"	*"Not a problem, Frank. What kind of a bag do you have there?"*
„Kein Problem, Frank. **Was** hast du da **für** eine Tasche?"	

This separation also occurs when **was für** is used in exclamatory statements of the type *What a surprise!*

„**Was für** dumme Ideen du hast!"	*"What stupid ideas you have!"*
„**Was** hast du **für** dumme Ideen!"	

E. Adverbs

The following adverbs are commonly used as interrogative elements.

wann   *when*
wo   *where*
wohin; woher   *to where; from where*
warum, weshalb   *why*
wie   *how*
wie lange   *how long*
wieso   *how is it that/why is it that*
wie viel   *how much*
wie viele   *how many*

Wohin gehst du denn? *(colloquial =* **Wo** gehst du denn **hin**?*)*	*Where are you going (to)?*
Woher kommt dieser Geruch?	*Where is this smell coming from?*
Wieso muss ich das Paket tragen?	*How is it that I have to carry the package? / Why do I ...?*
Wie viel hast du dabei?	*How much do you have with you?*

19.3 ▶ INDIRECT QUESTIONS

1. An indirect question is a direct question embedded in a main clause. If an information question is embedded, the interrogative word functions as a subordinating conjunction (see R.2.3), which transforms the direct question into a subordinate clause. As in all subordinate clauses, the conjugated verb (V_1) is normally in final position. The clause in which the direct question is embedded can be either a statement clause or a question clause, as illustrated in the examples below.

   COMPARE:

   Direct: Warum **hat** er ihr Geheimnis verraten?

   Indirect: <u>Ich möchte wissen</u>, warum er ihr Geheimnis verraten **hat.**

   Indirect: <u>Können Sie mir sagen</u>, warum er ihr Geheimnis verraten **hat?**

   Why did he betray her secret? (information question)

   I'd like to know why he betrayed her secret. (statement)

   Can you tell me why he betrayed her secret? (question)

2. If a yes-no question is embedded, **ob** *(if, whether)* is required as a subordinate conjunction.

   COMPARE:

   Direct: **Haben** Sie Ihren Ausweis dabei?

   Indirect: <u>Ich möchte wissen,</u> ob Sie Ihren Ausweis dabei **haben.**

   Indirect: <u>Können Sie mir sagen</u>, ob Sie Ihren Ausweis dabei **haben?**

   Do you have your ID on you? (yes-no question)

   I'd like to know if you have your ID on you. (statement)

   Can you tell me if you have your ID on you? (question)

Wortschatz
Wie sagt man *to stop?*

halten	auf·hören
an·halten	stehen bleiben
auf·halten	stoppen

1. **Halten** *(intransitive)* means *to come to a stop* (persons or vehicles).

   Hier wollen wir lieber nicht **halten.**

   Wissen Sie, wann der Zug **hält?**

   We'd rather not stop here.

   Do you know when the train is stopping?

2. **An·halten** is used with persons or vehicles and means *to come to a brief or temporary stop (intransitive)* or *to bring something to a brief or temporary stop (transitive)*. In the case of vehicles, such a stop is usually unscheduled.

Während der Zugfahrt haben wir mehrmals **angehalten.** *(intransitive)*	*During the train ride we stopped several times.*
Weil Kühe auf der Straße standen, **hielt** der Fahrer den Wagen **an.** *(transitive)*	*Because cows were standing in the road, the driver stopped the car.*

3. **Auf·halten** *(transitive)* means *to stop* or *hold up someone or something temporarily*.

Ich will dich nicht **aufhalten,** aber...	*I don't want to hold you up, but …*
Die Durchsuchung unseres Gepäcks war nicht länger **aufzuhalten.**	*The search through our luggage couldn't be put off any longer.*

4. **Auf·hören (mit etwas)** *(intransitive only)* means *to stop (doing something), cease*. If *someone* or *something* is stopping, this becomes the subject of a clause with **aufhören** as the verb, either V_1 or V_2. If the *stopping* is connected with a verb and its modifiers, the infinitive clause format is required, and all of these elements are grouped together into the clause (see 11.1).

Wann **hört** dieser Stress endlich **auf?**	*When is this stress finally going to stop?*
Dein Lügen muss sofort **aufhören!**	*Your lying has to stop right now!*
Wir müssen doch **aufhören,** dieses Zeug aus Berlin zu schmuggeln.	*We have just got to stop smuggling this stuff out of Berlin.*

If an *activity* is stopping, the verb expressing the activity becomes an infinitival noun and the object of **mit** (as in **mit dem Laufen**); or the verb is put into an infinitive clause, as described above.

Er hat mit **dem Rauchen** endlich aufgehört.	*He has finally stopped smoking.*
Er hat endlich aufgehört **zu rauchen.**	

5. **Stehen bleiben** (also **stehen·bleiben**) means *to (come to a) stop*, and is always intransitive. When used with vehicles and machinery, **stehen bleiben** can imply that the stopping occurs for mechanical reasons.

Einer der zwei Männer ging den Korridor entlang und **blieb** vorm Fenster **stehen.**	*One of the two men walked along the corridor and stopped (and stood) in front of the window.*
Hoffentlich **bleibt** der Zug nicht auf der Strecke **stehen.**	*I hope the train doesn't come to a stop (and stay standing) along the way.*

6. **Stoppen** *(intransitive)* means *to come to a stop* and is synonymous with **(an)halten**. **Stoppen** *(transitive)* means *to bring someone or something to a stop*.

Wir **stoppten** kurz vor der Grenze.	*We stopped just before the border.*
Die Grenzpolizei hat alle Autos an der Grenze **gestoppt.**	*The border police stopped all cars at the borders.*
Jahrelang versuchte das Regime, den Schwarzmarkt zu **stoppen.**	*For years, the regime tried to stop the black market.*

Übungen

A **Ja, nein oder doch?** Beantworten Sie diese Fragen. Vorsicht, manchmal ist mehr als eine Antwort möglich. Es kommt darauf an, wie Sie die Fragen verstehen und was Sie sagen wollen.

1. Lebt Ihr Großvater nicht mehr?
2. Wissen Sie nicht, wie die Hauptstadt von Togo heißt?
3. Trinken Sie gewöhnlich keinen Wein zum Abendessen?
4. Hat Goethe nicht das Drama *Wilhelm Tell* geschrieben?
5. Hat Mozart nicht *Die Zauberflöte* komponiert?
6. Würden Sie Ihre Kinder in den Ferien nach Cancun reisen lassen?
7. Halten Sie nie bei McDonald's an?
8. Finden Sie diese Aufgabe nicht lustig?

B **Fragen.** Ergänzen Sie die Fragen durch passende **wer**-Formen (**wer, wen, wem, wessen**).

BEISPIEL _____ hat das beste Examen geschrieben?
Wer hat das beste Examen geschrieben?

1. _____ ist da drüben stehen geblieben?
2. _____ stoppt der Polizist gerade?
3. Von _____ haben Sie von diesem Kurs erfahren?
4. Für _____ machen Sie Notizen?
5. _____ Aufsatz hat die Professorin für den besten gehalten?
6. _____ würden Sie in diesem Kurs gern näher kennenlernen?
7. _____ würden Sie diesen Kurs empfehlen?

C **Situationen.** Sagen Sie, was Sie in den folgenden Situationen machen. Verwenden Sie Vokabeln aus dem **Wortschatz.**

BEISPIEL Ein Freund fährt mit Ihnen in Ihrem Wagen. Er möchte an der nächsten Ecke aussteigen.
Ich halte den Wagen an der nächsten Ecke an.

1. Sie arbeiten seit Stunden und sind jetzt sehr müde.
2. Sie fahren in Ihrem Auto. Jemand, den Sie kennen, steht am Straßenrand und winkt Ihnen zu *(waves at you)*.
3. Beim Fußballspiel stehen Sie im Tor. Ein Gegenspieler schießt aufs Tor.
4. Sie gehen im Tiergarten spazieren. Plötzlich ruft ein Affe Ihnen zu: „Na? Wie geht's?"
5. Jemand hat sich tief in den Finger geschnitten und blutet stark.

D   **Bernds Entschluss.**   Sie können das, was Sie gerade über Bernd gehört haben, kaum glauben und fragen noch einmal nach dem fett gedruckten Satzteil.

BEISPIELE   Bernd hört jetzt **mit seinem Studium** auf.
Womit hört Bernd jetzt auf?

Er will **mit seiner Freundin** in eine Kommune ziehen.
Mit wem will er in eine Kommune ziehen?

1. Bernd interessiert sich **für einen radikal neuen Lebensstil.**
2. **Mit seinem Beruf** will er aufhören.
3. Er träumt **von einem idyllischen Leben auf dem Land.**
4. **Von einem Bauern** hat er ein Stück Land gepachtet *(leased)*.
5. Dort möchte er **ohne Stress und Verpflichtungen** *(obligations)* leben.
6. Natürlich will er noch Kontakt **zu seinen Freunden** haben.
7. **Über Besuche von Bekannten** wird er sich jederzeit freuen.
8. **Aber von seiner bisherigen** *(previous)* **Lebensweise** nimmt er jetzt Abschied.

E   **Gabis Eltern möchten einiges wissen.**   Gabi kommt während des Semesters auf kurzen Besuch nach Hause. Ihre Eltern möchten einiges wissen. Ergänzen Sie die Fragen ihrer Eltern durch **welch-.**

1. _____ Kurse hast du belegt?
2. _____ Kurs gefällt dir am besten?
3. An _____ Tagen hast du Deutsch?
4. _____ Kurs findest du am schwierigsten?
5. Mit _____ Leuten gehst du mittags ins Café?

F   **Mehr erfahren.**   Sie möchten mehr über jemanden im Kurs wissen. Stellen Sie Fragen.

BEISPIEL   In was für ... (Zimmer/Wohnung)
In was für einem Zimmer/einer Wohnung wohnst du?

1. Was für ...
2. In was für ... (Konzerte, Theaterstücke/gehen)
3. Mit was für ...
4. An was für ... (Interesse/haben)

G   **Fragen zu einem Thema stellen.**   Stellen Sie Fragen an jemanden im Kurs über eine interessante Reise oder schöne Ferien, die sie/er einmal gemacht hat. Verwenden Sie die folgenden Fragewörter.

1. wohin
2. wer
3. wen
4. *Präposition* + wem/wen
5. was
6. wo-
7. wo
8. wie lange
9. warum
10. was für (ein-)

H **Ja, das möchte ich mal wissen.** Beenden Sie die Sätze, so dass die Aussagen für Sie eine Bedeutung haben. Verwenden Sie einige der folgenden Fragewörter. Versuchen Sie dabei, Fragen und Informationen über ein Thema zu bilden, z.B. über Ihre Uni oder Schule; Ihre Lehrerin oder Ihren Lehrer; über die Familie einer Kollegin/eines Kollegen im Kurs.

BEISPIELE Ich möchte wissen, ...

Ich möchte wissen, warum man dieses Grundstück (piece of property) *für den Campus gewählt hat.*

Weiß jemand, ...

Weiß jemand, was unsere Professorin/unser Professor am Wochenende macht?

ob	was	wie viele
wann	wie	wer/wen/wem/wessen
warum	wie viel	wo/woher/wohin

1. Ich möchte gern wissen, ...
2. Manchmal frage ich mich, ...
3. Weißt du, ...
4. Wer weiß, ...
5. Ich weiß nicht, ...
6. Ich möchte gar nicht wissen, ...

Anwendung

A **Interview.** Sie sollen für die Studentenzeitung jemanden im Kurs interviewen. Versuchen Sie jetzt im Gespräch einiges über diese Person und ihre Interessen zu erfahren (etwa acht bis zehn Fragen). Gebrauchen Sie möglichst viele verschiedene Fragewörter! Verwenden Sie Redemittel in einigen Fragen und Reaktionen.

REDEMITTEL

Fragen

Sag mal: ... ?
Darf ich fragen, ... ?
Ich möchte (gern) fragen/wissen, ...
Kannst du sagen, ... ?
Ich hätte gern gewusst, ...
   (formal: I would very much like to know ...)
Stimmt es *(Is it true)*, dass ... ?

Reaktionen

Das ist aber interessant!
Erzähl doch mehr davon!
Wirklich?
Echt? *(colloquial: Really?)*
Ach was! *(Come on, really!)*
Das wusste ich gar nicht!

B **Gruppenarbeit: Fragen an Prominente.** Sie wollen in einer E-Mail einige Fragen an eine prominente Person stellen. Wem wollen Sie schreiben? Einigen Sie sich mit drei oder vier anderen Personen in einer Gruppe über acht bis zehn Fragen (mit acht bis zehn verschiedenen Fragewörtern!), die Sie an diese Person stellen könnten. Erzählen Sie im Kurs, welche Person Sie ausgewählt (*selected*) haben und welche Fragen Ihre Gruppe stellen möchte.

VORSCHLÄGE

Politiker	Geschäftsleute	Filmschauspieler
Wissenschaftler	Autoren	Sportler

C **Moment mal!** Als Hausaufgabe bereiten Sie eine kleine Geschichte oder Anekdote vor (*prepare*), die Sie einer Partnerin/einem Partner erzählen können. Beim Erzählen soll die Partnerin/der Partner Sie nach jedem Satz mit Fragen unterbrechen (*interrupt*).

BEISPIEL Sie sagen: „*Gestern habe ich draußen vor meinem Wohnheim einen komischen Mann gesehen.*"

Ihre Partnerin/Ihr Partner fragt: „*Moment mal! Wann war das genau? Wo ist dein Wohnheim? Wie hat dieser Mann ausgesehen? Warum hieltst du ihn für komisch?*" usw.

D **Ab jetzt nicht mehr!** Erzählen Sie, wann Sie in Ihrem bisherigen (*up till now*) Leben mit etwas Bestimmtem aufgehört haben.

BEISPIELE *Als ich 12 Jahre alt war, habe ich aufgehört, Geige zu spielen.*
Als ich 12 Jahre alt war, habe ich mit dem Geigespielen aufgehört.

Ein paar Tipps: Windeln (*diapers*) tragen • Nachmittagsschläfchen machen • Kindersendungen im Fernsehen sehen • in die Grundschule gehen • Sport treiben • ein Musikinstrument spielen • viel Milch trinken • immer vor 11 Uhr nachts ins Bett gehen usw.

Und womit wollen Sie nie im Leben aufhören?

E **Angenommen (*assuming*), Sie haben Zugang (*access*) zum Kurzfilm *Dufte*:** Sehen Sie sich den Film an, dann schreiben Sie fünf Ja-Nein-Fragen mit Fragewörtern aus diesem Kapitel und fünf Informationsfragen zum Film. Arbeiten Sie dann mit einer Partnerin/einem Partner im Kurs, stellen Sie ihm/ihr die Fragen, und antworten Sie auf ihre/seine Fragen.

BEISPIELE *Wie alt sind die jungen Männer, die zusammen reisen?*
Was hältst du am Anfang vom dritten Mann?
Was für eine Atmosphäre gibt es im Zugabteil?
Findest du die Anekdote plausibel?

Schriftliche Themen

<table>
<tr>
<td>**Tipps zum Schreiben**</td>
<td>

Asking Rhetorical Questions

When writing expository prose, you will normally formulate statements rather than pose questions. However, sometimes questions can be effective rhetorical devices, as they address readers directly, thus eliciting their involvement or response. With rhetorical questions, you should strive for a stylistic balance between direct and indirect questions.
</td>
</tr>
</table>

A **Das möchte ich gern wissen.** Im Leben gibt es viele Fragen aber wenige Antworten. Was für Fragen haben Sie? Erzählen Sie. Verwenden Sie direkte und indirekte Fragen dabei.

BEISPIEL *Ich möchte gern wissen, warum die Völker der Erde nicht friedlich zusammenleben können. Wieso müssen sie einander hassen und so oft Krieg gegeneinander führen? Ich verstehe auch nicht, wodurch man diese Situation vielleicht ändern könnte. Wie lange werden wir Menschen ...?* usw.

B **Standpunkt.** Äußern Sie sich zu einem Problem an Ihrer Universität/Schule, in Ihrer Stadt, in Ihrem Land oder in der Welt, das Sie für besonders dringend *(urgent)* halten. Bringen Sie Ihren Standpunkt durch den Gebrauch von rhetorischen Fragen und Fragen an die Leser ganz deutlich zum Ausdruck.

BEISPIEL *Ich halte die Kluft* (chasm) *zwischen Arm und Reich in vielen Ländern für ein großes Problem. Warum können wir dieses Problem nicht lösen? Manchmal muss ich mich fragen, ... Stimmt es also doch* (after all), *dass wir ... ? Zum Schluss* (in the end) *bleibt noch die große Frage: „Wann ...?"*

Zusammenfassung

Rules to Remember

1 Yes-no questions begin with a conjugated verb (V_1).

2 Information questions begin with an interrogative word + conjugated verb.

3　The word **doch** is a *yes* answer to a question posed negatively:

Verstehst du kein Deutsch?
—**Doch!** (Ich verstehe Deutsch.)

4　Indirect questions are subordinate clauses; the conjugated verb (V₁) normally comes last.

At a Glance

Forms of *wer?*		
	Persons	**Objects/Ideas**
Nom.	wer?	was?
Acc.	wen?	was?
Dat.	wem?	(mit) was?
Gen.	wessen?	(wegen) was?

Wo-compounds: Objects/Ideas		
wofür	woraus	woran
wodurch	wobei	worauf
wogegen	womit	worin
worum	wonach	worüber
	wovon	wovor
	wozu	

DO NOT combine with *wo-*
außer was?
gegenüber (von) was?
hinter was?
neben was?
ohne was?
seit was/wann?
zwischen was und was?

Word order for indirect question clauses
_____, warum _____ $\boxed{V_2}$ $\boxed{V_1}$.
wann
wo
(usw.)

Da-compounds ▪ Uses of *es*

Tagesschau

AP Images/Fabian Bimmer

Tagesschau: For many Germans, this 15-minute TV bulletin of national and international news is as much a part of daily life as breakfast, lunch, and dinner. The **Tagesschau** program has been broadcast regularly since December 26, 1952, and is now watched by 33% of the television audience in Germany, Monday through Saturday, at 8:00 PM. For many, it marks the beginning of the evening's TV entertainment, since prime time programming on all the major channels defers to its conclusion at 8:15 PM. The name derives from **Wochenschau,** the title of the weekly newsreels that used to be shown in cinemas prior to feature presentations. In addition to its TV presence, it is available online at **www.tagesschau.de,** and if you go to its home page you'll easily understand the categories of news it provides: **Inland, Ausland, Wirtschaft, Wetter, Ihre Meinung, Kontakt, Sport, Wissen, Kultur,** and **Kinder.** For the examples in this chapter, we refer to the program as the "evening news," since this is how many Germans have come to think of it.

Grammatik

German pronouns used as subjects, direct objects, and indirect objects refer to people, animals, things, and ideas with the same precision of case, number, and gender as do nouns. In the statement **Ich habe *ihn* gesehen,** the direct object pronoun **ihn** can refer to a donkey (**der Esel**), a mountain (**der Berg**), or a suggestion (**der Vorschlag**)—any singular masculine noun—as well as to a person. This is not true, however, when German pronouns are used with prepositions. A pronoun object of a preposition in German refers only to a living being, so that the **ihn** in the statement **Ich denke an ihn** can only signify a male person or an animate being with a masculine-gender name. To refer to inanimate objects or ideas in conjunction with most prepositions, German uses a shortcut known as a **da**-compound.

A. Forms

1. **Da**-compounds are formed like **wo**-compounds (see 19.2.B); the prefix **da(r)**- precedes the preposition. When the preposition begins with a vowel, an **-r-** is inserted to facilitate pronunciation. **Da**-compounds occur with many—but not all—prepositions. The following chart indicates which prepositions (accusative, dative, variable) can be combined with **da**- to form a compound, and which of these are sometimes used colloquially in a slightly reduced form.

preposition	*da*-compound	colloquial option
durch	dadurch	
für	dafür	
gegen	dagegen	
um	**darum**	drum
aus	**daraus**	draus
bei	dabei	
mit	damit[1]	
nach	danach	
von	davon	
zu	dazu	
an	**daran**	dran
auf	**darauf**	drauf
hinter	dahinter	
in	**darin**	drin
neben	daneben	

---

[1] There is also the *conjunction* **damit,** which means *so that, in order that* (see R.2.2).

preposition	*da*-compound	colloquial option
über	**darüber**	drüber
unter	**darunter**	drunter
vor	davor	
zwischen	dazwischen	

ALSO:

daher *(from there, from that)*
dahin *(to there)*

2. **Da**-compounds cannot be formed with **außer, gegenüber, ohne, seit,** or with genitive prepositions.

B. Use

1. The **da** in the **da**-compound stands conveniently for whatever is being referred to in conjunction with the preposition, regardless of its gender, case, or number. In the statement **Die Frau wartet darauf,** for example, **da** could mean *a taxi, a rainbow, a promotion,* or *the new contracts,* and the differences of gender and number (**das** Taxi, *der* Regenbogen, *die* Beförderung, *die* neuen Verträge), as well as the question of whether to use accusative or dative in this particular case with **auf,** all disappear behind **da.** Remember that this grammatical sleight of hand only applies to *inanimate* prepositional objects; where *animate* beings are concerned, care must be taken to indicate the gender and number of the referent, as well as the case governed by the preposition.

COMPARE:

Hat die Tagesschau schon angefangen?
—Nein, wir warten noch **darauf.**

Has the evening news already started?
—No, we're still waiting for it (to begin).

Will Papa mitschauen?
—Ja, wir warten **auf ihn.**

Does dad want to watch with us?
—Yes, we're waiting for him.

2. Occasionally a **da**-compound may be used to refer to living beings as belonging to a group, although the pronoun forms are usually preferred.

Die Tagesschau hat viele Sprecher und Moderatoren, **darunter/unter ihnen** Menschen aus verschiedenen Regionen Deutschlands.

The evening news has many presenters and anchors, among them people from various regions in Germany.

3. A **da**-compound can also refer to an entire previous clause.

Jeden Abend schauen wir zu, aber **danach** schalten wir den Fernseher ab.

We watch every evening, but after that we turn the TV off.

4. In addition to referring to specific inanimate things, **da**-compounds also appear in various idiomatic phrases and expressions. Here are some common examples.

Ich kann nichts **dafür**.	*It's not my fault. I can't do anything about it.*
Es kommt **darauf** an.	*It all depends.*
Darauf kommt es an.	*That's what counts.*
Dabei bleibt es.	*That's how it's going to be.*
Was sagen Sie **dazu?**	*What do you have to say about that?*
Es ist aus **damit**.	*It's over.*
Heraus **damit!**	*Out with it!*
Was haben wir **davon?**	*What good does it do us?*

20.2 ANTICIPATORY *DA*-COMPOUNDS

1. Many verbs and adjectives make use of prepositional phrases to complete their meanings (see 10.2, 13.5, and R.3).

Gestern Abend **handelte** der erste Beitrag **von schweren Unwettern im Süden Deutschlands.**

Last night, the first segment had to do with fierce storms in southern Germany.

2. In some cases, the object of such a preposition is not merely a noun phrase (i.e., a noun with modifiers, such as *severe weather*), but rather an entire clause, including a verb.

The second segment had to do with how…

To render this into German requires a special structure, since German prepositions cannot be simply joined to a clause as in English. Instead, a **da**-compound containing the preposition is inserted into the middle field of the main clause, while the information linked to the preposition follows directly after the main clause in the form of an additional clause. In other words, the **da**-compound signals or "anticipates" the clause to follow, alerting the reader or listener that information pertinent to the preposition is forthcoming.

Der zweite Beitrag handelte **davon, wie gewisse Politiker auf einen Skandal in ihrer Partei reagierten.**

The second segment had to do with how certain politicians reacted to a scandal in their party.

Ich interessiere mich **dafür, die Perspektive der Medien zu hören.**

I am interested in hearing the media's perspective.

3. The clause following the anticipatory **da**-compound can be an infinitive clause, or a subordinate clause introduced by **dass** or another conjunction, with a subject and a conjugated verb. If the subject of the anticipated clause is different from the subject of the main clause, a subordinate clause (rather than an infinitive clause) is required. The main clause is always separated from the anticipated clause by a comma.

Ich freue mich **darüber,** viele wichtige Informationen in kürzester Zeit **zu** bekommen. *(infinitive clause)*

I'm happy to get lots of important information in a very short time.

Man kann sich **darauf** verlassen, **dass** die Sendung genau 15 Minuten dauert. *(subordinate clause)*	*You can always depend on the program lasting exactly 15 minutes.*
Ich staune immer **darüber, wie viel** sie übers Ausland berichten. *(subordinate clause)*	*I'm always amazed at how much they report about foreign countries.*

4. Sometimes an optional anticipatory **da**-compound is added even when the prepositional phrase is not essential for completing the meaning of the verb.

Neulich wurde **(davon)** berichtet, wie langsam sich die Wirtschaft dort erholt.	*Recently it was reported (about) how slowly the economy there is recovering.*

5. The adverbs **dahin** and **daher** are used with **gehen** and **kommen** to anticipate subsequent clauses; they cannot be omitted.

Die Probleme kommen **daher,** dass einige Länder in der Eurozone sehr hohe Arbeitslosigkeit haben.	*The problems arise from the fact that several countries in the euro zone have very high unemployment.*
Die Tendenz geht **dahin,** diese Länder mit Hilfspaketen zu unterstützen.	*The tendency now is to support these countries with bail-out packages.*

6. **Da**-compounds can also be used with a number of adjectives that often take prepositional complements (see 13.5).

Die Perspektive ist immer **davon** abhängig, wer den Beitrag schreibt.	*The perspective is always dependent on who writes the segment.*

20.3 USES OF *ES*

A. Impersonal *es*

1. Impersonal **es,** like English *it,* can be used to indicate the occurrence of activities without any specific agent or "doer." It occurs frequently in weather and time expressions, as well as with numerous verbs that in English require an agent as the subject.

Es regnet (blitzt, donnert, friert, hagelt, schneit, stürmt).	*It is raining (lightning, thundering, freezing, hailing, snowing, storming).*
Es ist acht Uhr.	*It is eight o'clock.*
Es riecht (stinkt, duftet).	*It smells (stinks, gives off an aroma).*
Es klopft.	*Someone is knocking at the door. (lit., "it is knocking")*
Es brennt.	*There is a fire. Something is burning. (lit., "it is burning")*
Es zieht.	*There is a draft. (lit., "it pulls")*

2. **Es** also occurs in numerous so-called impersonal expressions in which *it* (**es**) is the subject of the German phrase or sentence but not of its English equivalent.

Wie geht **es** dir/Ihnen?	*How are you? How's it going?*
Es geht mir gut.	*I am fine.*
Es gelingt mir.	*I succeed.*
Es tut mir leid.	*I am sorry.*
Es fehlt mir an *(dative)* ...	*I am missing/lacking . . .*

In these examples, **es** functions as the subject of the clause and appears whether it is positioned in the front field or not (see 1.1.A).

Es ging mir das ganze Semester gut.	*I was fine/Things were good the whole*
Das ganze Semester ging **es** mir gut.	*semester.*

3. **Es** is also a factor—indirectly—in expressions of feeling and sensation, such as *I am cold, he became ill,* and *we're feeling dizzy.* But where English uses a personal pronoun and a predicate adjective, German uses a dative of reference (see 5.5.C), **sein** or **werden** in the third-person singular, a "disappearing" **es,** and an adjective. In a sentence with normal word order, **es** would appear in the front field, followed by these other elements.

Es ist *mir* heiß.	*I am (i.e., I feel) hot.*
Es war *uns* kalt.	*We were (i.e., we felt) cold.*
Es wurde *ihnen* übel/schlecht.	*They became ill/began to feel nauseated.*

But in everyday usage, the dative of reference in these sentences usually moves to the front field, and the **es** disappears after the verb. Notice that the verb is conjugated in the third-person singular regardless of whether the dative of reference is singular or plural.

Mir ist zu kalt.	*I'm (too) cold. / It's (too) cold for me.*
Uns war schwindlig.	*We felt dizzy.*
Ihr ist langweilig.	*She's bored.*
Ihm wurde übel/schlecht.	*He began to feel sick.*
Ihnen war viel zu heiß.	*It was much too hot for them. / They were too hot.*

Es likewise disappears when these statements are turned into questions.

Ist dir zu kalt?	*Are you (feeling) cold? / Is it too cold for you?*
War Ihnen schwindlig?	*Did you feel dizzy? / Did you get dizzy?*
Ist ihm langweilig?	*Is he (feeling) bored?*

Other elements may appear in the front field as well, similarly causing **es** to be dropped from the sentence.

COMPARE:

Es wird mir langsam schlecht.	
Mir wird langsam schlecht.	*I'm starting to feel sick.*
Langsam wird mir schlecht.	

4. In main clauses, **es** can introduce a sentence in which the true subject follows the conjugated verb. The verb agrees with this subject, not with **es**. This construction has a formal or literary flavor. (See also **es** with the passive, 12.1.B.)

Es folgen jetzt zwei Berichte über...	*Now follow two reports concerning . . .*
Es besuchte heute Nachmittag der Ministerpräsident ...	*There was a visit this afternoon by the prime minister . . .*

Here too, the impersonal **es** is not used if a different element is positioned in the front field.

COMPARE:

Es finden heute Wahlen statt.	*There are elections taking place today.*
Heute finden Wahlen statt.	*Elections are taking place today.*

B. *Es gibt; es ist/es sind*

1. The expression **es gibt** means *there is* or *there are* and normally refers to the *general existence* of something, to *permanent existence in a specific place*, or to *general consequences*. In this construction, **es** is the subject (not merely a placeholder), the verb form is always singular, and the object of the verb is always in the accusative case.

Für die Börse **gibt es** wieder einen Grund zu feiern.	*For the stock market there's reason to celebrate again. / The stock market has reason to celebrate again.*
Es gab für ganz Deutschland eine Unwetterwarnung.	*There was a severe weather warning for all of Germany.*
Es gibt noch nicht viele Schulen in Deutschland, die Chinesisch anbieten.	*There are not many schools yet in Germany that offer Chinese.*
Wegen der Preiserhöhungen **gab es** vor den Parlamentsgebäuden Proteste.	*Due to the price increases there were protests in front of the parliament buildings.*

2. The expression **es ist** (plural: **es sind**) also means *there is/are*, but **es ist/sind** denotes the presence of things or people in a specific place rather than in general. Since English *there is/are* does not make this distinction, many English speakers overuse **es gibt,** and should take care to consider which meaning of *there is/are* they wish to convey. Like **es gibt, es ist/sind** can be used in various tenses.

ES GIBT:

Es gibt in dieser Region noch viele Probleme.	*There are still many problems in this region.*
Nach dem Gipfeltreffen **gab es** nichts mehr zu diskutieren.	*After the summit meeting there was nothing more to discuss.*

ES IST:

Es waren schätzungsweise 500.000 Menschen beim Kölner Karneval dabei.	*There were an estimated 500,000 people participating in the Cologne "Karneval."*

Es war niemand in der Wohnung, als die Polizei ankam.	*There was no one in the apartment when the police arrived.*
Es sind heute drei Themen, denen wir uns widmen wollen.	*There are three topics today that we want to address.*

Unlike the **es** in **es gibt,** the **es** in **es ist/sind** is a front field placeholder and does not appear if another element occupies that position. In addition, **es ist/sind** is used only in main clauses rather than subordinate clauses or questions, where the movement of V_1 away from second position makes **es** unnecessary as a placeholder. Remember that the noun following **es gibt,** as the direct object of **gibt,** is always in the accusative, whereas the noun following **es ist/sind,** as the sentence subject, is in the nominative, and determines whether the phrase is singular (**es ist**) or plural (**es sind**).

COMPARE:

Es gibt in der Krebsforschung noch viel zu tun. *(statement)*	*There is still much to do in cancer research.*
Gibt es in der Krebsforschung noch viel zu tun? *(question)*	*Is there still much to do in cancer research?*
Auf der Tagung wurde gefragt, was **es** noch in der Krebsforschung zu tun **gibt.** *(dependent clause)*	*At the conference there were questions concerning what still needs to be done in cancer research.*

BUT:

Es war niemand in der Wohnung. *(statement)*	*There was no one in the apartment.*
War niemand in der Wohnung? *(question)*	*Was no one in the apartment?*
Es wurde festgestellt, dass niemand in der Wohnung **war.** *(dependent clause)*	*It was determined that no one was in the apartment.*

C. Anticipatory *es*

Es can be used to anticipate what will follow in a subsequent clause. It can be either a subject or a direct object and is often optional after a verb. The same usage occurs in English.

Es bleibt noch unklar, ob ...	*It still remains unclear if/whether . . .*
Es ist möglich/schade/wichtig, dass ...	*It is possible/too bad/important that . . .*
Wir haben (**es**) gewusst, dass ...	*We knew that . . .*
Viele können (**es**) nicht glauben, dass ...	*Many (people) cannot believe (it) that . . .*
Es freut/ärgert mich, dass ... **OR:** Mich freut/ärgert (**es**), dass ...	*It pleases/annoys me that . . .*
Es macht Spaß, wenn ...	*It is fun when . . .*

Wortschatz

es handelt sich um | es geht um | handeln von

1. The expressions **es handelt sich + um** and **es geht + um** are synonymous. They indicate what something *is about* and have a number of English equivalents. The subject of these expressions is always **es**, and they are often used with an anticipatory **da**-compound.

<table>
<tr>
<td>es handelt sich um
es geht um</td>
<td>it is a question of
it is a matter of
at issue is
at stake are
we are dealing with
we are talking about
it concerns</td>
</tr>
</table>

Es handelt sich hier **um** die Zukunft der Eurozone.	*What we are talking about/is at stake here is the future of the euro zone.*
Es geht darum, möglichst schnell die Terroristengruppen ausfindig zu machen.	*It's a matter of tracking down the terrorist groups as quickly as possible.*

2. **Handeln von** is used to express the idea that a text (book, article, poem, play) or other communicative medium (film, TV program) *is about* something.

Der Artikel **handelt von** deutsch-türkischen Beziehungen.	*The article is about German-Turkish relationships.*
Wovon handelt die Sendung?	*What is the TV program about?*

Übungen

A **Gegenstände *(objects)* des täglichen Lebens.** Was kann man mit diesen Gegenständen alles machen? Verwenden Sie Konstruktionen mit **da-**.

BEISPIELE ein Haus
*Man kann **darin** wohnen.*

ein Fernseher
*Man kann **davor** einschlafen.*

1. ein Stück Holz *(wood)*
2. Bleistift und Papier
3. ein Rucksack
4. Lebensmittel
5. ein Kompass
6. alte Bierflaschen
7. ein Fußballtor *(goal)*
8. ein Kühlschrank

Erzählen Sie von weiteren Gegenständen.

B   **Danach? Darüber? Nach ihnen? Über sie?**   Ergänzen Sie die folgenden Sätze mit einer **da**-Konstruktion oder einem Pronomen, je nachdem, mit welchem Wort die Idee anfängt und ...und welche Form (**da**- oder Pronomen) besser zu der Situation passt. Wenn Sie die Präpositionen für die Verben nicht wissen, können Sie sie bei R.3 nachschlagen *(look up)*.

> **BEISPIEL**   Das Wetter? Viele Leute ärgern sich _____.
> *Das Wetter? Viele Leute ärgern sich **darüber**.*

1. Die kommenden Ferien? Ja, ich denke sehr gern _____.
2. Meine Verwandten? Ich weiß, ich rede vielleicht zu viel _____.
3. Das Geburtstagsgeschenk? Ich habe Tante Isabel schon _____ gedankt.
4. Meine Freunde? Ich kann mich immer _____ verlassen *(depend on)*.
5. Mein Handy? Nein, ich kann nicht _____ verzichten *(do without)*.
6. Mein Aufsatz? Ich muss noch _____ arbeiten.
7. Die Wiedervereinigung? Dieser Film handelt ja _____.
8. Getränke für die Party? Keine Sorge – ich kümmere mich _____.
9. Der blaue Pulli? Nein, die Hose da passt gar nicht _____.
10. Deine Aufrichtigkeit *(sincerity)*? Tut mir leid, aber leider muss ich oft _____ zweifeln *(doubt)*.

C   **Fragen: Mit oder ohne *da*-Konstruktion?**   Antworten Sie bitte mit ganzen Sätzen (und ganz ehrlich!) auf die folgenden Fragen.

> **BEISPIELE**   Sind Sie mit der jetzigen Außenpolitik *(foreign policy)* in Ihrem Land einverstanden?
> *Ja, ich bin **damit** einverstanden.* [oder]
> *Nein, ich bin nicht **damit** einverstanden.*
>
> Haben Sie Respekt vor Anwälten *(lawyers)*?
> *Ja, ich habe Respekt vor **ihnen**.* [oder]
> *Nein, ich habe keinen Respekt vor **ihnen**.*

1. Freuen Sie sich über das Glück anderer Menschen?
2. Haben Sie etwas gegen Menschen, die anderer Meinung sind als Sie?
3. Interessieren Sie sich für Theater? Politik? Informatik *(computer programming)*?
4. Haben Sie Angst vor Ihren Professorinnen/Professoren?
5. Zählen Sie sich zu den Leuten, die fast jeden Tag etwas für die Umwelt tun?
6. Wären Sie bereit, ohne ein Auto zu leben?
7. Sind Sie mit Ihrem bisherigen Leben zufrieden?

D   **Knapper sagen.**   Drücken Sie die Ideen in den folgenden Sätzen knapper *(more succinctly)* und stärker aus. Verwenden Sie Ausdrücke mit **da**-Konstruktionen **(siehe oben, 1.B.4)**.

> **BEISPIEL**   Wir haben es so gemacht und wir können es jetzt nicht mehr ändern.
> *Dabei bleibt es.*

1. Ob ich morgen komme? Naja, wenn ich Zeit habe, komme ich vielleicht, aber ich weiß es noch nicht so genau.
2. Du hast meine Meinung gehört und jetzt möchte ich deine wissen.

3. Es hilft nichts, wenn Oliver sagt, es war nicht seine Schuld *(fault)*.
4. Ich bitte Sie jetzt noch einmal: Geben Sie mir die Information!
5. Ich möchte Ihnen helfen, aber ich hatte mit der Entscheidung nichts zu tun.
6. Was für einen Vorteil *(advantage)* soll mir das bringen?
7. Sie haben sich auf unsere Kosten gut amüsiert, aber jetzt hört der Spaß auf.

E **Anders formulieren.**   Drücken Sie die Sätze durch den Gebrauch von **da**-Konstruktionen anders aus.

BEISPIEL   Du kannst dich auf unsere Hilfe verlassen.
*Du kannst dich **darauf** verlassen, dass wir dir helfen werden.*

1. Wir möchten uns für eure Hilfe bedanken.
2. Unsere Professorin beklagt sich *(complains)* über unser schlechtes Benehmen.
3. Auswanderer haben oft Angst vor dem Verlust *(loss)* ihrer Muttersprache.
4. Ein Automechaniker hat uns zum Kauf eines neuen Autos geraten.
5. Einige Deutsche ärgern sich über die Arbeitslosigkeit im Nordosten des Landes.

F **Eigene Sätze bilden.**   Bilden Sie wahre Aussagen über sich selbst oder über Menschen, die Sie kennen. Verwenden Sie die angegebenen Verben mit **da**-Konstruktionen. (Erklärungen und Beispiele zu Verb + Präpositionen finden Sie bei R.3.)

BEISPIEL   sich freuen auf
*Ich freue mich **darauf**, nach dem Semester ausschlafen* (to sleep in) *zu können.*

1. Angst haben vor *(to be scared of)*
2. sich ärgern über *(to be annoyed at)*
3. überreden zu *(to persuade to do)*
4. sorgen für *(to see to something)*
5. zweifeln an *(to have doubts about)*
6. stimmen für *(to vote for)*
7. achten auf *(to pay attention to)*
8. streben nach *(to strive for)*
9. sich verlieben in *(to fall in love with)*
10. erzählen von *(to tell/talk about)*

G **Was gibt's?**   Drücken Sie die Sätze anders aus. Verwenden Sie die angegebenen Ausdrücke aus dem Kasten.

BEISPIEL   Man findet im Ruhrgebiet viele Großstädte.
Im Ruhrgebiet gibt es viele Großstädte.

es gibt   es fehlt   es ist/sind   es + [*verb*]

1. Ich habe im Moment leider kein Geld.
2. Ich höre draußen jemanden an die Tür klopfen.
3. In der Maximilianstraße in München befinden sich elegante Geschäfte.
4. Feuer!
5. Dass der Schnee vor morgen kommt, ist höchst unwahrscheinlich.
6. Kein Grund ist vorhanden *(exists)*, die Aussage dieses Polizisten zu bezweifeln.

Anwendung

A   Etwas vorführen (demonstrate).   Bringen Sie einen Gegenstand (oder ein Bild von einem Gegenstand) zum Unterricht mit. Erklären Sie, wie dieser Gegenstand funktioniert, was man damit machen kann usw. Verwenden Sie Kombinationen mit **da-**.

VORSCHLÄGE

ein altes Küchengerät *(kitchen utensil)*
Zubehör *(accessory)* für Xbox, Nintendo usw.
ein Gerät aus einem Chemie-/Biologielabor *(-laboratory)*
irgendeine Funktion auf Ihrem Handy
ein musikalisches Instrument, das Sie spielen
Zubehör für eine Sportart *(type of sport)*

REDEMITTEL

Das hier ist …
Ich möchte euch ein bisschen darüber informieren, wie …
Damit kann man …
Ich möchte euch zeigen, wie …
Habt ihr jetzt Fragen dazu?

B   Räumlich beschreiben.   Erkundigen Sie sich bei jemandem im Kurs danach, wie ein bestimmter Raum (z.B. ein Schlafzimmer, ein Garten, die Küche) bei ihr oder ihm aussieht. Benutzen Sie dabei viele Formen mit **da-**.

BEISPIEL   A: *Wie sieht dein Zimmer im Studentenwohnheim aus?*
                    B: *Mein Zimmer ist recht groß. In einer Ecke steht mein Arbeitstisch. Darauf steht mein Laptop und ich mache meine Aufgaben damit. Links davon … usw.*

C   Wovon handelt es?   Fragen Sie ein paar Studentinnen/Studenten in Ihrer Gruppe, was für Bücher sie in letzter Zeit *(recently)* gelesen oder welche Filme/Fernsehsendungen sie gesehen haben. Wenn Sie einen Titel hören, den Sie nicht kennen, fragen Sie danach: Wovon handelt dieses Buch? Worum geht es in diesem Film? Benutzen Sie in den Antworten Vokabeln aus dem **Wortschatz**.

BEISPIELE   *Also, am Anfang geht es hier um einen Jungen, der bei einer armen Familie lebt …*
                     Dieser Film handelt von zwei Menschen, die sich gegenseitig nicht ausstehen (stand) können …

Schriftliche Themen

Tipps zum Schreiben	**Avoiding Some Common Pitfalls**
	Use the first-person singular **ich** sparingly when presenting your views and opinions on a subject in writing. You can occasionally include your reader or other persons in the solutions you propose by using **wir.** Readers can become confused, however, if you shift between the pronouns **ich** and **wir** for no apparent reason. Also, make sure you have not used the neuter or impersonal pronoun **es** to refer to nouns that are masculine (*pronoun* **er**) or feminine (*pronoun* **sie**).
	After writing a first draft, reread it to see whether the use of an occasional **da**-compound instead of a preposition plus a previously mentioned noun will tighten your text without sacrificing its clarity.

D **Einen Standpunkt vertreten (*represent*).** Äußern Sie sich schriftlich zu einem Thema, zu dem es unterschiedliche Meinungen gibt. Versuchen Sie Ihre Argumente durch einige der folgenden Wendungen (*expressions*) einzuführen und zu betonen.

REDEMITTEL

Das Problem liegt meiner Meinung nach darin, dass …
Wir müssen uns vor allem darüber klar sein, wie/was/wer/inwiefern …
Ich möchte daran erinnern, dass …
Ich glaube, man kann sich nicht darauf verlassen (*rely upon*), dass …
Ja, das kommt daher/davon, dass …
Sind wir uns jetzt darüber einig, dass … ?
Ich halte es für wichtig/richtig, dass …
Daher gibt es keinen Grund … zu [tun].

THEMENVORSCHLÄGE

Weltpolitik
Umweltfragen
soziale Probleme
das Gesundheitswesen (*health care*)
Freizeit: lieber digital oder sportlich?
ideologische und politische Konfrontation an der Universität
Wirtschaftspolitik (*economic policy*)

Zusammenfassung

Rules to Remember

1   **Da**-compounds normally refer only to things, not to persons or other animate beings.

2   A **da**-compound is often used to anticipate an infinitive clause or subordinate clause.

3   **Es gibt** refers to general or permanent existence. **Es ist/es sind** refers to more localized, specific presence. The object of **es gibt** (*there is*) is always in the accusative.

4   The impersonal **es** can refer to an action (**es regnet**); it can be a placeholder (**es tut mir leid**); and it can anticipate a subordinate clause or infinitive clause that follows.

At a Glance

Preposition	
durch	an
für	auf
gegen	hinter
um	in
aus	neben
bei	über
mit	unter
nach	vor
von	zwischen
zu	

da-compound	
dadurch	daran (dran)
dafür	darauf (drauf)
dagegen	dahinter
darum (drum)	darin (drin)
daraus (draus)	daneben
dabei	darüber (drüber)
damit	darunter (drunter)
danach	davor
davon	dazwischen
dazu	

Noncombining prepositions	
außer	*(all genitive*
gegenüber	*prepositions)*
ohne	
seit	

Da-compounds: Sentence structure

_____ darauf (_____), dass _____ $\boxed{V_1}$

_____ darauf (_____), _____ zu $\boxed{\text{infinitive}}$

Uses of *es*	
Impersonal **es** (*es is the subject and always appears*)	• weather expressions (e.g., **es regnet**) • time expressions (e.g., **es ist drei Uhr**) • impersonal verbs (e.g., **es brennt, es zieht**)
Impersonal expressions	Wie geht **es** dir/Ihnen? **Es** tut mir leid. *(see 20.3.A for additional expressions)*
Feeling/sensation	**Es** is a placeholder in the front field, and disappears when the dative of reference moves to that position: **Es** ist mir kalt. → Mir ist kalt. **Es** wurde uns schlecht. → Uns wurde schlecht.
es gibt + *accusative* **es ist/es sind** + *nominative*	= *there is/there are*; refers to general *existence* = *there is/there are*; refers to more specific *presence*
Anticipatory **es**	**Es** _____, dass _____ $\boxed{V_1}$ _____ (es) (_____), dass _____ $\boxed{V_1}$

zum Beispiel

Fitness

Mathis Wienand/Getty Images

Fitness: If you're looking for fitness venues in Germany, Switzerland, or Austria, you're in luck: it's a thriving industry in all three countries. State-of-the-art fitness centers are springing up everywhere, as more and more people are joining—over 7 million in Germany, for example, or nearly 10% of the population. In Switzerland, you can find clubs such as **Eurofit, Club24, fitwork,** and **Fit-x** even in smaller cities. And for Austria, click through www.fitness-center.at to get a sense of how wide-ranging the offerings are there. But **Fitness-Clubs** are just one facet of the current emphasis on body culture and health. Marathons and half-marathons are growing steadily, as seen, for example, in the annual **Stadtläufe** organized in 20 cities by the sports outfitter Sportscheck ("Wir machen Sport"). And while traditional sports such as soccer and cycling remain as popular as ever, people are being drawn to trendier fitness options such as *Zumba* and *Bokwa* ("Der neue Kalorien-Killer aus den USA!").

329

Chapters 21 and 22 deal with the subjunctive mood and its role in two very different communicative situations: first, in expressing hypothetical (and sometimes "unreal") conditions, stating wishes, and making polite utterances and requests; and second, in signaling indirect discourse, in which one speaker wishes to indicate that he or she is conveying information expressed by someone else (and thus cannot vouch for its content). German uses two distinct grammatical forms in these two situations. The more common of these—the verb form used in conditional sentences, wishes, and polite expressions—is based on the second principal part of the verb (the simple past), and is therefore commonly referred to as *Subjunctive II*. The verb form used to signal indirect discourse is based on the first principal part of the verb (the infinitive), and is referred to as *Subjunctive I;* it is discussed in Chapter 22.

Grammatik

<table>
<tr><td>**21.1**</td><td>**THE SUBJUNCTIVE MOOD**</td></tr>
</table>

German verbs can be expressed in three different *moods*: the indicative, the imperative (see Chapter 23), and the subjunctive. These moods are used to make distinctions regarding how forcefully or tentatively the speaker or writer stands behind an utterance. The *indicative* is the most commonly used mood—both in everyday speech and in virtually all language registers discussed in this book so far—and simply shows that the speaker/writer wants to "indicate" or formulate an idea or a question. In other words, the speaker or writer wishes to express the comment or question directly. This can be qualified by a modal verb (see 9.2) or adverbs such as **vielleicht** *(perhaps)* or **vermutlich** *(probably)*, but the overall attitude is straightforward. The *imperative* mood is used to express commands, an even more direct (and sometimes even blunt) posture on the part of the speaker or writer.

Indicative

Ich **habe** zu viel zu tun.	*I've got too much to do.*
Also, ich **kann** wirklich nicht mit dir ins Fitnessstudio gehen.	*So I really can't go with you to the gym.*
Verstehst du das nicht?	*Don't you understand that?*

Imperative

Ach, **hör auf** mit deinen Ausreden. **Gehen wir!**	*Oh, quit making excuses. Let's go!*

The *subjunctive* mood, on the other hand, signals that the speaker or writer considers a statement or question to be conjecture, imagined, only a hypothetical possibility, a wish (something desired but not true at the moment of utterance), or speculation about what might have been (but did not in fact happen). The subjunctive mood is also used to convey a polite sense of distance, similar to its usage in English. (It is this sense of distance that ties the use of the subjunctive to indirect discourse, as mentioned above and discussed in detail in Chapter 22.)

Es **wäre** schön, wenn ich mitkommen **könnte**.	*It would be nice if I could come along.* (but it isn't possible)
Wenn ich nicht so viel Arbeit **hätte**, **würde** ich gern mitkommen.	*If I didn't have so much work, I'd really like to come along.* (but in fact I do, so I won't)
Wenn du nur am Wochenende **gefragt hättest!**	*If only you had asked on the weekend* (which you didn't do)
Könntest du mich jetzt bitte in Ruhe lassen?	*Now, could you please leave me alone?*

Notice the similarity between these forms (wäre/hätte/würde/könntest) and the second principal part of each verb, the simple past (war/hatte/wurde/konntest), which leads to their designation as *subjunctive II* (**der zweite Konjunktiv**).

21.2 ▶ PRESENT SUBJUNCTIVE II FORMS

A. *Würde* + infinitive

The most common subjunctive form in German, at least in spoken language, is **würde** *(would)* + **infinitive**. In this construction, **würde** functions like a modal verb as V_1, and the infinitive serves as V_2 in the verbal bracket (see 1.1.D). Like all present subjunctive verbs, **würde** is formed by adding the subjunctive endings **-e, -est, -e; -en, -et,** and **-en** to the simple past stem, modified with an umlaut (see 2.D below).

ich würd **e**	wir würd **en**
du würd **est**	ihr würd **et**
Sie würd **en**	Sie würd **en**
er/sie/es würd **e**	sie würd **en**

Würdest du wenigstens mit mir joggen gehen?	*Would you at least go jogging with me?*
—Joggen? Echt? Ich **würde** lieber in Eiswasser ertrinken.	*—Jogging? Really? I'd rather drown in ice water.*

In the following discussion, **würde** + infinitive forms will be distinguished from present subjunctive II single-word forms (such as **wäre** or **käme**), which likewise can translate as *would* _____.[1]

---

[1]Note that *would* _____ is not the only (and sometimes not the preferred) English translation for present subjunctive II forms or for **würde** + infinitive. English uses a variety of means to express the subjunctive:

Wenn wir Zeit **hätten**, ... $\left\{ \begin{array}{l} \textit{If we had time . . .} \\ \textit{If we did have time . . .} \\ \textit{If we were to have time . . .} \end{array} \right.$

B. Regular weak verbs

The present subjunctive II of regular weak verbs (such as **lernen, sagen,** and **spielen**; see 3.1.A) is formed by adding the subjunctive endings (**-e, -est, -e; -en, -et, -en**) to the simple past stem. Since these endings are identical to the past-tense endings, the present subjunctive II of regular weak verbs is indistinguishable from the simple past indicative of these verbs, and is therefore almost always replaced with **würde** + infinitive, unless the context makes the subjunctive mood of that verb obvious.

spielen	
Simple past	**Subjunctive II**
ich spielte	spielt **e**
du spieltest	spielt **est**
Sie spielten	spielt **en**
er/sie/es spielte	spielt **e**
wir spielten	spielt **en**
ihr spieltet	spielt **et**
Sie spielten	spielt **en**
sie spielten	spielt **en**

Wenn du Squash **spieltest,** ...
  (less common)

Wenn du Squash **spielen würdest,** ...
  (more common)

} *If you played /If you were to play squash, …*

C. Irregular verbs

1. The present subjunctive II of irregular verbs (see 3.1.C) is also formed by adding the subjunctive endings (**-e, -est, -e; -en, -et, -en**) to the simple past stem, but in addition these verbs alter the vowel of the stem either with an umlaut or by changing **a** to **e,** depending on the verb.

Infinitive	Simple past: *er/sie*	Subjunctive II: *er/sie*
brennen	brannte	**brennte**
bringen	brachte	**brächte**
denken	dachte	**dächte**
kennen	kannte	**kennte**
nennen	nannte	**nennte**
rennen	rannte	**rennte**
senden	sendete/sandte	**sendete**
wenden	wendete/wandte	**wendete**
wissen	wusste	**wüsste**

2. With the exception of **wissen** $\longrightarrow$ **wüsste,** these subjunctive forms are almost always replaced by **würde** + infinitive.

Wenn er bloß schneller **rennen würde,** ...   *If he would just run faster, . . .*

BUT:

Wenn ich das **wüsste,** ...   *If I knew that, . . .*

D. Strong verbs

1. The present subjunctive II of strong verbs is formed by adding the subjunctive endings (**-e, -est, -e; -en, -et,** and **-en**) to the simple past stem. In addition, the stem takes an umlaut when the stem vowel is **a, o,** or **u.** The charts below compare the simple past with the subjunctive II forms.

	gehen		kommen	
	Simple past	**Subjunctive II**	**Simple past**	**Subjunctive II**
ich	ging	ging **e**	kam	käm **e**
du	gingst	ging **est**	kamst	käm **est**
Sie	gingen	ging **en**	kamen	käm **en**
er/sie/es	ging	ging **e**	kam	käm **e**
wir	gingen	ging **en**	kamen	käm **en**
ihr	gingt	ging **et**	kamt	käm **et**
Sie	gingen	ging **en**	kamen	käm **en**
sie	gingen	ging **en**	kamen	käm **en**

OTHER EXAMPLES:

Infinitive	**Simple past:** *er/sie*	**Subjunctive II:** *er/sie*
bleiben	blieb	**bliebe**
fliegen	flog	**flöge**
schneiden	schnitt	**schnitte**
werden	wurde	**würde**

Wenn noch mehr Kunden **kämen, bliebe**   *If more customers were to come, the*
das Fitnessstudio noch länger auf.   *gym would stay open longer.*

2. With the exception of very common verbs such as **sein, werden, gehen, kommen,** and **tun,** the present subjunctive II of these verbs occurs mainly in written German. In spoken German, and even to some extent in written German, there is a strong tendency to use **würde** + infinitive.

Wenn du öfter *liefest,* könnte es dir sogar
 Spaß machen. *(less common)*

Wenn du öfter *laufen würdest,*   *If you ran (were to run, would run)*
 könnte es dir sogar Spaß machen.   *more often, it could even be fun for*
 (more common)   *you.*

3. A number of strong verbs with the simple past stem vowel **a** have alternative subjunctive forms with **ö** or **ü.** In some instances, **ö** or **ü** are the only forms. These forms are now considered obsolete and are normally replaced by **würde** + infinitive.

Infinitive	Simple past: *er/sie*	Subjunctive II: *er/sie*
beginnen	begann	**begönne** (*or* **begänne**)
empfehlen	empfahl	**empföhle** (*or* **empfähle**)
gewinnen	gewann	**gewönne** (*or* **gewänne**)
stehen	stand	**stünde** (*or* **stände**)
helfen	half	**hülfe**
sterben	starb	**stürbe**
werfen	warf	**würfe**

4. Remember that although these subjunctive II forms—weak, irregular, and strong—are derived from the simple past stem, they refer to present or future time, not the past.

COMPARE:

Das **war** aber schön.
  (*direct statement; in the past*)

That was really nice.

Das **wäre** aber schön.
  (*speculation; now or in the future*)

That would really be nice.

Wann immer ich zum Yogakurs **ging,** …
  (*direct statement; in the past*)

Whenever I went to the yoga course, …

Wenn ich zum Yogakurs **ginge,** …
  (*speculation; now or in the future*)

If I were to go to the yoga course, …

E. Modal verbs

1. Modal verbs with an umlaut in the infinitive take an umlaut in the present subjunctive II; only **sollen** and **wollen** do not. The subjunctive forms of these verbs are *not* normally replaced by **würde** + infinitive. Note the meanings of the modals in the subjunctive below.

Infinitive	Simple past: er/sie	Subjunctive II: er/sie	
dürfen	durfte	**dürfte**	*would/might be permitted to*
können	konnte	**könnte**	*could/would be able to*
mögen	mochte	**möchte**	*would like to*
müssen	musste	**müsste**	*would have to*

BUT:

sollen	sollte	**sollte**	*should*
wollen	wollte	**wollte**	*would want to*

2. Recall that **können** can express possibility and **müssen** can express probability (see 9.2). With these verbs, using the subjunctive shows that the inference of probability or uncertainty is itself uncertain. When the reference is to something happening in the *present* or *future*, the subjunctive modal + present infinitive is used; when the reference is to the *past*, a subjunctive modal + perfect infinitive (see 9.1.B and 24.2) is used.

Sie **müsste** eigentlich schon da **sein**.	*She really ought to be there by now.*
So etwas **könnte** schon **passiert sein**.	*Such a thing could actually have happened.*

F. *Haben, sein, werden*

Haben and **sein** (along with **würde**) are the most commonly used present subjunctive verbs and normally take the present subjunctive II form rather than **würde** + infinitive. Notice that they both require an umlaut.

Infinitive	Simple past: *er/sie*	Subjunctive II: *er/sie*
haben	hatte	**hätte**
sein	war	**wäre**

G. Summary: Subjunctive II forms vs. *würde* + infinitive

1. In spoken German, only the present subjunctive II forms of **haben, sein, werden, gehen, tun, wissen,** and the modal verbs are preferred over **würde** + infinitive and are commonly used. With most other verbs, **würde** + infinitive is substituted for present subjunctive II forms.

2. In written German, however, present subjunctive II forms appear more often, but even in writing, **würde** + infinitive is gradually replacing these forms. This poses a problem when one wants to avoid using two forms of **würde** back to back, which is especially prone to occur in a conditional sentence:

Wenn mir jemand mit dem Crosstrainer helfen **würde, würde** ich's versuchen.	*If someone would help me with the elliptical machine, I'd try it.*

The rule of thumb used to be that the **wenn**-clause should end with a present subjunctive II form, in order to avoid this repetition:

Wenn mir jemand mit dem Crosstrainer **hülfe, würde** ich's versuchen.

But the rule is becoming increasingly difficult to apply as present subjunctive II forms (like **hülfe**, for example) have for the most part fallen into disuse. To some German speakers, present subjunctive II forms such as **kennte** and **rennte** are so obsolete that they sound grammatically wrong. Other verbs, like **würfe** and **stürbe,** are acknowledged to be correct but are considered archaic, while some common verbs (such as **kommen** and **tun**) have present subjunctive II forms (**käme** and **täte**) that can substitute more or less equally for **würde kommen** and **würde tun,** especially in regional dialects. Modal verbs are often the best solution to the problem: Since their subjunctive II forms are almost always acceptable, it is usually preferable—when in doubt about a subjunctive II form—to use a **würde** + infinitive structure in one clause, and a modal verb in subjunctive II in the remaining clause.

Wenn mir jemand mit dem Crosstrainer helfen **würde, könnte** ich's versuchen.	*If someone would help me with the elliptical machine, I could try it.*

3. In summary: For writing or speaking, present subjunctive II forms are:

- preferred (some would say mandatory) for **haben, sein, werden,** and the modal verbs.

- stylistically proper for frequently used strong verbs such as **finden, gehen, kommen,** and **tun,** and for **wissen.**

- acceptable for weak verbs when the context makes the subjunctive meaning clear (usually in writing).

- almost never used for irregular verbs or the strong verbs listed in section D.3 above.

21.3 USES OF PRESENT SUBJUNCTIVE II

A. Hypothetical conditions and consequences

1. The present subjunctive II is used to express an unreal or contrary-to-fact condition and its consequence. Such "hypothetical" statements and questions consist of two parts: a **wenn**-clause (expressing the condition) and a consequence clause, following the English equivalent of *If…, then….* Since the **wenn**-clause is a dependent clause, the conjugated verb (V_1) appears at the end (see 1.3 and R.2). The consequence clause begins either with V_1 or—in the case of hypothetical statements—with an optional **dann** or **so,** followed by the conjugated verb. Hypothetical questions normally do not make use of **dann/so.**

Wenn nicht so viele Leute da **wären,** (dann/so) **würde** ich bestimmt öfter in den Club gehen.	*If there weren't so many people there, (then) I'd definitely go to the club more often.*
Wenn es ein Schwimmbad **hätte, wär's** für dich attraktiver?	*If it had a swimming pool, would it be more attractive for you?*

2. The order of the main clause and the **wenn**-clause can be reversed, just as in English, in which case **dann/so** is omitted.

Ja, es **wäre** attraktiver, wenn es ein Schwimmbad **hätte.** Und vielleicht auch noch eine Sauna.	*Yes, it would be more attractive if it had a swimming pool. And maybe a sauna too.*

3. Hypothetical statements can begin in German (as they also can in English) with a conjugated verb (V_1) that replaces **wenn** as the first element in the condition clause.

Hätte ich die richtigen Klamotten, (dann/so) …	*Had I the right things to wear, (then) …*
Wäre es draußen nicht so kalt, (dann/so) …	*Were it not so cold outdoors, (then)…*

The difference between German and English in this respect is one of range. Where English restricts this usage to the verbs *to have* and *to be*, German allows this construction for virtually all verbs.

Würde es nicht so viel kosten, (dann/so) …	*If it didn't cost so much, (then) …*
Könnte man vielleicht langsamer anfangen, (dann/so) …	*Maybe if one could start out more slowly, (then)…*

B. Conclusions without expressed conditions

Present subjunctives can appear with no condition expressed when the situation is not factually true, when one is speaking speculatively or with reference to a possibility, or when deferential politeness is in order (see also 21.3.D below).

Das **würde** ich nicht machen.	*I wouldn't do that.*
Das **wär's** für heute.	*That'll be it for today.*
An deiner Stelle **würde** ich das nicht tragen.	*If I were you* (lit., *in your place*), *I wouldn't wear that.*
Da **hätte** ich aber meine Bedenken.	*I'd have serious doubts about that.*
Ich **würde** lieber zu Hause bleiben.	*I'd rather stay at home.*
Ich **wüsste** nicht warum.	*I wouldn't know why.*

C. Wishes

1. Since wishes are inherently contrary to fact, they can also be expressed in the subjunctive mood. The intensifying adverb **nur** is added, sometimes in combination with the flavoring particle **doch** (see R.6.2.E).

Wenn er (doch) nur **mitmachen würde!**	*If only he would join in!* (fact: *he is not joining in*)

2. As in conditional statements, **wenn** can be omitted; the verb in first position then expresses the idea of *if*.

Wär(e)st[2] du (doch) nur nicht so faul!	*If only you weren't so lazy!* (fact: *you are lazy*)

3. Like English, German often prefaces contrary-to-fact wishes with the verbs **wollen** or **wünschen**. But unlike English, **wollen** or **wünschen** in this context are also expressed in the subjunctive mood.

Ich **wollte/wünschte,** ich **könnte** mehr als drei Klimmzüge machen.	*I wish I could do more than three chin-ups.* (fact: *I can't do more than three chin-ups*)

---

[2]As the chart in 2.F indicates, the subjunctive form of **sein**, conjugated with **du**, is **wärest**; but in spoken German, the abbreviated form **wärst** is much more common.

D. Polite requests

The sense of speculation and potentiality inherent in the subjunctive mood explains its connection with polite requests; by using it, the speaker implicitly suggests that it is up to the person addressed, rather than the speaker, to determine whether or not the wish will be fulfilled.

Wäre es möglich, das Laufband zu benutzen?	*Would it be possible to use the treadmill?*
Würden Sie mir bitte zeigen, wie es geht?	*Would you please show me how it works?*
Könnten Sie es mir bitte nochmal erklären?	*Could you please explain it to me one more time?*
Würden Sie bitte aufhören zu lachen?	*Would you please stop laughing?*

Subjunctive use in the first person similarly renders a sentence more deferential; rather than stating a demand, the speaker refers to something desired and potentially possible.

Ich **hätte** gern etwas zu trinken.	*I'd like to have something to drink.*

E. After *als (ob), als (wenn)*

1. A clause introduced by the conjunctions **als (ob)** or **als (wenn)** (see R.2) often describes a situation that *appears* to be the case but in the speaker's view may not be true. As long as the **als ob** clause refers to the same time as the main clause, the present subjunctive (subjunctive II or **würde** + infinitive) is used, regardless of the English tense of that verb.

Er tut (so), *als ob* er Arnold Schwarzenegger **wäre.**	*He's acting as if he were Arnold Schwarzenegger.*
Du tust manchmal (so), *als ob* du keine Ahnung **hättest.**	*Sometimes you act as if you didn't have a clue.*
Manche Leute tun (so), *als wenn* sie alles **wüssten.**	*Some people act as if they knew everything.*

2. The **ob** or **wenn** in this construction can be omitted, with V₁ placed directly after **als** (see R.2.3.D).

Sie sieht nur aus, *als ginge* ihr die Puste aus.	*She just looks as if she were out of breath.*
Der Trainer tut (so), *als wäre* diese Übung kinderleicht.	*The coach acts as if this exercise were child's play.*
Diese Leute tun (so), *als gäbe* es gar keine Gefahr.	*These people are acting as if there were no danger at all.*

3. In present time, the indicative is used instead of the subjunctive if in the speaker's view the impression is a correct one.

Er sieht aus, als ob er erschöpft **ist.**	*He looks as if he's exhausted* (i.e., he probably **is** exhausted).

21.4 PAST SUBJUNCTIVE FORMS AND USE

A. Forms

1. The past-time subjunctive is formed with the subjunctive auxiliary forms **hätte(n)** or **wäre(n)** + past participle.

Du *hättest* nicht **verstanden**.
You wouldn't have understood.

Wir *wären* länger **geblieben**.
We would have stayed longer.

2. Keep in mind that even though forms such as **käme** and **gäbe** are based on past-tense verbs, they refer to the present or future—not the past. Many English speakers mistakenly produce **gäbe**, for example, when trying to express a statement such as *I would have given anything to see that.* They understand that the idea refers to the past (as a past-tense, contrary-to-fact conclusion); and **gäbe** looks very much like **gab**, a past-tense form. But **gäbe** only means *gave* in the sense of *If I gave you* (i.e., *If I were to give you…*)—referring to the present or the future. To express an idea that refers to the past using the subjunctive, one must always use a compound form, with **hätte** or **wäre** as V$_1$, and a past participle (or variation thereof; see section C below) as V$_2$: **Ich hätte alles gegeben.**

B. Use

1. The past subjunctive is used to express unreal past conditions and imagined results that are contrary to fact.

COMPARE:

Wenn ich Zeit **hätte, würde** ich ins Fitnessstudio gehen. (*present*)
If I had time (hypothetical condition), *I'd go to the gym.*

Wenn ich Zeit **gehabt hätte, wäre** ich ins Fitnessstudio **gegangen**. (*past*)
If I had had time, I would have gone to the gym.

2. Past subjunctive and present subjunctive can be used in the same sentence.

COMPARE:

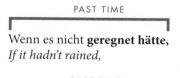

PAST TIME	PAST TIME
Wenn es nicht **geregnet hätte,**	**wäre** ich wohl joggen **gegangen.**
If it hadn't rained,	*I probably would have gone jogging.*

PAST TIME	PRESENT TIME
Hätte ich mit dem Joggen früher **angefangen,**	**wäre** es jetzt nicht so mühsam.
If I had started to jog earlier,	*it wouldn't be so tedious now.*

3. As with conditional sentences in the present, the order of the two clauses in a conditional sentence referring to the past may be reversed.

Ich **wäre** vielleicht, nee, ich **wäre** bestimmt joggen **gegangen,** wenn es nicht **geschneit hätte.**	*I would perhaps, no, I would <u>definitely</u> have gone jogging if it hadn't been snowing.*

4. The past subjunctive can also be used to describe hypothetical conclusions about the past.

Du **wär(e)st** auch nicht **gegangen!**	*You wouldn't have gone either!*

5. Wishes pertaining to the past require past subjunctive.

Wenn das Wetter nur besser **gewesen wäre!**	*If only the weather had been better!*

C. Modals in the past subjunctive

1. When no infinitive accompanies a modal verb, the past subjunctive of the modal is formed with the subjunctive auxiliary **hätte(n)** + past participle.

Das **hätte** sie nicht **gewollt.**	*She wouldn't have wanted that.*
Wir **hätten** es **gekonnt.**	*We would have been able to do that.*

2. If an infinitive accompanies the modal verb, the past subjunctive is formed with the auxiliary **hätte(n)** + a double infinitive (see 9.3). The subjunctive double infinitive construction is quite common with the three modals **können, müssen,** and **sollen** but less so with the others.

Common

Sie **hätte gehen können.**	*She could have gone (but didn't).*[3]
Sie **hätte gehen müssen.**	*She would have had to go (but didn't).*
Sie **hätte gehen sollen.**	*She should have gone (but didn't).*

Less common

Sie **hätte gehen dürfen.**	*She would have been permitted to go.*
Sie **hätte** nicht **gehen mögen.**	*She would not have liked to go.*
Sie **hätte gehen wollen.**	*She would have wanted to go.*

---

[3]The English sentence *She could have gone* is ambiguous. In the sense *She had the **ability** to go but didn't,* German uses the past subjunctive of the modal verb (since the question of ability lies in the past) with the double infinitive: **Sie hätte gehen können.** But in the sense *It is perhaps **possible** that she has gone,* German uses the present subjunctive of the modal verb (since the uncertain conjecture occurs in the present) and the perfect infinitive: **Sie könnte (schon) gegangen sein.**

3. In standard usage, double infinitives appear last in a clause, both in main clauses and dependent clauses. This means that **hätte** (V_1) precedes the double infinitive (V_2) in dependent clauses containing past subjunctive modal structures (see 1.3.A).

COMPARE:

Meinst du, dass ihr Freund *gegangen wäre?*

Do you think that her friend would have gone?

Meinst du, dass ihr Freund **hätte** *gehen sollen?*

Do you think that her friend should have gone?

4. Notice in the examples above that the parallel English structures *would have [gone]* and *could have [gone]* are not parallel in German. The phrase *could have [gone]* involves a modal verb and therefore requires a double infinitive structure, whereas *would have [gone]* is formed with **hätte/wäre** and a past participle.

COMPARE:

Hättest du diese Hanteln *heben können?*

Could you have lifted these dumbbells?

Hättest du diese Hanteln *gehoben?*

Would you have lifted these dumbbells?

OTHER EXAMPLES:

Du **hättest** es wenigstens *versuchen sollen.*

You should have at least tried.

Ich **hätte** es jedenfalls *versucht,* du Weichei.

I would have tried in any case, you wimp.

Weißt du, ich **hätte** es *schaffen können,* wenn du nicht *zugeschaut hättest.*

You know, I could have managed it if you hadn't been watching.

D. After *als (ob)/als (wenn)*

1. The past subjunctive is used after **als (ob)/als (wenn)** if the **als ob** clause refers to a time prior to that of the main clause.

Er machte einfach weiter, *als ob* ihn niemand **angesprochen hätte.**

He simply kept on going, as if no one had (just) spoken to him.

Sie tat (so), *als wenn* gar nichts **passiert wäre.**

She acted as if nothing had happened.

2. As with present subjunctive, **als** may stand alone in the subordinate clause, followed immediately by the auxiliary verb **hätte** or **wäre,** with the participle in final position.

Er machte einfach weiter, *als* **hätte** ihn niemand **angesprochen.**

Sie tat so, *als* **wäre** gar nichts **passiert.**

Wortschatz
Wie sagt man *to act?*

sich benehmen	tun, als ob …
sich auf·führen	handeln
sich verhalten	

1. **Sich benehmen** means *to act, behave (according to notions of socially good or bad behavior).* It is often used with adverbs such as **anständig** *(decently),* **gut, schlecht, unmöglich,** etc.

   Die meisten Zuschauer bei einem Tennisspiel **benehmen sich** anständig.

   Most spectators at a tennis match behave themselves well.

   Beim Fußball **benimmt sich** das Publikum nicht immer so gut.

   In the case of soccer, the crowd doesn't always behave so well.

   Benehmt euch, Leute!

   Behave, people!

2. **Sich auf·führen** means *to act, behave,* or *carry on,* in the sense of *conspicuous* behavior. It requires an adverb.

   Beim Tennis sind es die Spieler, die **sich** manchmal komisch **aufführen.**

   In the case of tennis, it's the players who sometimes behave strangely.

3. **Sich verhalten** means *to act, react, behave* in a given situation. It suggests *controlled* behavior.

   Aber wie würden Sie **sich** in so einer Stresssituation **verhalten?**

   But how would you behave in such a stressful situation?

   Wenn der Feueralarm mitten im letzten Satz klingelte, z.B., würde **sich** das Publikum ruhig **verhalten?**

   If the fire alarm went off during the final set, for example, would the crowd behave calmly?

4. **Tun, als ob…** means *to act* or *behave as if . . .*

   Einige Tennisspieler **tun** (so), **als ob** die Schiedsrichter blind wären.

   Some tennis players act as if the umpires were blind.

5. **Handeln** means *to act, take action.*

   Manche Leute **handeln** eben nur im eigenen Interesse.

   Some people just act in their own interest.

Übungen

A **Formen üben.** Sagen Sie es anders.

BEISPIELE er ginge
er würde gehen

sie würde uns schreiben
sie schriebe uns

1. du würdest denken
2. sie fielen
3. er würde sitzen
4. sie würde stehen
5. wir trügen es
6. sie würde sich verhalten
7. er schnitte sich
8. sie fänden uns
9. ich träfe ihn
10. ihr würdet froh sein
11. wir läsen es
12. ich würde mich benehmen
13. er würde laufen
14. es würde kalt werden
15. sie verließe ihn

B **Formen in der Vergangenheit (*past*).** Setzen Sie die Formen in **Übung A** in die Vergangenheit.

BEISPIELE er ginge
er wäre gegangen

sie würde uns schreiben
sie hätte uns geschrieben

C **Welche Verben passen?** Ergänzen Sie die Sätze durch passende Verben aus dem **Wortschatz.**

1. Während der Operation _____ sich der Patient ganz ruhig.
2. Wenn niemand seine Bitte erhört, dann muss er selber _____.
3. Während des Unterrichts hat sich das Kind unmöglich _____.
4. Du hast dich gestern Abend sehr seltsam _____. Warst du total ausgeflippt?
5. Die anderen Partygäste waren schockiert, weil Maximilian sich so unmöglich _____.
6. Gernot _____ immer sehr schnell, wenn er eine Entscheidung getroffen hat.
7. Sarah weiß nicht alles, sie _____ aber immer so.
8. Das Tier _____ sich ganz still, bis die Gefahr vorüber war.

D **Wie schön wäre das!** Leon denkt, wie schön es wäre, wenn er morgen keine Schule hätte. Setzen Sie seine E-Mail an Sofie in den Konjunktiv.

Hallo, Sofie!

Ach, wie schön wäre es, wenn wir morgen keinen Unterricht hätten!

Ich **stehe** erst gegen neun Uhr **auf.** Nach dem Frühstück **rufe** ich ein paar Freunde **an,** und wir **gehen** in der Stadt bummeln. Vielleicht **essen** wir zu Mittag in einem Straßencafé. Danach **kaufen** wir bei H&M ein paar neue Klamotten (*slang: clothes*), wenn wir noch genug Geld **haben.** Wenn nicht, dann machen wir etwas anderes. Wir **können** zum Beispiel ins Kino gehen. Du **darfst** mitkommen, wenn du **willst,** aber du **musst** schon um zehn Uhr bei mir sein. **Ist** das nicht ein toller Tag?

Dein Leon

E   **Wie schön wäre das gewesen!**   Setzen Sie Leons E-Mail von **Übung D** in den Konjunktiv der Vergangenheit.

BEISPIEL   *Ach, wie schön wäre es gewesen, wenn wir* **gestern** *keinen Unterricht gehabt hätten ...*

F   **Wie wäre es, wenn ... ?**   Erzählen Sie in ein bis zwei Sätzen davon.

BEISPIEL   wenn das Semester schon zu Ende wäre
Wenn das Semester schon zu Ende wäre, würde ich nach Hause fahren und arbeiten. Ich würde auch fast jeden Abend mit Freunden ausgehen (ginge ...aus).

1. wenn Sie mehr Zeit hätten
2. wenn Sie im Lotto viel Geld gewinnen würden
3. wenn Sie die Gelegenheit (*opportunity*) hätten ... [zu tun]
4. wenn Sie sich in einer Vorlesung sehr komisch aufführen würden
5. wenn Ihr Deutsch perfekt wäre
6. wenn Sie an einem Marathon teilnehmen (*take part*) könnten

Machen Sie fünf weitere Aussagen dieser Art (*type*) über sich selbst oder über Menschen, die Sie kennen.

G   **Situationen.**   Erklären Sie, was man in diesen Situationen machen muss oder soll. Es gibt manchmal mehr als nur eine Möglichkeit. Verwenden Sie Verben aus dem **Wortschatz.**

BEISPIEL   Man will einen guten Eindruck machen.
Man muss sich höflich (politely) *benehmen.*

1. Andere Leute im Bus wollen schlafen.
2. Jemand braucht dringend Hilfe.
3. Man will nicht zeigen, dass man Angst hat.
4. Man will jemand auf einer Party imponieren (*impress*).
5. Man hat sich um eine Stelle beworben (*applied*) und stellt sich jetzt beim Personalchef einer Firma vor.
6. Man will nicht für einen Dummkopf gehalten werden.

H   **Ach, diese Studenten!**   Der Professor überlegt, wie sein Kurs im vergangenen Jahr gewesen wäre, wenn die Studenten nur mehr gearbeitet hätten. Was denkt er?

BEISPIEL   Lukas lernte nicht fleißig und bekam deswegen eine schlechte Note.
Wenn Lukas fleißig gelernt hätte, hätte er sicher eine gute Note bekommen.

1. Anna schlief manchmal während der Stunde ein, weil sie vom Rugby-Training noch so müde war.
2. David hat seine Aufgaben nie rechtzeitig abgegeben *(handed in)* und verlor deswegen Punkte bei der Bewertung seiner Arbeit.
3. Jonas schwänzte *(cut class)* manchmal und machte deswegen oft die falschen Hausaufgaben.
4. Maria hat während der Stunde oft heimlich *(secretly)* SMS geschickt und hatte deswegen dauernd keine Ahnung, was gerade passierte.
5. Felix hörte oft nicht zu und wusste deshalb oft nicht, was andere gerade gesagt hatten.

I **Ach, wenn es nur anders wäre!** Denken Sie sich Wünsche zu den folgenden Themen aus. Verwenden Sie möglichst viele verschiedene Verben.

BEISPIEL   zu Ihrem Deutschkurs
Ach, wenn es im Deutschkurs nur nicht so viele Prüfungen gäbe!

1. zu Ihrem Wohnheim oder Ihrer Wohnsituation
2. zu Ihrer Heimatstadt *(hometown)*
3. zu einer Situation an Ihrer Uni oder in Ihrer Schule
4. zu einer Sportmannschaft oder Musik-Band
5. zu Ihren Job-Aussichten
6. zu Ihrem Hauptfach
7. zu Ihren Freunden oder Bekannten

J **O je.** Haben Sie als Kind manches (nicht) gemacht, was Sie jetzt bereuen *(regret)*? Machen Sie fünf Aussagen.

BEISPIELE   *Ich wünschte, ich hätte meine Eltern nicht so viel geärgert.*
Ach, wenn ich mich im Kindergarten nur besser benommen hätte!

K **Wir bitten höflichst.** Was sagen Sie in diesen Situationen?

BEISPIEL   Eine Frau, die neben Ihnen auf einer Parkbank sitzt, raucht eine Zigarette nach der anderen. Im Freien *(outdoors)* ist das Rauchen nicht verboten, aber Sie möchten, dass die Frau damit aufhört. Was sagen Sie ihr?
Könnten Sie bitte so nett sein und jetzt nicht rauchen? [oder]
Dürfte ich Sie bitten, nicht zu rauchen?

1. Sie essen mit anderen Leuten zusammen und brauchen Salz und Pfeffer vom anderen Ende des Tisches.
2. Sie wollen $ 20 von Ihrer Freundin/Ihrem Freund borgen.
3. Bei einer Prüfung haben Sie die Anweisungen Ihrer Professorin/Ihres Professors nicht verstanden.
4. Sie bitten am Informationsschalter im Bahnhof um Auskunft.
5. Sie sind in einer Buchhandlung und suchen ein bestimmtes Buch.

Berühmte Menschen. Erzählen Sie, was fünf berühmte Menschen (aus der Gegenwart und der Vergangenheit) vielleicht anders hätten machen können oder sollen.

BEISPIEL Napoleon
Er hätte nicht nach Russland marschieren sollen.

 Menschen, die so tun, als (ob)... Machen Sie fünf Aussagen über Menschen, die Sie kennen und die immer so tun, **als ob.** Machen Sie bitte ein paar Aussagen über die Gegenwart *(present)* und ein paar über die Vergangenheit *(past).*

BEISPIELE *Die Frau auf dem Crosstrainer tut so,* **als wäre** *sie ganz cool.*
Mein Bruder tat immer so, **als ob** *er alles besser wüsste als ich.*

Anwendung

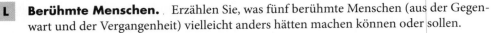

A **Ich?! Du!** Die Konjunktivformen lassen sich gut bei einem Streit (z.B. zwischen Mitbewohnern) verwenden:

BEISPIEL A: *Ich wäre nicht immer so sauer, wenn du wenigstens ab und zu mal deine Sachen aufräumen würdest.*
B: *Ich?! Tja, wenn du meine Sachen nicht immer tragen würdest, dann wüsste ich wenigstens, wo sie sind.*
A: *Was? Also, wenn du ... usw.*

Wie lange können Sie sich auf diese Weise mit einer Partnerin/einem Partner in so einem Rollenspiel streiten?

B **Was wäre, wenn ...** Diskutieren Sie mit anderen Leuten, wie die Welt und das Leben aussehen würde, wenn gewisse Dinge anders wären.

THEMENVORSCHLÄGE

Wenn Sie unsichtbar wären.
Wenn es keinen Strom mehr gäbe.
Wenn an einem Tag überhaupt keine Autos in Ihrer Stadt führen.
Wenn Sie nicht vernetzt *(digitally linked)* wären und Briefe schreiben müssten.
Wenn Instagram versehentlich *(by mistake)* alle Fotos löschen *(delete)* würde.

Wenn (das) so ... wäre, ja dann ...
Ja, erstens würde ich ...
Ich glaube, ich würde ...
Für mich wäre dann die Hauptsache/das Wichtigste ...
Dann müsste/könnte man auch ...
Und schließlich würde man/ich ...

Wenn der Strom nicht wäre.

C **Sagen Sie Ihre Meinung ...** Diskutieren Sie mit anderen Studentinnen/Studenten eine Situation im heutigen Leben, die anders werden sollte oder könnte. Sagen Sie Ihre Meinung darüber, wie man diese Situation ändern sollte, könnte oder müsste, damit alles besser wäre oder sein könnte.

Körperbild *(body image)* und Selbstbild
das Ausbildungssystem *(educational system)* in Ihrem Land
die Armut *(poverty)* auf der Welt
das Drogenproblem
die Zerstörung *(destruction)* der Umwelt
eine Situation an Ihrer Universität oder in Ihrer Schule
die politische Lage irgendwo auf der Welt

Meiner Meinung/Ansicht nach müsste/könnte/sollte man ...
Ich glaube, wir müssten/könnten ...
Ich bin der Meinung/Ansicht, dass ...
Es wäre besser, wenn ...
Ich wünschte, wir könnten ...
So wie ich die Sache sehe, müsste man ...
Man kann ja auch umgekehrt *(conversely)* argumentieren und sagen, dass ...

D **Wenn es anders gekommen wäre.**   Sprechen Sie mit anderen Studentinnen/ Studenten über ein großes politisches, kulturelles, historisches oder wissenschaftliches Ereignis – oder vielleicht über die Möglichkeit von irgendeinem großen Ereignis. Spekulieren sie darüber, was möglicherweise geschehen wäre, wenn das Ereignis nicht stattgefunden hätte, anders verlaufen oder anders ausgegangen wäre.

THEMENVORSCHLÄGE

Wenn Amerika 1776 den Unabhängigkeitskrieg nicht begonnen hätte.
Wenn jemand anders Präsidentin/Präsident der USA geworden wäre.
Wenn niemand das Fernsehen erfunden hätte.
Wenn es 2009 keine Rezession auf den Weltmärkten gegeben hätte.
Wenn Rosa Parks nicht den Mut gehabt hätte, im Bus sitzen zu bleiben.
Wenn soziale Netzwerke *(wie Facebook)* nicht existieren würde.
Wenn der Anschlag *(attack)* am 11. September 2001 nicht gewesen wäre.
Wenn die Mauer 1989 nicht gefallen wäre.

E **Ich hätte viel mehr machen sollen.**   Diskutieren Sie mit einer Partnerin/einem Partner über das letzte Jahr oder das letzte Semester: Was hätte sie/er mehr machen sollen? nicht so oft machen sollen? Was hätte diese Zeit besser/interessanter/produktiver/schöner gemacht? Da die Zeit ja schon vorbei ist, müssen Sie darüber im Vergangenheitskonjunktiv sprechen!

Schriftliche Themen

Tipps zum Schreiben

Using the Subjunctive

In speaking or writing, if you are presenting facts, you will use the indicative. If you are conjecturing, you *must* use the subjunctive. In your writing, strive for a stylistic balance between subjunctive forms and the alternate construction with **würde** + infinitive (see 2.G). As a rule, avoid the subjunctive of weak verbs and less commonly used strong verbs (for example, **hülfe, schöbe, löge,** etc.). Also avoid too many **hätte**'s and **wäre**'s since they add little to a composition. Finally, once you have initiated conjecture with a **wenn**-clause, there is no need to keep repeating this condition; continued use of the subjunctive signals continuing conjecture.
Wenn ich eine Uhr *wäre*, dann *würde* ich gern an einer Wand im Bahnhof *hängen*. Ich *dürfte* (*instead of* würde) nie *schlafen*, denn ich *müsste* (*instead of* würde) die Zeit *messen* und den Menschen *zeigen*, wie spät es ist.

A   **Wenn ich [X] wäre.**   Ihre Professorin/Ihr Professor wird Ihnen sagen, was (oder wer) in Ihrem Fall das X sein soll.

B   **Mal was anderes.**   Erzählen Sie, wie es wäre, wenn Sie einmal aus der Routine Ihres täglichen Alltags ausbrechen könnten. Was würden/könnten Sie anders machen? Wo? Mit wem? Warum?

C   **Ein Wunsch.**   In was für einer Welt würden Sie gern leben?

BEISPIEL   *Ich würde gern in einer Welt leben, in der alle Menschen in Frieden leben und arbeiten dürften. Alle wären glücklich, und niemand müsste sterben, weil er nicht genug zu essen bekäme. In einer solchen Welt gäbe es auch keine Rechtsanwälte* (lawyers), *denn niemand würde gegen andere Menschen einen Prozess führen und ein weiser Richter* (judge) *würde alle Streitfälle* (disputes) *schlichten* (settle) ... *usw.*

D   **Ein Bittbrief.**   Schreiben Sie einen kurzen aber höflichen Brief (Beispiel unten), in dem Sie eine Person, eine Firma, ein Fremdenverkehrsamt *(tourist bureau)* usw. um Auskunft über etwas bitten.

BEISPIEL

Messner-Verlag GmbH
Bismarckstraße 4
D-73765 Neuhausen

Ann Arbor, 1. März

Sehr geehrte Damen und Herren,

ich möchte Sie um Auskunft über ein Praktikum *(internship)* in Ihrer Firma bitten. Vor allem hätte ich gern nähere Informationen über die Tätigkeiten *(activities)*, die damit verbunden sind. Ich wäre Ihnen dankbar, wenn Sie mir ... usw.

Mit freundlichen Grüßen

Ihre/Ihr

[*Ihr Name*]

Zusammenfassung

Rules to Remember

1 The subjunctive expresses unreal, hypothetical, or contrary-to-fact conditional statements, as well as wishes and polite requests.

2 Subjunctive II has only two tenses: present (to refer to present and future time) and past (to refer to all past-time situations; no distinction is made between simple past, present perfect, and past perfect). **Würde** + infinitive expresses unreal or hypothetical situations only in the present or future.

3 Present subjunctive II forms are derived from the simple past form of the verb:

- For weak verbs, the simple past form is identical to the present subjunctive II (see chart below: **lernen** —→ **lernte**)

- For most irregular verbs, an umlaut is added to the simple past form (see chart below: **haben / werden / wissen** —→ **hätte / würde / wüsste**)

- For strong verbs, an umlaut (where possible) as well as subjunctive endings are added to the simple past form (see chart below: **sein / kommen** —→ **wäre / käme**)

4 **Würde** + infinitive is used more often than subjunctive II, though subjunctive II forms are preferred for the most commonly used verbs, such as **sein, haben, werden, wissen,** and the modal verbs. Subjunctive II forms can also be used for frequently occurring strong verbs such as **gehen, kommen,** and **tun.** Weak verbs are most often expressed in the subjunctive with **würde** + infinitive, unless the context makes it clear that the form is subjunctive rather than indicative.

5 The past subjunctive II is formed with an auxiliary (**hätte** or **wäre**) and a past participle.

6 Modal verbs with dependent infinitives in past subjunctive use a very distinct form: **hätte ... machen sollen** (*should have . . .*) or **hätte ... machen können** (*could have . . .*). A modal verb infinitive stands as the second element in a double infinitive structure; the double infinitive itself always stands at the end of a main or subordinate clause.

At a Glance

Würde + infinitive
Main clause
_____ würde *(middle field)* infinitive
Subordinate clause
_____, dass _____ infinitive würde

Subjunctive II: Present

	haben	sein	werden	lernen	wissen	kommen	können	sollen
ich	hätte	wäre	würde	lernte	wüsste	käme	könnte	sollte
du	hättest	wärest	würdest	lerntest	wüsstest	kämest	könntest	solltest
Sie	hätten	wären	würden	lernten	wüssten	kämen	könnten	sollten
er/sie/es	hätte	wäre	würde	lernte	wüsste	käme	könnte	sollte
wir	hätten	wären	würden	lernten	wüssten	kämen	könnten	sollten
ihr	hättet	wäret	würdet	lerntet	wüsstet	kämet	könntet	solltet
Sie	hätten	wären	würden	lernten	wüssten	kämen	könnten	sollten
sie	hätten	wären	würden	lernten	wüssten	kämen	könnten	sollten

Subjunctive II: Past

hätte
wäre } + past participle

Subjunctive II: Past-tense modals

hätte + | infinitive | | modal infinitive |

Past subjunctive: would/could/should have . . .

I would have helped.	→	Ich **hätte geholfen.**
I could have helped.	→	Ich **hätte helfen können.**
I should have helped.	→	Ich **hätte helfen sollen.**

22

Indirect discourse ▪ Subjunctive I

zum Beispiel

Metropolis

Metropolis (1927) is an expressionist science fiction film by Fritz Lang, a German-Austrian filmmaker who wrote and directed some of the best-known films of Weimar cinema. The plot of *Metropolis* revolves around Joh Fredersen, the elitist leader of a futuristic, dystopian world; his son Freder, who hopes to mediate between the capitalist caste to which he and his father belong and the oppressed workers who toil underground to make the lavish lifestyle of the capitalists possible; Maria, the prophetic leader of the workers; and Rotwang, a mad scientist in league with Joh who creates an evil *Maschinenmensch* identical to Maria, designed to sow discord among the workers. Like many silent films of its era, *Metropolis* uses intertitles, i.e., text on a black background appearing onscreen between scenes to supply dialogue. Since indirect discourse is the topic of this chapter, the examples throughout are actual quotes from these intertitles.

Grammatik

22.1 INDIRECT DISCOURSE

1. *Direct* discourse is, quite simply, what someone says.

   Rotwang sagt: „Endlich **bin ich** mit meiner Arbeit fertig.“

   Rotwang says: "Finally I'm finished with my work."

   The sentence above consists of two elements: a direct discourse statement („**Endlich bin ich ... fertig**“), introduced by a reference clause identifying the speaker (**Rotwang sagt: ...**). NOTE: German uses a colon at the end of the reference clause with direct discourse, rather than a comma as in English.

2. *Indirect* discourse, on the other hand, takes direct discourse and weaves it into the perspective of the reporting speaker or writer, while still retaining its informational content.

   Rotwang sagt, **dass er** mit seiner Arbeit endlich fertig ist.

   Rotwang says that he is finally finished with his work.

3. German has three ways to signal indirect discourse:

   a. a shift in pronouns and possessive adjectives (mandatory in the case of first- and second-person references in the direct discourse): **ich** $\longrightarrow$ **er** and **meiner** $\longrightarrow$ **seiner**

   b. the optional use of **dass** to introduce the indirectly quoted message

   c. the optional use of the subjunctive voice for the verb(s) in the indirectly quoted message

4. In spoken language, option (a) often suffices. Notice how pronouns can change the reference point.

   Rotwang sagt zu Joh: „Von jetzt an brauchen wir die Arbeiter nicht mehr.“

   Rotwang sagt, **sie** brauchen von jetzt an die Arbeiter nicht mehr.

   Rotwang sagt, **wir** brauchen von jetzt an die Arbeiter nicht mehr.

   Depending on the pronouns used, the perspective in the indirect version becomes either that of someone reporting on the proceedings from outside the group, with everyone mentioned in the third person (*they don't need the workers anymore*); or that of someone who identifies with the group (*we don't need the workers anymore*). In both cases, the direct discourse has been modified to indicate that a new speaker or writer is relating the original utterance indirectly to the reader or listener.

5. As for option (b), the indirect discourse can be introduced by the conjunction **dass,** but need not be. If **dass** is used, the indirect discourse becomes a subordinate clause, with V_1 in final position; if **dass** is not used, the word order remains that of a main clause. In either case, a comma separates the reference clause from the indirect discourse.

Rotwang sagt, **dass** er mit seiner Arbeit endlich fertig **ist.**

Rotwang sagt, er **ist** mit seiner Arbeit endlich fertig.

6. German can also use the subjunctive mood to indicate indirect discourse. This is optional: When speakers or writers have no need or desire to distance themselves from the message being indirectly conveyed, they often use the indicative mood of the verb, as in the examples above, which are typical of spoken language:

Rotwang sagt, er **ist** mit seiner Arbeit endlich fertig.

By using the subjunctive, however, the message bearer can emphasize the indirect nature of the message, as if to say: *"This is not my idea; I'm merely passing along what somebody else said."* German has a subjunctive form that is associated almost exclusively with indirect discourse; this form differs substantially from subjunctive II forms (see 21.2), as well as English subjunctive usage:

Rotwang sagt, er **sei** mit seiner Arbeit endlich fertig.

22.2   SUBJUNCTIVE I FORMS

A. Present subjunctive I

1. Subjunctive forms based on the infinitive—the first principal part of the verb—are known collectively as *subjunctive I.* Like subjunctive II[1] they use the subjunctive endings **-e, -est, -e; -en, -et, -en,** but for present subjunctive I verbs, these are attached to the infinitive stem. Notice that verbs such as **nehmen, werden,** and **wissen,** which change their stem vowel in the present-tense third-person singular, retain the vowel from the infinitive in subjunctive I.

Subjunctive I forms					
haben	**werden**	**müssen**	**wissen**	**lernen**	**nehmen**
ich habe	werde	müsse	wisse	lerne	nehme
du habest	werdest	müssest	wissest	lernest	nehmest
Sie haben	werden	müssen	wissen	lernen	nehmen
er/sie/es habe	werde	müsse	wisse	lerne	nehme
wir haben	werden	müssen	wissen	lernen	nehmen
ihr habet	werdet	müsset	wisset	lernet	nehmet
Sie haben	werden	müssen	wissen	lernen	nehmen
sie haben	werden	müssen	wissen	lernen	nehmen

---

[1]Subjunctive II forms are based on the second principal part of the verb: the simple past.

2. The present subjunctive I of **sein** is irregular in the first- and third-person singular.

Subjunctive I forms: *sein*	
ich sei	wir seien
du seiest	ihr seiet
Sie seien	Sie seien
er/sie/es sei	sie seien

3. Subjunctive I forms that are identical to the indicative are never used, and even subjunctive I forms that do deviate from the indicative, such as second-person singular and plural, sound stilted and are avoided by German speakers. Thus, aside from modal verbs and the verbs **wissen** and **sein,** the only subjunctive I form to occur with any regularity is the third-person singular: **er/sie/es.**

Indicative	Subjunctive I	
ich lerne	lerne	*(not used)*
du **lernst**	**lernest**	*(uncommon)*
Sie lernen	lernen	*(not used)*
er/sie/es **lernt**	lerne	*(used)*
wir lernen	lernen	*(not used)*
ihr **lernt**	**lernet**	*(uncommon)*
Sie lernen	lernen	*(not used)*
sie lernen	lernen	*(not used)*

When speakers or writers want to indicate indirect discourse for other persons (**ich / du / Sie / wir / ihr / sie,** pl.), subjunctive II and *würde* **+ infinitive** forms are used instead of subjunctive I (see 3.2 and 3.3 below).

Er sagte, du **hättest** (*not:* **habest**) kein Interesse an den Problemen der Arbeiter, Freder.   *He said you had no interest in the problems of the workers, Freder.*

B. Review: Present subjunctive II

Present subjunctive II verbs are formed with the stem of the second principal part of the verb (the simple past), followed by the subjunctive endings (see 21.2 and Appendix 3). Strong verbs take an umlaut if the stem vowel is **a, o,** or **u.**

Subjunctive II forms							
	sein	**haben**	**werden**	**müssen**	**wissen**	**lernen**	**nehmen**
ich	wäre	hätte	würde	müsste	wüsste	lernte	nähme
du	wärest	hättest	würdest	müsstest	wüsstest	lerntest	nähmest
Sie	wären	hätten	würden	müssten	wüssten	lernten	nähmen
er/sie/es	wäre	hätte	würde	müsste	wüsste	lernte	nähme
wir	wären	hätten	würden	müssten	wüssten	lernten	nähmen
ihr	wäret	hättet	würdet	müsstet	wüsstet	lerntet	nähmet
Sie	wären	hätten	würden	müssten	wüssten	lernten	nähmen
sie	wären	hätten	würden	müssten	wüssten	lernten	nähmen

C. Past subjunctive I

To express past time, subjunctive I (like subjunctive II—see 21.4) has only one structure: an auxiliary (**haben** or **sein**) in subjunctive I + the past participle. The most commonly used forms are highlighted below.

For verbs that take *haben*	For verbs that take *sein*
Ich **habe** das nicht gemacht.	Ich **sei** gestern nicht da geblieben.
Du **habest** … gemacht.	Du **sei(e)st** … geblieben.
Er/Sie **habe** … gemacht.	Er/Sie **sei** … geblieben.
Wir **haben** … gemacht.	Wir **seien** … geblieben.
Ihr **habet** … gemacht.	Ihr **seiet** … geblieben.
Sie/sie **haben** … gemacht.	Sie/sie **seien** … geblieben.

22.3 USING THE SUBJUNCTIVE IN INDIRECT DISCOURSE

1. Subjunctive I is used almost exclusively for indirect discourse, but the other subjunctive forms (subjunctive II and *würde* **+ infinitive**) can also take on this function. Whichever form one decides to use, *the tense of the subjunctive verb in the indirect discourse corresponds to the verb tense in the direct discourse,* regardless of the verb tense in the reference clause. In other words:

    a. If the direct discourse is in the *present tense,* the indirect-discourse version should use *present subjunctive* (I, II, or *würde* **+ infinitive**).

    Maria sagte: „Heute **will** ich euch eine Legende erzählen." *(present)*
    → Maria sagte, dass sie ihnen eine Legende erzählen **wolle.** *(present subjunctive I)*

b. If the direct discourse is in any *past tense* (simple past, perfect, or past perfect), then a *past subjunctive* is necessary (I or II).

Maria meinte: „Die Menschen **verstanden** sich nicht." *(simple past)*

⟶ Maria meinte, dass die Menschen sich nicht **verstanden hätten.** *(past subjunctive II)*

Freder sagte zu Maria: „Du **hast** mich **gerufen.**" *(perfect)*

⟶ Freder sagte zu Maria, sie **habe** ihn **gerufen.** *(past subjunctive I)*

c. If the direct discourse is in the *future tense*, a subjunctive form of **werden** (I or II) is used as the auxiliary (V₁) in the indirect version.

Rotwang versicherte Joh: „Du **wirst** den Rückweg ohne mich **finden.**" *(future)*

⟶ Rotwang versicherte Joh, er **werde** den Rückweg ohne ihn **finden.** *(subjunctive I of **werden**)*

d. If the direct discourse version contains a subjunctive II form, the indirect version must use subjunctive II or **würde** + infinitive.

Joh sagte: „Ich **möchte** herausbekommen, was meine Arbeiter in den Katakomben zu tun **haben.**" *(subjunctive II)*

⟶ Joh sagte, er **möchte** herausbekommen, was seine Arbeiter in den Katakomben zu tun **hätten.**

Notice that the decision whether or not to use **dass** is unrelated to the tense or mood of the direct discourse.

2. In the examples above, three of the five sentences use subjunctive I forms (rather than subjunctive II or **würde** + infinitive). But as indicated in 2.A above, there are many instances in which the subjunctive I form is identical to the indicative and therefore cannot function as a clear marker of reported speech. Subjunctive II forms can be substituted, but sometimes (as discussed in 21.2) these are archaic and obsolete. And very often, one hears German speakers using **würde**-constructions in indirect discourse where viable subjunctive I or II forms are available. To sort these options out, we will look first at the formal rules and then at current usage.

3. The formal rules for using the subjunctive in indirect discourse are quite simple: (a) Use subjunctive I whenever the form is distinct from the indicative; and (b) when subjunctive I is not distinct, use subjunctive II instead. This effectively restricts subjunctive I use to modal verbs, **wissen, sein,** exceptional forms such as **habest** (which are considered stilted and outdated), and the third-person singular of all other verbs. Under these rules, subjunctive II must be used for all other cases.

Maria erklärte: „Das **sind** eure Brüder."

Maria erklärte, das **seien** ihre Brüder. (subjunctive I **seien** *is distinct from the indicative here, so it can be used*)

Freder sagte: „Wir **bringen** die Kinder in den *Club der Söhne!*"

Freder sagte, sie **brächten** die Kinder in den *Club der Söhne.* (subjunctive I **bringen** *is not distinct from the indicative, so subjunctive II is used instead*)

This leads to an additional rule: (c) when subjunctive II forms are archaic or identical to the indicative, use **würde** + infinitive. For many speakers, this applies to **brächten,** so that they would say the following:

Freder sagte, sie **würden** die Kinder in den *Club der Söhne* **bringen.**

4. These rules are applied most consistently in print media and formal writing, where people are often quoted, where third-person verbs (the most distinctive subjunctive I form) are therefore plentiful, and where journalists must take pains (often for legal reasons) to show that they cannot vouch for the veracity of what someone else has said.

5. In spoken German, however, these rules rarely apply. Instead, one hears a mixture of very occasional subjunctive I forms, some common verbs (**sein, haben, kommen,** etc.) in subjunctive II, routine use of **würde** + infinitive, and very frequently the indicative. Speakers choose subjunctive and indicative forms depending on the distinctiveness of the subjunctive form available (**Sie sagten, sie *haben* keine Zeit** *vs.* **sie *hätten* keine Zeit**), and on the degree of formality, skepticism, or directness they wish to signal.

COMPARE:

Er sagte, er **hat** keine Zeit.   (implied: *That's what he said, and there's no reason to doubt it.*)

Er sagte, er **hätte** keine Zeit.   (implied: *I'm just telling you what he told me.*)

Er sagte, er **habe** keine Zeit.   (implied: *That's what he said, but I'm skeptical.*)

22.4 ▸ OTHER CONTEXTS FOR INDIRECT DISCOURSE

A. Extended direct discourse

As stated at the outset of the chapter, indirect discourse is usually accompanied by a reference clause that identifies the source of the utterance and includes a verb of speaking or thinking, such as **sagen** or **meinen** (see the **Wortschatz** in this chapter for more possibilities). In English, a reference clause must be provided each time an indirect quote is given—"Maria *remarked* . . . , and then she *added* . . . , and finally she *noted* . . . "—in order to make it clear that these are Maria's statements, and that the author is merely reporting them. In German, however, a writer can simply state the source at the outset, and then proceed to use subjunctive I verb forms (or subjunctive II substitutes when necessary; see 22.3) throughout an extended passage in which no further reference phrases are necessary.

Freder, der zwischen den zwei Welten vermitteln will, behauptet, er **wolle** den Menschen in die Gesichter sehen. Er **glaube** sogar, dass ihre kleinen Kinder seine Brüder und seine Schwestern **seien.** Deswegen **habe** er wissen wollen, wie seine Brüder **aussähen.** Seinem Vater gegenüber meint er, es **seien** ihre Hände gewesen, die die Stadt aufgebaut **hätten.** Was **werde** der Vater tun, wenn sie sich eines Tages gegen ihn wenden **würden?** Und ob der Vater **wisse,** was das **heiße,** entlassen zu werden?

Freder, who wants to mediate between the two worlds, claims that he wants to look those people in the face. [He says] he believes in fact that their little children are his brothers and sisters. That's why he wants to know [, he explains,] what his brothers look like. To his father he says that it was their hands that had built up the city. What will the father do [, he asks,] if they turn against him someday? [He asks as well] If the father knows what it means to be fired?

B. Indirect questions

1. Questions can be reported indirectly *(She wanted to know why he did it)*, and can likewise be expressed using the subjunctive. Once again, the question of which subjunctive to use (if any at all) changes according to context and intended level of formality. In writing, subjunctive I forms lend an aura of objectivity and distance.

   Der Vater fragte Freder, was er in den Maschinensälen zu suchen gehabt **habe**.

   The father asked Freder what he had been looking for in the machine rooms.

   By contrast, in colloquial speech one often hears the indicative, sometimes a **würde**-construction, and occasionally a subjunctive I or II, especially with modal verbs.

   Freder fragte sich erschöpft: „**Nehmen** zehn Stunden niemals ein Ende?"

   → Freder fragte sich erschöpft, ob zehn Stunden niemals ein Ende **nehmen würden**.

   Rotwang fragte Joh: „**Willst** du sie sehen?"

   → Rotwang fragte Joh, ob er sie sehen **wollte/wolle**. *(subjunctive II/I)*

2. The structure of the indirect clause depends on the type of question posed directly. With information questions, the question word (**wo, wie, warum, wann,** etc.) is repeated at the beginning of the indirect clause, while yes-no questions are expressed indirectly by using **ob** as a conjunction.

   Joh fragte verzweifelt: „Wo **ist** mein Sohn?"

   → Joh fragte verzweifelt, **wo** sein Sohn *sei*.

   Rotwang fragte Joh: „**Willst** du nach unten gehen?"

   → Rotwang fragte Joh, **ob** er nach unten gehen *wolle*.

C. Indirect commands

Commands are reported indirectly by stating what should or must be done, using the modal verb **sollen,** or sometimes **müssen**. In formal contexts, the subjunctive I form of the modal can be used, with less formal renditions using either subjunctive II or the indicative.

Der Maschinenmensch sagte den Arbeitern: „**Zerstört** *(destroy)* die Maschinen!"

→ Der Maschinenmensch sagte den Arbeitern, sie **sollten** die Maschinen **zerstören**.

22.5 OTHER USES OF SUBJUNCTIVE I

1. Subjunctive I can be used instead of subjunctive II in **als ob/als wenn** clauses (see 21.3.E), though subjunctive II is generally preferred. Here, subjunctive I takes on the role of conveying conjecture and speculation rather than signaling indirect discourse.

   Joh tat, als ob das Ganze ihn nichts
   angehe/anginge.

   Joh tat, als **gehe/ginge** ihn das Ganze nichts an.

   } *Joh acted as if the whole thing didn't concern him at all.*

2. Subjunctive I also functions as the so-called "exhortatory subjunctive," a very formal third-person imperative akin to English *Long live the Queen!* (**Es lebe die Königin!**). It is found mostly in older literature and conveys an elevated style.

   „Zwischen uns **sei** Wahrheit."
   [Goethe, *Iphigenie auf Tauris*]

   "May there be truth between us."

   „Dein Reich **komme,** dein Wille **geschehe** … " [Matthäusevangelium]

   "Thy kingdom come. Thy will be done. . . "
   [*The Gospel of Matthew*]

Wortschatz
Wie sagt man *to say?*

The following verbs of speaking can introduce indirect discourse. Many of them take a dative (indirect) object with people and an accusative (direct) object or a prepositional phrase with things.

an·deuten *to indicate*
an·kündigen *to declare, announce*
behaupten *to assert, maintain*
bekannt geben *to announce*
bemerken *to remark, say*
beteuern *to assure, swear*
betonen *to emphasize*
etwas ein·wenden (gegen) *to raise an objection (to)*
entgegnen (auf) *to reply (to)*
erläutern *to elucidate, elaborate*
erklären *to explain*
erwähnen *to mention*
erwidern (auf) *to reply (to)*
erzählen (von) *to tell (about)*

fragen (nach) *to inquire, ask (about)*
informieren *to inform*
leugnen *to deny*
meinen *to say, offer one's opinion*
mit·teilen *to inform*
raten *to advise*
reden (über/von) *to talk (about)*
sagen (von) *to say, tell (about)*
verkünden *to announce, proclaim*
versichern *to assure*
versprechen *to promise*
wissen wollen *to want to know*
zu·geben *to admit, confess*
zusammen·fassen *to summarize*

Übungen

A **Indirekte Rede in den Medien.** Die folgende Pressemeldung zeigt typische Beispiele für Verwendung des Konjunktivs. Markieren Sie zuerst **alle** Verben im Text: Umkreisen Sie alle Verben im Indikativ, unterstreichen Sie mit einem Einzelstrich alle Verben im Konjunktiv I, und dann mit einem Doppelstrich alle Verben im Konjunktiv II. Dann überlegen Sie in jedem Fall: Warum diese Form für dieses Verb? Und dann achten Sie auf die Vokabeln: Welche einleitenden Verben aus dem **Wortschatz** werden hier verwendet?

Interview mit Willy Brandt im Zweiten Deutschen Fernsehen am 25. August 1968[2]. Der Interviewer vom ZDF: „Herr Bundesminister, die Nachrichten aus der CSSR sind beeindruckend°, sehr beeindruckend. Die Bundesregierung hat zwar immer wieder betont, dass ihr Standpunkt der einer strikten Nichteinmischung° sei, aber das schließt doch einen persönlichen Kommentar nicht aus?" Als Antwort entgegnete Herr Brandt, er sei für diese erste Frage besonders dankbar: „Nichteinmischung vom Standpunkt der Regierung der Bundesrepublik Deutschland aus bedeutete und bedeutet, sich nicht einzumischen in die Verhältnisse° eines anderen Landes." Aber wenn er einmal den Außenminister jetzt außen[3] vorlassen dürfe, dann möchte er sagen, die Deutschen seien voll von Bewunderung°, Bewunderung, was die Würde° eines Nachbarvolks angehe, das es nicht leicht gehabt habe in der Vergangenheit und das seinen eigenen Weg bestimmen° wolle.

deeply moving
non-intervention

affairs

amazement, admira-tion/dignity/ determine

B **Von direkter Aussage zur indirekten Rede.** Geben Sie die Aussagen in indirekter Rede wieder.

BEISPIEL   Man lebt heutzutage sehr ungesund.
Sie meinte, …
Sie meinte, man lebe heutzutage sehr ungesund.

1. Im vergangenen Jahr hatten die Gastronomiebetriebe *(eating establishments)* höhere Besucherzahlen.
   Das Fremdenverkehrsamt *(office of tourism)* gab bekannt, dass …
2. Vermutlich *(presumably)* sind auch in diesem Sommer mehr Touristen zu erwarten.
   Gestern kündigte die Presse an, dass …
3. Es wird nicht mehr lange dauern, bis das Wohnungsproblem gelöst ist.
   Politiker gaben der Hoffnung Ausdruck, es …
4. Wenn man jetzt nichts dagegen tut, wird das Straßenverkehrssystem in der Bundesrepublik Deutschland in wenigen Jahren zusammenbrechen.
   Experten behaupten, …

---

[2]In this historic interview, Willy Brandt, then Foreign Secretary/Secretary of State of West Germany, responded on national TV to the Soviet invasion of Czechoslovakia, which was meant to crush the Prague Spring uprising. The interview took place four days after the invasion, as Europe saw itself potentially on the brink of another world war.

[3]**außen** is a play on words: **Außenminister** = *"outside" (foreign) minister;* **außen vorlassen** = *to leave outside*

5. Bleib fit, bleib gesund!
   Überall heißt es jetzt, man …

6. Früher brachten die Zeitungen meist schlechte Nachrichten.
   Viele sind der Meinung, …

7. Die besten Jahre sind jetzt.
   Manche denken, …

8. Die besten Jahre waren schon.
   Andere fragen, ob …

9. Wählervertrauen *(voter trust)* ist ein rohes Ei, man kann es nur einmal in die Pfanne hauen *(toss into the skillet)*.
   Der Redner betonte, …

10. Weil in der alten DDR die nötige Finanzierung fehlte, konnte der Staat viele Wohnhäuser nicht renovieren.
    Die Sache ließ sich so erklären: …

11. „Man soll den Tag nicht vor dem Abend loben *(praise)*.“ (Sprichwort)
    In einem Sprichwort heißt es, …

12. „Arbeite nur, die Freude kommt von selbst.“
    Der Dichter Goethe war der Meinung, …

C **Von direkter Aussage zur indirekten Rede: Angela Merkel.** Folgende Aussagen kommen direkt von Angela Merkel in ihrer Rolle als Bundeskanzlerin. Wie würde eine Journalistin/ein Journalist diese Zitate mit indirekter Rede umformulieren? Benutzen Sie dafür einige Verben vom Wortschatz in diesem Kapitel, z.B. *Frau Merkel meinte / verkündete / behauptete, …*

achieve
*support, benefit/
restrict/fence*

wins

allow

rumor/go bankrupt

civic engagement
successful

*enables/enemies/
opponents/danger*

1. „Die Frauenfußball-Nationalmannschaft ist ja schon Fußballweltmeister, und ich sehe keinen Grund, warum Männer nicht das Gleiche leisten° können wie Frauen.“ (2005)

2. „Der Staat muss fördern° und darf nicht einschränken°. In diesem Sinne muss er Gärtner sein und nicht Zaun°.“ (2006)

3. „Mit dem Kopf durch die Wand wird nicht gehen. Da siegt° zum Schluss immer die Wand.“ (2007)

4. „Wir werden nicht zulassen°, dass technisch manches möglich ist, aber der Staat es nicht nutzt.“ (2008)

5. „Es gibt ein Gerücht°, dass Staaten nicht pleitegehen° können. Dieses Gerücht stimmt nicht.“ (2009)

6. „Ich bin für Bürgerbeteiligung°. Ich bin für Transparenz.“ (2010)

7. „Ich bin hier, um zu sagen: Ich freue mich darüber, dass es gelungen° ist, bin Laden zu töten.“ (2011)

8. „Das Internet ist für uns alle Neuland, und es ermöglicht° auch Feinden° und Gegnern° […] unsere Art zu leben in Gefahr° zu bringen.“ (2013)

D **Jeder sagt es anders.** Drücken Sie den Inhalt der Sätze mit Verben aus dem **Wortschatz** anders und präziser aus.

BEISPIEL   Als er den Vorschlag *(suggestion)* machte, sagte niemand etwas.
                      Auf seinen Vorschlag erwiderte niemand etwas.

1. Er sagte genau, wie viel Geld er brauchte und wann.
2. Gegen diesen Plan kann ich nichts sagen.
3. Der Chef sagte den Angestellten, dass man 100 Arbeitskräfte würde entlassen müssen.
4. Von ihren Problemen sagte sie nichts.
5. Der Bürgermeister sagte seine Meinung über die städtischen Baupläne.
6. Nachdem sie so viel über die Talente des Kindes gesagt hatte, glaubten am Ende auch alle daran.
7. Der Polizist sagte, dass er mehr über den Unfall herausfinden wollte.

E   **Und dann meinte sie, ...**   Lesen Sie die direkten Aussagen unten und bilden Sie dann damit Sätze in der indirekten Rede (im Konjunktiv). Verwenden Sie dabei als Einleitung Verben aus dem **Wortschatz.** Achten Sie auf die Zeitstufe des Verbs in der direkten Rede.

BEISPIEL   „Ich habe gar nichts getrunken!"
                    *Benni hat uns **versichert**, er hätte gar nichts getrunken!*

1. „Diese Probleme haben wir wegen der Luftverschmutzung."
2. „Heute Abend um acht bin ich wieder zu Hause!"
3. „Man muss noch etwas Geduld haben."
4. „Als Bundeskanzler werde ich Ihr Vertrauen zurückgewinnen!"
5. „Ich habe *nie* Musik illegal heruntergeladen!"
6. „Unsere zwei Länder müssen besser zusammenarbeiten."
7. „Der Film war einfach zu lang."
8. „Ich habe sie wirklich nur gefragt, ob der Stuhl neben ihr frei ist."

Anwendung

A   **Worte der Woche.**   Geben Sie einige wichtige Zitate der letzten Woche zu politischen Ereignissen in der indirekten Rede wieder.

REDEMITTEL

Neulich habe ich im Internet gelesen, (dass) ...
Nach Angaben *(information)* [des Pressesprechers] ...
Die [Regierung] gab bekannt, (dass) ...
Es heißt/hieß *(is/was said)* auch, (dass) ...

B **Interview.** Interviewen Sie außerhalb des Kurses jemanden, die/der Deutsch spricht, und zwar über ihre/seine Meinung zu einem aktuellen politischen Ereignis *(event)* oder Thema. Stellen Sie etwa sieben Fragen. Berichten Sie über die Ergebnisse *(results)* Ihres Interviews im Kurs. Sagen Sie, welche Fragen Sie gestellt haben, und geben Sie die Meinung der befragten Person in der indirekten Rede wieder.

Fragen

Was halten Sie von … ?

Wie sehen Sie die Sache … ?

Darf ich Sie fragen, wie Sie zu den neuesten Ereignissen stehen?

Und wie beurteilen *(judge)* Sie … ?

Finden Sie es richtig/gut, dass … ?

Was für einen Eindruck hat … auf Sie gemacht?

Berichten

Sie/Er ist der Ansicht/Meinung, (dass) …

Sie/Er sagte auch, (dass) …

Bemerkt hat sie/er auch, (dass) …

Allerdings gab sie/er zu, (dass) …

Sie/Er gab der Hoffnung Ausdruck, (dass) …

C **Ratschläge *(pieces of advice).*** Sprechen Sie mit einer Partnerin/einem Partner über die besten und die dümmsten Ratschläge, die Sie je bekommen oder gehört haben – von Ihren Eltern, von Freunden, Lehrern, Trainern, Filmstars usw.

BEISPIEL   *Einmal sagte mir eine Freundin, man müsse/müsste sich jeden Tag Zeit nehmen, um an den Blumen zu riechen. Aber in der Stadt, wo wir damals wohnten …*

Schriftliche Themen

Tipps zum Schreiben

Using Quotations

Good journalistic prose usually contains a carefully balanced mixture of commentary and quotations (direct and indirect) from knowledgeable, interesting sources. Especially in written German, indirect quotations are routinely rendered with subjunctive forms—the more formal the tone, the more prevalent the use of subjunctive I, as long as those forms are distinctly subjunctive. Remember that subjunctive I can convey the idea of "quotedness" on its own, with no need to mention the quoted speaker in every instance (see 22.4.A). For the sake of style, writers should vary the use of **dass** in indirect quotations and use precise words for *say* to introduce both direct and indirect quotes.

A **So steht es geschrieben.** Lesen Sie einen Blog zu einem Online-Artikel oder Leserbriefe aus einer Zeitung oder Zeitschrift, um zu erfahren, was die Leute zu einem Thema so denken. Dann schreiben Sie einen Bericht über die Meinung dieser Leute, so wie man ihn in den deutschen Medien finden könnte.

BEISPIEL *Zum Thema „Philosophie als Hauptfach" meint Robert Wohl, ein Student im siebten Semester, dass man von den Studenten mehr fordern* (demand) *müsse, denn … usw.*

B **Lebensansichten *(views on life).*** Ihre Freunde haben bestimmt ein paar Ansichten über das Leben – über Beziehungen und Liebe, Arbeit und Jobs, die Zukunft und Weltpolitik. Sprechen Sie mit zwei oder drei Freunden (egal in welcher Sprache!) und dann schreiben Sie einen Bericht (auf Deutsch, natürlich!) über die Ansichten, die Sie erfahren haben, in der indirekten Rede im Konjunktiv.

BEISPIEL *Mein Freund Jonas ist der Ansicht, das Leben sei zu kurz, um mit gewissen Leuten zu tanzen. Er wolle sich doch pausenlos amüsieren, erklärt er, und deswegen sei es wichtig, dass … usw.*

Zusammenfassung

Rules to Remember

1 Present subjunctive I is used almost exclusively to express indirect discourse in formal, written settings.

2 Present subjunctive I is formed by attaching the subjunctive endings (**-e, -est, -e; -en, -et, -en**) to the unchanged stem of the infinitive; **sein** does not add **-e (ich sei, er/sie sei)**.

3 Past subjunctive I is formed with the auxiliary **haben** or **sein** in subjunctive I + the past participle. Future tense subjunctive I is formed with subjunctive I forms of **werden** + the infinitive.

4 The tense of the subjunctive verb in the indirect discourse corresponds to the verb tense in the direct discourse version, regardless of the verb tense in the reference clause: direct discourse verbs in any past tense (simple past, perfect, or past perfect) become past subjunctive in the indirect discourse; direct discourse verbs in the present tense are rendered in present subjunctive; and future tense verbs in the direct discourse use a subjunctive form of **werden** + infinitive in indirect discourse.

5 The formal rules for choice of subjunctive in indirect discourse are:

a. Use subjunctive I wherever possible, i.e., where subjunctive I forms are distinct from the indicative.

b. Where subjunctive I looks like the indicative, use subjunctive II forms.[4]

---

[4]An additional rule is used increasingly, even in formal contexts: Whenever these rules lead to an archaic or obsolete verb form, use the **würde** + infinitive construction.

6 These rules apply in practice only to formal reporting situations and written prose. In colloquial German, indirect speech is often conveyed with the indicative or, to suggest objectivity or distance between speaker and source, with **würde** + infinitive and subjunctive II for common verbs such as **kommen, tun, wissen,** etc. If subjunctive I forms are used in speaking, they can indicate an ironic or skeptical stance.

7 Subjunctive I can also be used in **als / als ob / als wenn** constructions and in very formal (and rare) "exhortatory" constructions such as **Es lebe die Königin!**

At a Glance

Subjunctive I forms							
	sein	**haben**	**werden**	**müssen**	**wissen**	**lernen**	**nehmen**
ich	sei	habe	werde	müsse	wisse	lerne	nehme
du	sei(e)st	habest	werdest	müssest	wissest	lernest	nehmest
Sie	seien	haben	werden	müssen	wissen	lernen	nehmen
er/sie/es	**sei**	**habe**	**werde**	**müsse**	**wisse**	**lerne**	**nehme**
wir	seien	haben	werden	müssen	wissen	lernen	nehmen
ihr	seiet	habet	werdet	müsset	wisset	lernet	nehmet
Sie	seien	haben	werden	müssen	wissen	lernen	nehmen
sie	seien	haben	werden	müssen	wissen	lernen	nehmen

Subjunctive I: Past time
haben
_____, er **habe** das gesagt
sein
_____, sie **sei** auch da gewesen

Subjunctive I: Tense agreement	Direct	Indirect	
Present	„Ich singe gern."	Er sagte,	er **singe** gern. dass er gern **singe.**
Past	„Ich bin eingeschlafen." „Ich schlief ein." „Ich war eingeschlafen."	Sie sagte,	sie **sei** eingeschlafen. dass sie eingeschlafen **sei.**
Future	„Ich werde das machen."	Er sagte,	er **werde** das machen. dass er das machen **werde.**

zum Beispiel

Knigge: Sir Adolph Franz Friedrich Ludwig Knigge (1752–1796), a German with an ample supply of names, would probably be surprised today at how well-known his has become. He was the author of many books, but is best known for his treatise, published in 1788, entitled *Über den Umgang mit Menschen* (*On Dealing with People*). There he offers advice, often with surprising nuance and sociological insight, on how to interact with people of diverse social standing, temperaments and commercial interests. Though the book does not concern itself with etiquette as such—which fork to use or the rules of precedence in introductions, for example—its widespread popularity has led people to make that connection, and today, the word **Knigge** is synonymous with *proper behavior*. A sampling of books, articles, and websites indicates its current wide range: *Der ultimative Büro-Knigge; Knigge für den richtigen Umgang mit E-Mails; Knigge für moderne Frauen; Knigge für Kinder; Business-Knigge; and Der kleine Facebook-Liebes-Knigge.*

367

Grammatik

23.1 **THE IMPERATIVE MOOD**

German conjugates verbs in three moods to convey various nuances of meaning and speaker intention—the indicative, the subjunctive (Chapters 21 and 22), and the imperative. One can connect certain forms of the subjunctive with particular kinds of speech (for example, indirect discourse with subjunctive I, or hypothetical conditionals with subjunctive II). But it would be an oversimplification to equate commands with the imperative mood. A more useful (and sociolinguistically more accurate) approach is to think of commands as a spectrum, ranging from suggestions and polite requests ("*Please pass the butter*") to forceful, blunt orders ("*Get away from the stove this instant!*") and official directives ("*Return all tray tables to their upright and locked position for landing*"), and to think of the imperative mood as one of several options for expressing commands along this spectrum. The goal is not merely to master the forms in German—they pose little difficulty in most cases—but to match the tone they convey with the intention of the command, and to deploy them along with other command-statement options in ways that are contextually appropriate.

A. Formation

1. The imperative mood (**der Imperativ**) has four forms in German, all derived from the present tense and relating to the person or persons being addressed.

    du-form   Familiar, singular: speaking to one friend or family member

    ihr-form   Familiar, plural: speaking to multiple friends or family members

    Sie-form   Formal, singular or plural: speaking to one or more persons with whom one uses **Sie** rather than **du**

    wir-form   First person plural: speaking to a group that includes oneself, as in *"Let's . . ."*

2. The **du**-imperative consists of the present-tense stem + an optional -**e** that is usually omitted, particularly in colloquial German.

    Schreib(e) bald!   *Write soon!*

    Bring(e) deine Freunde mit!   *Bring your friends along!*

    The final -**e** is *not* omitted if the infinitive stem ends in -**d**, -**t**, -**ig**, or in -**m** or -**n** preceded by a consonant other than **l** or **r**.

finden	**Finde** Zeit für Freunde!	*Find time for friends!*
warten	**Warte** geduldig!	*Wait patiently!*
entschuldigen	**Entschuldige** kleine Fehler!	*Excuse small mistakes!*
atmen	**Atme** tief, bevor du sprichst!	*Breathe deeply before speaking!*
öffnen	**Öffne** anderen die Tür!	*Open the door for others!*

3. Verb infinitives ending in **-eln** or **-ern** also add a final **-e** to the **du**-imperative, while the -e- preceding the -l or -r is sometimes dropped.

handeln	**Hand(e)le** zuversichtlich!	*Deal confidently!*
verwandeln	**Verwand(e)le** dich!	*Transform yourself!*
ändern	**Änd(e)re** deine Einstellung!	*Change your attitude!*
wandern	**Wand(e)re** so oft du kannst!	*Go hiking as often as you can!*

4. Verbs with the present-tense vowel shifts **e → i** or **e → ie** (see 2.1.B) also shift in the **du**-imperative. They do not add an **-e** after the verb stem.

sprechen	du sprichst → **Sprich** immer deutlich!	*Always speak clearly!*
lesen	du liest → **Lies** die Anweisungen!	*Read the instructions!*
essen	du isst → **Iss** deinen Teller leer!	*Eat your plate clean!*

EXCEPTION:

werden	du wirst → **Werde** schnell gesund!	*Get better quickly!*

However, verbs with the stem changes **a → ä, au → äu,** or **o → ö** do *not* have vowel shifts in the **du**-imperative and may take the optional **-e.**

tragen	du trägst → **Trag(e)** keine Jeans zum Interview!	*Don't wear jeans to the interview!*
laufen	du läufst → **Laufe** dich zuerst warm!	*Warm up first!*

5. The **ihr**-form imperative is the same as the **ihr**-form of the present tense, but the pronoun is omitted.

Kommt immer pünktlich zu Sitzungen!	*Always come to meetings punctually!*
Sprecht mit allen im Zimmer!	*Speak with everyone in the room!*

6. German occasionally includes the pronouns **du** and **ihr** with the familiar imperative for emphasis or clarification.

Ich habe dreimal aufgeräumt. **Mach <u>du</u> es mal! (Macht <u>ihr</u> es mal!)**	*I have cleaned up three times. You do it for a change! (You all do it for a change!)*

7. The **Sie**-form imperative is the same as the **Sie**-form of the present tense, with the verb in first position followed by the pronoun **Sie.**

Sprechen Sie nicht mit vollem Mund!	*Don't talk with your mouth full!*
Bleiben Sie stehen, bis Ihr Gastgeber Sie begrüßt!	*Remain standing until your host greets you!*
Lassen Sie Ihren Gesprächspartner zu Ende reden!	*Let your discussion partner finish talking!*
Sagen Sie nicht „Gesundheit" im Büro, wenn ein Kollege niest.	*Don't say "Gesundheit" in the office when a colleague sneezes.*

8. The **wir**-form imperative is the same as the **wir**-form of the present tense, with the verb in first position followed by the pronoun **wir**.

Reden wir nicht mehr darüber!	*Let's not talk about it anymore!*
Nehmen wir nun **an,** dass niemand die Antwort weiß.	*Let's assume now that no one knows the answer.*

9. The imperatives for the verb **sein** are irregular.

Sei **Seid** **Seien Sie**	vorsichtig!	*Be careful!*
Seien wir	vorsichtig!	*Let's be careful!*

10. Since imperative forms are only used in main clauses, separable-prefix verbs in the imperative voice always separate, with the prefix moving to the end of the clause.

auf·schreiben	**Schreiben Sie** immer bei Bewerbungsgesprächen alle wichtigen Details **auf.**	*Always write down all important details at job interviews.*
hin·setzen	**Setze** dich nicht bei einem Treffen als erste(r) **hin.**	*Don't be the first one to sit down at a meeting.*
auswendig· lernen	**Lernt** die Namen eurer Kollegen und Kolleginnen **auswendig!**	*Memorize the names of your (male and female) colleagues!*

B. Use

1. Traditional usage required an exclamation point for all commands in the imperative mood, much like a question mark is used to signal a question, but in current use the exclamation point is only required if particular emphasis is implied.

COMPARE:

Sag mir doch endlich, was du meinst!	*Tell me what you think for once!*
Sag mir einfach, wann das Meeting anfängt.	*Just tell me when the meeting will start.*

2. Depending on tone of voice and emphasis, the imperative mood can convey anything from a sense of urgency, blunt directive, or a warning, to an instruction or merely a suggestion.

Hör doch auf!	(spoken playfully, with emphasis on **auf**) *Oh, come on, stop it!* (spoken sharply) *Stop that immediately!*
Passen Sie auf!	(spoken kindly, with raised pitch on **auf**) *You'd better watch out!* (spoken sharply, with falling intonation overall) *Pay attention [you idiot]!*

Sagen Sie so was nie wieder!   *Never say anything like that again!*

Ach, essen wir jetzt.   *Oh, let's go ahead and eat now.*

3. Flavoring particles (see R.6) are often used along with intonation to establish or modify the tone of a command in the imperative mood.

- **Doch** can be used, along with sharp intonation, to intensify a command.

    Sag das **doch** nicht!   *Don't <u>say</u> that!*

    Doch can also add a sense of impatience or exasperation to imperatives.

    Hilf mir **doch!**   *Come on, help me!*

    Mach's **doch** einfach!   *Would you just <u>do</u> it!*

- **Mal** can be used in conjunction with relaxed intonation to soften the bluntness of a command in the imperative.

    Gehen wir **mal** einen trinken.   *Let's go have a drink sometime.*

    With certain verbs, and with raised pitch on the final element in the command, **mal** can add a sense of mild impatience that is best expressed by the English word *just.*

    Hört **mal** <u>zu</u>!   *Just <u>listen!</u>*

    Seien Sie **mal** <u>ruhig</u>!   *Just be <u>quiet!</u>*

- **Nur** can add a stipulative tone to imperatives, implying that consequences—either good or bad—will result.

    Versuchen Sie es **nur!**   *Just try it (and see)!*

- **Bitte**—although strictly speaking not a flavoring particle—is often used with commands to soften the tone and express a degree of deference. When it begins a sentence, it is set off by a comma only when stressed. It also occurs in other positions, but it cannot immediately precede pronouns.

    COMPARE:

    Bitte, tun Sie das!   *Please—<u>do</u> that!*
    Bitte vergesst die Nummer nicht!   *Please don't forget the number!*
    Zeig es ihnen **bitte** nicht!   *Please don't show it to them!*

4. Commands in the imperative sometimes include the comparative adverb **lieber** to convey the idea of *instead,* or what would be *preferable,* in response to a question, suggestion, or idea.

Sollte ich fürs Bewerbungsgespräch die rote Krawatte anziehen?   *Should I wear the red tie for the job interview?*
—Nein, nimm **lieber** die hellblaue.   *—No, take the light blue one (instead).*

Schau, da ist mein Chef im Café! Ich gehe ihn mal grüßen.   *Look, there's my boss in the café. I'll just go say Hi.*
—Spinnst du? Lass ihn **lieber** dich zuerst grüßen.   *—Are you crazy? [It's preferable if you] Let him greet you first.*

23.2 OTHER OPTIONS FOR EXPRESSING COMMANDS

A. Modals, subjunctives, and questions

1. In many social contexts, using the imperative mood with no modifications (as in **Gib mir die Butter!**) is inappropriately blunt. Inserting **bitte** into the command softens the authoritarian tone somewhat, but German speakers often make use of alternatives such as modal verbs (see 9.1.B) and subjunctive forms (see 21.3.D) to convey such requests. With rising intonation, they are perceived as questions (and are thus relatively deferential); with falling intonation, they have the effect of a polite command.

Kannst du mir die Butter geben?   *Can you give me the butter?*

Würden Sie mir bitte die Butter geben?   *Would you please give me the butter?*

2. In colloquial usage, one often hears such requests in the form of a question with rising intonation, which renders it a polite command.

Gibst du mir bitte die Butter?   *Could you please give me the butter?*

B. Impersonal commands

1. Directives for the general public such as signs, announcements, and warnings are often expressed with an infinitive rather than an imperative form, with the infinitive placed at the end of the phrase. The absence of a clearly marked addressee gives these commands an unfocused and therefore general, impersonal tone.

Einfach **ankreuzen,** komplett **ausfüllen** und **bestellen!**	*Simply check off [the box], fill out [the contact information] completely, and place your order!*
Bitte den Rasen nicht **betreten.**	*Please don't walk on the grass.*
Bitte an der Kasse **zahlen.**	*Please pay at the cash register.*

2. Instructions, such as those in recipes and technical manuals, are often expressed as infinitives.

Den Kopfsalat **waschen** und die Blätter in kleine Stücke **schneiden.** Die Eier hart **kochen** und **abschrecken.** Die Gurke **enthäuten** und in hauchdünne Scheiben **schneiden** ...	*Wash the lettuce and cut the leaves into small pieces. Boil the eggs until hard and chill in cold water. Peel the cucumber and cut into very thin slices . . .*
Den Datastick in den USB-Anschluss-Slot **hineinstecken** und aufs Display **schauen**...	*Insert the flash drive into the USB slot and look at the display . . .*

3. A passive construction without a subject (12.1.E) can carry the force of a command.

In dieser Sitzung **wird** nicht **gemailt!**	*No e-mailing at this meeting!*
In der Bahn **soll** nicht lang oder laut am Handy **gesprochen werden.**	*On trains, you shouldn't speak for a long time or loudly on your cell phone.*

Bei Tisch **wird** nicht **gesungen!**	*No singing at the dinner table!*
Im Seminar **wird** bitte nicht **gechattet** oder **gesurft.**	*Please, no online chatting or web surfing during the seminar.*

Wortschatz
Vokabeln zu „Social Media"

As you know, the world of technology features frequent use of commands and specialized vocabulary. This **Wortschatz** provides a list of terms that you may run across when dealing with a ubiquitous technical prop of contemporary culture: **das Handy** (*cell phone*)/**das Smartphone.** Note that English equivalents are provided only for noncognate words.

das Netz	*network*
das Festnetz, -e	*landline*
ins Festnetz an·rufen	*to call a landline phone*
das Mobilnetz, -e	*mobile/cell network*
der Apparat	*apparatus, gadget*
der Akku, -s	*rechargeable battery*
das [Touchscreen-] Display	
das Menü	
das Mikrofon, -e	
die Taste, -n	*button, key*
die Raute-Taste	*hash/pound key*
die Sternchen-Taste	*asterisk key*
Was man macht	
an·rufen	*to call up*
eine Nummer ein·geben	*to enter a number*
eine Nummer wählen	*to dial a number*
eine SMS schicken	*to send a text message*
auf die [Eins, Zwei] drücken	*to press [1, 2]*
die Extras	
der Klingelton, ̈-e	*ringtone*
das WLAN	*Wifi/wireless Internet*
im Netz/Internet surfen	*to surf the Internet*
die [Video-]Kamera	*[video] camera*
herunter·laden, downloaden	*to download*
hoch·laden, uploaden	*to upload*
… und dann bezahlen	
die Flatrate, -n	*flat-rate service*
die Gebühr, -en	*fee*
der Tarif, -e	*rate, tariff*
unbegrenzt	*unlimited*
der Vertrag	*contract*

> Die Bedienung ist ganz einfach: zuerst aufs Menü schauen, dann den Namen oder die Nummer finden, auf diese Taste drücken und dann …
>
> *It's easy to use: first look at the menu, find the name or the number, press this key, and then . . .*

Übungen

A **Nicht immer so höflich.** Drücken Sie diese Wünsche und Bitten durch den Imperativ der fett gedruckten Verben stärker aus.

BEISPIELE **Du sollst lauter sprechen.**
Sprich lauter!

Würdet ihr uns bitte **helfen?**
Helft uns bitte!

1. Herr Kollege, könnten Sie bitte einen Laptop **holen?**
2. Leute, bitte etwas lauter **reden!**
3. Du kannst mich heute Abend zu Hause **anrufen.**
4. Lena, könntest du bitte die Tür **öffnen?**
5. Herr Keller, darf ich Sie bitten, mir zu **helfen?**
6. Kinder, **seid** ihr bitte ruhig?
7. Max, ich hoffe, du **wirst** nicht böse.
8. Herr Professor, Sie sollen sich doch **beruhigen!**
9. Es wäre für uns gut, etwas fleißiger zu **sein.**

B **Situationen.** Was sagen Sie in der Situation? Verwenden Sie dabei passende Partikel, wie z.B. **doch, mal, nur, bitte, lieber.**

BEISPIEL Ein Freund von Ihnen will Eintrittskarten für ein Rockkonzert kaufen und fragt Sie, ob er Ihnen auch welche kaufen soll.
Ja, kauf(e) mir bitte auch eine Karte!

1. Studenten plaudern *(chat)* neben Ihnen in der Bibliothek, während Sie zu lesen versuchen.
2. Sie haben die Frage Ihrer Deutschprofessorin entweder nicht gehört oder nicht verstanden.
3. Sie wollen mit jemandem irgendwo gemütlich zusammensitzen und plaudern.
4. Sie wollen, dass niemand Sie in Ihrem Zimmer stört, und Sie hängen einen kleinen Zettel an die Tür.
5. Sie haben eine schwierige Hausaufgabe und möchten, dass ein paar Freunde Ihnen dabei helfen.
6. Sie haben Ihre Mutter beim Sprechen unterbrochen und wollen sich entschuldigen.
7. Ihr Hund bellt schon wieder und das wollen Sie sich nicht mehr anhören.
8. Ihre kleine Schwester kommt mit ganz schmutzigen Händen zum Essen.

C **Beim Skypen.** Sie skypen gerade mit einem Freund im Ausland (*overseas*), aber Sie haben dabei Probleme. Was sagen Sie Ihrem Gesprächspartner in Form eines Befehls?

1. Ihr Freund spricht zu leise.
2. Auf einmal hören Sie gar nichts, und 10 Sekunden später ist alles wieder OK – aber Sie haben nicht gehört, was der Freund in dieser Zeit gesagt hat.
3. Der Akku in Ihrem Laptop ist fast leer, und Sie wissen, dass Ihnen ganz wenig Zeit übrigbleibt.
4. Ihr Freund möchte Ihnen gerade ein lustiges YouTube-Video zeigen, aber er weiß nicht, ob das beim Skypen geht oder nicht.
5. Sie haben keine Zeit mehr zu sprechen und wollen das Gespräch beenden – aber auf höfliche Weise (*in a polite way*)!

D **Bitten!** Was für Bitten haben Sie an die folgenden Personen?

BEISPIEL an Ihren Vater
„*Papa, schick mir bitte mehr Geld!*"

1. an Ihre Eltern
2. an Ihre Geschwister (Schwester/Bruder)
3. an eine Freundin/einen Freund
4. an Ihre Deutschprofessorin/Ihren Deutschprofessor
5. an eine berühmte Person Ihrer Wahl (*of your choice*)

Anwendung

A **Ratschläge (*pieces of advice*).** In diesem Rollenspiel übernimmt eine Partnerin/ ein Partner die Rolle einer erfahrenen Studentin oder eines erfahrenen Studenten, und die/der andere die Rolle einer Person, die nächstes Jahr als Erstsemester(in) zur Uni kommt. Die erfahrene Studentin/Der erfahrene Student gibt dieser Person Ratschläge in Form von Imperativen (**du**-Form). Dabei ist es auch wichtig zu erwähnen, was man als Erstsemester(in) *nicht* machen sollte. Die Partnerin/Der Partner kann fragen, was hinter diesen Ratschlägen steckt.

BEISPIELE Belege keine Kurse vor dem Mittagessen!
(*Don't sign up for any classes before lunch!*)

Lerne deine Kommilitonen gut kennen!
(*Get to know your fellow students well!*)

Iss auf keinen Fall in der Mensa, wenn es Fisch gibt!
(*Whatever happens, don't eat in the cafeteria when they're serving fish!*)

B **Wie funktioniert dein Smartphone?** Nehmen wir an, Sie haben oder Ihr Partner hat ein Handy/Smartphone dabei: Eine Partnerin/Ein Partner tut, als ob sie/er gar nicht wüsste, was ein Handy ist oder wie es funktioniert. Die andere Person in der Gruppe zeigt und erklärt alles und antwortet auf die Fragen der Partnerin/des Partners.

Wozu dient diese Taste?	Wie gibt man eine Nummer ein?
Wie viele Telefonnummern kann man darauf speichern *(store)?*	Kann man Fotos und Musik herunterladen? Wie? Wie viel?
Was kann man alles im Menü finden?	Wie viel kostet das im Monat?
Wie lang kann man sprechen?	Wie kommt man ins Netz?
Kann man ins Ausland anrufen?	Wie schickt man SMS?

C   **Wer nicht hören will, muss fühlen.**   Das folgende Gedicht enthält Befehle *(commands)*, die manche Kinder sicher schon öfter gehört haben. Welche davon (**du**-Imperative) mussten *Sie* sich als Kind anhören? Welche Befehle werden Ihre Kinder später wohl von Ihnen zu hören bekommen? Wie deuten Sie die Zeilen: „Wer nicht hören will, muss fühlen?" Diskutieren Sie mit anderen Studenten darüber.

Erziehung

laß[1] das
komm sofort her
bring das hin
kannst du nicht hören
hol das sofort her
kannst du nicht verstehen
sei ruhig
faß das nicht an
sitz ruhig
nimm das nicht in den Mund
schrei nicht
stell das sofort wieder weg
paß auf
nimm die Finger weg
sitz ruhig
mach dich nicht schmutzig
bring das sofort wieder zurück
schmier dich nicht voll
sei ruhig
laß das
wer nicht hören will
muß fühlen

—Uwe Timm

Source: "Erziehung," by Uwe Timm from BUNDESDEUTSCH, LYRIK ZUR SACHE GRAMMATIK, ed. Rudolf Otto Wiemer. Reprinted by permission of Verlag Kiepenhauer and Witsch.

[1]This poem retains its original spelling, rather than the spelling of the recent **Rechtschreibreform** (see Appendix 2 for more details).

Schriftliche Themen

Tipps zum Schreiben	**Writing with the Imperative**
	Commands in the imperative mood are always directed at an audience: a friend (**du**); multiple family members (**ihr**); someone whom you address with **Sie**; or a group to which you yourself belong (**wir**). In writing, commands are usually found in correspondence, or perhaps in journalistic writing with a chatty (personal) tone, but only rarely in essays or research papers. If commands or instructions are written, they often take the infinitive-final constructions discussed in 2.B above. If you're writing a formal essay and wish to express something like "*Consider the effects . . . ,*" an imperative used in English in this context, you'll need to paraphrase it in German with a **wir**-imperative or a nonimperative form to make it sound less personal.

A **Tipps für neue Schüler/Studenten.**   Schreiben Sie 8–10 Tipps für jemand, der im kommenden Jahr an Ihrer Schule oder Uni lernt oder studiert. Dabei können Sie verschiedene Befehlsformen benutzen: **Man soll … / Es ist ganz wichtig, dass du … / usw.** Aber schreiben Sie ein paar Befehle mit dem Imperativ: **Vergiss nicht … / Nimm dir Zeit … / usw.**

B **Wie man schlechte Arbeiten (*research papers*) schreibt.**   In einem satirischen Artikel hat ein deutscher Uni-Student beschrieben, wie man am besten ganz schlechte Arbeiten schreibt[2]. Seine Befehle:

- Spät anfangen, die letzte Nacht durcharbeiten und alle Regeln wissenschaftlicher Arbeit ignorieren.

- Lassen Sie zunächst einige Wochen der Bearbeitungszeit verstreichen (*pass by*).

- Sprechen Sie niemals mit Ihren Studienkollegen über ihre Arbeiten, schon gar nicht über Ihre eigene.

- Seien Sie nicht zu streng (*hard, strict*) mit sich.

- Verwöhnen Sie Ihren Professor aber ruhig mit sinnfreien E-Mails, gern mit der Anrede „Hallöchen *(Hi!),* Herr Professor!"

Was für Ideen haben Sie noch dazu? Schreiben Sie noch 4–5 Sätze mit Befehlen in verschiedenen Formen (wie in diesem Text), entweder zu diesem Thema oder vielleicht zu einem anderen:

„Wie man bei Prüfungen garantiert durchfällt"

„Wie man Mitbewohnern/-bewohnerinnen am besten auf die Nerven gehen kann"

---

[2]*Der Spiegel,* 20 Februar 2008: Stefan Zimmermann, „Die perfekte Anleitung für schlechte Studienarbeiten." [URL: http://www.spiegel.de/unispiegel/studium/0,1518,534163,00.html]

C **Eine Anleitung** *(instructions for use).* Sie wissen ja schon, wie ein Handy/Smartphone funktioniert. Aber Sie kennen bestimmt irgendeinen technischen oder nichttechnischen Vorgang *(process)*, den nicht alle Leute kennen. Schreiben Sie einen Text mit einer Anleitung für diesen Prozess – Computerprogramm, Videospiel, Küchenrezept, Sporttraining – mit passenden Befehlen. Sie sollen sich ein Publikum ausdenken (generell, einige Freunde, jemand in Ihrer Familie) und die Befehle auf dieses Publikum zuschneiden *(tailor to fit)*. Versuchen Sie dabei, verschiedene Befehlsarten *(types)* zu verwenden!

Zusammenfassung

Rules to Remember

1 There are four imperative verb forms in German, corresponding to people addressed as **du, ihr, Sie, wir.**

2 The imperative conjugations are based on the *present tense* verb forms corresponding to these pronouns.

3 For the **du**-imperative, vowel shifts from **i** $\longrightarrow$ **e** and **i** $\longrightarrow$ **ie** are retained; **a** $\longrightarrow$ **ä** and **au** $\longrightarrow$ **äu** shifts are not retained.

4 In most cases, no pronoun is used after **du**- and **ihr**-imperatives: **Komm; Kommt.**

5 Pronouns are always used after **wir**- and **Sie**-imperatives: **Gehen wir; Gehen Sie.**

6 German uses several forms to express commands and requests besides the imperative: modal verbs; subjunctive forms such as **würde/könnte**; impersonal forms (with the infinitive in final position); and no-subject passives.

At a Glance

Imperative forms					
	gehen	**auf·schreiben**	**antworten**	**sprechen (e $\longrightarrow$ i)**	**tragen (a $\longrightarrow$ ä)**
du	Geh(e)	Schreib(e) … auf	Antworte	Sprich	Trag(e)
ihr	Geht	Schreibt … auf	Antwortet	Sprecht	Tragt
Sie	Gehen Sie	Schreiben Sie … auf	Antworten Sie	Sprechen Sie	Tragen Sie
wir	Gehen wir	Schreiben wir … auf	Antworten wir	Sprechen wir	Tragen wir

zum Beispiel

Herbsttag

Rainer Maria Rilke (1875–1926) is considered one of the great European poets of the 20th century. Throughout his life he lived, for varying periods of time, in Prague, Munich, Worpswede (an artist community in Lower Saxony), Paris, Italy, and Switzerland. The short poem "*Herbsttag*" was written in the autumn of 1902, just a few months after Rilke's move to Paris that summer. The poem begins with a reference to summer—"*der Sommer war sehr groß*"—and reflects in the following lines the transition from summer to autumn. While the initial stanzas convey a certain acquiescence, perhaps even contentment, the last stanza suggests the anxieties of someone with few roots or connections: "*Wer jetzt allein ist, wird es lange bleiben.*" The final lines, in turn, may express Rilke's own sense of melancholy at the prospect of autumn and winter in an unfamiliar place: "*…in den Alleen hin und her unruhig wandern, wenn die Blätter treiben.*"

379

Herbsttag

Herr, es ist Zeit. Der Sommer war sehr groß.
Leg deinen Schatten° auf die Sonnenuhren°,
und auf den Fluren° lass die Winde los.

Befiehl° den letzten Früchten, voll zu sein;
gib ihnen noch zwei südlichere Tage,
dränge° sie zur Vollendung° hin, und jage°
die letzte Süße° in den schweren Wein.

Wer jetzt kein Haus hat, baut sich keines mehr.
Wer jetzt allein ist, wird es lange bleiben,
wird wachen°, lesen, lange Briefe schreiben
und wird in den Alleen° hin und her
unruhig wandern, wenn die Blätter° treiben°.

—Rainer Maria Rilke [21.9.1902]

shadow / sundials
here: meadows

command

urge / completion / here: drive

sweetness

stay awake
boulevards, tree-lined roads
leaves / drift about

Grammatik

24.1   FUTURE TENSE

A. Formation

1. The future tense (**das Futur**) is formed with the conjugated present tense of the auxiliary **werden** (in this usage: *will*) + a verb infinitive.

werden + V₂ infinitive: *will* _____		
ich **werde**	*I*	
du **wirst**	*you* (sing. familiar)	
Sie **werden**	*you* (sing. formal)	
er/sie/es **wird**	*he/she/it*	
+ **gehen**		+ *will go*
wir **werden**	*we*	
ihr **werdet**	*you* (pl. familiar)	
Sie **werden**	*you* (pl. formal)	
sie **werden**	*they*	

2. In the future tense, **werden** functions as V_1 and the infinitive comes at the end of the main clause (V_2).

Hoffentlich **wird** das sonnige Wetter **andauern.**	*I hope the sunny weather will last.*

3. In a dependent clause, **werden** (V_1) moves to final position. However, if the dependent clause contains a double infinitive, as is the case with the future tense of modal verbs and some constructions with **lassen** (9.4 and 11.6), **werden** directly precedes the double infinitive.[1]

Meinst du, dass wir uns nach den Semesterferien *wiedersehen* **werden?**	*Do you think we'll see each other after the semester break?*

BUT:

Du, ich glaube nicht, dass wir uns **werden** *wiedersehen können.*	*You know, I really don't think we'll be able to see each other again.*

B. Use

1. Like other tenses in German (see 2.2.A; 3.2.C; 8.1.B), the future tense can be translated by multiple forms in English.

Er wird lange Briefe schreiben.	*He's going to write long letters.*
	He will write long letters.

2. German uses the future tense more sparingly than English. Both English and German use the present tense to convey future meaning when adverbial modifiers or other contextual clues make that meaning clear.

Ich **kaufe** den Wein *heute Abend.*	*I'm buying the wine tonight.*

But German much prefers the present tense in such cases, even where English may require a future tense form.

COMPARE:

Ich schreibe dir später.	*I'll write to you later.*
	I'm going to write to you later.

3. There are, however, several situations in which German favors the future tense.

a. To emphasize assumptions or intentions.

Er **wird wachen** und **lesen.**	*(I assume) He'll stay up and read.*
	He intends to stay up and read.

---

[1]As noted in 9.4.2, speakers in some parts of southern Germany and Austria handle this construction differently, by inserting the future auxiliary **(werden)** *between* the main verb and the modal verb, so that the example here would be rendered: … dass wir uns **wiedersehen** *werden* **können.**

Er **wird** bestimmt kein Haus **bauen.**   *He's definitely not going to build a house.*

b. To refer to states or actions in a relatively distant future.

COMPARE:

Was **macht** er das ganze Wochenende?   { *What is he doing all weekend?*
                                            { *What will he do all weekend?*

Was **wird** er wohl in den kommenden   *What will he do in the coming years?*
Jahren **machen?**

c. To distinguish future states or actions from present states or actions.

„Wer jetzt allein **ist, wird** es lange   *"Whoever is alone now will remain*
bleiben.“   *so for a long time."*

4. The German future tense is also used with the particles **wohl** or **schon** to express
present probability.

Das **wird** *schon* **stimmen.**   *That's probably right.*

Die Trauben **werden** *wohl* zum Ernten   *The grapes are probably ripe for the*
reif **sein.**   *harvest.*

24.2 ▸ FUTURE PERFECT TENSE

A. Formation

The future perfect tense (**Futur II**) is formed like the future tense—that is, with **werden**
(V_1) joined to an infinitive (V_2)—except that in the future perfect, the infinitive in question
is a *perfect infinitive* (see also 9.1.B) rather than the more commonly used *present infinitive.*
The perfect infinitive consists of the past participle and the appropriate auxiliary in present
infinitive form.

Present infinitive		Perfect infinitive	
tun	→	getan haben	*to have done*
sagen	→	gesagt haben	*to have said*
fahren	→	gefahren sein	*to have driven*
bleiben	→	geblieben sein	*to have stayed*

Notice how the sense of completion conveyed by the perfect tense characterizes the future
perfect tense as well.

Perfect: Er **hat** das Haus **gebaut.**   *He built the house.*

Future perfect: Er **wird** das Haus **gebaut haben.**   *He will have built the house.*

B. Use

1. The future perfect tense is used to express the idea that something *will have happened* by a specified point in the future, often with an adverbial modifier using **bis.**

Bis Oktober **wird** er sein Haus **gebaut haben.**	*He will have built his house by October.*
Und *bis* Ende Oktober **wird** er schon **umgezogen sein.**	*And by the end of October he'll have already moved in.*
Bis Ende November **wird** er wohl Hunderte von Briefen **geschrieben haben.**	*By the end of November he'll probably have written hundreds of letters.*

2. The future perfect can also be used to express probability concerning something that *has already happened,* often in conjunction with the particles **wohl** or **schon.**

Er **wird** *wohl* diesen Ort schon mal im Herbst **besucht haben.**	*He's probably already visited this place in autumn.*
Wird Rilke *wohl* alles selbst **erfahren haben,** was er in dem Gedicht beschreibt?	*Did Rilke experience everything himself that he describes in the poem?*

Wortschatz
weiter [machen] | fortfahren | fortsetzen

1. The most common way of expressing *to continue an activity,* especially in conversational settings, is to use the separable prefix **weiter.**

Mach (nur) **weiter!**	*(Just) keep on going!/Keep on doing it!*
Danach sind wir **weitergefahren.**	*After that we continued driving.*
Hör doch auf! Ich will **weiterlesen.**	*Stop that! I want to keep on reading/ continue reading.*

In this sense, **weiter** is often used without a verb to convey *encouragement to continue.*

Weiter so!	*You're doing great!/Keep on going!*

2. **Weiter** also functions as a comparative adverb, with the meaning of *further* (see R.5.1):

Rilke ist viel **weiter** gereist als ich.	*Rilke traveled much further than I (have).*

3. **Weiter·machen** + **mit** expresses *to continue* + a noun (as in "She's continuing her project").

Nach seinem Bruch mit Rodin **machte** Rilke mit dem Dichten **weiter.**	*After parting ways with Rodin, Rilke continued with writing poetry.*

4. The separable-prefix verb **fort·fahren** can be used to express a similar meaning, but is usually found in more formal settings (such as a meeting or lecture). It is intransitive, taking no direct object, but is normally complemented by a clause or phrase.

Wir **fahren fort,** wo wir gestern aufgehört haben.	*We'll continue where we left off yesterday.*
Er **fuhr** im Gedicht mit dieser Metapher **fort.**	*He continued with this metaphor in the poem.*

5. **Fort·setzen** also means *to continue something,* and is similarly formal, but it is transitive, requiring a direct object.

Nach dem Winter hat man die Arbeit am Haus **fortgesetzt.**	*After the winter, they continued the work on the house/working on the house.*

Übungen

A **Lottogewinner!** In einem Fernsehinterview erzählen Herr und Frau Lindemann, was sie mit ihrem Lottogewinn machen werden. Sie sprechen im Präsens. Erzählen Sie **im Futur** von den Plänen der Familie.

Herr und Frau Lindemann:
Mit unserem Lottogewinn von 500.000 Euro machen wir erst mal eine Reise nach Amerika. Unsere Tochter reist mit. In Boston kaufen wir uns einen Mercedes, denn dort kostet er weniger als bei uns, und wir fahren dann quer durch Amerika nach San Francisco. Wir fliegen nach Deutschland zurück, und wir bringen unseren neuen Mercedes mit!

B **Morgen.** Was werden Sie morgen tun? Was haben Sie vor zu machen? Ergänzen Sie die Sätze mit Verben im Futur und mit Beispielen von **weiter[machen, lesen, fahren usw.].**

BEISPIELE Am Nachmittag ...
Am Nachmittag werde ich an einem Aufsatz weiterarbeiten.

Um acht Uhr ...
Um acht Uhr werde ich aufstehen.

Um zehn Uhr ...
Um zehn Uhr wird meine Deutschstunde beginnen.

1. Um acht Uhr ...
2. Um halb zehn ...
3. Zu Mittag ...

4. Nach der Mittagspause ...
5. Am späteren Nachmittag ...
6. Am Abend ...

Und jetzt drei weitere Aussagen im Futur. **Sie** sollen einen Zeitpunkt wählen.

7. Ich denke, dass ...
8. Es ist möglich, dass ...
9. Ich weiß noch nicht, ob ...

C **Im Hörsaal: Was wird wohl geschehen sein?** Erklären Sie, warum die Leute sich wohl so benehmen *(behave)*.

BEISPIEL Georg hat heute Morgen Kopfschmerzen.
*Er **wird wohl** gestern Abend zu viel **gelernt haben.***

1. Jeff ist überglücklich. Er sitzt und strahlt *(beams)* und achtet *(pays attention)* auf gar nichts.
2. Stephanie ist heute bedrückt *(depressed)*. Sie weint leise während der Vorlesung.
3. Olivia döst *(is dozing)* in der letzten Reihe *(row)*, während alle anderen zuhören.
4. John sitzt ganz still auf seinem Platz. Er hat ein blaues Auge.
5. Katie kommt sonst immer pünktlich zur Vorlesung. Heute ist sie aber nicht da.

D **Futur II: Bis dahin.** Was wird bis dahin schon geschehen sein?

BEISPIEL Vor dem Ende dieses Jahres ...
werde ich mir ein Auto *gekauft haben.*
wird die Uni einen neuen Präsidenten *gefunden haben.*
werden Freunde von mir nach Europa *gereist sein.*

1. Bis zum nächsten Freitag ...
2. Vor dem Ende des Semesters ...
3. Bevor ich 30 werde, ...
4. Vor dem Jahre 2020 ...
5. Bis man Krebs *(cancer)* besiegt haben wird, ...

E **Weitermachen.** Beenden Sie die Sätze. Verwenden Sie die folgenden Verben.

fort·fahren   fort·setzen   weiter[·machen]

1. Es tut mir leid, dass ich Sie beim Lesen stören musste. Sie können jetzt ...
2. Die Stammzellforschung ist kontrovers. Meinen Sie, man sollte ... – oder nicht?
3. Wir werden diese Diskussion morgen ...
4. Wenn Sie zu der Brücke kommen, dann haben Sie den Campingplatz noch nicht erreicht. Sie müssen noch ein paar Kilometer ...
5. Bei der 20. Meile des Marathons konnte ich leider ...

Anwendung

A   **Was andere machen werden.**   Fragen Sie jemanden im Kurs nach ihren/seinen Plänen und berichten Sie darüber.

nächsten Sommer
nach dem Studium
im späteren Leben
wenn alles nach Plan geht

Weißt du schon, was du machen wirst, wenn … ?
Hast du dir überlegt *(thought about)*, was … ?
Was hast du für … vor *(have in mind)*?
Wenn alles nach Plan geht, dann werde ich …
Vielleicht wird es mir gelingen *(succeed)*… zu [tun].
Ich werde wohl …

B   **Prognosen für die Zukunft.**   Diskutieren Sie mit anderen Studenten, wie die Welt Ihrer Meinung nach in zwei, fünf, 10, 20 oder 30 Jahren aussehen wird. Was wird wohl anders sein als heute? Was wird es (nicht mehr) geben? Beginnen Sie mit einem Thema, und wenn Sie und Ihre Partnerin/Ihr Partner zwei bis drei Meinungen dazu ausgetauscht haben, machen Sie mit mindestens zwei Themen weiter.

Umwelt (Wasserversorgung, globale Erwärmung)
Medien (Fernsehen, Presse, Internet)
Technik und Informatik
Privatsphäre *(privacy)*
Wirtschaft (global und regional)
Film und Theater
Sport und Freizeit
Schule und Universität
Politik und Gesellschaft *(society)*
Übervölkerung *(overpopulation)*
Medizin und Gesundheitsfragen

REDEMITTEL

In … Jahren wird …
Höchstwahrscheinlich *(most likely)* werden wir (nicht) …
Ich denke, es wird wohl so sein: …
Es ist gut möglich *(quite possible)*, dass …
Vielleicht werden die Menschen …
Es würde mich (nicht) überraschen, wenn …
Es kann sein, dass wir in Zukunft[2] …
Es wird wahrscheinlich (keine) … (mehr) geben.

C **Voraussagungen (*predictions*).** Schreiben Sie eine Liste mit zehn bekannten (oder nicht sehr bekannten) Menschen auf. Dann lesen Sie die Liste einer Partnerin/einem Partner vor, die/der für jeden Namen eine (fiktive) Voraussage fürs Jahr 2020 macht.

BEISPIEL mein Onkel Fritz

Im Jahr 2020 wird mein Onkel Fritz wohl noch einmal mit seiner Band auf Tournee sein, und er wird wohl immer noch herumtanzen, als ob ein Teenager wäre.

Schriftliche Themen

Tipps zum Schreiben	**Qualifying Statements about the Future**
	There is a saying in English: *"Man proposes, God disposes."* **(Der Mensch denkt, Gott lenkt.)** In other words, things may not always turn out as planned. Thus, when conjecturing about the future or when telling of your own plans, you may want to qualify some of your statements with adverbial expressions such as the following:
	eventuell *(possibly, perhaps)*
	hoffentlich, unter Umständen *(under certain circumstances)*
	unter keinen Umständen *(under no circumstances)*
	vielleicht, wohl (schon) *(probably)*
	(höchst-)wahrscheinlich *([most] likely)*
	You can even stress the tentative nature of your future statements by beginning sentences with these qualifiers. Time expressions also work well in first position; they supply the reader with an immediate future context for what is to follow. Remember to use a mixture of present and future tense for the sake of stylistic variety, and be sure to vary your verbs.

---

[2]English speakers can say *in future* or *in the future*, though the latter form is preferred in the USA. German speakers can say **in Zukunft** and **in der Zukunft** as well, though the two forms have slightly different meanings. **In Zukunft** looks forward in general to a time *from now on*, while **die Zukunft** treats the future as an era, much like **die Vergangenheit** refers to the past.

A ***Herbsttag* – mal anders.** Werner Schneyder, der österreichische Kabarettist und TV-Kommentator, hat eine Parodie von Rilkes Gedicht geschrieben, und vermittelt dabei ein ziemlich anderes Bild vom Übergang *(transition)* zwischen Sommer und Herbst. Was steht im Mittelpunkt der Sommererfahrungen dieses lyrischen Ichs *(poetic persona)*? Woran denkt er am Ende des Sommers? Schreiben Sie darüber! Oder schreiben Sie …

- einen Vergleich zwischen Rilkes und Schneyders poetischem Ton.

- eine Analyse von Schneyders Vokabeln und Wortspielen.

- über Ihre eigenen Sommererfahrungen und -gedanken: Sind sie denen von Rilke oder von Schneyder ähnlicher?

- mit dem Futur: Was werden *Sie* nach den nächsten Sommerferien machen?

Herbsttag

(Nach° Rainer Maria Rilke)   here: *adapted from*

Herr: es ist Zeit. Der Sommer war sehr groß.
Leg deinen Schatten auf die Sonnenbrände°,   *sunburn*
nach Urlaubsende geht der Wirbel° los.   *hectic pace, craziness*

Befiehl den guten Zöllnern°, mild zu sein;   *customs agents*
gib ihnen noch zwei gütlichere° Tage,   *friendlier*
dränge sie zur Vollendung hin und jage
mich durch den Zoll° mit dem gepanschten° Wein.   *customs / spiked with sugar or other*
                                                                       enhancements, i.e., very cheap

Wer jetzt nach Haus kommt, riecht nach° Mittelmeer°.   *smells like / the Mediterranean*
Wer jetzt allein ist, wird es nicht lang bleiben,
wird viel erzählen und in Briefen schreiben,
wie man am Sandstrand° hin und her   *beach*
zu Mädchen wandert, wenn die Triebe° treiben°.   *appetites, urges / compel*

—Werner Schneyder [1985][3]

B **Meine Zukunftspläne.** Erzählen Sie in zehn Sätzen von Ihren Zukunftsplänen.

BEISPIEL *Ich bin jetzt im zweiten Studienjahr. In zwei Jahren werde ich mein Studium als Undergraduate abschließen. Was danach kommt, weiß ich noch nicht so genau. Vielleicht werde ich weiterstudieren. Es kann aber auch sein, dass ich zuerst ein paar Jahre arbeite oder einen Beruf erlerne. Auf jeden Fall werde ich … usw.*

---

[3]"Herbsttag," by Werner Schneyder from Karl Riha und Hans Wald, *Auf weißen Wiesen weiden grüne Schafe*. Parodien. Copyright © 2001. Reprinted by permission.

C   **Die Zukunft.**   Wie sehen Sie die Zukunft Ihres Landes? Ihrer Uni? Ihrer Heimatstadt? Schreiben Sie entweder aus positiver oder negativer Sicht.

Zusammenfassung

Rules to Remember

1   The future tense (**das Futur**) is formed with **werden** + present infinitive, using the same word order as modal verbs with infinitives.

2   The future perfect tense (**Futur II**) is formed with **werden** + perfect infinitive. Perfect infinitive = past participle + **haben** or **sein**.

3   German prefers the present tense in many cases where English uses the future tense. The future tense is used in German: (a) to emphasize intentions or assumptions, (b) to refer to a relatively distant future, and (c) to distinguish between the present and the future in contexts where this might not be clear.

4   The future perfect tense is used to relate what will have been done by some point in the future, or to speculate (often using **wohl** or **schon**) that something has probably happened or been done in the past.

At a Glance

***werden* + V₂ *infinitive: will* ___**
ich **werde**
du **wirst**
Sie **werden**
er/sie/es **wird**
wir **werden**
ihr **werdet**
Sie **werden**
sie **werden**

(alle mit: **gehen**)

Future I/Future II: Main clause word order				
	front field	V₁	*middle field*	V₂
Future I		werden		infinitive
Future I (with modal)		werden		infinitive + modal
Future II		werden		past participle + sein / haben

Reference
Chapters

Reference 1

NOUN GENDERS • NOUN PLURALS • WEAK NOUNS

All German nouns, whether they represent persons, things, or ideas, have a grammatical gender that is indicated by the definite article: masculine **der (männlich; das Maskulinum)**, feminine **die (weiblich; das Femininum)**, or neuter **das (sächlich; das Neutrum)**. While grammatical gender (**das Genus**) overlaps with sexual gender, so that male beings are usually grammatically masculine, and female beings feminine, for the great majority of nouns the designation follows no predictable pattern. Thus a tree (**der Baum**) consists of a trunk (**der Stamm**), covered with bark (**die Rinde**), which emanates into a branch (**der Ast**) and eventually a leaf (**das Blatt**). There are, however, several general guidelines for determining grammatical gender, based on meaning and characteristics of the word itself (suffixes, for example), and this section lists the most useful of these.

A. Masculine nouns

The following types of nouns are usually masculine:

1. Words designating male beings, their familial relationships, professions, and nationalities

der Mann, ⸚er	der Vater, ⸚	der Arzt, ⸚e	der Engländer, -
der Junge, -n	der Sohn, ⸚e	der Koch, ⸚e	der Franzose, -n
der Herr, -en	der Bruder, ⸚	der Pilot, -en	der Italiener, -
	der Onkel, -	der Professor, -en	der Kanadier, -
	der Vetter, -n		der Amerikaner, -

2. Agent nouns derived from verbs by adding the suffix **-er** to the infinitive stem

   arbeiten ⟶ der Arbeit**er**, -
   fahren ⟶ der Fahr**er**, -
   malen ⟶ der Mal**er**, -
   lehren ⟶ der Lehr**er**, -

3. Days of the week, months of the year, seasons, and most weather elements

(der) Montag	der Frühling	der Regen
(der) Mai	der Herbst	der Schnee

4. Names of cars, when referred to by the manufacturer's name, including foreign carmakers

der BMW	der Ford	der Opel	der Trabi
der Ferrari	der Mercedes	der Skoda	der VW

5. Names of most *non-German* rivers

der Mississippi	der Nil
der Mekong	der Delaware

EXCEPTIONS: die Wolga, die Themse, die Seine

6. Nouns ending in the suffixes **-ig, -ling, -or,** or **-us**

der Kä**fig,** -e *(cage)*	der Mot**or,** -en
der Hon**ig,** -e	der Fakt**or,** -en
der Lieb**ling,** -e	der Sozialism**us**
der Schwäch**ling,** -e *(weakling)*	der Zirk**us,** -se

7. Most nouns ending in **-en**

der Gart**en,** ⸚	der Krag**en,** - *(collar)*	der Ost**en**
der Haf**en,** ⸚ *(harbor)*	der Mag**en,** - *(stomach)*	der Süd**en**

B. Feminine nouns

The following types of nouns are usually feminine:

1. Words designating female beings and their familial relationships

die Frau, -en	die Mutter, ⸚	die Schwester, -n
die Tochter, ⸚	die Tante, -n	die Nichte, -n *(niece)*
die Kusine, -n		

2. Words designating professions and nationalities, using the suffix **-in** with masculine forms

die Ärzt**in,** -nen	die Engländer**in,** -nen
die Köch**in,** -nen	die Französ**in,** -nen
die Pilot**in,** -nen	die Italiener**in,** -nen
die Professor**in,** -nen	die Kanadier**in,** -nen
die Arbeiter**in,** -nen	die Amerikaner**in,** -nen
die Lehrer**in,** -nen	

3. Most nouns ending in **-e** (plural **-n**)

die Krawatt**e,** -n
die Maschin**e,** -n
die Sprach**e,** -n

EXCEPTION: der Gedanke *(thought)*

4. Nouns ending in the suffixes **-anz, -ei, -enz, -ie, -ik, -ion, -heit, -keit, -schaft, -tät, -ung,** or **-ur**

die Disson**anz,** -en	die Mus**ik**	die Land**schaft,** -en
die Kondito**rei,** -en	die Relig**ion,** -en	die Rival**ität,** -en
die Frequ**enz,** -en	die Dumm**heit,** -en	die Bedeu**tung,** -en
die Demokra**tie,** -n	die Schwierig**keit,** -en	die Proze**dur,** -en

    EXCEPTION: der Papagei, -en *(parrot)*

5. Names of many rivers in Germany, Austria, and Switzerland

die Donau	die Isar	die Weser
die Elbe	die Mosel	die Oder
die Havel	die Aare	

    EXCEPTIONS: der Rhein, der Inn, der Lech, der Main, der Neckar

6. Numerals used as nouns, as with test scores or competition results (see R.4.A)

    Ich habe eine Eins bekommen!   *I got a one! ("A" in the American grading system).*

C. Neuter nouns

The following types of nouns are usually neuter:

1. Names of continents, cities, and most countries. However, they only require an article when modified by adjectives.

    COMPARE:

    Berlin ist seit 1990 die neue Hauptstadt. *(no article)*
    Ein vereinigtes Berlin ist seit 1990 die neue Hauptstadt. *(article)*

2. Nouns for names of many metals

das Blei *(lead)*	das Gold	das Silber
das Eisen *(iron)*	das Metall	das Uran

    EXCEPTIONS: der Stahl, die Bronze

3. Letters of the alphabet, including designations for musical notes

ein kleines G	das Fis *(F-sharp)*
das große H	das Ges *(G-flat)*[1]
ein hohes C	

---

[1]In German, a sharp note is indicated with the **-is** suffix, a flat note with **-(e)s.** The chromatic scale beginning at C is thus written: C | Cis/Des | D | Dis/Es | E | F | Fis/Ges | G | Gis/As | A | B | H | C. Note that at the end of the scale, *B-flat* in English is named **B** in German, and *B* in English is **H** in German, hence the name of J.S. Bach's masterpiece: ***h-Moll-Messe*** *(B minor mass).* The **h** is lowercase here to indicate the minor key, as opposed to **H** (B major).

4. Infinitives and other parts of speech when used as nouns

(das) Lesen *(reading)*   das Ich *(ego)*

(das) Schreiben *(writing)*   das Für und Wider *(arguments for and against)*

5. Nouns ending in the suffix **-tum**

das Christen**tum**   das Juden**tum**   das Eigen**tum** *(possession)*

EXCEPTIONS: **der Reichtum, ¨er** *(wealth)*; **der Irrtum, ¨er** *(error)*

6. Nouns with the diminutive suffixes **-chen**, **-lein** (and their dialect variations **-erl**, **-el**, **-le**, **-li**). Also nouns with the suffixes **-ment** and **-(i)um**.

das Mäd**chen**, -   das Experi**ment**, -e

das Büch**lein**, -   das Dat**um**, *pl.* die Daten

das Buss**erl**, - *(kiss, smooch)*   das Muse**um**, *pl.* die Museen

das Häu**sle**, -   das Medi**um**, *pl.* die Medien

7. Most collective nouns beginning with the prefix **Ge-**

Berge ⟶ das **Ge**birge   Wolken ⟶ das **Ge**wölk

Büsche ⟶ das **Ge**büsch   Schreie ⟶ das **Ge**schrei *(screaming)*

EXCEPTIONS: der Gedanke *(thought, idea)*
der Gesang *(singing, vocal music)*
der Geschmack *(taste)*
der Gestank *(stench)*
der Gewinn *(profit)*

D. Compound nouns

In compound words, all gender and plural inflections are determined by the last word in the compound.

das Eisen, - *(iron)*

die Eisen**bahn**, -en *(railroad)*

der Eisenbahn**schaffner**, - *(railroad conductor)*

die Eisenbahnschaffner**uniform**, -en *(railroad conductor's uniform)*

E. Nouns with dual gender

1. Some words that look identical have different genders to distinguish their meaning. Here are some common examples:

der Band, ¨e	*volume*, i.e., *a book*		der Gefallen, -	*favor*
das Band, ¨er	*ribbon, tape*		das Gefallen	*pleasure*
die Band, -s	*band, music group*		der Gehalt, -e	*content(s)*
der Flur, -e	*hallway*		das Gehalt, ¨er	*salary, wages*
die Flur, -en	*meadow, pasture*			

der Kunde, -n	customer, client	das Schild, -er	sign, signboard
die Kunde	news, notice, information	der Schild, -e	shield
		der See, -n	lake
der Messer, -	gauge	die See, -n	sea
das Messer, -	knife		
		der Tor, -en	fool
der Moment, -e	moment	das Tor, -e	gate, portal; soccer goal
das Moment, -e	factor		

2. The word **Teil** (*part, element, share*) can be either masculine or neuter, but the respective meanings differ only slightly.

- ■ It is usually masculine (**der Teil**) when referring in general to a *part* of something (***ein großer Teil** der Bevölkerung* = *a large part of the population*).

- ■ It is neuter (**das Teil**) when referring to *mechanical parts* (**das Autoteil, -e**) or (colloquially) to articles of clothing (**Du, ich hab' *ein neues Teil* gekauft!**).

- ■ It can be either masculine or neuter in the more abstract meaning of *share*: **Die Frau hat wirklich *ihr(en) Teil* gegeben** = *That woman really did her share.*

- ■ Some compounds using **Teil** are masculine, as in **der Vorteil** (*advantange*) and **der Nachteil** (*disadvantage*); and some are neuter, as in **das Gegenteil** (*opposite*) and **das Urteil** (*verdict, judgment*).

3. **Meter** and its compounds and **Liter** are now usually treated as masculine, although some dictionaries still list neuter as the officially preferred gender (see R.4.2.B).

R.1.2 ▸ NOUN PLURALS

There are five basic plural endings for German nouns: **-, -e, -er, -en,** and **-s.** In some instances, the stem vowel of the noun also has an umlaut. In the plural, all nouns take the same article for any given case (i.e., **die** for nominative and accusative, **den** for dative, and **der** for genitive), regardless of the gender of the singular noun. The following guidelines should be considered rules of thumb only, for there are exceptions.

A. No plural ending (- or ¨)

Most masculine and neuter nouns ending in **-el, -en,** or **-er** take no plural ending, though many that are masculine do take an umlaut.

der Sessel, **die Sessel**	der Fahrer, **die Fahrer**
der Mantel, **die Mäntel**	der Vater, **die Väter**
der Wagen, **die Wagen**	das Fenster, **die Fenster**
der Garten, **die Gärten**	
das Kissen (*pillow*), **die Kissen**	

EXCEPTIONS: der Stachel, **die Stacheln** (*thorn, prickle, stinger*)

der Vetter, **die Vettern** (*male cousin*)

B. Plural ending -e or ̈e

1. A large number of monosyllabic masculine and neuter nouns take an **-e** ending in the plural. Some of these masculine nouns also take an umlaut.

   der Tisch, **die Tische**   der Bach, **die Bäche**
   das Jahr, **die Jahre**   der Stuhl, **die Stühle**

   EXCEPTIONS: der Mann, **die Männer;** der Wald, **die Wälder**

2. About thirty monosyllabic feminine nouns also take the plural ending **-e** and add an umlaut.

   die Angst, **die Ängste**   die Bank, **die Bänke**
   die Hand, **die Hände**   die Wand, **die Wände**

   ALSO:

   die Brust, die Faust *(fist),* die Frucht, die Haut *(skin; hide),* die Kraft *(strength),* die Kuh, die Kunst, die Laus, die Luft, die Macht *(power),* die Maus, die Nacht, die Wand, die Wurst, and a few others.

C. Plural ending -er or ̈er

Many monosyllabic neuter words take an **-er** plural ending and also have an umlaut when possible.

   das Bild, **die Bilder**   das Buch, **die Bücher**
   das Kleid, **die Kleider**   das Dorf, **die Dörfer**

D. Plural ending -(e)n

1. Almost all feminine nouns, including all those with feminine suffixes, take an **-(e)n** plural ending, but no umlaut.

   die Mauer, **die Mauern**   die Zeitung, **die Zeitungen**
   die Stunde, **die Stunden**   die Universität, **die Universitäten**

2. Nouns with the feminine suffix **-in** double the **-n** before the plural ending.

   die Autorin, **die Autorinnen**   die Polizistin, **die Polizistinnen**

E. Plural endings of foreign words

1. Many foreign words, particularly those ending in the vowels **-a** or **-o,** take an **-s** plural ending.

   das Büro, **die Büros**   die Kamera, **die Kameras**   das Sofa, **die Sofas**

2. German words borrowed from English ending in **-y** that require a vowel change in the English plural form do not normally show this change in their German equivalents:

   das Handy $\longrightarrow$ **die Handys**
   die Party $\longrightarrow$ **die Partys**[2]

---

[2]**Party:** Not to be confused with **die Partie** $\longrightarrow$ **die Partien,** which denotes a competitive *match,* as in **eine Bridgepartie,** or a *part* in a musical piece, as in **die Geigenpartie** *(violin part).*

3. German words borrowed from Latin with endings such as **-um** and **-us** often use **-en** in the plural.

> das Album —→ die Alb**en**
> das Museum —→ die Muse**en**
> der Rhythmus —→ die Rhythm**en**
> das Visum —→ die Vis**en** (*also*: Visa)
> das Universum —→ die Univers**en**
> das Zentrum —→ die Zentr**en**

F. Nouns without plurals

1. German nouns designating materials such as **Zucker** (*sugar*), **Wolle** (*wool*), and **Stahl** (*steel*), or abstract concepts like **Liebe** (*love*), **Hass** (*hatred*), and **Intelligenz** (*intelligence*) have no plural form.

2. Many collective nouns beginning with **Ge-** appear most often in the singular. Their English translations are often plural.

> das Gebirge (*mountains*)
> das Gebüsch (*bushes*)
> das Geschirr (*dishes*)

3. Certain English nouns always take a plural form, whereas their German equivalents have both singular and plural forms like most nouns.

> *eyeglasses* —→ die Brille (*one pair*); **die Brillen** (*multiple pairs*)
> *scissors* —→ die Schere (*one pair*); **die Scheren** (*multiple pairs*)
> *pants/trousers* —→ die Hose (*one pair*); **die Hosen** (*multiple pairs*); BUT: **die Jeans**
> (plural form can be used for both singular and plural meaning, as in English)

G. Nonstandard plural formations

A small number of nouns in both German and English have no plural form as such, yet the language has contrived a way to refer to multiple cases by manipulating or adding to the word, as in *jewelry* —→ *pieces of jewelry*, which parallels the German **der Schmuck** —→ **die Schmuckstücke.** As in English, the German word used for such plurals sometimes has a singular form of its own as well (for example, **das Schmuckstück**).

der Betrug (*deception*)		**die Betrügereien**
der Kaufmann (*businessman*)	}	**die Kaufleute**
die Kauffrau (*businesswoman*)		
der Kummer (*grief, sorrow*)		**die Kümmernisse**
der Rat (*advice*)		**die Ratschläge**
der Streit (*quarrel*)		**die Streitereien**

R.1.3 **WEAK NOUN DECLENSIONS**

1. A particular group of masculine nouns adds -**(e)n** to all cases singular and plural except the nominative singular. Except for a very small number of such nouns (see 3.d below), the -**(e)n** ending takes the place of the genitive singular -**(e)s** ending.

	Singular	**Plural**
Nom.	der Mensch	die Menschen
Acc.	den Mensch**en**	die Menschen
Dat.	dem Mensch**en**	des Menschen
Gen.	des Mensch**en**	der Menschen

2. The -**(e)n** suffix is required when the noun takes on any function other than the subject or predicate nominative of a sentence clause.

Unser **Nachbar** hat entweder keinen Rasenmäher oder keine Zeit zum Rasenmähen.	*Our neighbor has either no lawn mower or no time to mow the lawn.*
Kennst du den **Nachbarn,** den ich meine?	*Do you know the neighbor I mean?*
Ich muss mit diesem **Nachbarn** sprechen.	*I must speak with this neighbor.*

3. Nouns of this type include:

   a. Some nouns denoting male beings in general

der Bauer (*farmer*)	der Knabe (*boy*)
der Bote (*messenger*)	der Kunde (*customer*)
der Experte	der Nachbar
der Herr[3]	der Riese (*giant*)
der Junge	

   b. A number of nouns indicating nationality or religious affiliation

der Chinese	der Buddhist
der Grieche	der Jude
der Russe	der Katholik
der Türke	der Protestant

---

[3]**Herr** takes -**n** in the singular (**dem Herrn, des Herrn,** etc.), but -**en** in the plural (**den Herren, der Herren,** etc.).

c. All nouns designating male beings and ending in the foreign suffixes **-ant, -arch, -ast, -ege, -ent, -ist, -oge, -om, -oph, -ot**

der Komödi**ant**	der Poliz**ist**
der Mon**arch**	der Psychol**oge**
der Enthusi**ast**	der Astron**om**
der Koll**ege**	der Philos**oph**
der Stud**ent**	der Pil**ot**

d. A few weak nouns have a genitive singular ending in **-ens.**

	Singular	Plural
Nom.	der Name	die Namen
Acc.	den Namen	die Namen
Dat.	dem Namen	den Namen
Gen.	des Nam**ens**	der Namen

Other common nouns of this type include:

der Friede(n) *(peace)*
der Gedanke *(thought)*
der Glaube *(belief)*
der Wille *(will)*

e. The weak neuter noun **das Herz** is irregular in the singular.

	Singular	Plural
Nom.	das Herz	die Herzen
Acc.	das Herz	die Herzen
Dat.	dem Herzen	den Herzen
Gen.	des Herz**ens**	der Herzen

Since this suffix is identical to the plural form (except for **Herr,** see above), it is not added to the noun if the noun appears with no article or other modifier that can show case endings, in order to avoid confusion with the plural form of the noun.

COMPARE:

Mit dem Kopf versteht er das, **mit dem Herzen** aber nicht.	*He understands it with his head, but not with his heart.*
Sie hat die Rolle **mit viel Herz** gespielt.	*She played the role with a lot of heart.*

Übersicht

NOUN GENDERS • NOUN PLURALS • WEAK NOUNS

Masculine suffixes

-ig	der Honig
-ling	der Schwächling
-or	der Motor
-us	der Zirkus

Suffixes of weak masculine nouns

-ant	der Komödiant
-arch	der Patriarch
-ast	der Enthusiast
-ege	der Kollege
-ent	der Präsident
-ist	der Komponist
-oge	der Meteorologe
-om	der Astronom
-oph	der Philosoph
-ot	der Pilot

Neuter suffixes

-chen	das Mädchen
-lein	das Tischlein
-ment	das Testament
-um, -ium	das Datum
	das Studium
-erl	
-el	
-le	*(dialect variants)*
-li	

Feminine suffixes

-anz	die Toleranz
-ei	die Partei
-enz	die Frequenz
-ie	die Aristokratie
-ik	die Grammatik
-ion	die Religion
-heit	die Schönheit
-keit	die Freundlichkeit
-schaft	die Freundschaft
-tät	die Universität
-ung	die Vorlesung
-ur	die Prozedur

Plural formations

- or ¨	Fenster ⟶ **Fenster**
	Garten ⟶ **Gärten**
-e or ¨e	Tisch ⟶ **Tische**
	Stuhl ⟶ **Stühle**
-er *or* ¨er	Bild ⟶ **Bilder**
	Buch ⟶ **Bücher**
-(e)n	Tür ⟶ **Türen**
	Mauer ⟶ **Mauern**
-s	Büro ⟶ **Büros**

Reference 2

R.2.1 COORDINATING CONJUNCTIONS

A. Forms

German has five coordinating conjunctions.

aber	*but, however*
denn[1]	*for, because*
oder	*or*
sondern	*but rather*
und	*and*

B. Use

1. A coordinating conjunction (**die koordinierende Konjunktion, -en**) links words, phrases, or independent clauses by adding information (**und**), or by showing a contrast (**aber, sondern**), a reason (**denn**), or an alternative (**oder**). As far as word order goes, a coordinating conjunction is not considered part of the clauses or phrases that it connects. This means that main clauses following the conjunction show regular word order, with V_1 in second position—i.e., the conjunction is followed by a first element, then the conjugated verb. Dependent clauses after a conjunction likewise follow their usual order, with V_1 in final position.

Vor kurzem wurden *Hannabi* **und** *Augustus* zum Spiel des Jahres nominiert.	*Recently, Hannabi and Augustus were nominated for "Game of the Year."*
Viele Freunde von mir sind *Funkenschlag*-Fans, **aber** ich stehe eher auf *Die Siedler von Catan*.	*A lot of of my friends are Powergrid fans, but I am more into Settlers of Catan.*
Catan spiele ich oft, **denn** meine ganze Familie spielt es schon seit Jahren zusammen.	*I play Catan often, since my whole family has played it together for years now.*

---

[1]See the **Wortschatz** section of Chapter 3 for detailed information on how to use **denn**.

Oder wollt ihr *Stratego Fortress* spielen? Das habe ich auch da.

Or do you all want to play Stratego Fortress? *I've got that here too.*

Aber and **denn** can occur as flavoring particles (see R.6). In addition, **aber** can be used within a clause as an adverb meaning *however.*

Manche interessieren sich nicht für solche Spiele, ich meine **aber,** dass sie recht unterhaltsam sind.

Some people are just not interested in such games. I think, however, that they're quite entertaining.

2. A comma usually precedes clauses and phrases introduced by **aber, denn,** and **sondern.** No comma is necessary before **und** and **oder** when they join clauses, but in some cases a comma can help prevent a misreading.

Jedes Feld bei *Catan* ist eine Landschaft **und** jede Landschaft hat bestimmte Rohstoffe. *(no comma needed)*

With Catan, every tile is a land type and every land type has certain resources.

Manchmal spielen meine Geschwister **und** ich schaue nur zu.

BETTER:

Manchmal spielen meine Geschwister, **und** ich schaue nur zu.

Sometimes my siblings play, and I just watch.

3. **Aber** *(but)* links clauses or phrases by providing *contrasting additional* information. The first clause can be positive or negative.

Beim Handeln sind sie manchmal besser als ich, **aber** ich bin ihnen beim Bauen überlegen.

They're sometimes better at trading, but I'm superior to them in building.

4. **Sondern** *(but rather)* links clauses and phrases by providing *contrasting corrective* information regarding what was said in the first clause or phrase. The information to be corrected must contain a negating word such as **nicht, nie,** or **kein** (see 7.1 and 7.2). The corrective information following **sondern** can be limited to only those elements that require correction, or it can be a full clause.

Punkte bekommt man **nicht** fürs Kämpfen, **sondern** fürs strategische Denken und Bauen.

You don't get points for fighting, but rather for strategic thinking and building.

OR:

Man gewinnt also **nicht** durch Brutalität, **sondern** man muss zusammenarbeiten und erfolgreich planen.

So you don't win with violence, rather you have to cooperate and plan successfully.

R.2.2 **TWO-PART (CORRELATIVE) CONJUNCTIONS**

A. Forms

1. The following two-part (correlative) conjunctions link words, phrases, or clauses in parallel fashion.

entweder ... oder	*either . . . or*
nicht nur ... sondern auch	*not only . . . but also*
sowohl ... als/wie (auch)	*both . . . and, as well as*
weder ... noch	*neither . . . nor*

Bis 2011 mussten deutsche Männer im Alter von 18–23 **entweder** bei der Bundeswehr dienen **oder** Zivildienst leisten.	*Up until 2011, German men between the ages of 18 and 23 had to either serve in the military or perform community service.*
Das betraf **nicht nur** die, die sonst keine Pläne hatten, **sondern auch** diejenigen, die zur Arbeit oder zum Studium wollten.	*This applied not only to those who otherwise had no plans, but also to those who wanted to work or study.*
Und das Gesetz bestimmte, das **sowohl** Pazifisten **als auch** Nicht-Pazifisten dienen mussten.	*And the law saw to it that both pacifists and nonpacifists had to serve.*
Seit 2011 aber ist **weder** ein Wehrdienst **noch** ein Zivildienst erforderlich.	*Since 2011, however, neither military service nor community service is required.*

B. Use

1. When **entweder ... oder** is used to join two clauses, the position of **entweder** may vary, as well as the position of the finite verb in the first clause.

    Entweder ein junger Deutscher diente beim "Bund" **oder** als "Zivi."[2]
    Entweder diente ein junger Deutscher beim "Bund" **oder** als "Zivi."
    Ein junger Deutscher diente **entweder** beim "Bund" **oder** als "Zivi."
    *Either a young German man served in the **Bund** or he became a **Zivi**.*

2. Many non-German speakers make the mistake of assuming that *both* is equivalent to **beide** in all contexts. English uses *both* to modify plural nouns as well as to join two entities, singular or plural, in conjunction with *and*.

    Both men served as Zivis.
    Both Markus **and** his friend Lukas served as Zivis.
    But **beide** can only be used in German in the first case, that is, to modify a plural noun.
    Beide Männer haben als Zivis gedient.

---

[2]**Bund**, a shortened form of **Bundeswehr** (*federal armed forces*) was a well-known slang term for military service, and **Zivi** was an understandably shortened form of **Zivildienstleistender** (*a man performing community service in place of military service*).

In the second case, that is, to emphasize that the statement applies to two distinct entities, German requires the correlative conjunction **sowohl ... als auch.**

Sowohl Markus **als auch** sein Freund Lukas haben als Zivis gedient.

An additional example, by way of comparison:

Die Bundeswehr **und** der Zivildienst verlangten viel Einsatz.	The national defense **and** civil service required a high [degree of] commitment.
Sowohl die Bundeswehr **als auch** der Zivildienst verlangten viel Einsatz.	**Both** the national defense **and** civil service required a high commitment.

When speaking, one could stress the **und** of the first example above to make the desired emphasis clear. But in written German, **sowohl ... als auch** is necessary to underscore that both entities are included in the statement.

3. Correlative conjunctions can be used to link together multiple sentence subjects as well as other elements. In cases where the two subjects differ in person or number, the V_1 is conjugated to agree with the subject closest to it.

Sowohl einer, der als Zivi arbeitete, als auch Bundeswehrsoldaten **mussten** zuletzt sechs Monate dienen.	Both someone who worked as a **Zivi** as well as **Bundeswehr** soldiers had to serve at the end for six months.
Sowohl Bundeswehrsoldaten als auch einer, der als Zivi arbeitete, **musste** zuletzt sechs Monate dienen.	

R.2.3 SUBORDINATING CONJUNCTIONS

A. Forms

The following subordinating conjunctions are used frequently:

als	when, as	nachdem	after
als ob	as if, as though	ob	whether, if
bevor/ehe	before	obgleich/obschon/ obwohl	although, even though
bis	until, by		
da[3]	since, because	seit(dem)	since (temporal)
damit	so that (intent)	sobald	as soon as
dass	that	solange	as long as
anstatt dass	instead (of doing) (See also anstatt zu; 11.2.)	sooft	as often as
		während	while
ohne dass	without (doing) (See also ohne zu; 11.2.)	weil[3]	because
		wenn	when, if, whenever

[3]See the **Wortschatz** section of Chapter 3 for detailed information on how to use **da** and **weil**.

so dass/sodass	*so that (result)*	wenn ... auch	*even if, even though*
falls	*in case, if*	wenn ... nicht/	*unless*
indem	*by (doing)*	wenn ... kein-	

B. Use

1. A subordinating conjunction **(die subordinierende Konjunktion, -en)** connects a subordinate clause to a main clause. Subordinate clauses include noun clauses (beginning with **dass**), relative clauses (see 18.1), and adverbial clauses (14.4) that add information about when, how, why, or under what conditions the activity of the main clause occurs.

2. In a subordinate clause, the conjugated verb (V_1) is normally in final position (see 1.3). Notice that main and subordinate clauses in German are always separated by a comma.

Main clause	**Subordinate clause**
Der 1981 Film *Das Boot* ist spannend *(suspenseful)*,	**weil** *(because)* die Schauspieler, das Drehbuch *(script)* und die Filmtechnik alle überzeugend *(convincing)* **sind.**
	obwohl *(until)* man schon am Anfang das Ende **ahnt** *(suspects).*
	wenn man auch den Kontext der Handlung *(plot)* nicht **kennt.**

The only exception to this rule occurs when a subordinate clause contains a V_2 consisting of a double infinitive (see 9.3.A and 11.6), in which case V_1 stands immediately before the double infinitive.

Das Boot ist tief unter Wasser geblieben, weil es sich vor einem Zerstörer **hat verstecken müssen.**	*The boat remained deep underwater, because it had to hide from a destroyer.*

3. A subordinate clause can occur either before or after the main clause. If the sentence begins with a subordinate clause, the following main clause must begin with the conjugated verb (V_1). In other words, within the overall sentence structure a subordinate clause can occupy the front field, in which case V_1 stands as usual in second position.

Subordinate clause	**Main clause**
Weil es sich vor dem Zerstörer verstecken muss,	
Bis alles wieder repariert ist,	**bleibt** das U-Boot tief unter Wasser.
Falls der Zerstörer es noch einmal angreifen will,	

4. Interrogative words (see 19.2) can also function as subordinating conjunctions, creating subordinate clauses that follow the word order rules discussed above.

Niemand weiß, **wie lange** sie dort noch warten müssen.	*No one knows how long they have to wait there.*

C. *Als, wenn, wann*

1. English uses *when* in a variety of contexts:

   ■ one-time past events *(When he first arrived in town, . . .)*

   ■ repeated events *(When[ever] he ran into her in the park, . . .)*

   ■ future events *(When they get engaged, . . .)*

   ■ questions in all tenses *(When did they/When will they . . . ?).*

   German distinguishes among these uses of *when* with different words, so that English speakers must be especially careful to match context and meaning correctly.

2. To refer to *one-time* events or situations in the past—including states that existed over a period of time—German uses **als.**

Als der Krieg gerade angefangen hatte, ...	*When the war had just begun, . . .*
Als der Kapitän noch jünger war, ...	*When the captain was younger, . . .*
Als das U-Boot auf einmal tauchte, ...	*When the sub suddenly dove, . . .*

3. To refer to *recurring* events in the past or present (as in English *whenever*), German uses **wenn.**

Es ging immer etwas chaotisch zu, **wenn** jemand Alarm meldete.	*Things always became a little chaotic when(ever) someone sounded the alarm.*

   COMPARE:

Es ging aber besonders chaotisch zu, **als** der Kapitän zum ersten Mal Alarm meldete.	*Things were especially chaotic, however, when the captain sounded the alarm for the first time.*

4. German likewise uses **wenn** for *occurrences that have yet to happen* (but are related in the present tense).

Wenn das U-Boot wieder auftaucht, wissen sie nicht, was sie oben erwartet.	*When the sub surfaces again, they don't know what awaits them up there.*

5. **Wenn** also means *if (as a condition),* regardless of tense.

Wenn sie es nicht schaffen, an Gibraltar vorbeizukommen, werden sie den Einsatz aufgeben müssen.	*If they can't manage to get past Gibraltar, they'll have to give up the mission.*
Was wäre passiert, **wenn** die Torpedos ihre Ziele verfehlt hätten?	*What would have happened if the torpedoes had missed their targets?*

6. To ask a *when*-question referring to a *specific time*—either as a direct or indirect question—German uses **wann**.

„**Wann** kommt endlich unsere Verstärkung?" fragt der Kapitän.	*"When are our reinforcements finally going to get here?" asks the captain.*
Niemand weiß, **wann** die Reparaturen fertig werden.	*No one knows when the repairs will be finished.*

D. *Als ob, als wenn*

1. **Als ob** *(less common:* **als wenn**) means *as if* and is used to express conjecture or a contrary-to-fact condition. Clauses beginning with **als ob/als wenn** are normally in the subjunctive mood (see 21.3.E), and they frequently follow phrases such as **Es ist/war, Er tut/tat, Es scheint/schien**.

Am Anfang tut der Journalist so, **als ob** er keine Angst hätte.	*At first, the journalist acts as if he weren't scared.*

2. The word **ob** (or **wenn**) can be omitted while still retaining the meaning *as if*. In this case, the word order resembles that of a main clause, with **als** functioning as the first element, followed immediately by V_1, then the middle field and, if present, V_2.

Er tut, **als hätte** er keine Angst.	*He acts as if he weren't scared.*

E. *Bevor, ehe*

English *before* can be used as a preposition (***before** the meal*), as an adverb (*I did that **before**, but now, ...*), and as a conjunction to introduce a clause (***before** you go, ...*). German, however, has a different word for each of these uses: the preposition **vor** (see 6.4), adverbs such as **vorher** and **früher** (see 14.2), and the conjunction **bevor** (which is interchangeable with **ehe,** though **ehe** is more literary than colloquial).

COMPARE:

***Vor** der Ausfahrt* redete Thomsen sarkastisch über Hitler.	*Before the launch, Thomsen spoke sarcastically about Hitler.*
***Bevor** sie ausfuhren,* redete Thomsen sarkastisch über Hitler.	*Before they sailed, Thomsen spoke sarcastically about Hitler.*
Früher/Vorher hatte man an einen Sieg geglaubt, aber jetzt kamen bei der Marine Zweifel auf.	*Before (then) they had believed in a victory, but now doubts were arising in the navy.*

F. *Bis*

1. The conjunction **bis** *(until)* expresses the duration of an action *until* a certain time or place is reached. It also occurs as a preposition (see 6.2).

Der Ingenieur hört nicht auf, **bis** alles repariert ist.	*The engineer won't stop until everything is repaired.*

2. **Bis** is often used to indicate the time *by when* an action is completed.

Bis das U-Boot nach dem ersten Angriff wieder auftaucht, sind die englischen Schiffe schon weg.	*By the time the sub surfaces after the first attack, the English ships are already gone.*

G. *Damit, so dass (sodass)*

1. **Damit** *(so that)* signifies *a purpose* for doing something.

Sie fahren nach Vigo, **damit** der Journalist und der Ingenieur das U-Boot verlassen können.	*They sail to Vigo so that the journalist and the engineer can leave the sub.*

2. If both clauses have the same subject, German frequently uses a construction with **um** + **zu** + infinitive instead of **damit** (see 11.2).

Sie fahren dorthin auch, **um** mehr Brennstoff, Proviant und Torpedos **zu** laden.	*They sail there also in order to load more fuel, provisions, and torpedoes.*

3. **So dass** indicates the *result* of an action (as distinct from **damit**, which indicates the *purpose* of an action); as in English, the elements of this phrase can be used together, or spread over two clauses. When used together, they can be written as one word: **sodass.**

Den einen Tanker haben sie getroffen, **so dass/sodass** er zu sinken beginnt.	*They hit the one tanker, so that it begins to sink.*
Aber er sinkt **so** langsam, **dass** er 12 Stunden später noch im Wasser treibt.	*But it sinks so slowly that it is still floating in the water 12 hours later.*

H. *Dass*

1. **Dass** is equivalent to English *that* as an introduction to noun clauses. As in English, it can be omitted, which changes the word order to that of a main clause.

COMPARE:

Der Kapitän ging davon aus, **dass** die Engländer alle Überlebenden auf dem Tanker schon gerettet ***hatten.***	*The captain assumed that the English had already rescued all survivors on the tanker.*
Der Kapitän ging davon aus, die Engländer ***hatten*** alle Überlebenden auf dem Tanker schon gerettet.	

2. In English, it is permissible for one clause *(if they don't surface soon)* to be embedded within another *(that they will all suffocate),* with the two subordinating conjunctions positioned back to back:

He knows **that if** they don't surface soon, they will all suffocate.

But in German, the word order of such clauses makes this kind of embedding awkward. Instead, it is preferable to arrange the two clauses in linear succession:

Er weiß, **dass** sie alle ersticken werden, **wenn** sie nicht bald auftauchen.

I. Falls

Falls *(in case, if, providing)* is sometimes used instead of **wenn** to express possibility.

Sie haben ja Sauerstoffmasken, **falls** die Luftpumpe ausfällt.	*They have oxygen masks, of course, in case the air pump quits working.*

J. Indem

To express the English construction *by [_____]ing,* German uses a clause beginning with **indem** and repeats the subject from the first clause.

Der Kapitän will dem Journalisten und dem Ingenieur das Leben retten, **indem** er sie in Vigo absetzt.	*The captain wants to save the journalist's and the engineer's lives by dropping them off in Vigo.*

K. Nachdem

As in the case of *before,* German distinguishes among the grammatical contexts of *after* by using the preposition **nach,** the adverbs **nachher** and **danach,** and the conjunction **nachdem,** depending on the function of *after* in the sentence.

COMPARE:

Nach ihrer Ankunft in Vigo aber weiß er, dass sie alle wohl sterben werden.	*After their arrival in Vigo, however, he knows that they will probably all die.*
Nachdem sie aber in Vigo ankommen, weiß er, ...	*After they arrive in Vigo, however, he knows . . .*
Beim Festessen auf dem anderen deutschen Schiff geht alles lustig zu, aber **nachher** wird's gleich wieder ernst.	*At the banquet on the other German ship, there's laughter and fun, but after that things get serious again right away.*

L. *Ob*

1. **Ob** means *whether.*

   Bis zum Schluss ist man nicht ganz sicher, **ob** sie es schaffen werden oder nicht.

   One isn't completely sure until the end whether they're going to make it or not.

2. **Ob** can also be translated as *if,* but only when *if* is synonymous with *whether.* In cases where *if* introduces a condition, **wenn** is used.

   COMPARE:

   Wenn es neblig bleibt, können sie vielleicht an den Zerstörern unbemerkt vorbeifahren.

   If it stays foggy, perhaps they'll be able to steer unnoticed past the destroyers.

   Ob es so neblig bleibt, weiß natürlich keiner.

   Whether (if) it will stay so foggy—no one knows, of course.

M. *Obgleich, obschon, obwohl*

Obgleich, obschon, and **obwohl** all mean *although,* but **obwohl** is most common.

Der junge Seemann schreibt seiner Verlobten fast jeden Tag, **obwohl** er die Briefe gar nicht abschicken kann.

The young sailor writes to his fiancée almost every day, even though he can't send the letters.

N. *Seit, seitdem*

1. **Seitdem** (often abbreviated to **seit**) means *since* in a temporal sense. German uses the present tense with **seit(dem)** (see 2.2.B) to express an action that began in the past and continues into present time, for which English requires the present perfect.

2. If the action in the **seit(dem)** clause is not ongoing, then German uses the present perfect tense in that clause.

   COMPARE:

   Es ist das erste Mal, dass Johann durchdreht, **seit(dem)** er bei der Marine *ist.*

   *It's the first time that Johann has gone berserk since **he's been** in the navy.*

   Es ist das erste Mal, dass Johann durchdreht, **seit(dem)** er bei der Marine *angefangen hat.*

   *It's the first time that Johann has gone berserk since he **joined** the navy.*

3. In addition to the conjunction **seit(dem),** there is the dative *preposition* **seit** *(since, for)* (see 6.3) as well as the *adverbs* **seitdem** and **seither** (see 14.2).

Seit dem Vorfall mit den Läusen *benimmt sich* der Erste Offizier etwas anders.	*Ever since the incident with the lice, the first officer has been behaving differently.*
Sie erreichten Gibraltar ohne Probleme, aber **seitdem** *ist* die Spannung kaum zu ertragen.	*They reached Gibraltar without a problem, but since then the tension has been almost unbearable.*

O. *Sobald, solange, sooft*

The conjunctions **sobald** *(as soon as),* **solange** *(as long as),* and **sooft** *(as often as)* are often used to indicate the condition for doing an action.

Sobald die Engländer sie sehen, ist es vorbei.	*As soon as the English see them, it will all be over.*
Solange der Nebel hält, haben sie eine Chance.	*As long as the fog holds, they have a chance.*
Sie vermeiden die anderen Schiffe **sooft**[4] sie können.	*They avoid the other ships as often as they can.*

P. *Während*

1. The conjunction **während** *(while)* indicates the simultaneous occurrence of two actions or states. This conjunction should not be confused with the *preposition* **während** *(during)* (see 6.5).

COMPARE:

Während sie sinken, versuchen sie alles, um das U-Boot wieder in den Griff zu bekommen.	*While they're sinking, they try everything to get the sub back under control.*
Während der folgenden Szenen sieht man eine ganz andere Seite der Besatzung.	*During the following scenes, one sees a very different side of the crew.*

2. The conjunction **während** can also be used to contrast two actions.

Einige haben alle Hoffnung aufgegeben, **während** andere ums Überleben kämpfen.	*Some have lost all hope, while others fight to survive.*

---

[4]**Sooft** is pronounced as two words: **so** + **oft,** with a slight glottal stop between them.

Q. *Wenn ... auch, auch wenn*

Wenn ... auch and **auch wenn** mean *even if* or *even though*. **Wenn** and **auch** are normally separated by one or more words or phrases when **wenn** precedes **auch.** They normally occur together when **auch** comes first.

Der Ingenieur arbeitet stundenlang, **wenn** er **auch** ohne Schlaf und fast ohne Luft weitermachen muss (*or:* **auch wenn** er ... muss).	*The engineer works for hours, even though/even if he has to continue without sleep and almost without air.*

R. *Wenn ... nicht/wenn ... kein-*

1. The phrases **wenn ... nicht** and **wenn ... kein-** approximate English *unless.*

Wenn das U-Boot **nicht** innerhalb von sechs Stunden repariert ist, haben sie keine Chance mehr.	*Unless the sub is repaired within six hours, they have no chance [of survival].*

2. The phrase **es sei denn** can also be used to express *unless.*

Sie haben keine Chance mehr, **es sei denn,** das U-Boot ist innerhalb von sechs Stunden repariert.	*They have no chance [of survival] unless the sub is repaired within six hours.*

Übersicht

CONJUNCTIONS

Coordinating conjunctions
__ V₁ ____ V₂ [c] __ V₁ ____ V₂

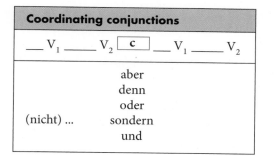

aber
denn
oder
(nicht) ...   sondern
und

Correlative conjunctions
sowohl ... als/wie auch ...
nicht nur ... sondern auch ...
entweder ... oder ...
weder ... noch ...

Subordinating conjunctions	
__ V₁ ____ V₂, [c] ____ V₂ V₁	
als	ob
als ob	obgleich
bevor	obschon
ehe	obwohl
bis	seit(dem)
da	sobald
damit	solange
dass	sooft
anstatt dass	während
ohne dass	weil
so dass/sodass	wenn
falls	wenn ... auch/auch wenn
indem	wenn ... nicht
nachdem	wenn ... kein-

Reference 3
PREPOSITIONAL PHRASES AS VERBAL COMPLEMENTS

CONCEPT AND USAGE

A. Prepositional phrases

1. German, like English, uses prepositional phrases in conjunction with certain verbs to create specific meanings. The very strength of these mental associations (*to believe **in**, to wait **for**,* for example) results in frequent mistakes among learners, since the combinations are often different across languages.

   Glaubst du **an** die Liebe auf den ersten Blick?

   *Do you believe **in** love at first sight?*

   Auf jemand(en) wie dich habe ich ja gewartet.

   *I was just waiting **for** someone like you.*

   In some cases, German uses prepositions with a verb to make distinctions not found in English.

   Der Mann stirbt **an** Hunger.

   *The man is dying **of** hunger.* (literally)

   Ich sterbe **vor** Hunger!

   *I'm dying **of** hunger!* (figuratively)

   In short, it is essential to learn the verb and preposition together for each desired meaning, and not assume a similarity between English and German combinations.

2. In some instances, verbs may have a direct or indirect object *and* a prepositional complement.

   Man erkennt **die Wise Guys**[1] leicht <u>**an ihrem Gesangsstil.**</u>

   One can recognize the Wise Guys easily by their style of singing.

   Was hindert **dich** <u>**an der Ausführung meines Befehls?**</u>

   What's hindering you from carrying out my order?

---

[1]The **Wise Guys** are a well-known *a capella* pop music group that began in the 1990s in Cologne and have toured and recorded extensively since then.

B. Prepositional *da*-compounds

When the prepositional object is expressed as a subordinate clause or an infinitive clause, a prepositional **da**-compound is used to link the verb with this object clause (see 20.2).

Ich freue mich **darüber,** dass es endlich wieder Sommer ist.	*I'm happy that it's finally summer again.*
Der Fußballspieler kämpft **darum,** bei seinem jetzigen Team zu bleiben.	*The soccer player is fighting to stay with his current team.*

Almost all of the verbs in the next section can occur with **da**-compounds. Some occur more often with **da**-compounds than with nouns and pronouns.

R.3.2 ▶ **EXAMPLES IN CONTEXT**

All of the prepositions listed below belong to one of three categories: prepositions that govern the accusative (see 6.2); prepositions that govern the dative (see 6.3), and variable prepositions that govern either the accusative or the dative (see 6.4). When used as verbal complements, variable prepositions govern a specific case for a specific meaning—e.g., the preposition **an** in **denken an,** with the meaning *to think about,* always governs the accusative. In the lists that follow, verb + preposition combinations will be grouped according to the case they govern.

A. *An*

Depending upon the verb with which it is used, **an** can govern either the accusative or dative case. Common examples include:

Accusative

denken an *to think of*	grenzen an *to border on*
(jmdn.[2]) erinnern an *to remind (s.o.) of*	sich richten an *to direct (a comment*
sich erinnern an[3] *to remember*	*or question) to*
sich gewöhnen an *to get accustomed to*	sich wenden an *to turn to, appeal to*
glauben an *to believe in*	

---

[2]The examples here and below make use of standard dictionary abbreviations:

jmdn. = jemanden (*someone*; accusative case)   **s.o.** = *someone*
jmdm. = jemandem (*someone*; dative case)   **s.th.** = *something*

[3]Notice that in some cases, a German verb + prepositional phrase is rendered in English with a verb + direct object.

Ich erinnere mich nicht **an alle Einzelheiten.**	*I don't remember **all the details.***
Sie zweifelte **an seiner Aufrichtigkeit.**	*She doubted **his sincerity.***

Dative

arbeiten an   *to work on/at*
(jmdn.) erkennen an   *to recognize (s.o.) by*
sich freuen an   *to delight in*
(jmdn.) hindern an   *to hinder/prevent (s.o.) from (doing s.th.)*
leiden an   *to suffer from*
sterben an   *to die of/from*
zweifeln an   *to doubt*

B. *Auf*

Auf occurs with many verbs expressing the idea of physically or mentally looking or aiming at or toward something. In such usage, it almost always governs the accusative. Common examples include:

Accusative

achten auf   *to pay heed to*
antworten auf   *to answer, respond to*
auf·passen auf   *to keep an eye on, watch out for*
sich beschränken auf   *to limit oneself to*
sich beziehen auf   *to refer to*
reagieren auf   *to react to*
schießen auf   *to shoot at*
sich verlassen auf   *to rely upon*
trinken auf   *to drink to*

blicken auf   *to glance at*
sich freuen auf   *to look forward to* (see also **über,** 2.H below)
(jmdn.) hin·weisen auf   *to refer (s.o.) to*
hoffen auf   *to hope for*
hören auf   *to listen to, heed*
sich konzentrieren auf   *to concentrate on*
vertrauen auf   *to trust in*
verzichten auf   *to forgo, renounce*
warten auf   *to wait for*
zeigen auf   *to point to/at*

Dative

beruhen auf   *to be based upon*
bestehen auf   *to insist upon*

C. *Aus*

Aus is not nearly as common as **an** and **auf** in prepositional complements. It usually means *of* or *from,* and always governs the dative case. Common examples include:

Dative

bestehen aus   *to consist of*
folgern aus   *to deduce from*
werden aus   *to become of*

D. *Für*

Für occurs with a number of common verbs and always governs the accusative case. Some common examples include:

Accusative

(jmdm.) danken für   *to thank (s.o.) for*
(jmdn./etwas) halten für   *to regard (s.o./s.th.) as*
sich entscheiden für   *to decide on* (see **Wortschatz** 10)
sich interessieren für   *to be interested in*
sorgen für   *to provide for, look after*
stimmen für   *to vote for*

E. *In*

In occurs in the accusative with a few verbs expressing *coming or getting into a situation or state.* It also occurs occasionally in the dative with certain verbs. Common examples include:

Accusative

ein·willigen in   *to agree to*
geraten in   *to get or fall into (danger, difficulty, etc.)*
sich verlieben in   *to fall in love with*
sich vertiefen in   *to delve into, become engrossed with*

Dative

sich irren in   *to err, be mistaken in/about*
sich täuschen in   *to be mistaken about*

F. *Mit*

Mit always governs the dative case, and in combination with verbs, it usually retains its basic meaning of *with.* Common examples include:

Dative

auf·hören mit   *to stop doing, cease*
sich befassen mit   *to deal with*
sich beschäftigen mit   *to occupy oneself with*
handeln mit   *to trade or deal in*
rechnen mit   *to count on*
telefonieren mit   *to speak on the phone with*
sich verabreden mit   *to make an appointment with*
verkehren mit   *to associate with, mix with*
sich vertragen mit   *to get along (well) with*

G. *Nach*

1. **Nach** governs the dative case and is used after several verbs that denote longing, inquiry, and reaching for. Some common examples include:

    ### Dative

    (be)urteilen nach   *to judge by/according to how*
    sich erkundigen nach   *to inquire about/after*
    (jmdn.) fragen nach   *to ask (s.o.) about*
    forschen nach   *to search for, investigate*
    greifen nach   *to reach for*
    schicken nach   *to send for*
    schreien nach   *to scream for*
    sich sehnen nach   *to long for*
    streben nach   *to strive for*
    suchen nach   *to search for*
    sich um·sehen nach   *to look around for*

2. **Nach** is also used after some verbs of perception. In these cases it means what something looks, sounds, smells, or tastes *like*.

    aus·sehen nach   *to look like (s.th. will happen); cf.* aus·sehen **wie** *to look like, be visually similar*
    klingen nach   *to sound like*
    riechen nach   *to smell like*
    schmecken nach   *to taste like*
    stinken nach   *to stink of*

H. *Über*

Über occurs with several verbs of speaking and usually expresses the idea of *about*. **Über** governs the accusative in these instances. Common examples include:

Accusative

sich ärgern über   *to be annoyed about/at*
sich beklagen über   *to complain about*
berichten über   *to report about/on*
sich beschweren über   *to complain about*
diskutieren über   *to discuss, talk about*
sich einigen über   *to agree upon*
sich freuen über   *to be happy about*
   (*cf.* sich freuen auf *to look forward to,* see **auf,** 2.B above)
sich lustig machen über   *to make fun of*

nach·denken über   *to think about, ponder*
reden über (*or* von)   *to speak about*
sich schämen über   *to be ashamed of*
spotten über   to joke about, ridicule
sprechen über (*or* von)   *to speak about*
staunen über   *to be amazed at*
(sich) streiten über   *to quarrel (with one another) about*
sich unterhalten über   *to converse about*

I. *Um*

Um is used with a number of verbs that describe activities where something is at stake or being requested. **Um** governs the accusative. Examples include:

Accusative

sich bemühen um   *to take pains with*
(jmdn.) beneiden um   *to envy (s.o.) for*
sich bewerben um   *to apply for*
(jmdn.) bitten um   *to ask (s.o.) for, request*
(jmdn.) bringen um   *to deprive or cause (s.o.) to lose*[4]
kämpfen um   *to fight for*
kommen um   *to lose, be deprived of*
sich kümmern um   *to look after, bother about*

sich sorgen um   *to be anxious/ worried about*
spielen um   *to play for (stakes)*
wetten um   *to bet for (stakes)*
es geht um   *it is a matter of* (see **Wortschatz** 20)
es handelt sich um   *it is a matter of* (see **Wortschatz** 20)

J. *Von*

Von always governs the dative. Examples include:

Dative

(jmdn.) ab·halten von   *to keep, prevent (s.o.) from (doing s.th.)*
ab·hängen von   *to depend upon*
(jmdm.) ab·raten von   *to advise (s.o.) against*
berichten von (*or* über)   *to report on*
sich erholen von   *to recover from*
erzählen von (*or* über)   *to tell about*
etwas fordern von   *to demand (s.th.) of/from*
halten (viel) von   *to think highly of*

handeln von   *to be about* (see **Wortschatz** 20)
leben von   *to live on*
reden von (*or* über)   *to speak about*
sprechen von   *to talk about*
sich unterscheiden von   *to differ from*
etwas verlangen von   *to demand (s.th.) from/of*
etwas verstehen von   *to understand (s.th.) about*
etwas wissen von   *to know (s.th.) about*

K. *Vor*

Vor occurs primarily with verbs denoting deference or fear. In such instances, **vor** always governs the dative. Common examples include:

Dative

Achtung/Respekt haben vor   *to have respect for*
Angst haben vor   *to have fear of*
erschrecken vor   *to shrink at, be frightened of*
fliehen vor   *to flee from*
sich fürchten vor   *to fear, be afraid of*

---

[4]**bringen um:** This verb should not be confused with the separable-prefix verb **um·bringen,** *to take a person's life.*

sich hüten vor   *to watch out for, be on guard against*
schreien vor   *to scream with/out of*
(jmdn.) schützen vor   *to protect (s.o.) from*
(sich) verstecken vor   *to hide from*
(jmdn.) warnen vor   *to warn (s.o.) of/against/about*
zittern vor   *to tremble with/from (fear, cold, etc.)*

L. *Zu*

In verbal complements, **zu** usually means *to, to the point of doing,* or *for the purpose of.* **Zu** always governs the dative. Common examples include:

Dative

(jmdn.) beglückwünschen zu   *to congratulate (s.o.) on*
(etwas) bei·tragen zu   *to contribute (s.th.) to*
(jmdn.) bringen zu   *to bring (s.o.) to the point of*
dienen zu   *to serve a purpose as*
sich entschließen zu   *to decide to* (see **Wortschatz** 10)
führen zu *to lead to*

(jmdm.) gratulieren zu   *to congratulate (s.o.) on*
etwas meinen zu   *to have an opinion (about s.th.)*
neigen zu   *to tend to/toward*
passen zu   *to match, be suited to*
(jmdm.) raten zu   *to advise (s.o.) to*
(jmdn.) überreden zu   *to persuade (s.o.)*
werden zu   *to become, turn into*
zwingen zu   *to force, compel to*

Übersicht

PREPOSITIONAL PHRASES AS VERBAL COMPLEMENTS

Verbal complements: Word order
Main clause
_____ V_1 _____ [verbal complement] V_2
Sie haben sich bestimmt [auf dieses letzte Beispiel] gefreut .
Subordinate clause
_____, dass _____ [verbal complement] V_2 V_1
Wussten Sie, dass ich mich auch [auf dieses letzte Beispiel] gefreut habe ?

R.4.1 ▸ NUMERALS

A. Cardinal numbers

1. German words for cardinal numbers (**die Grundzahl, -en**) are always single words, no matter how long the number, with the exception of numbers over a million. The irregular forms in the chart below are highlighted.

0	null				
1	eins	11	elf	21	**ein**undzwanzig
2	zwei	12	zwölf	22	zweiundzwanzig
3	drei	13	dreizehn	30	**dreiß**ig
4	vier	14	vierzehn	40	vierzig
5	fünf	15	fünfzehn	50	fünfzig
6	sechs	16	**sech**zehn	60	**sech**zig
7	sieben[1]	17	**sieb**zehn	70	**sieb**zig
8	acht	18	achtzehn	80	achtzig
9	neun	19	neunzehn	90	neunzig
10	zehn	20	zwanzig	99	neunundneunzig

---

[1]In German-speaking countries the numeral 7 is usually handwritten with a slash through the middle (7̶) to distinguish it from the numeral 1, which is usually written using two strokes rather than just one (1̸).

100	(ein)hundert
101	hunderteins
102	hundertzwei
200	zweihundert
999	neunhundertneunundneunzig
1.000	(ein)tausend
1100	elfhundert *(expressing years)*
1900	neunzehnhundert *(expressing years)*
2.000	zweitausend
9.999	neuntausendneunhundertneunundneunzig
100.000 *(or* 100 000*)*	hunderttausend
1.000.000 *(or* 1 000 000*)*	eine Million
2.000.000	zwei Million**en**
1.000.000.000	eine Milliarde *(billion)*
2.000.000.000	zwei Milliard**en**
1.000.000.000.000	eine Billion *(trillion)*
2.000.000.000.000	zwei Billion**en**

2. Notes on using **eins** in written form:

- When **1** stands by itself as a number, its written form ends with an -s: **eins**; when attached to another number (as in **21**), the -s is dropped: **einundzwanzig.**

- When used as a noun—for example, indicating a score on a test or in a competition—it is feminine, as are all such numbers: **eine Eins, eine Zwei.**

- Before a noun, meaning either *one* or *a*, **ein**- takes article endings (see 4.2). To distinguish **ein**- meaning *one* from **ein**- meaning *a*, the word is stressed when spoken to indicate the first meaning. In written texts, this stress can be indicated by italics, underlining, or spacing.[2]

Ich habe die Arbeit in **einer** Stunde fertig geschrieben.	*I finished the paper in one hour.*
Und stell dir vor, ich habe alles dafür auf **e i n e r** Webseite gefunden!	*And just think: I found everything for it on one website!*

- In German expressions equivalent to *one or two* or *one to two*, **ein** is used (without the **-s**), and takes no ending.

Wir fahren in **ein bis zwei Jahren** nach Deutschland zurück.	*We are traveling back to Germany in one to two years.*

---

[2]Notice the extra spacing between letters in the second example (e i n e r)—an orthographic convention used in German but not in English.

■ Before **hundert** and **tausend, ein** is optional. If used, the entire number is still written as one word.

125   (ein)hundertfünfundzwanzig
1.500   (ein)tausendfünfhundert

3. The following punctuation rules apply to numbers:

■ Either a period or a space can be used to separate thousands.

37.655 or 37 655 = *English 37,655*

■ In decimals and percents, German uses commas where English uses periods.

4,5 (*spoken:* vier Komma fünf)   *four point five (= 4.5)*

8,9% (*spoken:* acht Komma neun Prozent)   *eight point nine percent (= 8.9%)*

4. When **hundert** and **tausend** directly precede plural nouns, they do not take the plural form.

Seine Privatbibliothek umfasst mehr als **4.000 (viertausend) Bücher.**

His private library contains more than 4,000 books.

But when these numbers are used to express the idea *hundreds of . . .* or *thousands of . . . ,* they are plural nouns and thus capitalized. This is true whether a noun follows (as the object of **von**) or is only understood.

Ihre Bibliothek umfasst **Hunderte von** wertvollen Manuskripten.

Her library contains hundreds of valuable manuscripts.

Als 1906 das große Erdbeben kam, sind **Tausende** ums Leben gekommen.

When the big earthquake hit in 1906, thousands [of people] lost their lives.

5. **Million, Milliarde,** and **Billion** take endings in the plural: **Millionen, Milliarden,** and **Billionen.** Notice that English *billion* is expressed by German **Milliarde,** and that **Billion** in German means a *trillion* (that is, *a million million*).

Deutschland hat ungefähr 82 **Millionen** Einwohner.

Germany has about 80 million inhabitants.

Die Firma wurde für mehrere **Milliarden** verkauft.

The company was sold for several billions.

6. Whole numbers plus one-half have no endings and are written as follows:

anderthalb/eineinhalb   *one and a half*

zweieinhalb, dreieinhalb usw.   *two and a half, three and a half, etc.*

Der Film hat **anderthalb** Stunden gedauert.   *The film lasted one and a half hours.*

7. Numbers and amounts are approximated with words such as **etwa, rund, zirka,** or **ungefähr,** which all mean *roughly, around, about,* or *approximately.*

Es sind **etwa/rund/zirka/ungefähr** 800 Kilometer von München nach Hamburg.

It is about/around/approximately 800 kilometers from Munich to Hamburg.

8. The suffix **-erlei** indicates *kinds of* and is often used with numbers. This suffix takes no adjective ending.

zweierlei Bücher   *two kinds of books*
zehnerlei Bäume   *ten kinds of trees*
allerlei Probleme   *all kinds of problems*

9. The suffix **-fach** corresponds to English *-fold.* Words formed with it take endings when used as attributive adjectives. It can also be used as a neuter adjectival noun, which takes an ending and is capitalized.

eine **zweifache** Summe   *a twofold sum*
ein **zehnfacher** Gewinn   *a tenfold profit*
um **das Dreifache** vermehrt   *increased threefold*

10. The suffix **-er** is added to multiples of 10 to refer to decades, as in "*the 60s*" or "*the 80s.*" In this usage, no adjective endings are attached.

John F. Kennedy wurde Anfang der **sechziger (60er)** Jahre Präsident der USA.   *John F. Kennedy became president of the U.S.A. at the beginning of the sixties.*

11. Years up to 1999 are expressed with **-hundert,** followed by the final two digits (unlike English, which often deletes the word *hundred* when followed by other digits).

1124   *(spoken)* elf**hundert**vierundzwanzig
1848   *(spoken)* achtzehn**hundert**achtundvierzig
1989   *(spoken)* neunzehn**hundert**neunundachtzig

Beginning with 2000, years are expressed with **-tausend,** followed by the final two digits.

2001   *(spoken)* zwei**tausend**eins
2017   *(spoken)* zwei**tausend**siebzehn

B. Ordinal numbers

1. An ordinal number **(die Ordnungszahl, -en)** indicates relative position in a sequence, e.g., *first, second,* and *twenty-fifth,* as opposed to *one, two,* and *twenty-five.* The ordinal *first* is expressed in German with its own unique form, **erst-;** the ordinal numbers *second* through *nineteenth* are formed with the cardinal number followed by **-t-;** and from 20 on, ordinals are formed with the cardinal plus **-st-.** Several ordinal numbers are slightly irregular and are highlighted in the following chart.

1.	(der, die, das)	**erste**
2.	(der, die, das)	zweite
3.	(der, die, das)	**dritte**
4.	etc.	vierte
5.		fünfte
6.		sechste

7.	(der, die, das)	**siebte** (*less common:* **siebente**)
8.	etc.	**achte** (*no second* **t** *added*)
9.		neunte
10.		zehnte
11.		elfte
12.		zwölfte
19.		neunzehnte
20.		zwanzigste
21.		einundzwanzigste
30.		dreißigste
100.		hundertste
1.000.		tausendste

2. All ordinal numbers require an adjective ending following the final -t- or -st-, since they function as attributive adjectives, even when the noun they modify is understood, for example, **am fünften** [April].

das **erste** Mal *the first time*
ihr **zweites** Buch *her second book*

3. A period after a cardinal numeral (other than in a list) indicates that the number is to be read as an ordinal number, that is, with -t/-st plus an adjective ending.

Heute ist der **1.** Mai (*spoken:* der **erste** Mai). *Today is May 1st/the first of May.*

Wir begehen heute seinen **100.** Todestag *Today we are commemorating the*
(*spoken:* seinen **hundertsten** Todestag). *100th anniversary of his death.*

4. To enumerate points in a series, German uses the adverbial forms **erstens** (*first of all*), **zweitens** (*in the second place/secondly*), **drittens** (*in the third place/thirdly*), etc.

Lukas kann uns nicht helfen. **Erstens** ist *Lukas can't help us. First of all, he isn't*
er nicht hier, **zweitens** hätte er keine *here; secondly, he wouldn't want to;*
Lust dazu und **drittens** wüsste er *and thirdly, I guarantee he wouldn't*
garantiert nicht, was man tun sollte. *know what to do.*

5. Ordinal numbers can be used as nouns, and are capitalized according to the rules explained in 15.2.C.

Sie war **die Erste,** die es versucht hat. *She was the first (person) who tried it.*

Wir haben die Miete **am Zwanzigsten** *We paid the rent on the twentieth.*
bezahlt.

Jeder Fünfte musste das Zimmer verlassen. *Every fifth person had to leave the room.*

6. Ordinal numbers can serve as prefixes for adjectives (often superlative; see 15.1), forming one word where English uses two or more.

Sebastian ist der **zweitjüngste** Sänger in *Sebastian is the second youngest*
der Gruppe. *singer in the group.*

Was ist die **drittgrößte** Stadt der Schweiz? *What is Switzerland's third largest city?*

C. Fractional amounts

1. Fractions are nouns and are therefore capitalized. With the exception of **die Hälfte,** they are neuter and have no change in the plural. Fractions are formed by adding **-el** to the ordinal stem: ein **Viertel,** zwei **Drittel,** fünf **Achtel.**

2. *Half a(n)* is expressed in German by **ein- halb-.**

    Sie bestellten **ein halbes** Hähnchen.   *They ordered half a chicken.*

3. *Half (of) the* is most often expressed by **die Hälfte** + genitive, and less often by **die Hälfte + von.**

    Er verkaufte **die Hälfte** der Orangen.
    Er verkaufte **die Hälfte von** den Orangen. $\Big\}$ *He sold half (of) the oranges.*

4. German sometimes uses **d___ halb-** *(half the)* + noun instead of **die Hälfte** when referring to a single entity.

    Ich muss **den halben** Roman (*or:* **die**   *I have to read half (of) the novel by*
    Hälfte des Romans) bis Montag lesen.   *Monday.*

    Du hast ja schon **den halben** Tag (*or:* **die**   *You've already wasted half the day!*
    Hälfte des Tages) verschwendet!

R.4.2 ▶ **MEASUREMENTS**

A. Currencies and denominations

1. On January 1, 1999, the euro (**der Euro, -**[3]) became the official monetary unit of Germany and Austria for all electronic banking transactions, with euro currency replacing all bills and coins in January of 2002. Swiss currency remains the franc (**der Schweizer Franken, -**). **Der Euro** ($^1/_{100}$ = **der Cent, -s**), **der Franken** ($^1/_{100}$ = **der Rappen, -**), and **der Dollar** (like the former **Deutsche Mark** and **Schilling**) all remain singular when used with numbers to refer to amounts of money. Prices are read by stating any whole amount first, then the denomination (Euro/Dollar/Yuan/etc.) and then any fractional amount beyond the decimal point. In German speech, unlike English, nothing is inserted after the denomination.

€ 10,75	zehn Euro fünfundsiebzig	*ten euros **and** seventy-five cents*
€ –,82	zweiundachtzig Cent	*eighty-two cents*
sFr 6,50	sechs Franken fünfzig	*six francs **and** fifty rappen*
$7.99	sieben Dollar neunundneunzig	*seven dollars **and** ninety-nine cents*

---

[3]**Der Euro** actually has two plural forms: zwei **Euro,** zwei **Euros.** When citing amounts of money, the uninflected form is used: Das kostet 10 **Euro.** But when referring to the currency itself in the plural, **Euros** is correct: Diese **Euros** sind irgendwie schmutzig geworden. / Ich sammle (*collect*) **Euros.**

2. To indicate denominations of bills, coins, and stamps, German uses numbers with an -**er** suffix.

Bitte, drei **Sechziger** (Briefmarken) und eine[4] **Achtziger**.

Three sixties and an eighty, please.

Ich brauche hundert Euro: **einen**[5] **Fünfziger, zwei Zwanziger** und **einen Zehner.**

I need one hundred euros: a fifty, two twenties, and a ten.

B. Distances, weights, quantities, and temperatures

1. All German-speaking countries use the metric system.

   ■ **Distance**

   der Kilometer[6] (km) *(= 0.62 mile)*
   der Meter (m) *(= 39.37 inches)*
   der Zentimeter (cm) *(= 0.39 inch)*
   der Millimeter (mm) *(= 0.039 inch)*
   der Quadratmeter (m^2) *(= 10.76 square feet)*

   ■ **Weight**

   das Gramm (g) *(= 0.035 ounce)*
   das Kilogramm (kg) *(= 2.2 pounds)*

   ■ **Liquid measure**

   der/das Liter *(= 1.057 quarts)*

2. The following archaic measurements are occasionally found in set phrases: **Zollstock,** *measuring stick;* **meilenweit** laufen, *to walk for miles;* for grocery shopping: ein **Pfund** Käse *a pound of cheese;* for industrial measures: **Gallone** *gallon.*

   das Pfund *(= 500 grams)*
   der Zoll *(= 2.54 centimeters or 1 inch)*
   die Meile, -n *(= 1.6 kilometers)*
   die Gallone, -n *(= 3.79 liters)*

3. In German, masculine and neuter nouns of measurement used after numerals take no ending in the plural, while feminine nouns ending in -**e** do.

   der Kilometer ⟶ zwei Kilometer   *two kilometers*
   das Gramm ⟶ drei Gramm   *three grams*

   BUT:

   die Meile ⟶ vier Meile**n** *four miles*

---

[4]**Achtziger** is feminine because **die Briefmarke** is understood.
[5]**Fünfziger** is masculine because **der Schein** *(bill)* is understood.
[6]**Meter** and its compounds are generally considered masculine, although some dictionaries still list neuter as a possible gender. ***Das** Liter* is preferred by the German Institute for Standardization, but ***der** Liter* is commonly used as well.

4. Unlike English, German expressions of quantity do *not* use a word or structure equivalent to *of*, such as **von** or the genitive.

> vier Flaschen Wein *four bottles of wine (measure of quantity of wine)*
> drei Glas Bier *three glasses of beer (measure of quantity of beer)*

Instead, German nouns following quantifiers such as **Flaschen** and **Glas** are inflected according to their function in the clause, and any modifying adjectives must reflect the proper case for this function (see Chapters 5 and 13).

Nominative:	Hier sind vier Flaschen gut**er** Wein.
Accusative:	für vier Flaschen gut**en** Wein
Dative:	mit vier Flaschen gut**em** Wein
Genitive:	wegen vier Flaschen gut**en** Weines

5. Countries on the metric system use Celsius/Centigrade (°C) to measure temperatures. Thirty-two degrees Fahrenheit (°F) equals 0 degrees Celsius. To convert Fahrenheit to Centigrade, subtract 32 and multiply by 5/9. To convert Centigrade to Fahrenheit, multiply by 9/5 and add 32.

R.4.3 ▸ TIME

A. Units of time

1. The most common measurements of time are as follows:

die Sekunde, -n *second*	der Monat, -e *month*
die Minute, -n *minute*	die Jahreszeit, -en *season*
die Stunde, -n *hour*	das Jahr, -e *year*
der Tag, -e *day*	das Jahrzehnt, -e *decade*
die Woche, -n *week*	das Jahrhundert, -e *century*
das Wochenende, -n *weekend*	das Jahrtausend, -e *millennium*

2. To express *for hours, for days, for months,* etc., German adds the suffix **-lang** to the plural of units of time. As adverbs, such words are not capitalized.

Wir haben **stundenlang/tagelang/ monatelang** gewartet.   *We waited for hours/for days/for months.*

3. To indicate *how long ago* something happened, German precedes the time reference with the preposition **vor** (with the dative; see 6.3.J), where English places *ago* following the time reference.

Sie hat ihr Studium **vor einem Jahr** abgeschlossen.   *She completed her studies a year ago.*

Sie war **vor wenigen Stunden** da.   *She was here (just) a few hours ago.*

4. The following expressions with units of time are quite common:

tagsüber *during the day*
während/unter der Woche *during the week*
an Wochentagen *on weekdays*
am Wochenende *on the weekend*
im Laufe des Jahres *during the year*
alle zwei Tage/Wochen/Jahre *every other day/week/year*
alle drei Tage/Wochen/Jahre *every three days/weeks/years*

B. Talking about time: Minutes and hours

1. In colloquial language, the following expressions are used to tell time. Everything *before* the hour is **vor,** everything *after* the hour **nach.** In writing, a period has traditionally separated hours and minutes (8.00), though the use of a colon (8:00) is gaining acceptance in advertising.

Written	Spoken
8.00 Uhr	acht Uhr
8.10 Uhr	zehn (Minuten) nach acht
8.15 Uhr	(ein) Viertel nach acht (*regional usage in southern Germany also allows* [ein] Viertel neun, *i.e., a quarter of the way to nine*)
8.20 Uhr	zwanzig (Minuten) nach acht
8.25 Uhr	fünf vor halb neun
8.30 Uhr	halb neun (*i.e., halfway to nine*)
8.35 Uhr	fünf nach halb neun
8.40 Uhr	zwanzig (Minuten) vor neun
8.45 Uhr	(ein) Viertel vor neun (*regionally:* drei Viertel neun)
8.50 Uhr	zehn (Minuten) vor neun
8.55 Uhr	fünf (Minuten) vor neun

2. In addition to **vor** and **nach,** several other prepositions are used in expressing clock time.

- **Um** means *at.*

  Wir essen heute Abend **um** acht.　　　　　*We are eating this evening at eight.*

- Either **gegen** (*toward*) or **um ... herum** (*around*) can be used to mean *approximately.*

  Der Film endete **gegen** Mitternacht.　　　　*The film ended toward midnight.*

  Sie ging so **um** zehn **herum** nach Hause.　　*She went home at about 10 or so.*

- **In** is used with the dative case to refer to the endpoint of a duration.

  In einer Stunde ist Ihr Auto fertig.　　　　*Your car will be ready in an hour.*

3. To distinguish AM and PM in informal time expressions, German uses temporal adverbs referring to morning and evening; this context does not necessarily denote repeated occurrences.

Er kommt **um acht Uhr morgens/ abends.**	*He's coming at eight o'clock in the morning/evening.*

4. Official times (transportation schedules, concert performances, TV and radio times, official announcements, hours of business, etc.) are given according to a 24-hour clock without **Viertel, halb, vor,** or **nach.**

Written	Spoken
9.15 Uhr	neun Uhr fünfzehn/neun Uhr und fünfzehn Minuten
11.24 Uhr	elf Uhr vierundzwanzig/elf Uhr und vierundzwanzig Minuten
18.30 Uhr	achtzehn Uhr dreißig (= 6:30 PM)
22.45 Uhr	zweiundzwanzig Uhr fünfundvierzig/zweiundzwanzig Uhr und fünfundvierzig Minuten (= 10:45 PM)
0.15 Uhr	null Uhr fünfzehn/null Uhr und fünfzehn Minuten (= 12:15 AM)
English AM = 0.01 Uhr bis 12.00 Uhr *English* PM = 12.01 Uhr bis 24.00 Uhr	

C. Talking about time: Days of the week and parts of the day

1. Names of the days of the week and parts of the day are masculine, with the exception of **die Nacht/Mitternacht.** They take the dative contraction **am (an dem)** in time expressions (EXCEPT: **in der Nacht, zu Mittag, um Mitternacht**). With days only, **am** may be omitted.

(am) Montag	*on Monday*	am Morgen	*in the morning*
(am) Dienstag	*on Tuesday*	am Vormittag	*between morning and noon*
(am) Mittwoch	*on Wednesday*	zu Mittag	*at noon*
(am) Donnerstag	*on Thursday*	am Mittag	*at noontime (12-2)*
(am) Freitag	*on Friday*	am Nachmittag	*in the afternoon*
(am) Samstag[7]	*on Saturday*	am Abend	*in the evening (until bedtime)*
(am) Sonntag	*on Sunday*	in der Nacht	*at night (after bedtime)*
		um Mitternacht	*at midnight*

Das Spiel findet **(am) Samstag** statt.	*The game is taking place (on) Saturday.*
Sie hat einen Termin **am Vormittag.**	*She has a mid-morning appointment.*

---

[7]In northern Germany and throughout former East Germany, *Saturday* is more commonly referred to as **Sonnabend.**

2. To express parts of the day in conjunction with a day of the week, German combines the two to form one word.

Dienstagabend   *Tuesday evening*
Sonntagmorgen   *Sunday morning*
Donnerstagnachmittag   *Thursday afternoon*

Here as well, the contraction **am** is used to express *on* _____, but may be omitted.

(Am) Montagmorgen muss ich früh zur Arbeit.	*I've got to go to work early (on) Monday morning.*

3. Phrases with **Nacht** and **Abend** require further explanation.

- Notice that German distinguishes between **Abend** (the time between supper and bedtime) and **Nacht** (the time between bedtime and getting up). This means that a phrase such as *Friday night* (as in *Friday night we went to the movies*) translates properly to **Freitagabend,** while **Freitagnacht** refers to a later time frame, i.e., post-midnight.

- **Nachts** as a stand-alone adverb, however, is not so restricted in meaning, and can be used to refer to times prior to midnight, especially in conjunction with other time elements.

Um 9 Uhr **nachts** waren alle Restaurants schon zu.	*At 9 o'clock in the evening, all the restaurants were already closed.*

- The phrase **heute Nacht** depends on context for its meaning: spoken in the morning, it refers to the *previous night*; spoken later in the day, it denotes the *night to come*.

- English uses two prepositions in conjunction with *night*: *on* when there is intervening information, such as *on Tuesday night, on a windy night*; and *at* for general reference: *at night*. German uses **in** for both contexts. When used with **in, Nacht** stands alone or is followed by specific time references to avoid the ambiguity referred to above: **in der Nacht; in der Nacht von Freitag auf Samstag.** It can, however, combine with a day (as in **Samstagnacht**), but takes no preposition.

In der Nacht hörte jemand einen Schrei.	*Someone heard a scream at night.*
In der Nacht von Freitag auf Samstag ereignete sich ein Unfall.	*There was an accident (on) Friday night (i.e., during the night, not the evening).*
Wegen meiner Nachbarn konnte ich **Samstagnacht** gar nicht schlafen.	*Because of my neighbors, I couldn't sleep at all Saturday night.*

4. Adding an **-s** to the uncapitalized forms of days and parts of the day creates adverbs denoting repeated or habitual occurrences.

Diese Geschäfte sind **sonntags** zu.	*These stores are closed on Sunday(s).*
Sie arbeitet nur **nachmittags.**	*She only works afternoons./She works only in the afternoon.*

5. **Heute** *(today),* **gestern** *(yesterday),* **morgen** *(tomorrow),* and occasionally **vorgestern** *(the day before yesterday)* and **übermorgen** *(the day after tomorrow)* can be combined with parts of the day, as can the adverb **früh,** as in **morgen früh.** Notice that in

combinations such as *this morning*, German uses **heute** rather than *this*, as in **heute Morgen.** The parts of the days are still considered nouns in these phrases and therefore remain capitalized.

heute		**gestern**	
heute Morgen	*this morning*	gestern Morgen	*yesterday morning*
heute Vormittag	*today, between morning and noon*	gestern Vormittag	*yesterday, between morning and noon*
heute Mittag	*noon today*	gestern Mittag	*yesterday at noon*
heute Nachmittag	*this afternoon*	gestern Nachmittag	*yesterday afternoon*
heute Abend	*this evening, tonight*	gestern Abend	*yesterday evening, last night*
heute Nacht	*tonight (after bedtime)*	gestern Nacht	*last night (after bedtime)*

morgen[8]

morgen früh	*tomorrow morning*
morgen Vormittag	*tomorrow, between morning and noon*
morgen Mittag	*tomorrow at noon/noontime (12-2)*
morgen Nachmittag	*tomorrow afternoon*
morgen Abend	*tomorrow evening, tomorrow night*
morgen Nacht	*tomorrow night (after bedtime)*
vorgestern Abend	*the day before yesterday, in the evening*
übermorgen früh	*the day after tomorrow, in the morning*

D. Talking about time: Seasons and months

Seasons

der Frühling[9]	*spring*
der Sommer	*summer*
der Herbst	*fall, autumn*
der Winter	*winter*

Months

der Januar	der Juli
der Februar	der August
der März	der September
der April	der Oktober
der Mai	der November
der Juni	der Dezember

1. The names of the seasons and months are all masculine, and require the definite article in several instances where English does not: as the subject or direct object of a sentence, and with the prepositions **in** and **bis zu** (in contracted form with dative).

Der Herbst war dieses Jahr besonders mild.	*Fall was particularly mild this year.*
Ich kann **den** Februar hier nicht ausstehen.	*I can't stand February here.*
Hast du **im** April oder **im** Mai Geburtstag?	*Is your birthday in April or May?*
Wir bleiben **bis zum** Juli in der Schweiz.	*We're staying in Switzerland until July.*

---

[8]The adverb **morgen** by itself or before another time expression means *tomorrow* (as in **morgen früh**). Following other time expressions as a noun, it means *morning* (as in **heute Morgen**).

[9]**Das Frühjahr** can also be used for *spring*.

2. With other prepositions, after **sein** and **werden,** and following modifiers such as **Anfang, Mitte,** and **Ende,** no definite article is used.

Für August habe ich noch nichts geplant.	*I haven't planned anything yet for August.*
Von Januar **bis** März sieht man hier keine Sonne.	*You don't see any sun around here from January until March.*
Es **ist** endlich Juni!	*It's finally June!*
Anfang September fängt unser Semester an.	*Our semester starts at the beginning of September.*

E. Duration, specific time, *Zeit* vs. *Mal*

1. Duration of time is normally expressed using the accusative case with an article. The adjective **ganz** *(all, whole, entire)* is optional, but if included, it is preceded by an article.

Ich will **ein Jahr** in Berlin studieren.	*I want to study in Berlin for a year.*
Sie blieb **den ganzen Tag** in der Bibliothek.	*She stayed all day/the whole day in the library.*
Es hat **den ganzen Sommer** geregnet.	*It rained (for) the whole summer/ all summer.*

In the examples above, the duration of time refers to the activity denoted by the verb; in contexts where this is not the case, the preposition **für** can be used to show that the duration refers to another element in the sentence (see 6.2.E).

COMPARE:

Wir fahren **eine Woche** mit dem Schiff. (*eine Woche refers to the time spent traveling on the ship*)	*We're traveling for a week on the ship.*
Wir fahren mit dem Schiff **für eine Woche** auf Korsika. (*eine Woche refers to time spent on Corsica; we got there by ship*)	*We're traveling by ship for a week in Corsica.*

2. Specific time is also often expressed in the accusative case with words such as **jed-** *(every),* **letzt-** *(last),* **nächst-** *(next),* and **vorig-** *(previous).*

Jeden Tag muss ich eine Menge Hausaufgaben machen.	*Every day I have to do a huge amount of homework.*
Nächste Woche schreibe ich drei Prüfungen.	*Next week I have three exams.*
Und **letzten Freitag** waren zwei Aufsätze fällig!	*And last Friday two essays were due!*

3. There are several distinctions between the nouns **Zeit** and **Mal**.

a. The noun **die Zeit** refers to *specific time* or *duration of time*. It occurs in many time expressions, including the following:

in unserer Zeit *in our time (now)*	vor kurzer Zeit *a short time ago*
in früheren Zeiten *in earlier times*	vor langer Zeit *a long time ago*
in kurzer Zeit *in a short time*	zurzeit[10] *at the present time, now*
in letzter Zeit *lately, as of late*	zu jener Zeit *at that time, back*
in nächster Zeit/der nächsten Zeit	*then (also:* **damals***)*
in the near future	zu meiner/deiner/ihrer Zeit
nach einiger Zeit *after some time*	*in my/your/her day*
nach kurzer Zeit *after a brief time*	zu jeder Zeit (jederzeit) *(at) anytime*
nach langer Zeit *after a long time*	zu gewissen/bestimmten Zeiten *at certain*
von Zeit zu Zeit *from time to time*	*times*
vor der Zeit *prematurely*	zu gleicher Zeit *at the same time*
vor einiger Zeit *some time ago*	zu rechter Zeit *at the right moment*

b. The noun **das Mal** refers to a *singled-out occurrence*.

das erste/zweite/dritte/letzte Mal   *the first/second/third/last time*
zum ersten/zweiten/dritten/letzten Mal   *for the first/second/third/last time*
jedes Mal   *every (each) time*
ein anderes Mal   *another (i.e., different) time*

The suffix **-mal** (see 14.2) is used adverbially to express the *number of times* something happens. It occurs in the following common expressions:

einmal, zweimal, dreimal, ...   *once, twice, three times, . . .*
diesmal   *this time*
ein paarmal   *a few times*
manchmal   *sometimes*

F. Expressions of indefinite time

The genitive case is used with the word **Tag (eines Tages)** and parts of the day **(eines Morgens, eines Nachmittags, eines Nachts)**[11] to express indefinite time. This structure is common in narratives.

„Als Gregor Samsa **eines Morgens** aus unruhigen Träumen erwachte ...“	*"As Gregor Samsa awoke **one morning** from restless dreams . . ."*
Eines Tages werde ich einen Marathon laufen.	*Someday I'm going to run a marathon.*

---

[10]Both **zurzeit** and **zur Zeit** are legitimate forms, with different meanings: **zurzeit** *(at the moment)* is an adverb, and therefore not capitalized; **zur Zeit** is used when **Zeit** functions as a noun, as in **zur Zeit der Römer** *(at the time of the Romans)*.

[11]Although **Nacht** is feminine, German speakers say **des/eines Nachts** by analogy to **des/eines Tages**. This anomaly occurs only in this phrase.

G. Adjectives of time

1. Appended to a noun, the suffix **-lich** creates an adjective indicating *how often* something occurs. Except for **Monat,** the stem vowels of these nouns have an umlaut in this construction.

    ein **jährliches** Einkommen   *a yearly income*
    ein **monatliches** Treffen *(no umlaut)*   *a monthly meeting*
    eine **wöchentliche** Zeitung   *a weekly newspaper*
    ein **stündlicher** Glockenschlag   *an hourly chime, stroke of the hour*
    ein **zweimonatiger** Kurs *(no umlaut)*   *a two-month course*

2. With units of time, the suffix **-ig** creates adjectives expressing *how old* someone or something is or *how long* something occurs. The stem vowel of the noun takes an umlaut, except in **-monatig;** and in **-minutig/-minütig,** where it is optional.

    ein **zweijähriges** Kind   *a two-year-old child*
    eine **einstündige** Prüfung   *a one-hour exam*
    eine **sechstägige** Reise   *a six-day trip*
    ein **zweimonatiger** Urlaub   *a two-month vacation*
    ein **zehnminütiges/-minutiges** Schläfchen   *a ten-minute nap*

3. A number of adverbs of time form adjectives by adding the suffix **-ig.**
    heute: die **heutige** Deutschstunde   *today's German class*
    gestern: die **gestrige** Zeitung   *yesterday's newspaper*
    damals: die **damalige** Zeit   *(the) time back then*
    jetzt: die **jetzigen** Schwierigkeiten   *the present difficulties*
    ehemals: die **ehemalige** DDR   *the former GDR*
    vor: am **vorigen** Abend   *(on) the previous evening*

H. Dates and years

1. One asks for and gives dates in either of two ways in German.

    Der Wievielte ist heute?
    —Heute ist **der 4.** Juli.
    (*spoken:* der vierte Juli)

    Den Wievielten haben wir heute?
    —Heute haben wir **den 4.** Juli.
    (*spoken:* den vierten Juli)

    What's the date today?
    —Today is the 4th of July.

2. Dates after a day of the week preceded by **am** can be in either the dative or accusative case.

    Das Bach-Konzert findet **am** Sonntagabend, **dem** 20. Dezember, statt.

    The Bach concert is taking place on Sunday evening, the 20th of December.

    Und das Euroblast-Festival beginnt **am** Donnerstag, **den** 2. Oktober.

    And the Euroblast-Festival begins on Thursday, October 2.

3. Dates on forms and in letters are given in the order *day, month,* and *year.* If an article is used, it is in the accusative case.

   Geboren: 3.6.1998 (*spoken:* am dritten Juni / dritter sechster ...)

   Frankfurt, den 12. März 2015 (*spoken:* den zwölften März, ...)

4. Years are indicated by either **im Jahre** followed by the year or by the year alone—but never with the preposition *in* followed by the year, as in English.

   Der Erste Weltkrieg brach **1914** aus.
   Der Erste Weltkrieg brach **im Jahre 1914** aus. } *The First World War broke out in 1914.*

Übersicht

NUMERALS • MEASUREMENTS • TIME

Cardinal numbers: Irregular forms	
16	**sech**zehn
17	**sieb**zehn
21	**ein**undzwanzig
30	**drei**ßig
60	**sech**zig
70	**sieb**zig

Cardinal numbers: Suffixes		
-mal (*times*)	→	**dreimal**
-erlei (*kinds of*)	→	**zweierlei** Probleme
-fach (*-fold*)	→	ein **vierfacher** Gewinn

Ordinal numbers: Irregular forms	
1. (der, die, das)	**erste**
3. (der, die, das)	**dritte**
7. (der, die, das)	**siebte**
8. (der, die, das)	**achte**

Ordinal numbers: Fractions	
die	**Hälfte**
das	**Drittel**
	Viertel
	Fünftel
	Sechstel
	Siebtel
	Achtel
	(*etc.*)

Time: Units and names

die Sekunde, -n	der Sonntag	der Morgen	der Januar
die Minute, -n	der Montag	der Vormittag	der Februar
die Stunde, -n	der Dienstag	der Mittag	der März
der Tag, -e	der Mittwoch	der Nachmittag	der April
die Woche, -n	der Donnerstag	der Abend	der Mai
das Wochenende, -n	der Freitag	die Nacht	der Juni
der Monat, -e	der Samstag		der Juli
die Jahreszeit, -en			der August
das Jahr, -e	der Frühling		der September
das Jahrzehnt, -e	der Sommer		der Oktober
das Jahrhundert, -e	der Herbst		der November
das Jahrtausend, -e	der Winter		der Dezember

Cases used with time expressions

Specific time/ Duration of time	article *(accusative)* [+ **ganz**] + time unit: **einen Tag** **den ganzen Monat**
Indefinite time	article *(genitive)* + time unit: **eines Tages**

Time: Modifiers

How often	How long	When
jährlich	-jährig-	heutig-
monatlich	-monatig-	gestrig-
wöchentlich	-wöchig-	damalig-
täglich	-tägig-	jetzig-
stündlich	-stündig-	ehemalig-
		vorig-

Reference 5
VERB PREFIXES

German distinguishes between *separable* and *inseparable* prefixes. Separable prefixes attach to the front of the root verb in some situations, yet detach and stand alone in others. Inseparable prefixes, on the other hand, function as their name indicates and never separate from the root verb. A third category consists of prefixes that are inseparable with some verbs in specific meanings, but separable in other meanings. The following discussion deals in turn with these three kinds of prefix/verb-combinations and the ways they function in various grammatical contexts. Following the format of this edition, all separable-prefix verbs will be marked as such when they appear in lists as infinitives: **an·fangen.**

R.5.1	SEPARABLE PREFIXES

A. Separable prefixes and their meanings

1. Separable prefixes have a voiced stress and are usually prepositions or adverbs with specific meanings in their own right that either modify or completely change the meanings of the root verbs. Here are examples of the most common separable prefixes.

   NOTE: Prefixes marked with an asterisk can also be used inseparably (see R.5.3, below).

Prefix	Meaning	Example	
ab-	*off, away, down*	ab·nehmen *to lose weight*	
an-	*on, at, to(ward)*	an·sehen *to look at*	
auf-	*up, open, on*	auf·machen *to open up*	
aus-	*out*	aus·sterben *to die out*	
bei-	*by, with*	bei·stehen *to stand by someone, aid*	
ein-	*into*	ein·steigen *to get into, climb into*	
***durch-**	*through*	durch·setzen *to carry or put through*	
fort-	*away*	fort·gehen *to go away*	

Prefix	Meaning	Example
her-	*(to) here*	her·kommen *to come (to) here*
hin-	*(to) there*	hin·gehen *to go (to) there*
los-	*loose*	los·lassen *to turn loose, let go*
mit-	*with, along*	mit·singen *to sing along*
nach-	*after*	nach·blicken *to look or gaze after*
***über-**	*over, across*	über·fließen *to flow over*
***um-**	*around, about, over*	um·drehen *to turn over/around*
***unter-**	*under*	unter·gehen *to go down, set*
vor-	*before, ahead*	vor·arbeiten *to work ahead*
vorbei-	*by, past*	vorbei·laufen *to run by*
weg-	*away*	weg·gehen *to go away*
weiter-[1]	*keep on*	weiter·laufen *to keep running*
***wider-**	*against*	wider·hallen *to echo*
***wieder-**[1]	*back*	wieder·geben *to give back*
zu-	*to, toward; to a shut position*	zu·machen *to shut*
zurück-	*back*	zurück·rufen *to call back*
zusammen-	*together*	zusammen·stehen *to stand together*

2. Some separable prefixes should be learned as pairs, since they form antonyms when combined with the same verb.

an·drehen *to turn on*
ab·drehen *to turn off*

an·ziehen *to put on (clothes)*
aus·ziehen *to take off (clothes)*

auf·machen *to open*
zu·machen *to close*

---

[1]**Weiter** and **wieder** are separable prefixes only when they take these meanings. When used to mean *further* (comparative) and *again*, respectively, they become adverbs, and as such do not attach directly to the root verb.

COMPARE:

Wir können leider nicht **weitermachen.** *Unfortunately, we can't continue.*
Sie kann **weiter laufen** als ich. *She can run further than I (can).*

Ich hoffe, dass du alles bald **wiederbringst.** *I hope that you bring back everything soon.*
Er hofft, dass sie sich bald **wieder sehen.** *He hopes that they see each other again soon.*

auf·steigen   *to climb up*
ab·steigen   *to climb down*

ein·atmen   *to breathe in*
aus·atmen   *to breathe out*

vor·gehen   *to go ahead, precede*
nach·gehen   *to go after, follow*

zu·nehmen   *to increase, gain (weight)*
ab·nehmen   *to decrease, lose (weight)*

B. Use

1. When a separable-prefix verb is V_1 in a main clause, the prefix functions as a verbal complement and moves to the end of the middle field (see 1.1.C). This restricts the separation to contexts in which the separable-prefix verb is in the present or the simple past tense, and is not a dependent infinitive with a modal verb.

an·fangen: Das Konzert **fängt** um acht Uhr **an.**   *The concert begins at eight o'clock.*

weg·gehen: Nach der Pause **ging** er schnell **weg.**   *After the intermission he left quickly.*

2. A separable prefix also splits apart from the root verb in yes-no questions and imperatives, when the root verb is in first position.

mit·kommen: Kommst du heute Abend **mit?**   *Are you coming along tonight?*

aus·atmen: Atmen Sie langsam **aus!**   *Breathe out slowly!*

auf·hören: Hören Sie mit diesem Unsinn **auf!**   *Stop this nonsense!*

3. In a subordinate clause, the root verb moves to the end of the clause, and attaches directly to the prefix at the end of the middle field.

Weißt du, wann das Konzert **anfängt?**   *Do you know when the concert begins?*

Ich verstehe nicht, warum er so schnell **wegging.**   *I don't understand why he left so quickly.*

Du kannst entscheiden, ob du **mitkommst** oder nicht.   *You can decide if you're coming along or not.*

4. When separable-prefix verbs are used with modal verbs and in tenses that require an auxiliary verb as V_1, the root verb moves to V_2 position and attaches directly to its prefix. In conjunction with modal verbs (Chapter 9) or in the future tense (Chapter 24), the root verb remains an infinitive (**zurück·kommen, vorbei·marschieren**). In the perfect tense (Chapter 3) and past perfect tense (Chapter 8), the separable prefix attaches to the past participle of the root verb (**zurückgekommen, vorbeimarschiert**). Notice that in past participles formed with **ge-,** this element is inserted between the separable prefix and the root verb.

Ich **will** mir morgen das Museum **ansehen.**	*I want to take a look at the museum tomorrow.*
Dieses Restaurant **wird** bestimmt **zumachen.**	*This restaurant is definitely going to close.*
Nach langer Diskussion **haben** wir unseren Plan **durchgesetzt.**	*After a long discussion, we got our plan through.*

5. In infinitive clauses (see 11.1), the prefix and root verb remain together, with **zu** inserted between them to form one word.

Ich hatte keine Lust, noch einmal von vorne mit Physik **an<u>zu</u>fangen.**	*I didn't have any desire to start over again with physics.*
Also entschied ich mich, mit Deutsch **weiter<u>zu</u>machen.**	*So I decided to continue with German.*

6. The word order rules pertaining to separable-prefix verbs can also be applied to various verbal complements (see 1.1.C and 7.2.B), including infinitive complements (**stehen bleiben**[2]), adverb complements (**auswendig lernen**), and object noun complements (**Rad fahren**), with the important distinction that verbal complements do not attach directly to the root verb. Notice the similarity between the following sentences and separable-prefix verb structures:

Lernen Sie diese Vokabeln bitte **auswendig.**	*Please memorize these vocabulary words.*
Ich habe überhaupt keine Lust, alle diese Wörter **auswendig zu lernen.**	*I have absolutely no desire to memorize all these words.*
Sie **fährt** sehr gern **Rad.**	*She likes to go bike riding.*
Sie **wollte** letztes Jahr in Skandinavien **Rad fahren.**	*She wanted to go bike riding in Scandinavia last year.*

---

[2]According to the 2006 revision of the 1996 spelling reform, **stehen bleiben** (where **stehen** is a verbal complement, separate from **bleiben**) can also be written as **stehen·bleiben** (in which **stehen** functions as a separable prefix and attaches to **bleiben** in some contexts). The same holds true for **kennen(·)lernen** and several other verb + verb combinations.

C. *Hin-* and *her-*

1. The separable prefixes **hin-** and **her-** are used mainly in combination with other separable prefixes to indicate specific direction *away from* (**hin-**) or *toward* (**her-**) the observer.

Common combinations with *hin-* and *her-*	
hin(·gehen)	*(to go) to*
her(·kommen)	*(to come) from*
dorthin(·gehen)	*(to go) to there*
hierher(·kommen)	*(to come) to here*
hinein/hinaus(·gehen)	*(to go) in/out*
herein/heraus(·kommen)	*(to come) in/out*
hinauf/hinab(·gehen)	*(to go) up/down*
herauf/herab(·kommen)	*(to come) up/down*
hinüber(·gehen)	*(to go) over to*
herüber(·kommen)	*(to come) over to*
hinunter(·gehen)	*(to go) down to*
herunter(·kommen)	*(to come) down to*

2. Since they indicate direction, **hin-** and **her-** in combination with other prefixes usually make an action more specific than it would otherwise be.

    Er geht **aus.** *(general action)* He is going out.
    Sie geht **hinaus.** *(away from the observer)* She goes out *(of a room, house, etc.).*

    Er stieg aus dem Zug **(aus).** *(general action)* He got off the train.
    Sie stieg aus dem Zug **heraus.** *(toward the observer)* She got out of the train.

3. In colloquial usage, **her** can refer to motion away from (as well as toward) the observer. It frequently contracts to **r,** which is then connected to the root verb.

    Die Luft hier ist mir viel zu dick. Ich geh' mal **raus.** *It's too stuffy in here for me. I'm going outside.*
    Heraus/Raus aus meinem Haus! *(Get) out of my house!*

    Dieses Restaurant sieht gar nicht schlecht aus. Gehen wir mal **rein?** *This restaurant doesn't look bad at all. Shall we go in?*

4. Verbs of motion used with **hin-** and **her-** prefix combinations occasionally have an accusative noun that appears to be a direct object, but is really part of the adverbial expression.

    Das Kind läuft **die Treppe hinunter/ runter.** *The child runs down the stairs.*

R.5.2 INSEPARABLE PREFIXES

The following prefixes are inseparable:

be-	er-	miss-
emp-	ge-	ver-
ent-	hinter-	zer-

These prefixes take the place of **ge-** in forming the past participle: **hat besucht; haben verkauft.** These prefixes have no meanings by themselves, although several of them transform the meanings of root verbs in very specific ways.

A. Be-

1. A **be-** prefix verb is transitive, regardless of whether the root verb is transitive or intransitive.

antworten (auf)	*to answer*	**be**antworten	*to answer*
kämpfen (gegen)	*to fight against*	**be**kämpfen	*to fight against*
sprechen (über)	*to talk about*	**be**sprechen	*to discuss*

   Wir **sprechen über** diese Probleme. *We talk about these problems.*
   Wir **besprechen** diese Probleme. *We discuss these problems.*

2. The meaning of the verb may change considerably when a **be-** prefix is added.

kommen	*to come*	**be**kommen	*to receive*
sitzen	*to sit*	**be**sitzen	*to possess*
suchen	*to search*	**be**suchen	*to visit*

3. The prefix **be-** also creates transitive verbs from some nouns and adjectives.

der Freund	*friend*	**be**freunden	*to befriend*
die Frucht	*fruit*	**be**fruchten	*to fertilize, impregnate*
richtig	*correct*	**be**richtigen	*to correct*
ruhig	*calm*	**be**ruhigen	*to calm*

B. Ent-

When added to nouns, adjectives, or verbs, the prefix **ent-** expresses the idea of separation or removal. It is often equivalent to the English *de- (detach)*, *dis- (disconnect)*, or *un- (undo)*.

das Fett	*fat, grease*	**ent**fetten	*to remove the fat*
die Kraft	*strength*	**ent**kräften	*to weaken*
fern	*far*	**ent**fernen	*to remove*
decken	*to cover*	**ent**decken	*to discover*
falten	*to fold*	**ent**falten	*to unfold, develop*
heilig	*sacred*	**ent**heiligen	*to desecrate*
kommen	*to come*	**ent**kommen	*to escape, get away*

C. *Er-*

1. The prefix **er-** converts certain adjectives into verbs reflecting the quality expressed by the adjective.

hell	*bright*	**er**hellen	*to brighten*
hoch	*high*	**er**höhen	*to heighten*
möglich	*possible*	**er**möglichen	*to make possible*

2. The prefix **er-** also changes the meaning of certain root verbs to imply successful completion of an activity.

arbeiten	*to work*	**er**arbeiten	*to obtain through work*
finden	*to find*	**er**finden	*to invent*
raten	*to (take a) guess*	**er**raten	*to guess correctly*

    With certain verbs, the use of **er-** takes a potentially harmful action and makes it lethal.

schießen	*to shoot*	**er**schießen	*to shoot fatally*
schlagen	*to hit*	**er**schlagen	*to slay*
stechen	*to stab*	**er**stechen	*to stab to death*

D. *Hinter-*

1. The prefix **hinter-** can emphasize the idea of *behind* (as in *to leave behind*) in a root verb that already implies this.

Der Reiche hat seinen eigenen Kindern erstaunlich wenig **hinterlassen.**	*The wealthy man left his own children surprisingly little. (i.e., when he died)*
Sie wollte eine Nachricht für dich **hinterlassen.**	*She wanted to leave a message for you (i.e., before she departed)*
Als Kaution musste er eine Monatsmiete **hinterlegen.**	*He had to put down (i.e., leave) a month's rent as a security deposit.*

2. **Hinter-** can also convey a more abstract meaning of *behind,* as in the sense of getting behind a facade by way of investigation; or going behind someone's back—i.e., deceiving someone.

Ihre Behauptung, sie hätte das Geld einfach auf der Straße gefunden, muss **hinterfragt** werden.	*Her claim that she simply found the money on the street must be called into question (and/or investigated).*
Jahrelang hat der junge Mann die Bank mit seinen falschen Schecks **hintergangen.**	*For years, the young man deceived the bank with his fraudulent checks.*

E. *Miss-*

1. The prefix **miss-** indicates that something is done falsely or incorrectly. It often corresponds to English *mis-* or *dis-* and is only used with about fifteen verbs in German.

deuten	*to interpret*	**miss**deuten	*to misinterpret*
gefallen	*to be pleasing*	**miss**fallen	*to displease*
handeln	*to act (upon)*	**miss**handeln	*to mistreat*
trauen	*to trust*	**miss**trauen	*to distrust*

2. When used with verbs that already have an inseparable prefix, **miss-** becomes stressed.

    Er **missversteht** die Frage. *He misunderstands the question.*

F. *Ver-*

1. The prefix **ver-** has a wide variety of uses and meanings. Sometimes it adds the implication that the action of a root verb is done incorrectly, especially with reflexive verbs.

fahren	*to drive*	sich **ver**fahren	*to take the wrong road*
laufen	*to walk, run*	sich **ver**laufen	*to get lost (on foot)*
legen	*to lay*	**ver**legen	*to mislay, misplace*
rechnen	*to calculate*	sich **ver**rechnen	*to miscalculate*
spielen	*to play*	sich **ver**spielen	*to play a wrong note*
sprechen	*to speak*	sich **ver**sprechen	*to misspeak*

2. **Ver-** can also indicate that an action continues until something is used up or destroyed.

brauchen	*to use*	**ver**brauchen	*to use up*
brennen	*to burn*	**ver**brennen	*to burn up*
fallen	*to fall*	**ver**fallen	*to fall into ruin*
gehen	*to go*	**ver**gehen	*to pass or fade away*
schwinden	*to dwindle*	**ver**schwinden	*to disappear*
spielen	*to play*	**ver**spielen	*to gamble away, (i.e., to lose money by gambling)*

3. In some instances, **ver-** conveys the sense of *away*.

führen	*to lead*	**ver**führen	*to lead astray, seduce*
jagen	*to chase*	**ver**jagen	*to chase away*
reisen	*to travel*	**ver**reisen	*to go away on a trip*
schenken	*to give as a gift*	**ver**schenken	*to give away*
treiben	*to drive*	**ver**treiben	*to drive (someone) away*

4. Sometimes the prefix **ver-** simply intensifies, refines, or alters the action expressed by the root verb.

bergen	*to hide, cover*	**ver**bergen	*to hide, conceal*
gleichen	*to resemble*	**ver**gleichen	*to compare*
urteilen	*to judge*	**ver**urteilen	*to condemn*
zweifeln	*to doubt*	**ver**zweifeln	*to despair*

5. Finally, **ver-** converts many adjectives (often in the comparative form), a few adverbs, and an occasional noun into verbs.

größer	*larger*	**ver**größern	*to enlarge*
länger	*longer*	**ver**längern	*to lengthen*
mehr	*more*	**ver**mehren	*to increase*
nicht	*not*	**ver**nichten	*to annihilate*
die Ursache	*cause*	**ver**ursachen	*to cause*

G. Zer-

The prefix **zer-** indicates destruction or dissolution through the action denoted by the verb.

brechen	*to break*	**zer**brechen	*to break into pieces, shatter*
fallen	*to fall*	**zer**fallen	*to fall into pieces*
gehen	*to go*	**zer**gehen	*to dissolve (in a liquid)*
legen	*to lay*	**zer**legen	*to take apart, disassemble (usually irreparably)*
reißen	*to tear*	**zer**reißen	*to tear to pieces*
stören	*to disturb*	**zer**stören	*to destroy*

R.5.3 ▶ VARIABLE PREFIXES

A. Separable vs. inseparable

1. The prefixes **durch-** *(through)*, **über-** *(over, across)*, **um-** *(around, over)*, **unter-** *(under)*, **wider-** *(against)*, and **wieder-** *(back)* are used separably with some verbs and inseparably with others. In some instances, these prefixes may also be used either separably or inseparably with the same verb, depending upon the meaning implied. Used separably, prefix verbs tend to have a fairly literal meaning corresponding to the basic meaning of the verb + prefix. Used inseparably, the prefix often gives the verb a more abstract or figurative meaning. In the examples below, the underlined syllables receive intonational emphasis; notice how the prefixes are stressed differently depending on whether they are separable or inseparable.

Der Fährmann **setzte** die Reisenden einen nach dem anderen **über.**	*The ferryman carried the travelers across one by one.*
Sie **über<u>setzte</u>** den Aufsatz aus dem Französischen ins Deutsche.	*She translated the essay from French into German.*

2. In general, prefixes are stressed when used separably and unstressed when used inseparably.

Die Schule wurde während des Sommers **umgebaut.**	*The school was remodeled during the summer.*
Er hat seine Freundin **um<u>armt</u>.**	*He hugged his girlfriend.*

3. When prefix verbs are used inseparably, they generally make an intransitive verb transitive. In such instances, the auxiliary in the perfect tenses is **haben,** even when the verb without a prefix or with a separable prefix would take **sein.**

    COMPARE:

    Wir **sind** auf die andere Seite   *We jumped over onto the other side.*
       (hin)<u>über</u>gesprungen.

    Wir **haben** ein paar Kapitel im   *We skipped a few chapters in the book.*
       Buch **über**sprungen.

B. Use of the variable prefixes

1. Most (but not all) verbs with **durch-** are separable.

    Sie **macht** eine schlimme Zeit <u>durch</u>.   *She is going through a bad time.*

    BUT:

    Er **durch**<u>schaute</u> den Plan seines Feindes.   *He saw through the plan of his enemy.*

2. Most (but not all) verbs with **über-** are inseparable.

    Er hat einen Hund **über**<u>fahren.</u>   *He ran over a dog.*
    Wir **über**<u>lassen</u> Ihnen die Entscheidung.   *We leave the decision (up) to you.*

    BUT:

    Der Topf ist <u>über</u>gelaufen.   *The pot boiled over.*

3. Some verbs with **um-** are separable, others are inseparable. Some verbs with **um-** can be either separable or inseparable, depending upon the meaning.

    Sie versucht den Satz <u>umzuschreiben</u>.   *She's trying to rewrite/revise the sentence.*

    Er versucht den Satz zu **um**<u>schreiben</u>.   *He's trying to paraphrase the sentence.*

4. The same is true of verbs with **unter-** as a prefix: some are separable, some are inseparable, and some can be either, depending on the meaning.

    Der Junge wurde in einem Kinderheim   *The boy was lodged in a children's*
       <u>unter</u>gebracht.   *home.*

    Die schwere Arbeit hat seine Gesundheit   *The difficult work undermined his*
       unter<u>graben</u>.   *health.*

5. Most verbs beginning with **wider-** are inseparable.

    Seine Aussage **wider**<u>spricht</u> den Tatsachen.   *His statement contradicts the facts.*

    Niemand konnte sein Argument   *No one was able to refute his*
       wider<u>legen</u>.   *argument.*

    EXCEPTIONS:

    Das Wasser **spiegelt** die Lichter <u>wider</u>.   *The water reflects the lights.*

    Der Glockenton **hallte** <u>wider</u>.   *The sound of the bells echoed.*

6. **Wieder** can function three ways:

- As an inseparable prefix in **wieder**<u>holen</u> *(to repeat)*
- As a separable prefix, when combined with verbs to mean *back* (as in **wieder·bringen**)
- As an adverb meaning *again* (as in **wieder sehen**).

COMPARE:

Der Klavierspieler **wieder**<u>holte</u> die Stelle, bis er sie richtig spielen konnte.

The pianist repeated the passage until he could play it correctly.

Sie **bringt** uns morgen alles **wieder**.

She'll bring everything back to us tomorrow.

Du brauchst gar nicht **wieder<u>zu</u>kommen!**

Don't even bother coming back!

Hoffentlich kannst du deine Schlüssel **wieder** <u>finden</u>.

I hope you can find your keys again.

Übersicht

VERB PREFIXES

Separable prefixes: Forms	
Infinitive:	zurück·geben
Past participle:	zurückgegeben
With *zu*:	zurück<u>zu</u>geben

V_1 P

Ich **gebe** dir dein Geld **zurück**.

V_1 P

Ich **gab** dir dein Geld **zurück**.

P V_1

Du weißt ja, dass ich das Geld **zurückgab**.

Common separable prefixes	
ab-	*über-
an-	*um-
auf-	*unter-
aus-	vor-
bei-	vorbei-
ein-	weg-
*durch-	weiter-
fort-	*wider-
her-	*wieder-
hin-	zu-
los-	zurück-
mit-	zusammen-
nach-	

* Can also be used as inseparable prefixes.

Inseparable prefixes	
be-	hinter-
emp-	miss-
ent-	ver-
er-	zer-
ge-	

Reference 6

PARTICLES

CONCEPT

The information a speaker or writer conveys does not consist merely of statements, questions, and commands, but also of emotions and attitudes. Every language has unique ways of expressing such things as impatience, reassurance, outrage, or delight in tandem with the "facts" of an utterance. German does so by coupling intonation with certain words used expressly for this emotive function, often called "flavoring particles" (**die Abtönungspartikel, -n** or **die Modalpartikel, -n**). English speakers also make use of particles to add emotional color to their utterances, to be sure; but German has a much larger palette of such words, and this makes them notoriously difficult to translate.

The particles to be discussed are listed here:

aber	eigentlich	schon
also	halt	überhaupt
auch	ja	vielleicht
denn	mal	wohl
doch	nun	zwar
eben	nur/bloß	

Some of these have a literal meaning apart from their "flavoring" capacity; some have multiple "flavoring" meanings, depending on context and intonation. All should be used with care, following the (admittedly limited) explanations given here and the practical suggestions for usage provided by your instructor. In the examples below, take note of the intonational emphasis used for certain meanings, indicated by underlining. In many cases, the flavoring particles themselves are not emphasized, but rather the word or words that they are intended to "flavor."

R.6.2 PARTICLES IN USE

A. *Aber*

Besides the literal sense of **aber** as the coordinating conjunction *but* (see R.2.1), it serves as an intensifier in statements.

Das ist **aber** <u>nett</u> von dir.	*That's really nice of you.*
Hast du etwas dagegen? —**Aber** <u>nein</u>!	*Do you have a problem with that?* *—Of course not!*

B. *Also*

Also should not be confused with *also* (German: **auch**). It can mean *so* when introducing a consequence *(She said this, so I said that)*, but is used as well to connote reassurance or reinforcement of an idea expressed; to signal a reaction to something just said; or to introduce a summing up, much like English *Well, . . .*

Ich konnte nicht mehr lernen, **also**
  ging ich ins Bett.
	I couldn't study any more, so I went
	  to bed.

Du wirst uns **also** <u>helfen?</u>	*So you'll help us?*
Also, <u>gut</u> – wenn du willst.	*Well, all right—if you want to.*
<u>**Also**,</u> was willst du jetzt machen?	*So, (or: Well,) what do you want* *to do now?*

C. *Auch*

1. Besides its literal meaning of *also,* **auch** has a wide range of flavoring uses, many of which convey a sense of (or desire for) confirmation.

So schlecht war der Film (ja) <u>**auch**</u> nicht.	*The film wasn't really so bad.*
Bist du **auch** <u>sicher,</u> dass du es kannst?	*Are you really sure you can do it?*

2. **Auch** is sometimes used in the sense of *even*. With this meaning it is interchangeable with **sogar.**

Auch/Sogar in den <u>Alpen</u> fiel letztes Jahr weniger Schnee.	*Even in the Alps less snow fell last year.*

3. **Auch** can be used to intensify **nicht,** especially in certain commonly used phrases.

Vielleicht, vielleicht **auch** <u>nicht.</u> Warum **auch** <u>nicht?</u>	*Maybe, but (then again) maybe not.* *And (as a matter of fact) why not?*

D. *Denn*

Denn as a particle occurs only in questions; it adds a tone of either mild or strong impatience, surprise, or interest, depending on intonation. It also makes questions sound less abrupt.

Kommst du **denn** nicht **mit**?	*What? Aren't you coming along?*
Was habt ihr **denn** die ganze Zeit **gemacht**?	*So, what did you all do the whole time?*
Was ist **denn** hier **los**?	*What in the world is going on here?*

E. *Doch*

Doch is used in the following situations:

1. To stress validity (particularly in situations where one assumes a dissenting voice).

Das ist **doch** <u>Wahnsinn</u>!	*But that's crazy (no matter what anyone says)!*
Das <u>weißt</u> du **doch!**	*Come on, you know that!*

2. To convey surprise (in the face of previous expectations).

Sie hat <u>**doch**</u> Recht.	*So she's right after all.*

3. To stress disbelief (used in negative statements).

Das kann **doch** nicht dein <u>Ernst</u> sein!	*You can't really be serious!*

4. To intensify a sense of impatience or urgency in imperatives (assuming a negative reaction on the part of the person addressed), often with **mal** (see 23.1).

Hören Sie **doch** mal <u>zu</u>!	*Come on, listen!*

5. To respond positively to a statement or question with negative implications (see 19.1).

Du willst wohl nicht mitkommen, oder? —<u>**Doch**</u>!	*You don't want to come along, do you?* —*Oh yes, I do!*

F. *Eben*

1. As an adverb, **eben** means *just (now)/(then)*. It is synonymous with **gerade.**

Wo sind denn die anderen Gäste? —Die sind **eben** <u>weg</u>gegangen.	*Where are the other guests?* —*They just left.*

2. As a modifier, **eben** is roughly equivalent to English *just*, and can be used for both positive and negative statements.

Es <u>ist</u> **eben** so./So <u>ist</u> es **eben.**	*That's just the way it is.*
So ist es **eben** <u>nicht</u>!	*That's just not the way it is!*
Sie mag dich also? —**Eben** <u>nicht</u>!	*So she likes you, right?* —*That's just it: No!*

3. Used by itself as a response, **eben** implies agreement, the idea that a statement is *precisely* or *exactly* right.

    Das ist aber ein langes Kapitel.
    —<u>Eben</u>!/Ja <u>eben</u>!

    This is really a long chapter.
    —Precisely!/Exactly!

G. *Eigentlich*

1. **Eigentlich** can be used in statements and questions to soften and modify the tone, to imply that a question has not yet been fully answered, and as a discourse marker to change the topic of conversation.

    Weißt du **eigentlich,** wie sie <u>heißt</u>?

    Do you happen to know her name?

    Ich weiß **eigentlich** nicht, was ich <u>will</u>.

    I don't actually know what I want.

    Wo <u>wohnen</u> Sie denn **eigentlich**?

    So tell me, just where do you live?

2. This "flavoring" sense of **eigentlich** is concessive („Was ich **eigentlich** sagen wollte …"). To convey the stronger sense of *actually* ("*I'm <u>actually/really</u> going to do it!"),* German speakers tend to use an adverb such as **wirklich,** which implies that something *really* is the case, rather than **eigentlich.**

    COMPARE:

    Das ist **wirklich** sein Auto.
    Eigentlich ist das <u>sein</u> Auto.

    It really/actually is his car.
    Actually/To tell the truth, it is his car.

H. *Halt*

Halt is synonymous with **eben,** in the sense of *just,* but slightly more colloquial; it is used primarily in southern Germany, Austria and Switzerland.

Wir müssen **halt** <u>warten,</u> bis der Regen vorbei ist.

We'll just have to wait until the rain is over.

Ich möchte **halt** <u>wissen,</u> warum du nicht zurückgemailt hast.

I just want to know why you didn't email me back.

I. *Ja*

Ja can be used as a particle to mean the following:

1. To express the obviousness of a fact, with a hint of impatience; it is similar in this meaning to **doch.**

    Sie <u>wissen</u> **ja,** was ich meine.
    Das <u>tue</u> ich **ja** schon!

    Come on, you know what I mean.
    But I'm (obviously) already doing that!

2. To add a sense of urgency to imperatives; in this meaning, it is emphasized, and often preceded by **nur.**

> Komm (**nur**) <u>ja</u> nicht zu spät nach Hause!   *Don't you dare come home too late!*

3. To convey surprise, much like **doch.**

> Da <u>ist</u> sie **ja!**   *Well, there she is!*
>
> Das ist **ja** kaum zu <u>**glauben**</u>!   *That is really hard to believe!/I can hardly believe that!*

J. *Mal*

Mal softens a statement or command by adding a sense of casualness similar to English *hey* or *just,* rendering commands and suggestions less blunt. Almost any element in the sentence *except* **mal** can carry intonational stress, depending on the meaning one wants to convey.

> Ich muss dir **mal** was <u>**erzählen**</u>.   *I've just got to tell you something.*
>
> Komm **mal** <u>her</u>!   *(Hey,) come here!*
>
> Sieh dir das **mal** <u>an</u>!   *(Hey,) check this out!*

The same softening effect can be used to convey encouragement, or to lend an ironically casual tone to a threat.

Depending on intonation and pitch:

> <u>**Versuch**</u> es **mal!**   { *Just go ahead and try it!* (i.e., *come on, you can do it!*)
>
> *You just go ahead and try it!* (threatening)

K. *Nun*

Nun, often combined with **[ein]mal,** implies resigned acceptance of a situation. With this meaning it is virtually synonymous with **eben** and **halt.**

> Da konnte man **nun mal** nichts (weiter) <u>**machen**</u>.   *Well, there wasn't anything (further) to be done.*
>
> So sieht es im Moment **nun (ein)mal** <u>aus</u>.   *This just is the way things look at the moment.*

L. *Nur/bloß*

1. **Nur** lends a sense of urgency and emotion to questions.

> Wie konntest du das **nur** <u>**machen**</u>?   *How could you <u>do</u> that?*
>
> Wo <u>ist</u> sie **nur?**   *Where on earth <u>is</u> she?*

2. In commands, **nur** is roughly equivalent to *just:* threatening in some contexts, reassuring in others.

Denke **nur** nicht, dass ich das bald vergessen werde!	*Just don't think that I'll soon forget this!*
Rufen Sie mich **nur** nicht nach 10 Uhr an!	*Don't you dare/Just don't call me after 10!*
Warten Sie **nur**!	*Just wait!/Just you wait! (positive or negative, depending on intonation and pitch)*
Reden Sie **nur** <u>weiter</u>!	*Go on—keep talking! (i.e., you're doing fine!)*

3. Colloquially, **bloß** is often used instead of **nur,** and carries the same shades of meaning.

Sei **bloß/nur** nicht so <u>schüchtern</u>!	*Just don't be so shy!*
Warum hat sie das **bloß/nur** <u>gemacht</u>?	*Why on earth did she do that?*
Geh da <u>**bloß/nur**</u> nicht hin!	*Whatever you do, don't go there!*

M. Schon

1. As an adverb, **schon** means *already*.

Wir haben es **schon** <u>gemacht</u>.	*We have already done it.*

2. In adverbial usage, **schon** is often used with **mal** to mean *ever before*.

Waren Sie **schon mal** <u>Gast</u> in diesem Hotel?	*Have you ever been a guest in this hotel before?*

3. As a particle, **schon** expresses confidence or reassurance.

Ist alles fertig? —Ich glaube <u>**schon**</u>.	*Is everything ready? —Oh, I think so.*
Ich werde es <u>**schon**</u> machen.	*Don't worry, I'll do it.*

4. The particle **schon** can also convey hesitant or only partial agreement, the idea that although a statement is undoubtedly true, there might also be other considerations.

Du hast ja eine schöne Wohnung. —Das <u>**schon,**</u> aber noch keine Möbel.	*You have a nice apartment, you know. —Well, yes, but no furniture yet.*
Das ist <u>**schon**</u> richtig, was du sagst, aber ...	*What you say is true, but . . .*

5. **Schon** gives a sense of impatient encouragement to requests.

Setz dich **schon** <u>hin</u>!	*Come on now, sit down!*

6. **Schon** can also be used to add a sense of resignation to questions, and is not emphasized itself.

Was kann man in so einem Fall
schon <u>sagen</u>?

What can you possibly say in such
a case?

Wer möchte **schon** <u>allein</u> auf einer
Südseeinsel leben?

OR:

Wer möchte **schon** allein auf einer
<u>Südseeinsel</u> leben?

Who would ever want to live alone on
a South Sea island? (various
emphases are possible)

N. *Überhaupt*

1. In statements, **überhaupt** expresses generality regarding one or more of the sentence elements, and receives its own intonational emphasis.

Er sollte <u>überhaupt</u> mit seinen
Äußerungen vorsichtiger sein!

He should really (i.e., as an overarching
rule) be more careful about
what he says!

Sie interessiert sich für
Programmiersprachen, ja, für
Informatik <u>überhaupt</u>.

She's interested in programming
languages, in fact, in computer
science in general.

2. In questions, **überhaupt** can convey the idea of *at all,* in an absolute sense.

Hörst du mir **überhaupt** <u>zu</u>?

Are you listening to me at all?

Hast du **überhaupt** eine Ahnung,
was das **bedeutet**?

Do you have any idea at all what that
means?

3. Used with negatives, **überhaupt (nicht)** means *not, nothing, anything at all.* It is
synonymous in this usage with **gar (nicht)** (see **Wortschatz** 7).

Sie wissen <u>überhaupt/gar</u> nichts.

They don't know <u>anything at all</u>.

O. *Vielleicht*

1. **Vielleicht** has the literal meaning of *perhaps* or *maybe.*

Vielleicht mache ich mit, vielleicht nicht.   *Maybe I'll join in, maybe not.*

In this usage, it can also translate the English modal verb *might.*

Vielleicht klappt es dieses Mal.   *It might work this time.*

2. Used as a particle, **vielleicht** serves to underscore a sense of astonishment or an intense
reaction—the sort of sentiment that calls for an exclamation point—as expressed with
the English phrases *Let me tell you, . . . !* or *Boy, . . . !* In this usage it appears in the
middle field, never as the first element.

<u>Das</u> war **vielleicht** ein komischer Typ!
Da hatte ich **vielleicht** <u>Angst</u>, du!

Boy, that guy was weird!
I'll tell you, I was scared!

P. *Wohl*

1. In its literal sense, **wohl** suggests probability (see also 24.1.B). Its English equivalents are *no doubt, quite likely,* or *probably.*

Das wird **wohl** <u>lange</u> dauern.	*That will no doubt take a long time.*
Wenn sie es sagt, wird es **wohl** <u>stimmen</u>.	*If she says so, then it's probably true.*

2. As a particle, **wohl** conveys a sense of certainty.

Das kann man **wohl** <u>sagen</u>!	*You can say that again!*
Du bist **wohl** nicht bei <u>Sinnen</u>!	*You must be out of your mind!*

Q. *Zwar*

1. **Zwar** means *to be sure* or *of course* and is usually followed by an **aber** *(however)* in the subsequent clause.

Es gab **zwar** noch viel <u>Essen</u>, aber niemand hatte mehr Hunger.	*There was, to be sure, still a lot of food, but no one was hungry anymore.*

2. **Zwar** cannot be used as an affirmative response *("To be sure!")* to a question. Instead, German uses **allerdings** *(oh yes; by all means).*

COMPARE:

Haben Sie verstanden?	*Did you understand?*
—**Allerdings.**	*— Oh, yes!* (i.e., *I know what you're getting at*)

3. **Zwar** is also used to introduce details that follow a statement, in the sense of *namely* or *to wit,* moving from general to specific.

Das Konzert findet heute Abend statt, und **zwar** um 20 Uhr.	*The concert is taking place this evening, (namely) at 8 o'clock.*

R.6.3 **PARTICLES AS RESPONSES**

The following list provides some of the more commonly used phrases with particles as responses to something said or done. If no elements are underlined, this indicates that more than one element can be stressed in order to convey a particular meaning.

das ist aber wahr! *that sure(ly) is true!*
aber <u>nein</u>! *oh no! but of course not!*
also <u>gut</u>/also <u>schön</u> *well, OK (I'll do it)*
na <u>also</u>! *what did I tell you!*
also <u>doch</u>! *it's true what I said after all!*
eben! *precisely!*
eben <u>nicht</u>! *that's just it: No!*
na/nun ja *oh well, OK*
ich denke/glaube schon *I should think so*

was <u>ist</u> denn? *what's the matter?*
was ist denn hier <u>los</u>? *what's going on here?*
das darf doch nicht <u>wahr</u> sein! *that can't be (true)!*
das ist doch/ja <u>lächerlich</u>! *that's ridiculous!*
das <u>ist</u> es ja/eben! *that's just it, that's just what I mean*

ja, was ich sagen wollte, ...   *by the way, what I wanted to say . . .*
mal <u>sehen</u>   *we'll just have to (wait and) see*
das wird schon stimmen   *I'm (pretty) sure that's right*

so <u>ist</u> es eben   *that's just how it is*
es wird schon gehen/werden   *I'm (pretty) sure it'll work out*
das habe ich mir (auch) schon gedacht   *that's just what I figured (too)*

Übersicht

PARTICLES

Particle	Examples
aber	Das ist **aber** schön!
also	Du kommst **also?** **Also,** was machen wir nun?
auch	So viel kostet das ja **auch** nicht. Bist du **auch** sicher ?
denn	Was machst du **denn?**
doch	Das weißt du **doch!** Das ist **doch** nicht so schlecht. Kommst du nicht? —**Doch!**
eben	So ist es **eben.** Man muss **eben** warten.
eigentlich	Weißt du **eigentlich,** wann der Film beginnt?
halt	Ich möchte **halt** wissen, ob das stimmt oder nicht.
ja	Das denke ich **ja** auch. Das ist **ja** das Problem.
mal	Versuchen Sie es doch **mal!**
nun	So ist es **nun** mal.
nur/bloß	Wo warst du **nur?** Mach das **nur/bloß** nicht!
schon	Ja, **schon,** aber ... Setz dich **schon!**
überhaupt	Ich verstehe dich **überhaupt** nicht! Man soll **überhaupt** mehr zuhören und weniger reden.
vielleicht	Das war **vielleicht** dumm!
wohl	Das kann man **wohl** sagen.
zwar	Es ist **zwar** ziemlich alt, aber noch ganz gut. Ich will mein Geld zurück, und **zwar** sofort!

Reference
Section

Appendix 1
FORMATS FOR WRITTEN COMMUNICATION

Written communication comprises an increasingly wide range of styles, formats, and media—from tweets and Facebook wall-postings to journalistic blogs and formal business letters. The nature of these various media and registers makes it difficult to provide anything like a "correct" format or style. In the case of the formal business letter it is still possible to provide a model, since the format of such letters follows a formula that has changed relatively little in recent years. But at the other end of the spectrum, as in the case of texting or e-mail, the formats are more individualized and malleable, so that any guidelines must be taken as just that—guidelines, not a prescription. What follows is information pertaining to three modes of written personal communication, moving from informal to formal modes of writing, with information tailored to the media and register typical of each one.

A. Social networking sites

German speakers are connected on Facebook and LinkedIn, as one might expect, but also by means of more "local" social networking media such as Xing and Lokalisten. There's no particular "format" for messages posted on these sites, of course, but it helps to be familiar with the vocabulary that comes into play for users. Verb forms are included below for words borrowed directly from English.

auf [Facebook] sein   *to be on [Facebook]*
bei [Facebook] befreundet sein   *to be friends on [Facebook]*
(das) Mitglied von LinkedIn sein   *to be a member of LinkedIn*
der/das Link, -s verlinken   *link; to link (to)*
ein Foto taggen (taggte, getaggt)/markieren   *to tag a photo (be tagged)*
an·schubsen/zurück·schubsen   *to poke/to poke back*
an/auf die Pinnwand (*wall*) schreiben   *to write on a "wall"*
ein Foto hoch·laden/kopieren   *to upload/copy a photo*
eine Nachricht verschicken   *to send a message*

Here are a few additional terms pertaining to various kinds of postings and personal media.

das/der Blog, -s/das/der Mikro-Blog   *blog*
bloggen (bloggte, hat gebloggt)   *to blog*
chatten (chattete, hat gechattet)   *to chat online*
simsen (simste, hat gesimst)   *to send an SMS*
simsen (simste, hat gesimst)
texten (textete, hat getextet)   } *to text (via cell- or smart-phone)*
SMS senden (sendete, hat gesendet)
twittern (twitterte, hat getwittert)   *to send a message via Twitter*
sich vernetzen (vernetzte, hat vernetzt)   *to get connected via networking sites*

In these and related contexts (e.g., wall-posting, cell phone texting, instant messaging, etc.), the language used is characterized (as in English) by very casual regard for standard German spelling and punctuation, so that nouns are not capitalized, and abbreviations and phonetic shortcuts are common.[1]

B. E-mail

The level of formality in a German e-mail (**die E-Mail, -s**) is signaled immediately by the language used for the salutation, which should be consistent with the language used in the closing. Here are some guidelines for beginning and ending e-mail messages on various levels of formality.

1. Very informal (close friend, schoolmate, etc.)

COMMON SALUTATIONS:

Hi [*first name of addressee(s)*]!
Hey [*first name of addressee(s)*]!

[*message*]

SAMPLE CLOSINGS:

Ciao!
Mach's gut!
Bis dann!

[*your name*]

---

[1]Texting and e-mail abbreviations go in and out of style faster than the blink of an eye, but here's a current sampling:

3n - nie, niemals, nirgendwo (*no way in the world, never, impossible*)
BBB = Bis bald, Baby (*See you later, baby*)
fg = fett grins (*big fat grin*)/frech grins (*sassy grin*)
GN8 = Gute Nacht (*good night*)
G&K= Gruß und Kuss (*greeting and a kiss*)
lamito = Lache mich tot (*I'm dying laughing*)
ZuMioZuDi = zu mir oder zu dir (*my place or yours*)

2. Informal (family, older acquaintances)

COMMON SALUTATIONS:

```
Hallo [first name of addressee(s)]!/,²
Liebe Frau Schwarzenberger!/, (female)
Lieber Markus!/, (male)
Liebe Monika, lieber Frank!/, (two addressees, female and male)
Liebe Freunde!/, (plural)

[message]
```

SAMPLE CLOSINGS:

```
Beste Grüße!
Herzliche Grüße!
Liebe Grüße!

[your name]
```

---

3. For a formal e-mail (say, to contact a professor), titles and styles of address for the salutation are carried over from formal letters, while the date is of course already included in the e-mail address and therefore not repeated.

COMMON SALUTATIONS:

```
Sehr geehrte Frau Prof. Schnickschnack³,
Sehr geehrter Herr Prof. Schnickschnack,

[message]
```

STANDARD CLOSING:

```
Mit freundlichen Grüßen⁴

[your name]
```

---

[2]In contexts where "!/," is listed, either an exclamation point or a comma can be used after the salutation. The exclamation point is less formal and finalizes the salutation line, so that the subsequent message is considered a new sentence and begins with a capitalized first word. By contrast, the comma turns the salutation into an introductory phrase joined with the following sentence, so that the message continues with no capital letter on the first word.

[3]Here's a bit of sociolinguistic advice: No matter how informally you might address a professor via e-mail in a North American context ("Hi, Prof. Schnickschnack!"), this casual tone should be avoided in Germany, Switzerland, and Austria unless expressly encouraged.

[4]**Mit freundlichen Grüßen:** No punctuation follows this phrase when used as a closing.

C. Letters

1. In all but the most formal correspondence, the salutation usually consists of **Liebe(r)** ____, and the closing is chosen from a range of relatively informal to formal registers.

```
                                    Berlin, (den) 15. Januar 20...
                                    OR:
                                    Berlin, 15.1.20...
```

COMMON SALUTATIONS:

```
Liebe Frau Schwarzenberger,
Lieber Herr Schwarzenberger
Lieber Markus,
Liebe Monika, lieber Frank,(two addressees, female and male)
Liebe Freunde,
```

[*message*]

SAMPLE CLOSINGS:

| *Informal* | Herzlichst |
| | deine/eure |

| *More formal* | Herzliche Grüße |
| | dein/euer |

| *Most formal* | Mit freundlichen Grüßen |

---

2. In formal business correspondence, the headings, salutation and closing are arranged (and worded) as shown below. (If the sender is a business, the sender's information is normally already printed on letterhead.)

SENDER:

```
Andrea Möller
Ainmillerstraße 5
80801 München
(optional: email address/telephone number of sender)
```

DATE:
8. November 20…

ADDRESSEE:
(An)
Frau/Herrn
S. Markstädter
Süddeutsche Zeitung
Hultschiner Straße 8
81677 München
[D-81677 München *if sent from outside Germany*]

TOPIC:
Ihre Anfrage *(a single word or short phrase describing the subject of the letter)*

POSSIBLE SALUTATIONS:
Sehr geehrte Damen und Herren,

Sehr geehrte Frau (Dr.) Markstädter,

Sehr geehrter Herr (Dr.) Markstädter,

[all titles included]

[message]

STANDARD CLOSING:
Mit freundlichen Grüßen

[your name, with any titles included]

3. Note the following points regarding letters:

- In German dates, the day always precedes the month, and there is no comma between the month and the year.

- In addresses, the house number follows the street name.

- The title **Herrn** is an accusative object of the preposition **an.** The accusative form is retained in addresses even if **an** is omitted.

- The **D** before the postal code stands for Germany. Austria uses **A,** and Switzerland uses **CH.**

- Salutations in letters, being relatively formal, are normally followed by a comma rather than an exclamation point.

- There is no punctuation after the closing.

- There are no indentations until the closing, which may be indented or aligned with the left margin.

Appendix 2

SPELLING, CAPITALIZATION, AND PUNCTUATION: *RECHTSCHREIBREFORM* 2006

Beginning with the third edition of the *Handbuch zur deutschen Grammatik,* all explanations and examples have reflected the new rules for spelling, capitalization, and punctuation laid out in the **Rechtschreibreform** of 1996. That reform was conceived as a process that would continue through a transitional period until 2004, when a commission would decide which of the new rules to maintain on a permanent basis, and which should be revoked or amended. The "reform of the reform" that took place as planned in 2004 led to changes in a substantial number of the new rules, most often by returning to pre-1996 guidelines. But two years later, another commission was convened to "reform the reform" yet again—for the last time, it was hoped—and it is this set of rules, which went into effect officially on August 1, 2006, that now dictates conventions for spelling, capitalization, and punctuation in German, including their appearance in this edition of the *Handbuch*.

The information below is not meant to provide exhaustive coverage of the final reform, but rather to outline the basic categories of change in spelling (including capitalization) and punctuation that have been affected by the entire series of reforms. It focuses in particular on the "reform of the reforms" that occurred between 2004 and 2006—in other words, on the changes that may be new to teachers and students who are familiar with the initial 1996 reform but not with developments since then. In the examples below, this multi-year focus is indicated by the headings *pre-1996, 1996–2006,* and *post-2006,* showing rules as they existed before the reform process began, during the transitional period, and as they now stand. Changes made in 1996 and still in force will be shown under the headings *pre-1996* and *post-1996* to indicate that the rules adopted in the initial reform are still considered authoritative.

A. Spelling

1. Probably the most noticeable change initiated by the 1996 reform is the use of **ss** instead of **ß** in certain contexts. The new rule is simple: Use **ss** following short vowels and **ß** following long vowels and diphthongs. (Previously, **ß** was used after some short vowels as well as long.)

PRE-1996	POST-1996
Ich muß das lesen.	Ich **muss** das lessen.
Meinst du, daß es stimmt?	Meinst du, **dass** es stimmt?
Warum ißt du so wenig?	Warum **isst** du so wenig?

2. Where multiple consonants or clusters were sometimes dropped in compound words, the new rules stipulate that both words be written in their entirety. A hyphen may be used to make some compound nouns easier to read.

PRE-1996	POST-1996
selbständig (selbst + ständig)	selbstständig
Schiffahrt (Schiff + Fahrt)	Schifffahrt
Seelefant (See +Elefant)	Seeelefant/See-Elefant

3. The 1996/2004 reforms acknowledged that foreign words pass through phases of integration before they are felt to be "German" and require German spelling. At first, the foreign form feels more appropriate (**Telephon**); then the community begins adapting it by writing it both ways (**Telephon/Telefon**); and finally, when its "foreignness" is no longer felt, the local form predominates (**Telefon**). Hence the rules allow for the non-German and German versions of foreign-origin words that are felt to be in transition, such as **Joghurt/Jogurt; Portemonnaie/Portmonee;** and **Thunfisch/Tunfisch.** But now that **Telefon, Foto** and **fotografieren** are more or less fully integrated into everyday speech, the German spelling (with **f**) is now preferred over **ph.**

The 1996/2004 reforms also recognized that foreign words used in specific contexts, such as scientific or technical terms, and foreign words used internationally have a "specialized" feel and should therefore retain their foreign spelling to acknowledge their origin (e.g., Atmos**ph**äre, **J**ournalist, **Ph**iloso**ph**ie, Re**cy**cling, **Th**eater).

PRE-1996	1996–2006	POST-2006
Exposé	Exposee	**Exposé/Exposee**
Potential	Potenzial	**Potential/Potenzial**
Joghurt	Jogurt	**Joghurt/Jogurt**

B. Capitalization

1. The pre-1996 rule stated that formal pronouns of address (including possessive pronouns) should always be capitalized (**Sie/Ihnen/Ihr-**), and that **du** and **ihr** (and related forms) should be capitalized only in written correspondence. The 1996 reform maintained capitalization for all formal pronouns and possessive adjectives in all written contexts, as before, but called for uniformly lowercase pronouns for **du** and **ihr** (and related forms), including their use in correspondence. The 2006 reform maintains the capitalization rules for formal pronouns and possessive adjectives, but allows for either lower- or uppercase for familiar pronouns and possessive adjectives in correspondence: **Lieber Lukas, wie geht es dir/Dir? Und deiner/Deiner Familie?**

2. Following the 1996 reform, times of day following adverbs such as **gestern** or **heute** are now capitalized. In conjunction with days of the week, they now join with the day to form one word.

PRE-1996	POST-1996
heute abend	heute **Abend**
gestern nachmittag	gestern **Nachmittag**
Dienstag morgen	**Dienstagmorgen**

3. Adjectives that take on the function of a noun are likewise uniformly capitalized.

PRE-1996	POST-1996
Sie war die erste an Bord.	Sie war die **Erste** an Bord.
Ist das auf deutsch?	Ist das auf **Deutsch?**
Es war interessant für jung und alt.	Es war interessant für **Jung** und **Alt.**
Wir waren den ganzen Tag im freien *(outside)*.	Wir waren den ganzen Tag im **Freien** *(outside)*.

The only exceptions to this rule are **ander-**, **ein-**, **viel,** and **wenig.**[1]

Die **einen** denken das, die **anderen** denken das nicht.
Nur **wenige** verstehen das.
Das haben **viele** erlebt.

4. Nouns that are used in specific contexts as other parts of speech, such as adjectives, are once again written in lowercase to reflect that function. **Feind,** for example, is a noun meaning *enemy*; but **jemandem feind sein** means *to be at enmity with someone*. **Klasse** can mean *a class*, but also *very nice/good*.

PRE-1996	1996–2006	POST-2006
Er war mir feind.	... Feind.	... **feind.**
Alles war klasse.	... Klasse.	... **klasse.**

5. A special (and frequently used) application of this change is the German equivalent of *to be right/wrong*, which was altered in 1996, but now can be written either in upper- or lowercase.

PRE-1996	1996–2006	POST-2006
Sie hat recht *(she's right)*.	... Recht.	... **recht/Recht.**
Du hattest unrecht *(you were wrong)*.	... Unrecht.	... **unrecht/Unrecht.**

C. Words written together or separated

1. The overarching tendency of the 1996 reform with regard to compound words was to separate elements that had once been written together. Where the pre-1996 rules had once called for **rad·fahren** *(to ride a bicycle)* to be treated as a separable-prefix verb, in 1996 it became **Rad fahren** (and with the separation, in cases like this, came capitalization of the stand-alone noun). This was valid not only for noun-verb combinations, but also adjective-verb and verb-verb combinations (**frei·sprechen** ⟶ **frei sprechen; kennen·lernen** ⟶ **kennen lernen**) and adverb-adjective combinations such as **alleingültig** ⟶ **allein gültig** and **halbnackt** ⟶ **halb nackt.**

There was considerable protest from many quarters following this change, in large measure because it obliterated distinctions that had once been possible. How could

---

[1]While words like **viel-** and **ander-** are normally not capitalized, this can vary in practice. For example, the film mentioned throughout Chapter 5 (English: *The Lives of Others*), shows the title **Das Leben der Anderen** on movie posters and online references , while the published screenplay of the book is entitled **Das Leben der anderen** (Suhrkamp 2007).

one tell the difference, for example, between **frei sprechen** (*to acquit someone*) and **frei sprechen** (*to speak freely*), now that the fused form **freisprechen** (*to acquit someone*) was no longer available?

The 2006 reform addressed this issue in detail. Although it is not possible to cite all the resulting changes here, the general result is to have words that create a particular meaning through their fusion—a meaning other than that of the separate elements—to be treated (again) as a single word.

2. In noun-verb combinations where the noun's literal meaning is eclipsed by a new meaning in tandem with the verb, the noun is considered part of that verb, and is treated as a prefix, with no capitalization.

PRE-1996	1996–2006	POST-2006
eis·laufen (*to ice-skate*)	Eis laufen	**eis·laufen**
kopf·stehen (*to stand on one's head*)	Kopf stehen	**kopf·stehen**
leid·tun (*to be sorry*)	Leid tun	**leid·tun**

But in cases where the noun's meaning is largely retained, both versions are now acceptable.

PRE-1996	1996–2006	POST-2006
acht·geben (*to give/pay attention*)	Acht geben	**acht/Acht geben**
halt·machen (*to stop*)	Halt machen	**halt/Halt machen**

3. This new approach also applies to other words in combination with verbs.

PRE-1996	1996–2006	POST-2006
fertig·machen (*to wear down*)	fertig machen	**fertig·machen**
nahe·bringen (*to explain*)	nahe bringen	**nahe·bringen**
schwer·fallen (*to be difficult*)	schwer fallen	**schwer·fallen**

4. In certain adverb-adjective combinations, the 2004 reform allowed for more latitude than before, but the 2006 reform once again requires that the words be written together.

PRE-1996	1996–2006	POST-2006
hochgebildet (*highly educated*)	hochgebildet/hoch gebildet	**hochgebildet**
wohlverdient (*well-deserved*)	wohlverdient/wohl verdient	**wohlverdient**

D. Comma usage

1. In most respects, the rules for comma use have not changed in any of these reforms. Commas are still used in these instances:

■ To separate subordinate clauses from main clauses.

Weil du dich verspätet hast, haben wir den Zug verpasst!

■ To set off clauses linked by the coordinating conjunctions **denn, aber,** and **sondern.**

Katja wollte auf der Party bleiben, aber ich war wirklich zu müde dazu.

■ To set off appositions.

Thomas Bernhard, ein bekannter Autor, hielt gestern Abend einen Vortrag.

■ In place of a decimal point.

60,5%

REMEMBER: Commas are NOT used to set off adverbial sentence beginnings, as in English.

Leider habe ich meinen Führerschein nicht mit.	*Unfortunately, I don't have my driver's license with me.*

2. Commas were formerly required prior to clauses beginning with **und** and **oder,** but now they are optional, depending on readability.

PRE-1996

Michele liest ein Buch, und Stephan sieht fern.

POST-1996

Michele liest ein Buch und Stephan sieht fern.

BUT:

Ich denke oft an dich, und die Kinder fragen oft nach dir.

3. Commas were previously used in all cases to separate main clauses from infinitive clauses containing anything more than **zu** + infinitive. The rules have been relaxed to make these commas optional in some cases, depending on readability, but commas are still required to set off all infinitive clauses beginning with **um, ohne,** and **(an)statt,** regardless of readability.

PRE-1996

Ich habe keine Lust, ins Kino zu gehen.

Sie ist da, um uns zu helfen.

Er hat vor, ein Auto zu kaufen.

POST-1996

Ich habe keine Lust(,) ins Kino zu gehen.

Sie ist da, um uns zu helfen.

Er hat vor, ein Auto zu kaufen.
(**vor ein Auto** *could be misread as a prepositional phrase.*)

A comma is still required when the main clause includes an element that anticipates the infinitive clause, such as a **da**-compound or **es** (see 20.2–3).

E. Other punctuation marks

Other punctuation rules have been unchanged by the reforms.

1. A period (**der Punkt, -e**) is used with numerals to indicate an ordinal number + ending (see R.4.1.B).

den 5. Juli (spoken: den fünften Juli)	*the fifth of July*

2. An exclamation point (**das Ausrufezeichen, -**) is occasionally used after a salutation in a letter. It is also used after emphatic imperatives (see 23.2.B).

3. A question mark (**das Fragezeichen, -**) is used after questions, as in English.

4. Direct quotations (see 22.1) are preceded by a colon **(der Doppelpunkt, -e)** and enclosed by quotation marks **(die Anführungszeichen** *[pl.]***)**. In print and in handwriting, the initial quotation mark appears at the bottom of the line, while the final quotation mark is at the top of the line. The final quotation mark precedes a comma, but it follows a period.

Sisyphus sagte: „Es ist hoffnungslos."	*Sisyphus said, "It is hopeless."*
„Ich komme nicht", sagte sie.	*"I am not coming," she said.*

5. A hyphen **(der Bindestrich, -e)** is used to divide words at the end of a line. It is also used to indicate an omitted element common to two compound nouns in a pair.

eine Nacht- und Nebelaktion (= eine Nachtaktion und eine Nebelaktion)	*a covert operation* (lit. *a night and fog operation*)
Stadt- und Landbewohner (= Stadtbewohner und Landbewohner)	*city and country dwellers*

6. Semicolons **(das Semikolon)** are relatively rare, but can be used, as in English, to separate long elements in a series or to join main clauses.

In summary

It must be stressed that the topics and examples above provide only the most general overview of the details covered in the reforms from 1996 through 2006. If you are unsure whether a word should be written together or apart (is it **hoch begabt or hochbegabt? daran setzen** or **daransetzen?**) or whether certain nouns should be capitalized or not (**danksagen** or **Dank sagen?**), then you should consult the latest edition of *Duden: Die deutsche Rechtschreibung* (Dudenverlag) or www.duden.de.

Appendix 3
STRONG AND IRREGULAR WEAK VERBS

The irregular third-person singular forms are indicated in parentheses after the infinitive. Verbs requiring the auxiliary **sein** rather than **haben** are indicated by the word **ist** before the past participle. Past participles preceded by **ist/hat** are normally intransitive, but they can be used transitively with the auxiliary **haben**. For verbs that have multiple forms for the simple past, past participle, or subjunctive, the preferred form appears first.

Infinitive (3rd. pers. sing.)	Simple past	Past participle	Subjunctive II	Meaning
backen (bäckt)	backte/buk	gebacken	büke	to bake
befehlen (befiehlt)	befahl	befohlen	befähle/ beföhle	to command
beginnen	begann	begonnen	begänne/ begönne	to begin
beißen	biss	gebissen	bisse	to bite
bestechen (besticht)	bestach	bestochen	bestäche	to bribe, corrupt
bestreiten	bestritt	bestritten	bestritte	to contest, challenge
betrügen	betrog	betrogen	betröge	to deceive, cheat
beweisen	bewies	bewiesen	bewiese	to prove
biegen	bog	gebogen	böge	to bend
bieten	bot	geboten	böte	to offer
binden	band	gebunden	bände	to bind, tie
bitten	bat	gebeten	bäte	to ask (for), request
blasen (bläst)	blies	geblasen	bliese	to blow
bleiben	blieb	ist geblieben	bliebe	to stay, remain
braten (brät)	briet	gebraten	briete	to roast, fry
brechen (bricht)	brach	gebrochen	bräche	to break
brennen	brannte	gebrannt	brennte	to burn
bringen	brachte	gebracht	brächte	to bring
denken	dachte	gedacht	dächte	to think
dringen	drang	ist gedrungen	dränge	to penetrate, surge into
empfangen (empfängt)	empfing	empfangen	empfinge	to receive
empfehlen (empfiehlt)	empfahl	empfohlen	empfähle/ empföhle	to recommend
empfinden	empfand	empfunden	empfände	to feel

Infinitive (3rd. pers. sing.)	Simple past	Past participle	Subjunctive II	Meaning
erlöschen (erlischt)	erlosch	ist erloschen	erlösche	to go out, become extinguished
erschrecken (erschrickt)	erschrak	ist erschrocken	erschräke	to be startled
essen (isst)	aß	gegessen	äße	to eat
fahren (fährt)	fuhr	ist/hat gefahren	führe	to travel; to drive
fallen (fällt)	fiel	ist gefallen	fiele	to fall
fangen (fängt)	fing	gefangen	finge	to catch
finden	fand	gefunden	fände	to find
fliegen	flog	ist/hat geflogen	flöge	to fly
fliehen	floh	ist geflohen	flöhe	to flee
fließen	floss	ist geflossen	flösse	to flow
fressen (frisst)	fraß	gefressen	fräße	to eat (of animals)
frieren	fror	gefroren	fröre	to freeze, be cold
gebären (gebiert)	gebar	geboren	gebäre	to give birth
geben (gibt)	gab	gegeben	gäbe	to give
gehen	ging	ist gegangen	ginge	to go, walk
gelingen	gelang	ist gelungen	gelänge	to succeed
gelten (gilt)	galt	gegolten	gälte/gölte	to be valid
genießen	genoss	genossen	genösse	to enjoy
geraten (gerät)	geriet	geraten	geriete	to fall into, get into
geschehen (geschieht)	geschah	ist geschehen	geschähe	to happen
gewinnen	gewann	gewonnen	gewänne/ gewönne	to win
gießen	goss	gegossen	gösse	to pour
gleichen	glich	geglichen	gliche	to resemble; to equal
gleiten	glitt	ist geglitten	glitte	to glide, slide
graben (gräbt)	grub	gegraben	grübe	to dig
greifen	griff	gegriffen	griffe	to grip, grab, seize
haben (hat)	hatte	gehabt	hätte	to have
halten (hält)	hielt	gehalten	hielte	to hold; to stop
hängen	hing	gehangen	hinge	to hang (intransitive)
hauen	hieb; haute	gehauen	hiebe	to hew, cut; to hit
heben	hob	gehoben	höbe	to lift
heißen	hieß	geheißen	hieße	to be called; to bid (do)
helfen (hilft)	half	geholfen	hülfe	to help
kennen	kannte	gekannt	kennte	to know, be acquainted with

Infinitive (3rd. pers. sing.)	Simple past	Past participle	Subjunctive II	Meaning
klingen	klang	geklungen	klänge	to sound
kneifen	kniff	gekniffen	kniffe	to pinch
kommen	kam	ist gekommen	käme	to come
kriechen	kroch	ist gekrochen	kröche	to crawl
laden (lädt)	lud	geladen	lüde	to load
lassen (lässt)	ließ	gelassen	ließe	to let, leave
laufen (läuft)	lief	ist gelaufen	liefe	to run, walk
leiden	litt	gelitten	litte	to suffer
leihen	lieh	geliehen	liehe	to lend
lesen (liest)	las	gelesen	läse	to read
liegen	lag	gelegen	läge	to lie, be situated
lügen	log	gelogen	löge	to (tell a) lie
meiden	mied	gemieden	miede	to avoid
messen (misst)	maß	gemessen	mäße	to measure
nehmen (nimmt)	nahm	genommen	nähme	to take
nennen	nannte	genannt	nennte	to name, call
pfeifen	pfiff	gepfiffen	pfiffe	to whistle
raten (rät)	riet	geraten	riete	to advise; to (take a) guess
reiben	rieb	gerieben	riebe	to rub
reißen	riss	ist gerissen	risse	to tear
reiten	ritt	ist/hat geritten	ritte	to ride (on an animal)
rennen	rannte	ist gerannt	rennte	to run
riechen	roch	gerochen	röche	to smell
rinnen	rann	ist geronnen	ränne/rönne	to run, flow, trickle
rufen	rief	gerufen	riefe	to call
saufen (säuft)	soff	gesoffen	söffe	to drink (of animals)
saugen	saugte/sog	gesaugt/gesogen	söge	to suck
schaffen	schuf	geschaffen	schüfe	to create
	schaffte	geschafft	schaffte	to do, accomplish
scheiden	schied	geschieden	schiede	to separate
scheinen	schien	geschienen	schiene	to shine; to seem
schelten (schilt)	schalt	gescholten	schölte	to scold
schieben	schob	geschoben	schöbe	to shove, push
schießen	schoss	geschossen	schösse	to shoot
schlafen (schläft)	schlief	geschlafen	schliefe	to sleep
schlagen (schlägt)	schlug	geschlagen	schlüge	to strike, hit, beat
schleichen	schlich	ist geschlichen	schliche	to creep, sneak
schließen	schloss	geschlossen	schlösse	to close
schmeißen	schmiss	geschmissen	schmisse	to fling, hurl
schmelzen (schmilzt)	schmolz	ist/hat geschmolzen	schmölze	to melt

Infinitive (3rd. pers. sing.)	Simple past	Past participle	Subjunctive II	Meaning
schneiden	schnitt	geschnitten	schnitte	*to cut*
schreiben	schrieb	geschrieben	schriebe	*to write*
schreien	schrie	geschrien	schriee	*to shout, scream*
schreiten	schritt	ist geschritten	schritte	*to stride*
schweigen	schwieg	geschwiegen	schwiege	*to be silent*
schwellen (schwillt)	schwoll	ist geschwollen	schwölle	*to swell*
schwimmen	schwamm	hat/ist geschwommen	schwämme/ schwömme	*to swim*
schwingen	schwang	geschwungen	schwänge	*to swing*
schwören	schwor/ schwur	geschworen	schwüre	*to swear, vow*
sehen (sieht)	sah	gesehen	sähe	*to see*
sein (ist)	war	ist gewesen	wäre	*to be*
senden	sandte sendete	gesandt gesendet	sendete	*to send to transmit*
singen	sang	gesungen	sänge	*to sing*
sinken	sank	ist gesunken	sänke	*to sink*
sinnen	sann	gesonnen	sänne/sönne	*to think, reflect; to plot*
sitzen	saß	hat/ist[1] gesessen	säße	*to sit*
spinnen	spann	gesponnen	spänne/spönne	*to spin; to be crazy*
sprechen (spricht)	sprach	gesprochen	spräche	*to speak, talk*
springen	sprang	ist gesprungen	spränge	*to jump*
stechen (sticht)	stach	gestochen	stäche	*to prick, sting*
stehen	stand	hat/ist[1] gestanden	stände/stünde	*to stand*
stehlen (stiehlt)	stahl	gestohlen	stähle/stöhle	*to steal*
steigen	stieg	ist gestiegen	stiege	*to climb, rise*
sterben (stirbt)	starb	ist gestorben	stürbe	*to die*
stinken	stank	gestunken	stänke	*to stink*
stoßen (stößt)	stieß	gestoßen	stieße	*to push*
streichen	strich	gestrichen	striche	*to stroke; to paint*
streiten	stritt	gestritten	stritte	*to quarrel*
tragen (trägt)	trug	getragen	trüge	*to carry; to wear*
treffen (trifft)	traf	getroffen	träfe	*to meet; to hit (the target)*
treiben	trieb	getrieben	triebe	*to drive (cattle); to pursue (an activity)*

----

[1]The use of **sein** as an auxiliary for **sitzen** and **stehen** is common in southern Germany, Austria, and Switzerland.

Infinitive (3rd. pers. sing.)	Simple past	Past participle	Subjunctive II	Meaning
treten (tritt)	trat	ist/hat getreten	träte	to step, tread; to kick
trinken	trank	getrunken	tränke	to drink
tun	tat	getan	täte	to do
verbergen	verbarg	verborgen	verbärge/ verbürge	to hide, conceal
verderben (verdirbt)	verdarb	verdorben	verdürbe	to spoil
vergessen (vergisst)	vergaß	vergessen	vergäße	to forget
verlieren	verlor	verloren	verlöre	to lose
verschlingen	verschlang	verschlungen	verschlänge	to devour, gobble up
verschwinden	verschwand	ist verschwunden	verschwände	to disappear
verzeihen	verzieh	verziehen	verziehe	to forgive, pardon
wachsen (wächst)	wuchs	ist gewachsen	wüchse	to grow
waschen (wäscht)	wusch	gewaschen	wüsche	to wash
weisen	wies	gewiesen	wiese	to point
wenden	wandte	gewandt	wendete	to turn (towards)
	wendete	gewendet		to turn (i.e., to change direction)
werben (wirbt)	warb	geworben	würbe	to recruit, solicit
werden (wird)	wurde	ist geworden	würde	to become
werfen (wirft)	warf	geworfen	würfe	to throw
wiegen	wog	gewogen	wöge	to weigh
winden	wand	gewunden	wände	to wind, twist
wissen (weiß)	wusste	gewusst	wüsste	to know
ziehen	zog	gezogen	zöge	to pull, draw
		ist gezogen		to go, move
zwingen	zwang	gezwungen	zwänge	to force

German-English Vocabulary

This vocabulary contains all words from the exercises and activities in this text except for pronouns, possessive adjectives, and numbers. Also not included are obvious cognates and words for which the English translation is provided in the text.

- Nouns are listed with their plural endings: **die Auskunft, ⁻e; das Messer, -.**

- The genitive of weak nouns is given in parentheses before the plural: **der Experte, (-n), -n.**

- Adjective nouns are indicated as follows: **der Verwandte (ein Verwandter).**

- Strong and irregular verbs are listed with their principal parts: **tragen (trägt), trug, getragen.** Strong verbs requiring the auxiliary **sein** are indicated by an **ist** before the participle: **kommen, kam, ist gekommen.** Weak verbs requiring the auxiliary **sein** are shown by **(ist)** after the infinitive: **passieren (ist).**

- Separable prefixes are indicated by a raised dot: **ab·drehen.**

- Vowel changes for comparative forms of adjectives are indicated in parentheses: **warm (ä).**

- The following abbreviations are used:

abbrev.	abbreviation	*o.s.*	oneself
acc.	accusative	*part.*	particle
adj.	adjective	*pl.*	plural
adv.	adverb	*prep.*	preposition
coll.	colloquial	*sing.*	singular
coord. conj.	coordinating conjunction	*s.o.*	someone
dat.	dative	*s.th.*	something
fem.	feminine	*sub. conj.*	subordinating conjunction
gen.	genitive		

ab und zu now and then

ab·brechen (bricht ab), brach ab, abgebrochen to break off

ab·brennen, brannte ab, ist/hat abgebrannt to burn down

ab·bringen, brachte ab, abgebracht (von + *dat.*) to divert from, dissuade from

ab·drehen to turn off

der Abend, -e evening; **abends** in the evening(s)

das Abendessen, - evening meal

das Abenteuer, - adventure

aber *(coord. conj.)* but; *(adv.)* however

ab·geben (gibt ab), gab ab, abgegeben to hand in

das Abitur graduation diploma from a German *Gymnasium*

ab·nehmen (nimmt ab), nahm ab, abgenommen to take off, lose weight

ab·reißen, riss ab, abgerissen to tear down

ab·sacken to sink

ab·sagen to cancel, call off; to decline *(an invitation)*

der Abschied, -e departure; **Abschied nehmen** to take one's leave

ab·schließen, schloss ab, abgeschlossen to lock up, shut; to conclude, complete; **hat abgeschlossen** to finish (university study)

ab·schrecken to scare off; to chill with cold water (recipes)

das Abseits (soccer) offsides

die Absicht, -en intention

ab·springen, sprang ab, ist abgesprungen to jump off

ab·steigen, stieg ab, ist abgestiegen to move down, climb down

die Abtönungspartikel, -n modal ("flavoring") particle

ab·trocknen to dry off; dry the dishes

ab·warten to wait *(for something to happen)*

das Affenhirn, -e monkey's brain

ähneln *(dat.)* to resemble

der Akku, -s (rechargeable) battery

aktuell real, of current interest, relevant

all- all

die Allee, -n boulevard

allein alone

allerdings to be sure, by all means

alliiert allied

allmählich gradual(ly)

der Alltag everyday life

alltäglich everyday

die Alpen *(pl.)* the Alps

als when, as; than; **als ob** as if

also thus, so, therefore

alt (ä) old

das Alter age

ältlich elderly

die Altstadt, ¨e old section of a city

amtieren to hold an office

sich amüsieren to have a good time, amuse o.s.

an *(prep. with acc. or dat.)* on *(vertical surface)*, at, to

an·dauern to last, continue

ander- other; **unter anderem** among other things

and(e)rerseits on the other hand

ändern to change *(s.th.)*, modify; **sich ändern** to change

die Änderung, -en change

der Anfang, ¨e beginning; **am Anfang** in the beginning

an·fangen (fängt an), fing an, angefangen to begin, start

anfangs in/at the beginning

an·fassen to touch, take hold of

die Angabe, -n data, figure, statement

an·geben (gibt an), gab an, angegeben to indicate, give *(facts)*; to brag

das Angebot, -e offer, bid

der Angeklagte, -n (ein Angeklagter) defendant; *(fem.)* **die Angeklagte, -n**

angeln to fish

angenehm pleasant, agreeable

angespannt nervous, tense

der Angestellte, -n (ein Angestellter) employee; *(fem.)* **die Angestellte, -n**

an·greifen, griff an, angegriffen to attack

der Angriff, -e attack; **in Angriff nehmen** to tackle, take on

die Angst, ¨e fear

an·halten (hält an), hielt an, angehalten to stop, bring to a stop

an·hören to hear, listen to; **sich** *(dat.)* **etwas an·hören** to listen to s.th.

an·klagen to charge

an·kommen, kam an, ist angekommen to arrive; **an·kommen (auf** + *acc.*) to depend upon; **es kommt darauf an** it (all) depends

an·kreuzen to mark (a box or line) with an "x"; check off

an·lügen, log an, angelogen to lie (to)

an·machen to turn on (e.g., a light)

anmutend seeming

die Annonce, -n ad, announcement (newspaper)

der Anorak, -s parka

an·probieren to try on

an·reden to address, speak to

an·regen to encourage, prompt

an·rufen, rief an, angerufen to call up, telephone

die Anschaffung, -en purchase, acquisition

an·schalten to switch *or* turn on

der Anschlag, -schläge attack

an·sehen (sieht an), sah an, angesehen to see, look at; **sich** *(dat.)* **etwas an·sehen** to take a look at s.th.

die Ansicht, -en view, opinion

anstatt ... zu instead of (doing); **anstatt dass** instead of (doing)

an·stellen to hire, employ, sign on

anstrengend stressful, demanding

die Antwort, -en answer

antworten (auf + *acc.*) to answer

die Anweisung, -en instruction, direction

die Anwendung, -en application, use

an·ziehen, zog an, angezogen to dress; **sich an·ziehen** to get dressed

der Apfel, ¨ apple

die Arbeit, -en work, job

arbeiten to work

der Arbeiter, - worker; *(fem.)* **die Arbeiterin, -nen**

arbeitsam diligent, hardworking

das Arbeitsamt, ¨er employment office

die Arbeitskraft, ¨e worker; manpower

der Arbeitslohn, ¨e wage

die Arbeitsstelle, -n working place, job

der Arbeitstisch, -e desk

die Arbeitsweise, -n method of working

die Arche, -n ark

ärgern to annoy; **sich ärgern (über** + *acc.*) to be angry or annoyed with/ about

arm (ä) poor

die Armut poverty

die Art, -en type, kind

der Artikel, - article (grammatical; written)

der Arzt, ¨e doctor, physician; *(fem.)* **die Ärztin, -nen**

das Atomkraftwerk, -e nuclear power plant

die Atomwaffe, -n atomic weapon

auch too, also; even; **auch wenn** even if

auf *(prep. with acc. or dat.)* on *(horizontal surface)*, upon, at; **auf einmal** suddenly; **auf immer** forever, for good

auf·fordern to call upon; **zum Tanzen auf·fordern** to ask to dance

auf·fressen (frisst auf), fraß auf, aufgefressen to eat up *(of beasts)*, devour

die Aufgabe, -n assignment, task

auf·gehen, ging auf, ist aufgegangen to rise

auf·halten (hält auf), hielt auf, aufgehalten to stop, halt; to detain, delay; **sich auf·halten** to stay, spend time

auf·hören to stop, cease

auf·knöpfen to unbutton

das Aufkommen rise

auf·legen to put *or* lay on

auf·machen to open

die Aufmerksamkeit, -en attention

auf·passen to watch out, pay attention

auf·räumen to clean *or* tidy up

die Aufrichtigkeit (no pl.) sincerity

auf·rufen, rief auf, aufgerufen to exhort, call upon, call up

der Aufsatz, ∸e composition

auf·schneiden, schnitt auf, aufgeschnitten to cut open

auf·schreiben, schrieb auf, aufgeschrieben to write *or* jot down

auf·stehen, stand auf, ist aufgestanden to get up, stand up

auf·stellen to put *or* set up

der Auftrag, -träge commission

auf·wachen to wake up, awaken

auf·wachsen (wächst auf), wuchs auf, ist aufgewachsen to grow up

die Aufzeichnung, -en drawing

der Augenblick, -e moment

aus *(prep. with dat.)* out, out of, from

die Ausarbeitung completion, development

die Ausbeutung exploitation

aus·brechen (bricht aus), brach aus, ist ausgebrochen to break out

der Ausdruck, ∸e expression; **zum Ausdruck bringen** to express

aus·drücken to express

der Ausflug, ∸e excursion; **einen Ausflug machen** to take an excursion

aus·führen to carry out, undertake

ausführlich in detail, detailed

der Ausgang, -gänge exit; outcome

aus·geben (gibt aus), gab aus, ausgegeben to spend *(money)*

aus·gehen, ging aus, ist ausgegangen to go out

die Auskunft, ∸e information

das Ausland abroad

der Ausländer, - foreigner; *(fem.)* **die Ausländerin, -nen**

aus·lassen, ließ sich … aus, hat sich ausgelassen to rant and rave

aus·leihen, lieh aus, ausgeliehen to borrow; to lend (out)

aus·machen to turn off

aus·rechnen to calculate, figure out

die Ausrede, -n excuse

aus·reisen (ist) to leave *(a country)*

sich aus·ruhen to rest, take a rest

die Ausrüstung, -en outfit, equipment

die Aussage, -n statement

aus·schalten to switch *or* turn off

aus·schauen to look (like)

aus·sehen (sieht aus), sah aus, ausgesehen to look (like), appear

außer *(prep. with dat.)* except for, besides

außerdem moreover, in addition

außerhalb *(prep. with gen.)* outside of

äußern to express; **sich äußern** to express oneself *or* one's opinion

äußerst extremely

die Aussicht, -en prospect

aus·sprechen (spricht aus), sprach aus, ausgesprochen to express, enunciate

aus·steigen, stieg aus, ist ausgestiegen to climb out, get out

aus·strahlen to broadcast

aus·suchen to seek out, look for

aus·tauschen to exchange

aus·üben to practice (a trade, profession, or activity)

der Auswanderer, - emigrant

aus·weichen, wich aus, ist ausgewichen to get around, avoid

ausweichend evasive

der Ausweis, -e identification (ID)

auswendig by heart, by memory

aus·zeichnen to honor, award a prize to s.o.

die Auszeichnung, -en award, distinction

aus·ziehen, zog aus, ausgezogen to undress (s.o.); (with **sein**) to move out; **sich aus·ziehen** to get undressed

die Autobahn, -en expressway, superhighway

das Autogramm, -e autograph

der Autoreifen, - automobile tire

die Autowerkstatt, ∸en automobile service shop

der Bach, ∸e brook, small stream

backen (bäckt), buk (backte), gebacken to bake

der Backofen, ∸ oven

baden to bathe; **baden gehen** to go swimming

das Baggerschiff, -e dredging boat

die Bahn, -en track; railroad; **per Bahn** by rail

der Bahnhof, ∸e train station

balanciert balanced

bald (comparative: **eher**) soon

der Balkon balcony

der Ball, ∸e ball

der Band, ∸e volume; **das Band, ∸er** tape, ribbon

die Bank, ∸e bank; **die Bank, ∸e** bench

das Bankkonto, -konten bank account

basteln to do handicrafts; to putter

der Bau, -ten building

bauen to build, construct

der Bauer, (-n), -n peasant, farmer; *(fem.)* **die Bäuerin, -nen** farmer's wife

der Bauernhof, ∸e farm

der Baum, ∸e tree

der Bauplan, ∸e construction plan

die Baustelle, -n construction site

bayerisch Bavarian

(das) Bayern Bavaria

die Bazille, -n germ

beantworten (+ *acc.*) to answer

die Bearbeitung, -en editing, revision

sich bedanken (bei + *dat.***)** to express one's thanks to

bedauern to regret

die Bedeutung, -en meaning, significance, importance

sich bedienen to use, avail of something (+ *gen.*)

bedürfen, bedarf, bedurft *(gen.)* to need

sich beeilen to hurry

beenden to end, complete, conclude

befahren (befährt), befuhr, befahren to travel *or* drive on *or* along

der Befehl, -e command

sich befinden, befand, befunden to be, to be located

befreien to set free, rescue

befürchten to fear, suspect

begabt talented

begegnen *(dat.)* **(ist)** to meet, come across, encounter

die Begegnung, -en encounter

begehen, beging, begangen to commit

begeistert (von + *dat.)* enthusiastic about

begründen to provide a reason, substantiate

behandeln to deal with, to treat

behaupten to claim, maintain

die Behauptung, -en assertion, claim

die Behörde, -n authority

bei *(prep. with dat.)* by, near, at; while

bei·bringen, brachte bei, beigebracht *(dat.)* to teach, impart knowledge

beid- both

der Beifall, - applause

das Bein, -e leg

das Beispiel, -e example; **zum Beispiel** *(abbrev.* **z.B.)** for example

beißen, biss, gebissen to bite

bei·tragen (trägt bei), trug bei, beigetragen (zu + *dat.)* to contribute to

bekannt familiar, known, well-known

der Bekannte, -n (ein Bekannter) acquaintance; *(fem.)* **die Bekannte, -n**

bekannt geben (gibt bekannt), gab bekannt, bekannt gegeben to announce, make public

bekennen, bekannte, bekannt to confess

bekommen, bekam, bekommen to get, receive

belegen (einen Kurs) to enroll *or* register *(for a course)*

beleuchtet illuminated

beliebt popular

bellen to bark

sich bemächtigen to take control of *(+ gen.)*

bemerken to observe, note

die Bemerkung comment, remark

sich benehmen (benimmt), benahm, benommen to act, behave

benötigen to require, need

die Benotung grading

benutzen to use

das Benzin gasoline

der Bereich, -e district, region; *(topic)* area

bereit (zu + *dat.)* ready for, prepared

bereuen to regret

der Berg, -e mountain

die Bergbahn, -en mountain cable car

das Bergmassiv, -e mountain chain

der Bergschuh, -e climbing boot

der Bericht, -e report

berichten to report

der Beruf, -e profession

beruflich occupational

sich beruhigen to calm down

berühmt famous, renowned

sich beschäftigen (mit + *dat.)* to occupy oneself with

beschäftigt occupied, busy

bescheiden modest

beschreiben, beschrieb, beschrieben to describe

die Beschreibung, -en description

sich beschweren (über + *acc.)* to complain about

beseitigen to remove, put an end to, clear away

der Besen, - broom

besetzen to occupy

besichtigen to view, inspect

die Besichtigung, -en inspection; sightseeing

besiegen to conquer, overcome

besitzen, besaß, besessen to possess, own

der Besitzer, - owner

besonders especially

besser better

bestechen (besticht), bestach, bestochen to bribe

bestehen, bestand, bestanden to remain, exist, pass (a course, test); **bestehen (aus** + *dat.)* to consist of

besteigen, bestieg, bestiegen to ascend, climb (up)

bestellen to order

bestimmt definite; **bestimmter Artikel** definite article

bestreiten, bestritt, bestritten to contest

die Bestürzung, -en dismay, bewilderment

der Besuch, -e visit

besuchen to visit

der Besucher, - visitor

betonen to emphasize, stress

der Betrag, ¨e amount

betreiben, betrieb, betrieben to do, engage in

betreten (betritt), betrat, betreten to walk *or* step on *or* into

der Betrunkene (ein Betrunkener) drunk person; *(fem.)* **die Betrunkene**

sich betten to make a bed for oneself

die Bevölkerung, -en population

bewegen to move (s.o. or s.th.); **sich bewegen** to move, stir

beweisen, bewies, bewiesen to prove

sich bewerben (bewirbt), bewarb, beworben (um + *acc.)* to apply for

die Bewertung, -en evaluation

der Bewohner, - dweller, inhabitant

bewundern to admire

die Bewunderung, -en amazement, admiration

bezahlen to pay for

die Beziehung, -en relationship

bezweifeln to doubt

die Bibel, -n Bible

die Bibliothek, -en library

biegen, bog, gebogen to bend

die Biene, -n bee

der Bierdeckel, - beer coaster

bieten, bot, geboten to offer, bid

das Bild, -er picture

bilden to form, shape, construct; to constitute

die Bildgeschichte, -n picture story

der Bildschirm, -e (monitor) screen

billig cheap

binden, band, gebunden to tie

bis *(prep. with acc.)* until; *(sub. conj.)* until

bisherig prior, previous

bisschen: ein bisschen a bit, a little bit

bissig biting

der Bittbrief, -e letter of request

bitte please; you're welcome *(in response to thanks)*

die Bitte, -n request

blass pale

das Blatt, ¨er leaf; sheet *(of paper)*

blau blue; **blaues Auge** black eye

blau·machen to skip (class, school, work)

bleiben, blieb, ist geblieben to remain, stay

der Bleistift, -e pencil

der Blitzschlag, -schläge lightning bolt

die Blume, -n flower

die **Bluse, -n** blouse
die **Blüte, -n** blossom; blossoming
bluten bleed
der **Bluthochdruck** high blood pressure
der **Boden, ⸚** ground, earth, soil; floor
der **Bodensee** Lake Constance
(*in southern Germany*)
der **Bogen, -** *or* ⸚ bow, arch
die **Bohne, -n** bean
das **Boot, -e** boat
borgen to borrow; to lend
die **Börse, -n** stock exchange; stock
market
böse angry; evil; **böse (auf +** *acc.*)
angry at
die **Bowle, -n** (punch) bowl; punch
der **Brand, ⸚e** fire
das **Brandloch, ⸚er** hole caused by
something burning
brauchen to need; to use; **nicht zu tun
brauchen** to not have to do
die **Brauerei, -en** brewery
braun brown
der **Brei, -** porridge
breit wide, broad
bremsen to brake
brennen, brannte, gebrannt to burn
das **Brettspiel, -e** board game
der **Brief, -e** letter
der **Brieffreund, -e** pen pal; (*fem.*) die
Brieffreundin, -nen
die **Briefmarke, -n** stamp
die **Brieftasche, -n** (men's) wallet
der **Briefträger, -** mail(man); (*fem.*) die
Briefträgerin, -nen
die **Brille, -n** (eye)glasses, (pair of) glasses
der **Bruch, Brüche** break, breakup
die **Brücke, -n** bridge
der **Brunnen, -** fountain, well
das **Buch, ⸚er** book
die **Buchdruckerkunst** art of book
printing
buchen to book
das **Bücherregal, -e** bookcase
die **Buchhandlung, -en** bookstore
der **Buchstabe, -n** letter (*of alphabet*)
buchstabieren to spell
die **Buchung, -en** booking
der **Bundeskanzler** Federal Chancellor
of Germany
das **Bundesland, ⸚er** federal state
der **Bundesstaat, -en** federal state
der **Bürger, -** citizen; (*fem.*) die
Bürgerin, -nen
der **Bürgerkrieg, -e** civil war

der **Bürgermeister, -** mayor; (*fem.*) die
Bürgermeisterin, -nen
das **Büro, -s** office

die **Chance, -n** chance, opportunity
das **Chaos** chaos
chatten to chat online
der **Chef, -s** head, director, manager;
(*fem.*) die **Chefin, -nen**
der **Chinese, -n** Chinese (man); (*fem.*)
die **Chinesin**
der **Chorgesang** choir *or* chorus singing
das **Christentum** Christianity
der **Code** code

da (*adv.*) here, there; then; (*sub. conj.*)
since
dabei while doing (it); at the same time
das **Dach, ⸚er** roof
dafür for it/that; in return
dagegen on the other hand; against it/
that
daher therefore, for that reason
damalig of that time
damals then, in those days
damit (*adv.*) with that; (*sub. conj.*) so that
danach after it/that; afterward(s)
der **Dank** thanks
danken (*dat.*) to thank
daran on it/that
darauf thereafter, thereupon
dar·stellen to portray, depict
darüber about it/that
das **Dasein** existence, being
dass (*sub. conj.*) that
das **Datum, -ten** date (*of time*); (*pl.*)
data, facts
dauern to last, endure
dauernd continual(ly)
davon from *or* about it/that
dazu to it/that, for it/that; in addition
die **Decke, -n** blanket, ceiling, cover
decken to cover; **den Tisch decken** to
set the table
denkbar thinkable
denken, dachte, gedacht to think
die **Denkweite** expansive thought/
thinking

denn for, because
dennoch nevertheless
dergleichen the like
derselb- the same
deshalb therefore, for that reason
deswegen therefore, for that reason
deuten to interpret, explain
deutlich clear, distinct
deutsch German; **auf Deutsch** in
German
die **Deutschstunde, -n** German class
Diät halten to be/go on a diet
dick fat
der **Dieb, -e** thief
dienen to serve
der **Dienst, -e** service
dies- (*sing.*) this; (*pl.*) these
die **Diktatur, -en** dictatorship
das **Ding, -e** thing
die **Dirne, -n** prostitute
das **Display, -s** (computer) display
doch (*part.*) after all, really; oh, yes
das **Dorf, ⸚er** village
dort there
die **Dose, -n** (metal) can
der **Drache, (-n), -n** dragon
der **Drachen, -** kite
drängen to urge, coax
draußen outside
das **Drehbuch, -bücher** screenplay
dreschen, drosch, gedroschen to thresh;
pummel; fling; flail
dribbeln (soccer/basketball) dribble
dringend urgent, pressing
drücken to push
der **Drucker,-** printer
dumm (ü) stupid
die **Dummheit, -en** stupidity, stupid
thing
die **Dunkelheit** darkness
durch (*prep. with acc.*) through, by
durchaus nicht not at all, by no means
durchblättern (*sep. or insep.*) to page
through
durchdacht thought-out, considered
**durch·fallen, fiel durch, ist
durchgefallen** to fail (a test)
durch·führen to carry out
die **Durchsage, -n** broadcast
announcement
durch·setzen (seinen Willen) to get
one's way
dürfen (darf), durfte, gedurft to be
permitted to, may
(sich) duschen to take a shower

E

eben *(adv. and part.)* just, precisely
ebenso ... wie just as . . . as
echt real, genuine; (slang) really
die Ecke, -n corner
der Eckstoß, -stöße (soccer) corner kick
egal regardless, doesn't matter
ehe *(sub. conj.)* before
die Ehe, -n marriage
ehemalig former, previous
der Ehemann, ⸚er husband
ehrlich honest
das Ei, -er egg
eigen own
eigenartig peculiar, strange, queer
eigentlich actual(ly)
sich eignen to be suited
die Eile haste
ein paar a few
einander one another, each other
einäugig one-eyed
sich *(dat.)* **ein·bilden** to imagine
der Eindruck, ⸚e impression
einfach simple
ein·fallen (fiel ein), ist eingefallen to occur (to)
ein·führen to introduce, initiate
der Eingang, ⸚e entrance
ein·geben, gab ein, eingegeben to enter (a number)
ein·gehen, ging ... ein, ist eingegangen to enter (+ auf) into
die Einheit, -en unity; unit
einig in agreement
einig- *(pl.)* some, a few; **einiges** some things
sich einigen (über + acc.) to agree on
der Einkauf, ⸚e purchase
ein·kaufen to buy, purchase, shop for
die Einkaufstour, -en shopping trip
das Einkaufszentrum, -zentren shopping center
ein·laden (lädt ein), lud ein, eingeladen to invite
die Einladung, -en invitation
ein·leiten to begin, start
die Einleitung, -en introduction
einmal once; **noch einmal** once more
einmalig unique, one-time
ein·pflanzen to plant
sich *(dat.)* **ein·reiben (das Gesicht), rieb ein, eingerieben** to rub s.th. into one's face

ein·reichen to hand in
die Einrichtung, -en layout, setup; furnishings
ein·schlafen (schläft ein), schlief ein, ist eingeschlafen to fall asleep
einst once, one day *(past or future time)*
der Einsturz, ⸚e collapse
ein·treten (tritt ein), trat ein, ist eingetreten to step *or* walk in, enter
die Eintrittskarte, -n (admission) ticket
einverstanden in agreement
ein·wandern to immigrate
der Einwohner, - inhabitant; *(fem.)* **die Einwohnerin, -nen**
der Einwurf, -würfe (soccer) throw-in
ein·zeichnen to mark *or* draw in
ein·ziehen, zog ein, ist eingezogen to move in
einzig only, sole, single
das Eis ice; ice cream
der Eisverkäufer, - ice cream vendor; *(fem.)* **die Eisverkäuferin, -nen**
die Elfe, -n elf; also: **der Elf, -e**
die Eltern *(pl.)* parents
die E-Mail e-mail
empfehlen (empfiehlt), empfahl, empfohlen to recommend
das Ende, -n end; **zu Ende** at *or* to an end, over
endlich finally
die Endung, -en ending *(grammar)*
die Energiesparpolitik energy-saving policy
der Engländer, - Englishman; *(fem.)* **die Engländerin, -nen**
das Enkelkind, -er grandchild
die Enkeltochter, ⸚ granddaughter
entblättern to defoliate
entdecken to discover
die Entdeckung, -en discovery
enthalten (enthält), enthielt, enthalten to contain
enthäuten to peel, take off the outer skin
entkommen, entkam, ist entkommen to escape; to avoid
entlang *(prep. with acc. or dat.)* along
entlassen (entlässt), entließ, entlassen to dismiss, release, fire
entsagen *(dat.)* to renounce, give up
entsalzen to desalinate
(sich) entscheiden, entschied, entschieden to decide *(between options)*, settle, make up one's mind

die Entscheidung, -en decision; **eine Entscheidung treffen** to come to *or* make a decision
sich entschließen, entschloss, entschlossen (zu + dat.) to decide (to do)
entschlossen resolved, determined
der Entschluss, ⸚e decision, resolve; **einen Entschluss fassen** to make a decision
entschuldigen to excuse, pardon; **sich entschuldigen** to excuse o.s.
die Entschuldigung, -en apology, excuse
das Entsetzen fright, horror
sich entsinnen, entsann, entsonnen *(gen.)* to remember, recall
sich entspannen to relax, take it easy
entsprechend accordingly
entstammen (ist) *(dat.)* to be descended from
enttäuscht disappointed
entweder ... oder either . . . or
entwerten to devalue
entwickeln to develop s.th.; **sich entwickeln** to develop
die Entwicklung, -en development
erben to inherit
erblicken to see, catch sight of
die Erbschaft, -en inheritance
das Erdbeben, - earthquake
die Erde earth
sich ereignen to happen, occur, come to pass
das Ereignis, -se event, occurrence
erfahren (erfährt), erfuhr, erfahren to find out, hear, learn; to experience
die Erfahrung, -en (practical) experience
erfinden, erfand, erfunden to invent
die Erfindung, -en invention
der Erfolg, -e success
erfolgreich successful
sich erfreuen *(gen.)* to enjoy, be the beneficiary of
erfrieren, erfror, ist erfroren to freeze to death
erfunden imaginary, made-up
ergänzen to complete
ergeben, ergab, ergeben to result (in)
das Ergebnis, -se result
erhalten (erhält), erhielt, erhalten to receive, get
erhören to hear, answer *or* grant (a request)
sich erinnern (an + acc.) to remember, recall

sich erkälten to catch a cold
die Erkältung, -en cold *(illness)*
erkennen, erkannte, erkannt to recognize, discern
erklären to explain
die Erklärung, -en explanation; declaration
die Erkrankung, -en illness, affliction, disease
sich erkundigen (nach + *dat.***)** to inquire about
erlauben to allow, permit
die Erlaubnis, -se permission
erleben to experience
das Erlebnis, -se *(personal)* experience, event, occurrence
erledigen to take care of
-erlei kinds of
erlernen to learn, acquire
erlogen false, untrue
erlöschen, erlosch, ist erloschen to go out (light, fire)
ermitteln to investigate (a crime)
der Ermittler, - investigator
ermöglichen to make possible
ernten to harvest
erobern to conquer
eröffnen to open up
erraten (errät), erriet, erraten to guess correctly
erreichen to reach, attain
erscheinen, erschien, ist erschienen to appear
erschießen, erschoss, erschossen to shoot *(dead)*
erschlagen (erschlägt), erschlug, erschlagen to slay
erschweren to make more difficult
ersetzen to replace
erst only *(up to now)*; not until
erstaunlich amazing
der Erwachsene, -n (ein Erwachsener) adult; *(fem.)* **die Erwachsene, -n**
erwähnen to mention
Erwärmung (no pl.) warming (up)
erwarten to expect
erwehren to resist (doing) s.th. (+ *gen.*) sich
erweitert expanded
erzählen to tell, narrate
die Erzählskizze, -n narrative outline
die Erzählung, -en narrative, story
die Erziehung, -en upbringing, education
essen (isst), aß, gegessen to eat

der Essig vinegar
etwa approximately, about
etwas something; **etwas anderes** something else
die Eule, -n owl
eventuell possibly, perhaps
ewig eternal

F

fabelhaft fabulous, great
die Fabrik, -en factory
das Fach, ̈er field, subject, specialty
-fach -fold
fahren (fährt), fuhr, ist/hat gefahren to travel, ride; drive
der Fahrer, - driver; *(fem.)* **die Fahrerin, -nen**
das Fahrrad, ̈er bicycle
die Fahrt, -en ride, drive, trip
das Fahrzeug, -e vehicle
das Faktum, -ten fact
der Fall, ̈e case; **auf keinen Fall** by no means, in no case
das Fallbeispiel, -e case study
fallen (fällt), fiel, ist gefallen to fall
fällen to fell *(a tree)*
fällig due
der Fallrückzieher, - (soccer) bicycle kick
falls in case, in the event
der Fallschirm, -e parachute
das Familienmitglied, -er family member
das Familienverhältnis, -se family relationship
der Fan, -s (sports) fan
der Fänger, - catcher
die Farbe, -n color
farbenblind color blind
farbig in color, colorful
faul lazy, indolent; rotten
faxen to send a fax message
die Feder, -n feather; spring
fehlen to be missing, lacking
fehlend missing, lacking
der Fehler, - mistake, error
fehlerfrei error-free
feiern to celebrate
der Feiertag, -e public holiday
die Ferien *(pl.)* vacation
das Feriendorf, ̈er vacation resort
der Ferienort, -e vacation spot *or* village

die Ferienreise, -n vacation trip
die Ferienzeit vacation
das Ferienziel, -e vacation destination
das Fernglas, -gläser pair of binoculars
fern·sehen (sieht fern), sah fern, ferngesehen to watch TV
das Fernsehen television
der Fernseher, - television set
die Fernsehsendung, -en television program
fertig finished; ready
fest firm
das Fest, -e celebration, festive occasion, party
die Festbeleuchtung illumination, lighting
fest·halten (hält fest), hielt fest, festgehalten to keep a firm grip on
das Festnetz, -e landline (telephone)
der Fettdruck boldface type; **fett gedruckt** printed in boldface
der Feueralarm fire alarm/drill
das Fieber fever
die Filmrezension, -en film review
der Filmschauspieler, - movie actor; *(fem.)* **die Filmschauspielerin, -nen**
finden, fand, gefunden to find
die Firma, -men firm, company
flach flat, shallow
die Fläche, -n surface *(area)*
das Flachland flat country
die Flasche, -n bottle; *(slang)* wimp
die Flatrate flat-rate (cell phone) service
der Fleck, -en spot, stain
der Fleiß diligence, hard work
fleißig industrious, diligent
die Fliege, -n fly
fliegen, flog, ist/hat geflogen to fly
fliehen, floh, ist geflohen to flee
fließen, floss, ist geflossen to flow
flimmern to flicker
der Flug, ̈e *(air)* flight
der Flughafen, ̈ airport
das Flugzeug, -e airplane
die Flur, -en meadow, pasture; **der Flur, -e** hallway, corridor
der Fluss, ̈e river
die Flüssigkeit, -en fluid, liquid
die Folge, -n result
folgen (hat gefolgt) to obey
folgen (ist gefolgt) to follow
folgend following; **Folgendes** the following
die Fortbewegung (forward) motion

fort·fahren, fuhr fort, ist fortgefahren
(**+ mit**) to continue (to do)
fort·gehen, ging fort, ist fortgegangen
to go away
fort·setzen to continue (s.th.)
fort·ziehen, zog fort, ist fortgezogen to
go/move away
das Foto, -s picture, photograph
die Frage, -n question; **eine Frage**
stellen to ask a question
fragen to ask
das Fragewort, ¨er question word
die Frau, -en woman
frei free; **im Freien** outdoors
frei·geben (gibt frei), gab frei,
freigegeben to release, set free
die Freizeitbeschäftigung, -en
leisure-time activity
fremd foreign, strange
der Fremde (ein Fremder) stranger,
foreigner; *(fem.)* **die Fremde**
die Fremdsprache, -n foreign language
fressen (frisst), fraß, gefressen to eat
(animals)
die Freude, -n joy, delight
freuen to make happy; **sich freuen**
(**auf + acc.**) to look forward to; **sich**
freuen (über + acc.) to rejoice, be
happy about
der Freund, -e friend; *(fem.)* **die**
Freundin, -nen
der Freundeskreis, -e circle of friends
die Freundschaft friendship;
Freundschaft schließen to make
friends
der Friede(n), (-ns) peace
friedlich peaceful
frieren, fror, ist gefroren to freeze
der Friseur, -e barber; *(fem.)* **die**
Friseurin or **die Friseuse** hairdresser
fristen: ein Leben fristen to scrape by
in life
froh happy, glad
die Frucht, Früchte fruit
früher earlier, previous
der Frühling, -e spring
das Frühstück, -e breakfast
frühstücken to eat breakfast
fühlen to feel; **sich (wohl) fühlen** to feel
(fine)
führen to lead
für *(prep. with acc.)* for
sich fürchten (vor + dat.) to be afraid of
der Fuß, ¨e foot; **zu Fuß** on foot
die Fußsohle sole of a foot

ganz complete, whole, entire; quite
gar kein- not any at all; **gar nicht** not at
all; **gar nichts** nothing at all
die Gärtnerlehre, -n gardening
apprenticeship
die Gasse, -n street *(southern German)*
der Gast, ¨e guest
der Gastgeber, - host; *(fem.)* **die**
Gastgeberin, -nen
das Gasthaus, ¨er inn
die Gattung, -en genre
der Gaul, Gäule (old) horse
das Gebäck pastry
gebären (gebiert), gebar, geboren to
give birth, bear
das Gebäude, - building
geben (gibt), gab, gegeben to give; **es**
gibt there is/are
das Gebiet, -e area, territory, region
der Gebrauch, ¨e use, usage; custom
gebrauchen to use, make use of;
gebraucht used
die Gebühr, -en fee
das Geburtsjahr, -e birth year
der Geburtstag, -e birthday
die Geburtstagsfeier, -n birthday
celebration
gedenken (gen.), gedachte, gedacht to
remember, commemorate
das Gedicht, -e poem
geeignet suitable, appropriate
die Gefahr, -en danger
Gefahr laufen to run the danger of . . .
gefährlich dangerous
gefallen (gefällt), gefiel, gefallen *(dat.)*
to be pleasing
das Gefühl, -e feeling
gegen *(prep. with acc.)* toward; against
die Gegend, -en area, region
der Gegenspieler, - opponent
der Gegenstand, ¨e object, thing; subject
matter, topic
gegenüber *(dat.)* across from, opposite
die Gegenwart present *(time)*
der Gegner, - opponent, opposing player
der Gehalt contents, ingredients; **das**
Gehalt, ¨er salary
das Geheimnis, -se secret
gehen, ging, ist gegangen to go, walk;
es geht um *(acc.)* it is about, it deals
with, it is a matter of
gehorchen *(dat.)* to obey

gehören *(dat.)* to belong to
die Geige, -n fiddle, violin
das Geld, -er money
der Geldverdiener, - wage earner
die Gelegenheit, -en opportunity
gelingen, gelang, ist gelungen to
succeed; **es gelingt mir** I succeed
gelten (gilt), galt, gegolten to be valid
or worth; to be directed at; **gelten als**
to be considered (to be)
das Gemüse, - vegetable(s)
gemütlich cozy, snug; congenial, jolly
genau exact(ly), precise(ly)
genauso just as
genial brilliant; currently akin to
awesome as slang
genießen, genoss, genossen to enjoy
genug enough
genügen *(dat.)* to be enough, suffice
das Genus, -nera gender
gepanscht adulterated; spiked with
sugar (wine)
gerade *(adj.)* straight; upright, even
(numbers); *(adv.)* just, exactly
geradeaus straight ahead
geradezu downright
das Gerät, -e apparatus, device, piece of
equipment
die Gerechtigkeit justice
das Gericht, -e court
gering slight
die Germanistik German studies
gern gladly; **gern machen** to like to do;
gern haben to like (s.o. or s.th.)
das Geschäft, -e business, store
geschehen (geschieht), geschah, ist
geschehen to happen
das Geschenk, -e gift
die Geschichte, -n history, story
das Geschirr, - dishes, tableware
die Geschwister *(pl.)* brother(s) and
sister(s), siblings
die Gesellschaft, -en *(singular)* society,
company, association; *(plural)*
associations
das Gesicht, -er face
gestalten to shape, form, structure
gestern yesterday
gestrichen painted; called off, cancelled
gestrig yesterday's
gesund (comparative: **gesünder**) healthy
die Gesundheit health
das Gesundheitswesen health services
das Getränk, -e drink
die Getränkekarte, -n drinks menu

das Getreide grain
das Gewehr, -e rifle
das Gewicht, -e weight
gewinnen, gewann, gewonnen to win
gewiss (gen.) sure of
gewöhnlich usual(ly)
gewöhnt (an + acc.) accustomed to
gewölbt arched
gibt: es gibt there is/are
gießen, goss, gegossen to pour
der Gipfel, - peak, summit
glauben (an + acc.) to believe (in);
    glauben (+ dat.) to believe (a person)
gleich same, like; right away
gleichzeitig at the same time
das Gleis, -e track
gleiten, glitt, ist geglitten to glide, slip
das Glockenspiel, -e carillon, chime(s)
das Glück happiness, good fortune; zum
    Glück fortunately
glücklich happy; fortunate, lucky
glücklicherweise fortunately
die Glühbirne, -n light bulb
glühen to glow, be red hot
der Gott, -er god
der Graben, ⁇ ditch
gratulieren (dat.) to congratulate
die Grenze, -n border
grenzen (an + acc.) to border on
grob (ö) coarse, rough
groß (ö) big, large, great
die Größe, -n size
die Großeltern (pl.) grandparents
die Großmutter, ⁇ grandmother
die Großstadt, ⁇e major city (more than
    100,000 inhabitants)
der Großvater, ⁇ grandfather
der Grund, ⁇e reason; aus diesem
    Grunde for this reason
gründen to found
die Grundlage, -n beginning,
    foundation, basis
das Grundstück, -e piece of property
die Grundzahl, -en cardinal number
die Gruppe, -n group
der Gruß, ⁇e greeting
grüßen to greet
günstig favorable
gut (comparative: besser) (adj.) good;
    (adv.) well
gut aussehend/gutaussehend
    good-looking
gut bezahlt/gutbezahlt well paid
das Gymnasium, -sien university prep
    high school

H

das Haar, -e hair
haben (hat), hatte, gehabt to have
hacken to hack (into a computer)
der Hafen, ⁇ harbor
das Hafenviertel, - harbor district
der Häftling, -e prisoner
das Hallenbad, ⁇er indoor pool
halt (part.) just
halten (hält), hielt, gehalten to hold;
    stop; halten (für + acc.) to consider,
    regard as; halten (von + dat.) to have
    an opinion of/about
der Handel business deal
handeln to act, take action; handeln
    (von + dat.) to be about; es handelt
    sich um (acc.) it is about
die Handelsmetropole, -n trading
    metropolis
die Handlung, -n plot, action
die Handtasche, -n purse
das Handy cell phone
hängen, hängte, gehängt to hang
    s.th. (up)
hängen, hing, gehangen to be hanging
hängen bleiben, blieb hängen, ist
    hängen geblieben to get stuck
die Harfe, -n harp
hart (ä) hard
hassen to hate
hauchdünn extremely thin
häufig frequent
der Hauptbahnhof, ⁇e main train
    station
das Hauptfach, ⁇er major field of study
die Hauptrolle, -n leading role
der Hauptsatz, ⁇e main clause
die Hauptstadt, ⁇e capital (city)
das Haus, ⁇er house; zu Hause at home;
    nach Hause (to go) home
die Hausaufgabe, -n homework
    (assignment)
der Hausbesitzer, - homeowner; (fem.)
    die Hausbesitzerin
der Haushalt, -e household
der Hausherr, (-n), -en landlord; head
    of the house(hold)
das Haustier, -e house pet
die Haustür, -en front door
heben, hob, gehoben to lift, elevate, raise
das Heft, -e notebook
heim home, homewards
die Heimat, -en home; native land

der Heimatort, -e hometown
die Heimatstadt, -städte hometown,
    home city
heimlich secret(ly)
heimwärts towards home
heiraten to marry, get married
heiß hot
heißen, hieß, geheißen to be called or
    named; to mean, signify; bid, tell (s.o.)
    to; sie heißt her name is; das heißt
    that is (to say); es heißt it is said (that)
der Heißluftballon, -s hot air balloon
der Held, (-en), -en hero, (fem.) die
    Heldin, -nen
die Heldentat, -en heroic deed
helfen (hilft), half, geholfen (dat.) to
    help
das Hemd, -en shirt
herauf·holen to bring up, haul up
heraus·bekommen, bekam heraus,
    herausbekommen to find out
heraus·finden, fand heraus,
    herausgefunden to find out, discover
heraus·fischen to fish out
sich heraus·stellen to turn out to be
der Herbst, -e fall, autumn
der Herd, -e stove
herein in(to)
herein·kommen, kam herein, ist
    hereingekommen to come in
herein·lassen (lässt herein), ließ herein,
    hereingelassen to let in
der Herr, (-n), -en Mr., gentleman;
    (fem.) die Herrin, -nen lady, mistress
die Herrenboutique (-butike), -n men's
    clothing store
herrlich magnificent, splendid
herrschen to prevail; to rule
herum around
herum·kommen, kam herum, ist
    herumgekommen to get around
herum·schnüffeln to snoop/sniff/look
    around
herum·sitzen, saß herum, herumge-
    sessen to sit around
herum·surfen to surf around (on the
    Web)
herunter·laden, lud herunter,
    heruntergeladen to download
hervor·ragen to stand out
das Herz, (-ens), -en heart
herzlich cordial(ly)
heute today
heutig today's
heutzutage nowadays

die Hexe, -n witch
hier here
die Hilfe, -n help, assistance
die Himbeere, -n raspberry
der Himmel, - sky, heaven
das Himmelreich, -e heaven, heavenly
  kingdom
**hinauf·fahren (fährt hinauf), fuhr
  hinauf, ist/hat hinaufgefahren** to
  drive up
**hinauf·kommen, kam hinauf, ist
  hinaufgekommen** to come up
**hinauf·steigen, stieg hinauf, ist
  hinaufgestiegen** to climb up
hindurch through(out)
**hinein·schleichen, schlich hinein, ist
  hineingeschlichen** to sneak in
sich hin·setzen to sit down
hinter *(prep. with acc. or dat.)* behind
**hinterlassen (hinterlässt), hinterließ,
  hinterlassen** to leave behind
hinunter·schauen to look down
**hin·weisen, wies hin, hingewiesen
  (auf +acc.)** to indicate, point to
hinzu in addition, to this
hoch (höher) high; to the power of
das Hochhaus, ¨er skyscraper
**hoch industrialisiert/
  hochindustrialisiert** highly
  industrialized
hoch·laden, lud hoch, hochgeladen to
  upload
hoch qualifiziert/hochqualifiziert
  highly qualified
die Hochschule, -n university-level
  institution
höchst highly, very, extremely;
  höchstens at (the) most
höchstwahrscheinlich most likely
die Hochzeit, -en wedding
hoffen (auf + acc.) to hope for
hoffentlich hopefully
die Hoffnung, -en hope
höflich polite(ly)
die Höhe, -n height
die Höhenlage, -n elevation
die Höhensonne ultraviolet sunrays
holen to (go) fetch
das Holz wood
hören to hear
das Hörensagen hearsay
Horkrux, –e horcrux (from *Harry
  Potter*)
der Hörsaal, -säle lecture hall
das Hörverständnis listening
  comprehension

die Hose, -n trousers
die Hosentasche, -n trouser pocket
hübsch pretty, lovely
der Hügel, - hill
der Hund, -e dog
hupen to honk
der Hut, ¨e hat

ignorieren to ignore
im Ernst seriously
im Grunde genommen basically,
  fundamentally
im Laufe in the course of
immer always; **immer noch** still
imponieren *(dat.)* to impress
in *(prep. with acc. or dat.)* in, into, inside
indem by [—]ing
indessen in the meantime
der Index index
die Informatik computer science;
  computer programming
der Ingenieur, -e engineer; *(fem.)* **die
  Ingenieurin, -nen**
der Inhalt, -e content(s)
inline·skaten to rollerblade
innerhalb *(prep. with gen.)* inside of,
  within
installieren to install
der Intelligenzquotient IQ
das Interesse, -n interest
sich interessieren (für + acc.) to be
  interested in
interessiert (an + dat.) interested in
inzwischen meanwhile
der iPod iPod
irgend- some . . . or other; any . . . at all
irgendjemand someone or other
irgendwo(hin) (to) somewhere, anywhere
der Irrtum, ¨er error, mistake

ja yes; *(part.)* you know, of course
die Jacke, -n jacket
jagen to chase, hunt
das Jahr, -e year
der Jahresverlauf course of the year
die Jahreszeit, -en season of the year
das Jahrhundert, -e century
die Jahrtausendwende turn of the
  millennium

das Jahrzehnt, -e decade
je ever
je . . . desto/umso the more . . . the more
jed- each, every
jedenfalls in any event
jedermann everyone, everybody
jederzeit (at) any time
jedesmal each time, every time
jemand someone; **jemand anders**
  someone else
jen- that
jenseits *(prep. with gen.)* on the other
  side of
jetzig present
jetzt now
jeweils in each case, respectively
joggen to jog
der Jude, (-n), -n Jew; *(fem.)* **die Jüdin,
  -nen**
das Judentum Judaism
die Jugend youth
der Jugendliche (ein Jugendlicher)
  juvenile; *(fem.)* **die Jugendliche**
jung (ü) young
der Junge, (-n), -n boy, youth
der Junggeselle, (-n), –n bachelor

der Kaffee coffee
der Käfig, -e cage
kalt (ä) cold
die Kälte cold(ness)
kämmen to comb
die Kammer, -n chamber, room
kämpfen to battle, struggle
das Kanzleramt, -ämter Office of the
  Chancellor
das Kapitel, - chapter
kaputt broken, ruined, done for
die Karriere, -n career
die Karte, -n ticket; map
das Kartenspiel, -e card game; deck
  of cards
der Käse cheese
der Kassierer, - cashier; *(fem.)* **die
  Kassiererin, -nen**
die Katze, -n cat
der Kauf, ¨e purchase
kaufen to buy, purchase
das Kaufhaus, ¨er department store
kaum scarcely
keinesfalls by no means, not at all
der Keller, - cellar

der Kellner, - waiter; *(fem.)* **die Kellnerin, -nen** waitress

kennen, kannte, gekannt to know, be acquainted with

kennen lernen, lernte kennen, kennen gelernt to get to know, become acquainted with

das Kind, -er children

der Kinderwagen, - baby carriage

die Kindheit, -en childhood

das Kino, -s cinema, movie theater, the movies

die Kirche, -n church

die Kiste, -n crate

kitschig mawkish, trashy

klagen to lament, complain

der Kläger, - plaintiff; *(fem.)* **die Klägerin, -nen**

die Klammer, -n parenthesis

klar clear

die Klausur, -en test

das Klavier, -e piano

der Klavierbauer, - piano maker

die Kleiderabteilung, -en clothing department

die Kleidung clothes, clothing

das Kleidungsstück, -e piece of clothing

klein small, little; short *(in height)*

der Klempner, - plumber

klettern (ist) to climb, scramble

der Klingelton, -töne ringtone

klingen, klang, geklungen to sound

klug (ü) intelligent, clever, astute

die Klugheit intelligence, cleverness

die Kneipe, -n bar, pub

das Knie, - knee

der Knochen, - bone

der Koch, ̈e cook

kochen to cook

der Koffer, - suitcase, trunk, bag

der Kognat, -e cognate

die Kokospalme, -n coconut palm (tree)

der Kollege, (-n), -n colleague; *(fem.)* **die Kollegin, -nen**

komisch queer, strange, peculiar, comic(al)

kommen, kam, ist gekommen to come

der Kommissar, -e police inspector

der Kompass, -e compass

komponieren to compose

der Komponist, (-en), -en composer; *(fem.)* **die Komponistin, -nen**

der König, -e king; *(fem.)* **die Königin, -nen** queen

die Konjunktion, -en conjunction

können (kann), konnte, gekonnt to be able to, can

kontrollieren to check on

das Konzert, -e concert

der Kopf, ̈e head

der Kopfsalat, -e lettuce

der Korb, ̈e basket

der Körper, - body

der Krach (no pl.) controversy, fight, dissension

die Kraft, ̈e power

kräftig powerful, substantial, strong

krank (ä) sick, ill

das Krankenhaus, ̈er hospital

der Krankenwagen, - ambulance

krankhaft pathological, abnormal

der Krebs cancer

kreisen to circle

(das) Kreta Crete

die Kreuzung, -en crossing, intersection

der Krieg, -e war; **Krieg führen** to wage war

kriegen *(slang)* to get

die Kritik, -en criticism

krumm (comparative: **krümmer/krummer**) crooked, bent

die Küche, -n kitchen

der Kuchen, - cake

das Küchengerät, -e kitchen utensil *or* small appliance

die Kugel, -n ball, sphere

die Kuh, ̈e cow

der Kühlschrank, ̈e refrigerator

das Küken, - baby chicken

sich kümmern (um + *acc.*) to take care of, attend to

der Kunde, -n customer; *(fem.)* **die Kundin, -nen**

die Kunde news, notice, information

die Kunst, ̈e art; skill

künstlich artificial

die Kuppel, -n dome

der Kurs, -e course

kursiv (in) italics; **kursiv gedruckt** printed in italics

kurz (ü) short, brief

die Kürze brevity

kürzlich recently

der Kusin, -s male cousin; **die Kusine, -n** female cousin

der Kuss, ̈e kiss

L

lachen to laugh

laden, lud, geladen to load

die Lage, -n situation, position

lähmen to paralyze

die Lampe, -n lamp

das Land, ̈er land, country

die Landschaft, -en landscape

lang (ä) long

lange *(adv.)* for a long time

die Länge, -n length

langsam slow(ly)

sich langweilen to be bored

der Lärm noise

lassen (lässt), ließ, gelassen to let, leave

der Lastwagenfahrer, - truck driver

der Lauf, ̈e course, progress

laufen (läuft), lief, ist gelaufen to run, walk

der Läufer, - runner

das Laufwerk, -e (computer) drive

die Laune mood

läuten to ring

lauter *(adv.)* nothing but, purely

leben to live

das Leben life; **ums Leben kommen** to die, perish

der Lebenslauf, ̈e curriculum vitae

der Lebensstil, -e style of living

die Lebensweise, -n way of living

die Leber, -n liver

das Lebewesen, - creature

lecker tasty

der Ledermantel, ̈ leather coat

legen to lay, put; **sich legen** to lie down

die Legende, -n legend

das Lehrbuch, ̈er textbook

die Lehre, -n instruction, lesson, moral

lehren to teach

der Lehrer, - teacher; *(fem.)* **die Lehrerin, -nen**

lehrreich instructive

leicht easy, light

Leid tun: es tut mir Leid I am sorry

das Leiden, - sorrow, suffering

leider unfortunately

leihen, lieh, geliehen to loan, borrow

die Leine, -n leash

die Leistung, -en accomplishment

die Lektion, -en lesson

lesbar legible

die Leseaufgabe, -n reading assignment

lesen (liest), las, gelesen to read

der **Leserbrief, -e** letter to the editor
letzt- last
die **Leute** (*pl.*) people
lieb dear
die **Liebe** love
lieber preferably; **lieber tun** to prefer to do
der **Liebling, -e** darling, dear
die **Lieblingsspeise, -n** favorite dish
liebst: am liebsten most/best of all; **am liebsten tun** to like to do most/best of all
das **Lied, -er** song
liegen, lag, gelegen to be situated, lie
liegen lassen (lässt liegen), ließ liegen, liegen (ge) lassen to leave (lying about)
lila lilac (*color*)
links on the left; **nach links** to the left
das **Lob** praise
das **Loch, ¨er** hole
locker casually, nonchalantly
der **Lohn, ¨e** wage
das **Lokal, -e** premise; bar, restaurant
los: was ist los? what is the matter? What is going on?
löschen to delete, erase
lösen to loosen; to solve
los·schießen, schoss los, losgeschossen to shoot; to go ahead and start s.th.
los·werden (wird los), wurde los, ist losgeworden to get rid of
der **Lottogewinn, -e** lottery winnings
der **Löwe, (-n), -n** lion
die **Luft, ¨e** air
die **Lüge, -n** lie
lumpig paltry; (*slang*) stupid
die **Lunge, -n** lung
der **Lungenkrebs** lung cancer
der **Lungenzug, ¨e: einen Lungenzug machen** to inhale deeply
die **Lust** desire, inclination; **(keine) Lust haben ... zu tun** to have (no) desire to do
lustig merry, jolly, funny; **sich lustig machen (über + acc.)** to make fun of

machen to make; to do
die **Macht, ¨e** power, might
das **Mädchen, -** girl
mailen to send an e-mail

mal (*adv.*) times (*math*); (*part.*) just
das **Mal, -e** time; **zum ersten Mal** for the first time
der **Maler, -** painter; (*fem.*) die **Malerin, -nen**
manch- (*sing.*) many a; (*pl.*) some
manchmal sometimes
der **Mann, ¨er** man
die **Mannschaft, -en** team
der **Mantel, ¨** coat
das **Manuskript, -e** manuscript
das **Märchen, -** fairy tale
der **Markttag** market day
die **Maßeinheit, -en** unit of measurement
der **Massengeschmack** popular taste
maßlos utterly, beyond measure
die **Mauer, -n** (*masonry*) wall
der **Mauerfall** fall of the (Berlin) wall
das **Maul, ¨er** mouth (*of animals*)
das **Medikament, -e** medicine, drug
die **Medizin** (*science of*) medicine
das **Meer, -e** sea; ocean
der **Meer(es) blick, -e** view of the sea
mehr more
mehrere several
mehrmalig repeated
mehrmals several times
meinen to mean, think; to intend
die **Meinung, -en** opinion
die **Meinungsäußerung, -en** expression of opinion
meist- most; **meist** *or* **meistens** mostly
der **Meister, -** master; champion; (*fem.*) die **Meisterin, -nen**
melden to report
die **Meldung, -en** announcement
die **Menge, -n** a lot
der **Mensch, (-en), -en** human, man (*species*)
die **Menschheit** mankind, humankind
menschlich human
merken to notice; **sich** (*dat.*) **merken** to take note
merkwürdige strange, unusual
die **Messe, -n** convention, trade show
die **Metapher, -n** metaphor
die **Metropole, -n** metropolis
die **Miete, -n** rent
mieten to rent
das **Mikrofon, -e** microphone
die **Milch** milk
mild mild; amicable
die **Milliarde, -n** billion

mindestens at least (*with amounts*)
das **Missfallen** displeasure
mit (*prep. with dat.*) with
mit·bringen, brachte mit, mitgebracht to bring along
mit·kommen, kam mit, ist mitgekommen to come along
mit·machen to participate
mit·nehmen (nimmt mit), nahm mit, mitgenommen to take along
der **Mitspieler, -** fellow player, teammate
der **Mittag, -e** noon; **zu Mittag** at noon
mit·teilen to communicate, impart, tell
die **Mitteilung, -en** notification, communication, announcement
das **Mittel, -** means, medium
das **Mittelalter** Middle Ages
das **Mittelmeer** (no pl.) Mediterranean
mittlerweile in the meantime
das **Mobilnetz, -e** mobile/cell network
möchte(n) would like (to)
die **Modalpartikel, -n** modal particle
das **Modegeschäft, -e** fashion shop
das **Modell, -e** model
der **Moderator, -en** host, emcee
modisch fashionable (fashionably)
mögen (mag), mochte, gemocht to like; may
möglich possible
die **Möglichkeit, -en** possibility
möglichst as . . . as possible
der **Monat, -e** month
der **Mond, -e** moon
der **Morgen** morning; **heute Morgen** this morning
morgen tomorrow; **morgen früh** tomorrow morning
die **Moschee, -n** mosque
der **Motor, -en** motor
müde (*gen.*) tired of
die **Mühe** difficulty
der **Mund, ¨er** mouth
mündlich oral(ly)
die **Münze, -n** coin
das **Museum, -seen** museum
die **Musik** music
müssen (muss), musste, gemusst to have to, must
die **Musterkollektion, -en** sales samples
der **Mut** courage
die **Mutter, -** mother

nach *(prep. with dat.)* after; to(ward); according to

der Nachbar, (-s or-n), -n neighbor; *(fem.)* **die Nachbarin, -nen**

nachdem *(sub. conj.)* after

nacherzählen to retell

die Nacherzählung, -en adapted story

nachher afterward(s)

der Nachmittag, -e afternoon

die Nachricht, -en news, note, message, notice

nach·schlagen (schlägt nach), schlug nach, nachgeschlagen to look up *(in a book)*

nächst- next

die Nacht, ⁝e night

der Nachwuchs- up-and-coming, young

die Nähe proximity; **in der Nähe** near, nearby

der Name, (-ns), -n name

nämlich namely, that is

die Nase, -n nose

nass (comparative: **nässer/nasser**) wet

natürlich of course, natural(ly)

neben *(prep. with acc. or dat.)* beside, next to

nebenan next door, in the next room, alongside

das Nebenfach, ⁝er minor field of study

der Nebensatz, ⁝e dependent clause

der Neffe, (-n), -n nephew

nehmen (nimmt), nahm, genommen to take; **in Angriff nehmen** to tackle, take on

der Neinsager, - nay-sayer, negative person

nennen, nannte, genannt to name

nerven to get on one's nerves

nett nice

das Netz, -e network

neu new

neugierig curious

die Neujahrsansprache New Year's address

neulich recently

neuzeitlich modern, up-to-date

nicht not; **nicht einmal** not even; **nicht wahr** isn't it?, don't they?, etc.

die Nichte, -n niece

die Nichteinmischung, -en nonintervention

nichts nothing

nie never

nieder·gleiten, glitt nieder, ist niedergeglitten to slide down

die Niederlage, -n defeat

niedrig low

niemand no one, nobody; **niemand anders** no one else

noch still; **noch einmal** once more; **noch kein-** not any yet; **noch nicht** not yet; **noch nie** not ever (before)

normalerweise normally

die Note, -n grade

nötig necessary

die Notiz, -en note; **Notizen machen** to take notes

nur *(adv.)* only; *(part.)* just

nutzen *or* **nützen** to be of use

nützlich *(dat.)* useful

nutzlos useless

oberhalb *(prep. with gen.)* above

der Oberrichter, - high court judge

obgleich *(sub. conj.)* although

obig above

obwohl *(sub. conj.)* although

oder or

öffnen to open (s.th.); **sich öffnen** to open

oft (ö) often

öfter often; more often

ohne *(prep. with acc.)* without

ohne ... zu without [—]ing

ohne dass without [—]ing

das Ohr, -en ear

die Oma, -s granny

der Onkel, - uncle

der Opa, -s granddad, gramps

die Oper, -n opera

ordentlich neat, cleaned up

die Ordnung order, arrangement

die Ordnungszahl, -en ordinal number

der Ort, -e place

der Osten east

(das) Ostern Easter; **zu Ostern** at/for Easter

die Ostküste east coast

östlich eastern

die Ostsee Baltic Sea

paar: ein paar a few, several; **ein paar Mal** a few times

das Paar, -e pair, couple

packen to pack; to grasp, pounce on

das Paket, -e package

der Panoramablick, -e panoramic view

der Panzer, - tank, armor

der Papagei, (-s or-en), -en parrot

das Papier, -e paper

der Papst, ⁝e Pope

die Partei, -en faction, party

das Partizip, -ien participle

die Party, -s party

passen *(dat.)* to fit, suit

passend suitable, proper, fitting

passieren (ist) to happen, occur

die Pause, -n pause, break

das Pech bad luck *(literally:* pitch)

peinlich embarrassing

die Pension, -en bed and breakfast, inexpensive lodging

das Perfekt present perfect tense

per Hand by hand

pfeifen, pfiff, gepfiffen to whistle

der Pfeil, -e arrow

das Pferd, -e horse

die Pflanze, -n plant

der Pflichtkurs, -e required course

der Pförtner, - doorman

das Pfund, -e pound

pilgern (ist) to go on a pilgrimage

der Plan, ⁝e plan

das Pläsierchen little pleasure

der Plasmafernseher, - plasma TV

der Platz, ⁝e place, spot, site; room, space

platzen to explode, blow up

plaudern to chat

plötzlich sudden(ly)

das Plusquamperfekt past perfect tense

die Politik politics; policy

der Politiker, - politician; *(fem.)* **die Politikerin, -nen**

die Polizei police

der Polizist, (-en), -en policeman; *(fem.)* **die Polizistin, -nen**

das Portemonnaie, -s wallet

Position beziehen, bezog, bezogen to take a stand

die Post mail; post office
das Postamt, "er post office
der Posten, - post, position
das Präfix, -e prefix
das Präsens present tense
das Präteritum simple past tense
predigen to preach
der Preis, -e price; prize, award
preiswert good value for the money
prima great
der Prominente, -n (ein Prominenter) prominent person; *(fem.)* **die Prominente, -n**
das Pronomen, - pronoun
der Prosaband, "e volume of prose
die Protestaktion, -en protest march
der Protestierende, -n (ein Protestierender) protester; *(fem.)* **die Protestierende, -n**
der Proviant provisions, rations
der Prozess, -e lawsuit
die Prüfung, -en examination
der Psychiater, - psychiatrist; *(fem.)* **die Psychiaterin, -nen**
das Publikum audience
der Pullover, - sweater
der Punkt, -e point; period
pünktlich punctually
putzen to clean, polish; **die Zähne putzen** to brush one's teeth

die Qual, -en torment, misery
die Quelle, -n source
quer (durch) straight through, straight across
die Quote, -n (TV) rating

der Rabe, (-n), -n raven
das Rad, "er wheel; bike
Rad fahren (fährt Rad), fuhr Rad, ist Rad gefahren to ride a bicycle
der Rand, "er edge, side
rasch swift, speedy, rapid
der Rasen lawn, grass; **den Rasen betreten** to walk on the grass
rasieren to shave (s.o.)
der Rat advice

raten (rät), riet, geraten *(dat.)* to advise; to take a guess
das Rathaus, "er city hall
der Ratschlag, "e *(piece of)* advice, suggestion
das Rätsel, - riddle, puzzle
der Rattenfänger, - rat catcher
rauchen to smoke
räumlich spatial(ly)
die Raute-Taste, -n hash/pound key (telephone)
rechnen (mit + dat.) to calculate, figure on
recht right; quite
das Recht, -e right, privilege; justice
Recht haben to be right
rechts on the right; **nach rechts** to the right
der Rechtsanwalt, "e lawyer
rechtzeitig in time
die Redaktion editorial staff
die Rede, -n speech
das Redemittel, - verbal strategy; useful verbal expression or structure
reden to talk
der Redner, - speaker
die Regel, -n rule; **in der Regel** as a rule
regelmäßig regular
der Regen rain
regieren to rule, govern
die Regierung, -en government
der Regisseur, -e director (of a film, play, etc.)
regnen to rain
reich rich
das Reich, -e empire
reichen to reach (for), hand
das Reichstagsgebäude main building of the German parliament in Berlin
die Reihe, -n row; series
die Reise, -n trip, journey
das Reisebüro, -s travel agency
reisen to travel
der Reisende (ein Reisender) traveler; *(fem.)* **die Reisende**
der Reiseverkehr tourist travel
das Reiseziel travel/tourist destination
reißen, riss, gerissen to tear, rip
reiten, ritt, ist/hat geritten to ride *(an animal)*
die Reklame, -n advertisement; advertising
rennen, rannte, ist gerannt to run
das Restaurant, -s restaurant
das Rezept, -e recipe

die Rezession, -en recession
richten (an + acc.) to direct at
richtig correct, right
riechen, roch, gerochen to smell
das Rollenspiel, -e role-play
die Rolltreppe, -n escalator
der Roman, -e novel
rosten to rust
rot red
(das) Rotkäppchen Little Red Riding Hood
der Rotschopf, -schöpfe red-head
der Rücken, - back
der Rucksack, "e rucksack, backpack
der Rückweg, -e the way back/return
ruderlos without oars
der Ruf reputation
die Ruhe, -n peace, calm, rest
ruhig calm, quiet
das Ruhrgebiet Ruhr area *(industrial section of Germany)*
rund approximately, about, roughly, round; **rund um** around
der Rundbrief, -e a letter to be circulated
der Rundfunk radio

S

der Saal, Säle hall/large room
die Sache, -n thing, matter, subject
der Saft, "e juice
die Sage, -n legend, fable
die Säge, -n saw
sagen to say
sammeln to collect
die Sammlung, -en collection
der Satz, "e sentence
sauber clean, neat, tidy
sauer sour, mad, upset
das Schach chess
der Schäferhund, -e sheepdog
schaffen, schaffte, geschafft to do, accomplish, manage to do
schaffen, schuf, geschaffen to create
der Schal, -s scarf, shawl
die Schallplatte, -n record
der Schalter, - (ticket) window
sich schämen (über + acc.) to be ashamed of
die Schande disgrace
scharf (ä) sharp
der Schatten, - shadow
schauen to look

der **Scheibenwischer,** - windshield wiper

sich scheiden lassen, ließ, gelassen to get a divorce

der **Schein, -e** bill, banknote

scheinen, schien, geschienen to shine; to seem, appear

schenken to give *(as a present)*

schick stylish(ly)

schicken to send

schieben, schob, geschoben to shove, push

der **Schiedsrichter,** - referee

schief·gehen, ging schief, ist schiefgegangen to go wrong

schießen, schoss, geschossen to shoot

das **Schiff, -e** ship

schildern to depict, portray

der **Schirm, -e** screen

die **Schlacht, -en** battle

das **Schläfchen,** - nap

schlafen (schläft), schlief, geschlafen to sleep

das **Schlafzimmer,** - bedroom

schlagen (schlägt), schlug, geschlagen to strike, beat

der **Schlamassel** mess

die **Schlange, -n** snake; serpent

schlapp worn out, tired out

schlau clever, smart

schlecht bad(ly)

schleichen, schlich, ist geschlichen to creep, slink, sneak

schleppen to drag; **sich schleppen** to drag o.s.

schließen, schloss, geschlossen to close

schließlich in the final analysis, in the end

schlimm bad, evil; severe, grave

der **Schlips** necktie

der **Schluss, ¨-e** end; **zum Schluss** finally, in the end; **Schluss machen** to stop doing, put an end to

der **Schlüssel,** - key

schmal (comparative: **schmäler/ schmaler**) narrow

schmecken (nach + *dat.*) to taste like

schmeicheln *(dat.)* to flatter

schmelzen (schmilzt), schmolz, ist/hat geschmolzen to melt

schmieren to smear

sich schminken to put on make-up

schmutzig dirty, filthy

die **Schnauze, -n** snout (of an animal)

der **Schnee** snow

schnell fast

schon *(adv.)* already

schrecklich terrible, frightful

schreiben, schrieb, geschrieben to write

der **Schreiber,** - clerk, copyist; *(fem.)* die **Schreiberin, -nen**

die **Schreibmaschine, -n** typewriter

schreien, schrie, geschrien to shout, scream

schriftlich written, in writing

der **Schuh, -e** shoe

die **Schule, -n** school

der **Schüler,** - pupil; *(fem.)* die **Schülerin, -nen**

schützen to protect

schwach (ä) weak

die **Schwäche, -n** weakness

schwächlich weakly, feeble

schwachsinnig crazy, idiotic

schwarz (ä) black

schweigsam silent, taciturn

die **Schweiz** Switzerland

schwer heavy; difficult, hard

das **Schwert, -e** sword

die **Schwester, -n** sister

schwierig difficult

die **Schwierigkeit, -en** difficulty; **in Schwierigkeiten geraten** to get into difficulty

schwimmen, schwamm, ist/hat geschwommen to swim

schwindlig dizzy

schwören, schwur/schwor, geschworen to swear

sechsstellig six-digit

der **See, -n** lake; die **See, -n** sea

segeln to sail

sehen (sieht), sah, gesehen to see

sehnen + **nach** to yearn + for sich

sehenswert worth seeing

die **Sehenswürdigkeit, -en** attraction

sein (ist), war, ist gewesen to be

seit (prep. with dat.) since or for (temporal sense only)

seit(dem) *(sub. conj.)* since; **seitdem** *(adv.)* (ever) since then

die **Seite -n** page; side

seither (ever) since then

selber *(emphatic)* myself, yourself, themselves, etc.

selbst (one) self; even

die **Selbstaussage, -n** statement about oneself

selbstverständlich obvious(ly), self-evident; it goes without saying

selten seldom

die **Seltenheit, -en** rarity

seltsam strange(ly)

senden, sandte, gesandt to send

senden, sendete, gesendet to transmit

die **Sendung, -en** TV show

senken to lower, sink

setzen to set, put; **sich setzen** to sit down

sicher for sure; safe

die **Sicherheit** certainty, security

die **Sicht** sight, view, visibility

der **Sieg, -e** victory

siegen to conquer, be victorious

der **Sieger,** - winner, victor

simsen to text/text-message

die **Sinfonie, -n** symphony

singen, sang, gesungen to sing

das **Singspiel, -e** operetta, musical comedy

der **Sinn, -e** sense; **nicht bei Sinnen sein** to be out of one's mind

sinnlos pointless, senseless

sinnvoll meaningful; sensible

die **Sitte, -n** custom; **Sitten und Gebräuche** manners and customs

der **Sitz, -e** seat

sitzen, saß, gesessen to sit

der **Skat** skat *(card game)*

skeptisch skeptical

sobald as soon as

sofort immediately

sogar even

solange as long as

solch- such; **ein solch-** such a

sollen (soll), sollte, gesollt to be supposed to, ought to; to be said to

sondern but (rather)

der **Sonderpreis, -e** special price

die **Sonne, -n** sun

der **Sonnenbrand** sunburn

die **Sonnenuhr, -en** sundial

sonst otherwise

sooft as often as

die **Sorge, -n** worry, care

sorgen (für + *acc.*) to care *or* provide for

sorgenlos without worries

sowieso anyway

sowohl ... als auch both . . . and; as well as

spannend exciting

der **Spargel,** - asparagus

das **Sparkonto, -konten** savings account

sparsam thrifty, frugal

der Spaß fun; **Spaß machen** to be fun
spät late
spazieren gehen, ging spazieren, ist spazieren gegangen to take a walk
der Spaziergang, ¨**e** walk; **einen Spaziergang machen** to take a walk
speichern to store (in memory)
spendieren to treat someone to, pay for s.th. for s.o.
der Spiegel, - mirror
das Spiel, -e game
spielen to play
der Spielfilm, -e feature movie
der Spielplatz, ¨**e** playground, playing field
die Spielsache, -n toy
das Sportangebot, -e sports offerings
die Sportart, -en type of sport
das Sportgeschäft, -e sports store
die Sporthalle, -n gym
Sport treiben to do sports
der Sportler, - athlete; *(fem.)* **die Sportlerin, -nen**
der Sportverein, -e sports club
die Sprachkürze terseness
die Spraydose, -n spray can
sprechen (spricht), sprach, gesprochen to speak
das Sprichwort, ¨**er** saying, proverb
springen, sprang, ist gesprungen to jump, leap
der Spruch, ¨**e** saying, proverb
die Spülmaschine, -n dishwasher
spüren to feel, sense, perceive
der Staat, -en state
staatlich state, national
stabil rugged, sturdy
die Stadt, ¨**e** town, city
der Stadtplaner, - city planner; *(fem.)* **die Stadtplanerin, -nen**
der Stadtschreiber, - town clerk; *(fem.)* **die Stadtschreiberin, -nen**
der Stadtteil, -e section of a city
das Stadtzentrum, -zentren city center
die Stammzellenforschung stem cell research
der Standpunkt, -e view, position; **einen Standpunkt vertreten** to take a position/view
stark (ä) strong
die Stärke, -n strength
die Stasi short for "Ministerium für Staatssicherheit" (secret police of the GDR)
stattdessen instead (of that)

statt·finden, fand statt, stattgefunden to take place
stechen (sticht), stach, gestochen to prick; to sting, bite *(insect)*
stecken to stick, put
stehen, stand, gestanden to stand
stehlen (stiehlt), stahl, gestohlen to steal
die Steiermark Styria *(Austrian province)*
steigen, stieg, ist gestiegen to climb
der Stein, -e stone
die Stelle, -n position, spot, place; job
stellen to place; **eine Frage stellen** to ask a question
sterben (stirbt), starb, ist gestorben to die
die Sternchen-Taste, -n asterisk key (telephone)
die Steuern *(pl., fem.)* taxes
die Stilrichtung, -en (artistic) style
stimmen to be correct; to be true; **stimmen für** to vote for
die Stimmung, -en atmosphere
der Stock, ¨**e** stick, pole; story *or* floor of a building
stolz proud
die Stoppuhr, -en stopwatch
stören to disturb
stracks straight (away); without delay
der Strafraum, -räume penalty area
strahlen to beam, shine
der Strand, ¨**e** beach
die Straße, -n street
der Straßenarbeiter, - road repair worker
der Straßenrand, ¨**er** side of the road
der Straßenverkehr (road) traffic
der Streit fight, argument
sich streiten (stritt), gestritten to fight, argue
streng strict, harsh
der Strick, -e rope
der Strom, ¨**e** river, stream; electricity
das Stück, -e piece; a dramatic play
das Studentenheim, -e student dorm
das Studentenlokal, -e student tavern
das Studium, -ien studies, course of studies
die Stunde, -n hour, class (hour); **stundenlang** for hours
der Stundenplan, ¨**e** schedule
der Sturm, ¨**e** storm
der Stürmer, - (soccer) striker
stürzen (ist) to fall, plunge; **(hat)** overthrow

die Styroporpackung, -en Styrofoam packaging
das Substantiv, -e noun
suchen to seek, search
der Süden south
die Südseeinsel, -n South Sea island
summen to hum
die Süße, -n sweetness

der Tag, -e day; **eines Tages** one day
das Tagebuch, ¨**er** diary
die Tagesnachrichten *(pl.)* news of the day
die Tagesschau daily news program on German television
die Tageszeit, -en time of the day
täglich daily
tagsüber during the day
der Taler, - obsolete monetary unit
die Tankstelle, -n gas station
die Tante, -n aunt
der Tanz, ¨**e** dance
tanzen to dance
die Tapferkeit bravery
die Tasche, -n pocket
das Taschengeld spending money
die Taschenlampe, -n flashlight
der Taschenrechner, - pocket calculator
die Taschenuhr, -en pocket watch
die Tasse, -n cup
die Taste, -n button, key
die Tätigkeit, -en activity
der Tatort, -e scene of the crime
die Tatsache, -n fact
tatsächlich in fact, actually
taub deaf
taugen to be good for
tausend thousand
die Technik technology
der Teil, -e part, section
teilen to divide
teil·nehmen (nimmt teil), nahm teil, teilgenommen (an + *dat.*) to take part in, participate
der Tennisschläger, - tennis racket
der Teppich, -e rug, carpet
der Termin, -e fixed date; appointment
teuer expensive
der Teufel, - devil
das Thema, -men topic, subject, theme
die These, -n thesis
tief deep(ly)

die **Tiefe, -n** depth
die **Tiefenpsychologie** psychology of the subconscious
tief greifend/tiefgreifend profound, extensive
das **Tier, -e** animal
der **Tiergarten, ¨** zoo
tippen to type; to predict
der **Tisch, -e** table
der **Titel, -** title
die **Tochter, ¨** daughter
der **Tod, -e** death; **zu Tode** to death
toll crazy, insane; terrific, great
der **Ton, ¨e** tone
der **Topf, ¨e** pot
das **Tor, -e** gate, portal; goal (soccer)
der **Torwart, -warte** goalie, goalkeeper
tot dead
der **Tote (ein Toter)** dead person; *(fem.)* die **Tote**
töten to kill
der **Tourist, (-en), -en** tourist; *(fem.)* die **Touristin, -nen**
der **Touristenführer, -** tourist guide *or* guidebook
tragen (trägt), trug, getragen to carry; to wear
der **Trainer, -** (sport) coach
die **Traube, -n** grape
trauen *(dat.)* to trust
träumen to dream
traumhaft dreamlike, wonderful
traurig sad
treffen (trifft), traf, getroffen to meet; to hit; to affect
treffend apt, appropriate
treiben, trieb, getrieben to drive; to pursue an activity; **treiben (ist)** to drift, float
die **Treppe** stair(s)
das **Treppenhaus** stairwell
treten, trat, ist getreten to step
die **Tribüne, -n** (stadium) stands
der **Trick, -s** trick
der **Trieb, -e** appetite; drive
das **Trikot, -s** (sport) jersey
trinken, trank, getrunken to drink
trotz *(prep. with gen.)* in spite of
trotzdem *(adv.)* in spite of it/this, nevertheless; *(sub. conj.)* in spite of the fact that
trüb dreary
tun (tut), tat, getan to do, act
die **Tür, -en** door
türkisch Turkish
der **Typ, -en** type ; (slang) guy

übel nauseated, sick
über *(prep. with acc. or dat.)* over, across, above; about *(acc.)*
überall(hin) to everywhere
überein·stimmen to be in agreement
der **Übergang, -gänge** transition, crossing
die **Übergangsschwierigkeit, -en** transitional difficulty
übergeben, übergab, übergeben to hand over; **sich übergeben** to vomit
überglücklich overjoyed, exuberant
überhaupt in general, on the whole; **überhaupt nicht** not at all; **überhaupt nichts** nothing at all
überleben to survive
überlegen to ponder, consider; **sich etwas** *(dat.)* **überlegen** to think s.th. over; **überlegen sein** to be superior
überlisten to trick, outwit
übernachten to spend the night
überqueren to cross over
überraschen to surprise
die **Überraschung, -en** surprise
überreden to persuade
übersehen (übersieht), übersah, übersehen to overlook, ignore
übersetzen to translate
der **Übersetzer, -** translator; *(fem.)* die **Übersetzerin, -nen**
überspringen, übersprang, übersprungen to skip (over)
übertreiben, übertrieb, übertrieben to exaggerate
über·wechseln to change, go over
die **Überwindung, -en** conquest, break-through
überzeugen to convince; **überzeugt** convinced
die **Überzeugung** conviction
übrigens incidentally; **im Übrigen** in other respects
die **Übung, -en** exercise
um *(prep. with acc.)* around; by *(with quantities)*; **um sechs Uhr** at six o'clock
um ... zu in order to
um ... willen for . . . 's sake
umarmen to embrace, hug
um·bauen to remodel
um·fallen (fällt um), fiel um, ist umgefallen to fall over
der **Umfang, ¨e** girth, extension

umgeben (umgibt), umgab, umgeben to surround
umgekehrt vice versa, turned around
um·kippen to tip over
der **Umschlag, -schläge** envelope
um·schreiben, schrieb um, umgeschrieben to rewrite, revise
sich um·sehen (sieht um), sah um, umgesehen to look around
der **Umstand, ¨e** circumstance
die **Umwelt** environment
die **Umweltverschmutzung** environmental pollution
sich um·ziehen, zog um, umgezogen to change (clothes); **um·ziehen (ist)** to move, change one's residence
der **Unabhängigkeitskrieg, -e** war of independence
unbedingt absolutely
unbegrenzt without limitation
unbesonnen foolish
unbestimmter Artikel indefinite article
unergiebig unproductive, useless
unermüdlich untiring(ly)
unerwartet unexpected
der **Unfall, ¨e** accident
ungefähr approximately
das **Ungeheuer, -** monster
ungesund unhealthy
das **Ungeziefer** vermin
unglaublich unbelievable
die **Universität, -en** university *(coll.:* die **Uni, -s)**
unsäglich unspeakable/-bly
der **Unsinn** nonsense
unsterblich immortal
unten *(adv.)* below
unter *(prep. with acc. or dat.)* under, below, beneath; among; **unter anderem** among other things
unterbrechen (unterbricht), unterbrach, unterbrochen to interrupt
unterdessen meanwhile
unterdrücken to suppress, repress
unter·gehen, ging unter, ist untergegangen to set, go down; to perish
unterhalb *(prep. with gen.)* beneath
sich unterhalten (unterhält), unterhielt, unterhalten to converse (**über** + *acc.* about); to amuse o.s.
die **Unterhaltung, -en** amusement, conversation
die **Unterkunft, ¨e** lodging

**unternehmen (unternimmt), unter-
nahm, unternommen** to undertake;
to engage in an activity

das Unternehmen, - undertaking;
company, enterprise

der Unterricht instruction

unterrichten to instruct, teach

der Unterrichtsraum, ¨e instructional
room, classroom

unterschiedlich different, differing

**unterstreichen, unterstrich,
unterstrichen** to underline

unterstützen to support

die Unterstützung support

untersuchen to investigate, examine

der Untersuchungsbericht, -e
investigative report

unterwegs underway

die Untreue infidelity

unvergesslich unforgettable

unvergleichlich incomparable

unverständlich incomprehensible

unvorsichtig careless, not cautious

das Unwesen, - awful creature

unwiderstehlich irresistible

unzufrieden dissatisfied

der Urlaub, -e vacation

Urlaub machen to go on vacation

der Urlaubsort, -e vacation spot

die Ursache, -n cause

das Urteil, -e judgment, verdict

urteilen to judge

der USB-Anschluss, -schlüsse USB
connection

usw. (und so weiter) etc.

der Vater, ¨ father

die Vaterschaftsklage, -n paternity suit

der/die Vegetarier(in) vegetarian

sich verabschieden to take one's leave,
say good-bye

verändern to change s.th.; **sich
verändern** to become changed

die Veränderung, -en change

verantwortlich responsible

das Verb, -en verb

verbessern to improve

verbieten, verbot, verboten to forbid

verbinden, verband, verbunden to
connect, combine; to bandage

die Verbindung, -en connection

das Verbot, -e ban, prohibition

der Verbrecher, - criminal

verbrennen, verbrannte, verbrannt to
burn (up), scorch

verbringen, verbrachte, verbracht to
spend or pass (time)

der Verdacht suspicion

verdächtigen to suspect

verderben, verdarb, hat/ist verdorben
to ruin/go bad

verdeutlichen to make clear, illustrate

verdienen to earn, merit

vereinigt united

die Vereinigung unification

der Verfall, -fälle decline, drop

verfassen to write, compose

verfault rotten

verfließen, verfloss, ist verflossen
elapse, pass (of time)

vergangen past

die Vergangenheit past

vergessen (vergisst), vergaß, vergessen
to forget

der Vergleich, -e comparison

vergleichen, verglich, verglichen to
compare

vergleichend comparative

verhaften arrest, apprehend

sich verhalten to act, behave, react

das Verhältnis, -se relationship

verheiratet married

verhindern to stop, prevent

verjährt past the statute of limitations

verkaufen to sell

der Verkäufer, - salesperson; (fem.) **die
Verkäuferin, -nen**

der Verkehr traffic

die Verkehrsampel, -n traffic light

das Verkehrsmittel, - means of
transportation

verkehrt mixed up, not as it should be

verkünden to proclaim, announce

der Verlag, -e publishing house

verlängern to extend, lengthen

verlassen (verlässt), verließ, verlassen
(with dir. obj.) to leave, go away;
sich verlassen (auf + obj.) to
rely upon

der Verlauf, ¨e course

**verlaufen (verläuft), verlief, ist
verlaufen** to take its course, turn out;
sich verlaufen to get lost, lose
one's way

verletzen to injure, hurt; to insult, offend

die Verletzung, -en injury

sich verlieben (in + acc.) to fall in love
with

verlieren, verlor, verloren to lose

der Verlobte (ein Verlobter) fiancé;
(fem.) **die Verlobte** fiancée

der Verlust, -e loss

vermitteln to mediate

das Vermögen fortune

verneinen to answer in the negative

vernetzt digitally linked

verpassen to miss (a train; opportunity)

verpflanzen to transplant

der Verrat (no pl.) betrayal, treachery

verrostet rusted

verrückt crazy; **verrückt (auf + acc.)**
crazy about

versagen to fail

versäumen to miss, neglect to do

verschieden various, different

verschlechtern to make worse

verschwenden to waste, squander

die Verschwiegenheit discretion

**verschwinden, verschwand, ist
verschwunden** to disappear, vanish

versehentlich by mistake, accidentally

versichern to insure; to assure

die Versicherung, -en insurance,
assurance

die Versorgung (no pl.) supply,
maintenance

sich verspäten to be or arrive late

die Verspätung, -en delay

**versprechen (verspricht), versprach,
versprochen** to promise

verstaatlichen to nationalize

das Verständnis understanding,
comprehension

verstärken to strengthen

verstehen, verstand, verstanden to
understand

versuchen to try, attempt

die Verteidigung, -en defense

verteilen to distribute

der Vertrag, -träge contract

das Vertrauen trust, confidence

vertreiben, vertrieb, vertrieben to drive
away, scatter; **die Zeit vertreiben** to
pass the time

vertreten (vertritt), vertrat, vertreten to
represent, act on behalf of

der Verwandte (ein Verwandter)
relative; (fem.) **die Verwandte**

verwandtschaftlich pertaining to relatives

verwechseln to mix up, confuse

verwenden to use, make use of

verwirklichen to make come true,
realize (a goal)

verwöhnen to spoil, pamper

verzweifelt desperate(ly)
das Video, -s video
das Videospiel, -e video game
viel *(sing.)* much; **viel-** *(pl.)* many
vielleicht perhaps
vielmals often, many times
viel sagend/vielsagend significant, telling
viel versprechend/vielversprechend promising, encouraging
das Viertel, - quarter; section of a town or city
das Virus, Viren virus
der Vogel, ¨ bird
die Vokabel, -n (vocabulary) word
das Volk, ¨er people, nation, race
die Volkskrankheit, -en widespread illness
die Vollendung, -en completion, perfection
völlig total(ly), complete(ly)
vollkommen complete(ly)
die Vollpension lodging with all meals
von *(prep. with dat.)* from, of, by; about
vor *(prep. with dat. or acc.)* in front of, before; ago *(dat.)*; **vor allem** above all; **vor kurzem** recently
vorbei past; **an** *(dat.)* **... vorbei** (go) past
vor·bringen, brachte vor, vorgebracht to bring forward, bring up *(an argument)*
der Vorfahr, (-en), -en ancestor, forefather
vor·führen to demonstrate, display
der Vorgang, -gänge process
vor·gehen, ging vor, ist vorgegangen to be fast *(of clocks)*
die Vorgeschichte, -n prior history, prehistory
vor·haben to have in mind, intend
der Vorhang, ¨e curtain
vorher *(adv.)* before, previously
vorig previous
vor·lesen (liest vor), las vor, vorgelesen to read aloud
die Vorlesung, -en lecture *(course)*
der Vorschlag, ¨e suggestion
vor·schlagen (schlägt vor), schlug vor, vorgeschlagen to suggest
die Vorsicht caution, care
vorsichtig careful, cautious
vor·sprechen, sprach vor, vorgesprochen to audition (for a speaking part)

vor·stellen to introduce; **sich** *(dat.)* **vor·stellen** to imagine
die Vorstellung, -en performance, show; imagination
der Vortrag, ¨e lecture, talk
vorüber past, over
vorwärts forward
vorzüglich excellent, exquisite

wach awake
wachen to keep watch, to stay awake
wachsen (wächst), wuchs, ist gewachsen to grow
der Wagen, - car; wagon
die Wahl, -en choice
wählen to choose, select, vote
der Wähler, - voter; *(fem.)* **die Wählerin, -nen**
der Wahnsinn insanity
wahnsinnig crazy; *(adv.)* ridiculously
wahr true, real, genuine
während *(prep. with gen.)* during; *(sub. conj.)* while
die Wahrheit, -en truth
wahrscheinlich probably
der Wald, ¨er wood(s), forest
die Wanderausrüstung, -en hiking outfit
die Wanderkarte, -n trail map, hiking map
wandern to hike, wander, roam
die Wanderung, -en hike
wann *(interrog.)* when
die Ware, -n ware, product
warm (ä) warm
warten (auf + acc.) to wait for
warum why
was für what kind of
das Waschbecken, - wash basin, sink
waschen (wäscht), wusch, gewaschen to wash
das Waschpulver detergent
wasserdicht watertight, waterproof
der Wasserspiegel water surface
die Webseite, -n website
weder ... noch neither . . . nor
weg away
wegen *(prep. with gen.)* on account of
weg·gehen, ging weg, ist weggegangen to leave, go away
weg·stellen to put away, put down
weh! woe!

weh·tun, tat weh, weh getan to hurt, pain
weihen to devote
(das) Weihnachten *(or pl.)* Christmas; **zu Weihnachten** at/for Christmas
weil *(sub. conj.)* because
die Weile while, *(amount of)* time
der Wein, -e wine
weise wise
weiter additional, further
weiter·fahren (fährt weiter), fuhr weiter, ist weitergefahren) to drive on, continue driving, to drive further (than . . .)
weiter·gehen, ging weiter, ist weitergegangen to go on; to keep going
weiter·kommen, kam weiter, ist weitergekommen to make progress, to come/get further along
weiter·machen to keep doing
weit reichend/weitreichend far-reaching, extensive
welch- which
die Welt, -en world
der Weltkrieg, -e world war
der Weltmarkt, -märkte world market
die Weltmeisterschaft, -en world championship
der Weltraum outer space
der Weltrekord, -e world record
die Weltstadt, ¨e metropolis, major world city
die Wende turn, turning point
wenden, wandte, gewandt to turn
wenden, wendete, gewendet to turn (inside out)
wenig *(sing.)* little; **wenig-** *(pl.)* few
wenn *(sub. conj.)* when(ever), if; **wenn ... auch** even if, even though; **wenn ... kein/nicht** unless
die Werbeschrift, -en advertising brochure
die Werbung, -en advertisement, advertising
werden (wird), wurde, ist geworden to become, get
werfen (wirft), warf, geworfen to throw, toss
das Werk, -e book, work; works, factory
das Werkzeug, -e tool, implement
wert *(dat.)* worth, of value to; *(gen.)* worth, worthy of
das Wesen, - being, creature
der Westen west
der Wettanbieter person proposing a wager

wetten to bet, wager
das Wetter weather
der Wetterdienst weather service
der Wettkampf, ¨e competition
der/die Wettpate/-patin person
accepting a wager
wichtig important
wider (*prep. with acc.*) against
widersprechen (widerspricht),
widersprach, widersprochen (*dat.*) to
contradict
wie how; as
wieder again
wiederholen to repeat
die Wiedervereinigung, -en
reunification
wie lange how long
wieso how is it that
wie viel how much; **wie viele** how many
der Wille, (-ns), -n will
der Wirbel, - hectic pace, fuss, turmoil
wirken to have an effect, work
wirklich real(ly)
die Wirtschaft economy
der Wirtschaftsberater, - business
consultant
der Wirtschaftsplaner, -
economic planner; (*fem.*) **die**
Wirtschaftsplanerin, -nen
die Wirtschaftspolitik economic policy
wissen (weiß), wusste, gewusst to know
die Wissenschaft, -en science
der Wissenschaftler, - scientist; (*fem.*)
die Wissenschaftlerin, -nen
wissenschaftlich scientific
die Witwe, -n widow
der Witz, -e joke; wit
das WLAN Wifi/wireless Internet
woanders elsewhere
das Wochenende, -n weekend
der Wochentag, -e weekday
wohin to where
wohl probably
wohnen to live, dwell
der Wohnort, -e place of residence
der Wohnsitz, -e official residence
die Wohnung, -en apartment, dwelling
wollen (will), wollte, gewollt to want
to, intend
das Wort, ¨er individual word; **das**
Wort, -e connected words
der Wortschatz, ¨e vocabulary
die Wunde, -n wound
sich wundern to be amazed
das Wunderkind, -er child prodigy

der Wunsch, ¨e wish; **nach Wunsch** as
desired
wünschen to wish
der Wurfspieß javelin
die Würze, -n spice
die Wüste, -n desert
wütend (auf) enraged at

Z

die Zahl, -en number
zahlen to pay
der Zahn, ¨e tooth
der Zahnarzt, ¨e dentist; (*fem.*) **die**
Zahnärztin, -nen
der Zar, (-en), -en czar
der Zauberer, - wizard, magician
zauberhaft magical, enchanted
der Zaubertrank, - tränke magic
potion
der Zaun, ¨e fence
zeigen to show
die Zeile, -n line
die Zeit, -en time
die Zeitangabe, -n indication
of time
der Zeitausdruck, ¨e time expression
die Zeitform, -en verb tense
die Zeitschrift, -en magazine
die Zeitung, -en newspaper
das Zelt, -e tent
das Zentrum, Zentren center
zerbrechen (zerbricht), zerbrach,
zerbrochen to break (into pieces),
shatter
zerstören to destroy
die Zerstörung destruction
der Zettel, - scrap of paper; note
der Zeuge, -n witness; (*fem.*) **die**
Zeugin, -nen
ziehen, zog, gezogen to pull; **ziehen**
(ist) to move, go
ziemlich rather, fairly
das Zimmer, - room
der Zimmerschlüssel, - room key
der Zirkus, -se circus
das Zitat, -e quotation
der Zoll (no pl.) customs
der Zöllner, - customs agent
zornig angry
zu (*prep. with dat.*) to, at; too
der Zucker sugar
zuerst (at) first

zufällig per chance, by accident
zufrieden satisfied
der Zug, ¨e train
das Zugabteil, -e train compartment
zu·geben, gab zu, zugegeben to admit
die Zugverbindung, -en train connection
zu·hören (*dat.*) to listen to
der Zuhörer, - listener; (*fem.*) **die**
Zuhörerin
die Zukunft future
der Zukunftsplan, ¨e future plan
zuletzt at last, finally, in the end
zu·machen to close, shut
zunächst at first, first of all
die Zunge, -n tongue
zurück·bringen, brachte zurück,
zurückgebracht to bring back
zurück·führen (auf + acc.) to trace back
to, explain by
die Zurückhaltung reserve
zurück·kehren (ist) to return
zurück·kommen, kam zurück, ist
zurückgekommen to come back,
return
zu·rufen, rief zu, zugerufen (*dat.*) to
call to
zusammen together
der Zusammenbruch, ¨e collapse
zusammen·fassen to summarize
zusammen·halten (hält zusammen),
hielt zusammen, zusammengehalten
to hold *or* keep together
zusammen·stellen to put together
zusammen·wachsen (wächst
zusammen), wuchs zusammen,
ist zusammengewachsen to grow
together
zu·schauen to watch, observe
der Zuschauer, - spectator, onlooker;
(*fem.*) **die Zuschauerin, -nen**
zu·schneiden, schnitt zu, zugeschnitten
to tailor (+ auf) to
das Zustandspassiv, -e statal passive
zu viel too much
der Zweifel, - doubt
zu wenig too little
zu·winken (*dat.*) to wave at/to
zwar to be sure; namely
zweifeln (an + dat.) to doubt, have
doubts about
der Zwilling, -e twin
zwingen, zwang, gezwungen (zu + dat.)
to force, compel
zwischen (*prep. with acc. or dat.*)
between

Index

In the following grammatical index, the letter *n* after a page reference refers to material presented in a footnote.